HBJ LANGUAGE

8

Dorothy S. Strickland
Richard F. Abrahamson
Roger C. Farr
Nancy R. McGee
Nancy L. Roser

8

Karen S. Kutiper
Patricia Smith

HBJ LANGUAGE

HBJ HARCOURT BRACE JOVANOVICH, PUBLISHERS
Orlando San Diego Chicago Dallas

Printed in the United States of America

ISBN 0-15-316418-2

Acknowledgments

For permission to reprint copyrighted material, grateful acknowledgment is made to the following sources:

Atheneum Publishers, an imprint of Macmillan Publishing Company: From pp. 126–128 in *Plants That Changed History* by Joan Elma Rahn. Copyright © 1982 by Joan Elma Rahn.

The Berkley Publishing Group: From pp. 26–27 in *Tom Brown's Field Guide to Wilderness Survival* by Tom Brown, Jr., with Brandt Morgan. Copyright 1983 by Tom Brown, Jr.

Curtis Brown, Ltd.: From "Valentine Feelings" by Lee Bennett Hopkins. Copyright © 1975 by Lee Bennett Hopkins. Published in *Moments* by Harcourt Brace Jovanovich, Inc., 1980.

Children's Art Foundation: Adapted from "My First Assembly" by Jonathan Rosenbaum in *Stone Soup* Magazine, May/June 1986.

Don Congdon Associates, Inc.: From *Dandelion Wine* by Ray Bradbury. Copyright © 1953 by Ray Bradbury, renewed 1981 by Ray Bradbury.

The Dramatic Publishing Company: From *The Open Window* by H. H. Munro (Saki), dramatized by James Fuller. © MCMLXIV by The Dramatic Publishing Company. *Caution: The Open Window* is fully protected by copyright. It may not be acted by professionals or amateurs without written permission. All inquiries should be addressed to The Dramatic Publishing Company, 311 Washington St., Woodstock, IL 60098.

Ronald Everson: From "The Loaves" in *The Wind Has Wings: Poems from Canada,* edited by Mary Alice Downie and Barbara Robertson.

Tia Greenfield, on behalf of Lars Smith, and Marcy Castillo, on behalf of Marc Almond: From "Spirit of the Grizzly Bear" by Lars Smith and Marc Almond in *Paper of Life,* edited by Gail Newman. © 1985 by Lars Smith and Marc Almond.

Harcourt Brace Jovanovich, Inc.: "Study Steps to Learn a Word" from *HBJ Spelling,* Signature Edition, Level 8 (Gold) by Thorsten Carlson and Richard Madden. Copyright © 1988, 1983 by Harcourt Brace Jovanovich, Inc. Short pronunciation key and entries from *HBJ School Dictionary.* Copyright © 1985 by Harcourt Brace Jovanovich, Inc.

Alfred A. Knopf, Inc.: From "Dunkirk" in *Dunkirk* by Robert Nathan. Copyright 1941, 1945 by Robert Nathan.

Little, Brown and Company: From "The Tale of Custard the Dragon" in *Verses from 1929 On* by Ogden Nash. Copyright 1936 by Ogden Nash.

Macmillan Publishing Company: "The Main-Deep" from *Collected Poems* by James Stephens. Copyright 1925, 1926 by Macmillan Publishing Company, renewed 1953, 1954 by James Stephens.

Modern Curriculum Press, Inc.: From "A Modern Dragon" in *Songs from Around a Toadstool Table* by Rowena Bastin Bennett. Copyright © 1967 by Rowena Bastin Bennett.

Walter Dean Myers: From "The Cub" by Walter Dean Myers in *Cricket* Magazine, July 1987. © 1987 by Walter Dean Myers.

Oxford University Press: "A Misspelled Tail" by Elizabeth T. Corbett in *The Oxford Book of Children's Verse in America,* edited by Donald Hall.

Florence H. Pettit: From the introduction in *How to Make Whirligigs and Whimmy Diddles and Other American Folkcraft Objects* by Florence H. Pettit. Copyright © 1972 by Florence H. Pettit.

continued at the end of the book

Contents

2 Giving Instructions 54

3 Narrating Events

Reading ↔ Writing Connection

Composition Focus: Narrative Poem

Language Focus: Verbs

4 Explaining Related Ideas 154

Reading ↔ Writing Connection

Composition Focus: Paragraphs of Cause and Effect

Language Focus: More About Verbs

5 Persuading Others 202

Reading ↔ Writing Connection

Composition Focus: Persuasive Essay

Language Focus: Pronouns

6 Creating an Impression 250

7 Comparing and Contrasting 298

Reading ↔ Writing Connection

Composition Focus: Paragraphs of Comparison and Contrast

Language Focus: Prepositions, Conjunctions, Interjections

9 Creating Drama

Study Skills 471

Extra Practice 1

Dear Student,

Did you ever stop to think about how important English is in your everyday life? You may think of English only as a school subject, but you use English outside school all day long—when you listen to the radio, have a conversation, find a number in the phone book, flip through a magazine, or write a message.

English brings you information and entertainment. You use it to share with others your knowledge, ideas, and feelings. English, as you can see, is a very important part of your life.

We hope that HBJ Language will help you use English more effectively. We want you to discover the pleasure of being able to communicate with others whether you are listening, speaking, reading, or writing.

Sincerely,
The Editors

Understanding the Writing Process

Writing a story, a play, or an essay is like developing an invention. An inventor follows a plan—making adjustments along the way—to develop a bicycle, a light bulb, or any other new product to present to the public. In the same way, a writer follows a plan to develop a written piece for an audience. The plan a good writer follows is called the **writing process.** This process includes five stages:

1. Prewriting
2. Drafting
3. Responding and Revising
4. Proofreading
5. Publishing

A writer's progress from one stage to the next does not usually proceed in a straight line. Writers move backward and forward through the stages of the writing process because, like inventors, they make discoveries, happen upon new facts, or find gaps in their information as they work. This diagram shows the path a writer might take.

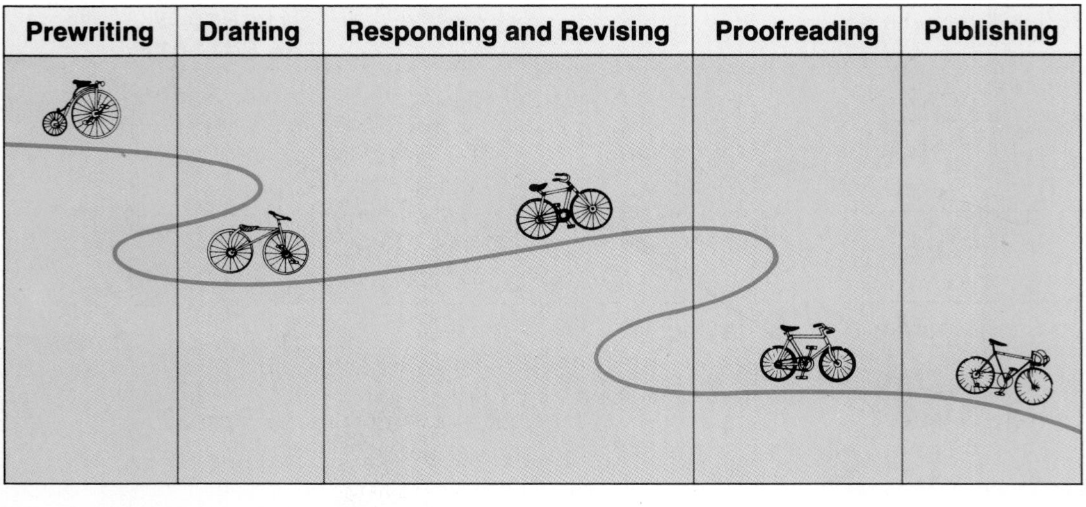

1 Prewriting

Getting started can be the most troublesome part of writing. That is why the prewriting stage is so important to the writing process. During the prewriting stage, you

- identify your audience, the individual or group for whom you are writing.
- define your purpose, or reason for writing, and decide on a writing form.
- brainstorm a list of possible topics about which you can write.
- select an appropriate topic for your audience and purpose.
- gather and organize information about this topic.

Examples of various writing forms, audiences, and purposes are listed in this chart.

Writing Form	Audience	Purpose
narrative poem	classmates	**to entertain** by telling a story in verse
business letter	store owner	**to persuade** to carry a product
how-to paragraph	campers	**to inform** about how to tie a square knot
friendly letter	cousin	**to express** feelings about an event

Graphic Organizers

Graphic organizers are tools to use in the prewriting stage of the writing process. Use them to generate ideas and to organize and focus on the information you will include.

Inverted Triangle Use an inverted triangle when you need to narrow your topic from a broad subject. This graphic organizer can be especially helpful when you are choosing a topic for a research report.

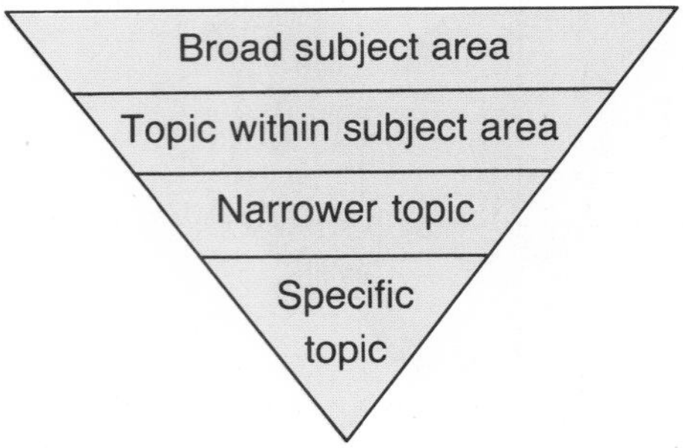

Time Line Use a time line to list events in the order in which they happen. A time line is useful when you are planning a story, a history report, or a biography.

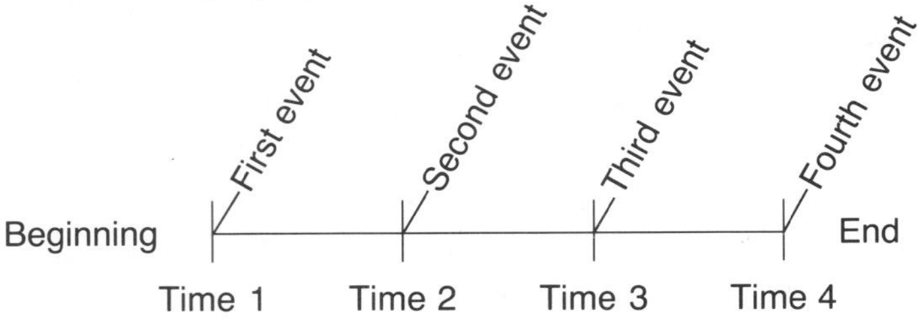

Cluster Use a cluster to help you think of ideas and details about your topic. This graphic organizer can be especially helpful when you are planning a description.

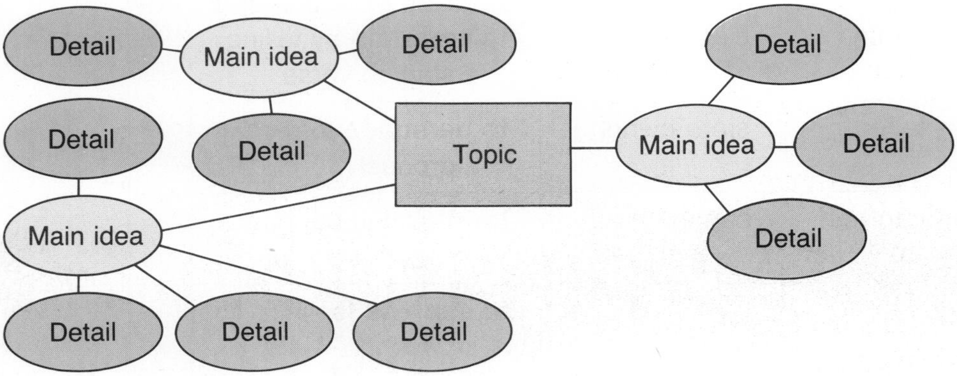

Chart Use a chart to arrange ideas that involve several categories of details and a process or actions that must be carried out in sequence. A chart helps you see all the parts of a process and the corresponding details at one time. This graphic organizer can be particularly helpful when you are planning a how-to paragraph.

	Category A	Category B	Category C
Step 1	Detail 1A	Detail 1B	Detail 1C
Step 2	Detail 2A	Detail 2B	Detail 2C
Step 3	Detail 3A	Detail 3B	Detail 3C

Venn Diagram Use a Venn diagram to identify the similarities and differences between two items. This graphic organizer can be helpful when you are planning paragraphs of comparison and contrast.

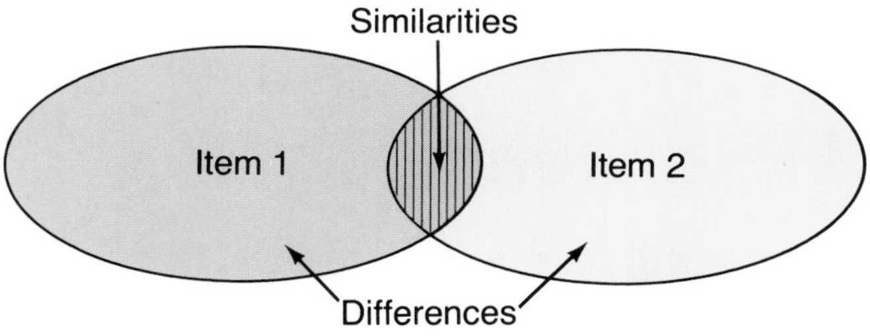

Outline Although an outline can be helpful in the planning of almost any form of writing, this graphic organizer is best suited to a composition that must include many main ideas and details. Use an outline to plan a composition that will include more than one paragraph, such as a research report.

Topic

I. Main idea
  A. Detail
  B. Detail
  C. Detail
II. Main idea
  A. Detail
  B. Detail
III. Main idea
  A. Detail
  B. Detail
  C. Detail

2 Drafting

In the drafting stage, you write the first version of your piece, using as a guide the ideas you gathered and organized in prewriting. Write freely, stating your ideas as clearly as possible without worrying about errors. As you write, you are likely to make discoveries that lead you back to the prewriting stage of the writing process to add, eliminate, or change ideas about your topic.

3 Responding and Revising

Responding and revising is the stage in which you evaluate your writing. By yourself or with a partner, respond to your writing by reviewing the organization, information, and language in your draft. Make sure your writing is appropriate for your audience and your purpose. Then revise your writing, making changes to improve it.

4 Proofreading

In the proofreading stage, you correct errors in grammar, spelling, capitalization, and punctuation. When you proofread, you polish your writing so that it is ready to publish.

5 Publishing

At the publishing stage, you share your writing with your audience. You might choose a written or an oral way of sharing. Consider your purpose and your audience as you decide on the best way in which to publish your work.

UNIT

1

Relating Personal Experiences

◆ COMPOSITION FOCUS: **Personal Narrative**
◆ LANGUAGE FOCUS: **Sentences**

A fire crackles under a starry sky, and you hear the sound of the familiar words *Gather round and you will hear a story.* Whose words are they, and to whom are they spoken? They are a storyteller's introduction to a type of communication that has been practiced throughout the ages. These words are spoken to listeners young and old. Through **narratives,** stories of actual or fictional events that take place over time, storytellers communicate experiences to their audience.

A story based on the storyteller's own experience is called a **personal narrative.** Writers of personal narratives use letters, magazine articles, or other forms of writing to relate what has happened to them. Jonathan Rosenbaum, for example, is a boy who used his own experience to write the magazine article "My First Assembly." He used details to show, not just tell, the reader what happened to him.

In this unit you will read "My First Assembly" and then learn how to write an effective personal narrative.

Jonathan Rosenbaum wrote "My First Assembly" *to express* his feelings about an event that happened to him.

Reading with a Writer's Eye
Personal Narrative

Jonathan Rosenbaum wrote a personal narrative in which he describes his first performance in a piano assembly. His narrative is personal because it is a story about his own experience and his feelings about that experience. Jonathan describes the assembly in a way that gives his readers the same feelings. As you read his narrative, notice the pictures it creates in your mind and the feelings it gives you.

My First Assembly
by Jonathan Rosenbaum

I COULDN'T BELIEVE IT. My first piano assembly. I would have to play a difficult Sonatina in front of hundreds of people. As I stared nervously at the crowd of parents, students, friends, and teachers, I wondered why I had ever consented to attend this. Yet, I was determined to prove to everyone, especially myself, that I could perform like a professional.

Soon the four head piano teachers announced the assembly would begin. Shakily I sat down with the other students who would be playing. Apparently, this must not have been the first assembly for the others since they seemed to be calmly awaiting their turn, whereas I was pale and fidgety. I hoped that the person playing before me did poorly so that if I made mistakes, it would not matter so much.

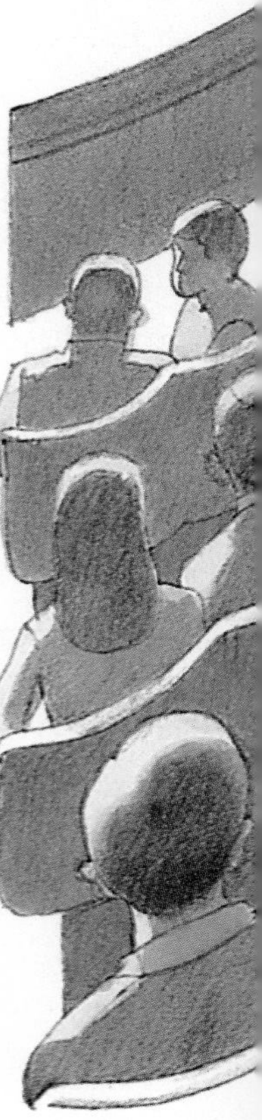

I was very anxious when the first student was called up to play. Articulately announcing her piece, the girl confidently adjusted the bench, warmed up her fingers, and began to do a finger dance on the keyboard. To my disappointment and terror, she played exceptionally well, making few errors in the notes. When her piece was finished, she regally bowed to the crowd's warm applause.

The next student was then called up to perform. He, too, did not make any mistakes, and so it proceeded, each student playing his material beautifully and professionally. The audience of relatives, friends, and teachers responded enthusiastically.

Both the expert performers and excited reactions increased my tension and anxiety. The standard of perfection set by those before me only made me more unsure and afraid of my own ability to perform.

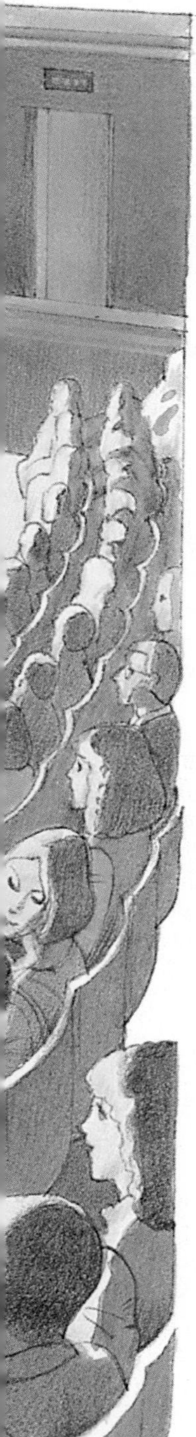

Finally, it was my turn. Hearing my name called paralyzed me. I felt like I do when I sit in the waiting room at the dentist's office, and the nurse calls me in for my examination. I knew that sooner or later I would have to go, but I really did not want to.

I tensely approached the mammoth piano. With sweat slithering down my neck, I stutteringly announced my piece. Fumbling, I adjusted the piano bench and limply sat down. I then gazed at the piano keys. They sneered back at me like the teeth of a monster about to gobble me up. I peered helplessly at the crowd. All eyes were fixed on me, impatiently waiting. A small internal struggle erupted. One side of me taunted, "You're going to make a muddle of it! Don't even try it!" The other side soothed, "No, try your best. That is all that is expected of you. However you play, if you honestly tried your best, you will always be a success."

I thought about this for a moment, took a deep breath, and then began to play. My hands quivered as they hit the ivory keys. As I got into the Sonatina, I realized that no rotten tomatoes were being thrown at me, no booing was echoing throughout the auditorium. The playing flowed till it became easy and natural. As my confidence built, so did the control of my fingers. Soon my total concentration and effort evaporated the audience, and I was alone with the piano and my Sonatina, enjoying the music I was creating. Finally, as I struck the finishing chord, the crowd rose in admiration and clapped approvingly. I happily and proudly bowed, and then I floated back to my seat.

The rest of the assembly was a blur. Outwardly I seemed to be concentrating on the music, but I was really thinking about what had just happened. I had almost let fear—the fear of failure, the fear of the ridicule of others—control me. I had forgotten that what mattered most of all was me and the way I felt about myself. With my new-found knowledge, I joined the other musicians in a final bow as my first piano assembly came to an end.

Respond

1. What feelings does Jonathan's narrative give you? Identify examples from his narrative that give you these feelings.

Discuss

2. Which parts of Jonathan's narrative can you picture in your mind? What details in the narrative create these pictures?

Thinking As a Writer
Analyzing a Personal Narrative

A personal narrative re-creates an experience that happened to the writer. Through the personal narrative, the writer attempts to share an experience with a reader. The writer tries to help the reader know what went through the mind of the writer.

With the writer as the main character, the story is told from the **first-person point of view.** To help the reader experience the event, the writer of a personal narrative presents what happened in **sequential order,** includes details, and shares his or her feelings.

Writer's Guide

A personal narrative
- uses the first-person point of view.
- presents events in sequential order.
- includes details and feelings.

I tensely approached the mammoth piano. With sweat slithering down my neck, I stutteringly announced my piece. Fumbling, I adjusted the piano bench and limply sat down. I then gazed at the piano keys. They sneered back at me like the teeth of a monster about to gobble me up. I peered helplessly at the crowd. All eyes were fixed on me, impatiently waiting. A small internal struggle erupted. One side of me taunted, "You're going to make a muddle of it! Don't even try it!" The other side soothed, "No, try your best. That is all that is expected of you. However you play, if you honestly tried your best, you will always be a success."

First-person point of view uses *I*, *me*, and *my* to present the event from the writer's point of view.

Sequential order arranges the event in time order. Words such as *then* help establish the order.

Details include clues that help the reader picture the event and that appeal to various senses—sight, taste, touch, smell, and hearing.

Discuss

1. What first-person words does the writer use in the paragraph above?
2. In your own words, describe what happened first, next, and last in the paragraph.
3. Which details in the paragraph help the reader picture what happened? How did the writer feel? Which details help show his feelings?

Try Your Hand

A. Analyze Personal Narratives Read the following personal narrative. List the events that happen in the narrative in sequential order.

> "Whoopee!" I yelled to no one in particular, running down the apartment stairway two steps at a time. "I won! I won the 'Trip Test' radio show contest for a free trip to Hawaii!" At the bottom step my pace slackened, and I strutted up the snow-filled street thoughtfully, my head spinning with visions of the hot sun and a week's vacation for two. Greeted by the sweet scent of piping hot apples, I quickened my gait as I crossed the threshold of the rich brownstone building. "Guess what, Charlene," I announced. "We are not going to have a white Christmas." How lucky I felt to be the one doing the giving for a change!

B. Identify Feelings Look back at the paragraph and write the feelings the writer expressed.

C. Add Details Add a sentence with details to the paragraph to show what might happen next.

D. Read Personal Narratives Choose a paragraph from "My First Assembly" on pages 10 and 11, or find another personal narrative in a magazine. Read the story, and then explain it to a partner, presenting the events in sequential order and identifying the writer's feelings. Include details to help your partner picture what happened.

Writer's Notebook

Collecting Emotion Words Did you notice emotion words such as *nervously* and *terror* in Jonathan Rosenbaum's story about his first piano assembly? Read the story again to find sentences with words that express feelings. Record each sentence in your *Writer's Notebook*, and circle the emotion word. If you don't know its exact meaning, look it up in a dictionary and record the meaning. Use emotion words to communicate feelings when you write and speak.

Thinking As a Writer
Visualizing Events and Feelings

Writer's Guide

To write a personal narrative, good writers
- picture in sequential order the things that happened.
- write details to show the reader what happened.

Good writers do not merely tell about an event. They include details that show what happened. To select details, writers **visualize,** or picture, what happened in time order. Read these sentences.

> I was very anxious when the first student was called up to play. Articulately announcing her piece, the girl confidently adjusted the bench, warmed up her fingers, and began to do a finger dance on the keyboard. To my disappointment and terror, she played exceptionally well, making few errors in the notes. When her piece was finished, she regally bowed to the crowd's warm applause.

To recall details, writers ask *who, what, when, where, why,* and *how* about an event. They try to remember what they saw, heard, smelled, tasted, and touched. When you write a narrative, you may want to use these charts to organize the details you visualize.

Questions	Answers
Who? What? When? Where?	

Senses	Sensory Details
Sight Hearing Smell Taste Touch	

Discuss

1. Which of the questions *who, what, where, when, why,* and *how* does the paragraph from "My First Assembly" answer?
2. Which details appeal to the senses? What feelings are recalled?
3. Read this sentence: *I squared my shoulders, caught hold of the Seeing Eye dog's hard leather harness, and took one trembling step forward.*

   Is this a good sentence for a personal narrative? Why or why not?

Try Your Hand

Visualize Details Think of an experience you had. Picture the details and recall your feelings. Use your senses to help you. Then write five sentences that include these details. Trade sentences with a partner, and discuss the picture your partner's sentences create in your mind.

Developing the Writer's Craft

Establishing a Point of View

Writer's Guide

Good writers

- craft their writing to reflect a point of view.

Skillful writers usually tell a story from a single point of view. Look at the following examples of three points of view.

1. I looked at Lim Sing despairingly. How could I make her understand? Leading her to the lake, I pantomimed drinking the water and doubled over as if it had made me sick.
2. Matthew looked at Lim Sing despairingly. "How can I make her understand?" he wondered. Leading her to the lake, he pantomimed drinking the water and doubled over as if it had made him sick.
3. Matthew looked at Lim Sing despairingly. He wondered how he could make her understand. Lim Sing furrowed her brow. She thought that he was upset with her. Leading her to the lake, Matthew pantomimed drinking the water and doubled over as if it had made him sick. Lim Sing's brow relaxed in sudden understanding.

In the first paragraph the writer uses *I* and *me* to write from the **first-person point of view.** The writer tells only the narrator's thoughts and feelings. In the second paragraph the writer uses the **limited third-person point of view.** The writer tells the reader what only one person, a character in the story, thinks and feels. The third paragraph uses the **omniscient third-person point of view.** Here the writer lets the audience know what each character thinks and feels. When you write personal narratives, remember always to use the first-person point of view.

Discuss

1. Look at the personal narrative on pages 10 and 11. What first-person words does the writer use?
2. Does the writer keep to the first-person point of view throughout the narrative? Give examples.

Try Your Hand

Use the First-Person Point of View Find a magazine article about an event. Imagine that you participated. Rewrite a paragraph in the story from the first-person point of view.

1 Prewriting
Personal Narrative

Writer's Guide

Prewriting Checklist

- ☑ Keep a journal.
- ☑ Select an event.
- ☑ Think about your audience and your purpose.
- ☑ Gather details.
- ☑ Organize the details.

Janice wanted to write a letter to her best friend, Rodney, who had recently moved to Georgia. Writers frequently use personal narratives in letters to tell about things that have happened to them. Janice used the information in the **Writer's Guide** to help her plan a personal narrative for her letter. Look at what she did.

◆ Brainstorming and Selecting an Event

First, Janice kept notes about her experiences in a journal. Then, she read over her recent entries to find news about herself that was likely to interest Rodney. Look at Janice's journal entries.

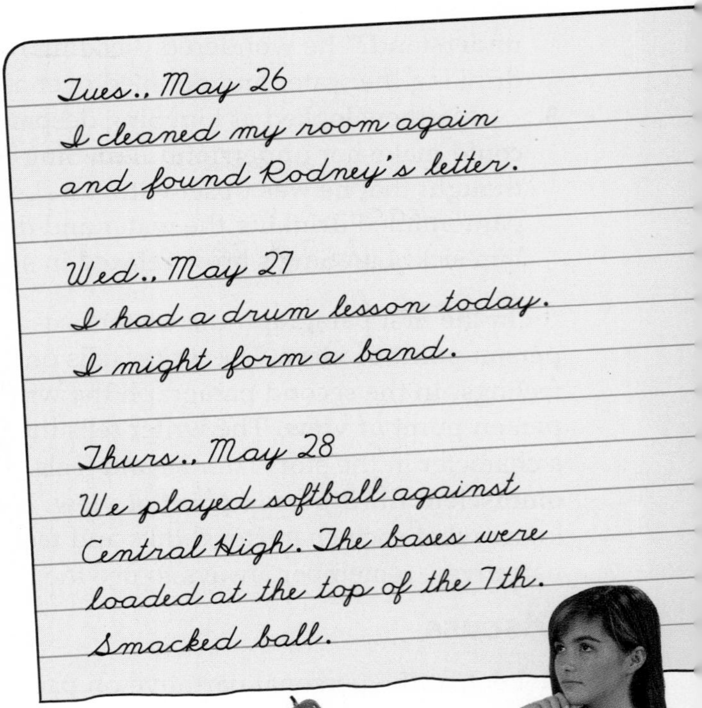

Tues., May 26
I cleaned my room again
and found Rodney's letter.
Wed., May 27
I had a drum lesson today.
I might form a band.
Thurs., May 28
We played softball against
Central High. The bases were
loaded at the top of the 7th.
Smacked ball.

Janice decided to write about the softball game because it had been an unusual experience and she wanted to share her excitement about it with Rodney. Since Rodney was a baseball fan, he was likely to be interested in the event. Janice saw that she had also noted details about the event in her journal. Therefore, she would be able to show rather than tell Rodney what had happened at the game.

Discuss

1. Look at each journal entry Janice wrote. Why do you think she entered these events in her journal? What did she include in every entry?
2. If Rodney took up drum lessons, which entry do you think Janice might have chosen? Why?

◆ Gathering Information

After Janice selected the event that she wanted to share with her friend Rodney, she gathered information for her personal narrative. Janice used the entry in her journal and talked to a friend on her team to help her remember details about the event. Janice wanted to include details that answered the questions *who, what, where, when, why,* and *how.* To do this, she first visualized the event in her mind. Next, she listed details that described what happened. Then, she remembered her feelings during the event and added them to her list. She noted as many sensory details as possible to show, not just tell, Rodney what happened and how it made her feel.

Coach said Carlota was hurt and I would hit instead.
top of the 7th inning
stood firmly in place, hands sweating, heart racing
kept my eye focused on off-white ball
swung—saw pitch curve
heard umpire yell strike one
felt pressured, nervous, dazed but determined
hands hot, clammy. Head pounding

Discuss

1. Look at Janice's details. Which of the questions *who, what, where, when, why,* and *how* do they answer? Does Janice need more details to answer the questions? If so, what are they?
2. Which senses did Janice use to gather details about the game? Give examples of other sensory details she could add.
3. Which notes describe Janice's feelings? What details does she include to support her feelings?

Organizing the Details

After Janice had gathered all the information she needed for her personal narrative, she was ready to organize her notes by using a diagram. Janice organized the details in sequential order.

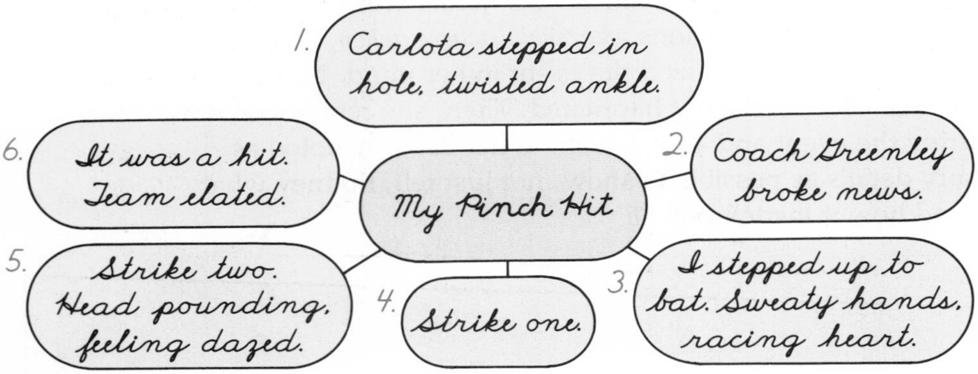

Discuss

1. What was the first detail Janice planned to write about? Why did she plan to write about it first?
2. What detail did Janice decide to tell about last? Why?

Try Your Hand

Now plan a personal narrative of your own.

A. Brainstorm and Select a Topic Make a list of events that happened to you recently. If you have a journal, use it for ideas.

- Cross out topics that are not important.
- Choose an event that is likely to interest your audience. Use this event for your personal narrative.

B. Gather Information Visualize your event. List details that answer the questions *who*, *what*, *where*, *when*, *why*, and *how*. Include sensory details, and list the feelings you experienced.

C. Organize the Details Look over your notes.

- Choose details that will help your audience picture the event.
- Arrange the details in sequential order. You may want to make a diagram like Janice's.

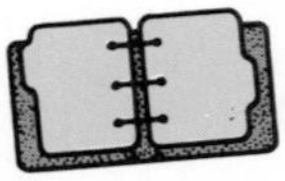

Save your notes and diagram in your *Writer's Notebook*. You will use them when you draft your personal narrative.

2 Drafting
Personal Narrative

Using her notes and diagram, Janice followed the checklist in the **Writer's Guide** to draft her personal narrative. Look at what she did.

> I know how much you enjoy baseball, so you should appreciate this story. You know I'm a pinch hitter on the Piermont softball team. Well, last Thursday was the big game against Central Junior High. We were losing 4 to 2 in the 7th inning.

Writer's Guide

Drafting Checklist

- ☑ Use your notes and diagram for ideas.
- ☑ Use details to show what happened to you.
- ☑ Arrange the details in sequential order.
- ☑ Include how you felt during the event.

Discuss

1. What details did Janice give to answer the questions *who, what, where, when, why,* and *how*?
2. Where might you add a detail about how Janice practiced? Why would you place it there?

Try Your Hand

Now you are ready to write a personal narrative.

A. Review Your Information Think about the information you organized in the last lesson. Decide if you need more details. If so, gather them.

B. Think About Your TAP Remember that your task is to write a personal narrative. Your purpose is to tell your audience what happened to you.

Task: What?
Audience: Who?
Purpose: Why?

C. Write Your First Draft Refer to the **Drafting Checklist.**

When you write your draft, put all your ideas on paper. Do not worry about spelling, punctuation, or grammar. You can correct the draft later.

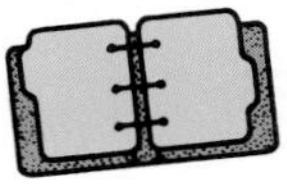

Save your first draft in your *Writer's Notebook.* You will use it when you revise your personal narrative.

3 Responding and Revising

Personal Narrative

Janice used the checklist in the **Writer's Guide** to revise her personal narrative. Look at what she did.

◆ Checking Information

When Janice read over her draft, she decided to cut an unnecessary sentence. To show her change, Janice used this mark ⸬. In the second paragraph, Janice added an interesting detail. To show her addition, she used this mark ^.

◆ Checking Organization

Janice moved a sentence because it was not in sequential order. To show that the sentence should be moved, she used this mark ○.

◆ Checking Language

In one sentence Janice replaced a word with a more exact word. She used this mark ^ to make her changes.

Writer's Guide

Revising Checklist

- ☑ Read your narrative to yourself or to a classmate.
- ☑ Think about your audience and your purpose. Add or cut information.
- ☑ Check to see that your personal narrative is in sequential order.
- ☑ Check your style. Decide if any words should be changed.

Replace — Thursday was the big game against Central Junior High. We were losing 4 to 2 in the 7th inning. Suddenly Carlota, our star hitter, hurt her ~~foot~~ ankle stepping in a hole while she ran to catch a fly ball. Then it was our turn to bat, bases were full, and Coach Greenley told me to hit for Carlota.

Move — I waited for the first pitch. I picked up my favorite bat and stood firmly in place with sweating hands and a racing heart.

Add — I kept my eye on the ball, but the first pitch was a curve. I swung early and missed badly. I should have been ready for the second pitch, another curve.

Cut — ~~My teammates groaned.~~ I prepared for the third pitch.

Discuss

1. Why do you think Janice added the detail about her first pitch? Do you agree with her decision to add it? Why or why not?
2. Could Janice have made other changes? Explain your answer.

Try Your Hand

Now revise your first draft.

A. Read Your First Draft As you read your narrative, think about your audience and your purpose. Ask yourself or a partner to respond, using the questions in the box. If you need help organizing a response group, refer to the **Tips on How to Speak and Listen in a Response Group** on page 23.

Responding and Revising Strategies

✔ Respond **Ask yourself or a partner:**	✔ Revise **Try these solutions:**
◆ Does my narrative show the event from the first-person point of view?	◆ **Add** details that tell how you felt during the event.
◆ Have I included the right number of details?	◆ **Cut** details that are unnecessary.
◆ Have I organized my personal narrative in sequential order?	◆ **Move** details that are out of order.
◆ Have I used exact words to tell what happened?	◆ **Replace** inexact words with synonyms that are more exact. See the **Revising Workshop** on page 22 and the **Writer's Thesaurus** at the back of the book.

B. Make Your Changes If the answer to any question in the box is *no*, try the solution. Use the **Editor's Marks** to show your changes.

C. Review Your Personal Narrative Again Keep revising until you feel it is well organized and complete.

EDITOR'S MARKS

- ∧ Add something.
- Cut something.
- Move something.
- Replace something.

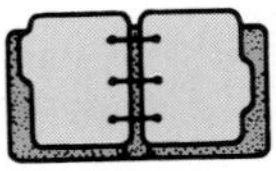

Save your revised personal narrative in your *Writer's Notebook*. You will use it when you proofread your narrative.

Revising Workshop
Using a Thesaurus

Good writers use words with just the right meanings to get their message across to their audience. If they cannot think of the exact word, they find it in a **thesaurus.** A thesaurus is a book of synonyms that are listed alphabetically. Sometimes antonyms are listed, too.

When you use a thesaurus, be aware of the **denotation** and the **connotation** of a word. The denotation of a word is the meaning that can be found in a dictionary. The connotation of a word is the positive or negative feeling that people associate with it.

Read these sentences.

1. With a strong sun and a <u>strong</u> wind, the weather was perfect for a hike.
2. With a strong sun and a <u>vigorous</u> wind, the weather was perfect for a hike.
3. The <u>mighty</u> wind whipped through my hair as I whistled my way toward the shore.

In the first sentence the writer repeats the word *strong*. To improve the sentence, the writer replaces one word in the second sentence with the more exact word *vigorous,* which has a positive connotation. In the third sentence, rather than repeat a word, the writer searched in a thesaurus for a synonym and found the word *mighty*. As you revise your writing, use a thesaurus to replace inexact or repeated words.

Practice

Rewrite each sentence, replacing the repeated word. Refer to your **Writer's Thesaurus** to find the word with the right connotation.

1. The painter was generally curt in interviews, so it was not surprising that his remarks to me were curt.
2. He is a man who detests reporters and detests publicity.
3. The artist happily prefers complete silence and happily works alone.
4. Although outsiders argue that he is aloof, his closest friends would contend that he is not aloof at all.
5. At night he gives his friends a tremendous welcome, setting his table with a tremendous variety of mouth-watering treats.

Listening and Speaking

Tips on How to Speak and Listen in a Response Group

There are several ways you can respond to your own and your classmates' writing. One way is to participate in a response group, a group of students who have come together to listen, respond, and share their writing. Response groups work best when they are limited in size. Three to five students is a good number. It is vital that all group members be active participants in the process of sharing and responding.

Speaking in a Response Group

1. Make copies of your work to distribute to group members.
2. Decide whether you want to read your material aloud or have each member of the group read it silently. Often, listening to your work can help you experience it objectively.
3. If you read your work aloud, read it twice. Allow at least a minute of silence between each reading so that your audience can organize their thoughts. When responding to your own work, make no apologies for it, and do not preface your reading with qualifying statements.
4. When responding to someone's work, you may want to use one of the following methods:
   a. List the main points and feelings it conveys.
   b. Summarize the work in one sentence that tells what it is about.
   c. Choose one word from the writing that describes the content.
   d. Choose one word that is not in the writing to summarize it.
5. Give specific reactions to specific parts. Avoid generalizations or meaningless comments such as "I really liked it, Sylvia, because it was really good." This says nothing.
6. Respect the authorship of the piece of writing. Realize that the writer owns that work and while you may give suggestions for improvement, you cannot impose your biases on the work.

Listening in a Response Group

1. Be quiet and listen while someone else's work is read.
2. Ask for specific feedback on your own work, but do not defend the work.
3. Do not reject what people tell you.
4. Try to understand the reasons for people's comments.

4 Proofreading
Personal Narrative

Writer's Guide

Proofreading Checklist

- ☑ Check for errors in capitalization.
- ☑ Check for errors in punctuation.
- ☑ Check to see that all your paragraphs are indented.
- ☑ Check for errors in grammar.
- ☑ Circle any words you think are misspelled. Find out how to spell them correctly.
- ⇨ For proofreading help, use the **Writer's Handbook.**

After revising her personal narrative, Janice used the **Writer's Guide** and the **Editor's Marks** to proofread it. Look at what she did.

Now imagine this. It was strike two, my head was pounding, and I felt dazed but determined. I swung my bat to meet the third pitch, a fast ball that sped towards me like (lightening) lightning Smack! My hit flew over first base and into right field. I only reached third, but (every one) everyone on base made it home, and the game ended 5 to 4 in our favor.

¶Write and tell me what you are doing on the fourth of july⊙ I wish we could spend it together. I really miss the fun we used to have here at Piermont.

EDITOR'S MARKS

- ≡ Capitalize.
- ⊙ Add a period.
- ∧ Add something.
- ∧ Add a comma.
- ∨ ∨ Add quotation marks.
- Cut something.
- Replace something.
- Transpose.
- ◯ Spell correctly.
- ¶ Indent paragraph.
- / Make a lowercase letter.

Discuss

1. Look at Janice's proofread narrative. What kinds of mistakes did she make?
2. Why did she start a new paragraph?

Try Your Hand

Proofread Your Personal Narrative Now use the **Writer's Guide** and the **Editor's Marks** to proofread your personal narrative.

Save your corrected personal narrative in your *Writer's Notebook*. You will use it when you publish your narrative.

5 Publishing
Personal Narrative

Janice made a clean copy of her personal narrative and checked it to be sure she had not left out anything. You can find Janice's personal narrative on page 49 of the **Writer's Handbook.**

Here's how Janice published her personal narrative in a friendly letter. If you need help writing a friendly letter, see the **Writer's Handbook.**

1. First, she added a heading, greeting, closing, and signature to her personal narrative.

Writer's Guide

Publishing Checklist

- ☑ Make a clean copy of your personal narrative.
- ☑ Check to see that nothing has been left out.
- ☑ Be sure there are no mistakes.
- ☑ Share your personal narrative in a special way.

2. Next, she addressed an envelope. (If you need help addressing an envelope properly, refer to the **Writer's Handbook.**) She mailed the letter and waited for a reply.

Discuss

1. What might happen if Janice forgot to gather all the information?
2. Why is placing the return address on the envelope important?

Try Your Hand

Publish Your Personal Narrative Follow the checklist in the **Writer's Guide.** If possible, write a friendly letter or try this idea for sharing your personal narrative:

- Collect the narratives of five classmates. Bind them into a book.

Writing in the Content Areas

Use what you learned to write about some kind of communication. You could write a personal narrative or another kind of paragraph. Use one of these ideas or an idea of your own.

Writer's Guide

When you write, remember the stages of the Writing Process.

- Prewriting
- Drafting
- Responding and Revising
- Proofreading
- Publishing

Social Studies

Even though modern languages contain hundreds of thousands of words, gestures or body movements are still useful in communicating. Think about some gestures you might use, such as those that mean "come here," "stop," or "be quiet." Describe some common gestures and their meanings, and tell in what situations they might be used.

Literature

Books and stories that tell about heroic acts are exciting to read. Readers often like to imagine they are the hero. Tell what happens in one of your favorite books of this type. Write the story as if you are the main character and the events are happening to *you*.

Health

To stay healthy in both body and mind, it is helpful to have someone you trust to listen to your everyday concerns. A trusted friend will listen without criticizing and will help you find solutions. Think about how close friends share their problems. Tell how someone can provide an understanding ear to a friend.

Science

Letters, telephone calls, sign language, and even smoke signals are ways to communicate. A more modern means of communication involves using computers and modems. Write about how you could send a message in one of these ways. Include diagrams to show how such a system works.

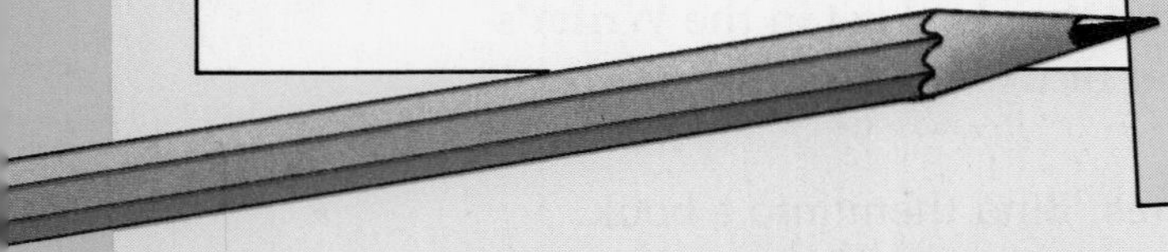

CONNECTING
WRITING ↔ LANGUAGE

Well-written paragraphs communicate thoughts and ideas to your reader. The following personal narrative illustrates one way to communicate with family or friends.

> Yesterday I discovered a new use for a roll of gray tape. As I toiled up the first big hill of the 10-kilometer bike race, my rear tire felt a little unstable. I quickly steered to the side of the road. There was a fat thumbtack in my brand-new tire. What could I do to fix it? Calm down and think, I said to myself. Then I remembered my favorite fix-all--the gray tape. In my bike bag I found a small roll. I ripped off a piece and wound it tightly around the puncture. Then I jumped back on my bike and pedaled faster than I ever had before. I streaked past the other riders and zoomed over the finish line first. What a surprising end that was for me!

◆ **Sentences in a Personal Narrative** The sentences highlighted in color are examples of declarative, interrogative, exclamatory, and imperative sentences. Some of the highlighted sentences are in natural word order, and some are in inverted word order. Using different kinds of sentences and inverted word order adds interest to writing.

◆ **Language Focus: Sentences** The following lessons will help you use different kinds of sentences in your own writing.

1 Four Kinds of Sentences

◆ **FOCUS** A **sentence** is a group of words that expresses a complete thought. There are four kinds of sentences: declarative, interrogative, imperative, and exclamatory.

A sentence expresses a complete thought. A sentence always begins with a capital letter and ends with a punctuation mark.

1. The stage is empty. sentence
2. Coming from behind the curtain.
   not a sentence

Every sentence must contain a subject and a predicate. The subject tells whom or what the sentence is about. The predicate tells what the subject is, does, or feels.

subject predicate

3. The mimes | bow to the audience.

There are four kinds of sentences. A **declarative sentence** makes a statement and ends with a period. An **interrogative sentence** asks a question and ends with a question mark. An **imperative sentence** gives a command or makes a request and ends with a period. An **exclamatory sentence** expresses strong feeling and ends with an exclamation point.

4. The performance is starting. declarative sentence
5. What will she do? interrogative sentence
6. Watch carefully. imperative sentence
7. How precisely she moves! exclamatory sentence

Guided Practice

A. Tell whether each word group is a *sentence* or *not a sentence.*

1. Performers study a lot.
2. In special classes.
3. Movement and imagination.

B. Identify what kind of sentence each is.

4. Will you watch me rehearse?
5. Tell me what you think.
6. What a good time we had!

THINK AND REMEMBER

- Be sure that each **sentence** expresses a complete thought and has a subject and a predicate. Begin a sentence with a capital letter, and end it with a punctuation mark.
- Remember that a **declarative sentence** makes a statement, an **interrogative sentence** asks a question, an **imperative sentence** gives a command or makes a request, and an **exclamatory sentence** shows strong feeling or surprise.

Independent Practice

C. Identifying Sentences Write *sentence* or *not a sentence* to identify each word group. For each sentence, write what kind of sentence it is.

7. Did you see my brother?

MODEL sentence—interrogative

8. Ryan just came back from the performance.
9. Jumping up and down and waving his arms.
10. What an amazing show the actors put on!
11. Quite a contrast to his usual self.
12. What does he usually do after a performance?
13. Drags himself in, discouraged and tired.
14. Listen to all the exciting details.
15. Have you ever seen such a big smile?
16. How different he looks when he's happy!

D. Proofreading: Capitalizing Sentences and Adding Punctuation Write each sentence correctly. Begin each with a capital letter, and end it with the correct punctuation.

17. the crowd was excited

MODEL The crowd was excited.

18. everyone applauded happily
19. they had seen an amazing show
20. how talented the mimes are
21. it is difficult to act out some emotions

Application — Writing

Pantomime Story Imagine that you are the person in the photograph. Write out a story you might communicate in mime. Include at least one declarative, one interrogative, one imperative, and one exclamatory sentence in your story.

2 Complete and Simple Subjects

◆ **FOCUS** The **subject** of a sentence names someone or something.

Remember that the subject names whom or what the sentence is about. The **complete subject** is all the words that make up the subject part of the sentence. It can be one word or many words. The words in color are the complete subjects.

1. A debate about a clean-air bill was held in the House of Representatives.
2. We watched the debate with interest.

The **simple subject** is the main, or key, word or words in the complete subject. The simple subject is usually a noun or a pronoun. If the complete subject is only one word or a name, the simple subject is the same as the complete subject. The words in color are the simple subjects.

3. A debate about a clean-air bill was held in the House of Representatives.
4. We watched the debate with interest.
5. Representative Michael Lee rose to respond.

In imperative sentences the subject is always *you* (understood). *You* refers to the person or persons to whom the command or request is given. *You* is only understood to be there. It is not actually written.

6. *(you)* Listen to both sides of the debate.

Guided Practice

A. Identify the complete subject in each sentence. If the subject is *you* (understood), answer *you*.

1. Members of the committee met today.
2. Our system of government works well.
3. Representative Thomas Crane stood up.
4. His two-year term of office is almost over.
5. A long debate took place.
6. Please vote for me.
7. Many voters applauded.
8. Tell me his name.

B. 9.–16. Identify the simple subject in each complete subject in **A.**

THINK AND REMEMBER

- Remember that the **complete subject** includes all the words in the subject.
- Remember that the **simple subject** is the main word in the complete subject.
- Remember that *you* (understood) is always the subject of an imperative sentence.

Independent Practice

C. Identifying Complete Subjects Write the complete subject in each sentence. If the subject is *you* (understood), write *you*.

17. The Speaker of the House called the meeting to order quickly and responsibly.

MODEL The Speaker of the House

18. Each state has representatives in the meeting.
19. This group of recently elected government officials meets often.
20. They discuss important issues concerning the rights of all citizens in our nation.
21. Each item is listed on a written agenda.
22. Every member votes on the items discussed.
23. Please listen carefully to the Speaker.
24. Representative Juan Perez was recognized by the Speaker of the House.
25. Each representative's words are carefully recorded and painstakingly documented.
26. Actions of the House of Representatives are recorded in the *Congressional Record*.

D. 27. – 36. Identifying Simple Subjects Write the simple subject from each complete subject in **C.**

27. The Speaker of the House called the meeting to order quickly and responsibly.

MODEL Speaker of the House

Application — Writing and Speaking

Speech Imagine that you are a politician. Choose a topic about which you feel strongly, and write a paragraph that you might deliver as a speech. Use at least one single-word or single-name simple subject and three complete subjects with details.

3 Complete and Simple Predicates

◆ **FOCUS** The **predicate** of a sentence tells what the subject is or does.

The **complete predicate** contains all the words and phrases in the predicate part of the sentence. Remember that the complete predicate must contain a **verb,** a word that tells what the subject does or is. The group of words in color is the complete predicate.

1. Denise is talking on the phone to her friend Mike.

The **simple predicate** is the verb of the sentence. It may be one word or several words. A simple predicate of more than one word is also known as a **verb phrase.**

2. Denise laughed at Mike's joke.

3. Denise's phone is ringing again.

If the complete predicate is made up of only one verb or a verb phrase, then the simple predicate is the same as the complete predicate.

4. Lauren is typing.

Sometimes one or more other words may separate the verb phrase in a simple predicate.

5. She can now call on a telephone device for deaf persons.

From now on in this text, the word *verb* will refer to the simple predicate in a sentence, and the word *subject* will refer to the simple subject.

Guided Practice

A. Identify the complete predicate in each sentence.

1. The telephone rang during the television show.
2. Dad is unhappily answering the phone.
3. Alex, the new soccer player, called.
4. Kim must return his call as quickly as possible.
5. Cliff will type a message for his sister.
6. Tell me about the newest suspense movie.
7. Nan has often told the ending to mysteries.
8. Sue does not reveal it very often.

B. 9.–16. Name the verb in each complete predicate in **A.**

THINK AND REMEMBER

- Remember that the **complete predicate** includes all the words in the predicate.
- Remember that the **simple predicate** is the verb or verbs in the complete predicate.

Independent Practice

C. Identifying Complete Predicates Write the complete predicate from each sentence.

17. The phone company provides a telephone device for the deaf.

MODEL provides a telephone device for the deaf

18. The initials TDD mean Telecommunications Device for the Deaf.
19. Users can connect their phones to the keyboard.
20. Messages are typed back and forth.
21. They can be printed on a screen or on paper.
22. A deaf person will not hear the ringing phone, of course.
23. A light flashes on and off instead.
24. Other devices have been created.
25. One is a type of smoke detector.
26. It is not much different from most alarms.
27. Yet it contains a special feature.
28. Most alarms make loud noises.
29. These sounds alert those around them.
30. Such sounds would not alert deaf persons.
31. A bright light alerts potential victims.
32. Many products have been created for the handicapped.
33. Many have assisted them in communicating.

D. 34.–50. Identifying Simple Predicates Write the verb from each complete predicate in **C.**

34. provides a telephone device for the deaf

MODEL provides

Application — Writing

Telephone Conversation Imagine that you are talking on a telephone. Write what you would tell a classmate about something that happened to you today. Add colorful details to help your classmate see the action just as it occurred. Use simple and complete predicates.

4 Word Order in Sentences

◆ **FOCUS** Words in sentences can be in natural or inverted word order.

In most sentences the subject precedes the verb. This is called **natural word order.** The word in color is the subject, and the verb is underlined.

1. The sailor walked ashore.

Imperative sentences are in natural word order.

2. (*you*) Find a shell.

Inverted word order occurs when a verb precedes the subject. Interrogative sentences are in inverted word order. If the verb in an interrogative sentence is two words, the subject may come between the two parts of the verb.

3. Away from the island swam the man .
4. Did he hear the ocean in the shell?

To find the subject in an inverted sentence, rearrange the sentence into natural word order.

5. The man swam away from the island.
6. He did hear the ocean in the shell.

Some inverted sentences begin with the word *here* or *there.* These words are never subjects.

7. Here is a deserted island .
8. There is only one person in the cartoon.

To find the subject in a sentence beginning with *here* or *there*, look for the verb and ask the question *Who?* or *What?* with it.

9. What is here?
10. Who is there in the cartoon?

To vary your sentences, you can sometimes put part of the complete predicate before the subject. These sentences are still in natural word order.

11. The water gushed into the huge ship.
12. Into the huge ship the water gushed.

Guided Practice

A. Identify whether each sentence is in *natural* or *inverted* word order.

1. Can you hear the ocean?
2. Two gulls flew above the beach.
3. There is a shell on the sand.
4. Look at that huge wave.

B. 5.–8. Identify the subject and the verb in each sentence in **A**. If the subject is *you* (understood), answer *you*.

> **THINK AND REMEMBER**
> - Remember that if the subject comes before the verb, the sentence is in **natural word order.**
> - Remember that if the subject comes after the verb, the sentence is in **inverted word order.**

Independent Practice

C. Identifying Word Order in Sentences Write *natural* or *inverted* to tell the word order of each sentence.

9. On the breakfast table was the newspaper.
MODEL inverted

10. Do you read comic strips?
11. Comics can be funny.
12. Here is today's paper.
13. On page 10 are the comics.
14. Read this cartoon aloud.
15. How silly that cartoon was!
16. Please pass the sports section.
17. Where are the baseball scores?
18. Here is the classified section.
19. The letters to the editor are amusing.

D. 20.–30. Identifying Subjects and Verbs Write the subject and the verb for each sentence in **C**. If the subject is *you* (understood), write *you*.

20. On the breakfast table was the newspaper.
MODEL subject—newspaper; verb—was

E. Writing Sentences in Natural and Inverted Word Order Write two sentences, each with the same complete subject and predicate. Write one sentence in natural word order and one in inverted word order. Remember to capitalize and to add end punctuation.

	Complete Subject	Complete Predicate
31.	this book	is a hystory of comic strips

MODEL *Natural:* This book is a history of comic strips.
Inverted: Is this book a history of comic strips?

	Complete Subjects	Complete Predicates
32.	the early comic strip "Hogan's Alley"	was among the most popular
33.	the famous strip "Krazy Kat"	came next
34.	the detective Dick Tracy	is still solving crimes
35.	my old favorite, "Peanuts,"	is here
36.	the characters Cathy and Garfield	are also popular today

F. Revising: Adding Variety to Sentences Rewrite each sentence, placing the subject in a new position. You may add words if you wish.

37. Samples of Rudi's drawings are in this sketchbook.

MODEL In this sketchbook are samples of Rudi's drawings.
Or Are samples of Rudi's drawings in this sketchbook?

38. Rudi has often thought about becoming an illustrator.
39. She drew pictures even as a child.
40. Some examples of her work hang on the bulletin board.
41. One of Rudi's picture stories is here.
42. Illustrating a children's book is among her ambitions.
43. You can tell a story through pictures.
44. Rudi will be a successful illustrator someday.
45. Successful illustrators are valued.
46. Pictures will illustrate her ideas.

Application — Writing

Cartoon Captions Imagine that you are the artist who drew the cartoon. Write what you think the man might be saying, thinking, and hearing. Try to write something that will be funny to readers of the cartoon. Use natural and inverted word order in your sentences.

5 Compound Subjects and Compound Verbs

FOCUS

- A **compound subject** is two or more subjects that have the same verb.
- A **compound verb** is two or more verbs that have the same subject.

Some sentences have two or more subjects that have the same verb. These subjects are called compound subjects. They are joined by the word *and* or *or.*

1. Lucia Diaz and Rita King are running in the 200-meter dash.

Some sentences have two or more verbs or verb phrases that have the same subject. These verbs are called compound verbs. They are joined by *and, or,* or *but.*

2. Diaz raced and won in the 100-meter dash earlier today.

A sentence may have a compound subject and a compound verb.

3. Diaz and King trained for longer races but did not enter them.

When a compound subject or verb is made up of three or more subjects or verbs, put a comma after each subject or verb except the last.

4. Kim Chu, Marty Bender, and Pat Hill are the best hurdlers.
5. They trained, practiced, and prepared for the event.

Guided Practice

A. Identify whether each sentence has a *compound subject,* a *compound verb,* or *both.* Name the subjects or the verbs in each compound.

1. The athletes and coaches are walking onto the field.
2. Fans, friends, and families are here for these exciting events.
3. Kim stretches her legs and shakes her arms before the event.
4. Marty looks at the large crowd and waves at his loyal friends.
5. Marty and Pat jump and run better than most athletes of their age.

THINK AND REMEMBER

- To form a **compound subject,** use two or more subjects that have the same verb, and join them with the word *and* or *or.*
- To form a **compound verb,** use two or more verbs that have the same subject, and join them with the word *and, or,* or *but.*
- With three or more compound subjects or verbs, use a comma after every subject or verb except the last.

Independent Practice

B. Identifying Compound Subjects and Verbs Write the compound subject, the compound verb, or both for each sentence. Write *compound subject, compound verb,* or *both* after each.

6. Reporters and broadcasters attend sports events.

MODEL Reporters, broadcasters—compound subject

7. Radio, television, and newspapers bring sports news to fans.
8. Writers and announcers report and describe major plays.
9. Television reporters and radio broadcasters sit in a special booth.
10. Photographers watch the action, focus their cameras, and shoot.
11. Television cameras record the action and provide replays.

C. Proofreading: Checking for Commas Write each sentence correctly. Add or delete commas where necessary.

12. Sports, news and entertainment are broadcast on television.

MODEL Sports, news, and entertainment are broadcast on television.

13. News announcer, and actor are only two of the many careers in television.
14. Writers conceive develop and produce scripts for shows.
15. Costumers artists and designers work behind the scenes.
16. Lights and scenery captivate audiences, and brighten a show.

Application — Writing and Speaking

Sports Bulletin Imagine that you are a radio sportscaster. Write a sports bulletin similar to the one in *Guided Practice.* Name the teams or athletes on the field, and describe what you see going on. Use at least two compound subjects and two compound verbs. Read your sports bulletin to a classmate as if you were broadcasting over the radio.

6 Simple and Compound Sentences

FOCUS

- A **simple sentence** contains one subject and one predicate.
- A **compound sentence** contains two or more related simple sentences.

A simple sentence contains one subject and one predicate.

1. Drivers wait.
2. The traffic is heavy on Dogwood Drive.

In a simple sentence the subject may be a compound subject, and the verb may be a compound verb.

3. The car and the van turned left. (compound subject)
4. Dad stopped and parked the car. (compound verb)

A simple sentence can also have both a compound subject and a compound verb.

5. The bus and the taxi turned the corner and headed east. (compound subject; compound verb)

A compound sentence contains two or more related simple sentences that are usually joined by a comma and the word *and, or,* or *but.*

6. You can turn here, or you can drive straight ahead.
7. The light changed, horns honked, and the cars moved forward.

Sometimes a semicolon joins the related simple sentences.

8. This street is one-way; you are going the wrong way.

Link to Speaking and Writing

Too many short sentences make writing dull to read, and short sentences sound monotonous when read aloud. As you revise your writing, combine related short, simple sentences into one compound sentence. What word joins the two sentences? What punctuation was added?

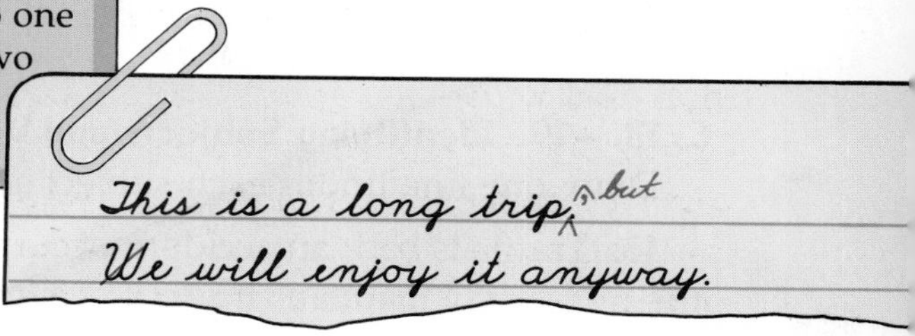
This is a long trip, but
We will enjoy it anyway.

Guided Practice

A. Identify whether each sentence is *simple* or *compound.*

1. Karim wrote to me and gave directions to his house.
2. I read them aloud, and Dad looked for signs.
3. Do we turn here, or should we ask for new directions?
4. Old River Drive is closed; we will follow Route 6.
5. Karim and his family live in that blue house.

THINK AND REMEMBER

- Use one complete subject and one complete predicate to form a **simple sentence.**
- Use two or more related simple sentences to form a **compound sentence.** To join the simple sentences, use a comma with the word *and, or,* or *but,* or use a semicolon.
- Combine related short, simple sentences in a compound sentence to avoid monotonous writing.

Independent Practice

B. Identifying Simple and Compound Sentences Write *simple sentence* or *compound sentence* for each sentence.

6. Traffic is bad; an accident occurred earlier.

MODEL compound sentence

7. Traffic reporting is an important job; many drivers depend on the reports.
8. Reporters in helicopters report traffic jams.
9. An accident or a stalled car could cause a jam.
10. Traffic reporters call in their reports to radio stations, and drivers listen for updates.
11. The drivers can then leave earlier, or they can take a different route.
12. Some traffic jams can be avoided; however, others cannot be escaped.

C. 13.–19. Identifying Subjects and Verbs Write each sentence in **B.** Draw one line under each subject and two lines under each verb.

13. Traffic is bad; an accident occurred earlier.

MODEL Traffic is bad; an accident occurred earlier.

D. Revising: Combining Sentences Combine each pair of sentences into one compound sentence. Join the sentences with a comma and *and*, *or*, or *but*, or use a semicolon.

20. Traveling is fun. An unfamiliar place can be confusing.

MODEL Traveling is fun, but an unfamiliar place can be confusing.

21. Many places have international signs. Anyone can read them.

22. These signs have no words. They have drawings instead.

23. You can find a restaurant. You can locate a telephone.

24. Some signs have a red slash. These signs mean "No."

25. International signs will guide you. You can always ask for help.

E. Writing Compound Sentences Think of another related simple sentence to combine with each of these sentences. Then write each pair as a compound sentence.

26. I want to visit Mexico.

MODEL I want to visit Mexico, but I do not speak Spanish.

27. I would like to travel.

28. You should learn a new language.

29. A foreign country is exciting.

30. The customs are different.

31. Vacation ideas need planning.

32. Climate and clothing must be considered.

33. Some people enjoy warm, tropical places.

34. Many travelers enjoy buses.

35. Trying new foods is an adventure.

36. Many tourists take photographs.

37. Some people enjoy traveling in groups.

Application — Writing

Directions Write directions for a classmate, telling the way from your school to your house. Point out landmarks along the way and any signs to be followed. Use at least three compound sentences in your directions.

7 Avoiding Sentence Fragments and Run-on Sentences

◆ **FOCUS** Two common sentence errors are sentence fragments and run-on sentences.

A sentence must have a subject and a verb and express a complete thought. To decide whether a group of words is a sentence, look for the subject and the verb, and ask yourself whether it expresses a complete thought. A **sentence fragment** may begin with a capital letter and end with an end punctuation mark, but it is not a sentence. It lacks either a subject or a verb and does not express a complete thought.

Fragment **1.** A strange coded message.
Correct **2.** A strange coded message arrived.
Fragment **3.** Delivered it.
Correct **4.** Someone in disguise delivered it.

Often, a sentence fragment should be part of the sentence before or after it.

5. You can read the message. If you break the code.
6. You can read the message if you break the code.
7. After dinner. We can figure it out.
8. After dinner we can figure it out.

A **run-on sentence** is a word group that should be written as two or more sentences or as a compound sentence.

Run-on **9.** I read the note now I will destroy it.
Correct **10.** I read the note. Now I will destroy it.
Correct **11.** I read the note, and now I will destroy it.

Guided Practice

A. Identify whether each group of words is a *complete sentence,* a *sentence fragment,* or a *run-on sentence.*

1. Coded messages during wartime.
2. Who wrote this it is confusing.
3. Elena found a message in code.
4. Deciphered the complicated code.

B. 5. – 8. Make sentences out of the fragments and run-on sentences in **A.**

THINK AND REMEMBER

- Avoid using **sentence fragments,** which lack either a subject or a verb and do not express a complete thought.
- Rewrite a run-on sentence as two or more sentences or as a compound sentence.

Independent Practice

C. Identifying Sentences, Sentence Fragments, and Run-on Sentences Write whether each group of words is a *sentence*, a *sentence fragment*, or a *run-on sentence*.

9. Solving puzzles one of my hobbies.

MODEL sentence fragment

10. A puzzle written in code is a cryptogram it is fun to solve.
11. Each letter of the alphabet is replaced by another letter.
12. Broken into groups just like words.
13. First, I look for short words, I find the words *a* and *I*.
14. Then I know what letters stand for *a* and *i*.
15. All the words with those letters.

D. Proofreading: Correcting Sentence Fragments and Run-on Sentences Rewrite each sentence. Correct each fragment by adding it to the sentence before or after it. Write each run-on sentence as either two simple sentences or one compound sentence.

16. Hieroglyphics is a kind of writing. In code.

MODEL Hieroglyphics is a kind of writing in code.

17. Ancient Egyptians used hieroglyphics American Indians did also.
18. In this writing system. The message is written in pictures.
19. Carved hieroglyphic writing was discovered. On a stone tablet.

Application — Writing and Reading

Coded Message Develop a code for a secret message. Write a message using your code. Write three or more sentences. Then exchange messages with a classmate, and solve each other's codes. Proofread the messages, and correct any sentence fragments or run-on sentences.

Building Vocabulary
The History of the English Language

The structure of your sentences in English owes its development to other languages. Knowing the history of the English language will help you understand this close relationship between English and other languages.

Language Families

The English language belongs to the Indo-European family of languages. Its words and sentence structures are like those of the major languages of Europe and the ancient languages of northern India. There is also a language family for each of these areas: northern Asia, southern Asia, China, Japan and Korea, northern Africa and the Middle East, southern Africa, and North and South America.

Old English

The history of modern English begins around A.D. 450. At that time the Germanic tribes of Angles, Saxons, and Jutes invaded Britain from Europe. The Germanic language of these groups largely replaced the Celtic dialects, which had been spoken by the people of Britain until then. Eventually the country and the language were known by the name of the tribe that conquered the most people—the Angles. **Old English** was primarily Germanic. A sentence in Old English is difficult for most people to understand today. Many of our most common English words, however, are derived from that Anglo-Saxon base, including *mother, father,* and *home.* Old English was also influenced to a lesser degree by invading Romans and Scandinavians.

Middle English

The Old English language lasted until the end of the eleventh century. In 1066 the Normans from France invaded Britain. Again, the invaders became the ruling class, and their language—a dialect of French—became the official language. The common people continued to speak English, though. After about 300 years English again became the chief language of the country, but it was quite different than before. Many French words had already been absorbed into English, and thousands more continued to come into the language. This form of English is called **Middle English,** and it lasted until about 1500.

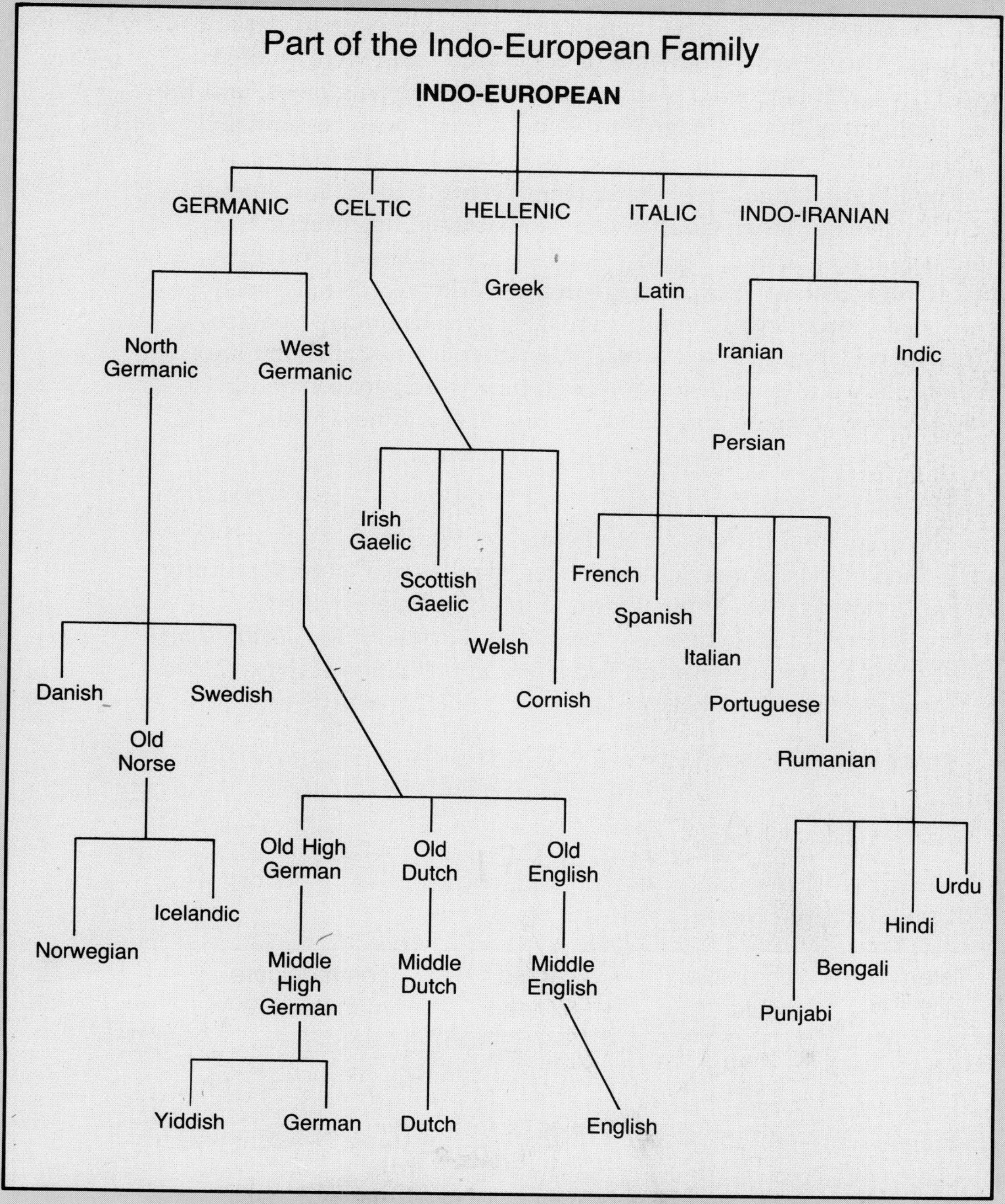
Part of the Indo-European Family
INDO-EUROPEAN
GERMANIC
CELTIC
HELLENIC
ITALIC
INDO-IRANIAN
Greek
Latin
North Germanic
West Germanic
Iranian
Indic
Persian
Irish Gaelic
Scottish Gaelic
Welsh
Cornish
French
Spanish
Italian
Portuguese
Rumanian
Danish
Swedish
Old Norse
Norwegian
Icelandic
Old High German
Old Dutch
Old English
Middle High German
Middle Dutch
Middle English
Yiddish
German
Dutch
English
Punjabi
Bengali
Hindi
Urdu

Modern English

The next major influence that affected the language was not an invasion of armies but an invasion of ideas. During the fourteenth through sixteenth centuries, there was renewed interest in classical learning. The classical languages of Greek and Latin were studied widely. English borrowed many words from these languages, and the development of the language into Modern English was essentially complete.

The English language of the sixteenth century looks and sounds basically like our language today. Since that time, however, the language has continued to grow. English has the largest and most varied vocabulary of any language in the world. Words have been borrowed from many different languages, such as Italian, Spanish, French, and languages of Africans and American Indians, and have been absorbed into English. Moreover, new words are constantly being created to name inventions, discoveries, and new ideas.

Etymology

The origin and history, or **etymology,** of words can be found in some dictionaries. An etymology traces changes in a word's meaning and structure from its original form to its contemporary form. Abbreviations for languages are used, such as *ME* for *Middle English, OFr* for *Old French,* and *Lat.* for *Latin.* The abbreviations are explained at the front of the dictionary.

peace [ME *pees,* fr. OFr *pais,* fr. Lat. *pac-, pax*]

Reading Practice

Write the word from the box that matches each word history. Use a dictionary with etymologies if you need help.

listen	chronicle	candid	communicate
skill	khaki	tornado	manufacture

1. Middle English *skil,* from Old Norse, meaning "distinction, knowledge"
2. French word *candide,* from Latin *candidus,* meaning "white," which came from *candere,* meaning "to shine"

3. Middle English word *listnen,* from Old English *hlysnan*
4. Urdu, from *khak,* meaning "dust," from Persian word *khak*
5. Variant of Spanish word *tronada,* meaning "thunderstorm," from *tronar,* meaning "to thunder," which came from the Latin *tonare*
6. Middle English word *cronicle,* from Norman French, variant of Old French *cronique,* from Latin *chronica,* from Greek *khronika,* meaning "annals," from *khronos,* meaning "time"
7. Old French word *manufactura* meaning "a making by hand," from Latin word parts, *manus,* meaning "hand," and *facere,* meaning "to make"
8. Latin word *communicatus,* from *communicare,* meaning "to impart," and from *communis,* meaning "common"

Writing Practice

Find each of the following words in a dictionary that gives information about etymologies. Then write a riddle for each word and an answer that relates to the word's origin. Write the answer on a separate sheet of paper. Have a classmate figure out the answer to your riddle.

Example: villain

Riddle: What kind of work should a villain do?

Answer: He should work on a farm. (from the Latin word *villanus,* meaning "farm tenant," and the Latin word *villa,* meaning "farmhouse or estate")

9. galaxy
10. comet
11. curfew
12. investigate
13. salary
14. muscle
15. discount
16. forecast
17. civilize

Project

As a class, brainstorm ideas about communication. Then make a list of thirty words relating to communication. Find each word in a dictionary, and write on separate index cards all the information given on each word's etymology. Sort the cards according to the most recent language given in the etymology. From what language are most of these words? Sort the cards again, this time according to the earliest language given in the etymology. From what language do most words come now?

Language Enrichment
Sentences

Use what you know about sentences to do these activities.

Tale Translation

The strange paragraph that follows is the beginning of an old folk tale. If you read it aloud to yourself, you will see that the writer used words that sound like the ones the story usually has. (Hint: The title is actually "Little Red Riding Hood.")

After you have figured out the story beginning, write it in correct English. Then find the simple subject and simple predicate of each sentence. Underline them and label them *S.S.* and *S.P.*

Ladle Rat Rotten Hot

Wants pawn term, a ladle gull lift wetter murder inner ladle card age honor itch offer beg, dock florist. Disk ladle gull worry ladle cluck wetter putty idle rat hot. Fur disk raisin, pimple colder ladle rat rotten hot. Wan moaning rotten hot's murder colder. "Tick disk basking winsome burden barter and shirker cockles to grown murder."

If you want to, try to continue the story with sound-alike words.

Noisy Punctuation

Victor Borge, a popular comedian, does a routine in which he makes sounds for the punctuation in a story as he reads the story aloud. If possible, listen to a recording of his act and notice the sounds he makes for end punctuation. Then use his punctuation sounds—or ones that you make up—as you read one of your favorite stories aloud to the class.

Fragments of Sense

Imagine that you find this torn-up message in your desk. Copy the sentence fragments on slips of paper. Arrange them however you like on a clean sheet of paper. Add a subject or a predicate to each fragment to make a sentence. Then complete the message.

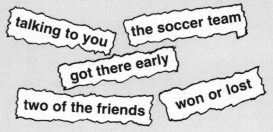

talking to you

the soccer team

got there early

two of the friends

won or lost

CONNECTING
LANGUAGE ↔ WRITING

In this unit you learned that sentences can make a statement, ask a question, give a command, or express strong feeling. You also learned that all sentences must have a subject and a predicate.

◆ **Using Sentences in Your Writing** Since sentences are the basic tools for communication, knowing how to vary them is an important writing skill. Pay special attention to the kinds of sentences you use as you do these activities.

I've Got It!

These people seem anxious to answer the telephone. Write three paragraphs describing the scene. Tell what each person is thinking as he or she rushes to the telephone. Try to use at least two sentences with compound verbs and two with compound subjects.

What's in a Word?

You learned about the history of some words on the **Building Vocabulary** pages. Now find out the etymologies of words that name tools used in communication.

Write a list of as many communication tools as you can. Remember to include reference books and inventions. Use a dictionary that contains word histories to find the etymologies.

Example:
pen—from the Latin word for *feather*
pencil—from the Latin word for *small brush* or *tail*
typewriter—from the Greek word for *dent* or *strike*

1 Unit Checkup

Think Back	Think Ahead
◆ What did you learn about a personal narrative in this unit? What did you do to write one?	◆ How will what you learned about personal narratives help you experience what another felt? ◆ How will knowing how to visualize events help you write a personal narrative?
◆ Look at the writing you did in this unit. How did knowing about the four kinds of sentences help you express your ideas?	◆ What is one way that you can use subjects and predicates to improve your writing?

Personal Narrative *pages 12 – 13*

Write the following events in sequential order.

1. The audience smiled, and they nodded in agreement as I spoke.
2. Why was I volunteering to speak at the school assembly?
3. I got my notes out to review one last time.
4. I tested the microphone, took a breath, picked up my notes, and began my speech.
5. The interviewing and note taking were the easy parts for me because I was not in front of an audience.

Visualizing Events and Feelings *page 14*

Write a sentence that shows an appropriate feeling for the event described.

6. Yesterday, my brother started his job at the newspaper.
7. My athletic brother had covered a ballet performance.
8. Today, his first article appeared.
9. Tom was not given a by-line for the article!
10. I asked him when he was going to cover a sporting event.

Establishing a Point of View *page 15*

Read each sentence. Write *yes* if it is from the first-person point of view. If it is not, rewrite the sentence in the first person.

11. With the thunderous applause echoing, he was pleased.
12. I could not believe how much they had enjoyed my song.
13. My teacher and I had worked very hard to evoke feelings.
14. They both worried about how to involve the audience.
15. As tears came to my eyes, the applause continued.

The Writing Process *pages 16 – 25*

Write the letter for the answer to each question.

16. When you plan a personal narrative, what type of event is best?
- **a.** An event that happened to you.
- **b.** An event in a famous person's life.
- **c.** An event without many details to clutter the narrative.

17. When drafting a personal narrative, what order should your writing follow?
- **a.** space order
- **b.** sequential order
- **c.** order of importance

18. What type of verb is more effective in a personal narrative?
- **a.** action verb
- **b.** verb in the future tense
- **c.** linking verb

19. What pronoun must be capitalized?
- **a.** We
- **b.** I
- **c.** He

20. Which is the best form for publishing a personal narrative?
- **a.** a news story
- **b.** a story
- **c.** a research report

Four Kinds of Sentences *pages 28 – 29*

Write *sentence* or *not a sentence* to identify each group of words. For each sentence, write what kind of sentence it is.

21. When a land stretches for thousands of miles.
22. The people have to communicate with each other.

23. What methods are available to us today?
24. What a variety!
25. Telephones and radios are the most common form of communication over long distances.
26. What the people will need for faster communication?

Complete and Simple Subjects *pages 30 – 31*

Write the complete subject in each sentence. Underline the simple subject. If the subject is *you* (understood), write (*you*).

27. Look at that rodeo clown's happy outfit!
28. People can express themselves with their clothes.
29. Sometimes clothes can show the season.
30. Styles frequently express a person's mood or attitude.
31. What clothes would you wear for a speech?
32. Do the slacks and the jersey fit the occasion?

Complete and Simple Predicates *pages 32 – 33*

Write the complete predicate from each sentence. Underline the simple predicate.

33. Telephone companies also have many devices for household telephones.
34. One common device is the mute button.
35. Telephones also may have a call-forwarding service.
36. Do you have any special services?
37. Try Dad's speaker attachment!

Word Order in Sentences *pages 34 – 36*

Write *natural* or *inverted* to tell what word order each sentence has.

38. What part of the newspaper do you read first?
39. Sports sections still are very popular in newspapers.
40. There are sports stories and scores for all readers.
41. The careful reader can follow golf, tennis, and swimming.
42. Slowly across the columns scan a fan's eyes.

Compound Subjects and Compound Verbs *pages 37 – 38*

For each sentence, write *compound subject, compound verb,* or *both.*

43. Newscasts inform and challenge audiences.
44. News, sports, and editorials are all parts of a newscast.
45. Men and women have starred and won honors as newscasters for decades on local and national broadcasts.
46. They write and present their own news stories.
47. Cameras and a set also are needed for a newscast.

Simple and Compound Sentences *pages 39 – 41*

Write *simple sentence* or *compound sentence* for each sentence below.

48. Maps are a form of communication.
49. Drawings show where to go, but numbers tell distance.
50. A map of a large state often is divided into two parts.
51. People make maps for personal use.
52. Some maps show roads; others show the terrain of the hills, lakes, valleys, and deserts.

Avoiding Sentence Fragments and Run-on Sentences *pages 42 – 43*

Write whether each group of words is a *sentence,* a *sentence fragment,* or a *run-on sentence.*

53. People in the armed forces with training.
54. First, they learn Morse code with flags then they use a radio.
55. Morse code is not a secret code.
56. Using dots and dashes to represent letters.
57. Code once dominated communications now it is rarely used.

The History of the English Language *pages 44 – 47*

Write the word from the box that matches each word history. Use a dictionary that provides etymologies if you need help.

talk	persuade	argue	word	woo

58. Middle French *persuader,* taken from Latin *persuadere*
59. Middle English *arguen,* derived from Old French and Latin
60. Middle and Old English, taken from German *wort*
61. Middle English *wowen,* from Old English *wogian*
62. Middle English *talken,* from Old English *talien*

UNIT

2

Giving Instructions

◆ COMPOSITION FOCUS: **How-to Paragraph**
◆ LANGUAGE FOCUS: **Nouns**

Do you know how to put up a tent? Would you like to learn how to play table tennis? Can you dig some clams and cook them for dinner?

If you want to learn any of these skills, someone can teach you. Another way to learn something is to follow written instructions.

Thousands of books, manuals, pamphlets, and instruction sheets are written and read every year. Experts who can explain clearly how to do or make something write these instructions. Tom Brown, for example, is an expert on survival and has written several books on the subject.

Tom learned some of his skills from his father and from a friend, and he taught himself other skills. He realized that people might be interested in learning his skills, and so he wrote his field guide on surviving in the wilderness. He wrote his instructions in a logical order so that anyone could follow them. Instructions on how to do or make something are found in **how-to paragraphs.** In this unit you will learn how to plan, write, and publish your own how-to paragraph.

Tom Brown wrote a survival guide *to inform* his audience about how to live in the wilderness.

Reading with a Writer's Eye
Information Article

In his book *Tom Brown's Field Guide to Wilderness Survival,* Tom Brown presents several simple shelters to build. Read this excerpt from *Tom Brown's Field Guide to Wilderness Survival* to learn how to construct emergency shelter.

from Tom Brown's Field Guide to Wilderness Survival

by Tom Brown

Natural Shelters

If you need a place to hole up quickly, you can find temporary protection in some kind of natural shelter. Almost anything that keeps out wind and weather will do. This might be a tree well, a fallen log, a matted clump of vegetation, a cave or rock outcropping—whatever you can squeeze into. If you are not sure what to look for, think about what animals use. Rabbits nestle into the thickest tangles of briars or bushes they can find. Foxes often den up in hollow logs or small rock caves. Birds usually roost beneath overhanging boughs. Almost all animals instinctively seek these natural shelters. You can do the same, keeping in mind some general guidelines.

First, make sure the shelter is safe. If you squeeze into a cave or under a fallen log, check to see that it won't collapse during the night. Try to make your natural shelter more habitable. Add sticks and boughs to "brush in" cave entries. Stuff hollow logs with a good supply of insulating leaves. Add protective brush and bark coverings to tangles of branches. Always line your shelter on the bottom so there is something between your body and the cold, wet ground. Also stay mindful of the fact that natural shelters are only temporary. If you have to spend a miserable night in the damp gloom under a fallen log, remember that tomorrow you can add on to it or construct a more permanent shelter from scratch.

The Wickiup

The wickiup is one of the simplest and quickest shelters to build. It was used extensively by the Indians of the plains and the Southwest—

especially in desert areas where building materials were scarce and warmth was not a critical factor. The name, appropriately, means "place of shelter."

To build a classic wickiup, find three strong ridgepoles and set them up tipi-fashion. If you have cordage, you can lash three ends together and open the poles like a tripod. If not, select ridgepoles with branches that will hook together at one end to form a sturdy base. Complete the skeleton by filling in the sides with branches.

Leave enough open space on the east side for an entryway. On top of the skeletal structure, pile any kind of brush you can find: sage, grasses, cactus pieces, bark slabs, creosote bush, rabbit bush, etc. Heap these materials into a dome. The more brush, the better the insulation. If grasses or similar materials are available, you can also create a loose thatchwork by bundling handfuls of it to plug into obvious holes.

For two people a wickiup six feet in diameter and five to six feet tall should be adequate. It can be made any size—even large enough to accommodate fifteen or twenty people. But remember that small is beautiful. For a cozy structure that still allows plenty of sleeping space, simply cut one of the ridgepoles shorter than the other two, forming a low, sloping, body-sized shelter.

Because of its low insulating properties, I recommend the wickiup primarily for desert and summer use. It provides good protection from sun and wind, but only marginal protection from rain and cold.

Respond

1. Would you be interested in reading the rest of Tom Brown's book?

Discuss

2. What natural animal shelters does Tom Brown suggest a person might use?

Thinking As a Writer

Analyzing a How-to Paragraph

Writer's Guide

A how-to paragraph
- names the process.
- identifies the materials used.
- lists the steps in the process.

A how-to paragraph explains how something is done or made. The steps must be stated so clearly that the audience can repeat the process.

Every how-to paragraph includes a statement that names the **process** it will explain. It also lists the **materials** to use and the **steps** to follow when performing the process. Note how Tom Brown has accomplished this in an excerpt from *Tom Brown's Field Guide to Wilderness Survival.*

The Wickiup

To build a classic wickiup, find three strong ridgepoles and set them up tipi-fashion. If you have cordage, you can lash three ends together and open the poles like a tripod. If not, select ridgepoles with branches that will hook together at one end to form a sturdy base. Complete the skeleton by filling in the sides with branches.

Leave enough open space on the east side for an entryway. On top of the skeletal structure, pile any kind of brush you can find: sage, grasses, cactus pieces, bark slabs, creosote bush, rabbit bush, etc. Heap these materials into a dome. The more brush, the better the insulation. If grasses or similar materials are available, you can also create a loose thatchwork by bundling handfuls of it to plug into obvious holes.

The **process statement** tells what the paragraphs will explain.

The **materials needed** are sometimes listed separately. Otherwise, they are included in the steps.

The **steps** explain step-by-step how to perform the process. The steps are arranged in sequential order.

Discuss

1. What process is explained by this paragraph?
2. What materials are needed to build a wickiup?
3. What are the steps for building a wickiup?

Try Your Hand

A. Analyze How-to Paragraphs Read these how-to paragraphs about other survival skills. Name the process that each begins to describe and list the steps given so far to perform the process.

1. A severe sunburn may cause fever, weakness, and chills. If the skin is reddened but there are no blisters, treat the burn with cool, wet compresses or cold water. Then apply moisturizing cream and a dry dressing.

2. To form a figure-eight bandage on the ankle, prepare to make several turns of the bandage. To begin, wrap the bandage two or three times around the middle of the foot. Next, carry the bandage in a diagonal path upward, across the foot, and around the ankle. To finish the first turn, carry the bandage diagonally downward across the front of the foot and under the arch.

B. List the Materials Look back at the paragraphs above. For each paragraph, make a list of materials needed to perform the process.

C. Read How-to Paragraphs Find a how-to paragraph on a product label or in a manual at home. Read the paragraph to a partner, pointing out the process and the materials. Identify the steps, listing them in sequential order.

Writer's Notebook

Collecting Wilderness Words Did you notice the words naming natural objects in the paragraphs on natural shelters? The writer used words such as *cave, outcropping,* and *briars* to refer to rock formations and vegetation. Read the selection again, and write in your *Writer's Notebook* the words that are unfamiliar to you. Look up the words in a dictionary and record their meanings. Remember to use these words when you write or speak about the wilderness.

Thinking As a Writer

Evaluating to Select Essential Information

Writer's Guide

To write a how-to paragraph, good writers
- evaluate the possible steps and details.
- include only the steps and details necessary to explain the process.

In a good how-to paragraph, a writer includes just the right amount of information to explain the process. The steps must be complete, but unnecessary information should be left out.

1. First, remove your helmet and empty your pockets.
2. ~~Items in your pockets take up unnecessary space.~~
3. Arrange to push the helmet and other gear in front of you.
4. ~~If water from above drips on your head, ignore it.~~
5. For assistance from the cave explorer ahead of you, attach your gear to that person's foot.

The writer of the list is planning a how-to paragraph about the process of crawling through a cave. The writer has evaluated which statements on the list are necessary and which are not.

Statements 1, 3, and 5 are necessary because they provide two steps and a detail that explain the process. The writer has crossed out statements 2 and 4 because they do not give necessary information. When you write a how-to paragraph, be sure to list necessary steps.

Discuss

1. Look at the second paragraph on how to build a wickiup on page 57. Is every sentence in the paragraph necessary? Why or why not?
2. Read this step: *To climb out of the cave, prepare a ladder.* Would you add it to the steps for crawling through a cave? Why or why not?

Try Your Hand

Evaluate to Select Essential Information Write only the steps that should be included in a paragraph with this topic sentence.

Even experts need to know how to act when their canoe capsizes.

1. If rescuers are nearby, hold onto the overturned canoe.
2. Then follow your rescuers' instructions.
3. To avoid capsizing, carry your canoe to safer water.

Developing the Writer's Craft
Using Precise Words

Writer's Guide

Good writers
- give the reader exact information by using precise words.

Because how-to paragraphs prepare the reader to perform a process, instructions must be exact and easy to follow. How-to paragraphs may contain technical information. They may list ingredients, materials, or steps. To give the reader a clear explanation, a good writer uses precise or specific words.

Read these sentences from "The Wickiup."

1. Leave enough open space on the east side for an entryway.
2. On top of the skeletal structure, pile any kind of brush you can find: sage, grasses, cactus pieces, bark slabs, creosote bush, rabbit bush, etc.

The writer carefully chose the underlined words to give the reader exact information. In the first sentence a specific adjective tells exactly where to place the entryway. The word is not especially technical or complicated, but it identifies an exact location. In the second sentence specific nouns tell readers exactly what kind of brush they might use. It gives specific possibilities and concrete suggestions. Because each sentence uses precise words, the steps are clear and easy for a reader to follow.

When you write your how-to paragraph, try to be as specific as possible. Use precise words to help your readers know exactly how to perform each step.

Discuss

1. Read this sentence from the second paragraph on page 57: *Heap these materials into a dome.* Which words in the sentence are precise words?
2. Look back at "The Wickiup" on pages 56 and 57. Which paragraph tells you how large to make the wickiup? What kind of precise words did the writer use in this paragraph? Why?

Try Your Hand

Use Precise Words Read again the section on natural shelters on page 56. Write four sentences for a paragraph on how to build a natural shelter. Use the most precise words you can in your sentences.

1 Prewriting
How-to Paragraph

Writer's Guide

Prewriting Checklist

- ☑ Brainstorm topics.
- ☑ Choose a process.
- ☑ Think about your audience and your purpose.
- ☑ Gather information.
- ☑ Organize the steps.

Phillip was an expert in outdoor living and wanted to share his skills with his classmates. He used the information in the **Writer's Guide** to help plan his how-to paragraph. Look at what he did.

◆ Brainstorming and Selecting a Topic

First, Phillip brainstormed a list of possible topics for a how-to paragraph. Look at Phillip's list. He thought of skills he knew how to perform, and he listed everything that came to mind.

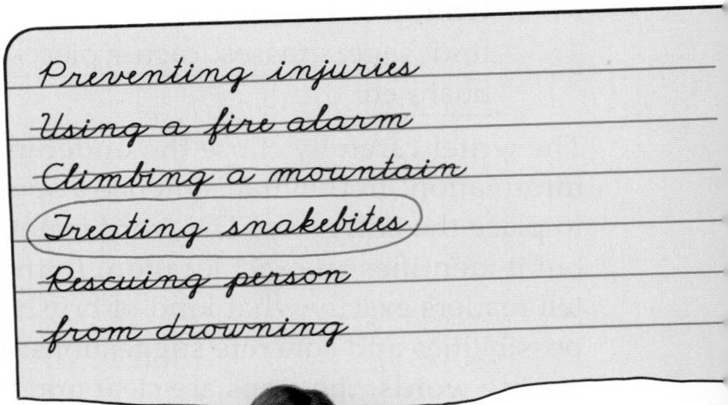

Next, Phillip looked at his list and crossed off topics for which he did not know every step or was uncertain of the correct order of the steps. He also crossed off topics that were too general for a paragraph and topics that would not interest his audience.

Finally, Phillip circled the most interesting topic that was left on his list. He decided to write about treating snakebites. Since his school was located in a desert area, home to several types of snakes, the subject was likely to be of high interest to his audience. Phillip also knew all the proper steps for treating the victim of a snakebite.

Discuss

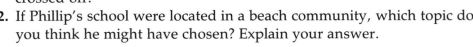

1. Look at each topic Phillip crossed off his list. Why do you think it was crossed off?
2. If Phillip's school were located in a beach community, which topic do you think he might have chosen? Explain your answer.

Gathering Information

After Phillip selected his topic, he gathered information for his how-to paragraph. He listed steps and materials needed for treating snakebites.

Notes for Steps

Calm victim.

Identify snake if possible; then retreat from snake's range.

Wear boots in snake areas.

Apply splint, keeping bitten part below heart.

Get to hospital. If over 2 hours away, pad bite and wrap with elastic wrap.

If necessary, get expert to draw out poison with snakebite kit.

Materials

splint, 2 inch by 2 inch cloth pad, elastic wrap, snakebite kit

Discuss

1. Look back at the notes Phillip prepared for his how-to paragraph. Which notes mention materials?
2. Read Phillip's steps. Are they written in a sensible order? Explain your answer.

Organizing Notes

After Phillip gathered all the information he needed for his how-to paragraph, he was ready to organize his notes. He knew his paragraph should include only steps for how to treat a snakebite victim. He selected those steps from his notes. Phillip listed the materials next to the step where that particular material would be used. Look at Phillip's list on the following page.

	Steps
	1. Identify snake.
	2. Calm victim.
Cloth, stick	3. Apply splint.
	4. Get to hospital.
Pad, elastic	5. Wrap bite.
Snakebite kit	6. Get expert to draw poison.

Discuss

1. Look back at Phillip's notes. Which notes were left out of his list? Why did he decide to leave them out?
2. Why did Phillip arrange the steps in the order shown?

Try Your Hand

Now plan a how-to paragraph of your own.

A. Brainstorm and Select a Topic Brainstorm a list of possible topics. Then think about each topic and your audience.

- Cross out topics that will not interest your audience.
- Cross out topics for which you do not know every step.
- Circle the topic left on your list that will be most useful to your audience. This will be the topic of your how-to paragraph.

B. Gather Information When you are satisfied with your topic, review the steps needed to perform the process. Make notes, listing everything that comes to mind. Let one step lead to the next. Recall the materials needed for the process.

C. Organize the Steps Look over your notes.

- A how-to paragraph should include only essential information; cross out any unnecessary steps or details.
- Think about your audience. Plan how to state the process. Organize the steps in sequential order. You may want to make a list like Phillip's.

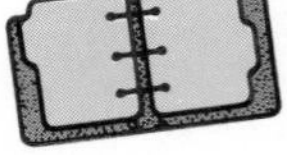

Save your notes and your list in your *Writer's Notebook*. You will use them when you draft your how-to paragraph.

2 Drafting
How-to Paragraph

Using his notes and his list, Phillip followed the **Writer's Guide** to draft his how-to paragraph. Look at what he did.

> **Writer's Guide**
>
> **Drafting Checklist**
>
> - ☑ Use your notes and list for ideas.
> - ☑ Name the process.
> - ☑ Write the steps in sequential order.
> - ☑ Identify the materials needed.

```
    Treating a snakebite victim requires quick
action and immediate medical attention. See if
you recognize the kind of snake before
retreating from its striking range. Calm the
victim, and splint the bitten body part.
```

Discuss

Did Phillip write a good topic sentence for his how-to paragraph? Explain your answer. What is another topic sentence he might use?

Try Your Hand

Now you are ready to write a how-to paragraph.

A. Review Your Information Think about the information you gathered and organized in the last lesson. Decide whether you need more information or whether you need to reorder the steps. If so, gather the information and make the changes.

B. Think About Your TAP Remember that your task is to write a how-to paragraph. Your purpose is to instruct your audience so that they could perform the process you have selected.

Task: What?
Audience: Who?
Purpose: Why?

C. Write Your First Draft Refer to the **Drafting Checklist.**

When you write your draft, just put all your ideas on paper. Do not worry about spelling, punctuation, or grammar. You can correct the draft later.

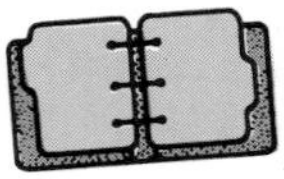

Save your first draft in your *Writer's Notebook.* You will use it when you revise your how-to paragraph.

3 Responding and Revising
How-to Paragraph

Phillip used the checklist in the **Writer's Guide** to help him revise his how-to paragraph. Look at what he did.

◆ Checking Information

Phillip decided to replace a vague phrase with a more exact word. To show his change, Phillip used this mark ^‾ . He also used this mark ⌐ to cut an unnecessary sentence from the paragraph.

◆ Checking Organization

Phillip found that his paragraph lacked **coherence,** the logical arrangement of detail sentences that allows one idea to flow smoothly to the next. One step was not in sequential order. To show that the step should be moved, Phillip used this mark ◯ . He also used this mark ^ to add some transitional words.

◆ Checking Language

When Phillip reread his paragraph, he found some inexact language. He used this mark ^‾ to replace it with a more precise word.

Writer's Guide

Revising Checklist

- ☑ Read your paragraph to yourself or to a partner.
- ☑ Think about your audience and your purpose. Add or take out information.
- ☑ Check to see that your paragraph is organized correctly and contains only essential information.
- ☑ Check your language for precise word choice.

Add — Cut — Replace — Move

Treating a snakebite victim requires quick action and immediate medical attention. ^First, See if you recognize the kind of snake before retreating from its striking range. ^Next, Calm the victim, and splint the bitten body part, remembering to keep the bitten area below the heart. ~~Splints are used for sprains and fractures as well as bites.~~ ^Then, Proceed to the hospital if one is less than ~~a few~~ ^two hours away. To make the splint, use a stick or other nearby object and a piece of cloth.

Discuss

1. What detail did Phillip delete? Why did he take it out?
2. Was it important for Phillip to use a more precise word in explaining when to proceed to a hospital? Explain your answer.

Try Your Hand

Now revise your first draft.

A. Read Your First Draft As you read your paragraph, think about your audience and your purpose. Read your paragraph silently or to a partner to see if it is complete and well organized. Ask yourself or your partner the questions in the box below.

Responding and Revising Strategies

✔ Respond **Ask yourself or a partner:**	✔ Revise **Try these solutions:**
◆ Do all the steps include essential information about the process?	◆ **Cut** information that is not essential.
◆ Have I included all necessary steps?	◆ **Add** any steps that may be missing.
◆ Are the steps in logical order?	◆ **Move** any steps that are not in sequential order.
◆ Is the order clear?	◆ **Add** transitional words or expressions to some of the sentences. See the **Revising Workshop** on page 68.
◆ Is the language precise?	◆ **Replace** general words with precise ones. See the **Writer's Thesaurus** at the back of the book.

B. Make Your Changes If the answer to any question in the box is *no,* try the solution. Use the **Editor's Marks** to show your changes.

C. Review Your How-to Paragraph Again Decide whether there is anything else you want to revise. Keep revising your paragraph until you feel it is well organized and complete.

EDITOR'S MARKS

- ∧ Add something.
- Cut something.
- Move something.
- Replace something.

Save your revised how-to paragraph in your *Writer's Notebook.* You will use it when you proofread your paragraph.

Revising Workshop
Achieving Coherence

A paragraph has **coherence** when its ideas are arranged in a clear order and each sentence flows smoothly to the next. Writers use **transitional words and expressions** as one way to achieve coherence. These words and expressions help the sentences in a paragraph flow in a logical order. Look at the boldfaced words in this paragraph.

> It's easy to estimate distance with a map. **First,** pinpoint a starting location. **Then,** pinpoint a destination. Place the straight edge of a piece of paper over the map in line with the starting and ending points. Mark the starting and ending points on the paper. **Finally,** match the marks on the paper to the scale on the map.

The writer used time-order words to help the writing flow from one sentence to the next. Various time-order words and phrases, such as those in this list, can be used to achieve coherence.

after	eventually	now
afterward	finally	not long after
as time passed	first, second, (etc.)	presently
at last	in the meantime	since
at the same time	later	soon
at this point	meanwhile	then
before	next	to begin with

Practice

Rewrite the following sentences, adding transitional words or expressions from the list.

1. Administer treatment for frostbite in a location where the frostbitten body part can be kept thawed. Submerge the hand or the foot in water warmed to between 102 and 105 degrees Fahrenheit.

2. Leave the hand or the foot submerged for at least 30 minutes. Keep stirring the water to speed thawing.

3. The body part should soon thaw. The skin will appear softened, and color and feeling will return.

4. Cover the thawed skin with fluffy bandages. Seek medical assistance.

4 Proofreading
How-to Paragraph

Writer's Guide

Proofreading Checklist

- Check for errors in capitalization.
- Check for errors in punctuation. Be sure that you have added commas to compound sentences.
- Be sure all your paragraphs are indented.
- Check for errors in your grammar.
- Circle any words you think are misspelled. Find out how to spell them correctly.
- ⇨ For proofreading help, use the **Writer's Handbook.**

After revising his second how-to paragraph, Phillip used the **Writer's Guide** and the **Editor's Marks** to proofread it. Look at what he did.

¶ Get an experienced person to draw out the poison with the snakebite kit⊙ this is only necessary if the bite is from a (rattle snake) and medical care is over an hour away. Then, wash the bite with soap and water, and get the victim to a doctor or a hospital. See that the victim gets an (antibiottic)

rattlesnake

antibiotic

EDITOR'S MARKS

- Capitalize.
- Add a period.
- Add something.
- Add a comma.
- Add quotation marks.
- Cut something.
- Replace something.
- Transpose.
- Spell correctly.
- Indent paragraph.
- Make a lowercase letter.

Discuss

1. Look at Phillip's proofread paragraph. What kinds of mistakes did he make?
2. Why did Phillip add commas in one sentence?

Try Your Hand

Proofread Your How-to Paragraph Now use the **Writer's Guide** and the **Editor's Marks** to proofread your paragraph.

Save your corrected how-to paragraph in your *Writer's Notebook.* You will use it when you publish your paragraph.

5 Publishing
How-to Paragraph

Phillip made a clean copy of his how-to paragraph and checked it to make sure none of the steps were left out. Then he shared the paragraph with his classmates by giving a demonstration speech. You can find Phillip's how-to paragraph on page 40 of the **Writer's Handbook.**

Here's how Phillip gave a demonstration speech based on his how-to paragraph.

1. First, he read over his paragraph and listed the steps on a notecard. He highlighted key words to help him remember the order of the steps. He got any materials needed to demonstrate the process.

Writer's Guide

Publishing Checklist

- ☑ Make a clean copy of your how-to paragraph.
- ☑ Check to see that no step has been left out.
- ☑ Check to see that there are no mistakes.
- ☑ Share your paragraph in a special way.

2. He practiced giving his speech and using his visual aids by himself and with a partner.

3. Before he gave his speech, he referred to the **Tips on How to Give and Follow Oral Directions** on page 71. These tips helped him to deliver his speech clearly and listen to other speeches attentively. After he delivered his speech, he answered questions from his audience.

Discuss

1. What might have happened if Phillip had not practiced giving the speech?
2. Why is it important to practice using visual aids?

Try Your Hand

Publish Your How-to Paragraph Follow the checklist in the **Writer's Guide.** If possible, give a demonstration speech, or try one of these ideas for sharing your how-to paragraph.

- Give the paragraph to a classmate to read. Then see if your classmate can perform the process correctly.
- Share your paragraph with classmates who have written their own how-to paragraphs. Gather the paragraphs together to form a how-to book. Make a copy of the book for everyone in the group.

Listening and Speaking

Tips on How to Give and Follow Oral Directions

Use the following guidelines for delivering or listening to a speech.

Giving Directions

1. Be sure to present your points in order, dividing them into steps.
2. Present complete information, using exact words and measures.
3. Define or illustrate difficult terms and concepts. You might use a diagram, such as a graph, or you might demonstrate a process, such as preparing an arm sling.
4. Talk confidently and enthusiastically when you speak. Look at the audience.

Following Directions

1. Place all of your attention on the person giving the directions.
2. Take notes on directions that are lengthy or complicated.
3. Listen for exact words and numbers, for example, *Find a triangular cloth for the arm sling; make two or three turns of the bandage.*
4. After the speaker is finished, ask questions for clarification.

Writing in the Content Areas

Use what you learned to tell how to do something. Write a how-to paragraph using one of these ideas or an idea of your own.

Writer's Guide

When you write, remember the stages of the Writing Process.

- Prewriting
- Drafting
- Responding and Revising
- Proofreading
- Publishing

Fine Arts

You do not need a radio or a fancy musical instrument to have music wherever you go. Tell how to make a homemade instrument, such as a kazoo, a drum, or something to strum. Try to use everyday materials in your instructions.

Physical Education

Your front steps or a trailside campfire are both places where you might want to play a game. Tell how to play one of your favorite games. It might be one you and your friends have made up. What are the rules? What equipment do you need? How many people can play?

Business

A sidewalk or garage sale is a good way to meet people in your neighborhood while your junk becomes someone else's bargains. Tell how to organize and set up a garage or sidewalk sale. Explain how you would attract customers.

Health

On a hike in the mountains or in a city park, a healthful snack stowed in your backpack is welcome. Tell how to prepare a take-along picnic. Try to include foods from each of these groups: meat (including poultry, fish, eggs, beans), vegetable-fruit, bread-cereal, and dairy.

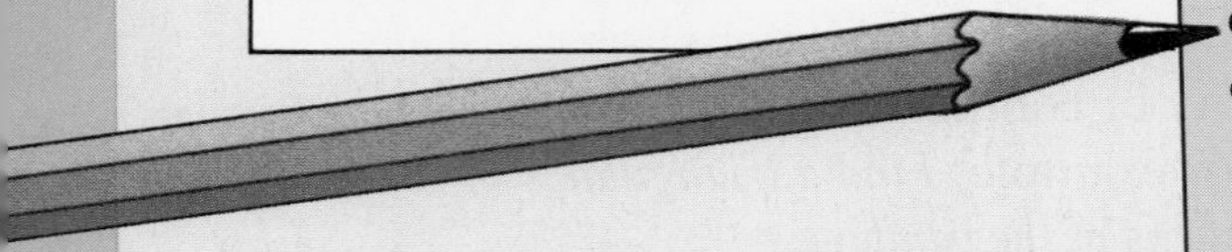

CONNECTING
WRITING ↔ LANGUAGE

A how-to paragraph gives you important information. Read the paragraph below. Why do you think the paragraph uses proper nouns?

> To find out how to get to somewhere in a city by bus, call the information department of the public transit system. Before you call, write down where you are and where you want to go. In San Francisco, for example, you might note that you are at the Academy of Science on Middle Drive in Golden Gate Park. You would also write that you want to go to the Exploratorium in the Palace of Fine Arts on Lyon Street. Next, call the telephone number for transit information and give the operator your locations. Write down the information the operator gives you, including the number of the bus and the streets where you get on and off the bus.

◆ **Nouns in a How-to Paragraph** The words highlighted in color are proper nouns. Using proper nouns makes it possible for you to understand how to get from one museum to the other.

◆ **Language Focus: Nouns** The following lessons will help you use different kinds of nouns in your own writing. You will learn how using precise nouns can make your writing clearer and more interesting to your audience.

1 Kinds of Nouns

FOCUS

- A **noun** names a person, a place, a thing, or an idea.
- There are several kinds of nouns: common, proper, concrete, abstract, and collective.

Nouns are words that name people, places, things, or ideas. A **common noun** names any person, place, thing, or idea. Common nouns are not capitalized. A **proper noun** names a particular person, place, thing, or idea. Proper nouns are always capitalized.

	Common Nouns	Proper Nouns
People	driver, parent, artist	Mr. Lloyd, Mom, Michelangelo
Places	country, state, island	Italy, Ohio, Jamaica
Things	store, language, award	Cy's Market, Dutch, Nobel prize
Ideas	thankfulness, justice	Christianity, Judaism

A **concrete noun** names a thing that can be seen, smelled, tasted, felt, or heard. An **abstract noun** names an idea, a quality, or a feeling that cannot be experienced with the senses.

A **collective noun** names a group of people, things, or animals.

Concrete Nouns	Abstract Nouns	Collective Nouns
child, laughter, heat, cheese, scent	faith, loyalty, sorrow, fear	flock, pack, audience

Guided Practice

A. Name the noun in each sentence. Tell whether each noun is *common* or *proper* and whether it is *concrete* or *abstract*.

1. Has the worker arrived?
2. That convenience is important.
3. This town has grown so fast.
4. Dr. Rios will live here.
5. Life here will be pleasant.
6. Mums were planted there.

THINK AND REMEMBER

- Remember that **nouns** name people, places, things, or ideas.
- Remember that **common nouns** name any person, place, thing, or idea, and **proper nouns** name particular persons, places, things, or ideas.
- Remember that **concrete nouns** name things that can be felt with the senses, and **abstract nouns** name qualities, feelings, or ideas that cannot be experienced with the senses.
- Remember that **collective nouns** name groups of people, things, or animals.

Independent Practice

B. Identifying Nouns Write the noun or nouns in each sentence. Then write *common* or *proper* and *concrete* or *abstract* for each noun.

7. Our new offices will be located here.

MODEL offices—common, concrete

8. Skyscrapers are expensive to build.
9. Great skill is required.
10. First, the foundation must be excavated and explored.
11. The builder then drives in steel pilings.
12. Next, girders are placed and fastened together.

C. Identifying Collective Nouns Write the collective noun from each sentence.

13. Our team is called the Easton Cougars.

MODEL team

14. We are sponsored by the hospital staff.
15. The group donates uniforms.
16. Two girls in my class are the best players.
17. For which school are you cheering?
18. Which squad has more players?
19. Which team won the state championship last year?
20. Which organization will win this year?

Application — Writing

Sketch Imagine that you live in what is now considered the country. Your home, however, is in an area undergoing a lot of growth and transition. Write a paragraph telling your neighbors how an area like this grows and changes into a big city. Use at least two of each kind of noun in your paragraph.

2 Capitalization of Proper Nouns

◆ **FOCUS** Each important word in a proper noun begins with a capital letter.

Remember that proper nouns are names of specific people, places, things, and ideas. Proper nouns are always capitalized. If a proper noun is more than one word, capitalize only the important words.

	Capitalization of Proper Nouns
Names and Titles of People	Mr. Evan Hall; Dr. Julia Martinez; John E. Ridd, Jr.; Captain Kelly; President Jefferson; Aunt Nancy
Languages	Chinese, English, Swahili, Korean, Spanish
Countries, Continents, Heavenly Bodies	Uganda, France, Asia, Europe, North Star, Earth *Exceptions:* sun, moon. The word *earth* is capitalized only when it refers to the planet Earth.
Geographical Terms	New England, Arctic Circle, Pacific Ocean, the West *Exceptions:* compass directions north, east, south, west
States, Provinces, Cities, Counties	Kansas; Ontario; Washington, D.C.; New Orleans; Stark County
Roads	Park Avenue, Main Street, Route 80
Buildings, Bridges, Monuments	World Trade Center, Wrigley Building, Golden Gate Bridge, Lincoln Memorial
Companies, Government Bodies, Organizations	Midwest Associates, Fred's Furniture, Congress, Senate, Cabinet, Explorers' Club, American Cancer Society
Calendar Items	Monday, August, Memorial Day, New Year's Eve *Exceptions:* fall, winter, spring, summer
Historical Events and Time Periods	Civil War, French Revolution, Industrial Revolution, Renaissance, Middle Ages
Documents	Gettysburg Address, Magna Charta
Awards	Nobel prize, Congressional Medal of Honor
Trademarks	Campbell's soup, Parker pens

Guided Practice

A. Identify which word or words in each item should be capitalized.

1. paris, france
2. president reagan
3. maple avenue
4. gulf of mexico
5. mr. peter ruis, sr.
6. american red cross

THINK AND REMEMBER

- Capitalize all proper nouns. If a proper noun is more than one word, do not capitalize unimportant words such as *of* or *the*.

Independent Practice

B. Capitalizing Proper Nouns Write each proper noun with correct capitalization.

7. congressman lee m. wayne

MODEL Congressman Lee M. Wayne

8. world trade center
9. lake shore drive
10. pinellas county, florida
11. veterans day
12. british columbia
13. freedom airlines
14. sudsbest soap

C. Proofreading: Checking for Capitalization Write each sentence correctly. Add capital letters where needed, and use lowercase letters where capitals should not be used.

15. On tuesday, september 4, exchange Students from mexico, japan, and nigeria arrived.

MODEL On Tuesday, September 4, exchange students from Mexico, Japan, and Nigeria arrived.

16. rosita lopez is in mrs. corbin's class.
17. My aunt drove kenji to his new home on fen road.
18. The students will study at the Museum.
19. They hope to visit the white house in washington, d.c.
20. They learned about many different Customs.

Application — Writing

Informative Paragraph Imagine that an exchange student is coming to stay in your home. Write a paragraph telling this person about the places you will visit together. Use at least ten proper nouns in your paragraph.

3 Abbreviations

◆ **FOCUS** An **abbreviation** is a shortened form of a word.

An abbreviation is a shortened form of a word. Most abbreviations are capitalized and are followed by a period.

Abbreviations	
Titles of People	Mister—Mr. Mistress—Mrs. Doctor—Dr. Junior—Jr. Senior—Sr. Captain—Capt.
Addresses	Street—St. Road—Rd. Boulevard—Blvd. Circle—Cir. Rural Route—R.R. Post Office—P.O.
States	Alaska—AK Vermont—VT Alabama—AL
Businesses	Company—Co. Corporation—Corp.
Organizations	North Atlantic Treaty Organization—NATO Parent-Teacher Association—PTA
Calendar Items	Saturday—Sat. Thursday—Thurs. August—Aug. January—Jan.
Times	midnight to noon—A.M. noon to midnight—P.M.
Units of Measure and Weight	quart—qt. pound—lb. kilogram—kg mile—mi. feet—ft. kilometer—km miles per hour—mph

Here are guidelines for abbreviating.

1. Use abbreviations for addresses on an envelope but not when writing an address in a sentence.
2. Do not use periods after abbreviations for organizations.
3. Use the standard United States Postal Service abbreviations, without periods, for state names.
4. Use periods after abbreviations for most English units of measure. Do not use periods after abbreviations for metric measurements.
5. Use an abbreviation for a unit of measure only when it has a numeral before it. If the number is spelled out, do not abbreviate the unit.
6. If you are unsure of how to abbreviate a word or a name, you should check in a dictionary.

Guided Practice

A. Tell what each abbreviation means.

1. ave.	3. FBI	5. NASA	7. CA
2. gal.	4. A.M.	6. in.	8. Jr.

B. Give the abbreviation for each word.

9. Hawaii	11. Senator	13. pound
10. Drive	12. Saturday	14. April

THINK AND REMEMBER

- Remember that an **abbreviation** is a shorter way to write a word.
- Do not capitalize abbreviations for common nouns.

Independent Practice

C. Spelling Out Abbreviations Write the meaning for each abbreviation.

15. Ave.

MODEL Avenue

16. R.R.	18. Dept.	20. Pl.
17. NATO	19. WV	21. Blvd.

D. Writing Abbreviations Write the abbreviation for each.

22. Sergeant Dixon

MODEL Sgt. Dixon

23. 55 miles per hour	29. Tasker & Company
24. Doctor Newman	30. United Nations
25. Power Corporation	31. March 17, 1990
26. 10:00 at night	32. 4 quarts
27. Post Office Box 9	33. Rural Delivery
28. Jones Fur Company	34. Dallas, Texas

Application — Writing

Advertisement Write an advertisement for an event you could hold to raise funds for your school. Decide whether your advertisement should be for the local newspaper or for a sign. Use abbreviations for the following information: address for the event, day, and time. Show your advertisement to the class.

4 Singular and Plural Nouns

FOCUS

- A **singular noun** names one person, place, thing, or idea.
- A **plural noun** names more than one person, place, thing, or idea.

The list below gives guidelines for spelling plural nouns.

1. Add *s* to form the plural of most nouns.
   tree—trees shovel—shovels log—logs
2. Add *es* to form the plural of nouns ending in *s, z, x, sh, ch,* or *ss.*
   branch—branches box—boxes bush—bushes
3. To form the plural of nouns that end in *y* preceded by a consonant, change the *y* to *i* and add *es.*
   agency—agencies variety—varieties family—families
4. Add *s* to form the plural of nouns that end in *y* preceded by a vowel.
   valley—valleys day—days decoy—decoys
5. For nouns that end in *o,*
   a. add *s* if the word ends in *o* preceded by a vowel or if the word is a musical term.
      radio—radios stereo—stereos
      piano—pianos alto—altos
   b. sometimes, *es* is added if the word ends in an *o* preceded by a consonant.
      tomato—tomatoes potato—potatoes
   Exceptions: taco—tacos avocado—avocados
6. For nouns that end in *f* or *fe,* change the *f* to *v* and add *s* or *es.*
   shelf—shelves half—halves life—lives
   Exceptions: safe—safes, roof—roofs, chief—chiefs, belief—beliefs
7. Add *s* to form the plural of nouns ending in *ff.*
   puff—puffs cuff—cuffs staff—staffs

There may be more than one correct plural form for some nouns. If you are unsure of the plural form of a noun, check in a dictionary.

Guided Practice

A. Spell the plural of each noun.

1. seed	**4.** ash	**7.** leaf	**10.** patio
2. trunk	**5.** berry	**8.** muff	**11.** toy
3. tax	**6.** mango	**9.** wolf	**12.** cypress

THINK AND REMEMBER

- Remember that a **singular noun** names one person, place, thing, or idea.
- Remember that a **plural noun** names more than one person, place, thing, or idea.

Independent Practice

B. Writing Plural Nouns Write the plural form of each noun.

13. ratio

MODEL ratios

14. index	18. mystery	22. beach
15. address	19. spoof	23. mosquito
16. calf	20. survey	24. soprano
17. knife	21. loaf	25. forest

C. Proofreading: Changing Singular Nouns to Plural The underlined noun in each sentence should be plural. Rewrite the word, using the correct plural form.

26. The lumber industry uses trees for various <u>purpose</u>.

MODEL purposes

27. Lumberjacks spend their <u>life</u> cutting trees for wood.
28. They fell selected trees and trim the <u>branch</u> in the forests.
29. <u>Pulley</u> are used to move logs.
30. They are moved through the sawmill on <u>carriage</u>.
31. Construction <u>company</u> buy mostly fir or pine lumber.
32. Lumber is only one of the many <u>product</u> of a tree.
33. Papermaking is one of the <u>industry</u> that depends on wood.
34. Some trees are harvested for their fruit or <u>nut</u>.
35. Walnuts and <u>pistachio</u> are actually seeds of trees.
36. Apples, pears, and <u>cherry</u> are favorite fruits from trees.

Application — Writing

Brochure Description Imagine that you are a promoter for a lumber company. Write a description of the products, from paper goods to furniture, that can be made from the trees your company harvests. Be specific about the names of the actual items manufactured. Be sure to use the correct forms of plural nouns.

5 More Plural Nouns

◆ **FOCUS** Some nouns form their plurals in special ways.

Some plural nouns are formed in special ways.

Guidelines for Spelling Some Plural Nouns
1. For some nouns you may have to change or add letters. man—men child—children alumnus—alumni
2. For some compound nouns that consist of a noun plus a modifier, add *s* to the noun or to the main word in the compound. sister-in-law—sisters-in-law passerby—passersby *Exceptions:* spoonful—spoonfuls cupful—cupfuls
3. Some nouns have the same form in the singular and in the plural. fish—fish sheep—sheep species—species
4. Some nouns have a plural form but a singular meaning. mumps physics gymnastics
5. To form the plurals of numerals, letters, symbols, and words used as words, add an apostrophe and *s*. three *r*'s in *surrender* two *110*'s in a row too many *which*'s the 1990's six &'s on this sign

Guided Practice

A. Tell how to spell the plural form of each noun.

1. woman
2. deer
3. *M*
4. cupful
5. tooth
6. left-hander
7. spoonful
8. measles
9. memorandum
10. father-in-law
11. headquarters
12. slacks
13. mouse
14. *250*
15. child
16. foot

THINK AND REMEMBER

- Follow the rules listed above to form the plurals of certain nouns.

Independent Practice

B. Writing Plural Nouns Write each plural form.

17. grandchild

MODEL grandchildren

18. cactus
19. editor in chief
20. salmon
21. foot
22. 1920
23. bacterium
24. teaspoonful
25. woman
26. &
27. jeans
28. goldfish
29. antenna
30. mumps
31. attorney-at-law
32. *212*
33. gladiolus
34. attorney general
35. octopus

C. Proofreading: Writing Plural Nouns Correctly The underlined noun in each sentence should be plural. Rewrite the word, using the correct plural form.

36. Those two <u>woman</u> are starting a catering business.

MODEL women

37. The one wearing the <u>suspender</u> is preparing a new dish.
38. She needs two <u>teaspoonful</u> of ginger.
39. Please wear your <u>eyeglass</u> to read that recipe.
40. We need several <u>cupsful</u> for tonight's meal.
41. Please slice eight mushrooms and clean two <u>fish</u>.
42. Did you know that mushrooms are actually <u>fungus</u>?
43. They sliced the apple rings in the shape of <u>*o*</u>.
44. My <u>sister-in-law</u> are learning to cook venison.
45. Meat from <u>deer</u> is plentiful in some regions.
46. The Pilgrims probably ate venison in the <u>1600</u>.
47. They frequently caught <u>salmons</u>.
48. Some <u>cattles</u> were raised for food.
49. Meat must be cooked to remove <u>bacterium</u>.

Application — Writing

Recipe Write a humorous recipe that students in a cooking class might prepare. Your recipe can be for a food you have just invented; it does not have to be a real recipe. Try to use some unusual plurals in your recipe.

6 Possessive Nouns

◆ **FOCUS** A **possessive noun** shows ownership or possession.

Possessive nouns tell to whom or to what something belongs.

1. Vince's plane **the plane that Vince owns**
2. the forecaster's report **the report from the forecaster**
3. the plane's instruments **the instruments of the plane**

Guidelines for Forming Possessive Nouns	
1. Add an apostrophe and *s* to a singular noun. Add an apostrophe and *s* to the end of compound words.	
Dolores's job	the airline's employees
Mike's cousins	my great-aunt's visit
2. Add just an apostrophe after most plural nouns ending in *s.*	
the passengers' tickets	the Wilsons' seats
the Dawsons' relatives	the Davises' luggage
3. For plural nouns that do not end in *s,* add an apostrophe and *s.*	
the people's flight	children's fares
4. To show possession for things owned by more than one person, add an apostrophe and *s* after the last noun.	
Jim and Jaclyn's bird	Bob and Ed's boat

Guided Practice

A. Tell how to form the possessive of each noun. Tell whether each possessive is a *singular possessive* or a *plural possessive.*

1. navigator
2. travelers
3. Jill
4. ten-year-old
5. James
6. the Martins
7. witnesses
8. children

THINK AND REMEMBER

- Remember that **possessive nouns** show ownership.
- Follow the rules listed above to form the possessives of nouns.

Independent Practice

B. Writing and Identifying Possessive Nouns Write the possessive form of each noun. Then write whether it is a *singular possessive* or a *plural possessive*.

9. airplane

MODEL airplane's—singular possessive

10. hurricane
11. Tony
12. computers
13. Douglas
14. gauge
15. Lopezes
16. Yoshi
17. mice
18. son-in-law
19. building
20. tornado
21. ladies
22. thief
23. neighbors
24. public
25. barometer

C. Revising: Replacing Phrases with Possessive Nouns Replace the underlined phrase with a phrase containing a possessive noun. Write the new phrase.

26. The weather report of Ms. Hicks called for rain.

MODEL Ms. Hicks's weather report

27. Ms. Hicks was a guest in our class today.
28. She answered all of the questions of the students.
29. The job of a weather forecaster sounds difficult.
30. We watched a weather report on the television that belongs to the school.
31. The weather report was from a broadcast of the local television station.
32. Ms. Hicks explained the meanings of symbols on weather maps.
33. She displayed a weather instrument that measures the velocity of the wind.

Application — Writing

Weather Report Imagine that you are an airport weather forecaster preparing a report for a pilot. Draw a map of the pilot's route. Create weather symbols to indicate rain, fog, snow, and sun. Then write a report describing special weather conditions that should be avoided. Use five possessive nouns in your weather report.

7 Appositives

◆ **FOCUS** An **appositive** identifies or renames the noun or pronoun that precedes it.

An appositive identifies or renames the noun or pronoun that precedes it. An appositive includes modifying words. It is usually set off from the preceding noun by a comma. The appositives in these sentences are highlighted.

1. I would like you to meet Ms. Collins, a fine musician.

If an appositive is used in the middle of a sentence, use a comma both before and after the appositive.

2. Our visitor, Ms. Collins, will play a piece on the piano.

No comma is used if the appositive is a single word that is closely related to the noun it renames or if the appositive is needed to identify the noun it follows.

3. Do you know the tune "Twinkle, Twinkle, Little Star"?

Guided Practice

A. Identify the appositive in each sentence and the word or words it renames.

1. I love art, my favorite subject.
2. I am painting my dog Skip.
3. Skip is a collie, a large dog.
4. Let me introduce Mr. Ash, the artist who helps me.
5. This is my friend Walt.
6. I use pastels, chalklike crayons.

B. Tell whether or not commas are needed in these appositives. If commas are needed, tell where they should be placed.

7. I enjoy math my favorite subject.
8. I am learning to speak Spanish a beautiful language.
9. My friend Steve works here.
10. The poem "Fog" is very short.
11. She plays tennis her favorite sport.

THINK AND REMEMBER

- Remember that an **appositive** identifies or renames the noun or pronoun that precedes it.
- Set off some appositives with commas.

Independent Practice

C. Identifying Appositives Write each sentence. Underline the appositive, and draw an arrow from the appositive to the word it explains.

12. Mr. Stern, this is my brother Ted.

MODEL Mr. Stern, this is my brother Ted.

13. Ted, meet Mr. Stern, a fine gardener.
14. We were admiring your garden, a splendid array of colors.
15. The iris, the state flower of Tennessee, is my favorite.
16. Irises are perennials, plants that bloom every year.
17. Annuals, plants that live only one year, require more work.
18. Mr. Stern, my friend Kitty would love to see your irises.

D. Proofreading: Checking for Commas with Appositives Write each sentence. Insert commas where needed to set off appositives. If the sentence is correct, write *correct*.

19. The International Club met on Monday the first of May.

MODEL The International Club met on Monday, the first of May.

20. We are studying Japan a group of islands in the Pacific.
21. Mr. Isao Shirai our guest speaker addressed the group.
22. He comes from Honshu the largest island.
23. We learned about bonsai the Japanese art of growing dwarf trees.
24. Mr. Shirai also discussed origami, the art of paper sculpture.
25. He made us a crane the Japanese symbol for good luck from folded paper.
26. My friend Sujan speaks some Japanese.

Application — Writing and Speaking

Speech Imagine that you must introduce a guest speaker to your class. Write a speech that tells who the speaker is, why he or she has been chosen to speak, and what the topic will be. Use appositives in your speech, and use commas if needed. Read your speech to a classmate.

Building Vocabulary
Multiple-Meaning Words: Specialized Vocabularies

Communicating clearly depends on using exact words. A subject area, such as science, mathematics, or social studies, has a specialized vocabulary (frequently nouns) to refer to specific concepts or objects within that area. Read through the lists of nouns below. How many do you recognize? How many can you define?

Hand me the whatchamacallit so I can measure this thingamabob.

Health	Science	Mathematics	Social Studies
antiseptic	molecule	decimal	legislature
infection	nucleus	equation	senate
splint	climate	triangle	amendment

Textbook writers usually define specialized vocabulary terms within the text. The term may also appear in a glossary at the back of the textbook. A **glossary** defines words as they are used in one particular subject. Compare these two entries for the word *degree*. The first entry is from a mathematics glossary and the second is from a dictionary. The dictionary entry shows the **multiple meanings** of the word *degree*. Remember that a word's meaning depends on the subject area in which it appears.

degree a unit of measure used for arcs and angles: *That is a 90-degree triangle.*

degree [di•grē] *n.* 1. A step in a series or a stage in a process. 2. A unit for measuring temperature: The normal temperature of the body is 98.6 *degrees* Fahrenheit. 3. A unit used for measuring arcs and angles: There are 360 *degrees* in a circle. 4. The number of times variables, as *x* and *y*, are used as factors in a term. 5. A measure of damage done to bodily tissue: a burn of the second *degree.* 6. A measure of guilt as fixed by law: murder in the first *degree.* 7. Amount, extent, or measure: There is only a small *degree* of difference between the twins. 8. Station; rank: a person of high *degree.* 9. A title awarded to a student who has completed a course of study or to a person as an honor.

Reading Practice

Write *health, education, mathematics, science, social studies,* or *common meaning* to identify the subject or general use of the word *degree* in each sentence. Then, use the dictionary entry for *degree* to write the definition number for each use.

1. Kelly suffered a burn of the first degree from the boiling water.
2. Please convert 68 degrees Fahrenheit into degrees Celsius.
3. Ramon earned his graduate degree in chemistry.
4. I think the plan will work to a certain degree.
5. Half a circle equals 180 degrees.
6. Kings and queens were considered members of the highest degree of nobility.

Writing Practice

Use a dictionary to find the meanings of the following words. Write a glossary entry for each word's particular subject area. Then write a general definition for each word. Use the word in one sentence to show its meaning in the subject area and in another sentence to show its general meaning.

Example: nucleus
Science: the central portion of an atom.
The nucleus of an atom consists of protons and neutrons.
Common meaning: a central point or group.
Bonita, Tim, and Kate make up the nucleus of the band.

7. cube **9.** constitution **11.** operation
8. vacuum **10.** pulse **12.** dividend

Project

Collect a number of pamphlets from the health field on how to cope with various emergencies. The Red Cross, a local hospital, and a health department are possible sources. Read through the pamphlets, and make a list of all the specialized vocabulary words. Write definitions for the words as used. With your classmates, put together a health glossary.

Language Enrichment
Nouns

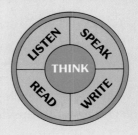

Use what you know about nouns to do these activities.

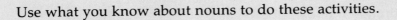

Light Show

Imagine that you have just bought this desk lamp. Write how to attach it to a desk, plug it in, and adjust it for reading. Use the labels to include specific nouns in your explanation. Present your information as a how-to speech to your classmates.

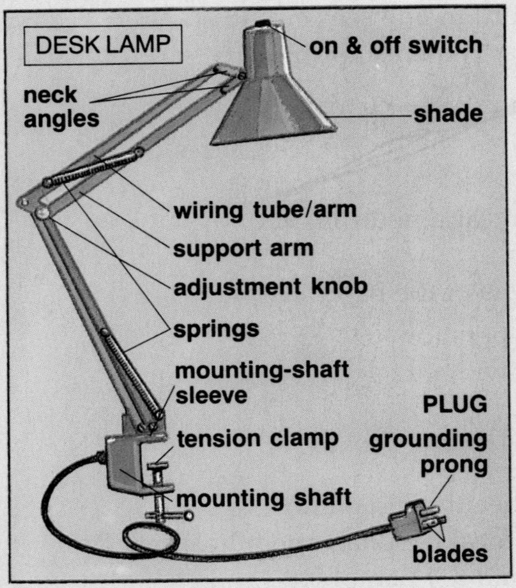

Promises, Promises

Mr. Talkalot makes promises that use abstract nouns. He says "If I'm elected, I promise you truth, beauty, and justice." Make up some questions that involve concrete problems. For example, you might write questions to ask him what he would do about traffic problems. Then suggest some solutions that use concrete rather than abstract nouns.

Possessives

In the comic strip "Peanuts," Snoopy's supper dish, Linus's blanket, and Schroeder's piano are possessions that go with the characters. With a partner, make up a chart that lists each classmate's name and an item that goes with him or her, such as a tuba or a pet. Then use the chart to play a game with the rest of your class. As you show and read each item on your chart, choose classmates to write on the chart the possessive form of the name that goes with each item.

CONNECTING
LANGUAGE ↔ WRITING

In this unit you learned that nouns can be common or proper and concrete or abstract. You also learned some of the rules about capitalizing, abbreviating, and spelling nouns.

◆ **Using Nouns in Your Writing** Knowing how to use nouns correctly can help you to write more precisely. Using specific nouns will provide your audience with a clearer picture of your thoughts. Pay special attention to the nouns you use as you do these activities.

Proper to Common

The common nouns used for many everyday things were once proper nouns. For example, the *saxophone* was named by its inventor, Adolphe Sax. Think about your own name. Write a paragraph to tell about how your name might become a common noun. Use your imagination. If you want, draw a picture of the object that has your name.

Zoom! Pow! Zip!

Cartoonists use a special vocabulary.

Be an apprentice cartoonist, and finish the cartoon. Write some dialogue for the speech balloons. Add more details, and label them with special vocabulary words.

2 Unit Checkup

Think Back	Think Ahead
◆ What did you learn about how-to paragraphs in this unit? What did you do to write one?	◆ How will what you learned about how-to paragraphs help you follow instructions? ◆ How will knowing how to select essential information help you write a how-to paragraph?
◆ Look at the writing you did in this unit. How did nouns help you express your ideas?	◆ What is one way you can use nouns to improve your writing?

How-to Paragraph *pages 58 – 59*

Read the following beginning sentences from how-to paragraphs. For each sentence, name the process that will be explained.

1. To choose a career, one should follow several steps.
2. Research shows that people learn in five stages.
3. When trying to fit into a new school, keep an open mind.

Evaluating to Select Essential Information *page 60*

Using the topic sentence, write *essential* or *not essential* for each detail.

When trying to fit into a new school, keep an open mind.

4. Be sure to write to friends at your old school.
5. Take part in classroom discussions.
6. Listen to the radio and enjoy the music.

Using Precise Words *page 61*

Write the following sentences, using precise words.

7. Turn the switch to the ________.
8. The library's ________ section gives job listings.
9. Open the computer manual to the ________ to begin.
10. Grasp the ________ firmly to drive in the nail.

The Writing Process *pages 62 – 71*

Write the letter for the answer to each question.

11. When you plan a how-to paragraph, what should you do first?
a. Organize the steps. **b.** Gather information. **c.** Brainstorm topics.

12. What should you do first when drafting a how-to paragraph?
a. Present the steps in order. **b.** Name the process.
c. List the materials needed.

13. What should you check last when revising the paragraph?
a. coherence **b.** completeness of information **c.** audience

Kinds of Nouns *pages 74 – 75*

Write the noun or nouns in each sentence. Then write *common* or *proper* and *concrete* or *abstract*.

14. The growth of our nation is happening in some surprising ways and in some surprising places.

15. The number of people over sixty has reached a record high and has changed how America views education, economics, and social organizations.

16. Cities in the southern regions are building skyscrapers, expanding to suburbs, and developing mass transportation systems.

17. Places such as Dallas, Houston, and Phoenix are experiencing economic rebirth.

18. The old Horace Greeley motto "Go west, young man" has changed to "Go south and west, all people."

Capitalization of Proper Nouns *pages 76 – 77*

Write each proper noun with correct capitalization.

19. galveston, texas
20. empire state building
21. new year's day
22. asia
23. mr. donald sloan
24. dallas–fort worth airport
25. spanish
26. world war II
27. monday, september 7

Abbreviations *pages 78 – 79*

Write the meaning of each abbreviation.

28. FL
29. S.
30. Dr.
31. W.

32. Apr.
33. U.S.A.
34. Inc.
35. mph
36. NY
37. Dec.

Singular and Plural Nouns *pages 80 – 81*

Write the plural form of each noun.

38. city
39. taco
40. cow
41. knife
42. door
43. play

More Plural Nouns *pages 82 – 83*

Write the plural form of each noun. Use a dictionary for help.

44. woman
45. focus
46. mother-in-law
47. 12
48. 1930
49. datum
50. man-of-war
51. louse
52. major general
53. medium
54. octopus
55. 1980
56. apparatus

Possessive Nouns *pages 84 – 85*

Write the possessive form of each noun. Write whether it is a *singular possessive* or a *plural possessive.*

57. Astrodome
58. men
59. workers
60. father-in-law
61. dog
62. cats
63. student
64. woman
65. relatives
66. slacks
67. cans
68. pupils
69. James
70. telegrams
71. city
72. American
73. agencies

74. towns

Appositives *pages 86 – 87*

Write each sentence. Underline the appositive and draw an arrow from the appositive to the noun or nouns it explains.

75. In 1746, José de Escando, a colonel in the Spanish army, was told to take soldiers across the Rio Grande and to set up new settlements.

76. He took two years to gather his band, a mixture of soldiers and colonists, and to train them in the skills necessary for survival.

77. Escando avoided settling the coast, an area known for deadly fevers.

78. Settlers, soldiers and natives alike, were forced to try to make a living by working rocky, barren ground.

79. As a result they could not depend on farming to support themselves and had to turn to cattle ranching, a now-familiar industry.

80. Escando, a native of Spanish Santander, called the new frontier by the name "New Santander."

81. The soldier-explorer earned a title, Count of Sierra Gorda, for his services.

82. As well as a new title, José de Escando had earned himself a name in American history, "the man who opened the Southwest."

Multiple-Meaning Words: Specialized Vocabularies *pages 88 – 89*

Look up the following words in a dictionary. For each word, write a glossary entry for each subject area the word is used in. Then write a general definition. Use the word in a sentence to show its meaning in one subject area and in another sentence to show its general meaning.

83. equivalent
84. infinite
85. latitude
86. orbit
87. tragedy

1-2 Cumulative Review

Four Kinds of Sentences *pages 28 – 29*

Write *sentence* or *not a sentence* to identify each group of words. For each sentence, write what kind of sentence it is.

1. A person uses movement as well as language to communicate in nearly every situation.
2. Sometimes what is said and what is merely implied by the speaker.
3. Who can tell what is the speaker's real message and what is inferred by the listener?
4. Give me the clear, spoken message over the implied message every time.
5. A broad smile, or a slight frown, or a hearty clap on the shoulder.
6. I will never know all of the things that a speaker is communicating!

Complete and Simple Subjects and Predicates *pages 30 – 33*

Write the complete subject of each sentence, and underline the simple subject once. Write the complete predicate, and underline the simple predicate twice.

7. Some people show their feelings on a grand scale, like actors on a stage.
8. Men and women use their faces and the rest of their bodies to show their emotions.
9. I watched my Aunt Elizabeth return a dress to the department store.
10. She moved her hands with increasing agitation and indignation.
11. Her eyes and eyebrows also expressed her emotions.
12. The manager of the department store did not know whether to give her a refund or an ovation.
13. Aunt Elizabeth attracted a crowd around her.
14. She asked for a refund and demanded an explanation.
15. The crowd around her and the cashier nearby watched in awe.
16. Few people would attempt to challenge her.
17. The manager of the store gave her the refund.
18. The crowd cheered and went back to their shopping.

Word Order in Sentences *pages 34–36*

Write *natural* or *inverted* to identify the word order of each sentence.

19. Will you be at the next press conference of the new city council?

20. Pick out someone from the group to study carefully.

21. There are always interesting types of people to observe.

22. Into the crowd and up to the first row walks the best person to study.

23. In many meetings, I have noticed that some interviewees wear a certain type of clothing.

24. They wear suits, dresses, ties, and accessories that set them apart from others.

Compound Subjects and Compound Verbs *pages 37–38*

Write each sentence. Underline compound subjects once and compound predicates twice. Write *compound subject, compound verb,* or *both.*

25. Males and females use their clothes to express themselves in many ways.

26. They mix and match a wide variety of clothing styles and colors.

27. Jeans and athletic shoes are comfortable and show that you are relaxed.

28. Ties, jackets, and dresses suggest a more formal or official mood.

29. Fashion-conscious people cut and style their hair.

30. Hats, scarves, and caps are worn not only for warmth but for style.

Simple and Compound Sentences *pages 39–41*

Write *simple sentence* or *compound sentence* for each sentence.

31. Tom and James do not seem to worry about their clothes or their personal appearance.

32. They do not think about what is in style, and their clothes show it.

33. They always wear the same things: jeans, a sweatshirt, and sneakers.

34. Their jeans are faded and beltless; their shoes don't have any laces.
35. Many brothers look alike, but their clothing styles are often different.
36. These brothers may stay the same, or one of them might decide to change.

Avoiding Sentence Fragments and Run-on Sentences *pages 42–43*

Write whether each group of words is a *sentence*, a *sentence fragment*, or a *run-on sentence*.

37. Some people change clothing styles, others refuse to change anything.
38. Unusual clothes or hairstyles that shock or amuse people.
39. Frequently, designers change styles more than consumers do.
40. Fashion designers with a need to create a new style and a new market.
41. I prefer to wear the same styles, I like the way my clothes look and I like to save money.
42. I also feel more comfortable in older clothing, but I know I am not in style.

Kinds of Nouns *pages 74–75*

Write the noun or nouns in each sentence. Then write *common* or *proper*.

43. When children are young, they have dreams about exciting adventures.
44. King Arthur and Cinderella are favorite characters of many children.
45. At a later age they go to middle school, and the dreams change.
46. They dream about things such as bicycles, clothes, and sports heroes.
47. Events such as the Olympics and the World Series are on their minds.
48. Each new year brings new hopes and dreams.

Possessive Nouns *pages 84 – 85*

Replace the underlined phrase with a phrase containing a possessive noun. Write the new phrase.

49. The dreams of older students are as different as each individual.

50. The hope of an athlete might be to be a star and to earn a scholarship to play in college.

51. Another student may yearn to be the best drummer in the band.

52. The wish of a serious student is often to earn marks that are high enough to get into a good college.

53. Most teenagers cannot wait until the day they get a license of a driver.

54. A few people want to have the careers that their parents have.

Appositives *pages 86 – 87*

Write each sentence. Underline the appositive, and draw an arrow to the noun or nouns it explains.

55. Mr. Dennis, the maintenance man at our school, really loves to fix things.

56. He prefers to repair radios and television sets, appliances he has learned a lot about.

57. This hobby is also part of his greatest dream in life, to own a fix-it shop.

58. Mr. Dennis saves money, hundreds of dollars, to buy all the tools that he will need.

59. Mrs. Connor, Mr. Dennis's banker, has agreed to finance the fix-it shop.

60. Everyone at school admires Mr. Dennis, a man who is working for a dream.

UNIT 3

Narrating Events

◆ COMPOSITION FOCUS: **Narrative Poem**
◆ LANGUAGE FOCUS: **Verbs**

"Listen, my children, and you shall hear/Of the midnight ride of Paul Revere." So begins a famous narrative poem about Paul Revere's historic midnight ride. A **narrative poem** tells a story in verse and may be historical, humorous, or autobiographical. It differs from other kinds of poetry. A **lyric poem,** for example, expresses a writer's thoughts and feelings about a subject rather than telling a story.

Any story you have ever read can become the subject of a narrative poem. If the narrative poem is historical, it may immortalize a heroic deed. "Paul Revere's Ride," for instance, has kept alive the famous deed of a Revolutionary War hero.

In writing this narrative poem, Henry Wadsworth Longfellow had two main tasks. One was to create a story and the other was to use all the elements of poetry. In this unit you will learn how to combine the elements of stories and poems to create a narrative poem.

Henry Wadsworth Longfellow created "Paul Revere's Ride" *to entertain* readers with a poetic telling of a historic event.

Reading with a Writer's Eye
Narrative Poem

When the British march at night toward Lexington and Concord, it's time to rouse the Americans to action, and Paul Revere is impatient to do so. Will the British take the shorter water route or the longer land route? Read Henry Wadsworth Longfellow's poem to find out.

Paul Revere's Ride

by Henry Wadsworth Longfellow

Listen, my children, and you shall hear
Of the midnight ride of Paul Revere,
On the eighteenth of April, in Seventy-five;
Hardly a man is now alive
Who remembers that famous day and year.
He said to his friend, "If the British march
By land or sea from the town tonight,
Hang a lantern aloft in the belfry arch
Of the North Church tower as a signal light,—
One, if by land, and two, if by sea;
And I on the opposite shore will be,
Ready to ride and spread the alarm
Through every Middlesex village and farm,
For the country folk to be up and to arm."

Then he said, "Good night!" and with muffled oar
Silently rowed to the Charlestown shore,
Just as the moon rose over the bay,
Where swinging wide at her moorings lay
The *Somerset,* British man-of-war;
A phantom ship, with each mast and spar
Across the moon like a prison bar,
And a huge black hulk, that was magnified
By its own reflection in the tide.
Meanwhile, his friend through alley and street
Wanders and watches, with eager ears,
Till in the silence around him he hears

The muster of men at the barrack door,
The sound of arms, and the tramp of feet,
And the measured tread of the grenadiers,
Marching down to their boats on the shore.
Then he climbed the tower of the Old North Church,
By the wooden stairs, with stealthy tread,
To the belfry-chamber overhead,
And startled the pigeons from their perch
On the somber rafters, that round him made
Masses and moving shapes of shade,—
By the trembling ladder, steep and tall,
To the highest window in the wall,
Where he paused to listen and look down
A moment on the roofs of the town
And the moonlight flowing over all.

Beneath in the churchyard, lay the dead,
In their night-encampment on the hill,
Wrapped in silence so deep and still
That he could hear, like a sentinel's tread,
The watchful night-wind, as it went
Creeping along from tent to tent,
And seeming to whisper, "All is well!"
A moment only he feels the spell
Of the place and the hour, and the secret dread
Of the lonely belfry and the dead;
For suddenly all his thoughts are bent
On a shadowy something far away,
Where the river widens to meet the bay,—
A line of black that bends and floats
On the rising tide, like a bridge of boats.
Meanwhile, impatient to mount and ride,
Booted and spurred, with a heavy stride
On the opposite shore walked Paul Revere.
Now he patted his horse's side,
Now gazed at the landscape far and near,
Then, impetuous, stamped the earth,
And turned and tightened his saddle girth;
But mostly he watched with eager search

The belfry tower of the Old North Church,
Lonely and spectral and somber and still.
And lo! as he looks, on the belfry height
A glimmer, and then a gleam of light!
He springs to the saddle, the bridle he turns,
But lingers and gazes, till full on his sight
A second lamp in the belfry burns!

A hurry of hoofs in a village street,
A shape in the moonlight, a bulk in the dark,
And beneath, from the pebbles, in passing, a spark
Struck out by a steed flying fearless and fleet;
That was all! And yet, through the gloom and the light,
The fate of a nation was riding that night;
And the spark struck out by that steed, in his flight,
Kindled the land into flame with its heat.
He has left the village and mounted the steep,
And beneath him, tranquil and broad and deep,
Is the Mystic, meeting the ocean tides;
And under the alders that skirt its edge,
Now soft on the sand, now loud on the ledge,
Is heard the tramp of his steed as he rides.

It was twelve by the village clock,
When he crossed the bridge into Medford town.
He heard the crowing of the cock,
And the barking of the farmer's dog,
And he felt the damp of the river fog,
That rises after the sun goes down.

It was one by the village clock
When he galloped into Lexington.
He saw the gilded weathercock
Swim in the moonlight as he passed,
And the meeting house windows, blank and bare,
Gaze at him with a spectral glare,
As if they already stood aghast
At the bloody work they would look upon.

It was two by the village clock,
When he came to the bridge in Concord town.
He heard the bleating of the flock,
And the twitter of birds among the trees,
And felt the breath of the morning breeze
Blowing over the meadows brown.
And one was safe and asleep in his bed
Who at the bridge would be first to fall,
Who that day would be lying dead,
Pierced by a British musket-ball.
You know the rest. In books you have read,
How the British Regulars fired and fled,—
How the farmers gave them ball for ball,
From behind each fence and farmyard wall,
Chasing the redcoats down the lane,
Then crossing the fields to emerge again
Under the trees at the turn of the road,
And only pausing to fire and load.

So through the night rode Paul Revere;
And so through the night went his cry of alarm
To every Middlesex village and farm,—
A cry of defiance, and not of fear,
A voice in the darkness, a knock at the door,
And a word that shall echo for evermore!
For, borne on the night-wind of the Past,
Through all our history, to the last,
In the hour of darkness and peril and need,
The people will waken and listen to hear
The hurrying hoof-beats of that steed,
And the midnight message of Paul Revere.

Respond

1. How does the sound of the words in this poem make you feel about the story?

Discuss

2. What happens in the beginning of the poem? What occurs in the middle? What happens at the ending?
3. How do you know which route the British chose?

Thinking As a Writer
Analyzing a Narrative Poem

Writer's Guide

A narrative poem
- may be about a heroic event or a mock-heroic event.
- has narrative and poetic elements.

A narrative poem is a poem in which a narrator tells a story. Sometimes the poem is mock-heroic: the poet tells about a minor event using heroic language to treat it in a humorous way.

Every narrative poem contains **narrative elements** and **poetic elements.**

The Narrative Elements

In a narrative poem, the narrative elements include the **introduction,** the **complication,** and the **resolution.**

Paul Revere's Ride

Listen, my children, and you shall hear
Of the midnight ride of Paul Revere,
On the eighteenth of April, in Seventy-five;
Hardly a man is now alive
Who remembers that famous day and year.

The **introduction** sets up the situation and informs the reader of what is to come. It should capture the reader's attention and make the reader want to continue.

* * *

Then he said, "Good night!" and with muffled oar
Silently rowed to the Charlestown shore,
Just as the moon rose over the bay,
Where swinging wide at her moorings lay
The *Somerset,* British man-of-war;
A phantom ship, with each mast and spar
Across the moon like a prison bar,
And a huge black hulk, that was magnified
By its own reflection in the tide.

The **complication** introduces elements of conflict. It provides a basis for a story line or a plot in the narrative poem.

* * *

You know the rest. In books you have read,
How the British Regulars fired and fled,—
How the farmers gave them ball for ball,
From behind each fence and farmyard wall,
Chasing the redcoats down the lane,

The **resolution** ends the story line in the narrative poem. It resolves the conflict and concludes the plot.

The Poetic Elements

Narrative poems have strong rhyme and rhythm. Also, their lines are usually grouped into sets called **stanzas.** Here are some traditional stanzas from narrative poems.

> Abou Ben Adhem (may his tribe increase!)
> Awoke one night from a deep dream of peace,
> —Leigh Hunt

A **couplet** is formed by two rhyming lines. Couplets are usually not set off by space above and below.

> Belinda lived in a little white house,
> With a little black kitten and a little gray mouse,
> And a little yellow dog and a little red wagon,
> And a realio, trulio, little pet dragon.
> —Ogden Nash

A **quatrain** has four lines and is a common stanza form in narrative poems.

> She looked at him, and he looked at her.
> They were English children, born and bred.
> He frowned her down, but she wouldn't stir.
> She shook her proud young head.
> "You'll need a crew," she said.
> —Robert Nathan

A **cinquain** has five lines and is less common in narrative poems.

Rhyme is the repetition of syllable sounds especially at the ends of lines of poetry. In this excerpt from Ernest Lawrence Thayer's "Casey at the Bat," each matching end rhyme has been labeled with the same letter.

It looked extremely rocky for the Mudville nine that day;	*a*
The score stood two to four, with but one inning left to play.	*a*
So, when Cooney died at second, and Burrows did the same,	*b*
A pallor wreathed the features of the patrons of the game.	*b*

The pattern of beats is called the **meter**. A ´ indicates a heavily stressed syllable, and ˘ indicates a lightly stressed syllable. Look at the meter in Lewis Carroll's "The Walrus and the Carpenter."

The sun was shining on the sea,
  Shining with all his might:
He did his very best to make
  The billows smooth and bright—
And this was odd, because it was
  The middle of the night.

Discuss

1. What in "Paul Revere's Ride" indicates that the narrator was probably a witness to the events? What can you tell about the story line from the part of the poem on page 106?
2. What kind of feeling does the resolution of the poem leave you with?
3. Why are the lines in "Casey at the Bat" labeled *aabb*? If the rhyme scheme were *abab*, which lines in the poem would rhyme?

Try Your Hand

A. Analyze Story Line Look back at the first stanza of "Casey at the Bat." Explain what you can tell about the story line from this stanza.

B. Identify Stanzas Write *couplet, quatrain,* or *cinquain* to identify each of the following.

1. At midnight in the month of June
   I stand beneath the mystic moon.
2. "You are old, Father William," the young man said.
      "And your hair has become very white;
   And yet you incessantly stand on your head—
      Do you think at your age, it is right?"
3. A Beetle, a Bat, and a Bee
   Were wrecked on the Isle of Boree,
   With a barrel of gum
   And a tom-tom drum
   And a hammock for each of the three.

C. Identify Rhythm and Rhyme Scheme Copy the stanza in item 3. Write the rhyme scheme. Then mark the meter.

D. Analyze Narrative and Poetic Elements Choose one stanza from "Paul Revere's Ride" on pages 102–105. Write what happens in that part of the story. Then write the rhyme scheme.

Writer's Notebook

Collecting Vivid Verbs Did you notice vivid verbs such as *stamped* and *springs* in "Paul Revere's Ride"? These verbs paint a vivid picture of the action. Read "Paul Revere's Ride" again. Record in your *Writer's Notebook* any vivid verbs. Look up the words in the dictionary and record their meanings as verbs. Try to use these and other vivid verbs when you speak and write.

Developing the Writer's Craft
Choosing Words to Create a Mood

Writer's Guide

Good writers
- use dramatic language to create a mood.

Mood is the atmosphere a reader gets from a story or a poem. In a poem about a heroic deed, the poet uses dramatic language to establish a dramatic mood. In a mock-heroic poem, the poet uses dramatic language to create a frivolous mood.

Read these lines from "Paul Revere's Ride."

A moment only he feels the spell
Of the place and the hour, and the secret dread
Of the lonely belfry and the dead;

Now read these lines from "Casey at the Bat."

He pounds with cruel vengeance his bat upon the plate;
And now the pitcher holds the ball, and now he lets it go,
And now the air is shattered by the force of Casey's blow.

In the first example, the underlined words create a solemn atmosphere of a churchyard at night. In the second example, the words are used humorously to treat a minor event in a mock-heroic way.

When you write your narrative poem, choose words to create your mood.

Discuss

What feeling do the underlined words from "Casey at the Bat" give you? What other dramatic words might the poet have used?

Try Your Hand

Create a Mood Rewrite the last stanza of "Casey at the Bat." Use different dramatic words, but keep the same mood as the original.

Oh, somewhere in this favored land the sun is shining bright,
The band is playing somewhere, and somewhere hearts are light;
And somewhere men are laughing, and somewhere children shout,
But there is no joy in Mudville—Mighty Casey has struck out.

1 Prewriting
Narrative Poem

Kimiko wanted to write a narrative poem for a poetry contest advertised in a magazine. She used the information in the **Writer's Guide** to help plan her poem. Look at what she did.

Writer's Guide

Prewriting Checklist

- ☑ Brainstorm topics.
- ☑ Select a topic.
- ☑ Think about your audience and your purpose.
- ☑ Gather words and images.

Brainstorming and Selecting a Topic

First, Kimiko decided on a story for her poem. She knew that she wanted her poem to be mock-heroic, so she brainstormed suitable topics for a humorous narrative poem.

Next, Kimiko looked down her list. She selected the topic she liked best, choosing a present for a father who is difficult to please.

a dream of being chased by a crocodile

trying to choose a gift for a difficult father for Father's Day

a day when everything went wrong

a day in the life of a wacky inventor

Discuss

1. How was Kimiko's process of selecting a topic different from the way you have selected topics for other assignments?
2. If Kimiko had listed the topic "why I like my room," might she have used it for her narrative poem? Why or why not?

Gathering Words and Images

After Kimiko selected her topic, she gathered information. She knew that the main part of her poem would be the many fruitless attempts by the narrator to solve her problem. She made a cluster diagram listing gifts that might be considered. Next to each gift, she wrote precise, vivid words and sensory details.

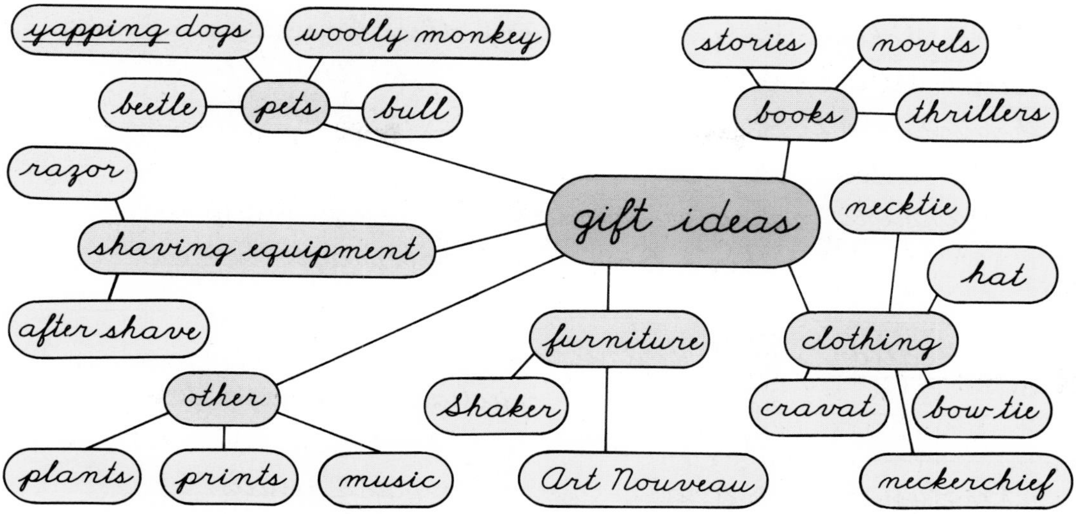

She decided that in her poem she would use **onomatopoetic** words, words that imitate the sound of what they name, like *buzz* for the sound of a bee. She also decided to use **alliteration,** a series of words with the same beginning sound. She included examples of both in her cluster.

Kimiko thought about ways of showing humor in a narrative poem. She knew that her mock-heroic quest for a present would be funny. She remembered that words can be used in humorous ways and she made a list of humorous uses of words.

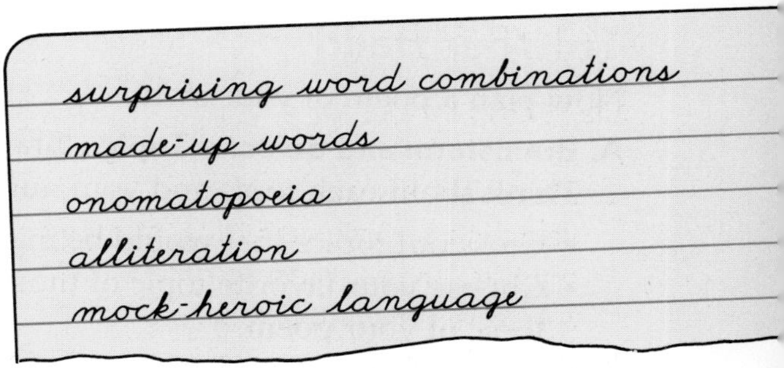

Discuss

1. Kimiko's diagram is not complete. Tell five words she could add.
2. Do you think Kimiko will use every word in her diagram in her poem? Why or why not?

Organizing Information

Before Kimiko started to draft her poem, she thought about the best way to organize her material. She noted the stanza form she would use, the rhyme scheme, and the meter, and she planned the story outline. She made a chart to show the introduction, the complication, and the resolution of her poem.

Stanzas—quatrains

Rhyme Scheme—rhyme for every other line

Meter—same meter as poem "Aged Aged Man" from Through the Looking Glass

Story Outline

Beginning narrator wants a gift for father for Father's Day; keep short, maybe two or three stanzas

Complication search begins and each gift is considered and rejected; one stanza for each gift idea

Resolution gift finally chosen and the results; maybe two stanzas

Discuss

How can thinking of a poem with a meter you want to imitate be helpful?

Try Your Hand

Now plan a poem of your own.

A. Brainstorm and Select a Topic Brainstorm a list of possible topics. Think about each topic and your audience.

- Cross out topics that would be inappropriate for a narrative poem.
- Choose your favorite topic of those left on the list. This will be the topic of your poem.

B. Gather Words and Images When you are satisfied with your topic, plan how to gather information about the event. You may wish to draw a cluster diagram. Include precise, vivid words and sensory details.

C. Organize Information Look over your notes.

- Make some initial decisions about stanza form, rhyme scheme, and rhythm. Jot down some rhyming words you might use.
- Plan an outline of the story events for the introduction, complication, and resolution. You may wish to make a chart like Kimiko's.

Save your diagram and your chart in your *Writer's Notebook.* You will use them when you draft your poem.

2 Drafting
Narrative Poem

Using her diagram and her chart, Kimiko followed the checklist in the **Writer's Guide** to draft her poem. Look at what she did.

Writer's Guide

Drafting Checklist

- ☑ Use your diagram and your chart for ideas.
- ☑ Write your stanzas in sequential order.
- ☑ Develop an introduction, a complication, and a resolution.
- ☑ Give your poem a title.

```
                 The Quest
             by Kimiko Hanaka

It's very hard to choose a gift
  For Dad on Father's Day --
A present that is adequate
  For all I want to say,

A present that conveys respect
  And filial devotion,
But will not cost too much to keep,
  Or cause a big commotion.
```

Discuss

What are some additional details you might expect to find in Kimiko's poem? Where would you expect to find them? Why?

Try Your Hand

Now you are ready to write a poem.

A. Review Your Information Think about the information you gathered and organized in the last lesson. Decide whether you need more information. If so, gather it.

B. Think About Your TAP Remember that your task is to write a narrative poem. Your purpose is to entertain your audience with your topic.

Task: What?
Audience: Who?
Purpose: Why?

C. Write Your First Draft Use the **Drafting Checklist** to help you write your poem.

When you write your draft, just put all your ideas on paper. Do not worry about spelling, grammar, or punctuation. You can correct the draft later.

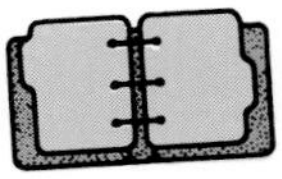

Save your first draft in your *Writer's Notebook*. You will use it when you revise your narrative poem.

3 Responding and Revising

Narrative Poem

Kimiko used the checklist in the **Writer's Guide** to revise her poem. Look at what she did.

Checking Information

Kimiko saw that she had to add some words and cut others to make the two lines fit the meter. The number of syllables needed to be rearranged. To show the additions, she used this mark ∧ . She cut two words from the next line, using this mark ℘ .

Checking Organization

Kimiko saw that the story would flow better if she moved two stanzas to the beginning of the search for the gift. She used this mark ↺ to move them.

Checking Language

In one stanza Kimiko replaced several words with one word. She used this mark ∧‾ to make her change.

Writer's Guide

Revising Checklist

- ☑ Read your poem to yourself or to a partner.
- ☑ Think about your audience and your purpose. Add or cut information.
- ☑ Check to see that your poem has an introduction, a complication, and a resolution.
- ☑ Check for dramatic words that give the right mood.
- ☑ Check for wordy language.

```
My dad hates noise; he cringes if
  There's buzzing, clacking, squawking.
My dad wears earplugs so he won't
  Be bothered by my talking.

So pets are out--from yapping dog
  To soft and woolly monkey.
They take up room, make [lots of] noise,        ← Add
  And special feed costs ~~lots of~~ money.      ← Cut

my dad dislikes my taste in books,               ← Move
  So I save hard-earned cash,
And do not give him my great finds,
  Which he'd burn with the trash.

And music's just as bad, as are
  Fine prints, and plants, and art.
It's best that I ~~get rid of~~ [eliminate] all
  Such items from the start.
```

Discuss

1. Kimiko moved two stanzas. Why did she make this change?
2. Look at the words Kimiko replaced. Explain why she replaced them.
3. Are there other changes Kimiko should make? Explain your answer.

Try Your Hand

Now revise your first draft.

A. Read Your First Draft As you read your poem, think about your audience and your purpose. Read your poem silently or to a partner to see if it is complete and well organized. Ask yourself or your partner the questions in the box.

Responding and Revising Strategies

✔ Respond **Ask yourself or a partner:**	✔ Revise **Try these solutions:**
◆ Have I included in my poem the features of a narrative?	◆ **Add** or rewrite to make sure that these elements are included.
◆ Have I used rhyme, meter, imagery, and vivid language?	◆ **Add** or rewrite to include these elements.
◆ Have I followed the stanza form I chose?	◆ **Cut** or **replace** any stanzas or lines that do not fit the pattern.
◆ Does each word in my poem add to its meaning?	◆ **Cut** or **replace** wordy language. See the **Revising Workshop** on page 116.

B. Make Your Changes If the answer to any question in the box is *no*, try the solution. Use the **Editor's Marks** to show your changes.

C. Review Your Poem Again Decide whether there is anything else you want to revise. Keep revising your narrative poem until you feel it is well organized and complete.

EDITOR'S MARKS

- ∧ Add something.
- Cut something.
- Move something.
- Replace something.

Save your revised narrative poem in your *Writer's Notebook*. You will use it when you proofread your poem.

Revising Workshop
Avoiding Wordy Language

In poems and in other forms of writing, experienced writers revise their work to remove wordy language. They make their writing concise by taking out unnecessary words or phrases and by substituting single words for long-winded phrases.

Look at the underlined words in these sentences.

1. "John Henry" is a story handed down through the ages about a man who works on the first railroad for trains to travel across America.
2. "John Henry" is a legend about a worker on the first railroad across America.

In the first sentence the writer used wordy language. In the second sentence the writer made some changes to say the same thing in fewer words. The phrases *a story handed down through the ages* and *man who works* were replaced with *legend* and *worker*. The phrase *for trains to travel* was left out because it is unnecessary. The second sentence communicates the same message as the first one, but in fewer words.

Practice

Rewrite each sentence. Take out the words in parentheses ( ) or replace them with fewer words that mean the same thing.

1. According to the legend, John Henry was born with (a tool that hammers) in his hand.
2. When he was (a person who was grown up), he joined a crew of workers to help build the railroad from the Atlantic to the Pacific.
3. One day the foreman came into the tunnel with a strange (odd) machine that he called a steam drill.
4. "This drill can dig faster than six workers at once," claimed the (man who was in charge of all the workers).
5. John Henry said he could beat it in a contest (to see if he or the steam drill would win) and set to work with his 14-pound hammer.
6. At the end of day two, John Henry had broken through the cave ahead of the steam drill, but then he dropped from exhaustion (because he was so tired).

Listening and Speaking
Tips on How to Read Aloud and Listen to Poetry

Reading Poetry Aloud

1. Prepare to read a poem aloud. Read the poem over to yourself several times. Note the following:
   - the rhythm
   - the rhyme scheme or the sound of the lines where the stanzas end
   - the words that are most important to the poet's ideas
   - the mood and the meaning of the poem
2. Your voice is capable of many different sounds. Keep the following variations in mind as you read.
   a. **pitch**—how high or low you speak. By varying pitch you can show emotion and create different voices for different characters.
   b. **volume**—how loudly or softly you speak. By varying volume you can create a mood or emphasize important parts of the poem. You can also stress words that emphasize the poem's meter.
   c. **tone**—your attitude toward the poem's subject, expressed by your voice. By varying the tone of your voice, you can help the listener interpret the poem's meaning as you express feelings.
   d. **tempo**—how quickly or slowly you read. You can speed up the tempo to show a rush of quick, exciting events or slow it down for a serious, difficult, or suspenseful part.
   e. **pausing**—stopping for a short or a long period between sentences or stanzas and after lines with punctuation at the end.
3. Use gestures when appropriate.

Listening to Poetry

1. Listen carefully to the title so that you have an idea of what is to come.
2. Try to get an idea of the poem's stanza form, meter, and rhyme scheme as you hear it read. Identify the subject, the narrator, and the characters (if any). Listen for the story line if the poem is narrative. Listen for words that are repeated and emphasized.
3. If possible, listen to a poem several times.
4. Think about how the poet used the elements of poetry to express meaning.

4 Proofreading
Narrative Poem

After revising her poem, Kimiko used the **Writer's Guide** and the **Editor's Marks** to proofread it. Look at what she did.

Writer's Guide

Proofreading Checklist

- ☑ Check for errors in capitalization. Be sure that you've capitalized people's names correctly.
- ☑ Check for errors in punctuation.
- ☑ Check for errors in grammar.
- ☑ Circle any words you think are misspelled. Find out how to spell them correctly.
- ⇨ For proofreading help, use the **Writer's Handbook.**

```
But mom has let me know that, since,
 He's used them for a rag.
Next father's Day, I'll give a card
 Wrapped in a store-bought bag

And then, just as I left The mall,
 Above the parking lot      balloon
I saw a bright hot-air baloon--
 and thought, of course! Why not?"
```

EDITOR'S MARKS

- Capitalize.
- Add a period.
- Add something.
- Add a comma.
- Add quotation marks.
- Cut something.
- Replace something.
- Transpose.
- Spell correctly.
- Indent paragraph.
- Make a lowercase letter.

Discuss

1. What kinds of corrections did Kimiko make?
2. Why did she capitalize *Father's Day* and *Mom*?

Try Your Hand

Proofread Your Narrative Poem Now use the **Writer's Guide** and the **Editor's Marks** to proofread your poem.

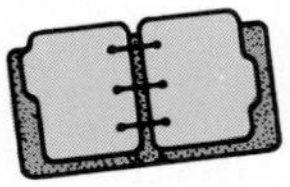

Save your corrected poem in your *Writer's Notebook*. You will use it when you publish your narrative poem.

5 Publishing
Narrative Poem

Kimiko made a clean copy of her narrative poem and checked it to be sure she had not left out anything. Then she and her classmates published their poems by entering them in a poetry contest. You can find Kimiko's poem on page 54 of the **Writer's Handbook.**

Here's how Kimiko and her classmates published their narrative poems for a poetry contest.

Writer's Guide

Publishing Checklist

- ☑ Make a clean copy of your poem.
- ☑ Check to see that nothing has been left out.
- ☑ Be sure that there are no mistakes.
- ☑ Share your poem in a special way.

1. They read, or listened to their teacher read, the contest directions. They took notes on any special contest requirements, such as typing the poem with double spacing, obtaining a parent's or a guardian's signature, and mailing the entry before a deadline.

2. They made final copies of their poems, following the contest instructions. They addressed their envelopes. They wrote neatly and clearly, making sure to include their return addresses.

Discuss

1. What might happen if contestants did not follow the contest directions?
2. Why should each contestant include his or her return address?

Try Your Hand

Publish Your Narrative Poem Follow the checklist in the **Writer's Guide.** If possible, enter your poem in a contest or try one of these ideas for sharing your narrative poem.

- Share your poem with your family.
- Make a class poetry magazine.
- Send your poem to a children's magazine, such as *Stone Soup.*

Writing in the Content Areas

Use what you have learned to write a narrative poem. You can make it humorous or serious. Use one of these ideas or an idea of your own.

Writer's Guide

When you write, remember the stages of the Writing Process.

- Prewriting
- Drafting
- Responding and Revising
- Proofreading
- Publishing

Literature

A frigate is a small, fast ship. Emily Dickinson compared this kind of ship to a book in her poem "There Is No Frigate Like a Book." Think of a book that, like a boat, has taken you away to a foreign or imaginary land. Describe the place so that someone else can enjoy the journey.

Physical Education

The narrative poem "Casey at the Bat," written by Ernest L. Thayer, is about baseball. Think of a sport you enjoy, and put your name in the title of a poem or a story about that sport. Tell what happens one day when you play the sport.

Mathematics

Do you have trouble understanding math sometimes? Have you ever wished that one of those triangles, squares, or rectangles in a math problem would whisper the answer to you? Write a fanciful narrative poem telling about such an event.

Science

Many scientists find wonder in the world they see through a microscope or a telescope or in a tide pool or a field. Take a close look at one of these environments and describe what you discover in a narrative poem. You may wish to read the poem "To Look at Any Thing" by John Moffit for ideas.

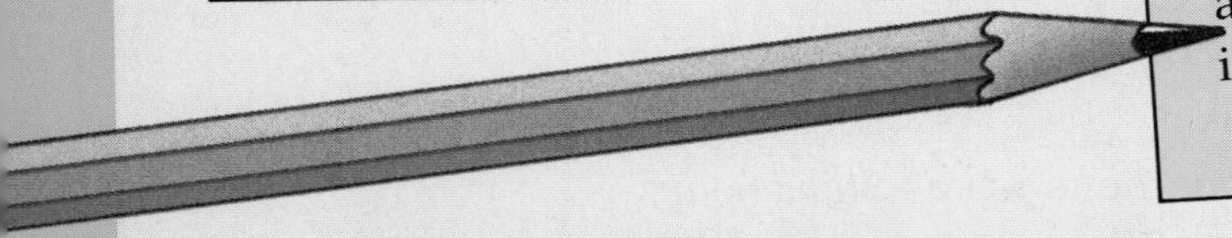

CONNECTING
WRITING ↔ LANGUAGE

As you know, poetry can tell stories. These verses continue the story of "Casey at the Bat." How does the poet's choice of words help you picture the frenzied crowd and feel the tension of the game?

> And now the leather-covered sphere came hurtling through the air.
> And Casey stood a-watching it in haughty grandeur there.
> Close by the sturdy batsman the ball unheeded sped —
> "That ain't my style," said Casey. "Strike one," the umpire said.
>
> From the benches, black with people, there went up a muffled roar,
> Like the beating of the storm-waves on a stern and distant shore.
> "Kill him! Kill the umpire!" shouted someone on the stand;
> And it's likely they'd have killed him had not Casey raised his hand.
>
> With a smile of Christian charity great Casey's visage shone;
> He stilled the rising tumult; he bade the game go on;
> He signaled to the pitcher, and once more the spheroid flew;
> But Casey still ignored it, and the umpire said, "Strike two."

- **Verbs in a Narrative Poem** "Casey at the Bat" contains verbs that help the reader picture the action. The highlighted verbs tell about this event that took place in the past. Some past-tense verbs, such as *ignored,* end in *ed*. Others, such as *said,* have irregular spellings.
- **Language Focus: Verbs** The following lessons will help you use different kinds of verbs in your own writing.

1 Verbs

FOCUS

- A **verb** expresses action or being.
- A **linking verb** connects the subject to a word or words in the predicate.

Remember that a verb tells what the subject of a sentence does (its action) or what it is (its state of being). The words in color are verbs.

1. The captain commands the starship.
2. It is one of the finest vessels in the fleet.

An **action verb** expresses physical or mental action. The words in color are action verbs.

3. The ship streaks into space. physical action
4. The crew trusts the captain. mental action

Linking verbs connect the subject of a sentence with a word in the predicate that describes the subject. The words in color are linking verbs.

5. The planet Earth is far away now.

Some linking verbs can also be used as action verbs.

6. The crew felt calm. linking verb
7. Jamal felt the cover of the book. action verb

To tell whether a verb is an action verb or a linking verb, replace it with a form of the verb *be*. If the meaning does not change, the verb is a linking verb.

8. The command deck grew silent. linking verb

   The command deck was silent.

Linking Verbs
Some Forms of *Be*
am, is, are, was, were, will be, could be, has been
Other Verbs
appear, seem, look, sound, taste, feel, smell, become, grow, remain, stay, turn

Guided Practice

A. Identify each verb. Tell whether it is an *action verb* or a *linking verb*.

1. Science fiction fascinates me.
2. Space movies are the best.
3. The special effects are superb.
4. The captain vanishes.
5. We find him on a planet.
6. His ship flashes past stars.

THINK AND REMEMBER

- Remember that **action verbs** express physical or mental action.
- Remember that **linking verbs** link the subject of a sentence with a word in the predicate that describes the subject.
- Use vivid action verbs for lively writing.

Independent Practice

B. Identifying Verbs Write the verb from each sentence. Write *action verb* or *linking verb* to show how the verb is used in each sentence.

7. Paula gazed at the stars through the telescope.

MODEL gazed—action verb

8. I often wondered about the names of the stars.
9. Paula explained some of them to me.
10. Her favorite subject is astronomy.
11. Astronomy teaches us about Greek and Roman heroes.
12. The names of these giants became the names of stars.

C. Identifying Action Verbs Write the action verb from each sentence. Write *mental action* or *physical action* to show how the verb is used in each sentence.

13. I consider astronauts modern-day heroes.

MODEL consider—mental action

14. Astronaut Neil Armstrong first walked on the moon.
15. Millions of Americans watched his historic accomplishment.
16. We admire the courage of all astronauts.
17. We realize the unique dangers.
18. Some Americans observe shuttle liftoffs.
19. Sally Ride led the way for American women in space.

Application — Writing

Movie Scene Write a description of a heroic or courageous act for a movie scene. Tell enough about the scene so that a producer can decide whether to use it. Use your **Writer's Thesaurus** at the back of this book to locate vivid action verbs.

2 Main Verbs and Helping Verbs

FOCUS

- The **main verb** is the most important verb in a verb phrase.
- A **helping verb** works with the main verb to express action or being.

Helping Verbs
am, are, is, was, were, can, could, would, should, have, has, had, do, does, did, will, shall, be, being, been, may, might, must

Remember that a verb may be made up of one word or more than one word. A verb that consists of more than one word is called a **verb phrase.** The word group in color is a verb phrase.

1. The archaeologists are looking for old objects.

The main verb is the most important verb in a verb phrase. It is always the last verb in the verb phrase. The other verbs are helping verbs.

helping verbs — main verb

2. Mrs. Lyons has been recording the findings.

Sometimes a verb that looks like a helping verb is actually the main verb in a sentence.

3. They might be digging for more pots. **helping**
4. This bracelet might be very old. **main**

A verb phrase may sometimes be interrupted by other words. A **contraction** is the shortened form of two words. Sometimes there are helping verbs within contractions. In these sentences, the verb phrases are shown in color.

5. Some ancient cups have just been found.
6. Could this have been the site of a house?
7. The archaeologists couldn't be sure.

Guided Practice

A. Identify the *main verb* and the *helping verb or verbs* in each underlined verb phrase.

1. An exhibit of Egyptian artifacts will be shown here.
2. The exhibit should arrive at our local museum in April.
3. Our teacher is taking the whole class to see it.
4. It'll be a rare opportunity to see such ancient objects.
5. Egyptian kings may have worn those very garments.

THINK AND REMEMBER

- Remember that a **verb phrase** is made up of a **main verb,** the most important verb in a verb phrase, and one or more **helping verbs.**

Independent Practice

B. Identifying Main Verbs and Helping Verbs Write the verb phrase from each sentence. Underline the helping verb or verbs once. Underline the main verb twice.

6. The pyramids of Egypt have been standing since 2800 B.C.

MODEL have been standing

7. They've been called one of the Seven Wonders of the World.
8. Thousands of workers must have labored on these tombs.
9. The tomb of Pharaoh Khufu is named the Great Pyramid.
10. It can be found near the city of Cairo.
11. The Great Pyramid may contain over 2 million blocks.
12. Each block would have weighed 5,000 pounds.
13. Layers of blocks were placed on top of each other.
14. How could the workers have built the pyramids?
15. We'll never be sure.

C. Adding Helping Verbs Write each sentence, adding one or more helping verbs to the main verb in parentheses ( ).

16. Divers (find) treasures on sunken ships.

MODEL Divers may find treasures on sunken ships.

17. Tons of sand (buried) one Roman ship.
18. It (taking) its cargo across the Mediterranean.
19. Centuries ago a storm (destroyed) the vessel.
20. A coin in the wreck (reveal) its age.
21. Some treasure (salvaged) by divers.
22. Much more (hidden) beneath the sea.

Application — Writing

Journal Entry Pretend that you are on an archaeological dig. Write a journal entry describing what you discovered during one day. Use main verbs and helping verbs to describe your actions. If you need help writing a journal entry, see page 48 of the **Writer's Handbook.**

3 Principal Parts of Regular Verbs

◆ **FOCUS** The **principal parts** of a verb are the *present*, the *present participle*, the *past*, and the *past participle*.

Verbs do more than simply show action or being. Verbs also express time by changing tenses. The **tense** of a verb shows when the action or being takes place. The words in color show tense change.

1. The pioneers travel all day
2. The pioneers are traveling west.
3. The pioneers traveled through St. Louis.
4. The pioneers will travel all the way to California.

You use the principal parts of a verb to form the tenses. Each verb has four principal parts.

Present	Present Participle	Past	Past Participle
cross	(is, are) crossing	crossed	(have, has, had) crossed

To form the present participle of regular verbs, add *ing* to the present. Use forms of the verb *be* (*am, is, are*) with the present participle.

For regular verbs, add *ed* to form the past and the past participle. Use the helping verbs *have, has,* or *had* with the past participle.

Some words undergo spelling changes to form the principal parts.

1. If a one-syllable verb ends in a single consonant and that consonant is preceded by a single vowel, double the final consonant before adding *ed* or *ing.* **Example:** drop, dropped, dropping
2. If a verb ends in a consonant plus *y*, change the *y* to *i* before adding *ed.* **Example:** study, studied
3. If a verb ends in *e*, drop the *e* before adding *ed* or *ing.* **Example:** like, liked, liking

Guided Practice

A. Name and spell the four principal parts of each verb.

1. live
2. try
3. want
4. struggle
5. read
6. hurry

THINK AND REMEMBER

- Remember that the **principal parts** of a verb express time by changing tenses.
- Remember that there are four principal parts of a verb—*present, present participle, past,* and *past participle.*

Independent Practice

B. Writing Principal Parts Write the principal parts of each verb.

7. save

MODEL save, (is, are) saving, saved, (have, has, had) saved

8. walk
9. remind
10. donate
11. clean
12. deserve
13. knot
14. worry
15. watch

C. Completing Sentences Write the correct principal part of the verb in parentheses ( ).

16. Early explorers (map—past) our country.

MODEL mapped

17. Fremont (survey—past) the West.
18. In 1842 he was (explore—present participle) the Rockies.
19. There he (befriend—past) Kit Carson.
20. He (hire—past) Kit Carson as a guide.
21. Fremont (record—past) his memoirs.

D. Writing Sentences Write four sentences for each verb, using each principal part.

22. plan

MODEL We plan a trip out West.
We are planning to fly from Pittsburgh.
We planned one stop at Sequoia National Park.
We have planned other stops also.

23. hike 24. cook 25. stop 26. hurry 27. camp

Application — Writing

Diary Imagine that you are a member of a pioneer family heading west. Keep a diary about your trip, and write about four or five days on the trail. Describe what you have seen and your feelings about the trip. Try to use all the principal parts of verbs in your writing.

4 Principal Parts of Irregular Verbs

FOCUS

- An **irregular verb** does not have *ed* or *d* added to the present to form the past or the past participle.
- The principal parts of some irregular verbs are formed according to certain patterns.

Although irregular verbs do not have *ed* added to the present to form the past and past participle, many of these verbs do follow certain patterns. Learning the patterns will help you remember the principal parts.

Group 1

For some irregular verbs, the vowel changes to *a* to form the past.

Present	Present Participle	Past	Past Participle
become	(is, are) becoming	became	(have, has, had) become
come	(is, are) coming	came	(have, has, had) come
run	(is, are) running	ran	(have, has, had) run

Group 2

The vowel in some irregular verbs changes to *a* to form the past and to *u* to form the past participle.

Present	Present Participle	Past	Past Participle
begin	(is, are) beginning	began	(have, has, had) begun
drink	(is, are) drinking	drank	(have, has, had) drunk
ring	(is, are) ringing	rang	(have, has, had) rung
sing	(is, are) singing	sang	(have, has, had) sung
sink	(is, are) sinking	sank	(have, has, had) sunk
spring	(is, are) springing	sprang	(have, has, had) sprung
swim	(is, are) swimming	swam	(have, has, had) swum

Group 3

The past and the past participle are the same for some irregular verbs.

Present	Present Participle	Past	Past Participle
bend	(is, are) bending	bent	(have, has, had) bent
bring	(is, are) bringing	brought	(have, has, had) brought
buy	(is, are) buying	bought	(have, has, had) bought
creep	(is, are) creeping	crept	(have, has, had) crept
fling	(is, are) flinging	flung	(have, has, had) flung
lay	(is, are) laying	laid	(have, has, had) laid
lead	(is, are) leading	led	(have, has, had) led
leave	(is, are) leaving	left	(have, has, had) left
lend	(is, are) lending	lent	(have, has, had) lent
seek	(is, are) seeking	sought	(have, has, had) sought
shine	(is, are) shining	shone	(have, has, had) shone
sit	(is, are) sitting	sat	(have, has, had) sat
sting	(is, are) stinging	stung	(have, has, had) stung
swing	(is, are) swinging	swung	(have, has, had) swung
think	(is, are) thinking	thought	(have, has, had) thought

Group 4

For some irregular verbs, the present, the past, and the past participle all have the same spelling.

Present	Present Participle	Past	Past Participle
bet	(is, are) betting	bet	(have, has, had) bet
burst	(is, are) bursting	burst	(have, has, had) burst
cost	(is, are) costing	cost	(have, has, had) cost
hurt	(is, are) hurting	hurt	(have, has, had) hurt
put	(is, are) putting	put	(have, has, had) put
set	(is, are) setting	set	(have, has, had) set
shut	(is, are) shutting	shut	(have, has, had) shut
spread	(is, are) spreading	spread	(have, has, had) spread

Guided Practice

A. Give the four principal parts of each verb.

1. sing
2. sit
3. make
4. burst
5. begin
6. spread
7. cost
8. drink

THINK AND REMEMBER

- Remember that **irregular verbs** do not have *ed* added to form the past and the past participle.
- Follow certain patterns to form the principal parts of some irregular verbs.

Independent Practice

B. Writing Principal Parts of Irregular Verbs Set up a chart as shown. Fill in the chart with the principal parts of each verb.

9. ring

MODEL

Present	Present Participle	Past	Past Participle
ring	(is, are) ringing	rang	(have, has, had) rung

10. melt **12.** sell **14.** spend **16.** lose
11. run **13.** leave **15.** spring **17.** sing

C. Checking Irregular Verbs in Sentences Write the correct form of the verb in parentheses ( ).

18. The captain (tell, told) us not to dive.

MODEL told

19. He (said, say) he had the latest weather reports.
20. A storm had (brought, bring) rough seas.
21. He (think, thought) that the storm would be over soon.
22. That afternoon we (made, make) our preparations for the long-awaited dive.
23. Clear weather and calm seas had (came, come).
24. After the bad weather cleared, we (swam, swim) carefully over the reef.
25. We then (sought, seek) rare coral formations.

Application — Writing and Speaking

Oral Report Imagine that you are a diver on a quest for a sunken ship. You must describe your work in an oral report to a group of oceanographers. Write your report in a paragraph, giving detailed observations of what you have found on your dives. Use at least four irregular verbs in your writing. Present your report to your classmates.

5 More Irregular Verbs

◆ **FOCUS** Some irregular verbs do not follow a pattern when they change form.

Remember that irregular verbs do not form the past and the past participle by adding *ed* to the present form.

Group 5

To form the past participle of some irregular verbs, add *n, en,* or *ne* to the present.

Present	Present Participle	Past	Past Participle
do	(is, are) doing	did	(have, has, had) done
drive	(is, are) driving	drove	(have, has, had) driven
give	(is, are) giving	gave	(have, has, had) given
go	(is, are) going	went	(have, has, had) gone
grow	(is, are) growing	grew	(have, has, had) grown
know	(is, are) knowing	knew	(have, has, had) known
ride	(is, are) riding	rode	(have, has, had) ridden
rise	(is, are) rising	rose	(have, has, had) risen
throw	(is, are) throwing	threw	(have, has, had) thrown
write	(is, are) writing	wrote	(have, has, had) written

Group 6

For other irregular verbs, add *n* or *en* to the past to form the past participle. The spelling may change slightly.

Present	Present Participle	Past	Past Participle
break	(is, are) breaking	broke	(have, has, had) broken
choose	(is, are) choosing	chose	(have, has, had) chosen
fly	(is, are) flying	flew	(have, has, had) flown
forget	(is, are) forgetting	forgot	(have, has, had) forgotten
freeze	(is, are) freezing	froze	(have, has, had) frozen
lie	(is, are) lying	lay	(have, has, had) lain
speak	(is, are) speaking	spoke	(have, has, had) spoken
tear	(is, are) tearing	tore	(have, has, had) torn
wear	(is, are) wearing	wore	(have, has, had) worn

Guided Practice

A. Give the principal parts of each verb.

1. eat	**3.** rise	**5.** throw	**7.** sew
2. write	**4.** break	**6.** freeze	**8.** tear

THINK AND REMEMBER

- Remember that the past participle of some irregular verbs is formed by adding *n*, *en*, or *ne* to the present or the past.

Independent Practice

B. Writing Principal Parts of Irregular Verbs Set up a chart as shown. Fill in the chart with the principal parts of each verb.

9. break

MODEL

Present	Present Participle	Past	Past Participle
break	(is, are) breaking	broke	(have, has, had) broken

10. steal	**12.** ride	**14.** hide	**16.** bite
11. wear	**13.** see	**15.** know	**17.** beat

C. Revising: Adding Irregular Verbs in Sentences Write the correct form of the verb in parentheses ( ).

18. Joni (drew, drawn) a sketch to illustrate a myth.

MODEL drew

19. She had (chose, chosen) to invent an imaginary bird.
20. Everyone (see, saw) the resemblance to an eagle.
21. The eagle was (flown, flying) across the sky.
22. Joni has never (forgot, forgotten) how pleased she was.
23. Few would have (knew, known) of her talent.

Application — Writing

Movie Cartoon Imagine that you are creating a movie or a television cartoon character who can perform superhuman acts. Describe your character's abilities. Tell about an event in which the character must use these abilities. Use the principal parts of irregular verbs correctly.

6 Verb Tenses

◆ **FOCUS** The six verb tenses are the present, the past, the future, the present perfect, the past perfect, and the future perfect.

Six tenses of verbs are used to express time.

The **present tense** expresses action that is happening now.

1. People explore their world.
2. They discover places and things.

The **past tense** expresses action that happened in the past.

3. Sailors in the fifteenth century explored the world in wooden ships.
4. They discovered new shipping routes.

The **future tense** expresses action that will occur in the future.

5. One day scientists and technicians will explore other planets in space.
6. They will discover places far away.

The **present perfect tense** expresses action that began in the past and is still continuing.

7. For years we have explored the wonders of the universe with telescopes.
8. We have discovered many new ideas.

The **past perfect tense** expresses action that occurred in the past before some other action.

9. When Magellan had explored for three years, he returned to Spain.
10. He told his countrymen about many interesting things that he had discovered.

The **future perfect tense** expresses action that will take place in the future before some other future action.

11. By the year 2010, spacecraft will have explored the mysterious surface of Mars.
12. By that time, they will have discovered clues to that planet's mysteries.

A list of all the forms of a verb, grouped by tense, is a **conjugation.** This table shows a partial conjugation of the verb *explore.* Remember that you use some of the principal parts of verbs to form all the tenses.

Conjugation of the Verb *Explore*	
Principal Parts: explore, (is, are) exploring, explored, (have, has, had) explored	
Present Tense	
Singular I explore you explore he, she, it explores	*Plural* we explore you explore they explore
Past Tense	
Singular I explored you explored he, she, it explored	*Plural* we explored you explored they explored
Future Tense	
Singular I will (shall) explore you will explore he, she, it will explore	*Plural* we will (shall) explore you will explore they will explore
Present Perfect Tense	
Singular I have explored you have explored he, she, it has explored	*Plural* we have explored you have explored they have explored
Past Perfect Tense	
Singular I had explored you had explored he, she, it had explored	*Plural* we had explored you had explored they had explored
Future Perfect Tense	
Singular I will (shall) have explored you will have explored he, she, it will have explored	*Plural* we will (shall) have explored you will have explored they will have explored

Guided Practice

A. Identify the tense of each verb.

1. learn
2. will travel
3. had imagined
4. blasts
5. described
6. observed
7. had examined
8. has predicted
9. will orbit
10. will determine
11. will have circled
12. notices
13. have scouted
14. looked
15. will have searched

> **THINK AND REMEMBER**
> - Remember that there are six tenses for every verb: **present, past, future, present perfect, past perfect,** and **future perfect.**

Independent Practice

B. Identifying Verb Tenses Write each verb or verb phrase from each sentence. Next to each, write its tense.

16. Medical science constantly seeks improvements.

MODEL seeks—present

17. Improvements in medicine have advanced rapidly.
18. A fiber-optic arthroscope provides fast, easy diagnosis.
19. Its invention has allowed doctors to view inside the body without cutting.
20. Once, a knee injury signaled the end of an athletic career.
21. Now, surgeons completely repair torn ligaments.
22. Years ago they thought this impossible.
23. Someday artificial ligaments will replace torn ones.
24. Doctors also have explored the body with lasers.
25. Laser surgery uses a beam of light instead of a knife.
26. The light will reach into very small places.
27. By the year 2030 the laser will have progressed even more.

C. Writing Verb Tenses Write each sentence using the correct tense of the verb in parentheses ( ).

28. Ferdinand Magellan (sail—past) around the earth.

MODEL Ferdinand Magellan sailed around the earth.

29. He (enlist—past perfect) as a soldier before he turned 26.
30. However, Magellan later (decide—past) to become a navigator.

31. We (name—present perfect) Magellan's route around South America the Strait of Magellan.
32. Today we (explore—present) the ocean for other purposes.
33. Food supplies (improve—future) when we harvest the ocean.
34. By the year 2000, perhaps we (solve—future perfect) the problem of world hunger.

D. Proofreading: Correcting Verb Tenses Rewrite each sentence using the correct tense for each underlined verb.

35. Our knowledge of the universe had increased daily.

MODEL Our knowledge of the universe increases daily.

36. *Pioneer* probes will have passed by Saturn in 1981.
37. Since that time scientists will analyze *Pioneer*'s photographs.
38. By 1976 *Viking* space probes already land on Mars.
39. At that time they have conducted tests of the atmosphere.
40. By the year 2000 the probes traveled on toward the stars.
41. Analysis of the data had continued for years to come.
42. Now the scientific community considered future options.

E. 43.–60. Writing Sentences Choose two of the verbs in this list:
pull pack invent discover launch land
For each, write sentences about a topic using the six tenses.

MODEL I work at a NASA laboratory.
I worked on designs for the space probes.
My sister will work on special effects for films.
She has worked on similar projects.
She said she had worked very hard.
By June, we will have worked in the realms of fact and fiction.

Application — Writing

Friendly Letter Imagine that you are exploring an unknown territory or experimenting with a new scientific instrument. Write a letter describing your exploration or experiment to a friend. Tell what you have seen and done, what is happening now, and what you expect to discover. Try to use in your writing all six verb tenses discussed in this lesson. If you need help writing a friendly letter, see page 62 of the **Writer's Handbook.**

7 Be, Have, Do

◆ **FOCUS** The verbs *be, have,* and *do* are irregular.

Irregular verbs do not form their past and past participle by adding *ed*. The verbs *be, have,* and *do* are irregular.

1. Maria is in position on the court. **form of *be***
2. She now has the ball over the net. **form of *have***
3. She did well in the last match. **form of *do***

You can use the verbs *be, have,* and *do* as main verbs or as helping verbs.

	Main Verbs	Helping Verbs
4.	Maria is ready for the ball.	She is standing at the baseline.
5.	She has the serve.	The match has lasted one hour.
6.	The players did their best.	They did please the crowd.

Study the conjugations for *be, have,* and *do*. Notice the different forms used with singular and plural subjects.

Conjugation of the Verb *Be*			
Principal Parts: be, being, was, been			
	Present	**Past**	**Future**
I	am	was	will be
he, she, it	is	was	will be
we, you, they	are	were	will be
	Present Perfect	**Past Perfect**	**Future Perfect**
I	have been	had been	will have been
he, she, it	has been	had been	will have been
we, you, they	have been	had been	will have been

Conjugation of the Verb *Have*			
Principal Parts: have, having, had, had			
	Present	**Past**	**Future**
I, we, you, they	have	had	will have
he, she, it	has	had	will have
	Present Perfect	**Past Perfect**	**Future Perfect**
I, we, you, they	have had	had had	will have had
he, she, it	has had	had had	will have had

Conjugation of the Verb *Do*			
Principal Parts: do, doing, did, done			
	Present	**Past**	**Future**
I, we, you, they	do	did	will do
he, she, it	does	did	will do
	Present Perfect	**Past Perfect**	**Future Perfect**
I, we, you, they	have done	had done	will have done
he, she, it	has done	had done	will have done

Link to Speaking and Writing

The verbs *be, have,* and *do* can be used in contractions. Be sure to use the correct contraction with the subject of the sentence. Why is the contraction *hasn't* used instead of *haven't* in this sentence?

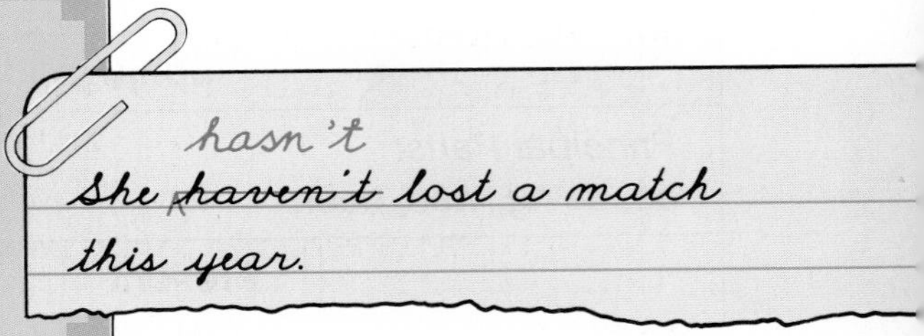

hasn't
She haven't lost a match
this year.

Guided Practice

A. Identify the correct form of the verb in parentheses ( ) to complete each sentence.

1. Tennis (is, are) my best sport.
2. I (has, have) a good backhand.
3. Luis (am, is) my tennis partner.
4. We have (been, be) playing often.
5. Luis has not (have, had) lessons.
6. Lessons (was, were) costly.
7. Playing has (does, done) him good.
8. He (is, are) doing as well as I.
9. Luis (has, have) beaten me.
10. We (does, do) not play daily.

B. Name the correct contraction in parentheses ( ) for each sentence.

11. He (hasn't, haven't) forgotten good sportsmanship.
12. It (aren't, isn't) hard to achieve.
13. They (weren't, wasn't) angry with each other.
14. We (doesn't, don't) enjoy a game with poor losers.
15. You (haven't, hasn't) seen a better game than this.

THINK AND REMEMBER

- Remember that irregular verbs do not form the past or past participle by adding *ed*.
- Remember that the irregular verbs *be, have,* and *do* can be used as main verbs or as helping verbs.
- Use the correct contractions for the verbs *be, have,* and *do.*

Independent Practice

C. Writing Verb Forms Write the correct form of the verb in parentheses ( ).

16. Interviewer: (Do, Does) you have time for a few questions?
MODEL Do
17. Maria: I will (been, be) right with you.
18. Interviewer: How (does, did) you get ready for the match this afternoon?
19. Maria: I (had, has) a light workout this morning.
20. Interviewer: (Was, Were) it your normal workout routine?
21. Maria: Yes. I lifted weights, and I (did, done) some stretching exercises.
22. Interviewer: You (have, had) a knee injury last week. How (are, is) your knee now?
23. Maria: It is feeling much better. It has (be, been) improving every day.
24. Interviewer: (Were, Was) you worried today that it would slow you down?
25. Maria: No. It (did, do) not affect my playing today at all.
26. Interviewer: Will you (been, be) training to play in the U.S. Open?
27. Maria: Yes. By August I will have (been, be) working out for three months.

dentifying Correct Verbs and Contractions Write the correct form of the verb or contraction in parentheses ( ).

28. Exercise (is, are) the most efficient way to improve your tennis game.

MODEL is

29. Fitness (doesn't, don't) require a lot of time or expensive equipment.
30. Daily practice (aren't, isn't) the only part of a good training regimen.
31. Exercise (are, is) helpful for building strong muscle groups throughout the body.
32. Weight lifting (has, have) given many players more strength in the arms and legs.
33. A healthful diet (is, are) of major importance to every athlete.
34. The best players (doesn't, don't) eat excessive amounts of junk food.
35. Fruits and vegetables (is, are) good sources of vitamins, minerals, and fiber.
36. A tennis player (don't, doesn't) want to lose stamina during a game.
37. You will (be, been) able to gain a much greater speed through sprinting.
38. After a 220-yard sprint, you will (has, have) been exercising your heart.

E. Writing Sentences Write a sentence, using each verb phrase.

39. will be

MODEL She will be at the park tomorrow.

40. do have
41. won't
42. hasn't been
43. were
44. have done
45. will have
46. doesn't do
47. had done
48. is having
49. shall do

Application — Writing

Interview Continue the interview started in **C.** Write five questions the interviewer might ask Maria about her match and the answer Maria might give for each question. Use different forms of the verbs *be, have,* and *do* in your interview.

8 Subject-Verb Agreement

◆ **FOCUS** A subject and a verb should agree in number.

The subjects and verbs of your sentences should agree in number. **Agreement** in number means using a singular verb with a singular subject and a plural verb with a plural subject.

1. A lightning bolt streaks across the sky. singular
2. Three lightning bolts streak across the sky. plural

The chart will help you see when to use a singular or a plural verb.

Use a Singular Verb	Use a Plural Verb
I, you (singular) he, she, it	we, you (plural) they

Sometimes your sentences may have more than one subject. If you combine sentences and form compound subjects, be sure that the verb agrees with the compound subject. Study these rules for agreement.

If you join the subjects with *and,* use a plural verb.

3. The lightning and thunder frighten the children.

If you join singular subjects with *or,* use a singular verb. If you join plural subjects with *or,* use a plural verb.

4. A lightning rod or a closed car guards you from lightning.
5. Trees or buildings attract electric charges.

If you join a singular and a plural subject with *or* or *nor,* use a verb that agrees with the subject that is nearest the verb.

6. The twins or John knows what to do. singular
7. Neither television nor telephones are to be used. plural

Guided Practice

A. Identify the present-tense form of the verb in parentheses ( ) that would agree with each subject.

1. it (fly)
2. he (close)
3. they (have)
4. an atom (carry)
5. ice and hail (swirl)
6. forests or a field (offer)

THINK AND REMEMBER

- Remember that the subject and the verb of a sentence agree in number. Use singular verbs with singular subjects and plural verbs with plural subjects.
- Remember that compound subjects may take singular or plural verbs.

Independent Practice

B. Writing Correct Verb Forms Write the correct form of the verb in parentheses ( ).

7. A lightning flash (lights, light) the sky.

MODEL lights

8. The thunderclaps (are, is) deafening.
9. Neither we nor my brothers (likes, like) storms.
10. Violent thunderstorms (terrifies, terrify) me too.
11. Wu and I (creeps, creep) quietly upstairs.
12. A slamming window (makes, make) us jump.

C. Revising: Combining Sentences Combine each set of sentences to make one sentence with two or more subjects. Use the conjunction given in parentheses ( ). Be sure the verb agrees with the subject.

13. Lightning causes forest fires.
    Careless people cause forest fires. (or)

MODEL Lightning or careless people cause forest fires.

14. Volunteers combat the blazes.
    Paid fire fighters combat the blazes. (and)
15. Water restrains the fire.
    A fire line restrains the fire. (or)
16. Lookouts sight and report the fires.
    Forest rangers sight and report the fires.
    Airplane pilots sight and report the fires. (or)
17. Insects destroy millions of trees annually.
    Disease destroys millions of trees annually. (and)

Application — Writing and Speaking

Storytelling Many people make up stories to explain unusual happenings. Write a story that you think could explain why thunder and lightning occur. Try to use two compound subjects. Be sure that your verbs agree with your subjects. Tell your story to a young child.

9 Tense Changes

◆ **FOCUS** Verb tenses change to indicate that events happen at different times.

Remember that you use tenses to tell the time of events. Unnecessary tense changes make it difficult for your audience to understand when events take place. When writing, keep these points in mind.

Keep the tense of the verbs in your writing consistent within sentences and from one sentence to the next. The words in color are verbs.

Incorrect: **1.** Sequoyah invented an alphabet that he teaches to the Cherokees.

Correct: **2.** Sequoyah invented an alphabet that he taught to the Cherokees.

Incorrect: **3.** Willa Cather was an author. She writes about pioneers.

Correct: **4.** Willa Cather was an author. She wrote about pioneers.

When events occur at different times, change the verb tense to convey the correct sequence.

5. Many people think of pioneers as those who traveled west.

6. I have enjoyed stories about the West, and someday my children will read these same stories.

7. The pioneers had courage that has inspired others.

8. After they had journeyed west, they built new lives for themselves.

Remember that if you are writing about something that has already happened, you should use verbs in the past tense. If you are writing about events happening now, use verbs in the present tense.

9. James Michener portrayed the growth of a town when he wrote the book *Centennial*.

10. The book gives the reader historical information and weaves it in with the story.

Guided Practice

A. In each sentence, identify which tense of the verb in parentheses ( ) you would need to use to keep the verb tense consistent.

1. A pioneer is a person who (advance) into unknown territory.
2. There were pioneers of the land and pioneers of ideas whose courage (help) to build this country.
3. Willa Cather and James Michener both wrote about pioneers, but they (start) with different points of view.
4. Willa Cather had moved west early in her life, and she (use) her experiences in many of her stories.
5. James Michener bases his detailed stories on research that he (do).
6. Michener studied and (write) about Maryland, Colorado, Hawaii, and Texas.

THINK AND REMEMBER

- Remember to keep verb tenses consistent within sentences and from sentence to sentence.
- Change verb tenses only to show that the time of events changes.

Independent Practice

B. Using Consistent Tense Write each sentence with the correct form of the verb in parentheses ( ). Keep the tense in each item consistent.

7. Willa Cather met pioneers who (face) life with courage.

MODEL Willa Cather met pioneers who faced life with courage.

8. Her family (live) in Virginia before they moved to the state of Nebraska.
9. She rode horseback when she (visit) settlers in their houses made of sod.
10. Cather studied literature and (graduate) from college in 1895.
11. She had worked for newspapers and magazines before she (write) her own novels.
12. During her career, she wrote play reviews. As a result, she (develop) a taste for the theater.
13. Many people read her books now and (appreciate) the quality and strength of the pioneers she portrayed.
14. People (read) her stories for years to come. They will be rewarded with an insight into our American heritage.

C. Proofreading: Correcting Tense Changes Rewrite each sentence so that the verb tense is consistent.

15. Sequoyah was one of the greatest Cherokees because he teaches his people reading and writing.

MODEL Sequoyah was one of the greatest Cherokees because he taught his people reading and writing.

16. Sequoyah had a serious disease as a child that will leave him with a weak leg.
17. He does not hunt much, but he made many things with his hands.
18. In 1812 he leaves his family and fought with American soldiers at war against the British.
19. He watched an army captain as he will read little black marks on white sheets of paper.
20. Sequoyah is fascinated by the symbols that "talked" to the man. His people had never written anything down.
21. After Sequoyah had returned to his tribe, he will develop a system of writing for the Cherokees.
22. Sequoyah worked for twelve years before he is finished with the system of writing.
23. The others in his tribe become suspicious because they did not understand Sequoyah's ideas.
24. With his ten-year-old daughter, Ah-yoka, Sequoyah proved that his written symbols work.
25. Soon children, parents, and grandparents were learning the new written symbols, and the Cherokees are printing a newspaper.
26. The newspaper teach the members of the Cherokee tribe to communicate through writing.
27. The Cherokees see the printed word pass down legends, stories, and other thoughts to future generations.
28. Sequoyah will be remembered because he brings the wisdom of written language to many.

Application — Writing

Biographical Sketch Imagine that you are a biographer who writes about the lives of famous people. Write a biographical sketch about your next subject. Choose an important event in the person's life. Describe the most important details of the event. Write your sketch for someone who knows nothing about the person. After you write, check for consistent use of tense.

Building Vocabulary
Prefixes

Many English words can be divided into two or more parts that have meanings of their own. The words *interstate* and *detour* can be divided into *inter* + *state* and *de* + *tour*. The parts *inter* and *de* are prefixes. The parts *state* and *tour* are base words.

A **base word** is a complete word that cannot be separated into smaller parts and still retain its meaning. A **prefix** is a syllable that is added to the beginning of a base word to change its meaning.

You can add prefixes to many words to form new words. Study the chart of prefixes. Notice how the meaning of the base word is changed by the prefix.

Prefix	Meaning	Examples
de	down, from	depress, defrost
dis	reverse of, not	disagree, distrust
ex	out of, former	export, exchange
extra	outside of	extraterrestrial
fore	before, in front	foremost, forehead
il, im, in, ir	not	illogical, improbable, incorrect, irregular
inter	between, among	intersect, international
mis	wrong, badly	misinterpret, misjudge
non	not	nonstop, nonslip
over	too much, above	overcrowded, overhear
post	after	postdate, postwar
pre	before	prehistoric, pretest
re	back, again	retrace, reconsider
un	not, opposite of	unpack, unhappy

Recognizing prefixes can help you understand the meanings of words. In some words, the beginning letters may seem to be prefixes but are not. Check in a dictionary if you are unsure.

Reading Practice

Read each sentence. Write the word or words that have a prefix, and underline the prefix. Use the chart on page 146 for help. Then write your own brief definition of each word.

Example: Our vacation ended in disorder on the very first day.
disorder—not in order, confusion

1. My family went through quite an extraordinary happening.
2. We had been driving down the interstate highway in our car.
3. Suddenly a flash flood hit and a stream overflowed onto the road.
4. Dad misjudged how deep the water was.
5. Our car was disabled by the water, and it floated away.
6. The rushing water deposited our car on a steep bank.
7. A truck driver reassured us that he would unload the car safely.

Writing Practice

Add a prefix from the chart to each of the following base words to form a new word. Write a sentence for each new word.

8. cast
9. ordinary
10. place
11. do
12. claim
13. press
14. legal
15. head
16. formal
17. view
18. war
19. paid

Project

Sometimes, trying to figure out word meaning from a prefix and base word may cause trouble. Some words may trick you. Remember, the beginning letters of a word may look like a prefix, but they may not be a prefix at all. Look through textbooks and stories and make a list of words whose beginnings are spelled like the prefixes in the chart. Use what you have learned about prefix meanings to write what you think is the definition of each word. When you are finished, check the words in a dictionary.

fore + ign?
dis + approve?
re + mark?
re + sign?

Language Enrichment
More Verbs

Use what you know about verbs to do these activities.

Lights! Camera! Action!

Pretend that you are the director of this movie scene. Write what you want the actors to do. Use vivid present-tense action verbs. Choose actors from the class to pantomime your directions.

Speaking Initially

Do students in your class know your middle name or initial? If they don't, see if they can guess your middle initial from the clues you give. (If you have no middle name, make up one for yourself.) First, think of verbs that begin with the same letter as your middle name. Write down those verbs, and use as many as you can in a paragraph. Read it to your classmates, and have them figure out your middle initial.

Help Wanted

Helping verbs are looking for work. Employ the helping verbs by writing a "Help Wanted" ad. (Refer to page 124 to see what verbs to use.)

Help Wanted

Truck Driver. This job *will* take you to new places. You *might* travel all over the country. If you *can* drive a car, you *should* call today:
555-5555

CONNECTING
LANGUAGE ↔ WRITING

In this unit you learned that verbs show action and can also play other roles. They can link the subject of a sentence with a word that describes or explains it. In addition, verbs can have helping verbs, and they can express time through various tenses.

◆ **Using Verbs in Your Writing** If you know how to use verbs correctly, you can make your writing flow. With the right verb, a sentence can invite your readers to continue. Pay special attention to the verbs you use as you do these activities.

Prefix Puzzles

You learned about prefixes on the **Building Vocabulary** pages. Here is a way to use prefixes to challenge yourself—or to challenge others—in a game of word skill.

Use the seven prefixes in the left column and the base words in the right column. Matching prefixes and base words, make a list of as many *new* words as you can. *Do not use a dictionary* to form the words. If you are challenging a classmate, a judge (using a dictionary) will determine the winner and read the winning word list.

Prefixes	Base Words	
re	stand	view
dis	write	sign
under	pose	take
pre	play	appear
inter	cover	
ex	state	
over	tend	

Wish You Were Here

Imagine that you are sending a postcard from a vacation spot. First, cut out a postcard-size shape from heavy paper. Describe to a classmate a scene from your imagined vacation spot. Write a message that uses some of these linking verbs: *look, sound, taste, smell, feel.* Draw your scene on the other side. Then, send the card to your classmate.

3 Unit Checkup

Think Back	Think Ahead
◆ What did you learn about a narrative poem in this unit? What did you do to write one?	◆ How will what you learned about narrative poems help you recognize narrative and poetic elements? ◆ How will knowing how to analyze story lines help you write a narrative poem?
◆ Look at the writing you did in this unit. How did verbs help you express your ideas?	◆ What is one way you can use verbs to improve your writing?

Narrative Poem *pages 106 – 108*

Read the following lines from narrative poems. For each line, write whether it is from a *heroic* or a *mock-heroic* poem.

1. But hark! My gentle sister/Bids me slop yon pigs.
2. The knights, banners and heraldry aloft/March out to war.
3. A kingly grand repast was that/Of ants and worms and beetles fat.

Choosing Words to Create a Mood *page 109*

Write the following sentences. Add dramatic words that communicate a certain mood.

4. The ________ knight climbed the stairs to the ________ chamber.
5. He drew his ________ sword from its ________ casing.
6. The knight entered the ________ room.
7. A strange and ________ force engulfed the ________, armored hero.

The Writing Process *pages 110 – 119*

Write the letter for the answer to each question.

8. When you plan a narrative poem, what should you do first?

   a. Brainstorm topics. **b.** Outline events. **c.** Draw a cluster.

9. What should dramatic words give in a narrative poem?
   a. a mood **b.** sequence of events **c.** rhyme scheme

10. Which would be the best magazine in which to publish narrative poems?
   a. *Adventurer* **b.** *Good Housekeeping* **c.** *Newsweek*

Verbs *pages 122 – 123*

Write the verb from each sentence. Write whether it is an *action* verb or a *linking* verb.

11. In mythology, a hero is a person of courage.
12. Some heroes descended from the gods.
13. These heroes ran long distances and fought battles.
14. Two of these heroes are Hercules and Jason.
15. Not all of the ancient heroes were from mythology.

Main Verbs and Helping Verbs *pages 124 – 125*

Write the verb phrase from each sentence. Underline the helping verb once and the main verb twice.

16. Students should seize the opportunity to be a hero.
17. They will be exposed to new challenges.
18. Each challenge can develop into an unknown quest.
19. The quest has always demanded courage.
20. Such courage can produce happiness.

Principal Parts of Regular Verbs *pages 126 – 127*

Write the four principal parts of each verb.

21. embarrass	**24.** laugh	**27.** believe
22. look	**25.** sneeze	**28.** jump
23. drop	**26.** talk	**29.** memorize

Principal Parts of Irregular Verbs *pages 128 – 130*

Set up a chart as shown. Fill in the chart with the principal parts of each verb on the next page.

Example:

Present	Present Participle	Past	Past Participle
ring	ringing	rang	(have) rung

30. sit
31. become
32. choose
33. begin
34. rise
35. set
36. cost
37. seek
38. feel

More Irregular Verbs *pages 131 – 132*

Write the correct form of the verb in parentheses ( ).

39. Winifred has (began, begun) a community program.
40. She (drove, driven) through her neighborhood last year and noticed a large number of stray cats.
41. Winifred has (wrote, written) to the mayor and has received a grant to set up a pet shelter.
42. Communities throughout her county have (saw, seen) this idea in action and have copied it.
43. Winifred (spoke, spoken) on television about the pet crisis.

Verb Tenses *pages 133 – 136*

Write the verb from each sentence below. Next to each verb, write its tense.

44. Heart disease killed thousands last year.
45. Research scientists have looked for the disease's causes.
46. They have investigated nutrition and daily stress.
47. Doctors recommend exercise, relaxation, and a proper diet.
48. Most people, however, will ignore good advice.

Be, Have, Do *pages 137 – 140*

Write the correct form of the verb in parentheses ( ).

49. (Do, Does) you have a favorite hero?
50. I (has, have) had one since first grade.
51. Who (is, are) he or she?
52. She (is, am) Amelia Earhart.
53. She has always (be, been) my hero.

Subject-Verb Agreement *pages 141 – 142*

Write the correct form of the verb in parentheses ( ).

54. Life in the oceans (include, includes) plants and animals.

55. Many forms of sea life (seems, seem) mysterious and beautiful.

56. Men, women, and children (enjoy, enjoys) the water.

57. The ocean's movement and smell (relax, relaxes) people.

58. Surfing, scuba diving, and deep-sea fishing (bring, brings) many people to the sea.

Tense Changes *pages 143 – 145*

Rewrite each sentence so that the verb tense is consistent.

59. Beth's grandfather was a rodeo rider when he is a young man just out of school.

60. Once her grandfather was riding a horse that will hurt him when it banged against a fence.

61. The horse reared back and rolls onto its rider.

62. The saddle hit Beth's grandfather in the leg and breaks the thigh bone in two places.

63. Beth's grandmother put splints on the leg and wraps rags around the splints.

Prefixes *pages 146 – 147*

Read each sentence. Write the word or words that have a prefix from the chart on page 146, and underline the prefix. Then write your own definition of each word.

64. The knight departed from his king's castle.

65. Merlin had had a forewarning of the coming adventure.

66. The knight would meet a dishonorable person on the road.

67. The evil opponent would unseat the knight.

68. But, finally, the knight would overcome his enemy and return to the castle.

UNIT 4

Explaining Related Ideas

◆ COMPOSITION FOCUS: **Paragraphs of Cause and Effect**
◆ LANGUAGE FOCUS: **More About Verbs**

What goes up must come down. Did you know that water evaporates into the air and then comes down as rain? Have you ever wondered why rain falls *down*? Gravity accounts for the fall. Gravity, the force that pulls an object toward the center of the earth, is the *cause*. The fall is one *effect;* another is the increase in speed as the object falls. Frequently, writers explain an event by identifying its causes or its effects.

Paragraphs of cause and effect appear in news stories, magazine and encyclopedia articles, and nonfiction books. Joan Elma Rahn wrote *Plants That Changed History,* a nonfiction book that explains the influence of plants on industry. In explaining a plant's influence, the writer sometimes isolated an event and investigated the reasons that it happened. At other times she isolated an event and investigated the results that occurred because of the event. In this unit you will read an excerpt from *Plants That Changed History* and then learn how to explain events by writing paragraphs of cause and effect.

Reading with a Writer's Eye
Information Article

When fuel starts disappearing, civilization has a problem! In this article, Joan Elma Rahn explains how coal mining developed as a result of an early fuel crisis. Read to discover why there was a fuel crisis and what happened because of fuel shortages.

from Plants That Changed History
by Joan Elma Rahn

In about 1750 in England, and somewhat later in other countries, a great change took place. Before then most clothes and furniture and many other things people needed were made by hand, or at the most with very simple tools. But now, some things began to be made with more complex machines. Before, people had walked or used animals or the wind to transport themselves or their goods. Now they began to use machines. This time was called the Industrial Revolution, and in England it lasted about a hundred years. It began when it did because England was experiencing a fuel crisis. This had been developing slowly for a few hundred years, and it was now coming to a head. The Industrial Revolution began where it did because England had a solution to her problem within her own borders.

The problem was a lack of wood, which was needed both for fuel and for structural timbers. Many of the other countries of Europe were experiencing the same problem, but to a lesser degree. The human population was growing, and more houses and public buildings were being built and more lumber was needed for them. All these people also had to be kept warm in winter, and wood was the standard fuel. People also had to be fed, and as more forests were cut down to make room for farms, there might be a temporary increase in the amount of lumber on the market, but when no new trees were planted in the places of the old ones, eventually, there was less. Since the days of the first great voyages of discovery several of the nations of Europe had been building great empires, with colonies all over the world. Merchant ships were needed for transporting goods and people to and from these places, and armed ships were needed to maintain control over the colonies and the sea routes to them. The nations of Europe frequently went to war with each other over disputes about many things, including their empires, and navies were needed to conduct the battles at sea. Great Britain, especially, being an island nation, required a strong navy. Ships in those days were all wooden, and whole forests were cut down for the sake of building ships.

Some nations, including Great Britain, were beginning to import lumber from overseas colonies with forested land. But this made wood expensive.

It was apparent that burning wood as fuel was becoming a luxury, and that wood would have to be conserved primarily for use as lumber.

England's solution to the fuel problem was to use coal. Up until then coal had been considered a rather poor choice of fuel. Not that it didn't burn well or give adequate warmth—in that respect it was as good as wood. The trouble with it was that it was dirty. It produced a sooty smoke that left a fine black covering over everything. Foods or manufactured goods that ordinarily were dried over wood or charcoal fires were ruined over coal.

Despite this problem coal began to be used more and more in private homes and in industry. At first surface mining was sufficient to supply the demand, but when the surface coal was used up, mines had to be dug into the earth to get at deeper and deeper deposits. As the mines became deeper, a new problem arose. Water seeped into the mines, making the already not-very-agreeable occupation of mining even more disagreeable or even impossible. The problem was worse in mines along the seashore. Some coal seams, which were exposed well up on the dry land surface, tilted downward and seaward. The miners who followed these seams soon found themselves working under the sea, where leakage was severe. Carrying water up in buckets or even raising it with hand-operated pumps simply would not do. Some mines maintained a hundred or more horses just to keep the pumps working. Something better was needed.

Respond

1. What is one new idea that you learned from this excerpt? Why does that new information interest you?

Discuss

2. Who might find the information in Joan Elma Rahn's book useful? Why might they need this information?
3. Why did England experience a shortage of wood? Why did England turn to coal for fuel?

Thinking As a Writer

Analyzing Paragraphs of Cause and Effect

Writer's Guide

A paragraph of cause and effect
- may begin with a cause and list its effects.
- may begin with an effect and list its causes.

A paragraph of cause and effect explains what happened as a result of an event. It may begin with a **cause** (a reason) or with an **effect** (a result).

This paragraph begins with an **effect.** It names a situation or an event caused by all the other events in the paragraph.

> The problem was a lack of wood, which was needed both for fuel and for structural timbers. Many of the other countries of Europe were experiencing the same problem, but to a lesser degree. The human population was growing, and more houses and public buildings were being built and more lumber was needed for them. All these people also had to be kept warm in winter, and wood was the standard fuel.

The **topic sentence** states the effect.

The **detail sentences** list the causes that explain why the first event happened.

This paragraph begins with a **cause.** It names a situation or an event that caused all the other events in the paragraph to happen.

> Despite this problem coal began to be used more and more in private homes and in industry. At first surface mining was sufficient to supply the demand, but when the surface coal was used up, mines had to be dug into the earth to get at deeper and deeper deposits. As the mines became deeper, a new problem arose. Water seeped into the mines, making the already not-very-agreeable occupation of mining even more disagreeable or even impossible.

The **topic sentence** states the cause.

The **detail sentences** list the effects that explain what happened as a result of the first event.

Discuss

1. In what order are cause and effect given in each of the paragraphs?
2. What event or situation is being explained by the first paragraph?

Try Your Hand

A. Analyze Paragraphs of Cause and Effect Read these paragraphs about natural phenomena. Name the one event each paragraph is about, and write whether it is a *cause* or an *effect*.

1. During high tide the ocean water rises to the greatest levels and washes up farthest onto shore. The movement of the high tide's flood and ebb currents may affect the time schedules for fishermen in large vessels.
2. Steam and a rush of hot water shoot out of a geyser to relieve pressure that has accumulated underground. Since there are openings in the earth's surface, water can seep underground. The underground rocks heat the water. Pressure builds until the water boils and shoots through an opening in the earth.
3. The trembling that people feel during an earthquake is due to vibrations that occur when rocks slip along a fault.

B. List Causes and Effects Look back at the topic sentence in each paragraph. Then list the events given in the other sentences and write whether they are *causes* or *effects*.

C. Write Causes and Effects Write a topic sentence that states a cause or an effect. Then write a detail sentence that might follow the topic sentence.

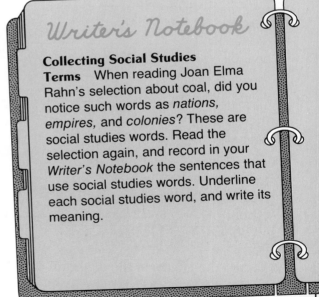

Writer's Notebook

Collecting Social Studies Terms When reading Joan Elma Rahn's selection about coal, did you notice such words as *nations*, *empires*, and *colonies*? These are social studies words. Read the selection again, and record in your *Writer's Notebook* the sentences that use social studies words. Underline each social studies word, and write its meaning.

Thinking As a Writer
Connecting Cause and Effect

An **effect** is an event that results from other events. To connect an effect to a series of causes, good writers ask themselves *why* an event happened.

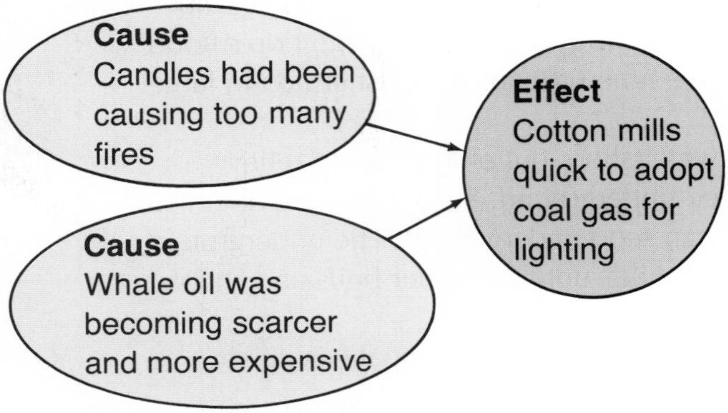

Cause
Candles had been causing too many fires
Cause
Whale oil was becoming scarcer and more expensive
Effect
Cotton mills quick to adopt coal gas for lighting

Writer's Guide

To write a cause-and-effect paragraph, good writers

- connect in their minds one event to a series of other events.
- ask themselves *why* or *what happened* to connect the events.

A **cause** is an event that leads to other events. To connect a cause to a series of effects, writers ask themselves *what happened* as a result of an event. In some cause-and-effect paragraphs, writers may link events in a causal chain.

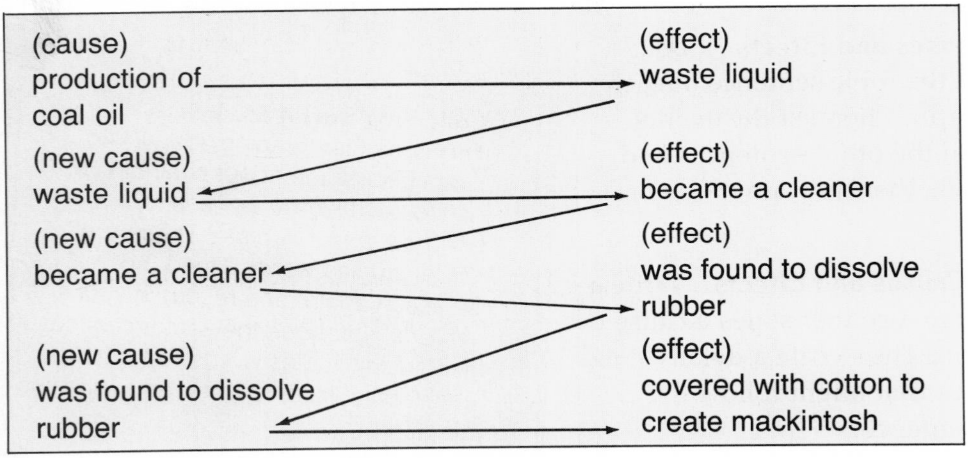

(cause)
production of coal oil
(effect)
waste liquid
(new cause)
waste liquid
(effect)
became a cleaner
(new cause)
became a cleaner
(effect)
was found to dissolve rubber
(new cause)
was found to dissolve rubber
(effect)
covered with cotton to create mackintosh

Discuss
What are the effects in the diagram? What are the causes?

Try Your Hand
Connect Causes and Effects Think of an event that happened to you, and list two causes or two effects of the event.

Developing the Writer's Craft
Using Formal and Informal Language

Writer's Guide

Good writers
- use formal language for science or research reports.
- use informal language for friendly letters or stories.

To communicate a message clearly, a writer uses a specific tone in writing. **Tone** is the attitude a writer wants to bring to a reader. If the tone is serious or factual, writers use formal language. If the tone is casual, writers may use informal wording.

Read the first sentence. Then read the sentence from *Plants That Changed History* that communicates the same information.

1. There'd be frequent showdowns between European nations over run-ins about many things, including their empires, and navies were needed for the rumbles at sea.
2. The nations of Europe frequently went to war with each other over disputes about many things, including their empires, and navies were needed to conduct the battles at sea.

In the first sentence, the underlined nouns and the contraction *there'd* make the writing informal. The tone is inappropriate for the subject. In the second sentence, the writer avoids using a contraction and uses the underlined words, which communicate the same meaning.

When you write paragraphs of cause and effect, choose words that provide an appropriate tone. Use formal language to help your readers understand your attitude toward your topic.

Discuss

1. Read this statement. *When water seeped into the mines, the miners had a new gripe about the problems they'd have.* Should the statement be added to a research report? Why or why not?
2. Why is there no contraction in sentence 2?

Try Your Hand

Use Formal Language Think about how certain plants and animals depend on each other in a tidal pool, tropical reef, or another ecosystem that interests you. Write some ideas that show causes and some that show effects about the ecosystem. Use formal language.

1 Prewriting
Paragraphs of Cause and Effect

Writer's Guide

Prewriting Checklist

- ☑ Select an event.
- ☑ Think about your audience and your purpose.
- ☑ Gather information.
- ☑ Organize the details.

Steve wanted to write about an event in outer space for his classmates. He used the checklist in the **Writer's Guide** to help him plan his paragraphs. Look at what he did.

Brainstorming and Selecting a Topic

First, Steve brainstormed a list of possible ideas for his paragraphs of cause and effect. He looked down his list and crossed out ideas that did not have an easily identifiable cause-and-effect relationship.

Steve decided to write about the supernova and circled *exploding star* from his list because it interested him. Since his class happened to be studying stars, Steve felt that his audience was likely to be interested as well.

solar eclipse
space walk
exploding star
space flight
the first telescope

Gathering Information

After selecting a topic, Steve used the library to gather information for his paragraphs of cause and effect. He did not use the fiction section, because he needed factual information. Instead, he concentrated his research in the nonfiction and reference sections of the library.

In the reference section, Steve consulted several encyclopedias. Steve knew that encyclopedias were a good place to start for general information. He found his subject in the *Encyclopedia Americana,* the *World Book Encyclopedia,* and the *Illustrated Encyclopedia for Astronomy and Space.*

Steve consulted an almanac to see if he could find statistics about the supernova his brother had seen. He was especially interested in looking for cause-and-effect relationships. He used the *Information Please Almanac* and the *World Almanac and Book of Facts.*

Steve wanted to locate the star in the night sky. He used the *Cambridge Atlas of Astronomy* and other special atlases to find maps of the night sky. Steve talked to another person to get more information about exploding stars. He interviewed Professor Chisholm from the city planetarium and got valuable insights. He carefully took notes during the interview and added them to the notes he gathered in the library.

Discuss

1. What other space-related topics might Steve have considered? Remember that they would have to involve a cause and an effect.
2. Steve looked up *supernova* in the encyclopedia. What other topic might he have looked up to find information about his subject?

Organizing the Causes and Effects

After Steve had gathered all the information he needed and had taken notes, he was ready to organize the events that had taken place. He arranged his causes and effects on a chart so that he would know in which order they had occurred. Then he put the events for each paragraph in order.

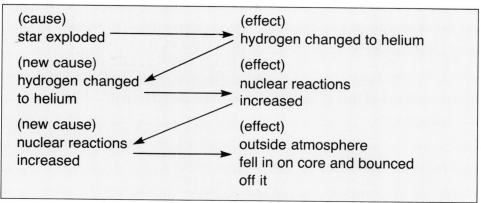

(cause) star exploded	→	(effect) hydrogen changed to helium
(new cause) hydrogen changed to helium	→	(effect) nuclear reactions increased
(new cause) nuclear reactions increased	→	(effect) outside atmosphere fell in on core and bounced off it

Discuss

1. What was the cause of the increase of nuclear reactions?
2. What was the effect of this increase?
3. Why are the events on the diagram shown in a chain?

Try Your Hand

Now plan a paragraph of cause and effect of your own.

A. Brainstorm and Select a Topic Brainstorm a list of possible topics. Think about cause-and-effect relationships around you. If you cannot think of an appropriate topic, think of a subject that interests you. Then talk to people who know about the subject to find events for topics. Think about each topic and your audience.

- Cross out topics that are not interesting.
- Cross out topics that do not involve cause and effect.
- Circle the event that is most likely to interest you and your audience.

B. Gather Information Use library resources to find information about your topic. Concentrate on the nonfiction section. Also, use reference books for valuable information. Note facts that explain why the event happened (causes) and what happened because of the event (effects). If possible, try to interview people who have knowledge about your topic. Take notes carefully.

C. Organize the Facts Look over your notes.

- Choose the main causes and the main effects. Select the details that will make your explanation as simple and as clear as possible.
- Arrange the details for each paragraph. Decide whether you will begin a paragraph with a cause or with an effect. Pay particular attention to the possibility of causal chains. You may want to make a chart like Steve's.

Save your notes and your chart in your *Writer's Notebook*. You will use them when you draft your paragraphs of cause and effect.

2 Drafting
Paragraphs of Cause and Effect

Using his notes and his chart, Steve followed the **Writer's Guide** to draft his paragraphs. Look at what he did.

Writer's Guide

Drafting Checklist

- Use your notes and chart for ideas.
- Write the cause or the effect first.
- After a cause, list its effects.
- After an effect, list its causes.

A star called Supernova 1987A exploded in a blast that was visible from Earth on February 25, 1987. Supernova 1987A began as a very large star. Hydrogen in the star changed to helium. Other nuclear reactions occurred and increased until the outside atmosphere fell in on the core and bounced off it.

The explosion of Supernova 1987A affected the universe in a number of ways. It shone as brightly as 100,000 suns.

Discuss

Look at Steve's first paragraph. Is the event in the topic sentence a cause or is it an effect? What are the other events in the paragraph?

Try Your Hand

Now you are ready to write a paragraph of cause and effect.

A. Review Your Information Think about the causes and the effects you gathered and organized in the last lesson. Gather more information if necessary.

B. Think About Your TAP Remember that your task is to write paragraphs of cause and effect. Your purpose is to explain your topic to your audience.

Task: What?
Audience: Who?
Purpose: Why?

C. Write Your First Draft Use the **Drafting Checklist** to help you. When you write your draft, just put all your ideas on paper. Do not worry about spelling, punctuation, or grammar. You can correct the draft later.

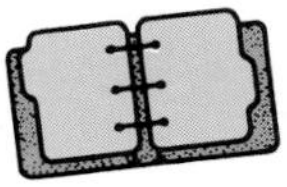

Save your first draft in your *Writer's Notebook*. You will use it when you revise your paragraphs.

3 Responding and Revising
Paragraphs of Cause and Effect

Steve used the checklist in the **Writer's Guide** to revise his paragraphs of cause and effect. Look at what he did.

Writer's Guide

Revising Checklist

- ☑ Read your paragraphs to yourself or a partner.
- ☑ Think about your audience and your purpose. Add or cut information.
- ☑ Be sure that your paragraphs are organized correctly.
- ☑ Check to see that you have used appropriate language.

◆ Checking Information

Steve checked the information in his paragraphs to make sure it was accurate. To replace words that gave inaccurate information, he used this mark ⁀. Steve also added an interesting detail. To show addition, he used this mark ∧ .

◆ Checking Organization

In his second paragraph Steve found a sentence that did not keep to the topic. He used this mark ℓ to cut the sentence. He also moved a sentence so that the sequence of events was clear. To show that the sentence should be moved, he used this mark ↻ .

◆ Checking Language

Steve replaced some informal wording with formal language. He used this mark ⁀ to make his change.

Add ☐ Cut ☐ Move ☐ Replace ☐

A star called Supernova 1987A exploded in a blast that was visible from Earth on February 25, 1987. Supernova 1987A began as a very large star. Hydrogen in the star changed to helium. Other nuclear reactions occurred and increased until the outside atmosphere fell in on the core and bounced off it. ∧ *The color of the star changed from blue to red to blue again before it collapsed.*

The explosion of Supernova 1987A affected the universe in a number of ways. It shone as brightly as 100,000 suns. ~~You can't imagine how bright it was.~~ It blew off its outside atmosphere. The exploding star sent off a blinding light. ~~Tiny bits~~ *Particles* of the atmosphere formed into a cloudlike mass of dust and gas.

Discuss

1. Steve thought his audience would be interested in the detail he added about brightness. Why might that interest an audience?
2. What other changes could Steve have made?

Try Your Hand

Now revise your first draft.

A. Read Your First Draft As you read your paragraphs, think about your audience and purpose. Read your paragraphs silently or to a partner to see if they are complete and well organized. Ask yourself or your partner the questions in the box.

Responding and Revising Strategies

✔ Respond **Ask yourself or a partner:**	✔ Revise **Try these solutions:**
• Do my paragraphs begin with a cause or with an effect?	• **Replace** your first sentence with one that states the cause or the effect of all other events in the paragraph.
• Have I used formal language throughout?	• **Replace** informal language with formal language.
• If I have presented a chain of events, are they in sequential order?	• **Move** any sentences that seem out of place.
• Does each sentence keep to the topic?	• **Cut** sentences that do not explain why something happened or what happened. See the **Revising Workshop** on page 168.

B. Make Your Changes If the answer to any question in the box is *no*, try the solution. Use the **Editor's Marks** to show your changes.

C. Review Your Cause-and-Effect Paragraphs Again Decide whether there is anything else you want to revise. Keep revising your paragraphs until you feel they are well organized.

EDITOR'S MARKS

- ∧ Add something.
- Cut something.
- Move something.
- Replace something.

Save your revised paragraphs of cause and effect in your *Writer's Notebook*. You will use them when you proofread your paragraphs.

Revising Workshop
Keeping to the Topic

Good writers include only sentences that support the main idea in a paragraph. Look at this paragraph about the northern and southern lights. The third sentence should be cut because it is about a different topic. Although the fourth sentence is related, it is not about the topic either and must be cut.

> The northern and southern lights form red and green spectacles in the sky, growing brighter and dimmer as they change shape. Known as *auroras,* they begin as electrified particles of the sun. From there the particles travel to Earth, guided by its magnetic field toward the north and south poles. The earth is a magnet with a magnetic field that extends beyond its atmosphere. When the charged particles fall into the earth's atmosphere, the lights occur.

Practice

Rewrite the sentences as a paragraph. Leave out any sentences that do not keep to the topic.

1. Temperature changes in the sun make its surface as uneven as the surface of boiling water.
2. The temperature at which water boils is 100 degrees Centigrade if the air pressure is normal.
3. One effect of the changes is *sunspots,* areas that appear darker than the rest of the sun.
4. Another result is tongue-like clouds of bright gases called *prominences* that reach far above the surface and may form an arch.
5. Arched doorways are copies of a shape found in nature.
6. A third effect is *solar flares,* streams of bright gases that shoot up from the surface, usually near sunspots.
7. Finally, invisible particles shoot from the surface to the earth's atmosphere where we see them as the northern and southern lights.

4 Proofreading
Paragraphs of Cause and Effect

Writer's Guide

Proofreading Checklist

- Check for errors in capitalization.
- Check for errors in punctuation.
- Be sure that all your paragraphs are indented.
- Check for errors in grammar. Be sure your verb tenses are consistent.
- Circle any words you think are misspelled. Find out how to spell them correctly.

⇨ For proofreading help, use the **Writer's Handbook.**

After revising his cause-and-effect paragraphs, Steve used the **Writer's Guide** and the **Editor's Marks** to proofread them. Look at what he did.

¶ The cloudlike mass grew as the explosion of the star continued. the supernova hurled more debri (debris) into space, sent X rays and gamma rays to Earth, and ~~forms~~ formed into a dense star at the core. In this way the large star left a small remnent (remnant) of itself at the center.

EDITOR'S MARKS

- Capitalize.
- Add a period.
- Add something.
- Add a comma.
- Add quotation marks.
- Cut something.
- Replace something.
- Transpose.
- Spell correctly.
- Indent paragraph.
- Make a lowercase letter.

Discuss

1. Look at Steve's proofread paragraph. Why did he change the verb *forms* to *formed*?
2. Why did Steve add a comma in one sentence? What other punctuation mistake did Steve make?

Try Your Hand

Proofread Your Paragraphs of Cause and Effect
Now use the **Writer's Guide** and the **Editor's Marks** to proofread your paragraphs.

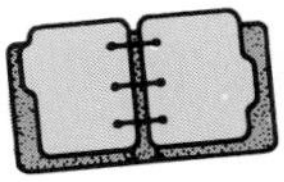

Save your corrected paragraphs in your *Writer's Notebook.* You will use them when you publish your paragraphs.

5 Publishing
Paragraphs of Cause and Effect

Writer's Guide

Publishing Checklist

- Make a clean copy of your paragraphs.
- Check to see that nothing has been left out.
- Be sure that there are no mistakes.
- Share your paragraphs of cause and effect in a special way.

Steve made a clean copy of his paragraphs of cause and effect and checked them to be sure he had not left out anything. Then he and his classmates decided to publish their cause-and-effect paragraphs by making an encyclopedia. You can find Steve's paragraphs on page 43 of the **Writer's Handbook.**

Here's how Steve and his classmates published their paragraphs in an encyclopedia.

1. They reviewed several encyclopedias to study their organization and design. They conducted a class meeting to name their encyclopedia and to assign jobs. They followed the **Tips on How to Conduct a Meeting** on page 171.
2. They formed their paragraphs into encyclopedia articles. They titled the articles by naming the topic and briefly defining it. Steve and his friends used the titles to arrange all the articles in alphabetical order.
3. They laid out each page of the encyclopedia. They showed the columns and planned where to place each article. They added illustrations that helped clarify an event.

4. Next, they typed their articles to fit the columns on the page layout. At the end of his article, Steve wrote his name to show that he was the author. Steve and his classmates pasted the articles and illustrations onto the layout. Then, they numbered the pages.

5. Once the pages were complete, they duplicated them. Then, they made a title page and a copyright page for their encyclopedia. They bound the pages together. Finally, they made a cover that displayed the encyclopedia title.

Discuss

1. Why did they arrange the articles in alphabetical order?
2. What might happen if the layout were not planned for each page?

Try Your Hand

Publish Your Article Follow the checklist in the **Writer's Guide.** If possible, create an encyclopedia of your own, or try one of these ideas.

- Exchange your paragraphs of cause and effect with a partner. Read your partner's paragraphs to see if you can come up with a cause or an effect your partner forgot to list.
- Create a television quiz show called *The Main Event*. Read the detail sentences from each of your paragraphs, and let a panel of two to three classmates name the event in the topic sentence.

Listening and Speaking
Tips on How to Conduct a Meeting

When a large group of people must meet to make decisions, parliamentary procedure can help the meeting run smoothly. Follow these tips.

1. Elect a chairperson to run the meeting.
2. Have the chairperson follow an *agenda,* or list of items to cover.
3. Ask a secretary to take notes, or *minutes,* of the meeting.
4. Have another participant second a *motion,* or suggestion, before discussing it.
5. Nominate candidates for various jobs.
6. Have the chairperson *adjourn,* or close, the meeting.

Writing in the Content Areas

Writer's Guide

When you write, remember the stages of the Writing Process.

- Prewriting
- Drafting
- Responding and Revising
- Proofreading
- Publishing

Use what you learned to explain some causes and effects. Write your explanation in one or more paragraphs, and use references for information if necessary. Use one of these ideas or an idea of your own.

Physical Education

Every year American athletes seem to be getting faster, stronger, and, in some cases, bigger. Explain some effects these changes might have on the rules for professional sports such as basketball and baseball.

Social Studies

Many towns and cities are facing problems in disposing of household waste. Research the causes for this problem in your area or your state. Then explain them. What could be done to remove or lessen some of those causes?

Science

The use of aerosol propellants is being phased out in the United States. Many scientists believe that aerosol propellants have caused damage to the earth's ozone layer. Do research to find out what the damaging effects are. Have aerosols started a chain of cause-and-effect problems?

Literature

To solve a crime, a detective in a mystery novel has to figure out what caused a suspect to commit the crime, or what the person's *motive* was. Read a short mystery, and tell your class about it. Include in your report the effect (the crime committed) and the cause (why the person did it).

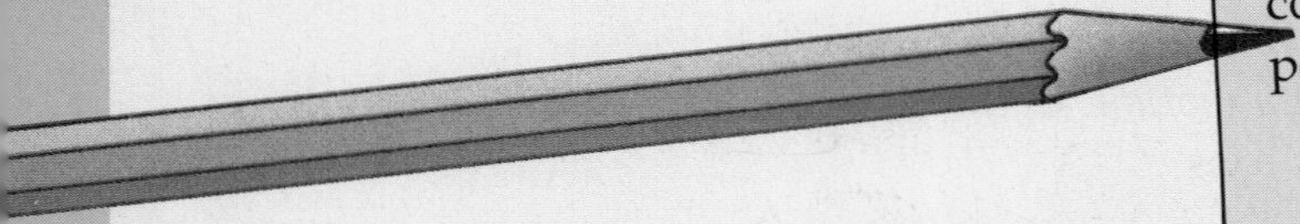

CONNECTING
WRITING ↔ LANGUAGE

Paragraphs of cause and effect tell what happens and why it happens. What causes and effect do you learn about in this science article?

> The sea is a noisy place. Just swim near the parrot fish on a coral reef. You can hear them chewing, *crunch, crunch*. All through the water world, there are grunts, deep moans, snaps, drummings, squeaks, roars, clatters, bangs, and from time to time through the corridors of water, the calling of the great whales.
>
> The crustaceans crack their claws and clap their bony legs. When there are thousands of snapping shrimp in a school, they make a noise that is like very loud static on a radio.

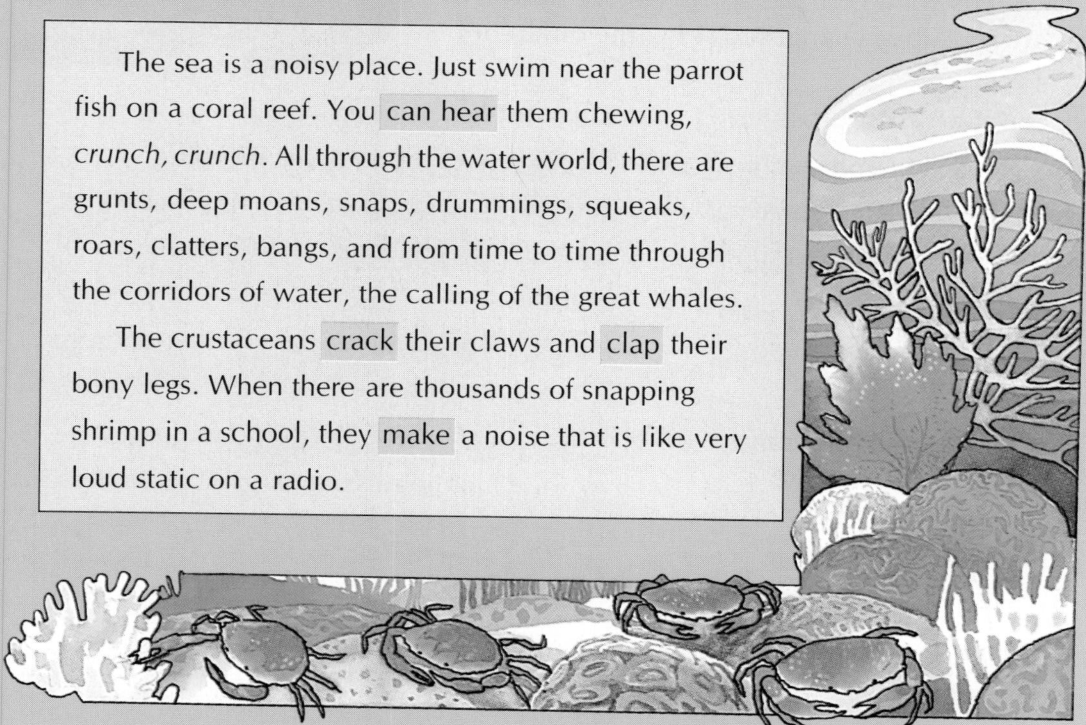

◆ **Verbs in Paragraphs of Cause and Effect** The words highlighted in color are **transitive verbs,** verbs which have **direct objects.** The verbs in the first and fourth sentences are **intransitive** verbs, verbs that do not have direct objects. By using different kinds of verbs, the author varied the style of her writing.

◆ **Language Focus: More About Verbs** The following lessons will help you use different kinds of verbs in your own writing.

1 Progressive Forms of Verbs

◆ FOCUS A **progressive verb** expresses action that continues.

The progressive form of a verb shows action that is *in progress.* It is made up of a form of the helping verb *be* plus the present participle of the main verb. The verb in color is in the progressive form.

A spacecraft is orbiting the planet Mars.

Each tense of a verb has a progressive form. The form of the verb *be* changes to show the different tenses.

Present Progressive	**1.** The craft is collecting data now.
Past Progressive	**2.** It was collecting data this morning.
Future Progressive	**3.** It will be collecting data all this week.
Present Perfect Progressive	**4.** It has been collecting data for at least two months.
Past Perfect Progressive	**5.** It had been collecting data for two months before it landed.
Future Perfect Progressive	**6.** It will have been collecting data for a year by the time the mission is over.

Guided Practice

A. Identify the tense of each progressive form.

1. is landing
2. had been launching
3. will be receiving
4. will have been going
5. has been probing
6. was producing

THINK AND REMEMBER

- Remember that the progressive form of a verb shows continuing action.
- Remember that a form of the verb *be* plus the present participle forms the progressive.

Independent Practice

B. Identifying Verb Tenses Write the tense of each progressive form.

7. are scheduling

MODEL present progressive

8. will be scanning
9. had been ascending
10. will have been roaming
11. were delaying
12. have been occupying
13. is exploring

C. Writing Progressive Forms For each verb, write the progressive form given in parentheses ( ).

14. encourage (present progressive)

MODEL are encouraging

15. refuel (past progressive)
16. grow (present progressive)
17. wonder (past perfect progressive)
18. hover (future perfect progressive)
19. imagine (present progressive)
20. plan (present perfect progressive)
21. roam (future progressive)

D. 22. – 29. Writing Sentences Write sentences using the verbs you formed in **C.**

22. are encouraging

MODEL They are encouraging me to learn about space.

E. Revising: Replacing Verbs Replace each underlined verb with a progressive form of the verb that makes sense in the sentence. Write the verb and the name of its progressive form.

30. By the year 2010 humans will establish an outpost on Mars.

MODEL will be establishing—future progressive

31. U.S. *Viking I* and *II* scouted the surface of Mars in 1976.
32. Other American spacecraft had monitored Mars five years earlier.
33. Now the Soviets have devised ships to explore one of Mars's moons.
34. In the 1990's Soviet vehicles will rove the planet's surface.
35. Since exploration began, dust storms obscured the surface.

Application — Writing

Story Write a brief story to tell the people of Earth about the colonists who will first inhabit the planet Mars. Describe the conditions on the planet that they will have to overcome and how they will do so. Use progressive verb forms in your story. If you need help writing a story, see page 50 of the **Writer's Handbook.**

2 Direct Objects

◆ **FOCUS** A **direct object** receives the action of a verb.

Every sentence has a subject and a verb, but it may need something else to complete the thought. A **complement** is an element in a sentence that completes the thought started by the subject and the verb.

One kind of complement is a direct object. A direct object usually follows an action verb and receives the action of a verb. It can be a noun or a pronoun. It answers the questions *whom* or *what.* The words in color are direct objects.

1. The Coast Guard crew tracks icebergs. **tracks *what?* icebergs**
2. Patrol planes carry members of the crew. **carry *whom?* members**

Direct objects may be compound. When there are three or more direct objects in a series, use a comma after each one except the last.

3. The Coast Guard uses ships and airplanes on patrol.
4. Icebergs command fear, awe, and fascination in people.

When identifying direct objects, do not be confused by modifying words or phrases. Such words may come between the verb and the direct object, or they may appear after verbs with no direct object. Remember that direct objects answer only the questions *whom* or *what.*

5. The captain steered the ship. **direct object—answers the question *what***
6. The captain steered the specially equipped ship. **direct object—other words modify *ship***

Link to Speaking and Writing

To avoid repetitive sentences, combine sentences that have the same subject and verb but different direct objects.

The crew assignment listed the captain, and the first mate, ~~for the next voyage.~~ ~~The crew assignment listed~~ a radio operator, and an oceanographer for the next voyage.

Guided Practice

A. Identify the *subject*, the *verb*, and the *direct object* in each sentence. If there is no direct object, answer *none*.

1. Icebergs pose a danger to ships.
2. They separate from glaciers.
3. The noise splits the air.
4. The icebergs drift at sea.
5. Only part of an iceberg shows.
6. Some icebergs last for two years.
7. Finally the sun melts them.

B. Combine each pair of sentences into one sentence with a compound direct object.

8. Icebergs often carry boulders.
   Icebergs often carry seals.
9. The Coast Guard uses ships.
   The Coast Guard uses planes.
10. Crew members examine the radar screen and satellite photos.
    Crew members examine a range finder.
11. The Coast Guard patrol charts an iceberg's location.
    The Coast Guard patrol charts its course.
12. This information saves lives.
    This information saves ships.

THINK AND REMEMBER

- Remember that a **complement** completes the meaning of the sentence.
- Remember that a **direct object** receives the action of the verb.
- Remember to combine sentences to form compound direct objects.

Independent Practice

C. Identifying Sentence Parts Write each sentence. Underline the subject once and the verb twice. Then write the direct object. If there is no direct object, write *none*.

13. The Coast Guard patrols the United States waterways.

MODEL The Coast Guard patrols the United States waterways. waterways

14. The members rescue men, women, and children from disasters.
15. They must face floods and shipwrecks.
16. Their duties also include the enforcement of sea laws.
17. The Coast Guard operates the International Ice Patrol.
18. The patrol reports the position and direction of drifting icebergs.
19. A radio center warns ships at sea of the icebergs.
20. Crews often mark certain icebergs as part of the tracking.
21. They shoot colored dye at the tips of icebergs.
22. The marked iceberg can be easily followed.
23. Icebergs can cover distances of five to forty miles per day.

D. Revising: Combining Sentences Combine each pair of sentences into one sentence with a compound direct object. Remember to punctuate compound direct objects correctly.

24. The South Pole has always interested explorers.
The South Pole has always interested scholars.

MODEL The South Pole has always interested explorers and scholars.

25. Roald Amundsen discovered the South Pole.
Roald Amundsen discovered the Northwest Passage.
26. He crossed plateaus.
He crossed mountains and glaciers.
27. He battled fierce winds.
He battled bitter cold.
28. The crew set up a small tent at the South Pole.
The crew set up a Norwegian flag at the South Pole.
29. Amundsen explored the Antarctic region.
Amundsen explored the Arctic region.

Application — Writing

Expository Paragraph Imagine that you are a crew member on a ship tracking an iceberg. Write a one-paragraph report for your superior officers, recording your observations of how the iceberg looks, whether any melting occurs, and where you follow it. Use direct objects in your paragraph. Write at least one sentence with a compound direct object. If you need help writing an expository paragraph, see the **Writer's Handbook.**

3 Indirect Objects

◆ **FOCUS** An **indirect object** tells to whom or what or for whom or what the action of the verb is done.

An indirect object does not receive the action of a verb. It tells *to whom* or *to what* or *for whom* or *for what* some action is done. An indirect object comes after the verb and before the direct object. It is always a noun or a pronoun. A sentence that has an indirect object must have a direct object as well.

verb — indirect object — direct object

1. The trainer is throwing the dolphin a fish .

verb — indirect object — direct object

2. He brought it a special treat today.

A sentence may have a compound indirect object. Use commas after each indirect object in a series except the last.

3. Dan handed Tim, Joan, and Amy some dolphin food.

Link to Speaking and Writing

An indirect object can also be used with the preposition *to* or *for*. Then it is not an indirect object but the object of a preposition. To make your sentences less wordy, try to replace some prepositional phrases with indirect objects.

Marine parks offer a thrilling spectacle to visitors.

Guided Practice

A. Identify the direct object and the indirect object in each sentence.

1. At one time whaling offered people many valuable raw materials.
2. Whale oil gave them fuel for lamps and cooking.
3. Spermaceti gave manufacturers a lubricating oil.
4. Ambergris gave perfume a long-lasting odor.
5. Conservationists can show us substitutes for whale products.

THINK AND REMEMBER

- Remember that an **indirect object** tells *to whom, to what, for whom,* or *for what* the action of the verb is done.

Independent Practice

B. Identifying Indirect Objects and Direct Objects Write the indirect object and the direct object from each sentence.

6. I must show you my gift.

MODEL indirect object—you direct object—gift

7. Judy bought me a wonderful book about marine fowl.
8. This chapter tells the reader many details about penguins.
9. Living in colonies affords them protection from enemies.
10. Male penguins give females help in hatching eggs.
11. The mother passes the father the egg across the ice.
12. Together they find the young penguin some food.
13. May I read you this quote about Macquarie Island?
14. This rocky island offers penguins sanctuary.
15. I must get Judy a special gift in return for the book.

C. Revising: Replacing Phrases with Indirect Objects Rewrite each sentence, replacing the underlined phrase with an indirect object.

16. Please give these tickets to your teacher.

MODEL Please give your teacher these tickets.

17. They will allow passage for your class on a whale watch.
18. The boat's captain will give life vests to you.
19. He will give information to us about the humpback whale.
20. The trip will teach respect to boaters for the whale.
21. After the voyage the crew will serve lunch to the students.
22. Please give this information about the trip to your teacher, your parents, and your classmates.

Application — Writing

Commercial Imagine that you are the owner of a marine park. Write a commercial that will make tourists want to come to visit the park. Describe what the tourists will see and learn. Use indirect objects in your commercial.

4 Predicate Nominatives

◆ **FOCUS** A **predicate nominative** is a noun or a pronoun that follows a linking verb and renames the subject.

A predicate nominative is a noun or a pronoun that renames or identifies the subject of the sentence. It always follows a linking verb.

	subject	verb	predicate nominative	
1. This model	airplane	is	a Flying Tiger	.

Remember that a direct object receives the action of the verb. A predicate nominative renames the subject of the sentence.

	subject	verb	direct object	
2. Model	airplanes	require	power	for flying.

	subject	verb		predicate nominative	
3. Model	airplanes	are	exact	copies	of larger planes.

A predicate nominative may be compound. If there are three or more predicate nominatives, use commas after each predicate nominative in the series except the last.

4. The power source for a model plane may be a rubber band, a gasoline engine, a jet engine, a rocket, or a battery.

Guided Practice

A. Identify the predicate nominative and the subject to which it refers in each sentence.

1. Amelia Earhart was a famous airplane pilot.
2. In 1928 she was the first woman to cross the Atlantic Ocean.
3. On that flight the future pilot was only a passenger.
4. Four years later she was the pilot of her own plane.
5. Her final attempt was a flight around the world.

THINK AND REMEMBER

- Remember that a **predicate nominative** is a noun or pronoun that follows a linking verb and identifies or renames the subject.

Independent Practice

B. Identifying Predicate Nominatives Write each sentence. Underline the predicate nominative. Draw an arrow to the subject to which it refers.

6. A model builder must be a very patient person.

MODEL A model builder must be a very patient person.

7. Model building is a widely enjoyed hobby.
8. It is also an interesting career.
9. Models are tests made before the final product.
10. He is the architect and builder of this model building.
11. The small building is an exact replica of the real project.
12. The material may be wood or plastic.

C. Distinguishing Between Direct Objects and Predicate Nominatives Write *direct object* or *predicate nominative* to identify each underlined word.

13. I heard the phone in the hall.

MODEL direct object

14. The person calling was Sue.
15. She persuaded me to enter the meet.
16. The first two people at the meet were Sue and I.
17. Last year's winners were Jim Parker and Sue.
18. Every meet has two judges.
19. The judges for this meet were Mr. Rios and his wife.
20. Sue was the first person to fly her plane.
21. At the end of its flight, it developed engine trouble.
22. The owners of the fastest model planes were Jim and I.
23. The judges announced the names of the winners.
24. Jim and I had both won first prize.

Application — Writing

Biography Imagine that you are a writer for an aviation reference book. Write a one-paragraph biography about a real or imaginary pilot. Tell who the pilot was and what event made him or her famous. Use predicate nominatives in your paragraph.

5 Transitive and Intransitive Verbs

FOCUS

- A **transitive verb** has a direct object.
- An **intransitive verb** does not have a direct object.

A verb that has a direct object is called a transitive verb. The verb expresses action that is carried across to a receiver of the action.

1. Astronomers study the stars. **transitive verb with direct object**

A verb that has no direct object is called an intransitive verb. There is no receiver of the action. Words that follow an intransitive verb often tell *how, where,* or *when.*

2. The star twinkles brightly. **twinkles *how?* brightly**
3. Dr. Murray gazes at the sky. **gazes *where?* at the sky**
4. The telescope operates every evening. **operates *when?* every evening**

Action verbs can be either transitive or intransitive depending on their use in the sentence. Remember that modifying words or objects of phrases that follow a verb cannot be direct objects.

5. I am reading the book. **transitive**
6. I am reading about the universe. **intransitive**

Linking verbs are always intransitive. They do not express action, and they do not have direct objects. Remember that predicate nominatives sometimes follow linking verbs, but they do not receive any action.

7. Our universe is a vast expanse of space. **linking verb with predicate nominative**

Guided Practice

A. Identify the action verb in each sentence, and tell whether it is *transitive* or *intransitive.*

1. Galileo first used a simple refractor telescope in 1609.
2. Isaac Newton invented the reflecting telescope.
3. Giant modern telescopes reveal new galaxies.
4. Astronomers must look through Earth's atmosphere.
5. Telescopes in space will work without that barrier.

THINK AND REMEMBER

- Remember that a **transitive verb** has a direct object and an **intransitive verb** does not.

Independent Practice

B. Identifying Transitive and Intransitive Verbs Write the verb in each sentence, and label it *transitive* or *intransitive*. If it is transitive, write the direct object.

6. Scientists find new stars all the time.

MODEL find—transitive; stars

7. New stars form from clouds of dust and gas.

8. Gravity pulls these clouds together.

9. The contracting cloud matter becomes hot.

10. A star will burn its hydrogen for millions of years.

11. In the end, some stars explode in an enormous bright light.

C. Writing Sentences Write two sentences for each verb. In one sentence the verb should be transitive, and in the other it should be intransitive.

12. – 13. point

MODEL Ryan pointed his pen toward me.
Lisa pointed at the planet Venus.

14. – 15. ring
16. – 17. drive
18. – 19. leave
20. – 21. spin
22. – 23. sail
24. – 25. focus
26. – 27. move
28. – 29. play
30. – 31. drop
32. – 33. touch
34. – 35. jump
36. – 37. skate

Application — Writing and Speaking

Speech Imagine that you are an astronomer who has just discovered a new star or a comet. Give your discovery a name, and write a brief report on what it looks like and how you discovered it. Share your observations with your classmates in an informal speech. Be sure to explain why you chose that particular name for your discovery. Use five transitive verbs and five intransitive verbs in your speech.

6 Active and Passive Voice

FOCUS

- A transitive verb is in the **active voice** when the subject performs the action.
- A transitive verb is in the **passive voice** when the subject receives the action.

When the subject of a sentence performs the action, the verb is in the active voice. When the subject receives the action, the verb is in the passive voice. The passive voice is made up of a form of the verb *be* and the past participle.

1. The girls steer the canoe through the rapids. active
2. The canoe is steered through the rapids by the girls. passive

When you change a sentence from active voice to passive voice, the direct object in the active voice becomes the subject in the passive voice.

3. The water splashes the sides of the canoe. active
4. The sides of the canoe are splashed by the water. passive

Use active verbs wherever possible in speaking and writing. To change a verb from passive voice to active voice, find the word in the predicate that tells who performs the action. This word becomes the subject.

5. The rules of safe canoeing should be learned by beginners. passive
6. Beginners should learn the rules of safe canoeing. active

You will sometimes use the passive voice when the performer of the action is unknown or unimportant.

7. This canoe was made for shooting through rapids. passive

Guided Practice

A. Identify the verb in each sentence. Tell whether it is in the *active voice* or the *passive voice.*

1. The paddles are held by the girls.
2. Rosita paddles the canoe.
3. Lora watches the current.
4. Waves rock the boat.
5. The canoe is hurled forward.
6. A shout is heard on shore.

THINK AND REMEMBER

- Remember that when a verb is in the **active voice,** the subject performs the action. When a verb is in the **passive voice,** the subject receives the action.
- Use the active voice more than the passive voice, since active verbs are stronger than passive verbs.

Independent Practice

B. Identifying Active and Passive Voice Write the verb in each sentence. Write *active voice* or *passive voice.*

7. Irrigation, transportation, and recreation are provided by rivers.

MODEL are provided—passive voice

8. Rivers are formed by springs and smaller streams of water.
9. These streams bring water from mountaintops and hills.
10. The slope of the channel causes swift currents.
11. Mud and stones are carried along by the current.
12. White water is created by the rush of the water over rocks.

C. Revising: Changing Passive Voice to Active Voice Rewrite each sentence in the active voice to make it stronger and more direct.

13. Canoe camping is enjoyed by many families.

MODEL Many families enjoy canoe camping.

14. As many as four people can be carried by a canoe.
15. Life preservers or vests should be worn by everyone.
16. Some of the gear can be rented by beginning campers.
17. Warm, lightweight sleeping bags should be used by campers.
18. Travelers will be insulated from the cold by warm clothing.
19. When you canoe, you will be kept warm by a wet suit.
20. Wool is worn by most campers in wet, cold weather.
21. Backpacks can be held in the canoe bottom by a strong piece of rope.
22. Food can be kept dry by a waterproof bag.

Application — Writing

Postcard Imagine that you just finished canoeing down a river. Write a postcard message to your classmates telling them about your trip. Be sure to tell them about all the things you did. Use the active voice throughout your message.

7 Easily Confused Verb Pairs

◆ **FOCUS** Sometimes a verb is confused with another verb.

Sometimes pairs of verbs are confused. To learn how to use these pairs of verbs correctly, study this chart for their meanings and usage.

Principal Parts	Meaning and Usage	Sentence Example
lie, (is) lying, lay, (have) lain	"to rest" or "to recline"; has no direct object	In summer, Skipper *lies* in the shade.
lay, (is) laying, laid, (have) laid	"to put down"; may have a direct object	Skipper *laid* the bone at my feet.
bring, (is) bringing, brought, (have) brought	"to come carrying something"; has a direct object	Please *bring* the pitchfork to me.
take, (is) taking, took, (have) taken	"to go carrying something"; has a direct object	*Take* this carton of eggs to Mrs. Rush.
rise, (is) rising, rose, (have) risen	"to get up" or "to go up"; never has a direct object	The family *rises* before dawn each morning
raise, (is) raising, raised, (have raised)	"to lift" or "to grow"; has a direct object	They *raise* corn, wheat, alfalfa, and barley.
leave, (is) leaving, left, (have) left	"to go away from" or "to go without taking"; sometimes has a direct object	Rosa *leaves* for school after doing her chores.
let, (is) letting, let, (have) let	"to allow"; may have a direct object	Rosa's father *lets* her feed the chickens.

Guided Practice

A. Choose the correct verb to complete each sentence.

1. The temperature has (raised, risen) since this morning.
2. (Rise, Raise) the window to let in some fresh air.
3. Earlier today Frank (took, brought) the cows to that field.
4. He (let, left) them there to graze all morning.
5. Four of the cows are (lying, laying) under the trees.
6. When will you (bring, take) them back here for milking?
7. Frank (leaves, lets) her in charge of feeding the cows.
8. Frank (raised, rose) the farm hand's pay two weeks ago.

B. Use each pair of words in a sentence that illustrates the meanings of both words. You may use other forms of the words.

9. – 10. lay, lie
11. – 12. raise, rise
13. – 14. bring, take
15. – 16. leave, let

> **THINK AND REMEMBER**
> - Remember always to check troublesome verb pairs. To use them correctly, study which words should have or usually have direct objects.

Independent Practice

C. Identifying Correct Verb Forms Write the verb in parentheses ( ) that correctly completes each sentence.

17. The invention of the reaper (took, brought) new techniques to farming.

MODEL brought

18. Modern tractors have (raised, risen) farm productivity.
19. Haying machines (leave, let) farmers hay the fields quickly.
20. The machine (lays, lies) the hay down in the field in even piles.
21. Farmers do not worry about the hay (laying, lying) in the fields.
22. Farmers can (leave, let) the hay bales outside.
23. From the hilltop, we watched one farmer (bring, take) some bales into the barn.
24. As we watched, I asked my dad, "Will you (bring, take) me here again next week?"
25. Farm income has (raised, risen) because of modern technology.

D. Using the Correct Troublesome Verb Choose the correct verb in parentheses ( ) to use in each sentence. Then, write the correct present-tense form of that verb.

26. The hens (lay, lie) at least ten dozen eggs every week.

MODEL lay

27. Jorge (raise, rise) very early in the morning when visiting the farm to gather the eggs.

28. The hen house (lie, lay) near the silo and the barn, in the center of the farm.

29. Jorge slowly and carefully (bring, take) one egg out of each of the hens' nests.

30. He skillfully (rise, raise) each egg in front of a light for the purpose of candling.

31. He (leave, let) any of the eggs that are not fresh and suitable for the family.

32. He (leave, let) the rest of the eggs from each nest stay where they are.

33. Jorge (bring, take) us some fresh eggs almost every morning.

E. Writing Sentences Write sentences for each pair of verbs. You may use other forms of the verbs.

34. – 35. lie, lay

MODEL Many cattle ranches lie in the Midwest.
The dog laid the bone in the hole.

36. – 37. bring, take

38. – 39. rise, raise

40. – 41. leave, let

Application — Writing

Paragraph of Cause and Effect Imagine that you are a farmer or a person involved in another business. Write a paragraph of cause and effect telling how you think your business will change in the future as large companies continue to take over small businesses. Tell about the role that technology will play in these changes. Remember to use troublesome verbs correctly in your paragraph. If you need help writing a paragraph of cause and effect, see page 43 of the **Writer's Handbook.**

Building Vocabulary
Latin and Greek Prefixes and Roots

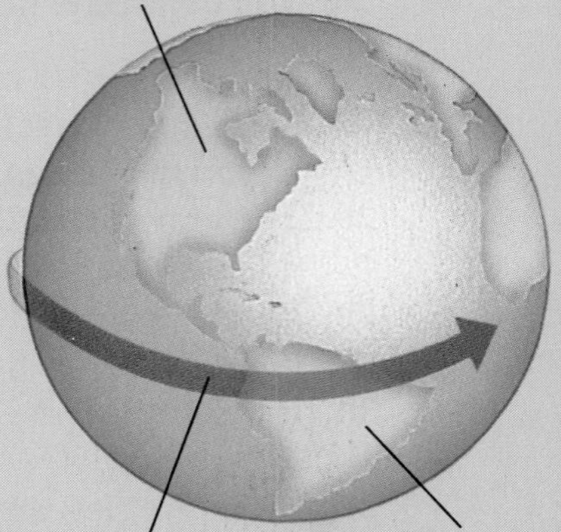

Suppose you found the word *circumference* on a diagram in your social studies textbook. If you did not know the word's meaning, you might figure it out from its word parts if you knew that *circum* is a Latin prefix meaning "around."

Many scientific terms and common English words are formed by combining word parts derived from Latin or Greek. Knowing the meaning of a certain Latin or Greek prefix or root can help you figure out the meaning of a new word that has the same word part.

Study the charts of Latin and Greek prefixes and roots.

Prefix	Meaning	Example
ante	before	antedate
anti	against	antifreeze
circum	around	circumnavigate
hemi, semi	half; half, partly	hemisphere; semicircle
sub	under, below	subsoil
super	over, above	supersonic
uni, bi, tri	one; two; three	unique; bisect; tripod

Root	Meaning	Example
auto	self	autograph
bio	life	biology
dic, dict	say	dictate
gram, graph, grav	write	engrave
meter	measure	centimeter
micro	small	microfilm
photo	light	photograph
scope, scopy	see	microscope
tele	distant	telescope
therm, thermo	heat	thermometer

Reading Practice

Read each sentence. Write the letter of the correct definition of the underlined word. Use the charts of prefixes and roots for help.

1. The planet Earth is unique in this galaxy.
   a. one of a kind b. uninteresting c. inhabited
2. We study Earth's plant and animal life in biology.
   a. a study of life b. a study of space c. a study of germs
3. The equator divides the Earth into two hemispheres.
   a. continents b. half spheres c. climates
4. Our geography class collected photographs of Puerto Rico.
   a. something "written" in rock b. something "written" by hand
   c. something "written" with light
5. Puerto Rico's climate is semitropical.
   a. not tropical b. partly tropical c. above tropical
6. Antarctica has almost constant subzero temperatures.
   a. above zero b. between zero c. below zero
7. In subzero temperatures cars will not run without antifreeze.
   a. protection against freezing b. frozen water c. frozen earth

Writing Practice

Rewrite the following sentences. Replace each underlined phrase with a word that has a root or a prefix from the charts.

8. The field of geography makes into one many sciences.
9. Early geographers were explorers such as Ferdinand Magellan, whose ship navigated around the globe in two years.
10. Now, above-the-speed-of-sound jets circle the Earth in hours.
11. The geographical records of the Greeks date before all others.
12. Ships use devices for seeing distant things to sight land.
13. We use heat-measuring devices to record daily temperatures.

Project

Many prefixes and roots have been combined to form words for new means of transportation, such as *super*sonic jet, *auto*mobile, *bi*cycle, or *sub*marine. Work with your classmates to invent future forms of transportation. Create the names for these new vehicles by combining prefixes and roots from the charts. Write a paragraph describing each new vehicle, and draw a picture of it. Be sure to include what effects these vehicles might have on people.

Language Enrichment
More About Verbs

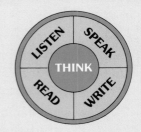

Use what you know about verbs to do these activities.

Al Active and Paul Passive

Two friends, Al Active and Paul Passive, went camping together. When they returned home, they told friends about the trip. Al described their adventures using the active voice. In contrast, Paul described the trip using the passive voice.

Pretend that you are either Al or Paul, and tell about an incident from the trip in the way he would tell it. Have your classmates guess which of the campers is speaking.

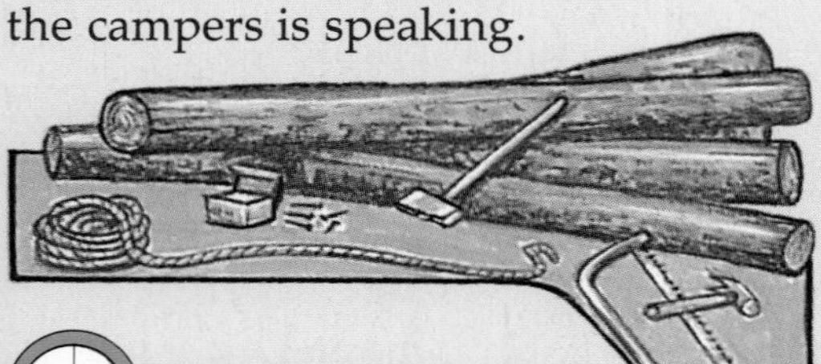

Building a Raft

How would you use the materials in the picture to build a raft? Write a paragraph explaining how to do it. Use sentences with direct objects, such as "Saw the logs into even lengths." Remember that a direct object usually follows an action verb and receives the action of the verb. Make drawings to go with your explanation if you wish.

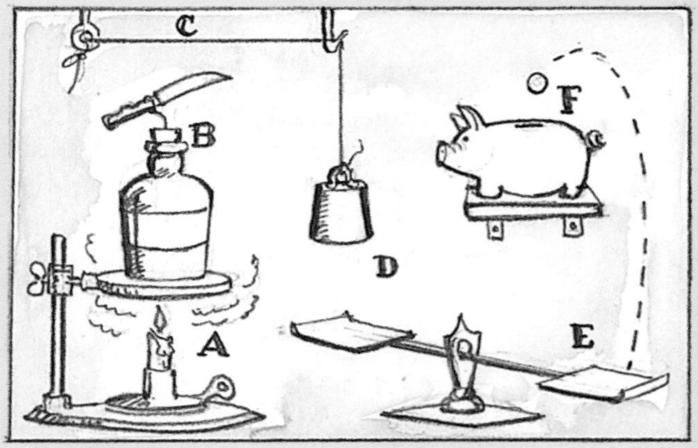

Wacky Inventions

Cartoonist Rube Goldberg created a character who loved to invent things. Professor Lucifer Gorgonzola Butts always made doing simple things as complicated as possible. You might read Steven Caney's *Invention Book* (Workman, 1984) for examples of the professor's inventions.

Think of something that is simple to do, such as sharpening a pencil. Think like the professor, and invent a new machine to do that task. Draw a diagram of your invention. Then write a paragraph explaining how it works. Use several direct objects in your explanation. Explain your invention as you display your diagram to the class.

CONNECTING
LANGUAGE ↔ WRITING

In this unit you learned more about verbs. You learned the difference between transitive and intransitive verbs and between passive and active verbs.

◆ **Using Verbs in Your Writing** Knowing how to use different kinds of verbs can add variety to your writing. By using the right verbs, you will avoid confusing your audience. Pay special attention to the verbs you use as you do these activities.

Underwater Exploration

Imagine that you are an underwater explorer viewing a scene from your submarine. Write one or two paragraphs telling about what you see. Since you want to make the reader feel as if he or she is right there with you, use the present progressive tense.

Tools of the Trade?

You learned about Latin and Greek roots on the **Building Vocabulary** pages. An important word, *scientist,* comes from the Latin root *scien,* which means "knowing."

Match each piece of scientific equipment with the Latin or Greek root or roots related to its name. Then make a list of ways a scientist might use the equipment. (Note: *Mar* is the Latin root for "sea." *Aqu* is the Latin root for "water.")

4 Unit Checkup

Think Back	Think Ahead
◆ What did you learn about paragraphs of cause and effect in this unit? What did you do to write one?	◆ How will what you learned about paragraphs of cause and effect help you explain problems or find solutions? ◆ How will knowing how to see what happened or why it happened help you write a cause-and-effect paragraph?
◆ Look at the writing you did in this unit. How did progressive verb forms help you express your ideas?	◆ What is one way you can use progressive forms of verbs to improve your writing?

Paragraphs of Cause and Effect *pages 158 – 159*

Read the following sentences. Add a cause if the sentence is an effect. Add an effect if the sentence is a cause.

1. Days are longer in the summer and shorter in the winter.
2. A solar eclipse is rare.
3. The meeting of high and low pressure systems is dangerous.

Connecting Cause and Effect *page 160*

Rewrite each sentence so it is clearly a cause or an effect. Then add another sentence that would logically follow the rewritten sentence.

4. We ran out of drinking water.
5. The sun evaporated the surface moisture.
6. It had not rained for months.

Using Formal and Informal Language *page 161*

Write the following sentences, using words that create a serious or factual tone.

7. Storms ________ the construction.

8. Many states ________ the sea for business.
9. The sea ________ every coastline in the world.

The Writing Process *pages 162 – 171*

Write the letter for the answer to each question.

10. When gathering information for a paragraph of cause and effect, which reference source would you use?
    a. encyclopedia **b.** novel **c.** editorial page
11. When drafting a paragraph of cause and effect, what should you write first?
    a. causes **b.** effects **c.** topic sentence
12. What type of language must you use in a paragraph of cause and effect for a research paper?
    a. informal language **b.** formal language **c.** poetic language

Progressive Forms of Verbs *pages 174 – 175*

Write the progressive form of each verb.

13. they sail (present progressive)
14. he walked (past progressive)
15. they study (past perfect progressive)
16. we unearthed (past perfect progressive)
17. he will fly (future perfect progressive)

Direct Objects *pages 176 – 178*

Write each sentence. Underline the subject once and the verb twice. Circle the direct object. Some sentences may have more than one direct object. If there is no direct object, write *none.*

18. Hurricanes dump rain wherever they go.
19. They generate gale winds that may exceed 150 mph.
20. The weather bureau uses airplanes, radar, and satellites to track hurricanes.
21. People who live in the Gulf states fear the damage and injuries that often result from the storms.
22. A hurricane has an eye of about 15 miles in width.

Indirect Objects *pages 179 – 180*

Write the indirect object and the direct object from each sentence.

23. I must show you the souvenirs from my vacation.
24. I brought Mother a set of postcards from Houston.
25. They'll show her the sights of a famous city.
26. This book offers tourists a guided tour of Dallas.
27. Vacations can provide us an education as well as a rest.

Predicate Nominatives *pages 181 – 182*

Write each sentence. Underline the predicate nominative. Draw an arrow to the subject to which it refers.

28. A stalactite is a rock formation.
29. It is an interesting sight to see in a cave.
30. A stalactite is the counterpart of a stalagmite.
31. They both are frequently objects of study.
32. They are opposite images of one another.
33. Scientists become stalactite and stalagmite students to learn about geological history.

Transitive and Intransitive Verbs *page 183 – 184*

Write each sentence. Underline the verb and label it *transitive* or *intransitive*. If it is transitive, underline the direct object twice.

34. Astronauts are the explorers of this century.
35. They fly their spaceships into unknown places.
36. Astronauts operate complex computers and machines.
37. They look into the future as well as into space.
38. They are testing equipment and procedures.

Active and Passive Voice *pages 185 – 186*

Write the verb in each sentence. Write *active voice* or *passive voice*.

39. The oceans on earth are influenced by the moon.
40. The moon's position affects the earth's gravitational pull.

41. Tides are changed by the location of the moon.
42. The moon has been studied by scientists for a long time.
43. In 1969, a man first stepped on the moon's surface.

Easily Confused Verb Pairs *pages 187–189*

Write the correct form of the verb in parentheses ( ).

44. The earth rarely (leaves, lets) us be careless.
45. To stay in the desert as the sun (rises, raises) is deadly.
46. A person should (set, sit) in the shade.
47. At night, a person should (bring, take) a jacket for warmth.
48. The setting sun (leaves, lets) the unwary shivering.
49. When you return, please (bring, take) my canteen back to me.

Latin and Greek Prefixes and Roots *pages 190–191*

Read each sentence. Write the correct definition of the underlined word. Use the chart of prefixes and roots on page 190 for help.

50. Land and water can be antagonists.
    a. friends
    b. opponents
    c. painful
51. Their conflict is usually subterranean.
    a. underground
    b. underwater
    c. above ground
52. These traffic signs are nearly universal.
    a. devastating
    b. worldwide
    c. finished
53. A seismograph will not show how much land is lost.
    a. device for recording wind
    b. device for recording earthquakes
    c. device for recording erosion
54. Starfish can be studied in a biology class.
    a. a kind of math
    b. map-making
    c. study of living things

1-4 Cumulative Review

Compound Subjects and Compound Verbs *pages 37 – 38*

For each sentence write *compound subject, compound verb,* or *both.*

1. The boy found an envelope and brought it home to his family.
2. A list of directions and a treasure map were in the faded envelope.
3. The boy, his friends, and his relatives tried but did not understand either the map or the directions.
4. He went with his family to the museum and asked for help.
5. The museum curator decoded the map and gave them an explanation.
6. The map and the directions were written in Spanish and were part of an elaborate joke.

Simple and Compound Sentences *pages 39 – 41*

Write *simple sentence* or *compound sentence* for each sentence.

7. The boy and his friends laughed and laughed for hours.
8. The members of his family were not amused, but they did not scold him.
9. The boy decided to study and to learn the Spanish language.
10. First, he learned the most common verbs, and then he moved to the most common nouns.
11. The mystery about the envelope also sparked his curiosity about maps.
12. The situation made him laugh; it had introduced him to two new subjects.

Avoiding Sentence Fragments and Run-on Sentences *pages 42 – 43*

Write whether each group of words is a *sentence,* a *sentence fragment,* or a *run-on sentence.*

13. Reading a map and speaking a new language for a change.
14. A map is a visual form of communication a language is an oral form of communication.
15. Both systems of communication work.
16. When a person cannot talk or when a person cannot hear.
17. Both words and pictures are symbols that stand for things or ideas.
18. They stand for ideas or objects they suggest ideas or objects.

Possessive Nouns *pages 84 – 85*

Rewrite each sentence, replacing the underlined phrase with a phrase containing a singular or a plural possessive noun.

19. Learning <u>the language of a country</u> teaches one about people and culture.
20. <u>A report of the education commission</u> emphasizes learning the language of another country.
21. It agrees with <u>the thinking of most teachers</u> that students grow by experiencing other cultures.
22. <u>The opinion of Neal</u> is quite different.
23. To him, <u>the languages of other countries</u> are just fun to learn to speak.
24. <u>The enjoyment by Neal</u> is in understanding and saying words others do not know.

Verbs *pages 122 – 123*

Write the verb or verb phrase from each sentence. Write whether it is an *action verb* or a *linking verb*.

25. Mother Teresa has become a symbol of help for the poor.
26. She is a heroine to the sick and the impoverished.
27. She insists that the fortunate should help the unfortunate.
28. Corporations and individuals alike feel pity for the poor.
29. She collects their donations and buys food and medical supplies.
30. For the whole world, she has become a symbol of charity in action.

Principal Parts of Verbs *pages 126 – 132*

Change the verb to show the form called for in parentheses ( ).

31. Early wagon trains (leave—past) the East with passengers who were filled with hope.
32. A wagon master and a guide (take—past) total responsibility for the people and their belongings.
33. Historians (label—past participle) these people "pioneers."
34. The government (open—past participle) vast areas of the West to statehood.
35. The wagon masters (lead—past) the pioneers to a new land.
36. Our class (read—present participle) about the pioneers.

Verb Tenses *pages 133 – 136*

Write the verb from each sentence. Next to each verb, write its tense.

37. The wagon trains to the West were like little cities on wooden wheels.

38. Before reaching their new homes, the surviving pioneers had triumphed over the deadly pitfalls of the trail.

39. Today's "wagon trains" are the convoys of recreational vehicles on the road.

40. You can often see a string of these huge, gleaming vehicles rolling down the highway.

41. They have changed the definition of camping in America.

42. Will future historians see the drivers of recreational vehicles as pioneers?

Be, Have, Do *pages 137–140*

Write the correct form of the verb in parentheses ( ).

43. People (do, does) not want to believe that what a person (do, does) for a living can be heroic.

44. (Do, Does) you think that a heroic job has to be a dangerous job?

45. I (has, have) been uncertain for some time about this.

46. What (is, are) your view on this matter?

47. Heroes (have, has) a reputation for being different from others.

48. Their image has (be, been) changing in movies and in books.

49. It seems that anyone can (be, been) a hero nowadays.

50. I admire people who (do, does) their best, day in and day out.

Subject-Verb Agreement *pages 141 – 142*

Write the correct form of the verb in parentheses ( ).

51. Truck drivers (is, are) not all the same.

52. The open road (calls, call) to them for many different reasons.

53. The travel, the money, and the freedom (appeals, appeal) to some who sit in the huge truck.

54. Truck drivers with families often (leaves, leave) them for long stretches of time.

55. A woman with her citizens-band radio and her dog (rides, ride) happily toward the west.

56. An independent driver or a company employee (drives, drive) for reasons as diverse as the products that truckers carry.

Direct and Indirect Objects *pages 176 – 180*

Write the direct object and the indirect object from each sentence.

57. We must give the natural environment our full and complete attention.
58. It gives us the air we breathe, the water we drink, and the food we eat.
59. Keeping the environment clean gives people a healthy place to live.
60. Fostering unpolluted water, air, and soil also offers other life forms a better chance to live.
61. If we respect it, nature will give everyone a lifelong reward.

Active and Passive Voice *pages 185–186*

Rewrite each sentence in the active voice. If the sentence cannot be rewritten in the active voice, write *cannot be rewritten.*

62. All elements in nature are sustained by the other parts of the natural order.
63. Many varieties of plants, flowers, and trees are brought forth by the earth.
64. The ponds, lakes, and inland seas are surrounded by land.
65. Rocks and other objects are kept in place by the force of gravity.
66. All plants and animals are nurtured by air, water, and soil.
67. Even the smallest living thing should be considered a miracle.

Easily Confused Verb Pairs *pages 187 – 189*

Write the verb in parentheses ( ) that correctly completes each sentence.

68. The responsibility for good government no longer (lies, lays) in someone else's hands.
69. We cannot (sit, set) in our chairs and hope that others will make the right decisions for us.
70. Our schools will (raise, rise) students' awareness of this problem.
71. Television cannot (leave, let) this all-important issue go unnoticed.
72. Our democratic form of government will long endure if all voters (raise, rise) up to participate.

UNIT 5

Persuading Others

◆ COMPOSITION FOCUS: **Persuasive Essay**
◆ LANGUAGE FOCUS: **Pronouns**

Imagine that you are on the jury in a courtroom. A lawyer is summing up a case, arguing that the other side is wrong and that her side is right. Your decision will hinge on how strong this evidence is and how persuasively the lawyer presents it. You make the same kind of decision when you read persuasive writing, writing that attempts to convince you to take one side of an issue.

People use persuasive writing in newspaper editorials, speeches, business letters, and essays— forms of writing that present the personal views of the author.

In preparing to write his essay "Is There Life on Mars?", Peter Roop did research to learn about both sides of the issue. Then he took a position and created a convincing argument. In this unit you will learn how to write a convincing persuasive essay.

Peter Roop wrote "Is There Life on Mars?" *to persuade* others to share his viewpoint on an issue.

Reading with a Writer's Eye
Persuasive Essay

Is there finally an answer to the age-old controversy over whether there is life on Mars? After examining the evidence, Peter Roop has an opinion. Read his persuasive essay to find out what his position is on this issue. As you read, notice what arguments he makes in favor of his position, and review the evidence to decide whether you agree.

Is There Life on Mars?

by Peter Roop

Is there life on Mars? For centuries, people have asked this question. Some have answered yes, just look at the canals. Others have concluded no, Mars is too cold for life. No one has had any scientific evidence, however, to support an accurate answer. That is, not until 1975, when three experiments aboard the *Viking I* lander detected signs of life on Mars. For the first time we had evidence.

Did the *Viking I* lander really find evidence of life on Mars? Scientific controversy continues to rage over this question. However, a close examination of the results of the Viking mission leads to only one conclusion. Yes, we have evidence of life on Mars.

That Mars is a cold, dry, desert-like planet scientists knew from photographs taken during spacecraft flybys. But in order to determine if life actually exists on Mars, life-seeking experiments had to be conducted on the surface of the planet.

Eight years of intensive planning took place before *Viking I* journeyed to Mars. Scientists from around the world contributed ideas and experiments on the best ways to search for life. Would Martian life be small or large? If it were large, then cameras could spot it. If life were

small, even microscopic, then highly specialized instruments would be needed to detect life.

Three life-seeking instruments were designed and successfully tested here on Earth before *Viking* blasted off. How, though, would scientists judge if the instruments actually found signs of life on Mars? Scientists agreed that if just one experiment showed positive signs of life, signs that could only be created by living organisms, that would be convincing evidence.

When *Viking I* landed on Mars on July 20, 1976, the temperature was −122°F. Only once before had such a low temperature been recorded on Earth. This was in Antarctica where life indeed survives such extreme temperatures. Scientists were increasingly optimistic that they might find life on Mars.

Viking's first photographs showed a dry, red, rock-covered plain much like a desert on Earth except that there were no visible signs of life. "There was not a hint of life—no bushes, no trees, no cactuses, no giraffes, antelopes, or rabbits," said one disappointed scientist, adding, "So far, no rock has obviously gotten up and walked away either."

The scientists then turned to the biological and chemical experiments in their search for Martian life. First, the *Viking*'s long sampler arm scooped up samples of the red Martian soil. The dirt was divided, a measured portion going to each of the three chambers holding the three experiments. Nothing happened for 72 hours. Then suddenly, each experiment showed signs of life.

Dr. Vance Oyama created the first experiment that indicated life. Dr. Oyama was optimistic about finding life on Mars, placing the chances of success at 50 percent. His experiment injected nutrient-rich water into a sample of the superdry Martian soil. He reasoned that the more food and water he gave any microbes, the more gases they would release. If life was present, the experiment would show an increase in oxygen.

Much to his surprise, Dr. Oyama's experiment showed an increase of twenty times the normal amount of oxygen in the Martian atmosphere.

The second life-seeking experiment also showed signs of being alive. This experiment, designed by Dr. Norman Horowitz, looked for evidence of photosynthesis, the process in which plants use water, sunlight, and carbon dioxide to create food. If carbon dioxide was absorbed, it meant that plant life was present in the Martian soil. Much to the surprise of the scientists, carbon dioxide was absorbed at a rapid rate.

"You could have knocked me over with one of those Martian cobbles," Dr. Horowitz said when the results first came in.

The third experiment, designed by Dr. Gilbert Levin, found signs of life, too. Dr. Levin's experiment was intended to detect signs of *microbes*, or tiny animals. An instrument injected radioactive "food"—liquid chemicals—into samples of Martian soil. "If the microorganisms are present," Dr. Levin stated, "they consume the food and give off radioactive breath, or gas, which is then very easily detected because of the instrument's sensitivity." This is exactly what happened. Several hours after the soil sample was injected with the food, radioactive gas was released. More evidence of life on Mars had been found.

Later investigations, however, showed flaws in two of the experiments. In the first experiment, scientists demonstrated that the oxygen had been released, not from any living thing, but from the reaction of the water with the iron-rich soil. In the second experiment, the experiment itself absorbed carbon dioxide, creating its own signs of life.

Was something wrong with the third experiment, too? Was the *Viking* mission another dead end in the search for life? To make certain that his instruments were working properly, Dr. Levin conducted a second experiment. He injected the same soil sample with the liquid food again. Then he heated the sample to kill any microbes. This time no radioactive gas was released because the heat killed all life in the soil.

Scientists tried to disprove Dr. Levin's conclusions, arguing that Mars is too cold for life or that life cannot exist without water. Dr. Levin set out to prove them wrong. In a laboratory on Earth he performed the same three experiments that Viking had done on Mars. Instead of using Martian soil, however, he used samples of cold, waterless soil from Antarctica. Levin knew these samples had microscopic life in them, life that survived in the extremely dry and cold soil.

Dr. Levin's experiment detected the life in the samples. Dr. Oyama's and Dr. Horowitz's experiments, though, indicated that no type of life was present in the samples. These two experiments had failed to find life even on Earth!

Was Dr. Levin's experiment the only way life was detected on Mars? No, there was other evidence, photographic evidence. The cameras aboard the *Viking* lander operated for over 600 days (almost two Earth years) taking 40,000 photographs. Many of these photographs were taken at exactly the same time of day and of the same landscape. Scientists closely examined the pictures for any changes. One rock, right in front of the lander, had a green patch on it in 1976. Over the two years the patch changed in shape and color. Similar photographic experiments on Earth reveal that lichen or moss behave in exactly this same way.

Scientists who reject this photographic evidence argue that the patch seems changed because of dust from a Martian storm or from dirt dropped on it by the *Viking* scooper. Levin argues, "The greenish spot penetrates through the dust and appears displaced slightly from its original position. Everybody who's looked at it in detail agrees there's some change."

All signs point to life on Mars. New missions to Mars will find more evidence of life. Manned and unmanned missions are already underway by the United States and the Soviet Union. Who knows what additional evidence they might find during their explorations—fossils, hibernating microbes, microscopic plants?

For now we know that *Viking*'s explorations were successful. As Dr. Levin concludes, "It's more likely than not that we detected life." We do have neighbors on Mars, even if they are extremely small.

Respond

1. What is Peter Roop's position on this issue? Do you agree with him? Explain your answer.

Discuss

2. What evidence does the writer give to support his position? In your opinion, is it strong evidence? Why or why not?
3. What is the opposite position on this issue? What evidence is given to support this side? How strong is this evidence?

Thinking As a Writer

Analyzing a Persuasive Essay

In a persuasive essay the writer presents a position on an issue to convince readers to agree. In building the argument, the writer discusses both sides of the issue in unemotional language.

Persuasive essays usually have an **introduction, supporting arguments,** and a **conclusion.**

Writer's Guide

A persuasive essay
- presents evidence to support one side of an issue.
- has an introduction, supporting arguments, and a conclusion.

Is there life on Mars? For centuries, people have asked this question. Some have answered yes, just look at the canals. Others have concluded no, Mars is too cold for life. No one has had any scientific evidence, however, to support an accurate answer. That is, not until 1975, when three experiments aboard the *Viking 1* lander detected signs of life on Mars.

The **introduction** captures the interest of the reader and provides a **thesis statement** that indicates the writer's position on the issue.

* * *

Scientists who reject this photographic evidence argue that the patch seems changed because of dust from a Martian storm or from dirt dropped on it by the *Viking* scooper. Levin argues, "The greenish spot penetrates through the dust and appears displaced slightly from its original position. Everybody who's looked at it in detail agrees there's some change."

The **supporting arguments** mention the opposite side of the issue, but most importantly present evidence in favor of the writer's side. The evidence includes reasons backed up by facts and quotations from experts. The reasons are often presented in order of importance, the most important reason appearing last.

* * *

For now we know that *Viking*'s explorations were successful. As Dr. Levin concludes, "It's more likely than not that we detected life." We do have neighbors on Mars, even if they are extremely small.

The **conclusion** restates the writer's position. It may also summarize the reasons for the position. Strongly persuasive essays usually end with a call for action.

Discuss

1. In the persuasive essay "Is There Life on Mars?" what is the purpose of the introduction of the supporting arguments?
2. Which sentence in the introduction is the thesis statement? Why do you think this?
3. Dr. Levin's statement supports the photographic evidence for life on Mars. Why do you think he is a good person to quote?

Try Your Hand

A. Analyze a Persuasive Essay Read the following sections of a persuasive essay. For each section write *introduction, supporting argument,* or *conclusion* to identify where in the essay it belongs.

1. "If something isn't done soon, we will simply have to build a new shelter," claims Officer Tracy Patterson. In addition to raising money, the campaign saves the expense of building a new shelter, since emptying the old one makes room for strays.
2. Should being homeless cost a dog its life? This is the price too many dogs pay for the "crime" of having no home. Greenleaf Village should begin a campaign to place homeless dogs with families.
3. Opponents argue that a campaign would cost too much money and that Greenleaf has more pressing problems. In fact, a campaign could actually raise money for the community. Workers would donate their time and materials and charge a small fee to the buyer for their services.
4. The public, then, should join in this campaign because it will raise money and cancel the need to kill unwanted dogs.
5. A campaign to place homeless dogs with families can save thousands of lives. According to Officer Patterson, "Of the two thousand dogs that passed through our shelter last year, seventy-five percent had to be killed."

B. Organize Arguments Organize the supporting arguments in **A** from least to most important. Write the numbers of the arguments in the order in which they should appear in the essay. Then write reasons for the order you chose.

C. Read Persuasive Essays Turn to the editorial section of a daily newspaper. Choose an editorial or a letter to the editor, and read it to a partner, identifying the parts of the essay.

Writer's Notebook

Collecting Science Words Did you notice the science words such as *organism* and *radioactive* in the essay "Is There Life on Mars?" Read the essay again. Record in your *Writer's Notebook* any sentences with science words with which you are unfamiliar. Look up the words in a dictionary and record their meanings. Try to use the words when you write and speak.

Thinking As a Writer
Evaluating Reasons to Support a Conclusion

Writer's Guide

To write persuasive essays, good writers
- develop conclusions based on reasons.
- must have enough evidence to support their conclusions.

In good persuasive essays, writers present their positions, or opinions, on issues. An **opinion** is a statement of beliefs that cannot be proved true or false. To give worthwhile opinions, writers must make **generalizations,** or draw logical conclusions about the issues. For a conclusion to be logical, it must be based on reasons supported by **facts.** Facts are statements that can be proved true or false.

Before writing a persuasive essay, a writer may create a diagram like this:

Opinion: Automobiles should be required to have seat belts with shoulder straps.

↓

Reasons Supported by Facts

1. Wearing seat belts with shoulder straps can save lives.
2. More people wear seat belts if required to do so by law.
3. Seat belts are a less expensive safety device than air bags.

When you write a persuasive essay, you might want to use charts to organize your support materials.

Discuss

1. Look at the persuasive essay on pages 204 – 207. Is the writer's conclusion logical? Explain your answer.
2. What facts does the writer present to support his reasons?

Try Your Hand

Evaluate Reasons Take a position on an issue that interests you. Write your position and list five strong reasons for it. Trade sentences with a partner and decide how each of you could support your reasons with facts.

Developing the Writer's Craft
Using Vivid Language

Writer's Guide

Good writers
- help a reader picture the facts by using vivid words that apply to their subject.

To be convincing, good writers use vivid words that help a reader focus on the facts in a persuasive essay. Since persuasive essays are based on logic, writers are careful about their choice of words.

Read these sentences from the persuasive essay.

1. Dr. Levin's experiment was intended to detect signs of *microbes*, or tiny animals.
2. An instrument injected radioactive "food"—liquid chemicals—into samples of Martian soil.

The writer chose the underlined words carefully to clarify Dr. Levin's experiment. Besides helping the reader to visualize it, the scientific words suggest that the writer is knowledgeable in this field. Therefore, his arguments become more believable.

When you write your persuasive essay, provide visual details for your reader. Use vivid words that make your subject clear.

Discuss

1. Look back at page 205 of the persuasive essay. What vivid words does the writer use to describe the first experiment that indicated life on Mars? Which words are scientific?
2. Read this statement. *In the second experiment, the test itself absorbed carbon dioxide, creating its own signs of life.* Is *absorbed* a good verb for the sentence?

Try Your Hand

Use Vivid Language Look at both pictures of the earth. Take either position on what shape the earth is. Write three sentences that give facts to support your position. Use vivid words that apply to the subject.

Round

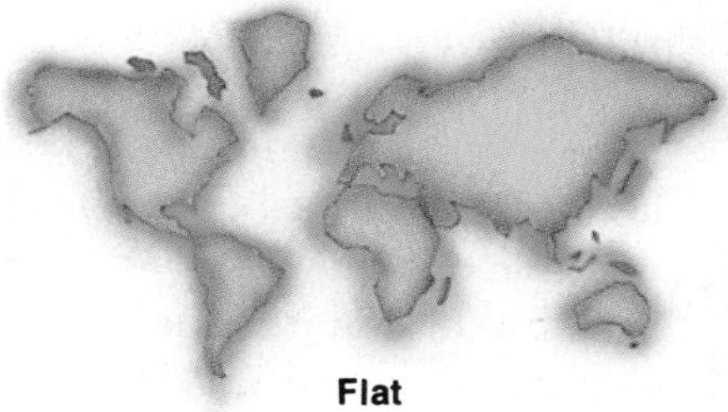
Flat

1 Prewriting
Persuasive Essay

Writer's Guide

Prewriting Checklist

- ☑ Brainstorm topics.
- ☑ Select an issue.
- ☑ Think about your audience and your purpose.
- ☑ Gather information.
- ☑ Organize the essay.

Michael was president of a school achievement club. The club was about to begin raising funds by selling T-shirts. Michael had to convince club members to agree with his advertising decision. He wanted to write a persuasive essay for club members. He used the information in the **Writer's Guide** to help him plan his essay. Look at what he did.

◆ Brainstorming and Selecting a Topic

First, Michael brainstormed a list of possible issues for his persuasive essay. The club's members had decided to sell school T-shirts in an effort to raise extra money, and they had some important decisions to make. By thinking about the decisions, Michael came up with a list of issues. He listed every issue relating to the fund-raising plan that occurred to him.

Next, Michael looked down his list and crossed out every issue that did not have two sides to it. He also crossed off an issue that needed no further discussion because it had already been decided.

Finally, Michael circled the remaining issue that was most likely to interest his audience. He decided to write about the best way to advertise, because all the members were concerned about spending their money wisely.

Sell by mail or phone
Decide on the sizes
What words to print
Find out about sales laws
Decide on the price
Use radio or magazine ads
Sell T-shirts or fruit baskets

Discuss

1. Study each item Michael crossed off his list. Which was not an issue because it had already been decided?
2. Which ideas were tasks to be done by individual buyers rather than issues? Would they be good topics for a persuasive essay? Explain your answer.
3. Which issue should have been decided at an earlier date?
4. If Michael's club was concerned about the best way to deliver T-shirts to small and large organizations, what might be a good issue for his essay?

Stating a Position and Gathering Information

After Michael selected the issue, he had to decide what his position would be. To help him decide, he listed some *pros,* or advantages, and some *cons,* or disadvantages, for both radio and magazine advertising. He also did a little research. Through his research and his lists, he came to a logical conclusion on his position, and he wrote a clear, precise thesis statement.

Then Michael listed reasons for his position, considering advantages for his side of the issue and disadvantages for the other side. These reasons would strengthen his thesis statement and allow him to present the issue clearly.

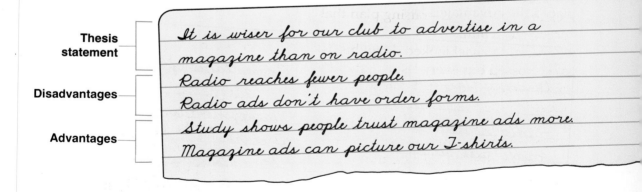

Thesis statement	It is wiser for our club to advertise in a magazine than on radio.
Disadvantages	Radio reaches fewer people. Radio ads don't have order forms.
Advantages	Study shows people trust magazine ads more. Magazine ads can picture our T-shirts.

Next, Michael gathered information on both sides of the issue. He wanted to have at least three advantages and three disadvantages. An advertising book gave him several additional reasons. He added them to his list.

When Michael read over his reasons, he saw that some of them needed facts or examples to reinforce them. Michael used books and listened to local businesspeople to find appropriate facts. He added the facts to his notes.

Radio reaches fewer people.

KGIS radio station
-average listeners: 10,000
Lexington Outlook
--28,000 readers

Discuss

1. Look back at Michael's list of advantages and disadvantages. How do these points support his thesis statement?
2. Why is it important for Michael to support with facts the reason *Radio reaches fewer people*?

◆ Organizing the Reasons

Once Michael had gathered all the evidence he needed for his persuasive essay, he was ready to organize it. He grouped the disadvantages for one side of the issue and the advantages for the other side in order from least to most important. Michael knew he would build the strongest argument by ending with his side of the issue, so he placed the advantages last.

Disadvantages of Radio	Advantages of Magazines
Radio reaches fewer people.	Magazine ads can picture our T-shirts.
Radio ads don't have order forms.	Study shows people trust magazine ads more.
It is more costly to reach people through radio.	Magazines last; people can read ads again.

Discuss

1. Look at Michael's first list of advantages and disadvantages. Which will he discuss first? Why do you think this is the best way to build a strong argument for his side of the issue?
2. What disadvantage should appear last? Why do you think this?

Try Your Hand

Now plan a persuasive essay of your own.

A. Brainstorm and Select a Topic Brainstorm a list of possible issues. Listen to discussion around you, and list issues that matter to you. Think about each issue and your audience.

- Cross out issues that do not have two sides.
- Cross out any issues that have already been decided.
- Circle the most important issue left on your list. This will be the topic of your essay.

B. State a Position and Gather Information When you are satisfied with your topic, list the pros and cons for both sides of the issue, and come to a conclusion about your position. Write a thesis statement. Then list three advantages for your side of the issue and three disadvantages for the other side. If you have trouble thinking of enough advantages or disadvantages, read books or listen to people to find more. Gather facts to support each reason. Make sure you are gathering facts, not propaganda. If you need help, follow the **Tips on How to Recognize Propaganda** on page 216.

C. Organize the Information Look over your notes.

- In a persuasive essay, reasons should be supported by facts or examples. Cross out any opinions.
- Think about your audience. Choose reasons in which your audience would be most interested.
- Plan to place your thesis statement in the introduction. Next, list the supporting facts, including both sides of the issue. Place the advantages for your side last. Arrange each set of reasons in order of importance from least to most important.

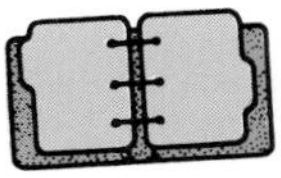

Save your notes and lists in your *Writer's Notebook*. You will use them when you draft your persuasive essay.

Listening and Speaking

Tips on How to Recognize Propaganda

When listening for facts, be aware of propaganda techniques. Listen for the facts, and make sure they are logical. Base your reactions on common sense, not emotion. Ask yourself whether the speaker or the writer is trying to convince you by using methods such as these, which are not based on facts.

1. **Bandwagon** *Everyone wants a Tyson ten-speed.*
   You are being asked to do or believe something to be like everyone else.

2. **Either-Or** *You'll look frumpy if you don't wear Supercool jeans.*
   You are told that your only choice is either to accept the speaker's product or idea or to settle for something distasteful. The speaker fails to mention all the other choices. The speaker implies that if you don't accept what he or she has to offer, you will be compromising.

3. **Emotional Words** *Don't look old and dull in eyeglasses. Get on the fast track to popularity in contact lenses.*
   The attempt is to convince you through words that appeal to your emotions rather than to your ability to reason.

4. **False Cause** *You caught your cold because you didn't wear a raincoat.*
   The speaker tries to convice you that one event caused another just because it happened first.

5. **Name-Calling** *Don't vote for that no-good Representative Lynch. Just look at that suit he's wearing.*
   The speaker criticizes someone and then gives you weak evidence or no evidence for the criticism. Frequently, connotative words, words with emotional implications, are used.

6. **Testimonial** *Actress Cheryl Simpson says, "Tony's trucks are best!"*
   You are told that because an expert or a famous person supports an idea or uses a product, you should also support it or use it. Perhaps people think that if they buy this product or support the idea, they will be more like this admirable person.

2 Drafting
Persuasive Essay

Using his organized notes, Michael followed the checklist in the **Writer's Guide** to draft his essay. Look at what he did.

Writer's Guide

Drafting Checklist

- Use your notes and lists for ideas.
- Include your thesis statement in the introduction.
- Follow the order of the notes you organized.
- Conclude the essay by calling on the audience to act on your recommendation.

The Advertising Choice: Radio or Magazine?

What is the difference between 28,000 and 10,000? The answer, of course, is a number, the number of people we can reach for the same price through radio or magazine advertising. Research indicates that, for our needs, advertising through a magazine is wiser.

For our purposes, a major disadvantage of radio advertising is that it does not leave people with an order form they can use.

Discuss

Which part of Michael's first paragraph is his thesis statement?

Try Your Hand

Now you are ready to write a persuasive essay.

A. Review Your Information Think about the information you gathered and organized in the last lesson. Gather more information, if needed.

B. Think About Your TAP Remember that your task is to write a persuasive essay. Your purpose is to persuade your audience to accept your side of the issue you have chosen.

Task: What?
Audience: Who?
Purpose: Why?

C. Write Your First Draft Refer to the **Drafting Checklist.**

When you write your draft, just put all your ideas on paper. Do not worry about spelling, punctuation, or grammar. You can correct the draft later.

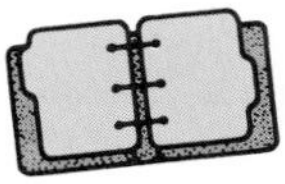

Save your first draft in your *Writer's Notebook.* You will use it when you revise your essay.

3 Responding and Revising
Persuasive Essay

Michael used the checklist in the **Writer's Guide** to revise his persuasive essay. Look at what he did.

◆ Checking Information

Michael decided to take away a detail that did not keep to his topic. To show his change, he used this mark ℘. In the same paragraph, Michael added a detail to support a reason. To show the addition, he used this mark ∧ .

◆ Checking Organization

Michael moved the most important reason to the end of a paragraph. To show that it should be moved, he used this mark ↻ .

◆ Checking Language

To make his writing less choppy, Michael decided to combine two sentences. He used this mark ∧‾ to make his change.

Writer's Guide

Revising Checklist

- ☑ Read your essay to yourself or to a partner.
- ☑ Think about your audience and your purpose. Add or cut information.
- ☑ Check that your essay is organized correctly and has a logical conclusion.
- ☑ Check for choppy language. Combine some sentences to improve your style.

Replace
Cut
Move
Add

Also, the expense of reaching a single individual through radio is higher than through magazines. It would cost 2½ cents to reach one person through a 60-second commercial, according to KISP radio. A commercial is a radio spot. For less than a penny, a ⅓-page magazine ad would reach one reader, says Advertising News.

A magazine advertisement would have an order form and ~~A magazine advertisement~~ could picture the Lexington Lions T-shirt and logo. In this way we would set up an image of ourselves. ~~People would see how attractive the lion on our T-shirts looks.~~ Most important, magazines are a permanent medium. Another advantage is that people think of magazine advertisements as more truthful than radio commercials. In the poll conducted by our club, out of 300 individuals, 239 preferred magazine advertisements for this reason.

Discuss

1. Why was it important for Michael to add the detail about how many people favored magazine advertisements in the club's poll?
2. Michael moved one of his reasons. Do you agree with his change? Why or why not? Explain your answer.

Try Your Hand

Now revise your first draft.

A. Read Your First Draft As you read your essay, think about your audience and your purpose. Ask yourself or your partner the questions in the box.

Responding and Revising Strategies

✔ Respond **Ask yourself or a partner:**	✔ Revise **Try these solutions:**
• Have I stated my position in the introduction?	• **Add** a thesis statement that declares your position.
• Do I give strong reasons that lead to a logical conclusion?	• **Replace** any reasons that are weak or **add** facts to support them.
• Are my reasons arranged in order of importance?	• **Move** any reasons that seem out of place.
• Is my writing smooth?	• Combine two short sentences into one sentence. See the **Revising Workshop** on page 220.
• Have I revised language?	• **Add** visual details to your work.

B. Make Your Changes If the answer to any question in the box is *no*, try the solution. Use the **Editor's Marks** to show your changes.

EDITOR'S MARKS

- ∧ Add something.
- Cut something.
- Move something.
- Replace something.

C. Review Your Persuasive Essay Again Decide whether there is anything else you want to revise. Keep revising your essay until you feel it is complete.

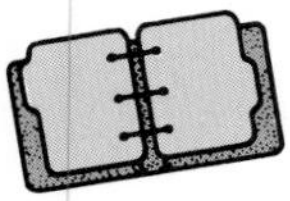

Save your revised draft in your *Writer's Notebook*. You will use it when you proofread your essay.

Revising Workshop
Combining Sentences to Avoid Choppy Writing

Good writers make their writing interesting by combining some of their sentences. They avoid the continuous use of short, choppy sentences. Look at three ways a writer might combine sentences.

1. Emily is an eighth-grade student. Emily delivers newspapers every afternoon.
2. Emily, <u>an eighth-grade student</u>, delivers newspapers every afternoon.

The writer combined the first set of sentences by forming an appositive in sentence 2.

3. Her employer arrived. Her employer announced a contest. Her employer urged everyone to participate.
4. Her employer <u>arrived, announced a contest, and urged everyone to participate</u>.

To combine this set of sentences, the writer formed a compound predicate in sentence 4.

5. Emily wanted to win. Fernando wanted to win. Cecilia wanted to win.
6. <u>Emily, Fernando, and Cecilia</u> wanted to win.

To combine the last set of sentences, the writer formed a compound subject in sentence 6.

The longer sentences avoid the choppy effect of the shorter ones and add variety to the writing.

Practice

Combine each set of sentences. Follow the directions in parentheses ( ). Remember to use the proper punctuation in your new sentences.

1. Emily's employer was Mr. Acuña. Emily's employer believed such contests were beneficial. (Form an appositive.)
2. They increased newspaper sales. They helped employees improve their work skills. (Form a compound predicate.)
3. Employee morale increased. Efficiency increased. (Form a compound subject.)
4. The workers earned more money. The workers were happier. (Form a compound predicate.)

4 Proofreading
Persuasive Essay

Writer's Guide

Proofreading Checklist

- Check for errors in capitalization.
- Check for errors in punctuation.
- Check to see that all your paragraphs are indented.
- Check for errors in grammar. Be sure that you have written comparisons with adjectives and adverbs correctly.
- Circle any words that you think are misspelled. Find out how to spell them correctly.
- ⇨ For proofreading help, use the **Writer's Handbook.**

After revising his persuasive essay, Michael used the **Writer's Guide** and the **Editor's Marks** to proofread it. Look at what he did.

> Most important, magazines are a permanent medium. Because they last, the advertisements can be read by people again. Also our club has the opportunity to attract even more customers by clipping (cliping) the advertisements and posting them on, for example, supermarket bulletin boards.
>
> ¶ In conclusion, magazine Advertising is the most ~~more~~ effective (affective) way of all for our club to spend the money that it has set aside to attract customers.

EDITOR'S MARKS

- ≡ Capitalize.
- ⊙ Add a period.
- ∧ Add something.
- ∧ Add a comma.
- ∨∨ Add quotation marks.
- Cut something.
- Replace something.
- Transpose.
- ◯ Spell correctly.
- ¶ Indent paragraph.
- / Make a lowercase letter.

Discuss

1. Look at Michael's proofread essay. What kinds of mistakes did he correct?
2. Why did he change *more* to *most*?

Try Your Hand

Proofread Your Persuasive Essay Use the **Writer's Guide** and the **Editor's Marks** to proofread your essay.

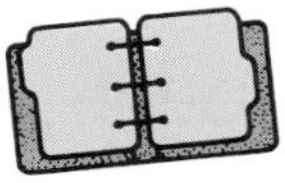

Save your corrected essay in your *Writer's Notebook*. You will use it when you publish your essay.

5 Publishing
Persuasive Essay

Michael made a clean copy of his persuasive essay and checked it to be sure he had not left out anything. Then he published his essay by presenting it as a business report to the members of his club. You can find Michael's essay on page 44 of the **Writer's Handbook.**

Here's how Michael published his persuasive essay by presenting it as a report.

Writer's Guide

Publishing Checklist

- ☑ Make a clean copy of your persuasive essay.
- ☑ Be sure that nothing has been left out.
- ☑ Be sure there are no mistakes.
- ☑ Share your persuasive essay in a special way.

1. After he typed his essay, Michael made enough copies for everyone in his audience. Then, he placed each copy in a file folder.

2. At a meeting, he passed out his essay to the officers and other members of the club. Michael asked all the members to read it.

3. Michael discussed the contents of the report with his audience and helped them follow his recommendations. He was prepared to answer questions and was ready to defend his position.

Discuss

1. Why should the writer make and distribute copies of his essay to club members?
2. What might the audience want to discuss about a persuasive essay after reading it?

Try Your Hand

Publish Your Persuasive Essay Follow the checklist in the **Writer's Guide.** If possible, present your persuasive essay as a report, or try one of these ideas for sharing it.

- Send your persuasive essay to a newspaper or a magazine and ask to have it published as a letter to the editor.
- Turn your essay into a speech directed at a group of classmates, and try to convince them to share your position. Invite a classmate to speak in favor of the opposing side. Ask your audience which speech is more convincing.

Writing in the Content Areas

Use what you learned to write a persuasive essay. Support your feelings and ideas with convincing reasons. Use one of these ideas or an idea of your own.

Writer's Guide

When you write, remember the stages of the Writing Process.

- Prewriting
- Drafting
- Responding and Revising
- Proofreading
- Publishing

Mathematics

The inches, pounds, and other units of measure that people commonly use in the United States differ from the units used in the metric system, which is common in most other nations. A proposal several years ago to "go metric" has not been carried out successfully. Tell what you think the United States government should do in regard to the metric system.

Fine Arts

When money is tight, families, businesses, and even schools have to make some hard decisions. In recent years many schools have decided to eliminate some of their fine arts courses in order to afford to continue their academic courses. Tell why you agree or disagree with such a decision.

Physical Education

Professional sports is big business in the United States and involves millions of dollars. Do you feel that this fact has influenced players and fans in a positive or a negative way? Tell what role you would like to see professional sports play in American society.

Literature

In the comic strip *Peanuts,* Sally once spent an entire summer hoping that a program based on the book she was assigned to read would be on television; that way, she would not have to read the book. You may have found yourself in somewhat the same situation. Tell what you think about the practice of assigning books for students to read during vacation.

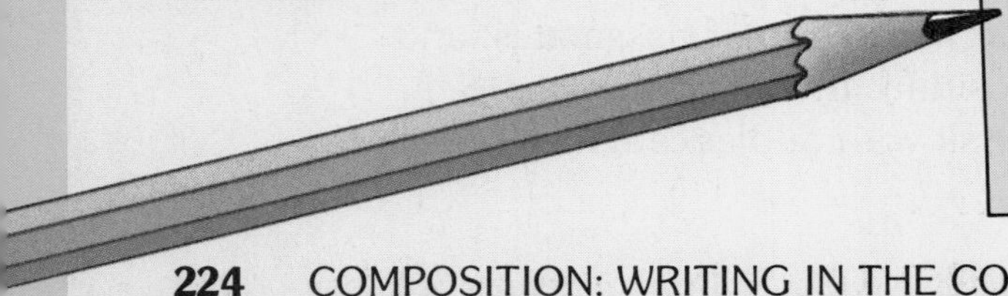

CONNECTING
WRITING ↔ LANGUAGE

A persuasive essay presents the writer's opinion on an issue and supports that point of view with reasons. In the following essay what reasons do you agree with or disagree with?

> It happened again. I went to see the movie version of a book and left the theater feeling disappointed. Why, I asked myself, did neither the hero nor the ship he commanded appear as I had imagined? Where was the cabin boy, my favorite character? Had the fight on the beach been forgotten by the producer? I have concluded that reading a book is much more enjoyable than seeing the movie version of that book.
>
> When you read, your imagination can have free rein. The book's author usually describes the characters and settings, but your imagination fills in the details. Just as important, the length of a book is in its favor. A movie can rarely include all the incidents in a book.
>
> Watching movies can be fun, but for a number of reasons, reading a book is more satisfying. I will choose a book over a movie any day.

◆ **Pronouns in a Persuasive Essay** The words highlighted in color are **pronouns.** They take the place of nouns and avoid the unnecessary repetition of nouns. There are several different kinds of pronouns. They can show person, number, gender, and possession. They can also be used to point out things and to ask questions.

◆ **Language Focus: Pronouns** The following lessons will help you use different kinds of pronouns in your own writing.

1 Personal Pronouns

◆ **FOCUS** A **pronoun** takes the place of a noun or nouns.

The pronouns *I, me, you, he, him, she, her, it, we, us, you, they,* and *them* are personal pronouns.

1. Erin and Carol helped Kevin plan the walkathon.

   They helped him plan it .

Personal pronouns show **number.** They can be singular or plural. Remember that singular means "one" and plural means "more than one."

2. Lew caught up with the twins and walked beside them . plural
3. Where did the dog come from? It is so funny! singular

Personal pronouns also show **person** (first, second, or third). **First-person pronouns** stand for the person speaking, **second-person pronouns** stand for the person being spoken to, and **third-person pronouns** stand for the person or thing spoken about.

4. I will walk for ten miles in the walkathon. first person
5. Barb, did you get a pledge from your parents? second person
6. The leader talked to spectators as he walked. third person

Third-person singular personal pronouns show **gender** (masculine, feminine, or neuter).

7. Kevin hopes he can raise fifty dollars. masculine
8. Each girl knows she is walking for a good cause. feminine
9. The day will be memorable when it is over. neuter

Guided Practice

A. Identify the pronoun or pronouns in each sentence.

1. He and I wore special sweatshirts.
2. Will you wear the hat or carry it?
3. Scott knows we can finish with them.
4. Sandy's feet hurt her.
5. They have a radio.
6. Sandy, would you carry it?

B. 7. – 12. Tell the number, person, and gender for the personal pronouns in each sentence in **A.**

THINK AND REMEMBER

- Remember that a **pronoun** takes the place of a noun or nouns.
- Remember that personal pronouns show number, person, and gender.

Independent Practice

C. Identifying Personal Pronouns Write the personal pronoun in each sentence. Then write its number and person, and write its gender if possible.

13. Volunteers understand that charities need them.

MODEL them—plural, third person

14. Charities earn money when they hold events.
15. An event is successful only if it is well planned.
16. She donated time for a sale held yesterday.
17. They will help by picking up items.
18. Many people helped us.

D. Revising: Replacing Nouns with Pronouns Rewrite each sentence, replacing the underlined word or words with a personal pronoun.

19. Don thinks Don will take part in a fund-raiser in March.

MODEL Don thinks he will take part in a fund-raiser in March.

20. People like flowers because flowers symbolize spring.
21. Don, I heard Don say that flowers are also said to stand for feelings of hope.
22. You and I raise money, which you and I know funds important and necessary research.
23. One way that research helps cancer patients is by giving the patients hope.
24. Ask Mrs. Green if Mrs. Green will buy some daffodils.

Application — Writing and Speaking

Questions Imagine that you are a news reporter who has just observed the walkathon. Write a list of ten questions that you would like to ask the participants. Find out important details by asking *who, what, when, where,* and *why.* Use as many different personal pronouns as possible in your questions. Ask a classmate your questions. He or she should respond as one of the walkers would respond. Write the answers.

2 Pronouns and Antecedents

◆ **FOCUS** A pronoun should agree with its antecedent in number, in person, and in gender.

An **antecedent** is the noun or nouns to which a pronoun refers. An antecedent may precede or follow the pronoun that refers to it. A pronoun agrees with its antecedent in number (singular or plural) and in person (first, second, or third).

1. Rita learned to ride when she was five.
2. Kim and I will meet at the park when we finish.
3. Do you want to meet there, Rita ?

Third-person singular pronouns agree with their antecedents in gender (masculine, feminine, or neuter), in number, and in person.

4. Matt can control the bicycle because he has practiced riding it .

Use a plural pronoun with a compound antecedent joined by *and*.

5. Dad and I found a place we had never seen before.

Link to Speaking and Writing

Using pronouns makes your writing and speaking more interesting. However, each pronoun must have a clear antecedent. Why is the first sentence confusing?

They applauded for the riders when they went by.

As the riders went by, the spectators in the park applauded for them.

Guided Practice

A. In each sentence, identify the pronoun and its antecedent. Tell the number, person, and gender of each pronoun.

1. Bill said he could change a tire.
2. Mom and Sharon help when they can.
3. Sharon took lunch with her.
4. Check the tire; it has a hole.
5. Take these helmets and wear them.

THINK AND REMEMBER

- Remember that an **antecedent** is the noun to which a pronoun refers.
- Be sure that a pronoun agrees with its antecedent in number and in person.
- Make pronouns agree with their antecedents in gender.

Independent Practice

B. Identifying Pronouns and Antecedents Write the pronoun and the antecedent from each sentence. Write the person, number, and gender of each pronoun.

6. David showed the group a bicycling book he had read.

MODEL he—David; third person, singular, masculine

7. Lisa Austin wrote an article about a trip she had taken.
8. After it was written, the story was published.
9. Lisa's father had said he would map the route.
10. The roads curved as they went up.
11. Lisa had dreaded them, but the hills were easy.

C. Adding Pronouns That Agree with Antecedents Write the pronoun that agrees with its underlined antecedent in number, in person, and in gender.

12. Cyclists have a skill ________ enjoy.

MODEL they

13. Thirty young people entered the race; ________ were all fast.
14. That girl thinks ________ has a good chance of winning.
15. Although ________ is young, Al is the fastest rider.
16. The racers hope ________ can win trophies.
17. Because ________ is the first prize, this trophy is the largest.

Application — Writing

Personal Narrative Remember a time when you first learned a skill. Write a description for someone who is just learning the same skill. Tell how you learned it and how you felt about your accomplishment. Use at least eight pronouns in your paragraph. Be sure that the pronouns have clear antecedents.

3 Subject and Object Pronouns

◆ **FOCUS** Personal pronouns can be in the nominative case or in the objective case.

Case is the form of a pronoun that shows how it is being used. Pronouns used as subjects are in the **nominative case.**

1. They are members of the Junior Achievement Club.

Pronouns used as objects are in the **objective case.**

2. The club adviser supervises them .

	Nominative Case		Objective Case	
	Singular	Plural	Singular	Plural
First Person	I	we	me	us
Second Person	you	you	you	you
Third Person	he, she, it	they	him, her, it	them

A **subject pronoun** is used as a subject or as a predicate nominative. Remember that subjects or predicate nominatives may be compound. As with noun subjects, pronouns used as subjects—whether single subjects or compound—must agree with the verb in number.

3. They own this company. **subject**

4. The shareholders are they . **predicate nominative**

5. She and I make the computer screens. **compound subject**

An **object pronoun** can be used as a direct object, as an indirect object, or as an object of a preposition. Remember that direct or indirect objects may be compound.

6. Susan's partners need her . **direct object**

7. The workers' adviser gives them assistance. **indirect object**

8. Today, he is helping her and me . **compound direct object**

The word *I* is always used for the subject or the predicate nominative in the first person. If *I* is part of a compound subject or a compound predicate nominative, put the word *I* last. *I* is always capitalized.

The word *me* is always used as a direct or an indirect object in the first person. If there is more than one object, put the word *me* last.

9. Cheryl and I keep the records.

10. Dan gave Cheryl and me the checkbook.

Guided Practice

A. Name the pronoun or pronouns in each sentence. Tell whether each pronoun is in the *nominative case* or in the *objective case.*

1. She and Andy are bankers.
2. He gave me the reports.
3. They have already seen them.
4. You should balance the checkbook.
5. Will you call me?
6. I found an error and corrected it.

B. Replace the underlined words with a subject or an object pronoun.

7. <u>The employees</u> gain valuable experience in their company.
8. <u>The experience</u> teaches them about business methods.
9. <u>Juan</u> and his company publish a newspaper.
10. He helps <u>Carina</u> with the paper's layout.
11. Juan positions <u>the articles</u> carefully.
12. <u>The salespeople</u> sell advertising space in the paper.
13. The best salespeople are <u>Jim and I</u>.

THINK AND REMEMBER

- Remember that subject pronouns are in the nominative case and object pronouns are in the objective case.
- Use subject pronouns as subjects and as predicate nominatives.
- Use object pronouns as direct and indirect objects, and as objects of prepositions.

Independent Practice

C. Identifying Pronouns and Case Write the pronoun or pronouns from each sentence. Next to each pronoun, write *nominative* or *objective.*

14. What career interests you most?
MODEL you—objective
15. I admire Andrew Carnegie and have always respected him.
16. He made a great deal of money in the steel industry.
17. It was mostly given to schools and libraries.
18. They established educational foundations with the money.
19. College professors all over the country have used them.

D. Revising: Replacing Words with Pronouns Rewrite each sentence, replacing the underlined word or words with a subject pronoun or an object pronoun.

20. Executives work for the corporation.

MODEL They work for the corporation.

21. Ken Black and his brother manage the company.

22. The company sold the brothers some of its stock.

23. This conglomerate is a business that owns several other companies.

24. It needs the companies to make a profit.

25. The employees are part of an enormous corporation.

26. The president is Ms. Lois Heller.

27. Today, we are going to be meeting Ms. Heller and her assistant.

E. 28.–35. Identifying Pronouns by Their Use in a Sentence Write the pronouns you wrote to replace words in **D.** Write whether each is the *subject,* the *predicate nominative,* the *direct object,* or the *indirect object* of the sentence.

28. They work for the corporation.

MODEL They—subject

F. Adding Correct Pronouns For each sentence, write the correct subject pronoun or object pronoun in parentheses ( ).

36. The other members of my business club and (I, me) manufacture paperweights.

MODEL I

37. The fastest workers in the group are Shawn and (me, I).

38. Ms. Robbins told (he and I, him and me) the secret of a good sales talk.

39. (Me and Ms. Robbins, Ms. Robbins and I) practiced my sales pitch a few times.

40. I might even sell (her, she) or Shawn a paperweight.

Application — Writing

Business Proposal Imagine that you need funds to start a business. Write a persuasive business letter to someone who might lend you the money. Describe the business that you would like to start and your product or service. Tell why you feel your business would be a worthwhile investment. Use subject and object pronouns correctly in your letter.

4 Possessive Pronouns

◆ **FOCUS** A **possessive pronoun** shows ownership or possession.

The possessive case shows ownership. You have already studied possessive nouns. Possessive pronouns replace possessive nouns.

	Possessive Pronouns	
	Singular	Plural
First Person	my, mine	our, ours
Second Person	your, yours	your, yours
Third Person	his, her, hers, its	their, theirs

1. Florence Griffith Joyner is receiving her medal.
2. The athletes have earned their honors.
3. I cannot believe the gold medal is mine .
4. His training and effort have been rewarded.
5. The bronze medal is his .

Guided Practice

A. Identify the possessive pronoun or pronouns in each sentence.

1. David is proud of his swimming.
2. Our brother is quite talented.
3. His dream is to enter the Olympics.
4. His coach showed him her medal.
5. He held it up by its ribbon.
6. A medal may one day be his.

B. Identify the possessive pronoun that correctly completes each sentence.

7. Women ran ________ first Olympic marathon in 1984.
8. Joan Benoit made up ________ mind to enter the marathon.
9. Weeks before, she had injured ________ knee.
10. Dr. Stan James used ________ skill to repair it.
11. The knee quickly regained ________ strength.

THINK AND REMEMBER

- Remember that **possessive pronouns** show ownership and replace possessive nouns.

Independent Practice

C. Identifying Possessive Pronouns Write the possessive pronoun or pronouns from each sentence.

12. Mom volunteered her time to coach for the Special Olympics.

MODEL her

13. Our cousin will be participating in the wheelchair events.
14. Special Olympians are proud of their skills.
15. Each athlete trains for his or her specialty.
16. The group receives its funding from the Joseph P. Kennedy, Jr., Foundation.
17. If you will volunteer time, I will give some of mine.

D. Revising: Replacing Phrases with Possessive Pronouns Rewrite each sentence, replacing the underlined words with a possessive pronoun.

18. The Olympic games had <u>the games'</u> beginning in 776 B.C.

MODEL The Olympic games had their beginning in 776 B.C.

19. The Greeks started the games to honor <u>the Greeks'</u> gods.
20. A pentathlete tested <u>the pentathlete's</u> skill in the pentathlon.
21. <u>The pentathlon's</u> events combined track and field sports.
22. The Greeks' Olympics were similar to <u>our Olympics</u>.
23. The games owe <u>the games'</u> preservation to us all.

E. Completing Sentences Write a possessive pronoun to complete each sentence.

24. Jim Thorpe gained ________ fame during the 1912 Olympics.

MODEL his

25. ________ gold medals were won in the decathlon and pentathlon events.
26. One month later the Olympic Committee took ________ medals.
27. The committee said that allowing a paid athlete to participate was against ________ rules.
28. Earlier, Jim had earned ________ living by playing baseball.
29. Jim's medals have now been returned to ________ rightful place.

Application — Writing

Friendly Letter Imagine that you are training for the Olympics. Write a letter to a classmate describing the training. Use possessive pronouns in your letter. If you need help, see page 62 of the **Writer's Handbook.**

5 Reflexive, Intensive, and Demonstrative Pronouns

Compound Personal Pronouns

Singular

First Person
myself
Second Person
yourself
Third Person
himself
herself
itself

Plural

First Person
ourselves
Second Person
yourselves
Third Person
themselves

FOCUS

- A **reflexive pronoun** refers to the subject.
- An **intensive pronoun** emphasizes a noun or a pronoun.
- A **demonstrative pronoun** points out a particular person, place, or thing.

When you add the word *self* or *selves* to pronouns, you form **compound personal pronouns.**

Compound personal pronouns can be reflexive or intensive. Reflexive pronouns refer to the subject.

1. Miyoshi sees herself as a future surgeon.

Compound personal pronouns that emphasize their antecedents are intensive pronouns.

2. Bert can carry the knapsack himself.

Reflexive and intensive pronouns must agree with their antecedents in number, in person, and in gender.

	singular	plural
reflexive	Did Bert hurt himself?	We saw ourselves on tape.
intensive	The race itself is short.	The runners themselves are fine.

The demonstrative pronouns *this, that, these,* and *those* point out particular people, places, and things. They must agree with their antecedents in number.

3. That is the best sweatband for me. singular
4. These are the sturdiest track shoes we have. plural

Guided Practice

A. Tell whether each underlined pronoun is *intensive, reflexive,* or *demonstrative.*

1. What career goals have you set for yourself?
2. That is hard to say, but I might be a photographer.
3. These are some of the pictures I've taken.
4. Do you develop the film yourself or take it to a store?
5. Usually, I do the developing myself at home.

THINK AND REMEMBER

- Remember that a **reflexive pronoun** refers to the subject.
- Use an **intensive pronoun** to emphasize its antecedent.
- Use a **demonstrative pronoun** to point out a specific person, place, or thing.

Independent Practice

B. Identifying Reflexive, Intensive, and Demonstrative Pronouns
Write the pronoun from each sentence. Then write *reflexive, intensive,* or *demonstrative* to show what kind of pronoun it is.

6. Todd himself has entered the science fair.

MODEL himself—intensive

7. The project shows how cells reproduce by themselves.
8. This is an excellent model of cell division.
9. Todd created and assembled the entire model himself.
10. The cell is duplicating itself exactly.

C. Completing Sentences Write the reflexive, intensive, or demonstrative pronoun that would complete each sentence.

11. We need money to buy ________ a stereo.

MODEL ourselves

12. Beth has gotten ________ a job at Gateway Cinema.
13. ________ is a great job because she gets to watch the movies.
14. She helps customers find seats for ________.
15. ________ can be quite helpful in a dark theater.

D. Proofreading: Correcting Reflexive and Intensive Pronouns Write each incorrect pronoun correctly.

16. Why are those people congratulating themself?

MODEL themselves

17. Seth and Julie are really proud of herself.
18. You herself saw their softball team win the game.
19. Seth made two home runs themselves.
20. Afterward, Seth and his friends bought yourself a snack.

Application — Writing

Advice Column Imagine that you are an advice columnist and someone has asked about achieving a goal. Write a paragraph telling that person how to accomplish the goal. Use at least two reflexive, two intensive, and two demonstrative pronouns.

6 Indefinite Pronouns

◆ **FOCUS** An **indefinite pronoun** does not refer to a particular person, place, or thing.

Remember that most pronouns refer to a definite person, place, or thing. An indefinite pronoun does not indicate a particular person, place, or thing. Indefinite pronouns may or may not have antecedents. The words in color are indefinite pronouns.

1. Everyone rehearsed last night. **no antecedent**
2. Much of the stage was hidden behind its heavy curtain. **antecedent *stage***
3. All of the risers are now in position. **antecedent *risers***

Indefinite pronouns can be singular or plural.

Indefinite Pronouns				
Singular			Plural	
all	everybody	no one	all	most
another	everyone	nothing	any	none
any	everything	one	both	several
anybody	most	some	few	some
anyone	much	somebody	many	
anything	neither	someone		
each	nobody	something		
either	none	such		

When used as subjects, indefinite pronouns must agree with verbs in number. Notice that the pronouns *all, any, most, none,* and *some* may be singular or plural. Their number depends on their meaning in the sentence. If the antecedent names something that cannot be counted, the indefinite pronoun is singular. If the antecedent names something that can be counted, the indefinite pronoun is plural.

4. Some of the music is from an old traditional songbook. **singular**
5. Some of the singers are in the rehearsal room warming up. **plural**
6. Most of the students are seated now. **plural**

Possessive pronouns agree in number and in gender with indefinite pronouns. Look at the antecedent to tell whether the possessive pronoun should be masculine or feminine.

7. Each of the girls has brought **her** own music book.
8. All of the singers invited **their** guests.

Sometimes when you use an indefinite pronoun, you do not know the gender of the subject. If you need to use a possessive pronoun to refer back to the subject, you may need to use these guidelines.

Possessive Pronouns with Indefinite Pronouns
1. Use the words *his or her* as possessive pronouns. Example: Everybody practiced his or her part for the show.
2. Rewrite the sentence to avoid referring to gender. Example: The chorus had practiced each part for the show.
3. Change the subject to a plural form. Example: All of the singers practiced their parts for the show.

Guided Practice

A. Identify the indefinite pronoun in each sentence. Tell whether it is *singular* or *plural*.

1. Most of the students who came from that academy read music.
2. Few may like singing.
3. Somebody mentioned having a class play sometime after final examinations.
4. Everyone is welcome at the tryouts for the play.
5. Many of the songs are easy.
6. Someone will make the costumes.

B. Choose the word in parentheses ( ) that agrees in number and in gender with each indefinite pronoun.

7. Each of the performances (were, was) videotaped.
8. Some of the harmony (is, are) unclear on the tapes.
9. One of the mothers brought (her, their) camera.
10. All of the students did (their, his) best.
11. Everybody (was, were) pleased with the results.

THINK AND REMEMBER

- Remember that **indefinite pronouns** do not indicate a particular person, place, or thing.
- Be sure that indefinite pronouns used as subjects agree with their verbs in number.
- Be sure that possessive pronouns agree with indefinite pronouns in number and in gender.

Independent Practice

C. Identifying Indefinite Pronouns Write the indefinite pronoun from each sentence. Write *singular* or *plural* to identify it.

12. All of the parents attended our choral concert.

MODEL All—plural

13. Most of the students had made every rehearsal.
14. Backstage everyone was a little nervous.
15. Someone had sent us a large bouquet of flowers.
16. At eight o'clock everybody filed onto the stage.
17. All of the singers carried music books.

D. Revising: Changing Indefinite Pronouns Rewrite each sentence by rewording it. Change a singular indefinite pronoun to a plural one and a plural indefinite pronoun to a singular one. Be sure to make any other changes needed.

18. Everyone invited his or her friends to go to the football game.

MODEL All of the students invited their friends to go to the football game.

19. One of the teachers had dismissed his class early.
20. Several of them had taught their students to play the school song.
21. Each of the band members is ready.
22. Some of the players were already wearing their uniforms.

Application — Writing

Song Imagine that you are a songwriter writing the words to a song for a choral group. Write one verse for a song that promotes world peace and understanding. Use indefinite pronouns in your verse.

7 Interrogative and Relative Pronouns

FOCUS

- An **interrogative pronoun** is used to ask a question.
- A **relative pronoun** connects a group of words to a noun or a pronoun antecedent.

An interrogative pronoun introduces a question. The words *who, whose, whom, what,* and *which* are interrogative pronouns. The antecedent of an interrogative pronoun is usually in the answer to the question.

1. Who are the residents of this apartment?

   Mr. and Mrs. Rodriguez are the residents of this apartment.

A relative pronoun connects a group of words to an antecedent. The words *that, which, who, whom,* and *whose* act as relative pronouns.

2. Seven towns participated in the survey that was taken.

Notice that the words *who, whom, which,* and *whose* can be either relative or interrogative pronouns, depending on how they are used in the sentence.

3. Which is the best source of energy? **interrogative pronoun**
4. Here are other questions which ask about fuel. **relative pronoun**

To decide whether to use *who* or *whom* in a question, answer the question using *he* or *she* or *him* or *her*. If the answer can include *he* or *she*, use *who*. If the answer can include *him* or *her*, use *whom*.

5. Who has the results? She has the results.
6. To whom shall I give this? You should give it to her .

Guided Practice

A. Tell whether each underlined pronoun is a *relative pronoun* or an *interrogative pronoun*. Identify the antecedent for each relative pronoun.

1. A public opinion poll is a survey <u>that</u> reviews current problems.
2. People <u>who</u> participate share their feelings on the issues.
3. <u>Which</u> of the candidates do people prefer?
4. <u>Whose</u> are the most popular?
5. <u>Whom</u> does the interviewer choose for polling?

B. Tell whether you would choose *who* or *whom* to complete each question.

6. ________ would be the best judge for your county?
7. ________ will the voters prefer, Conway or Bianco?
8. ________ are the local lawyers supporting?

THINK AND REMEMBER

- Use an **interrogative pronoun** to begin a question.
- Use a **relative pronoun** to link a group of words to a preceding noun or pronoun.

Independent Practice

C. Identifying Relative and Interrogative Pronouns Write the relative or interrogative pronoun from each sentence; tell which type it is. If it is a relative pronoun, write its antecedent.

9. Candidates who run for office need poll results.

MODEL who—relative pronoun; Candidates

10. A student who runs for class president may have a poll taken.
11. Students whose opinions are recorded should remain anonymous.
12. Whom do you favor for your next class officers?
13. Who is the most qualified student?
14. Whose was the idea of a nationwide survey?

D. Proofreading: Correcting Questions with *Who* and *Whom* Read each sentence. If the word *who* or *whom* is used correctly, write *correct*. If the word is used incorrectly, rewrite the sentence correctly.

15. Whom is responsible for the river cleanup?

MODEL Who is responsible for the river cleanup?

16. Who did the townspeople blame for the water pollution?
17. Whom went to the town meeting last night?
18. Who will you enlist as helpers for the project?
19. Who has the best plan for cleaning up the pollution?
20. Who will the town hire for the cleanup operation?

Application — Speaking and Writing

Survey Write five survey questions on a topic of current interest. Use interrogative and relative pronouns. Ask a classmate your questions, and record the answers. Write a paragraph summarizing your survey.

Building Vocabulary
Homophones and Homographs

Words such as *our* and *hour* or *some* and *sum* are examples of homophones (from the Greek for "same sound"). **Homophones** are words that sound alike but have different meanings and spellings.

It is easy to tell the difference between homophones when you see the written words. However, homophones can cause confusion when you hear them spoken. Usually, the sense of the sentence determines which meaning and which spelling are intended.

The words *wind* (movement of air, pronounced /wind/) and *wind* (to turn or crank, pronounced /wīnd/) are examples of homographs (from the Greek for "written the same"). **Homographs** are words spelled alike but having different meanings and sometimes different pronunciations.

As with homophones, the sense of the sentence will help you determine which meaning and pronunciation of a homograph are correct. If you need help with homophones or homographs, check meanings and pronunciations in a dictionary.

Reading and Writing Practice

1. – 62. Read the following poem. Write all the words that should be replaced with their homophones. Rewrite the poem with the correct spelling of each homophone. Use a dictionary when needed.

A Misspelled Tail

by Elizabeth T. Corbett

A little buoy said, "Mother, deer,
May I go out to play?
The son is bright, the heir is clear,
Owe, mother, don't say neigh!"

"Go fourth, my sun," the mother said,
The ant said, "Take ewer slay,
Your gneiss knew sled, awl painted read,
Butt dew knot lose your weigh."

"Ah, know," he cried, and sought the street
With hart sew full of glee—
The whether changed—and snow and sleet,
And reign, fell steadily.

Threw snowdrifts grate, threw watery pool,
He flue with mite and mane—
Said he, "Though I wood walk by rule,
I am not rite, 'tis plane.

"I'd like to meat sum kindly sole,
For hear gnu dangers weight,
And yonder stairs a treacherous whole—
Two sloe has been my gate.

"A peace of bred, a nice hot stake,
I'd chews if I were home,
This crewel fête my hart will brake,
Eye love knot thus to roam.

"I'm week and pail, I've mist my rode,"
But here a carte came past,
He and his sled were safely toad
Back two his home at last.

Writing Practice

Write two sentences for each pair of words. The sense of the sentence should clearly indicate the correct meaning and pronunciation for each homograph. Use a dictionary if you need help.

Example: content, content

Healthy snacks have a low sodium and sugar content.
The cat was quite content curled up on the windowsill.

63. close, close
64. stable, stable
65. compact, compact
66. meter, meter
67. sound, sound
68. well, well
69. console, console
70. object, object
71. bat, bat

Project

With a partner, list as many homophones as you can think of, including the ones from this lesson. Write your own nonsense poem or silly story, using the homophones to create confusion.

Language Enrichment
Pronouns

Use what you know about pronouns to do these activities.

Who's on First?

The famous comedians Abbott and Costello acted out a classic baseball routine called "Who's on First?" If you can, listen to a recording or read a copy of the routine. Notice how using interrogative and indefinite pronouns for the players' names adds to the humorous confusion. Organize your own pronoun baseball team. Write a paragraph in which you tell who plays each position, but instead of using proper names, identify each player with a singular indefinite pronoun.

It's Greek to Me!

Languages other than English also contain pronouns. To find out what some of them are, ask classmates, friends, teachers, and relatives who can speak other languages. Compare these pronouns with English pronouns by making charts similar to the chart in Lesson 3 of this unit. Share your information with the class.

Fix It

Imagine that you own a repair shop. Write a paragraph telling about the various things people have brought to be repaired. Use as many personal pronouns as you can, but do not use any antecedents for these pronouns. Then trade paragraphs with a classmate. Ask him or her to fix your paragraph by crossing out some of the pronouns and replacing them with nouns that clarify who the people are and what items need repair.

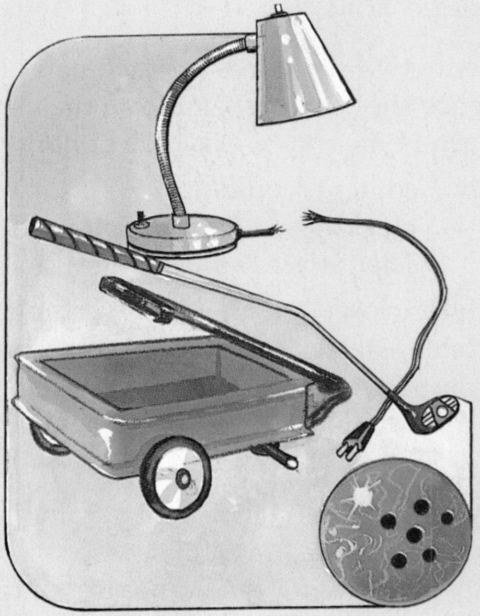

CONNECTING
LANGUAGE ↔ WRITING

In this unit you learned about different kinds of pronouns. You learned how to use subject, object, and possessive pronouns to replace nouns. You learned to use interrogative pronouns to frame questions properly.

◆ **Using Pronouns in Your Writing** Knowing how to use pronouns is important for speaking and writing. Knowing when to use a pronoun and when to use a noun will help you write more clearly. Pay special attention to the pronouns you use and their antecedents as you do these activities.

Greeting Card

You learned about homophones and homographs on the **Building Vocabulary** pages. Some personal pronouns are homophones: *I/eye; we/wee; you/ewe; him/hymn.* You might see these homophones used on birthday cards. Write a birthday card message using some of the personal-pronoun homophones.

Hippo Birdie two Ewe

Time Capsule

Often, people put special possessions in a time capsule. Use your imagination to write a paragraph telling what possessions you would add to a time capsule. Remember to use possessive pronouns.

5 Unit Checkup

Think Back	Think Ahead
◆ What did you learn about persuasive essays in this unit? What did you do to write one?	◆ How will what you learned about persuasive essays help you to convince others? ◆ How will knowing how to select evidence help you write a persuasive essay?
◆ Look at the writing you did in this unit. How did pronouns help you express your ideas?	◆ What is one way you can use pronouns to improve your writing?

Persuasive Essay *pages 208–209*

Rewrite these sentences to make them suitable issues for persuasive essays.

1. I like orange juice.
2. This is an important mathematics lesson.
3. My cat is a wonderful pet.

Reasons and Support *page 210*

Read the thesis sentence. Write *yes* or *no* to indicate whether or not each reason strongly supports it.

Students should take more risks in their school work.

4. All the teachers and our parents say we should take chances.
5. Risk-taking is great fun!
6. By taking risks, students learn not to be passive.

Using Vivid Language *page 211*

Rewrite the following sentences. Use vivid words to present the facts in the original sentence.

7. The tall man is a basketball player.
8. She is a fast runner.
9. That dress is unattractive.

The Writing Process *pages 212 – 223*

Write the letter for the answer to each question.

10. What must be included in the draft of your first paragraph?
  a. a summary **b.** a thesis statement **c.** detail sentences

11. When organizing information, in what order should the supporting reasons be given?
  a. no special order **b.** most to least important **c.** least to most important

12. Where would a persuasive essay be published in a newspaper?
  a. the front page **b.** the editorial page **c.** the local news page

Personal Pronouns *pages 226 – 227*

Write the personal pronoun in each sentence. Then write its gender, number, and person.

13. The Johnsons are advocates of progress; they want our state to develop its industry.

14. They do not believe a state should be all agricultural.

15. Some citizens hope to keep things as they are.

16. Both groups believe they are helping.

17. I believe that both sides have useful ideas.

Pronouns and Antecedents *pages 228 – 229*

Write the pronoun from each sentence and its antecedent. Write the person, number, and gender of each antecedent.

18. Thad hopes to fulfill a dream that he has.

19. Mr. and Mrs. Sitton want him to go into the family business.

20. Thad has another goal to tell them about.

21. Thad thought of it while writing a story.

22. Ms. Lobo, the artist, thinks she knows Thad's abilities.

Subject and Object Pronouns *pages 230 – 232*

Write the pronoun or pronouns from each sentence. Next to each pronoun write *nominative* or *objective*.

23. I like to talk about setting goals.

24. They give me a focus for working on a project.

25. Few people establish them without help.
26. One goal for me is to try hard to meet any challenge.
27. Goals also provide us a way of judging personal progress.

Possessive Pronouns *pages 233 – 234*

Write the possessive pronoun or pronouns from each sentence.

28. Each sport has its own measure of achievement.
29. Many athletes want their teams to win championships.
30. Arnold Palmer wanted to win his first U.S. Open.
31. A coach wants his or her team to play its best.
32. In your favorite sport, what would be your goal?

Reflexive, Intensive, and Demonstrative Pronouns *pages 235 – 236*

Write the reflexive, intensive, or demonstrative pronoun or pronouns from each sentence. Then write *reflexive, intensive,* or *demonstrative* to show what kind of pronoun each is.

33. Writing teachers themselves want to be successful writers.
34. This is an excellent attribute for a teacher of writing.
35. They themselves have worked with the writing process.
36. Teachers then know that writing itself is difficult.
37. A student can often find himself or herself listening more carefully to an experienced writer-teacher.
38. Those are the lessons that make a lasting impression.

Indefinite Pronouns *pages 237 – 239*

Write the indefinite pronoun or pronouns from each sentence. Write *S* for singular or *P* for plural.

39. All of the cattle will not win blue ribbons.
40. Anyone at a livestock fair can see why not.
41. Most of the entrants usually have at least one flaw.

42. Everyone is welcome to watch the judging.
43. All should remember that someone has to win.
44. Few of the judges don't enjoy a livestock competition.

Interrogative and Relative Pronouns

pages 240 – 241

Write the relative or interrogative pronoun from each sentence. Write *relative pronoun* or *interrogative pronoun*. For each relative pronoun, write its antecedent.

45. Pulitzer Prizes, which have been awarded since 1917, are given for achievements in literature, journalism, and music.
46. Who won the Pulitzer Prize in fiction last year?
47. The winner is often someone who writes about American values.
48. To whom would you have given your vote?
49. A writer who wins a Pulitzer Prize receives money and recognition.
50. Which would seem more important to you?

Homophones and Homographs *pages 242 – 243*

Write two sentences for each pair of words. The sense of the sentence should clearly indicate the correct meaning and pronunciation for each word. Use a dictionary if you need help.

51. principle—principal
52. lead—lead
53. past—passed
54. new—knew
55. can—can

UNIT 6

Creating an Impression

◆ COMPOSITION FOCUS: **Character Sketch**
◆ LANGUAGE FOCUS: **Adjectives and Adverbs**

If a painter uses brushes to create a visual picture, what would you use to paint a mental picture? Just as brushes help create visual images on canvas, there are tools to help you create word pictures in a description. Instead of brushes, the person creating the word pictures uses sensory words and comparisons.

Where are you likely to encounter descriptions? You might find them on television, on the radio, or in print. A description may appear in any form of writing, from a friendly letter to an essay or a novel.

Ray Bradbury, for example, wrote a description of a character in the novel *Dandelion Wine.* Through the character sketch, Ray Bradbury gives his readers an impression of the great-grandmother in his novel. He creates the impression with details about the character's physical activity, using words and comparisons to paint a mental sketch or image of the character. In this unit you will learn how to describe someone through a character sketch.

Ray Bradbury created *Dandelion Wine* primarily *to entertain* his readers.

Reading with a Writer's Eye
Character Sketch

When Great-grandma stops bustling her way through the day, something is dreadfully wrong. Ray Bradbury describes Great-grandma's movements in a way that reveals her personality. Read his character sketch to discover what seems to have gone wrong. As you read, try to picture Great-grandma in your mind and form an impression of her.

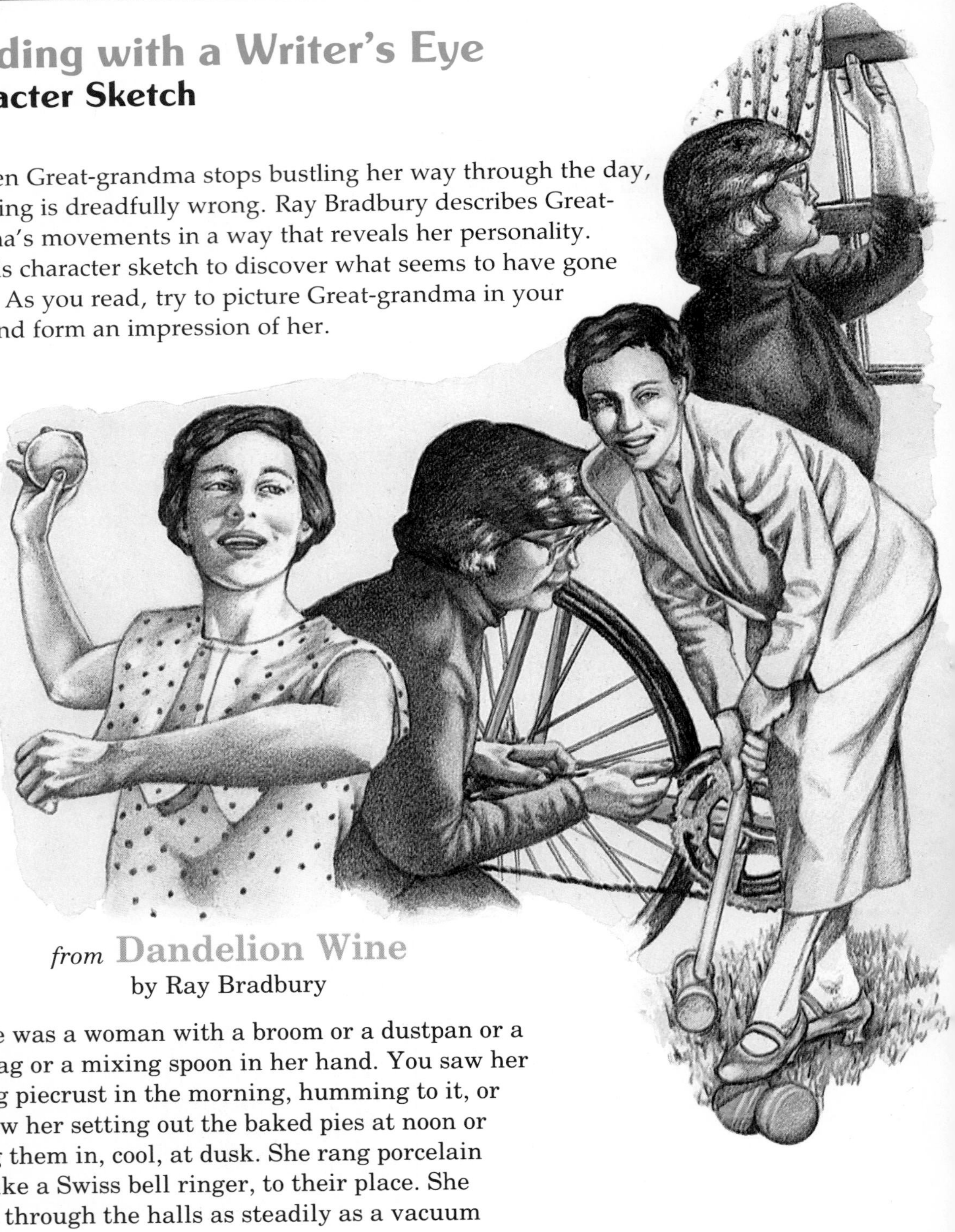

from Dandelion Wine
by Ray Bradbury

She was a woman with a broom or a dustpan or a washrag or a mixing spoon in her hand. You saw her cutting piecrust in the morning, humming to it, or you saw her setting out the baked pies at noon or taking them in, cool, at dusk. She rang porcelain cups like a Swiss bell ringer, to their place. She glided through the halls as steadily as a vacuum machine, seeking, finding, and setting to rights. She made mirrors of every window, to catch the sun. She strolled but twice through any garden, trowel in hand, and the flowers raised their quivering fires upon the warm air in her wake. She slept quietly and turned no more than three times in a night, as relaxed as a white glove to which, at dawn, a brisk hand will return. Waking, she touched people like pictures, to set their frames straight.

But, now. . . ?

"Grandma," said everyone. "Great-grandma."

Now it was as if a huge sum in arithmetic were finally drawing to an end. She had stuffed turkeys, chickens, squabs, gentlemen, and boys. She had washed ceilings, walls, invalids, and children. She had laid linoleum, repaired bicycles, wound clocks, stoked furnaces, swabbed iodine on ten thousand grievous wounds. Her hands had flown all around about and down, gentling this, holding that, throwing baseballs, swinging bright croquet mallets, seeding black earth, or fixing covers over dumplings, ragouts, and children wildly strewn by slumber. She had pulled down shades, pinched out candles, turned switches, and—grown old. Looking back on thirty billions of things started, carried, finished and done, it all summed up, totaled out; the last decimal was placed, the final zero swung slowly into line. Now, chalk in hand, she stood back from life a silent hour before reaching for the eraser.

Respond

1. What is happening to Great-grandma? Does it seem wrong or right to you? Why?

Discuss

2. What is your impression of Great-grandma? Describe her in your own words.
3. What details does Ray Bradbury include to give you this impression?

Thinking As a Writer
Analyzing a Character Sketch

> **Writer's Guide**
>
> A character sketch
> - includes sensory details.
> - usually includes some figures of speech.

A character sketch, like any other description, creates in the reader's mind an image, or a mental picture, of a person or an object. To paint the picture, the writer uses sensory details and **figures of speech.**

Figures of speech make comparisons to suggest what a person or an object is like. **Simile, metaphor,** and **personification** are three kinds of figures of speech.

> She was a woman with a broom or a dustpan or a washrag or a mixing spoon in her hand. You saw her cutting piecrust in the morning, humming to it, or you saw her setting out the baked pies at noon or taking them in, cool, at dusk. She rang porcelain cups like a Swiss bell ringer, to their place. She glided through the halls as steadily as a vacuum machine, seeking, finding, and setting to rights. She made mirrors of every window, to catch the sun. She strolled but twice through any garden, trowel in hand, and the flowers raised their quivering fires upon the warm air in her wake. She slept quietly and turned no more than three times in a night, as relaxed as a white glove to which, at dawn, a brisk hand will return. Waking, she touched people like pictures, to set their frames straight.
>
> But, now...?
>
> "Grandma," said everyone. "Great-grandma."
>
> Now it was as if a huge sum in arithmetic were finally drawing to an end.

Sensory details appeal to sight, sound, smell, taste, or touch, using exact words to help the reader picture or experience a scene.

A **simile** uses *like* or *as* to make a comparison.

A **metaphor** states or suggests that one object is the same as another. Metaphors often use forms of the verb *be* to make a comparison.

Personification gives human abilities to something not human, such as an animal, an object, or an idea.

Discuss

What pictures does Ray Bradbury's description of Great-grandma create in your mind? To which of your senses does his description appeal?

Try Your Hand

A. Analyze Sensory Details Read the following descriptions of people. For each description, write the senses that are used: sight, sound, smell, taste, or touch. Write the words from the description that appeal to each sense.

1. Mrs. Winston glared at me from behind the register. Her scolding was as shrill as a siren's blare. "Don't touch what you won't buy," she barked, her breath reeking of peppermint in sharp contrast to her sour temper.
2. Sometimes Chet would unexpectedly run into a friend from the past, and then he'd greet the friend with a warm, firm handshake, as if the chance meeting were the greatest of gifts. Even his spectacles reached out to welcome the friend.
3. Laing had been born on the houseboat. It was the only home the boy had ever known, and he meant to grow old there, preferring his life alone. Sometimes, like a squirrel darting forward to capture a nut, he would venture ashore for an abrupt visit to a relative or two. Greeting them with a salty kiss, Laing seemed to wear the sea. It was a comfortable coat he never discarded.

B. Identify Figures of Speech Write every figure of speech in the descriptions in **A.** Label the figures of speech *simile, metaphor,* or *personification.*

C. Add Sensory Details Reread each description in **A.** Write the next sentence that might appear. Try to write sentences that appeal to the senses and use figures of speech.

D. Read Descriptions Choose a section of the character sketch on pages 252–253 or a novel excerpt that describes a favorite character. Read the description aloud to a partner, pointing out sensory details and figures of speech.

Writer's Notebook

Collecting Indirect Comparisons
Did you notice the indirect comparisons in the description of Great-grandma's accomplishments? For example, the writer says that Great-grandma stuffed gentlemen and boys as well as turkeys and chickens. Read the character sketch again, and record in your *Writer's Notebook* any indirect comparisons you find. Try to use your own original indirect comparisons when you describe someone's personality or accomplishments.

Thinking As a Writer
Visualizing Comparisons

In a good character sketch, writers make comparisons between the character and other objects to create pictures in the reader's mind.

After imagining the character and the object, writers can make an **analogy,** or word comparison, to organize the comparison.

Writer's Guide

To write a character sketch, good writers often
- visualize the person mentally.
- isolate a feature or a personality trait.
- compare the person to something with the same trait.

Person	:	Feature	: :	Object	:	Feature
Great-grandma	:	moved	: :	vacuum	:	glided

An analogy helps a writer isolate the common feature of two items that are otherwise quite different. Notice how the analogy leads to the verb *glided* in the sentence from the character sketch.

> She glided through the halls as steadily as a vacuum machine, seeking, finding, and setting to rights.

When you write a character sketch, visualize the two items you are comparing to find out what they have in common.

Discuss

1. Look back at the other comparisons in the character sketch on pages 252–253. What mental pictures do you think Ray Bradbury had before writing each comparison?
2. Read this sentence. "His steel-blue eyes clouded over like a threatening thunderstorm." What analogy could you make for the sentence? Why did the writer use the verb *clouded*?

Try Your Hand

Visualize Comparisons Think of a person you admire. Write three comparisons that would help a reader picture the person's features or personality traits. Trade your work with a partner. Identify the feature or the trait in each of your partner's comparisons.

Developing the Writer's Craft
Avoiding Overused Words and Clichés

Writer's Guide

Good writers help a reader picture a character by

- using fresh words and original comparisons.

Clichés are phrases that have been worn out by overuse. Skillful writers avoid the automatic use of this type of phrase.

> **1.** She was as busy as a bee.
> **2.** She was a woman with a broom or a dustpan or a washrag or a mixing spoon in her hand.

The first sentence uses a worn-out simile to describe Great-grandma. In the second sentence, the writer uses specific words that show what kept Great-grandma busy, helping the reader to picture the character.

> **3.** Great-grandma's days were numbered.
> **4.** Now it was as if a huge sum in arithmetic were finally drawing to an end.

Sentence 3 uses a worn-out expression to describe the end of Great-grandma's life. In sentence 4, the writer creates a fresh comparison between the character's life and a sum in arithmetic.

When you write your character sketch, be sure to avoid clichés and overused words. Instead, create fresh comparisons and use specific words that will help a reader picture the character.

Discuss

1. Instead of a cliché like *never a dull moment,* what specific words does the writer use to show how active Great-grandma's life was? Look back at page 253 to find them.
2. Read this sentence: *At parties, he always stuck out like a sore thumb.* Should the sentence be used in a character sketch? Why or why not?

Try Your Hand

Avoid Overused Words and Clichés Write two sentences for each of these phrases. First, write a sentence that includes the overused words. Then, write a sentence that avoids them by using specific words or by making a fresh comparison.

1. generous to a fault
2. green with envy
3. cool as a cucumber
4. red as a beet
5. fit as a fiddle
6. tower of strength

1 Prewriting
Character Sketch

Sara wanted to write a character sketch for a classmate. She used the information in the **Writer's Guide** to help her plan her description. Look at what she did.

Writer's Guide

Prewriting Checklist

- ☑ Brainstorm subjects.
- ☑ Select a person to write about.
- ☑ Think about your audience and your purpose.
- ☑ Gather traits.
- ☑ Organize the details.

◆ Brainstorming and Selecting a Topic

First, Sara brainstormed a list of possible subjects for her character sketch. Look at Sara's list. Sara listed the name of everyone who seemed interesting to her.

Next, Sara looked down her list, trying to recall how each person looked and acted. Sara crossed off the name of everyone she did not know well. Then, she crossed off the name of anyone who did not make a strong impression on her.

Finally, Sara circled the best subject that was left on her list. She decided to describe her father for her classmate Heather because Heather was about to meet him for the first time.

my neighbor, Tanya
Dad
Dr. Yoko Arimoto
Uncle Theo
my gymnastics coach, Sugi
Cousin Rick

Discuss

1. Look at each name Sara crossed off her list. Why do you think she did not choose each person?
2. When choosing a person to describe, what questions should you ask to find the best subject for your description?

Gathering Information

After Sara selected her topic, she gathered information for her character sketch. Sara observed her father at work and during his leisure time activities, and she examined old photographs to help her detail his character traits. She made clusters, placing all the traits that came to mind in two diagrams.

Next, Sara looked over her diagrams and thought about each trait. To gather images that would help her classmate picture her father, Sara asked herself what else shared the same traits. She added a few comparisons and made several analogies.

Then, Sara looked over her diagrams and thought about her main impression of her father. She wanted to create a mood in her character sketch that would give her classmate the same impression. Sara decided that her father was energetic. She noted her impression and highlighted the details that would help her create the mood.

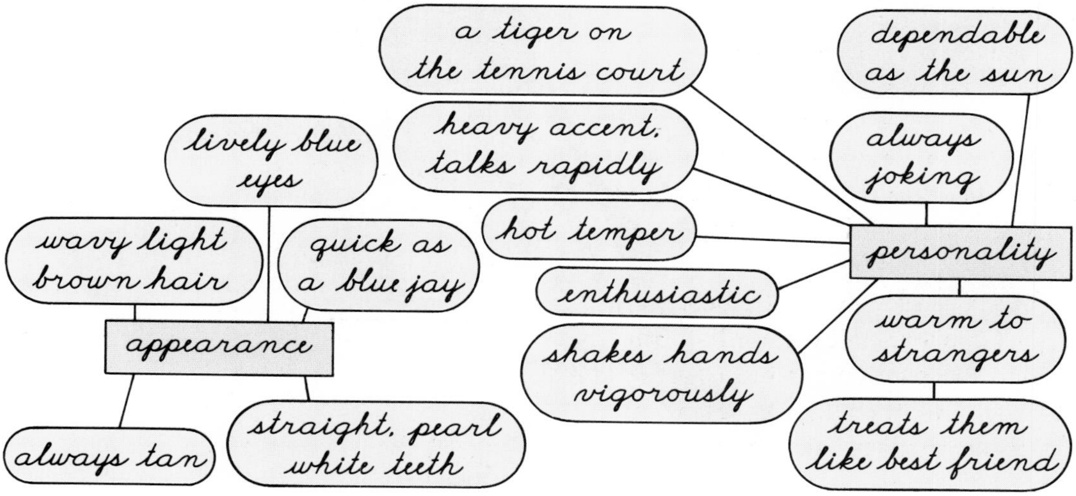

Discuss

1. Look at the first diagram. What physical traits does Sara include? Why do you think she chose these traits?
2. What comparisons does Sara make in her diagrams? Which ones can she use to create similes? Which can she use to create metaphors?
3. Think about the mood Sara wants to establish in her character sketch. Which words in her diagrams will help her establish this mood?
4. Which senses will Sara appeal to in her character sketch—sight, sound, taste, touch, or smell? Give examples from her diagrams.

Organizing Details

After Sara had gathered all the information for her character sketch, she was ready to organize her notes. Sara knew she could use space order in some descriptions. For example, she could describe her father's face by starting with his wavy hair and moving down to his rugged chin. Otherwise, she could begin with the most noticeable or obvious detail, the one that struck her first. Sara drew a plan for beginning each paragraph with the most noticeable detail.

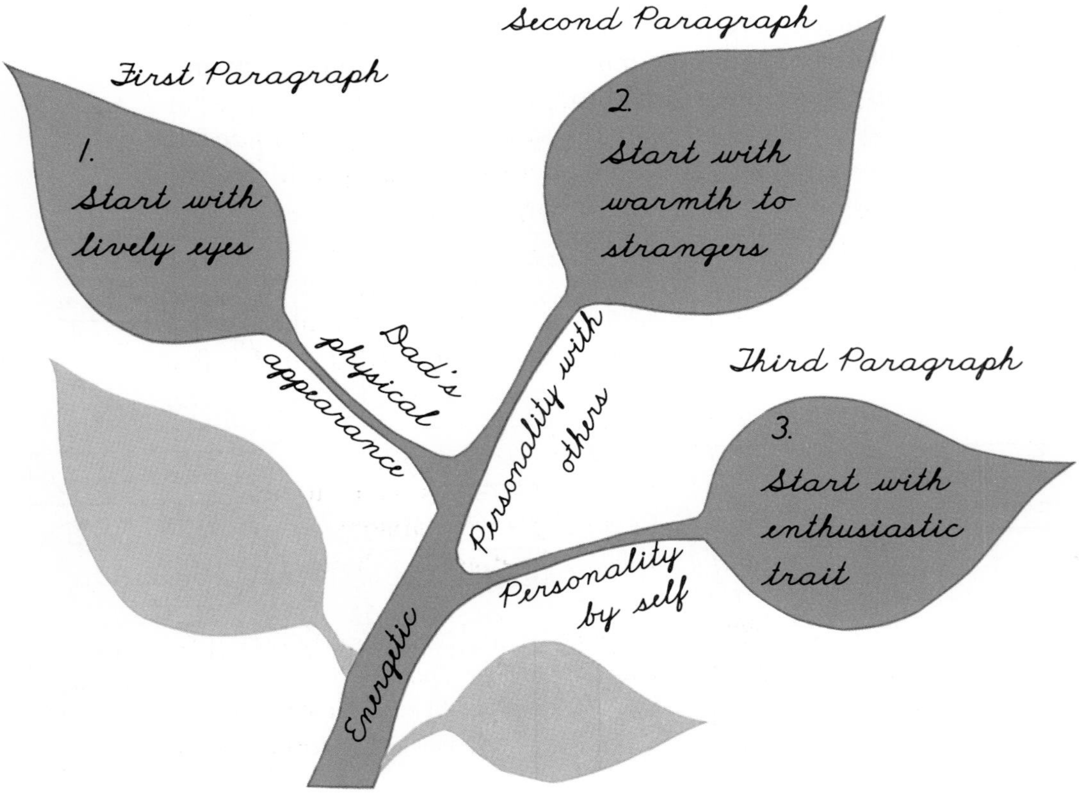

Discuss

1. What will Sara describe first, second, and third in her character sketch? Why?
2. Do you agree with the detail she has chosen to start each part of her description with? Why or why not?
3. Sara's father listens to the radio often. If she decides to add this detail, in which part should she place it? Why?

Try Your Hand

Now plan a character sketch of your own.

A. Brainstorm and Select a Topic Brainstorm a list of possible people to describe. Include all the interesting people who come to mind. Think about each person and your audience. Try to recall the physical features and personality traits of each person you listed.

- Cross out the name of anyone you do not know well.
- Cross out the name of anyone who has not made a strong impression on you.
- Circle the name of the most interesting person left on your list that you can easily observe.

B. Gather Information When you are satisfied with the person you chose for your character sketch, make notes about how the person looks and acts. You may want to draw diagrams like Sara's. Try to include some comparisons in your notes. Visualize the feature or the trait that you are describing. Then think of something with the same trait. Now is also the time to decide how you feel about your subject. What is your main impression of the person? Think about the mood you want to create. Highlight notes that will help you establish this mood.

C. Organize the Details Look over your notes.

- A character sketch should have enough comparisons to help the audience picture the person. Add some comparisons if more are needed, but do not include so many that your audience becomes confused or distracted.
- Think about your audience. Choose the details that will give him or her the same impression you have of the person.
- Think about the mood you want to create. Plan to use carefully chosen words and expressions that will convey this mood to your audience.
- Plan to use space order or to begin with the most noticeable or obvious feature or trait. Divide your description into parts, and decide which detail you will use to start each part. You may want to make diagrams like Sara's.

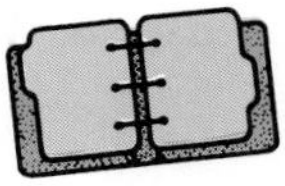

Save your notes and your diagrams in your *Writer's Notebook*. You will use them when you draft your character sketch.

2 Drafting
Character Sketch

Using her notes and her diagrams, Sara followed the checklist in the **Writer's Guide** to draft her description. Look at what she did.

> "Is everyone ready?" asks Dad, his lively eyes expecting a yes. He smiles warmly with a quick flash of his pearl-white teeth. That is Father for you, always on the move, with eyes as quick as a blue jay's and legs that propel him as rapidly as wings. His energy is visible in a tan that never leaves his well-bronzed skin and waves that ripple tirelessly through his brown hair. Always rushing, he dresses somewhat haphazardly. Sometimes the colors don't match, or a shirttail hangs out like an untied bow.

Writer's Guide

Drafting Checklist

- ☑ Use your notes and diagrams for ideas.
- ☑ Set the mood.
- ☑ Move from the most noticeable detail to the least.
- ☑ Use sensory words and figures of speech.
- ☑ Include physical features and personality traits.

Discuss

1. Look at the way Sara began her description. Do you think it is a good way to establish the mood? Why or why not?
2. Which sentences include figures of speech? Are they effective?

Try Your Hand

Now you are ready to write a character sketch.

A. Review Your Information Think about the details you gathered and organized in the last lesson. Decide whether you need more details. If so, gather them.

B. Think About Your TAP Remember that your task is to write a character sketch. Your purpose is to describe to your audience the person you have selected.

Task: What?
Audience: Who?
Purpose: Why?

C. Write Your First Draft Refer to the **Drafting Checklist** as you draft your character sketch.

When you write your draft, just put all your ideas on paper. Do not worry about spelling, punctuation, or grammar. You can correct the draft later.

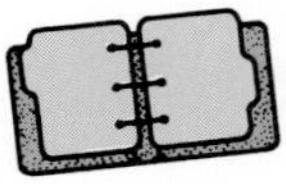

Save your first draft in your *Writer's Notebook*. You will use it when you revise your character sketch.

3 Responding and Revising

Character Sketch

Sara used the checklist in the **Writer's Guide** to revise her character sketch. Look at what she did.

Checking Information

Sara decided to take out an unnecessary detail. To show her change, she used this mark ℯ .

Checking Organization

Sara decided to move a group of words to the beginning of a sentence to make her sentence clearer. To show that the words should be moved, she used this mark .

Checking Language

To make her description more vivid, Sara added an adjective to describe her father's handshake. She used this mark ∧ to show her change. She also replaced an overused expression. To show this change, she used this mark .

Writer's Guide

Revising Checklist

- ☑ Read your character sketch to yourself or to a partner.
- ☑ Think about your audience and your purpose. Add or cut information.
- ☑ Check to be sure that your description is organized in some logical way.
- ☑ Check for places to add adjectives or adverbs to make your writing vivid.

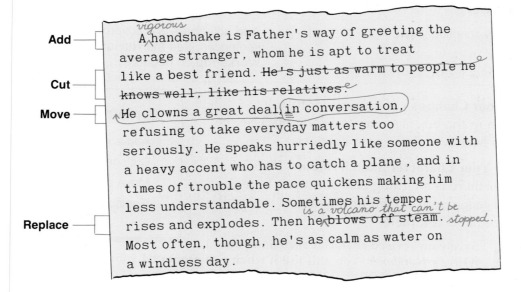

Add — A *vigorous* handshake is Father's way of greeting the average stranger, whom he is apt to treat

Cut — like a best friend. ~~He's just as warm to people he knows well, like his relatives.~~

Move — He clowns a great deal, in conversation, refusing to take everyday matters too seriously. He speaks hurriedly like someone with a heavy accent who has to catch a plane, and in times of trouble the pace quickens making him less understandable. Sometimes his temper

Replace — rises and explodes. Then he ~~blows off steam~~ *is a volcano that can't be stopped*. Most often, though, he's as calm as water on a windless day.

Discuss

1. Why did Sara move words in the second sentence? Where do you think the words sound better? Why?
2. Are there other changes Sara could make? Explain your answer.

Try Your Hand

Now revise your first draft.

A. Read Your First Draft As you read your character sketch, think about your audience and your purpose. Read your draft silently or to a partner to see whether it is complete and well organized. Ask yourself or your partner the questions in the box.

Responding and Revising Strategies

✔ Respond **Ask yourself or a partner:**	✔ Revise **Try these solutions:**
• Have I created a specific mood?	• **Add** words that will help establish mood.
• Have I used imagery to create pictures in the reader's mind?	• Find figures of speech in your notes and **add** them to your description.
• Have I used fresh descriptive language?	• **Replace** clichés. See the **Writer's Thesaurus** at the back of the book.
• Are my details organized in some logical way?	• **Move** any details that seem out of place.
• Is my description vivid?	• **Add** adjectives and adverbs to some sentences. See the **Revising Workshop** on page 265.

B. Make Your Changes If the answer to any question in the box is *no,* try the solution. Use the **Editor's Marks** to show your changes.

C. Review Your Character Sketch Again Decide whether there is anything else you want to revise. Keep revising your sketch until you feel it is well organized and complete.

EDITOR'S MARKS

- ∧ Add something.
- Cut something.
- Move something.
- Replace something.

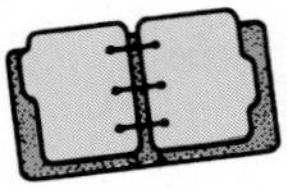

Save your revised character sketch in your *Writer's Notebook.* You will use it when you proofread your sketch.

Revising Workshop
Expanding Sentences with Adjectives and Adverbs

Good writers use adjectives and adverbs to make the sentences in a description as vivid as possible. Sometimes their sentences begin as a short, general thought.

1. Rachel joined the team.
2. Rachel eagerly joined the basketball team.

In the first sentence, the writer makes a general statement that does not give readers enough information to paint a specific picture in their minds. In the second sentence, the writer has added descriptive words that give more information so that a reader can picture Rachel.

The word *eagerly* is an adverb that tells *how* Rachel joined the team. An adverb can also add information to a sentence by answering the question *where, when, how often,* or *to what extent.*

The word *basketball* is used as an adjective to tell *what kind* of team Rachel joined. An adjective can also add information to a sentence by answering the question *which one* or *how many.*

A sentence may need more than one adjective or adverb to paint a clear picture.

3. Rachel eagerly joined the school basketball team.

In the third sentence, the word *school* was added as an adjective to describe the team more exactly. This adjective sharpens the sentence by giving a clearer picture of the team Rachel joined.

Practice

Rewrite each sentence. Add descriptive words that give readers more information or help paint a clearer picture in their minds.

1. Rachel was shorter than the other players.
2. She knew how to handle the ball on the court.
3. The girl observed players in action to learn their moves.
4. To compensate for her height, she practiced.
5. She scored points for the team.
6. Unfortunately, she lost her temper.
7. The coach had warned Rachel not to display such behavior again.

4 Proofreading
Character Sketch

After revising her sketch, Sara used the **Writer's Guide** and the **Editor's Marks** to proofread it. Look at what she did.

Writer's Guide

Proofreading Checklist

- ☑ Check for errors in capitalization.
- ☑ Check for errors in punctuation.
- ☑ Check that your paragraphs are indented.
- ☑ Check for errors in your grammar. Be sure that you used pronouns correctly.
- ⇨ For proofreading help, use the **Writer's Handbook.**

¶ The energy Father has for others spills over into his own activities, too. His (enthusiasem) enthusiasm and continual interest in people ~~makes~~ make him the perfect (sales man) salesman. I ask myself if he ever feels depressed or dispirited because his energy seems as dependable as the sun. On the tennis court, the man is a tiger, ready to pounce on his (pray) prey. Afterward, the person ~~who~~ whom he beats gets some friendly advice on how to strengthen his or her game, and then my father suggests a rematch.

EDITOR'S MARKS

- Capitalize.
- Add a period.
- Add something.
- Add a comma.
- Add quotation marks.
- Cut something.
- Replace something.
- Transpose.
- Spell correctly.
- Indent paragraph.
- Make a lowercase letter.

Discuss

1. Look at Sara's proofread sketch. What kinds of mistakes did she make?
2. Why did Sara make the pronoun changes in her last sentence?

Try Your Hand

Proofread Your Character Sketch Now use the **Writer's Guide** and the **Editor's Marks** to proofread your own character sketch.

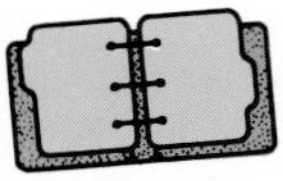

Save your revised character sketch in your *Writer's Notebook.* You will use it when you publish your sketch.

5 Publishing
Character Sketch

Sara made a clean copy of her character sketch and checked it to be sure she had not left anything out. Then she published her character sketch by sharing it with her classmate Heather. You can find Sara's character sketch on page 56 of the **Writer's Handbook.**

Here's how Sara published her character sketch.

1. Sara found photographs of the person her sketch described. She looked for pictures that illustrated the mood she was trying to create in her character sketch. Sara pasted the photographs she found on a separate sheet of paper.
2. Sara showed the photographs and read her character sketch to her classmate Heather.

Writer's Guide

Publishing Checklist

- ☑ Make a clean copy of your character sketch.
- ☑ Check to be sure that nothing has been left out.
- ☑ Check to see that there are no mistakes.
- ☑ Share your character sketch in a special way.

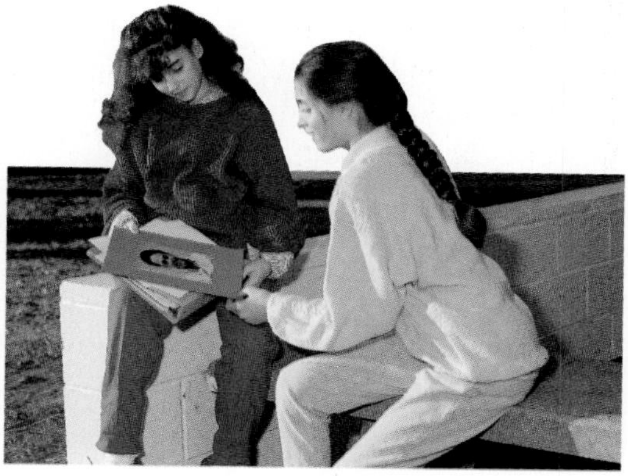

Discuss

1. Why are photographs helpful with a character sketch?
2. What main idea should a character sketch bring out?

Try Your Hand

Publish Your Character Sketch Follow the checklist in the **Writer's Guide.** If possible, present your character sketch to a partner, or try one of these ideas for sharing your sketch.

- Write sketches of other people familiar to you. Bind the sketches into a character sketchbook.
- Use your character sketch to make up lyrics for a song. Sing or present the song to the person it describes.

Writing in the Content Areas

Writer's Guide

When you write, remember the stages of the Writing Process.

- Prewriting
- Drafting
- Responding and Revising
- Proofreading
- Publishing

Use what you learned to write about people in the past, the present, or the future. You can write a description or choose another form of writing. Use one of these ideas or an idea of your own.

Fine Arts

Although musical styles change, some topics treated musically remain the same. One such topic is descriptions of people. Think of songs that describe people. Look through folk-song collections and other music books. Choose one song, and write a description of its main character.

Science

Many scientists are brimming with ideas about what the future will hold. Some of these ideas have been about inventions or transportation; some have been about changes in ways of living. Such changes cause changes in styles of clothing. Predict what you think the people of the future will be wearing.

Literature

Do you have a favorite book that was written long ago, perhaps even before the twentieth century? Tell about how the appearance and actions of the characters reflect a different way of life. For example, you might describe how the main characters dressed, what they did for fun, and how they traveled.

Social Studies

Restored villages, such as the historic district in Williamsburg, Virginia, give people of today a taste of yesterday. Imagine that you are living in the future and want to set up a town to give people an idea of what it was like to live in the twentieth century. Describe what people in your restored town would be wearing and doing.

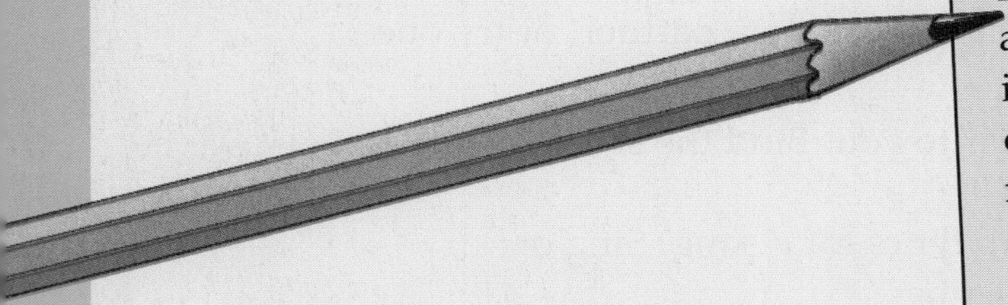

CONNECTING
WRITING ↔ LANGUAGE

People enjoy reading about other people. Good writers take great care to make their characters come alive for their audiences. Besides describing the characters' features, the authors describe the characters' accomplishments and their effects on other people. What effect did this singer have on her audience?

> Coretta tossed her snaky arms toward the sky so hard that they pulled her onto her toes. Her powerful singing rushed forward surely and steadily like lava flowing from a volcano. No one and nothing would stop her now. She could hit a high note and hold it, her voice sharper than a knife, piercing through molecules of sky. On the next note, her warbling tones sounded like a night bird calling sorrowfully for its mate. Glistening tears streaked the cheeks of her spellbound listeners.

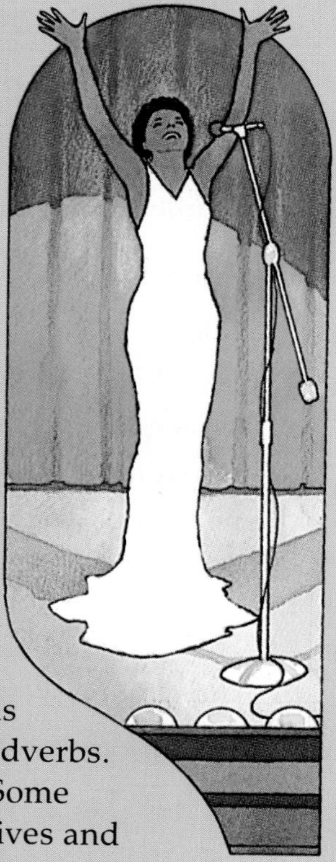

- **Adjectives and Adverbs in a Character Sketch** The words highlighted in color are different kinds of adjectives and adverbs. Some adjectives such as *sharper* help make comparisons. Some adverbs, such as *now,* have no comparative forms. Adjectives and adverbs make a description more vivid.
- **Language Focus: Adjectives and Adverbs** The following lessons will help you use different kinds of adjectives and adverbs in your own writing.

1 Adjectives

◆ **FOCUS** An **adjective** modifies a noun or a pronoun.

An adjective modifies a noun or a pronoun by answering one of these questions: *What kind? Which one? How much?* or *How many?*

1. The actors wore medieval costumes. **What kind?**
2. Today is the last day of the fair. **Which one?**
3. Four jugglers performed on stage. **How many?**
4. Visitors spent the whole day at the fair. **How much?**

Adjectives usually precede the word they modify. When adjectives follow the word they modify they are usually set off by commas.

5. The children, wide-eyed and shy , stared at the costumes.

The words, *a, an,* and *the* are special adjectives called **articles.** *The* is called a **definite article** because it refers to a particular person, place, or thing. *A* and *an* are called **indefinite articles** because they refer to any one of a number of persons, places, or things.

6. A man was dressed up like an ogre.
7. The chariot races were scheduled for two o'clock.

Proper adjectives come from proper nouns; they are capitalized.

8. We ate several European foods.

When you use two or more adjectives to describe a noun, a comma may be needed between them. To see if a comma is needed, try these tests. If you can put the word *and* between the adjectives, use a comma. If the adjectives can be reversed without affecting the meaning, use a comma.

9. The women wore long, flowing dresses.
10. An old elm tree provided shade.

Guided Practice

A. Identify the adjective or adjectives in each sentence, including articles. Identify the word each adjective modifies.

1. An expert glassblower was at the fair.
2. She dipped a pipe into molten glass.
3. She blew into a long tube.
4. A clear bulb grew at the end.
5. She shaped the fiery glass.
6. It became an elegant bottle.

THINK AND REMEMBER

- Remember that an **adjective** modifies a noun or a pronoun.
- Remember that *a* and *an* are indefinite articles and *the* is a definite article.
- Capitalize proper adjectives.
- Use a comma between two or more adjectives if each modifies the noun by itself or if the order can be reversed.

Independent Practice

B. Identifying Adjectives and the Words They Modify Write each sentence. Underline the adjectives, including articles. Then draw two lines under the words the adjectives modify.

7. The Renaissance lasted for three centuries.

MODEL The Renaissance lasted for three centuries.

8. The Renaissance inspired great writing.
9. William Shakespeare was an English writer.
10. He wrote three kinds of plays—comedy, tragedy, and history.
11. His lovely sonnets show his skill in poetry.
12. Do you understand the message of the last sonnet?
13. The first plays by Shakespeare were published in 1594.
14. A repertory company performed the plays.

C. Proofreading: Capitalizing Proper Adjectives Write the proper adjectives that should be capitalized.

15. The painter Giotto was a skilled italian artist.

MODEL Italian

16. Great works were produced by italian artists and sculptors.
17. Michelangelo painted the fresco of the sistine Chapel.
18. The venetian artist Titian painted with brilliant colors.
19. Soon the Renaissance was to reach french artists.
20. Sculptors and other european artists flourished.

Application — Writing

Poster Create a poster to advertise a fair in your city or town. Write a slogan on the poster. Then write a sentence describing each of six events to be held. Use at least one adjective in each sentence.

2 Other Parts of Speech as Adjectives

◆ **FOCUS** Other parts of speech can be used as adjectives.

Many indefinite pronouns can be used as adjectives.

1. All flights are on time. **adjective**

The interrogative pronouns *whose, which,* and *what* can be used as adjectives.

2. What time is your flight? **adjective**

The words *this, that, these,* and *those* may be pronouns in some sentences but adjectives in others. These demonstrative adjectives point out specific persons, places, or things.

Adjective	**Pronoun**
3. This gate will open soon.	**4.** This is your ticket.

Nouns can also be used as adjectives.

5. Everyone must go through airport security. **adjective**

You can sometimes use the present or past participles of verbs as adjectives.

6. A moving belt carries the luggage to a truck. **adjective**

You may sometimes be unsure whether a word is an adjective or another part of speech. Remember that adjectives modify nouns or pronouns.

Guided Practice

A. Identify whether each underlined word being used as an adjective is an *adjective,* a *pronoun,* a *noun,* or a *verb.*

1. Many intelligent passengers take advantage of lower airline fares.
2. Some airlines offer special weekend rates.
3. Hundreds of flights from all over the world service American cities each day.
4. A 747 is designed to carry more than 450 people on long flights.
5. Shorter flights hop between cities with few passengers.
6. Which flight has reduced fares for qualified travelers?
7. A growing part of this industry is air freight.

THINK AND REMEMBER

- Remember that other parts of speech can also function as adjectives.

Independent Practice

B. Identifying Parts of Speech Write the underlined word or words that are used as adjectives in each sentence. Next to each word write *adjective, pronoun, noun,* or *verb.*

8. What problem is a pressing concern in aviation?

MODEL What—pronoun; pressing—verb

9. Most airports are located near large cities.
10. Departing and arriving planes are noisy.
11. This annoying noise can very easily be heard by city residents.
12. Airport designers place the runways in the most remote area.
13. What choice do the planners have?
14. All scheduled flights could be rescheduled at reasonable hours.
15. Much noise could be controlled in that way.

C. 16.–23. Identifying Modified Words Write the underlined words from **B.** Next to each, write the word it modifies.

MODEL 16. What—problem; pressing—concern

D. Writing Sentences Write a sentence for each word, using the word as an adjective.

24. kitchen

MODEL The kitchen staff prepared a meal.

25. rattling
26. which
27. several
28. these
29. security
30. spoken
31. open

Application — Writing and Speaking

Speech Imagine that you are a flight attendant or a pilot on an international flight. Write a speech welcoming the passengers and giving them some advice on how to enjoy the flight. Include some information on safety and precautionary measures. Try to use two adjectives in each sentence of your speech.

3 Predicate Adjectives

◆ **FOCUS** A **predicate adjective** is an adjective that follows a linking verb and describes the subject of the sentence.

Like a predicate nominative, a predicate adjective follows a linking verb. A predicate nominative can be a noun or a pronoun, but a predicate adjective is always an adjective.

1. Wolfgang Amadeus Mozart was a composer. predicate nominative
2. His music is famous. predicate adjective

A sentence may have a compound predicate adjective. If there are three or more adjectives, use a comma after each one except the last.

3. This opera is harmonious, upbeat, and lively.

Be careful not to mistake a present participle for a predicate adjective. A present participle may also follow a linking verb as part of a verb phrase.

4. The whole audience was restless. predicate adjective
5. The whole audience was applauding. present participle

Guided Practice

A. Identify the predicate adjective in each sentence.

1. Even today classical music sounds timeless.
2. Mozart and other classical musicians were Austrian.
3. Music is important to the Austrian people.
4. The Vienna Boys' Choir has become famous.
5. Salzburg is notable for its annual music festival.
6. The festival seems appropriate as a tribute to Mozart.

B. Identify whether each underlined word is a *predicate nominative* or a *predicate adjective*.

7. You seemed spellbound during the movie.
8. It was a tribute to my favorite composer, Irving Berlin.
9. His music will always remain an American treasure.
10. It still sounds wonderful to today's audiences.
11. The color and choreography were outstanding.

THINK AND REMEMBER

- Remember that a **predicate adjective** is a word that follows a linking verb and describes the subject of the sentence.
- Use commas in compound predicate adjectives containing more than two adjectives.

Independent Practice

C. Identifying Predicate Adjectives and the Words They Modify Write each sentence. Underline the predicate adjective(s). Draw an arrow from each predicate adjective to the word it modifies.

12. Operatic music sometimes sounds quite serious.

MODEL Operatic music sometimes sounds quite serious.

13. Opera can also be dramatic, humorous, or lighthearted.
14. The music is often lively during comical scenes.
15. Light opera is usually funny and romantic.
16. Most operas are French, German, or Italian.
17. The plot of an opera may become very complicated.

D. Distinguishing Predicate Nominatives from Predicate Adjectives Write each underlined word. Then write *predicate nominative* or *predicate adjective.*

18. *Amadeus* was a movie about Wolfgang Amadeus Mozart.

MODEL movie—predicate nominative

19. The scenes were colorful and lavish.
20. Mozart was a musical genius all of his life.
21. He had become a virtuoso by age six.
22. He seemed arrogant.
23. Mozart's music, however, sounded brilliant and inspired.

Application — Writing

Character Sketch Write a character sketch of an imaginary musician. Tell people about his or her personality, voice or instrument, and musical talent. Use predicate adjectives to describe these aspects of the musician's character. If you need help writing a character sketch, see page 56 of the **Writer's Handbook.**

4 Comparisons with Adjectives

◆ **FOCUS** Adjectives can be used to compare nouns. The three degrees of comparison are positive, comparative, and superlative.

The **positive degree** describes only one thing, the **comparative degree** compares two things, and the **superlative degree** compares three or more things.

Forming the Comparative and Superlative Degrees			
Rule	**Positive**	**Comparative**	**Superlative**
1. For one-syllable words, add *er* or *est* to the positive form.	thin	thinner	thinnest
2. For some two-syllable words, add *er* and *est* to the positive form.	heavy	heavier	heaviest
For other two-syllable words, add *more/less* and *most/least.*	frequent	more/less frequent	most/least frequent
3. For three-syllable words, add *more/less* and *most/least.*	difficult	more/less difficult	most/least difficult

Spelling Guidelines		
1. Double the final consonant in words with a short vowel sound.		
sad	sadder	saddest
2. Change final *y* to *i* in words that end in a consonant plus *y*.		
hardy	hardier	hardiest
3. Drop the final *e* before adding *er* or *est.*		
pale	paler	palest

Guided Practice

A. Identify whether each adjective is in the *positive, comparative,* or *superlative* degree.

1. grand
2. hilliest
3. stately
4. braver
5. more visible
6. less fashionable
7. strong
8. icy

THINK AND REMEMBER

- Remember that the **positive degree** describes only one thing.
- Use the **comparative degree** to compare two things.
- Use the **superlative degree** to compare three or more things.

Independent Practice

B. Identifying Degrees of Comparison Write the adjective of comparison from each sentence. Next to each adjective write its degree of comparison.

9. The design of a house is more important than its size.

MODEL more important—comparative

10. Architecture is one of the oldest forms of art.
11. Some of the greatest works are still standing in Greece.
12. These buildings are even more ancient than the Roman ruins.
13. Gothic design is the most common choice for churches.
14. An architect must be a skillful artist and engineer.
15. Frank Lloyd Wright was one of the most famous architects.
16. His houses are sturdier than many others of the same age.

C. Using the Correct Form of Comparison Write each sentence with the correct comparative form of the adjective in parentheses ( ).

17. Are you (interested) in a new house than in an old one?

MODEL Are you more interested in a new house than in an old one?

18. A new house is usually (expensive) than an old one.
19. It will also have (few) structural problems.
20. The (important) factor of all may be the house's location.
21. Moving might be the (troublesome) experience in anyone's life.
22. For others it is the (exciting) adventure.

Application — Writing

Real Estate Ad Imagine that you are trying to sell an old house. Write a newspaper advertisement that would make a potential homeowner want to buy the home. Use positive, comparative, and superlative adjectives in your ad.

5 Irregular Comparisons with Adjectives

◆ **FOCUS** Some adjectives have irregular forms of comparison.

Some adjectives have unusual comparative and superlative forms. Study the chart to learn these comparative and superlative forms.

Positive	Comparative	Superlative
good, well	better	best
bad, ill	worse	worst
much, many	more	most
little (amount)	less, lesser	least

Use *little, less, least,* or *much* when referring to things that cannot be counted. Use *few, fewer, fewest,* or *many* when referring to things that can be counted.

1. I have less anxiety about the meet than I expected.
2. Fewer gymnasts participated in this meet than in the last one.
3. Our coach has much patience with the many team members.

Some adjectives, such as *perfect, daily, right,* and *square,* have no comparative or superlative forms because they cannot be compared.

4. Donna has perfect form on the balance beam.

(If something is perfect, it cannot be more perfect or less perfect.)

Link to Speaking and Writing

Do not add *er, est, more,* or *most* to irregular comparatives or superlatives.

Donna is the ~~most~~ best gymnast on our team.

Guided Practice

A. Tell the comparative *(C)* or superlative *(S)* form of each adjective.

1. good (C)
2. little (S)
3. bad (S)
4. much (C)
5. many (S)
6. ill (C)

B. Tell whether each adjective can be compared.

7. unique
8. endless
9. few
10. empty
11. absolute
12. instant

THINK AND REMEMBER

- Remember that some adjectives have unusual comparative and superlative forms.
- Remember that some adjectives cannot be used to compare.

Independent Practice

C. Identifying Positive, Comparative, and Superlative Adjectives
Write the adjective from each sentence. Next to the adjective, write *positive, comparative,* or *superlative.*

13. We use the best equipment available for gym meets.

MODEL best—superlative

14. Bouncing on a trampoline is a good way to get exercise.
15. Bouncing is better than jumping.
16. Many movements can be completed in the air.
17. The best gymnasts can turn somersaults in midair.
18. A mat gives better protection than does the floor.
19. This means a gymnast has less chance of injury.
20. More protection comes from tumbling correctly.
21. The worst falls can occur when a gymnast lands incorrectly.

D. Choosing Correct Adjective Forms Choose the correct form of the adjective in parentheses ( ).

22. Ellen is (an excellent, the most excellent) skater.

MODEL an excellent

23. Her (best, most best) jump is the flip jump.
24. Ellen's form is (perfect, more perfect).
25. Which girl has (an unusual, a more unusual) routine for the competition?
26. The skater whose routine has the (most, mostest) variety will win.
27. What could be (worse, more worse) for a skater than a sprained ankle?

Application — Writing

World Record In 1976 Nadia Comaneci set an Olympic record by receiving a perfect score in gymnastics. Invent a sports hero who sets an imaginary Olympic record. Write a paragraph that tells sports fans about the athlete. Identify the sport, and tell how the record was set. Use comparative forms of adjectives such as *good, bad,* and *many.*

6 Adverbs

◆ **FOCUS** An **adverb** modifies a verb, an adjective, or another adverb.

Adverbs add to the meaning of other words in a sentence. They modify verbs, adjectives, or other adverbs.

1. The explorers walked slowly into the cave. verb
2. The inside was quite clammy. adjective
3. The leader peered ahead very carefully. adverb

Adverbs answer the questions *Where? When? How? How often?* or *To what extent?* Notice that many adverbs end with *ly*.

Where? here there upstairs away outside
When? today soon yesterday now already
How? slowly sadly angrily loudly neatly
How often? once frequently often usually always
To what extent? just far little altogether

An adverb can be placed before or after the verb it modifies.

4. Our eyes gradually adjusted to the darkness.
5. The small group crept forward .

An adverb can be placed before an adjective or another adverb.

6. A frequently heard sound is the flutter of bat wings.
7. Hearing it just once is enough for me.

An adverb can be placed at the beginning or end of a sentence.

8. Reluctantly Kim agreed to lead the way.
9. She grasped her flashlight firmly .

Adverbs that answer the question *To what extent?* are called **intensifiers.**

Common Intensifiers				
almost	least	most	quite	somewhat
entirely	less	nearly	rather	too
extremely	more	not	really	very

Notice that some adverbs do not end with *ly*.

down	here	now	thus	upstairs
fast	never	still	up	near

The words *how, when, where,* and *why* can be used as adverbs.

10. How close did you get to the underground pool?

11. When did you first see it?

12. Where did you find the fossils?

13. Why did you think to look here?

Link to Speaking and Writing

To make your speaking and writing vigorous, use a strong, specific verb rather than a verb and an adverb. Why does the verb *murmured* better convey the mood of the sentence than *spoke softly*?

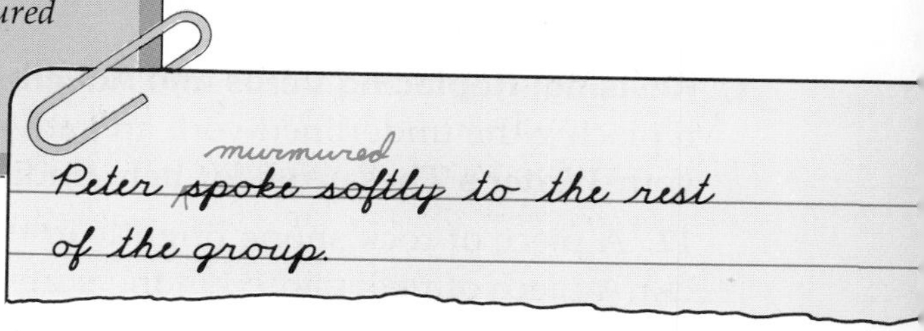

murmured
Peter spoke softly to the rest
of the group.

Guided Practice

A. Identify the adverb or adverbs in each sentence and the word each modifies. Tell which adverbs are intensifiers.

1. Caves form very slowly over time.
2. Water trickles downward.
3. It wears away the rock.
4. Rather large and brilliantly colorful rooms may be created.
5. How deep is the deepest cave?

THINK AND REMEMBER

- Remember that an **adverb** modifies a verb, an adjective, or another adverb.
- Remember that **intensifiers** answer the question *To what extent?*
- Use specific verbs to strengthen your speaking and your writing.

Independent Practice

B. Identifying Adverbs and the Words They Modify Write each sentence. Underline the adverb or adverbs, and draw an arrow from each adverb to the word it modifies. Draw two lines under any adverbs used as intensifiers.

6. Very eager tourists visit Carlsbad Caverns annually.

MODEL Very eager tourists visit Carlsbad Caverns annually.

7. Come explore underground in a most beautiful national park.
8. Look deep inside the miles of passages.
9. Walk alone through almost untouched caverns.
10. Look up at the unusually shaped stalactites.
11. Very friendly guides take visitors to the Big Room daily.

C. Revising: Replacing Verbs and Adverbs Rewrite each sentence, replacing the underlined verb and adverb with a specific verb. Use your **Writer's Thesaurus** for help finding specific verbs.

12. A piece of rock shone brightly in the sunlight.

MODEL A piece of rock glinted in the sunlight.

13. Kim quickly took the shiny rock.
14. She looked curiously at the tiny fossil.
15. She lightly felt the outline of a wing on one side.
16. Kim gently gave the strange rock to Mrs. Wei.
17. Mrs. Wei proudly showed the fossil to the other diggers.

D. Writing Sentences Use each word in a sentence. Write whether the word is an *adjective* or an *adverb*.

18. then

MODEL We planned to climb the cliff, but then we changed our minds. adverb

19. tomorrow
20. homely
21. lonely
22. costly
23. sometimes
24. deadly

Application — Writing

Personal Narrative *Spelunking* is the exploring of caves. Imagine that you are on a spelunking team. Write a paragraph describing what you found. Use adverbs to describe your explorations. If you need help writing the narrative, see page 49 of the **Writer's Handbook.**

7 Comparisons with Adverbs

◆ **FOCUS** Some adverbs have three degrees of comparison: positive, comparative, and superlative.

Like adjectives, adverbs can be compared by degrees.
Use the **positive degree** when there is no comparison.

1. Jorge herded the cows fast .

Use the **comparative degree** to compare two things.

2. He rode faster than his brother.

Use the **superlative degree** to compare three or more things.

3. Of all the cowhands, Jorge rode the fastest .

Forming the Comparative and Superlative Degrees

Rule	Positive	Comparative	Superlative
1. For some words add *er* and *est* to the positive form.	hard	harder	hardest
2. For most adverbs ending in *ly*, add *more, less, most, least.*	steadily	more steadily less steadily	most steadily least steadily

Spelling Guidelines

To add *er* or *est* to adverbs, you must:

1. Change final *y* to *i* before adding endings.
early earlier earliest

2. Drop the final *e* before adding endings.
late later latest

Some adverbs form comparative or superlative degrees irregularly.

Positive	Comparative	Superlative
well	better	best
badly, ill	worse	worst
much	more	most
little	less	least
far	farther	farthest

Most adverbs that indicate time, place, or degree cannot be compared. There is no comparative or superlative degree for *now, there, nearby, really, away, anywhere, once, first, next, never, always*, and *usually*.

Link to Speaking and Writing

Use *farther* and *farthest* to refer to distance. *Further* and *furthest* refer to time, quantity, or degree.

You must throw the lasso farther to rope the steer. Research your topic further before writing your paper.

Guided Practice

A. Identify the comparative and superlative degrees of each adverb. If the adverb cannot be compared, answer *none*.

1. highly	**3.** smoothly	**5.** rather	**7.** clearly	**9.** hard
2. soon	**4.** well	**6.** deep	**8.** loud	**10.** only

B. Tell whether you would use *farther* or *further* to complete each sentence.

11. Jorge rode ________ than his father rode that day.
12. Mr. Nieto has thought ________ about sending Jorge to college.
13. It is ________ from home than Jorge has ever traveled before.
14. Jorge has ridden on a bus to ________ destinations than his brothers have ridden.
15. He has considered ________ travel plans.

THINK AND REMEMBER

- Remember that adverbs have three degrees of comparison—positive, comparative, and superlative.
- Remember that some adverbs cannot be compared.
- Use *farther* and *farthest* to compare distances. Use *further* and *furthest* to compare quantity, time, or degree.

Independent Practice

C. Identifying Degrees of Comparison Write the adverb or adverbs in each sentence. Next to the adverb write *positive, comparative,* or *superlative* to identify its degree of comparison.

16. Long ago Spain had slowly colonized Texas.

MODEL slowly—positive

17. In 1821 Mexico finally broke free from Spain.
18. Mexico more readily opened the land to colonists.
19. The settlement grew faster each year.
20. Then officials tried to govern the settlers unfairly.
21. The new Texans fought most fiercely for their independence.
22. The Alamo stands proudly as a reminder of that battle.

D. Using *Farther* and *Further* Correctly Write *farther* or *further* to complete each sentence.

23. I have examined this book ________.

MODEL further

24. Have you read ________ about the Cattle Queen of Texas?
25. Lizzie Johnson traveled ________ on the Chisholm Trail than some men.
26. Did the Chisholm Trail extend ________ than San Antonio?
27. Selling stray cows kept cowhands from going ________ into debt.
28. As railroads went ________ across Texas, cattle drives ended.

E. Adding Adverbs in the Positive, Comparative, and Superlative Degrees Write each sentence correctly. If necessary, change the adverb in parentheses ( ) to the comparative or superlative degree.

29. Ranch life was (frequently) dangerous than safe.

MODEL Ranch life was more frequently dangerous than safe.

30. By 1850 Texas longhorns roamed (freely) on the range.
31. These dangerous cattle would charge (quickly) than buffalo.
32. Cowhands rose (early) in the morning to tend cattle.
33. Of all the riders on the range, they rode (well).
34. They handled their horses (skillfully) than anyone else.

Application — Writing

An Adventure Write one or two paragraphs about Jorge. Tell how he learned to throw the lasso and about an adventure he had when he needed this skill. Use positive, comparative, and superlative degrees of adverbs in your story.

8 Negatives

◆ **FOCUS** Two negative words should not be used together.

Negative adverbs are almost always used to modify verbs.

1. The raven would not say anything but one word.
2. It never left its perch above the door.

Common Negative Adverbs

not (*n't*)	never	hardly	barely
rarely	seldom	nowhere	scarcely

Do not confuse negative adverbs with other negative words such as *nobody, nothing, none, no one,* or *neither.* These words function as pronouns.

3. No one was there when I answered the door.

Avoid using two or more negative words in the same sentence. This is called a **double negative.**

Guidelines for Using Negative Words
1. Replace one part of a double negative with its opposite, an affirmative word. Negatives: none — no one — nowhere — never Affirmatives: any — anyone — anywhere — ever INCORRECT: Andy never read none of Edgar Allan Poe's writing.
2. Do not use the negative adverbs *barely, hardly,* or *scarcely* with other negative words. INCORRECT: She couldn't hardly put the book down.

Guided Practice

A. Identify the negative word in each sentence.

1. I can hardly stand the suspense in Poe's poetry.
2. Not one line in "The Raven" lacks excitement.
3. I never read the poem "Annabel Lee."
4. There was no finer poet than Edgar Allan Poe.
5. None of his short stories end in a predictable way.

THINK AND REMEMBER

- Remember that most negative adverbs are used to to modify verbs.
- Never use double negatives in your writing.

Independent Practice

B. Identifying Negative Adverbs Write the negative word in each sentence.

6. Sally has barely begun reading "The Purloined Letter."

MODEL barely

7. She will never guess the ending.
8. You can't miss any of the clues as you read.
9. The missing letter isn't easy to locate.
10. Dupin seldom fails to solve a mystery.
11. You can hardly fail to feel the suspense.

C. Revising: Eliminating Double Negatives Rewrite each sentence, eliminating the double negative.

12. I haven't known of no one with a sadder life than Poe's.

MODEL I haven't known of anyone with a sadder life than Poe's.
OR I have known of no one with a sadder life than Poe's.

13. He didn't never know his parents.
14. Neither of them never lived very long.
15. He did not make no close friends as a child.
16. Before long he didn't have nowhere to live.
17. He hardly had nobody who could help him.

Application — Writing

Friendly Letter Read "The Raven." Imagine that you are a friend of the narrator. Write a letter to him explaining why you think he should get rid of the raven in his room. Use at least three negative adverbs in your letter. If you need help writing a friendly letter, see page 62 of the **Writer's Handbook.**

9 Adverb or Adjective?

FOCUS

- An **adverb** modifies a verb, an adjective, or another adverb.
- An **adjective** modifies a noun or a pronoun.

Some words can be used as both adjectives and adverbs. To tell whether a word is an adverb or an adjective, find the word it modifies. Remember, an adverb modifies a verb, an adjective, or another adverb, and an adjective modifies a noun or a pronoun. Remember also that adjectives can follow linking verbs.

Study the following pairs of troublesome adverbs and adjectives to learn how to use them properly.

Word	Part of Speech	Sentence Example
real	adjective	These boots are made of *real* leather.
really	adverb	The lamb's wool was *really* clean.
good	adjective	The grange had a *good* exhibit of crops.
well	adverb	Corn grew especially *well* this year.
well	adjective	Maria was ill, but now she is *well* again.
bad	adjective	A blight caused a *bad* potato crop.
badly	adverb	Squash had also grown *badly.*
sure	adjective	Tomás is *sure* to win a prize.
surely	adverb	He *surely* has worked hard enough.
most	adjective	*Most* county fairs have agricultural exhibits.
most (very)	adverb	The naming of the winners is *most* exciting.
almost	adverb	You can *almost* feel the anticipation.

Guided Practice

A. Identify the correct word to complete each sentence.

1. A 4-H Club teaches members to become (good, well) citizens.
2. Young people become (real, really) involved in a project.
3. (Most, Almost) clubs teach home and community skills.
4. (Most, Almost) every member enters an exhibit at a fair.
5. It is (sure, surely) hard work to raise a crop or an animal.
6. Those who do (good, well) at a local fair might enter a state fair.

THINK AND REMEMBER

- Remember that some words can be used as either adverbs or adjectives.
- Remember that words modifying nouns or pronouns can only be adjectives (*real, good, bad, sure*).
- Remember that some words can only be adverbs (*really, badly, surely, almost*).

Independent Practice

B. Using Troublesome Adjectives and Adverbs Write the correct word to complete the sentence.

7. The Green County Fair has a (real, really) fine craft show.

MODEL really

8. The entrants made (almost, the most) unusual items.
9. Julie did a very (good, well) job on her afghan.
10. It had (very, real) tiny rosebuds in the center.
11. She (most, almost) yelled when she saw a blue ribbon on it.
12. The judges (surely, sure) must have felt she deserved it.
13. I saw a red ribbon on a (real, really) beautiful quilt.
14. Many of the other crafts (sure, surely) could have won.
15. The judge felt (bad, badly) that she had only three prizes to give.

C. Proofreading: Checking for Correct Use of Adjectives and Adverbs Each sentence contains one error. Write each sentence correctly.

16. Fairs are held in most every part of the world.

MODEL Fairs are held in almost every part of the world.

17. People have a real good time at the exhibits.
18. Merchants do good selling souvenirs and food.
19. Cornhuskers or sheepshearers may do good in the contests.
20. Some fairs have real tough athletic contests.
21. The best fair of all is sure a World's Fair.
22. I would feel badly if I missed the chance to attend one.
23. Most everyone can learn something from the displays.

Application — Writing

Paragraph of Contrast Imagine that you are a judge at a county fair. Write a paragraph to contrast animals that you had to judge at the fair. Use troublesome adjectives and adverbs correctly. If you need help writing a paragraph of contrast, see page 42 of the **Writer's Handbook.**

Building Vocabulary
Suffixes

You can make new words by adding a syllable to the end of base words. These syllables are called **suffixes.** When a suffix is added, the new word is usually a different part of speech.

Adjective Suffix	Meaning	Examples
able, ible	able to be	enjoyable, sensible
al	belonging to	national, seasonal
en	made of, like	wooden, golden
esque	like	picturesque
ful	full, full of	armful, hopeful
ish	like	selfish, ticklish
ive	tending to	productive, massive
less	without	restless, timeless
ous	having the quality of	religious
some	like or tending to	irksome
y	showing	healthy, windy

Noun Suffix	Meaning	Examples
ance, ence	act, state	resistance, dependence
er, or	doer	builder, auditor
hood	condition	childhood, adulthood
ion, tion	state, action	reaction, introduction
ity, ty	quality	equality, loyalty
ment	action, result	agreement, shipment
ness	state, quality	eagerness, thickness

Verb Suffix	Meaning	Examples
ate	cause to become	operate
en	become, make	fasten, frighten
ify, fy	cause, make	testify, notify
ize	cause to be	summarize, mobilize

Adding suffixes to root words sometimes causes spelling problems. Keep the following in mind:

1. When adding a suffix beginning with a vowel to a root word ending in *e*, drop the final *e* before adding the suffix. imagine—imaginable For words ending in *ce* or *ge*, keep the final *e*. outrage—outrageous
2. When adding a suffix beginning with a consonant to a root word ending in *e*, keep the final *e* and add the suffix. force—forceful
3. When adding a suffix to a word ending with a consonant + *y*, change the *y* to *i* before adding the suffix. mystery—mysterious

Reading Practice

Read each sentence and find the word or words that contain a suffix from the chart. Write each word, underline its suffix, and write what part of speech the word is.

1. The bald eagle is the national emblem of the United States.
2. The United States government chose this emblem in 1782.
3. The eagle stands for independence, skill, and strength.
4. In the United States, it is unlawful to hunt or kill bald eagles.
5. At one point the bald eagle was in danger of extinction.

Writing Practice

Add two different suffixes from the chart to each base word to form two new words. Write each word, label its part of speech, and use the word in a sentence.

6. agree
7. doubt
8. magnet
9. bright
10. intense
11. accept
12. respect
13. final
14. industry

Project

Think of as many descriptive words as possible that contain suffixes. Make a chart similar to this one, and categorize your descriptive words according to the five senses. Use these words in your writing.

Sight	Sound	Taste	Smell	Touch
spotless	audible	bitterness	smoky	roughness

Language Enrichment
Adjectives and Adverbs

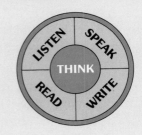

Use what you know about adjectives and adverbs to do these activities.

Tom Swifties

In a Tom Swifty, adverbs are used in an amusing way. The way in which Tom says something is a pun on what he says. ("I got a blue ribbon," said Tom winningly.) Make up a Tom Swifty of your own, and try it out on your classmates. If they groan, which is the usual response to a clever pun, you have a winner!

"Waffle Words" in Advertisements

Many advertisers use adjectives and adverbs to describe their products. Some make comparisons such as "makes your teeth whiter," "tastes better," or "runs smoother." These advertisers use comparisons with adjectives and adverbs but never complete the comparison. Your teeth are made whiter than what? Something tastes better than what? Look in old magazines and newspapers for advertisements that contain these "waffle words." Rewrite them, and make the comparison complete.

Sharing Adjectives and Adverbs

With a partner, put together a list of ten adjectives and ten adverbs. Then trade that list with another pair of classmates. Working separately, write a paragraph that contains all or most of the words on the list. Read your paragraphs to one another. Notice how the same set of adjectives and adverbs can be used to produce entirely different paragraphs.

CONNECTING
LANGUAGE ↔ WRITING

In this unit you learned that adjectives can be formed from verbs, pronouns, and nouns. You learned that predicate adjectives help describe the subjects of sentences. You found out that adverbs give a reader more complete information. You saw that both adjectives and adverbs can help you compare two or more things.

◆ **Using Adjectives and Adverbs in Your Writing** Knowing how to use adjectives and adverbs is an important writing skill. Precise adjectives help your readers visualize what you describe in your writing. Carefully chosen adverbs can make your writing more lively. Pay special attention to the adjectives and adverbs you use as you do these activities.

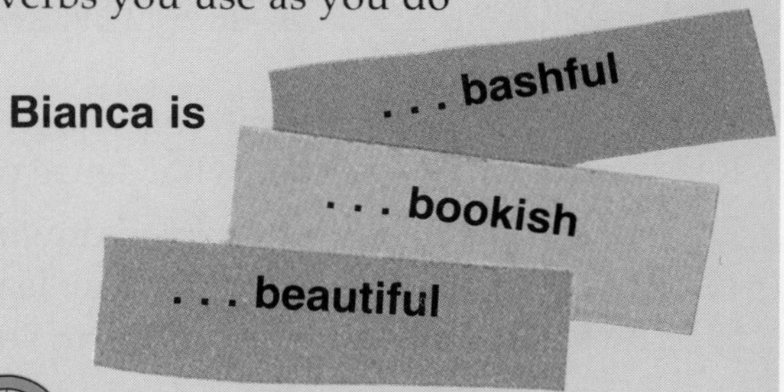
Bianca is
. . . bashful
. . . bookish
. . . beautiful

A Wild Ride

To make sure customers return, the Harum-Scarum Amusement Park adds a new scary ride each year. This year the park has hired you to design its new ride. Write a business letter to the park's owner describing the ride you propose. To interest the owner use lively adjectives and adverbs in your description.

If you want, draw a diagram to accompany your description. Then read your letter aloud to the class and ask who would be brave enough to try your ride.

A, My Name Is Alice

Use the list of suffixes on the **Building Vocabulary** pages to create adjectives for a game. Each player thinks of adjectives that begin with the letter of his or her first name and that end with a suffix. For each player's turn, he or she should complete this sentence: *(Name)* is *(adjective)*. Continue the game until the players run out of adjectives.

6 Unit Checkup

Think Back	Think Ahead
◆ What did you learn about character sketches in this unit? What did you do to write one?	◆ How will what you learned about character sketches help you to create a visual picture? ◆ How will knowing how to visualize comparisons help you write a description?
◆ Look at the writing you did in this unit. How did adjectives and adverbs help you express your ideas?	◆ What is one way you can use adjectives and adverbs to improve your writing?

Character Sketch *pages 254 – 255*

Read each sentence. Write what sense or senses each sentence appeals to.

1. The blood-red sports car sped down the interstate highway.
2. The passengers enjoyed the new leather seats and upholstery.
3. The salty ocean air and the warm sun made the drive pleasant.

Visualizing Comparisons *page 256*

Write a word or words that convey a meaning similar to that of each underlined comparison.

4. Balboa yelled <u>like a child</u> when he saw the Pacific Ocean.
5. His famous sighting filled Balboa <u>with sunshine</u>.
6. The explorer is known as "<u>the Father of the Pacific</u>."

Avoiding Overused Words and Clichés *page 257*

Rewrite each sentence. Use fresh words or original comparisons to replace overused words and clichés.

7. The woodsman was as tall as a tree.
8. He was as quick as a cat running through the trees.
9. The woodsman was usually as quiet as a mouse.

The Writing Process *pages 258 – 267*

Write the letter for the answer to each question.

10. When organizing details in a character sketch, what should be used to help the audience picture the person?
- **a.** comparisons
- **b.** general labels
- **c.** an opinion

11. In revising, how can nouns be made more descriptive?
- **a.** Capitalize them.
- **b.** Add specific adjectives.
- **c.** Use pronouns in place of the nouns.

12. How must the person's picture match your published sketch?
- **a.** to provide a visual aid
- **b.** to attract readers
- **c.** to show the person's most memorable trait described in the sketch

Adjectives *pages 270 – 271*

Write each sentence. Underline the adjectives, including articles, once. Underline twice the words the adjectives modify.

13. The heritage of the old Southwest attracts many different types of people.

14. American citizens enjoy the study of the many diverse cultural influences.

15. Three influences were the American Indians, the Spanish, and the blacks.

16. Each diverse group has had a decisive impact on the cultural and economic development of the region.

17. The Spanish colonization of America began in the early eighteenth century.

Other Parts of Speech as Adjectives *pages 272 – 273*

Write each underlined word or phrase used as an adjective. Next to each, write *adjective*, *pronoun*, *noun*, or *verb*.

18. What will be a developing focus in education in the years to come?

19. Most schools now are focused on courses of studies that were developed decades ago.

20. A growing trend in education is the connection of work experience with academic training.

21. What choice did educational planners have?

22. All courses probably should be redesigned with such an ideal.

Predicate Adjectives *pages 274 – 275*

Write each sentence. Underline the predicate adjective. Draw an arrow from the predicate adjective to the word it modifies.

23. Today, modern music can be romantic or philosophical.

24. The music is almost always fast paced and highly technical.

25. Many popular rock stars are British, Swedish, or American.

26. The charts may become filled with groups from all over the world.

27. The competition for the music consumer's dollar is very tight.

Comparisons with Adjectives *pages 276 – 277*

Write the adjective of comparison from each sentence. Next to each adjective, write its degree of comparison.

28. Automobile design has become more important than price.

29. Transportation efficiency is our newest concern.

30. One of the greatest improvements has been made in efficiency.

31. These cars are even more luxurious than their predecessors.

32. Henry Ford is the man most responsible for the idea of making modern changes in car design.

Irregular Comparisons with Adjectives *pages 278 – 279*

Write the adjective of comparison from each sentence. Next to the adjective, write *positive, comparative,* or *superlative.*

33. America produces the best food available for the cost.

34. Visiting a supermarket is a good way to get an idea of how advanced the industry is.

35. Not many food products are immediately ready for the marketplace.

36. The best food products may go through several processing steps.

37. The better supermarkets offer a variety of foodstuffs.

Adverbs *pages 280 – 282*

Write each sentence. Underline the adverb or adverbs, and draw an arrow from each adverb to the word it modifies. Underline twice any adverb used as an intensifier.

38. Very eager computer programmers discover new challenges daily.

39. They enjoy the adventures of exploring the most complex programming systems.

40. They look deep inside the loops of adventure games.

41. Avid programmers seem to seek the unusually designed programs.
42. Really intensive "hackers" spend hours and hours at work.

Comparisons with Adverbs *pages 283 – 285*

Write the adverb that compares in each sentence. Next to the adverb, write *positive, comparative,* or *superlative* to identify its degree of comparison.

43. People had cautiously declined to get involved in crime prevention.
44. In the 1980's police more freely invited public participation.
45. Law enforcement more openly admitted the need for help.
46. The programs spread faster each year with rising crime.
47. The Neighborhood Watch program works most efficiently.

Negatives *pages 286 – 287*

Write the negative word in each sentence.

48. Few true adventurers haven't experienced some form of fear.
49. It is scarcely realistic to expect everyone to be brave.
50. Even though something hasn't happened before, it still may.
51. An experienced adventurer seldom escapes all types of close calls.
52. One can never tell how any adventure will turn out.

Adverb or Adjective? *pages 288 – 289*

Write the correct word in parentheses ( ) to complete the sentence.

53. The Boy Scouts have a (real, really) exciting challenge.
54. They did a very (good, well) job of developing a ranch.
55. The mountains have (real, really) dangerous cliffs.
56. The new campers (most, almost) yell when they first see Philmont.
57. After a hiker has been away, a bed looks (well, good).

Suffixes *pages 290 – 291*

Read each sentence and find the word or words that contain a suffix from the charts on page 290. Write each word, underline its suffix, and write what part of speech the word is.

58. Progress has never been a regional goal.
59. It has been an endless goal since the beginning of history.
60. The continuous search for progress enlivens our arts.
61. Progressive people have always stepped forward to lead.
62. The pursuit of happiness includes the urge for progress.

UNIT 7

Comparing and Contrasting

◆ COMPOSITION FOCUS: **Paragraphs of Comparison/Contrast**
◆ LANGUAGE FOCUS: **Prepositions, Conjunctions, Interjections**

Suppose you have a choice of whether to spend your free time watching a movie or reading a book. Both are new, but the movie is a comedy and the book is a mystery. You need to make a decision. We often have to compare and contrast objects, recognizing similarities and differences in order to make everyday decisions.

Writers use comparison and contrast to give their audience a thorough understanding of their subjects. Kim Choi (chôi), for example, includes paragraphs that compare and contrast ideas in her essay on leisure time.

To write her essay, Kim Choi identified the similarities and differences between leisure time in the past and leisure time today. By contrasting them, she helps her audience understand the subjects. In this unit you will learn how to share your understanding of subjects by writing paragraphs of comparison and contrast.

Kim Choi wrote "What Is Leisure?" *to inform* others about past and present ideas.

Reading with a Writer's Eye

Paragraphs of Comparison and Contrast

When the ancient Greeks took a break from shipbuilding, pottery, and other forms of labor, how did they spend their free time? Kim Choi discovered what the Greeks and other peoples of the past chose to do in their leisure time. Read this essay by Kim Choi to find out what past ideas of leisure time were and how they compare with our ideas today.

What Is Leisure?

by Kim Choi

What do you do after you return home from school and finish your homework? What do you do for fun and enjoyment during that time? That block of time that is left over after your work, the free time left over for you to enjoy, is called **leisure time.**

To most people, leisure simply means recreation that provides escape from the strains of their everyday work-world. In order to find out how this modern definition of leisure compares with definitions of the past, the role of leisure in the past needs to be examined.

As the nature and quantity of work changed over time, people in different periods of history had varying definitions of leisure. To the Greeks, leisure meant time to use their minds to expand their intellectual horizons. It was a time to further their education so that they could contribute to society by becoming better citizens. In contrast, the Romans regarded leisure primarily as a time when people were permitted to rest from hard, physical work. The Pilgrims, instead of believing that leisure was in some way beneficial, viewed it as a disgraceful state of laziness that promoted mischief. As a result, they advocated hard work from sunrise to sunset.

The role that leisure plays in a young person's life today is similar to the role that it plays in an adult's life. It provides both with pleasure, amusement, and sometimes friendship. A youngster can spend it in whatever way he or she chooses, just as an adult can. In the same way that it offers youth freedom from the rigors of school work, it provides adults relief from the rigors of a job.

However, leisure time serves a more significant purpose in a young person's life. In childhood and in youth, it is a time away from school work during which youngsters are free to explore the world around them. Through sports activities such as baseball, basketball, and football, they strengthen their bodies and, at the same time, learn ways to interact with others. By pursuing such hobbies as reading, computing, rocketry, cooking, photography, quilting, or playing a musical instrument, youngsters can find out more about their abilities. Leisure time, if used well, helps the youngsters discover and develop the interests, talents, and feelings that will give shape to their future lives.

As a person reaches adulthood, life becomes more complicated and work becomes more demanding. With the responsibility of making a living, a person has less leisure time. Precisely because it is so precious, many adults take great care in choosing and planning their leisure activities.

The kinds of activities individual adults prefer vary according to the person's job, temperament, and physical ability. People who work at physically demanding jobs, such as construction work or dance, may find spectator sports or movies relaxing. On the other hand, those who sit at a desk all day, may find physical activities, such as tennis or jogging, more appealing. A person who enjoys being alone would prefer reading or painting over going to parties. Strenuous sports such as marathon running and mountain climbing may be more suitable for those who are in good physical shape.

With the rapid advance of technology, machines are taking over much of what we call "hard work." By the time today's youth reach adulthood, they will undoubtedly have more leisure time than today's adults. They will probably be able to take advantage of shorter workweeks and longer vacations. They will be able to enjoy more free time away from jobs. This is delightful news—but only for those who are prepared to take advantage of more leisure time.

How can people today prepare themselves for this increase in leisure time? They can begin by defining the word for themselves. How people define leisure will determine how they will use it. Each one's personal definition will help in the search for meaningful ways to spend leisure time.

Respond

1. Do you agree or disagree with Kim Choi's ideas about leisure time today and in the future? Explain your answers.

Discuss

2. Does this essay give you a better understanding of leisure time? If so, what does it make you realize?
3. In what way is today's idea of leisure time different from past ideas? Is it like any idea in the past? If so, which one?

Thinking As a Writer

Analyzing Paragraphs of Comparison and Contrast

Writer's Guide

A paragraph of comparison or contrast

- points out similarities or differences.
- describes the same features for both subjects.

A paragraph of comparison points out the similarities between two or more subjects; a paragraph of contrast points out the differences. The topic sentence usually indicates whether the subjects will be compared or contrasted. The detail sentences describe the same features of both.

Paragraphs of comparison and contrast can be organized using the **point-by-point method** or the **block method.**

The role that leisure plays in a young person's life today is similar to the role that it plays in an adult's life. It provides both with pleasure, amusement, and sometimes friendship. A youngster can spend it in whatever way he or she chooses, just as an adult can. In the same way that it offers youth freedom from the rigors of school work, it provides adults relief from the rigors of a job.

As the nature and quantity of work changed over time, people in different periods of history had varying definitions of leisure. To the Greeks, leisure meant time to use their minds to expand their intellectual horizons. It was a time to further their education so that they could contribute to society by becoming better citizens. In contrast, the Romans regarded leisure primarily as a time when people were permitted to rest from hard, physical work. The Pilgrims, instead of believing that leisure time was in some way beneficial, viewed it as a disgraceful state of laziness that promoted mischief. As a result, they advocated hard work from sunrise to sunset.

A **paragraph of comparison** shows how subjects are alike. The topic sentence states what subjects will be compared.

The **point-by-point method** describes one feature at a time for each subject. Transitional words and expressions underlined in the detail sentences point out each new feature.

A **paragraph of contrast** shows how subjects are different. The topic sentence states what will be contrasted.

The **block method** describes fully all of one group's views, features, or qualities. It then describes all of the same points for the next group.

Transitional words and expressions are used here to signal the introduction of the next group's points.

Discuss

1. Look at the topic sentence in each paragraph. Which words indicate to the reader whether the paragraph will compare or contrast more than one thing?
2. Which transitional words are used to compare two details? Which transitional words are used to contrast two details? What other words would be possible?
3. Why is the point-by-point method effective in the first paragraph?
4. Do you think the block method, used in the second paragraph, is as effective? Explain your answer.

Try Your Hand

A. Analyze Topic Sentences Read the following unfinished paragraphs of comparison and contrast. For each, write *compare* or *contrast* to indicate the purpose of the paragraph.

1. Swimming and running are sports that have a number of characteristics in common. Swimmers and runners can both enjoy their activities alone rather than as members of teams.
2. Astronauts are different from athletes in a number of ways. Astronauts perform their jobs in a sitting position for extended periods of time, but athletes change positions frequently.

B. Add Detail Sentences Look back at the paragraphs in **A.** Write one detail sentence that might appear in each paragraph.

C. Order Detail Sentences Rewrite paragraph 2 in **A,** using the block method. Include the sentence you added.

D. Using Transitional Expressions Read the paragraph you just wrote for **C.** Circle the transitional words and expressions used to signal the introduction of new points. Replace these expressions with other words that would also be effective.

Writer's Notebook

Collecting Synonyms and Antonyms Did you notice the synonyms and antonyms, such as *leisure time* and *free time, rest* and *work,* and *sunrise* and *sunset,* in the essay on leisure? Read the essay again and record in your *Writer's Notebook* the synonyms and antonyms you find. Try to think of other synonyms and antonyms for these words and record them, too. Try to use synonyms and antonyms when you compare or contrast things.

Thinking As a Writer

Evaluating Whether to Compare or Contrast

> **Writer's Guide**
>
> To write paragraphs of comparison and contrast, good writers
> - group their details into categories.
> - evaluate the categories to decide which kind of paragraph to write and which details to include.

In good paragraphs of comparison and contrast, a writer discusses features that both subjects have in common.

In planning a paragraph comparing airplane pilots and truck drivers, a writer first listed a mixture of details and then grouped the details into classes, or categories labeled to show how the details are related.

To **evaluate,** or judge, whether the two subjects are mostly alike or mostly different, the writer made a circle diagram, which shows the degrees of similarity and difference between the two subjects. The size of the overlapping section indicates whether the writer should write a paragraph of comparison or a paragraph of contrast. You may want to use a circle diagram to help you decide which kind of paragraph to write.

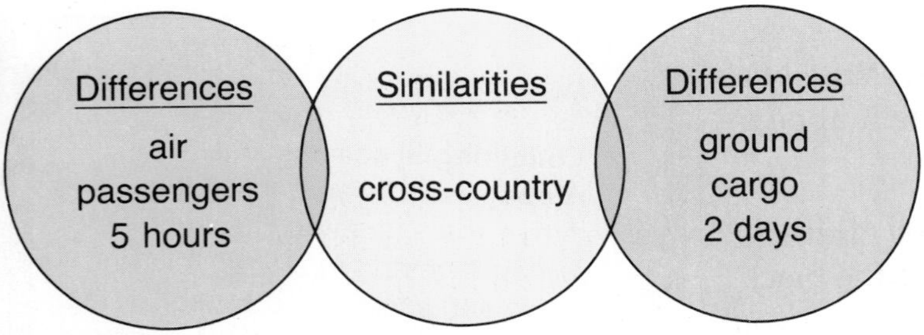

Discuss

Should the writer's paragraph compare airplane pilots to truck drivers, or should it contrast the two subjects? Why?

Try Your Hand

Evaluate Details Choose two related subjects that interest you. Make a list of details for each of them, and then make a circle diagram. Trade diagrams with a partner. Decide whether your partner should compare or contrast his or her subjects.

Developing the Writer's Craft
Writing for an Audience and a Purpose

> **Writer's Guide**
>
> Good writers
> - craft their writing to match the audience.
> - remember their purpose.

Good writers adjust their writing to suit their audience and their purpose.

The writer's purpose may be to express ideas and feelings, as in a journal; to inform readers of facts; to persuade them to accept an opinion; or simply to entertain them with a poem or a story. Here are two examples of writing for different purposes.

1. A person who enjoys being alone would prefer reading or painting over going to parties.

2. My stomach does somersaults when I attend parties.

Along with matching their writing to their purpose, good writers adjust their language to suit their audience. If their writing includes difficult or special vocabulary, they define unusual terms.

When you write your paragraphs of comparison and contrast, match your writing to your purpose and your audience.

Discuss

Look back at sentences 1 and 2. What is the purpose of each sentence—to express, to inform, to persuade, or to entertain?

Try Your Hand

Match Your Writing to Your Audience and Your Purpose Look at the pictures and the caption about the events in a triathlon. Choose two different audiences. Write an original definition of the term *triathlon* for each audience. Identify the audience for each definition.

A contestant performs all three sports in succession.

1 Prewriting
Paragraphs of Comparison and Contrast

> **Writer's Guide**
>
> **Prewriting Checklist**
> - ☑ Brainstorm topics.
> - ☑ Select a topic.
> - ☑ Think about your audience and your purpose.
> - ☑ Gather information.
> - ☑ Organize the features.

Cora wanted to write a composition several paragraphs long that would compare and contrast two or more items. She used the information in the **Writer's Guide** to help plan her paragraphs. Look at what she did.

◆ Brainstorming and Selecting a Topic

First, Cora brainstormed a list of possible topics. Then, she looked through books to find more topics for her paragraphs of comparison and contrast. Look at Cora's list.

~~African safaris~~
~~mystery stories~~
three underwater tunnels
~~spaceships and astronauts~~
~~Mt. Vesuvius and Mt. Rainier~~
sharks and whales

Next, Cora looked at her list and crossed off topics that were too broad for her paragraphs.

Then, she checked in books to see which of the remaining topics had items she could compare and contrast. Cora crossed all other topics off her list.

Finally, Cora circled the most interesting topic that was left on her list. She decided to write about the underwater tunnels because one of them was located in Japan, a country her teacher was about to visit. Cora also knew she could gather information on this topic.

Discuss

1. Which topics on Cora's list were too broad for her paragraphs? What might she have done instead of crossing them off the list?
2. Which topic includes two items that would probably be difficult to compare and contrast? Why?

◆ Gathering Information and Organizing the Features

After Cora selected her topic, she gathered information for her paragraphs of comparison and contrast. Cora made notes of the features to use when comparing and contrasting the tunnels.

Features of the tunnels

location, safeguards, accidents, construction, lining, year built

Next, Cora used these categories and filled in the information for the Thames, the Hudson, and the Seikan tunnels.

	Thames Tunnel	*Hudson Tunnel*	*Seikan Tunnel*
Location	*under Thames*	*under Hudson*	*under Pacific*
Safeguards	*shield*	*air pressure*	*shield*
Accidents	*no fatalities*	*20 fatalities*	*34 fatalities*
Construction	*pick & shovel*	*drill & dynamite*	*boring machine*
Year built	*1843*	*1904*	*1988*

After completing this chart, Cora entered her information on a circle diagram. The circle diagram shows the similarities and differences among the three tunnels.

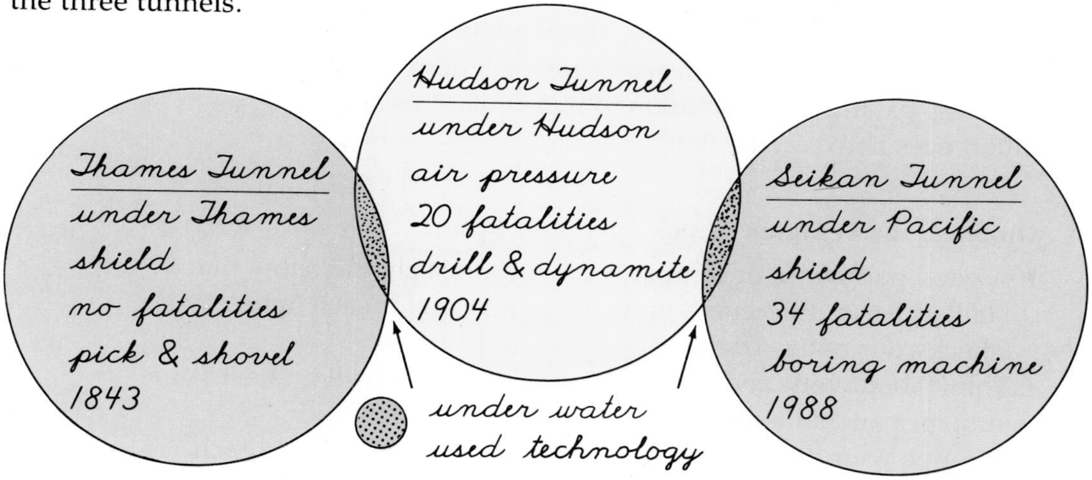

Cora decided to write her paragraph of comparison first, because she wanted to emphasize the similarities among the three tunnels. She also decided to make her contrast paragraph clear by describing the differences point by point.

Discuss

1. Look back at Cora's first notes. Which one did she leave out of her chart? Why do you think she left it out?
2. Should Cora write a paragraph of comparison or a paragraph of contrast about the Hudson and Seikan tunnels? Why?
3. If you were Cora, would you use the point-by-point method or the block method to discuss the Hudson and Seikan tunnels? Why?

Try Your Hand

A. Brainstorm and Select a Topic Brainstorm a list of possible topics. You might also look in books and magazines to find topics with items to compare and contrast. List every topic that interests you. Think about each topic and your audience.

- Cross out topics that are too broad.
- Look in books to see which topics have items with enough features to compare and contrast. Cross out topics lacking items with enough features.
- Circle the remaining topic that interests you most and is most likely to interest your audience. This will be the topic for your paragraphs of comparison and contrast.

B. Gather Information When you are satisfied with your topic, plan how you can gather information about the items you are comparing and contrasting. Note the features for each item you will compare and contrast, paying close attention to the similarities and the differences between the items.

C. Organize the Features Look over your notes.

- A good paragraph of comparison or contrast should show the similarities or differences in the same feature for each item. Check your notes for the same types of features.
- Think about your audience. Include details that will interest your audience and suit your purpose.
- Arrange your notes, listing the matching features next to each other. You may want to make a circle diagram like Cora's.

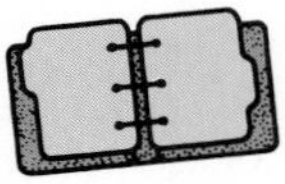

Save your notes and your circle diagram in your *Writer's Notebook*. You will use them when you draft your paragraphs of comparison and contrast.

2 Drafting

Paragraphs of Comparison and Contrast

Using her chart and her circle diagram, Cora followed the **Writer's Guide** to draft her paragraphs. Look at what she did.

> The Thames and Hudson tunnels are alike in several significant ways. Just as the first tunnel lies under a river, the Thames, the second one is under a river, the Hudson. In both cases new methods were used to safeguard the builders who bored through the silt and clay. A cast-iron shield protected the Thames workers, while a shaft filled with compressed air was designed to protect the Hudson crew. Yet a dangerous accident occurred in each tunnel, and each accident led to a heroic rescue.

Writer's Guide

Drafting Checklist

- ☑ Write the topic sentence of your paragraph first.
- ☑ Point out similarities or differences next.

Discuss

1. Does Cora's topic sentence introduce a paragraph of comparison or of contrast? How do you know?
2. In what ways are the two tunnels similar and different?

Try Your Hand

Now you are ready to write paragraphs of comparison and contrast.

A. Review Your Information Think about the information you gathered and organized. Decide whether you need more information. If so, gather it.

B. Think About Your TAP Remember that your task is to write paragraphs of comparison and contrast. Your purpose is to inform your audience about the similarities and differences between items.

Task: What?
Audience: Who?
Purpose: Why?

C. Write Your First Draft Refer to your **Drafting Checklist** to write your paragraphs.

When you write your draft, just put all your ideas on paper. Do not worry about spelling, grammar, or punctuation. You can correct the draft later.

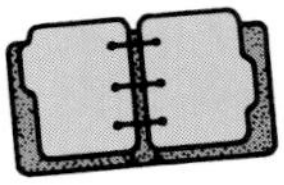

Save your first draft in your *Writer's Notebook*. You will use it when you revise your paragraphs.

3 Responding and Revising
Paragraphs of Comparison and Contrast

Cora used the checklist in the **Writer's Guide** to revise her paragraphs of comparison and contrast. Look at what she did.

◆ Checking Information

Cora decided to take away a detail. To show her change, she used this mark. Cora added a fact to match one in a previous sentence. She used this mark ∧ .

◆ Checking Organization

Cora moved a sentence that was out of order in this second paragraph. She used this mark.

◆ Checking Language

Cora found two sentences that could be combined to show contrast. She used this mark ∧. She also replaced an inappropriate word with a better one. She used this mark ∧‾ .

Writer's Guide

Revising Checklist

- ☑ Read your paragraphs to yourself or to a partner.
- ☑ Think about your audience and your purpose. Add or cut information.
- ☑ Be sure that your paragraphs are organized correctly.
- ☑ Check for sentences that can be combined to show contrast.

Cut — Add — Replace — Move — Add

In other ways the Thames and Hudson tunnels had little in common. ~~Twenty-eight men were originally trapped in the Hudson Tunnel.~~ The Thames accident ended happily without a single death; however, ~~. T~~twenty perished in the Hudson disaster. The Thames workers used picks and shovels, but the Hudson ~~guys~~ workers used drills and dynamite. After the accident, they, like the Thames workers, had a shield to protect them as they finished the tunnel. The first underwater tunnel ever constructed, the Thames opened formally in 1843. Last, there was a sixty-one-year difference between the dates on which the two tunnels opened. The ceremonial opening of the Hudson occurred in 1904.

Discuss

1. Cora cut one sentence. Would you have cut it? Why or why not?
2. Why might Cora have added the sentence at the end?

Try Your Hand

Now revise your first draft.

A. Read Your First Draft As you read your paragraphs, think about your audience and your purpose. Read your paragraphs silently or to a partner to see if they are complete and well organized. Ask yourself or your partner the questions in the box.

Responding and Revising Strategies

✔ Respond **Ask yourself or a partner:**	✔ Revise **Try these solutions:**
• Does each topic sentence introduce the comparison or the contrast paragraph?	• **Add** a key word such as *common* to show the comparison or the contrast.
• Does every point support each topic sentence?	• **Cut** similarities or differences that seem out of place in each paragraph.
• Is my word choice appropriate for my audience?	• **Replace** any words or sentences that are too simple or too difficult.
• Can any of my sentences be combined to strengthen a contrast?	• **Replace** the two sentences with one sentence that combines them, using words that show contrast. See the **Revising Workshop** on page 314.

B. Make Your Changes If the answer to any question in the box is *no,* try the solution. Use the **Editor's Marks** to show your changes.

C. Review Your Paragraphs Again Decide whether there is anything else you want to revise. Keep revising your paragraphs until you feel they are well organized and complete.

EDITOR'S MARKS

- ∧ Add something.
- Cut something.
- Move something.
- Replace something.

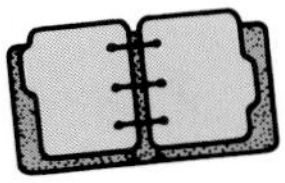

Save your revised paragraphs in your *Writer's Notebook.* You will use them when you proofread your paragraphs of comparison and contrast.

Revising Workshop
Combining Sentences to Show Contrast

Attentive writers combine contrasting ideas, using key words to point out the contrast. Read these sentences.

1. Most downhill skiers wear specially designed clothes. Cross-country skiers wear various types of clothing.
2. Most downhill skiers wear specially designed clothes; <u>on the other hand</u>, cross-country skiers wear various types of clothing.

The writer combined the two sentences by adding a semicolon and a short expression. The expression *on the other hand* establishes the contrast. Notice the comma that follows the expression.

Other words can be used to combine sentences and establish a contrast.

although	however	on the contrary	whereas
but	instead	still	while
even though	nevertheless	though	yet

Practice

Choose the best word or phrase in parentheses ( ) to combine each pair of sentences. Rewrite the sentences as one sentence, using the correct word or phrase and punctuation.

1. A movie uses music to create suspense. A novel uses only words. (; however,) (; nevertheless,)
2. Movies usually run for about two hours. Books may take many more hours to read. (, but) (; still,)
3. Movies show you exactly how characters look and act. Novels let you use your imagination. (; on the contrary,) (,even though)
4. In movies the rest of the audience may influence your response. You are a solitary audience for a novel. (, whereas) (, even though,)
5. You have to notice clues in a movie as they occur. You can reread the pages of a novel if you missed a clue. (, while) (; still,)
6. Movies may have spectacular special effects. Books can be exciting too. (, although) (, instead)
7. You can read a book anywhere. With a movie you must go to a theater or watch it on television. (, whereas) (, even though)

4 Proofreading
Paragraphs of Comparison and Contrast

Writer's Guide

Proofreading Checklist

- ☑ Check for errors in capitalization.
- ☑ Check for errors in punctuation.
- ☑ Be sure that all your paragraphs are indented.
- ☑ Check your grammar. Be sure that subjects and verbs agree.
- ☑ Circle any words you think are misspelled. Find out how to spell them correctly.
- ⇨ For proofreading help, use the **Writer's Handbook.**

After revising her paragraphs of comparison and contrast, Cora used the **Writer's Guide** and the **Editor's Marks** to proofread her paragraphs. Look at what she did.

> ¶ There are even more diffrences (differences) between the Hudson Tunnel and the Seikan Tunnel, a Japanese passageway opened in 1988. The Hudson Tunnel lies under a river; however, the Seikan crosses the Pacific ocean from the mainland to Hokkaido. Instead of the Hudson's iron-and-brick lining, cement lines the Seikan Tunnel. Finally, a compressed air shaft that failed the Hudson workers was replaced by a shield in the Seikan project. Its representatives ~~says~~ say their losses are considerable, though.

Discuss

1. Look at Cora's proofread paragraph. What kinds of mistakes did she make?
2. Which sentence had a subject and verb that did not agree? How did Cora make them agree?

Try Your Hand

Proofread Your Paragraphs Use the **Writer's Guide** and the **Editor's Marks** to proofread your paragraphs.

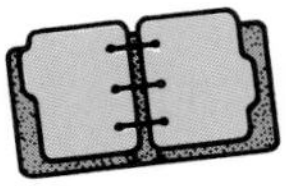

Save your corrected paragraphs in your *Writer's Notebook.* You will use them when you publish your paragraphs.

EDITOR'S MARKS

- ≡ Capitalize.
- ⊙ Add a period.
- ∧ Add something.
- ∧ Add a comma.
- ∨∨ Add quotation marks.
- Cut something.
- Replace something.
- Transpose.
- ◯ Spell correctly.
- ¶ Indent paragraph.
- / Make a lowercase letter.

5 Publishing
Paragraphs of Comparison and Contrast

Writer's Guide

Publishing Checklist

- Make a clean copy of your paragraphs.
- Check to see that nothing has been left out.
- Share your paragraphs in a special way.

Cora made a clean copy of her paragraphs and checked them to be sure she had not left out anything. Then she and her classmates made a bulletin board display of their paragraphs for their teacher. You can find Cora's paragraphs on pages 41 and 42 of the **Writer's Handbook.**

Here's how Cora and her classmates published their paragraphs of comparison and contrast.

1. First, they gave their paragraphs titles. Then, they met with other students and classified their paragraphs into categories. They planned space on the bulletin board for each student's paragraphs and for pictures. They wrote a caption for each picture.

2. Cora created a banner for her category and placed it on the bulletin board along with her paragraphs according to the plan. Then the students invited another class to come and look at their display.

Discuss

1. What might happen if the students had not planned where to place their paragraphs on the bulletin board?
2. Why is it important to write captions for the pictures in step 1?

Try Your Hand

Publish Your Paragraphs of Comparison and Contrast Follow the checklist in the **Writer's Guide.** If possible, create a bulletin board display, or try one of these ideas for sharing your paragraphs.

- Present your paragraphs in an oral report, using nonverbal cues in the presentation. If you need help, follow the **Tips on How to Use Nonverbal Cues.**
- With your classmates, classify your paragraphs into categories. Bind each group of paragraphs into a booklet, using the category label for the title. Make a cover and a title page listing all the writers. Present the booklet to your teacher.

Listening and Speaking

Tips on How to Use Nonverbal Cues

Listening

1. Pay close attention to facial expressions, matching them to what the speaker says. Facial expressions can reveal a speaker's feelings.
2. Notice the speaker's hand and arm gestures. He or she may be using them to signal important points.
3. Pay attention to pauses and silences. Decide whether the speaker is using them to emphasize or to introduce a point in the speech.

Speaking

1. Look at the audience while you speak. Avoid staring at the floor or at your notes.
2. Match your facial expressions and gestures to the words you say.
3. Avoid nervous gestures. Place your hands by your sides or on the speaker's stand, not in your pockets.
4. Maintain comfortable posture. Hold your head up and stand straight, relaxing your shoulders to avoid a stiff appearance.
5. Include pauses. Break up the flow of your words with silences to stress important points or to introduce new points.

Writing in the Content Areas

Use what you have learned to write several paragraphs that include comparisons and contrasts. Use one of these ideas or an idea of your own.

Writer's Guide

When you write, remember the stages of the Writing Process.

- Prewriting
- Drafting
- Responding and Revising
- Proofreading
- Publishing

Physical Education

Most sports seem to involve a ball of some kind, although that ball can be as small as a table-tennis ball or as large as a basketball. Think of two sports you enjoy, and compare and contrast them. Two features you could consider are rules and equipment.

Social Studies

Life in other countries is in some ways like life in the United States but is very different in other ways. Choose a country that you have studied. Compare and contrast what you think the life of a student your age in that country would be like with what your own life is like.

Science

You may have noticed that the leaves of trees come in many shapes, sizes, and colors. Collect leaves from two or three different kinds of trees and mount the leaves on paper, identifying the kind of tree from which each leaf came. Then compare and contrast the size, shape, and color of the leaves.

Fine Arts

Someone once said that the reason an artist paints a picture of a tree is because *another* artist has painted a tree. The person who said that probably thought that artists tend to compare their work and get ideas from each other. Find paintings of trees or some other common subject, and compare and contrast how two artists have painted their subjects.

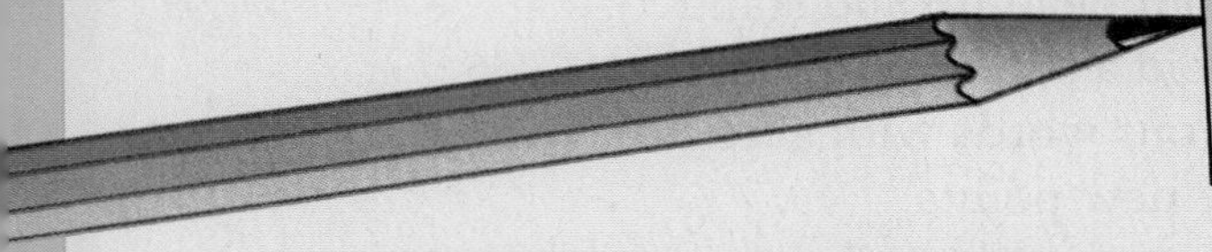

CONNECTING

WRITING ↔ LANGUAGE

Stories set in places that are meant for play and relaxation often include moments of suspense. A writer makes the surprise more intense by including comparisons and contrasts. How do the comparisons in the paragraphs below add to the suspense?

> "Hey! Who's there?" Kate's words came out shakily. The scraping noise stopped abruptly, but Kate crept farther under her covers. She wondered if nights were always this frightening in the little cabin she had just rented for the summer. Morning HAS to come soon, she thought.
>
> How different the little cabin had seemed earlier that evening! With her friends gathered inside, it was easy to joke about monsters and other fantasy creatures of the night. The cabin had felt cozy and safe as the threesome sang their favorite songs.

◆ **Prepositions, Conjunctions, and Interjections**
The words highlighted in color are commonly used prepositions, conjunctions, and interjections. Prepositions and conjunctions help connect other words in sentences. Interjections help the reader feel the emotions the writer wants to express.

◆ **Language Focus: Prepositions, Conjunctions, and Interjections** The following lessons will help you use prepositions, conjunctions, and interjections in your own writing.

1 Prepositions and Prepositional Phrases

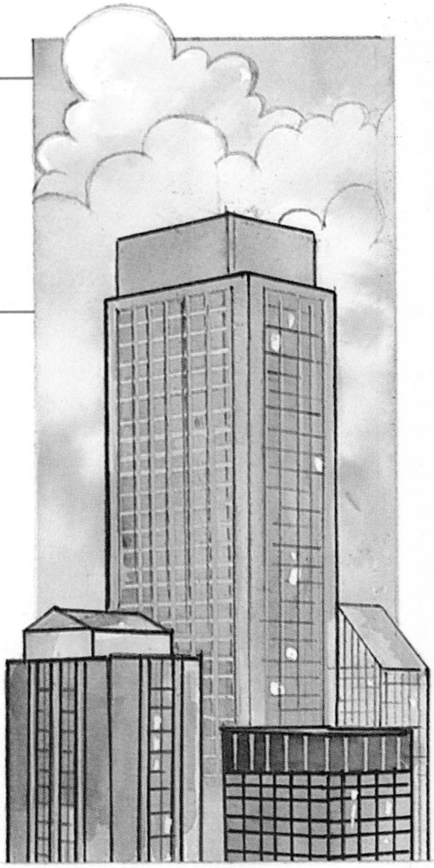

FOCUS

- A **preposition** relates a noun or a pronoun to another word in the sentence.
- A **prepositional phrase** is made up of a preposition, the object of the preposition, and all the words in between.

Prepositions connect words in a sentence. A preposition relates a noun or a pronoun to another word in the sentence. The highlighted words are prepositions.

1. Mr. Erland walked into the office.
   Into connects walked and office.
2. He had an interview for a new job.
   For connects interview and job.

A prepositional phrase is made up of a preposition, the object of the preposition, and all the words in between. The noun or the pronoun in the prepositional phrase is the object of the preposition.

prepositional phrase

3. Mrs. Ward's office is in a modern skyscraper.

preposition object of the preposition

When the object of a preposition is a pronoun, it must be in the objective case.

4. Mr. Erland shook hands with her.

A sentence may have more than one prepositional phrase. When a long prepositional phrase or a series of prepositional phrases introduces a sentence, use a comma after the last word in the prepositional phrase.

5. In the corner office near the supply room for the computer department, Mr. Erland found an empty desk.

A preposition may have a compound object.

6. Complete the application with a pencil or a pen.

Study the prepositions in the chart.

aboard	before	during	near	till
about	behind	except	of	to
above	below	for	off	toward
according to	beneath	from	on	under
across	beside	in	onto	underneath
after	besides	in back of	out	until
against	between	in front of	out of	unto
along	beyond	in place of	outside	up
among	but	in spite of	over	upon
around	by	instead	past	with
as	concerning	instead of	since	within
at	despite	into	through	without
because of	down	like	throughout	

Notice that some words can be either adverbs or prepositions, depending on their use in sentences. Adverbs, however, never have objects.

7. Please come in and sit down. adverb
8. The secretary hurried down the hall. preposition

Guided Practice

A. Identify the preposition and its object in each sentence.

1. I applied for a waiter's job.
2. How did you hear about it?
3. I read an ad in the paper.
4. One of my friends works here.
5. I enjoy this kind of work.
6. Carry the tray above your head.

B. Tell whether each underlined word is a *preposition* or an *adverb*.

7. Can you work <u>during</u> lunch hour?
8. I will bring your menus <u>over</u>.
9. We want a table <u>near</u> a window.
10. We have a few tables <u>outside</u>.
11. They sat <u>down</u> for their meal.

THINK AND REMEMBER

- Use a **preposition** to relate a noun or a pronoun (the **object of the preposition**) to another word in the sentence.
- Remember that a **prepositional phrase** includes a preposition, its object, and all the words in between.

Independent Practice

C. Identifying Prepositions and Prepositional Phrases Write the prepositional phrase or phrases from each sentence. Underline each preposition once, and draw two lines under its object or objects.

12. Always be pleasant during a job interview.

MODEL during a job interview

13. Getting the job may depend on an interviewer's first impression.
14. Because of the competition for good jobs today, you must prepare for an interview.
15. Dress in neat and clean clothing.
16. Be sure that you arrive at the interview on time.
17. Smile at the interviewer and speak clearly to him or her.
18. Talk about your previous jobs and volunteer work.
19. After the interview, thank the interviewer for his or her time.

D. Distinguishing Between Adverbs and Prepositions Write *adverb* or *preposition* to identify each underlined word.

20. This letter arrived in today's mail.

MODEL preposition

21. It says that postal rates will go up next week.
22. Circulate the letter to all employees.
23. A copy will be posted near the mail room.
24. Everyone who walks by will see it.
25. This system has always worked before.

E. Revising: Expanding Sentences Add two prepositional phrases to each sentence. Be sure to use both nouns and pronouns as objects of prepositions. Write the expanded sentences.

26. I work.

MODEL I work in a department store with her.

27. We sell lamps.
28. The mall is busy.
29. A customer arrived.
30. The telephone rang.
31. Two more people entered.
32. It became noisy.

Application — Writing

Journal Entry Imagine that you have just been interviewed for a job. Write a journal entry that describes what happened during the interview and your feelings about the job. Use at least six prepositional phrases. If you need help writing a journal entry, see page 48 of the **Writer's Handbook.**

2 Prepositional Phrases Used as Adjectives or Adverbs

FOCUS

- A prepositional phrase that modifies a noun or a pronoun is an **adjective phrase.**
- A prepositional phrase that modifies a verb, an adjective, or an adverb is an **adverb phrase.**

Like an adjective, an adjective phrase modifies a noun or a pronoun. It tells *what kind, which one, how much,* or *how many.* The words in color are adjective phrases.

1. Lucy is a comic strip character of many talents.
   modifies noun, tells *what kind*
2. She advises those with personal problems.
   modifies pronoun, tells *which ones*

An adjective phrase can modify a noun used as the object of a preposition.

3. Lucy is ready with good advice for her patients.

Like an adverb, an adverb phrase modifies a verb, an adjective, or an adverb. It tells *when, where, how, how often,* or *to what extent.* The words in color are adverb phrases.

4. Lucy waited for a patient all morning.
   modifies verb, tells *how*
5. The office was open until noon.
   modifies adjective, tells *when*
6. The doctor will return immediately after lunch.
   modifies adverb, tells *when*
7. Lucy's office is located near an apple tree.
   modifies verb, tells *where*

A word or a phrase may separate the prepositional phrase and the word it modifies.

8. Above the desk Lucy's sign listed her rates.
9. She walked slowly around the desk.

Guided Practice

A. Identify the adjective phrase and the word it modifies.

1. Some carefully trained doctors treat only certain kinds of disorders.
2. Those with particular expertise and advanced training are called specialists.
3. Patients with serious problems may need a specialist.
4. Treatment by a specialist should solve the problem.
5. People from far away may see a specialist.

B. Identify the adverb phrase and the word it modifies.

6. On some occasions general practitioners are needed.
7. These doctors are familiar with many medical areas.
8. In their offices they treat various illnesses.
9. Their work and advice are invaluable to many families.
10. They may refer patients to a specialist.
11. The general practitioner works with many other health professionals.

> **THINK AND REMEMBER**
> - Remember that an **adjective phrase** is used to modify a noun or a pronoun.
> - Remember that an **adverb phrase** modifies a verb, an adjective, or an adverb.

Independent Practice

C. Identifying Adjective Phrases and the Words They Modify Write each sentence. Underline the adjective phrase once. Draw two lines under the word it modifies.

12. Mike has a new job in a doctor's office.

MODEL › Mike has a new job in a doctor's office.

13. He is an assistant to the doctor.
14. A well-trained physician's assistant knows much about medicine.
15. Some of the patients see Mike regularly.
16. He can treat many of the ailments himself.
17. The office near the front door is his.

D. Identifying Adverb Phrases and the Words They Modify Write each sentence. Underline the adverb phrase once. Draw two lines under the word it modifies.

18. Teri took four psychology classes during college.

MODEL Teri took four psychology classes during college.

19. She brought her tape recorder to every class.
20. Teri enjoyed the lab work on Wednesdays.
21. She worked with a lab partner.
22. In the laboratory students made psychological experiments.
23. In their reports they described a rat's learning behavior.
24. They trained the rat with cheese.
25. The rat ran successfully through a maze.
26. Teri wrote her report with her lab partner.

E. Distinguishing Between Adverb Phrases and Adjective Phrases Write the prepositional phrase. Then write *adjective phrase* or *adverb phrase* to identify it.

27. Do you know the difference between psychology and psychiatry?

MODEL between psychology and psychiatry—adjective phrase

28. Psychiatry is practiced by a medical doctor.
29. Psychologists study the behavior of people and animals.
30. Each of these sciences treats emotional problems.
31. In schools and businesses, psychology is frequently used.
32. Early in the school year, teachers can test students.
33. The tests can identify the interests of each student.
34. Some of the students may discover a career choice.
35. Industries use psychology in many ways.
36. Psychologists help businesses make the workplace more efficient for employees.

Application — Writing

Paragraphs of Comparison and Contrast Write a humorous article for your school paper in which you compare a visit to the dentist with a visit to a physician. Describe what you like and dislike about each. Use three adverb phrases and three adjective phrases in your paragraphs. If you need help writing paragraphs of comparison and contrast, see pages 41 and 42 of the **Writer's Handbook.**

3 Using Prepositions Correctly

◆ **FOCUS** Some prepositions are frequently misused.

Many people become confused when using certain prepositions. Study these pairs to learn which to use.

Between refers to two people or items. *Among* refers to three or more people or items.

1. Please sit between Wayne and Carol.
2. Among the five of them were three different opinions.

In means "within" or "inside." *Into* shows movement from the outside to the inside.

3. We jumped up and down in the pool.
4. The lifeguard stood up and jumped into the pool.

At shows that someone or something is already in place. *To* shows movement toward someone or something.

5. Diego has been at the pool for two hours.
6. He walks two miles to the pool every day.

Beside means "next to." *Besides* means "in addition to."

7. The juice machine is beside the locker room.
8. Besides apple juice, it also has orange juice and grapefruit juice.

Guided Practice

A. Choose the correct preposition in parentheses ( ) to complete each sentence.

1. Water safety classes are given (at, to) many pools in the community.
2. Swimmers can choose (between, among) public and private lessons.
3. Sign up for lessons (at, to) a Red Cross office near your home.
4. Never jump (into, in) a pool unless you can swim.
5. When you are at the beach, always swim (among, between) lifeguard stands.
6. Be especially careful (into, in) deep water.
7. (Beside, Besides) swimming rules, you should also know about boat safety.

THINK AND REMEMBER

- Learn to use troublesome pairs of prepositions correctly.

Independent Practice

B. Choosing Prepositions Write the correct preposition in parentheses ( ) to complete the sentence.

8. My family sits together (at, to) every swim meet.

MODEL at

9. Ho is racing (in, into) the next swim meet.
10. He has trained (at, to) the pool every day for the past three weeks.
11. Ho will be taking part (in, into) the medley race.
12. (Beside, Besides) him, there are three other strong swimmers on his team.
13. The swimmers divided the four strokes (between, among) themselves.
14. Larry is the fastest swimmer (between, among) the four.
15. When he gets (at, to) the end of his lane, the next racer starts.
16. Their lane is the one (beside, besides) mine.

C. Proofreading: Using Prepositions Correctly Each sentence contains one error. Rewrite the sentence correctly.

17. Lee spent his vacation to a resort in Florida.

MODEL Lee spent his vacation at a resort in Florida.

18. Snorkeling is one way to enjoy a vacation to the beach.
19. Snorkelers can see the varieties of fish into the ocean.
20. A careful diver surfaces periodically among dives.
21. The diver fits a breathing tube in his or her mouth.
22. Beside the tube and the mask, you may need a neoprene wet suit for cold water.
23. Divers must take care not to get caught between the weeds.

Application — Writing

Safety Rules Imagine that you are a lifeguard at a community pool. Write five safety rules for swimmers to follow when they are at the pool. Use the prepositions *between/among, in/into, at/to,* and *beside/besides* correctly.

4 Conjunctions

◆ **FOCUS** A **conjunction** connects words or groups of words in a sentence.

The words *and, but, or, so, yet, for,* and *nor* are common conjunctions. These words are called **coordinating conjunctions.** They connect words or groups of words that have the same function in sentences. When three or more words in a series are joined, use a comma after every word except the last.

Coordinating conjunctions can also be used to join sentences. Remember to use a comma before a coordinating conjunction when you join sentences.

1. The word *lacrosse* is French, but the game is American Indian.

Correlative conjunctions are pairs of words that, like coordinating conjunctions, join individual words, groups of words, or sentences. The words these conjunctions join should be parallel—two words, two phrases, or two sentences. Notice where the correlative conjunctions are placed in these examples.

2. Both Dad and I cheered for the Panthers.
3. The Panthers won not only the game but also the championship.
4. Either we will attend the game or we will watch it on television.

These are some common correlative conjunctions.

either. . . or	not only. . . but also	neither. . . nor
both . . . and	whether. . . or	just as . . . so

Guided Practice

A. Identify the conjunction in each sentence. Tell whether each conjunction is a *coordinating conjunction* or a *correlative conjunction.*

1. The stadium was small but crowded.
2. We stood and cheered.
3. Neither Sam nor I had eaten.
4. I found a busy but fast vendor.
5. She sold both nuts and milk.
6. He or I would stand in line.

THINK AND REMEMBER

- Use a **conjunction** to join words or groups of words.
- Use a **coordinating conjunction** to join words that have the same function in a sentence.
- Remember that **correlative conjunctions** are pairs of words that join individual words, groups of words, or sentences.

Independent Practice

B. Identifying Conjunctions Write each sentence. Underline the conjunctions once. Draw two lines under the words, phrases, or sentences they join.

7. Our gym class plays lacrosse and softball.

MODEL Our gym class plays lacrosse and softball.

8. Each squad has both a captain and a co-captain.
9. The blue team or the red team usually wins at hockey.
10. The blue team has stronger players, but the red team is quicker.
11. In cold or rainy weather, we usually stay inside.

C. Revising: Combining Sentences Combine each pair of sentences by using the coordinating conjunction or the pair of correlative conjunctions in parentheses ( ). Write each new sentence.

12. Professional athletes need daily practice. Competent coaches must help them train. (and)

MODEL Professional athletes need daily practice, and competent coaches must help them train.

13. Traveling may be exciting. It might be tiring. (or)
14. Fans love to watch their favorite team perform. They are proud when their team wins. (not only. . . but also)
15. People will cheer for a player. They may become angry when the player makes a mistake. (but)
16. The noise can distract the players. They learn to ignore it. (yet)
17. A player's life is rewarding. It is stressful. (yet)

Application — Writing

History Lacrosse was invented by North American Indians in the 1700's. Write a two-paragraph imaginary history for modern sports fans telling how the game developed. Use conjunctions in your paragraphs.

5 Interjections

◆ **FOCUS** An **interjection** is a word or a group of words that expresses feeling or emotion.

An interjection has no grammatical relationship to the rest of the sentence. It expresses feeling or emotion. When an interjection expresses strong emotion, use an exclamation point after it. When it expresses mild emotion, use a comma.

1. Well! I've never seen such strange writing.
2. Well, I think I know how to read it.

Common Interjections

ah	bravo	hush	oh, dear	oops	well
aha	gee	my	oh, my	ouch	whew
alas	hey	my goodness	oh, no	ugh	whoa
boo	hurrah	oh	say	uh oh	wow

You can also use adjectives and nouns as interjections.

Nonsense! Impossible! Good!

Guided Practice

A. Identify the interjection in each sentence.

1. Wow! This is a great idea!
2. Hey! Where did you get that?
3. Ouch! The plates are hot.
4. Oh, I know that.
5. Aha! I finally found it.

B. Complete each sentence of the conversation with an interjection.

6. DAVID: ________! What do you think of this invitation?
7. MOM: ________, I'm not sure what it says.
8. DAVID: ________! It's written backwards.
9. MOM: ________! Let's hold it up next to a mirror.
10. DAVID: ________! It's an invitation to a "backwards party"!

THINK AND REMEMBER

- Use an **interjection** to express feeling or emotion.
- Use an exclamation point or a comma after an interjection.

Independent Practice

C. Identifying Interjections Write each interjection and its punctuation.

11. Hurrah! I got permission to have a party!

MODEL Hurrah!

12. Whew! Planning a successful party can really be a lot of hard and detailed work.
13. Gee, how will we ever finish so many invitations in time for the big event?
14. Aha! We can use my new computer to put address labels on all of the envelopes.
15. Wow! That will save hours of work!
16. My, your plans are moving along rapidly.

D. Using Interjections in Sentences Write an interjection and its punctuation to complete each sentence.

17. ________ How long has it been since I've seen you?

MODEL My!

18. ________ we moved to New Orleans nearly three years ago.
19. ________ Has it really been that long?
20. ________ Living in New Orleans must be wonderful.
21. ________ my homework keeps me too busy to see all the sights of the city.
22. ________ You should do some sightseeing one weekend.

E. Writing Sentences Use each interjection in a sentence.

23. Hey!

MODEL Hey! Look at that old car!

24. Ouch!
25. Wow!
26. Nonsense!
27. Aha!
28. Good!
29. Look!
30. Oh!
31. Gosh!
32. Ugh!

Application — Writing

Dialogue Imagine that David is at a party where everything is done in reverse. People pronounce their names backward, say hello when someone leaves, and eat dessert before dinner. Write five lines of conversation overheard at the party. Write your conversation like the one in **B.** Use at least five interjections.

Building Vocabulary
Idioms

The argument between the two players got out of hand.

Fortunately, a referee was on hand to settle things.

To understand the two sentences with the cartoon, you have to go beyond the usual meaning of each word. The phrases *out of hand* and *on hand* are called idioms. Taken as a whole, each phrase means something different from the words by themselves.

An **idiom** is a commonly used expression that means something other than the meaning of its individual words. Many idioms are so familiar that most people do not even recognize them as such. Often, idioms are metaphors. If a sentence refers to a new policy *taking root,* it does not mean someone planted the policy and it is growing. It means that it is becoming established

Idioms generally are considered *informal* or *slang* and are, therefore, not standard for formal writing. If you find an informal idiom in your formal writing, you should find a way to rephrase the sentence.

1. The guests are due to *show up* at eight P.M.
2. The guests are due to *arrive* at eight P.M.

Some idioms include prepositions, and people can have difficulty choosing the correct preposition to use. Check the idiom in a dictionary if you are unsure of its use.

Idiom	Meaning	Example Sentence
in the doghouse	in disfavor	Boy, was I in the doghouse after I broke Mom's pitcher!
fed up	disgusted	I'm fed up with this project.
spill the beans	reveal a secret	Don't spill the beans about the surprise party for Denny.
the cat's pajamas	especially nice	Irwin's new skateboard is the cat's pajamas.

Reading Practice

Read each sentence. Write *standard* if there is no idiom in the sentence. Otherwise, write the idiom from the sentence, and label it *incorrect* or *informal*. Rewrite the sentence, replacing the idiom with an acceptable word or phrase. Use a dictionary if you need help.

1. Stop beating around the bush and tell me what you really think.
2. First of all, the old equipment will be no go.
3. I've got to hand it to you; you did a good job assembling the new equipment.
4. Don't let the compliment go to your head.
5. If you two agree to work together, the job can be done faster.
6. Keep an ear on their progress.

Writing Practice

Idioms can be difficult to learn. Many people use the wrong prepositions and other words on occasion. Rewrite the following conversation. Replace each mixed-up idiom with the correct idiom. Use a dictionary if you need help.

"By my watch, it is tall time for lunch," said Sam. "Let's fly the hatch and go for a picnic this afternoon. We can live it off. I'll buy our lunch at the sandwich bar."

"I have to think once about doing that," replied Terry. "I don't want to face the musician for skipping my chores. My sister said she'd put the hand on us."

"Come in; take me down on my offer."

"Will you pitch out and help me do the chores before we go?" asked Terry.

Project

See how many idioms you can find in everyday language. Listen carefully to your own conversations and to dialogues on radio and television. Look through magazine and newspaper articles and books. With your classmates, make a chart of the idioms you identify. Write a definition for each idiom.

Language Enrichment
Prepositions, Conjunctions, Interjections

LISTEN SPEAK THINK READ WRITE

Use what you know about prepositions, conjunctions, and interjections to do these activities.

Obstacle Course

Imagine that you are a radio sports commentator, and describe to your classmates a race along the pictured obstacle course. Try to describe the race vividly so that your listeners can imagine the excitement. Use prepositions in your commentary.

Creature Communication

Look through some magazines to find some photographs of various kinds of wild and domestic animals. Cut out speech balloons from paper and add dialogue to express their concerns. Use interjections. Decorate a bulletin board with the pictures.

Conjunction Junction

Play a game of "Conjunction Junction" with a small group of classmates. Make up sentences like the one below. Have each group member add to the sentence by using a conjunction.

Dad may never let me loose in the kitchen again . . . .

CONNECTING
LANGUAGE ↔ WRITING

In this unit you learned that some "little" words—prepositions, conjunctions, and interjections—can make a big difference in your writing.

◆ **Using Prepositions, Conjunctions, and Interjections in Your Writing** Knowing how to use these "little" words can make your writing more precise. Without them, a reader might not understand the connections between your thoughts. Pay special attention to the prepositions, conjunctions, and interjections you use as you do these activities.

Idioms at Play

You learned about idioms on the **Building Vocabulary** pages.

The musician in the picture could probably make better music if she understood the idiom *play by ear.* Draw a cartoon to illustrate the meaning of one of the following idioms with the word *play*: *play cat and mouse, play down, play one's cards right.* Write a caption for your cartoon.

And So On

Almost everyone overuses the word *and* when speaking. See if you belong to that majority. Use a tape recorder as you tell about what you did to get ready for school this morning. Play back the recording, and count the number of times you used the word *and.* Then write down your words, eliminating the unnecessary *and*'s and other conjunctions.

7 Unit Checkup

Think Back	Think Ahead
◆ What did you learn about paragraphs of comparison and contrast in this unit? What did you do to write one?	◆ How will what you learned about paragraphs of comparison and contrast help you to make decisions? ◆ How will knowing how to see likenesses and differences help you write paragraphs of comparison and contrast?
◆ Look at the writing you did in this unit. How did prepositions, conjunctions, and interjections help you express your ideas?	◆ What is one way you can use prepositions, conjunctions, and interjections to improve your writing?

Paragraphs of Comparison and Contrast *pages 304–305*

Read each topic sentence. Write *comparison* or *contrast* to tell the topic sentence's purpose.

1. Movies and television shows share many characteristics.
2. Jogging is much harder on the knees than walking.
3. The stresses placed on attorneys and physicians are very similar.
4. Mowing a lawn usually requires more strength than washing dishes.

Evaluating Whether to Compare or Contrast *page 306*

Read the topic sentence. Write whether each detail sentence would be useful in a paragraph of comparison or a paragraph of contrast.

Reading a book is different from watching television.

5. Books require the reader to turn pages.
6. Books are always portable, but not all televisions are.
7. To read a book, one must pay attention to the words.

Writing for an Audience and a Purpose *page 307*

Write a purpose for each of the following sentences.

8. Managing a store is a difficult occupation.
9. As Jenny danced across the floor, Bob's eyes lit up.
10. Work can be very challenging, so it is important to relax.

The Writing Process *pages 308 – 317*

Write the letter for the answer to each question.

11. What characteristic should the topic for your paragraph have?
    a. It should be narrow. **b.** It should be simple.
    c. It should be diverse.
12. When drafting, what type of details should be developed after the topic sentence?
    a. similarities **b.** differences **c.** similarities and differences
13. When revising your paragraph, what should be deleted?
    a. points that support the topic sentence **b.** details that aren't matched
    c. words used in transition

Prepositions and Prepositional Phrases *pages 320 – 322*

Write the prepositional phrase or phrases from each sentence. Underline the preposition once, and underline its object or objects twice.

14. People from the beginning of their careers have realized that it is important to balance work with recreation.
15. The ability to release tension is frequently a key to career success.
16. Workers must recognize that they are influenced indirectly by work pressures.
17. Stress in the workplace or in the home can harm a worker's job performance.
18. Employers should be sure that their workers can recognize the signs of stress.

Prepositional Phrases Used as Adjectives or Adverbs *pages 323 – 325*

Write each sentence. Underline each prepositional phrase once.

Underline twice the word it modifies.

19. Some people join clubs with exercise equipment.

20. Others become runners of very long road races.
21. People in areas where there is cable television relax as they watch professional and college sports.
22. Employees in this department are club members.
23. Most clubs have members with a desire for the social life.
24. Helping people control tension has become a concern during the last decade.
25. Employers have learned from university studies regarding stress management.
26. In these studies, scientists showed that decreased stress means increased productivity.
27. Employees produced more in calmer workplaces.
28. Now stress management is practiced by large corporations.
29. People realize in these times that handling stress is very important.

Using Prepositions Correctly *pages 326–327*

Write the correct preposition in parentheses ( ) to complete each sentence.

30. Employees should come (at, to) their job sites with the desire to work.
31. All should strive to work (in, into) the same direction.
32. They should divide all tasks (among, between) themselves.
33. A group leader should avoid a separation (between, among) himself or herself and another employee.
34. The idea is to get everyone to dive (in, into) the work.
35. A group effort helps the whole team and the company (beside, besides) those lacking ambition.
36. We should all learn to work (beside, besides) each other if we are to consider ourselves part of a team.

Conjunctions *pages 328–329*

Write each sentence. Underline the conjunctions once. Underline twice the words, phrases, or sentences they join.

37. Our tennis team plays for the fun and the exercise, not purely for the victory.
38. Even on match days, we make jokes and laugh out loud.

39. Neither the captain nor the co-captain takes the league standings very seriously.
40. The singles players are somewhat serious, but the doubles teams are very casual.
41. In practice or at matches, the emphasis is on relaxing and enjoying the team's company.
42. I am happy with that attitude, and I think most of the others on the team are satisfied also.
43. Some of our opponents are very competitive, but we think that we have enough pressures in the rest of our lives.
44. To me tennis isn't a life or death game.

Interjections *pages 330 – 331*

Write each interjection and its punctuation.

45. Wow! What a great pass she threw; it went right out of sight!
46. Aha! The coach has changed his mind about his original estimation of the team.
47. Boy, I wonder what he will do now that our team is so far ahead of the opposing team.
48. Hurrah! Coach is finally letting the second string play in an important game!
49. Oh, my! The quarterback fumbled the snap!
50. Ouch! That running back was hit hard by that linebacker.

Idioms *pages 332 – 333*

Read each sentence. Write the idiom from each sentence. Then rewrite the sentence, replacing the idiom with an acceptable word or phrase. Use a dictionary if you need help.

51. I ran into an old friend.
52. I didn't have the heart to face another Monday morning.
53. Many teenagers' ideas fly in the face of adult beliefs.
54. Let's fly the coop now while we have a chance!
55. We would be up the creek without school or work.

1-7 Cumulative Review

Four Kinds of Sentences *pages 28 – 29*

Write *sentence* or *not a sentence* to identify each group of words. For each sentence, write what kind of sentence it is.

1. Writing letters for reaching out to new business contacts.
2. Write a letter to the firm, and ask about its new line of products.
3. Did you know that there are a variety of uses for the business letter?
4. Not only for sales, persuasion, inquiries, replies, and applications, but also as contracts and permanent records.
5. Oh, what a valuable tool a letter is!
6. Some firms depend solely on letters to conduct business.

Compound Subjects and Compound Verbs *pages 37 – 38*

Write each sentence. Draw one line under each compound subject and two lines under each compound verb. Write *compound subject, compound verb,* or *both* after each sentence.

7. I never hide my feelings or pretend to be unemotional.
8. My mother and father have always communicated their emotions.
9. Parents and children should allow their true feelings to show.
10. Adults and children have the same kinds of feelings and should share them.
11. Without sharing, we develop barriers between us and prevent honest communication.
12. Good feelings and bad feelings are equally valuable and should be communicated.

Appositives *pages 86 – 87*

Write each sentence. Underline the appositive, and draw an arrow from the appositive to the noun it explains.

13. Today, Thursday, May 1, would be a good day to start my father's biography.
14. It will focus on his great dream in life, to invent a new chemical.
15. The chemical, X25-123, would make gasoline work more efficiently.

16. Consumers all across America, ordinary drivers, would save money.

17. Dad's chemical, a water derivative, would cost only pennies to manufacture.

18. It would help to conserve one of our most precious resources, our oil reserves.

Principal Parts of Verbs *pages 126 – 132*

Write each sentence, using the correct principal part of the verb in parentheses ( ).

19. Dad (stay—past) in school until he earned a master's degree in applied science.
20. He (know—past) he had to learn all the basic sciences and mathematics to reach his goal.
21. Students are (realize—present participle) that science is a basic requirement for success.
22. They have been (show—past participle) the way by their parents and teachers.
23. The successes of the past (dictate—present) the ways of the future.
24. Students are (remain—present participle) in school for longer durations of time.
25. The abilities of students (show—present) in their willingness to take on greater challenges.

Verb Tenses *pages 133 – 136*

Write the verb or verbs from each sentence below. Next to each verb, write its tense.

26. Many of today's engineers believe strongly in the study of liberal arts.
27. They had studied mathematics, chemistry, and other sciences before they went to college.
28. Now they are sorry that they have missed some of the more creative courses.
29. How will they ever imagine new concepts, innovations and designs?
30. Studies in liberal arts have assisted many to be receptive to new ideas.

Subject and Object Pronouns *pages 230 – 232*

Write the pronoun or pronouns from each sentence. Next to each pronoun, write *nominative* or *objective.*

31. He wants to be President of the United States sometime before growing old.
32. I believe that holding a national office was an idea developed in him as a child.
33. A beloved, insightful grandmother gave him that noble ambition.
34. What might she have seen in him when he was just a young schoolboy?
35. That intuition about him held secretly for so many years seems to have been right.
36. They will surely nominate him to be President of the United States on the first ballot.

Pronouns and Antecedents *pages 228 – 229*

Write each sentence. Add the pronoun in parentheses ( ) that agrees with its antecedent in number, person, and gender.

37. Alfred Nobel provided for the annual awarding of the various Nobel Prizes in (their, his) will.
38. Winners earn awards in (his/her, their) fields of expertise.
39. William Faulkner won one for (his, their) novels and short stories.
40. Faulkner shows (its, his) view of life in the southern United States in his writing.
41. Another well known American author, John Steinbeck, won (his, hers) in 1962.
42. Did Steinbeck ever imagine that (it, he) would win a Nobel Prize?

Reflexive, Intensive, and Demonstrative Pronouns *pages 235 – 236*

Write the reflexive, intensive, or demonstrative pronoun from each sentence. Then write *reflexive, intensive,* or *demonstrative* to show what kind of pronoun it is.

43. We need to make ourselves a plan for the upcoming holidays.
44. Jane herself has several good ideas.
45. The best part of her plan is that it lets us choose activities ourselves.

46. Those are the kind of easy-to-understand plans anyone can follow.
47. Jane's exciting holiday activities themselves are simple and easy.
48. The participants in the activities are all responsible for themselves.

Subject-Verb Agreement *pages 141 – 142*

Write the correct form of the verb in parentheses ( ).

49. Humanities (is, are) a required academic course at many liberal arts schools.
50. These schools (require, requires) their students to have a broad education.
51. A knowledge of languages, creative writing, and philosophy (attract, attracts) many businesses.
52. Businesses with a technical focus still (hire, hires) liberal arts majors for various departments.
53. A firm with many employees (want, wants) creativity as well as technical know-how.
54. In successful companies, managers and product designers (use, uses) abstract ideas as easily as slide rules.

Predicate Adjectives *pages 274 – 275*

Write each sentence. Underline the predicate adjective or adjectives. Draw an arrow from each predicate adjective to the word it modifies.

55. Karl Bodmer was relatively unknown before he came to work in America.
56. His career as a painter in Europe was ordinary.
57. His paintings of landscapes had been trite, typical, and monotonous.
58. Bodmer's two-year visit to the American West was lucky because it gave him a chance to do something well.
59. His paintings of American Indians were vivid and realistic.
60. The paintings Bodmer produced while in America became famous throughout the world.

Comparisons with Adjectives *pages 276 – 279*

Write the adjective of comparison from each sentence. Next to the adjective, write *positive, comparative,* or *superlative.*

61. Karl Bodmer's best paintings are of the Indians.
62. The paintings are in one of the world's finest museums.
63. Prior to his trip to America, his works received little attention.
64. Most of them are ordinary landscapes.
65. Bodmer's better works were done in the United States.
66. The change gave him a fresher outlook on his work.

Comparisons with Adverbs *pages 283 – 285*

Write each sentence. Underline each adverb. Write its degree of comparison. Draw an arrow from the adverb to the word it modifies.

67. In the early days of television, shows usually lasted thirty minutes.

68. The total programming for a day rarely exceeded twelve hours.

69. The length of a programming day has steadily increased.

70. With twenty-four-hour service, people turn on their sets more readily.

71. Cable has increased a viewer's choices dramatically.

72. Of all the possibilities, people watch sports, movies, and drama the most avidly.

73. Television has taken over entertainment more quickly than any other medium in history.

Adverb or Adjective? *pages 288 – 289*

Write the adjective or adverb from each sentence. Identify it by writing *adjective* or *adverb.* Do not write articles.

74. The idea of adventure has changed recently.
75. People used to think that adventure came solely from dangerous activities.
76. The more dangerous an activity seemed to be, the more appealing it was.

77. People are less willing now to take foolish risks.
78. Today, games have given us a different idea of danger.
79. These activities create suspense more quietly.
80. The most suspenseful games can be more exciting than reality.

Prepositions and Prepositional Phrases *pages 320 – 322*

Write the prepositional phrase or phrases from each sentence. Underline each preposition.

81. The man or woman with a smile is happy whether at work or at play.
82. These people go to work assuming that it will be fun.
83. Work is not something they do merely to put food on the table or clothes on their backs.
84. On the other hand, they put as much effort into play as they do into work.
85. They work very hard at their leisure activities, believing that they serve a purpose.
86. They get as much benefit from work as they do from play.
87. Clearly, both activities can be part of a well-balanced lifestyle.

Conjunctions and Interjections *pages 328 – 331*

Write the conjunctions and interjections. Then, write *conjunction* or *interjection* to identify them.

88. Whoa! Is that large black and white horse yours or your little sister's?
89. Most of the people that I know ride horses for pleasure or for exercise.
90. Their reasons are both obvious and not-so-obvious.
91. Right! It is an expensive sport, but it is worth it.
92. Sure! People consider their valuable horses to be either pets or investments.
93. Many people like to dress like cowboys whether they are or not.
94. Hey! Could I come over and ride that horse someday?
95. No! Neither my horse nor I would like that.
96. I will work very hard on my riding. Really!

UNIT

8

Reporting Information

◆ **COMPOSITION FOCUS: Research Report**
◆ **LANGUAGE FOCUS: Complex Sentences and Verbals**

Who invented the piano? Why did the buffalo disappear from the American frontier? Something sparks our interest, raising questions about the past and the present. To find answers, we investigate a topic. Sometimes we record the responses in a **research report,** a factual account of the topic that is based on several sources.

Research reports are written by professionals such as doctors, historians, and journalists as well as by students. Mary C. Lewis, for example, is a professional writer whose interest in education prompted her to ask, "Who started the first schools for black students?"

To answer that question, Lewis looked through books and magazines for information on black education. She took notes and then organized them to write a research report. In this unit you will learn how to get information from many different sources and how to shape it into a research report.

Mary C. Lewis wrote "Three Who Looked Ahead" *to inform* others about a topic that interested her.

Reading with a Writer's Eye
Research Report

Was there really a school in which the students used burnt splinters for pencils and mashed elderberries for ink? Mary C. Lewis, prompted by tales she heard in her childhood, found the answer to this question and others when she did research to discover who established the first black American schools. As you read her research report, notice the details she includes to keep her readers interested in her subject.

Three Who Looked Ahead

by Mary C. Lewis

During the late nineteenth century, the idea of educating black people was still so new that schools for them were rare. In many areas there were no public schools at all for blacks to attend. Nevertheless, black Americans viewed education reverently as the tool that would prepare them for better lives. Fortunately, a few pioneers stepped in and founded their own schools for black youth. Among the pioneering educators were three black women: Lucy C. Laney, Mary McLeod Bethune, and Nannie Helen Burroughs. Their experiences and motives provide important clues to anyone who seeks to understand American education.

Lucy C. Laney could appreciate education. Her parents planned many years ahead for her to attend school. Born in Macon, Georgia, in 1854, Laney obtained enough schooling to qualify for entrance to college. When she got her degree from Atlanta University in 1873, she was one of its first graduates. For the next ten years, Laney taught at several elementary schools in Georgia. Then, in 1883, a group of black parents asked her to open a private school in Augusta, Georgia. The parents were disturbed by the lack of high schools for blacks, and they didn't want limits placed on their children's future. Laney accepted their offer and opened her school in 1886.

The new school began on a small scale but grew quickly. At first, one teacher and six students were housed in a Presbyterian church basement. By its second year, the Haines Normal and Industrial Institute had 234 students. In 1914, 900 young people took classes in such fields as education, nursing, and carpentry. Laney devoted herself tirelessly to the

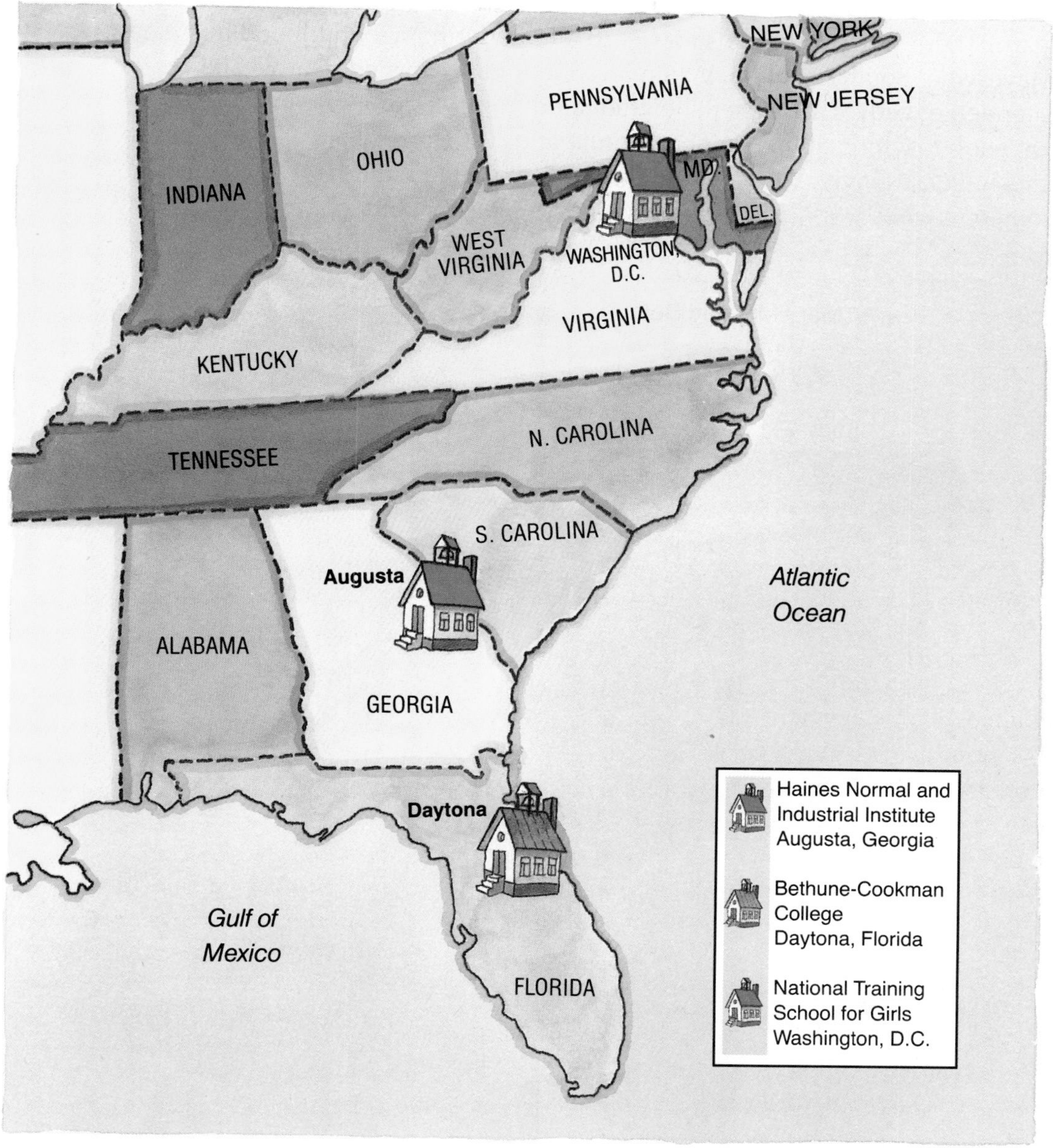

Haines Institute's growth. Throughout the years, teacher training was her main purpose. Laney wanted to prepare students to teach others, to reach out to children as Laney had reached out to them. Until her death in 1933, Lucy Laney helped the Haines Institute and its students to flourish.

Supposedly, when Mary McLeod Bethune was born in 1875, her eyes were wide open, and thus she could see into the future. If that is true, her vision was of a future in which all children would get an opportunity to learn. There were no schools for her to attend during her childhood in Mayesville, South Carolina. When a school finally opened nearby, she attended eagerly. Later, after she graduated from Moody Bible Institute, she got a job teaching at the Haines Institute and was strongly affected by Lucy Laney. Interestingly, her view of her future sharpened under the guidance of someone whose work and achievements she was to parallel.

Mary McLeod Bethune

Lucy C. Laney

In 1904, Bethune moved to Florida and established the Daytona School for Girls in Daytona Beach. Bethune found the money to open the doors and keep the school running, as she would continue to do for many years to come. The cash supply was so low at first that the students used burnt splinters for pencils and mashed elderberries for ink. Bethune's desk was really a packing crate. However, the financial struggle was only part of her challenge. Once the school was on firmer ground, many board members preferred to focus on vocational and industrial education, which would steer its students toward manual labor. Bethune insisted, at the risk of losing financial support, that Daytona's students should receive large doses of subjects such as history, foreign languages, and English literature, so that they would be prepared for future leadership. Her determination was rewarded when she convinced the board to support her approach. Many years later, in 1922, the school merged with nearby Cookman Institute and became Bethune-Cookman College.

Bethune continued as president of the college until 1942 and was on its board until her death in 1955. During the 1930s and 1940s, as she became active in national affairs, she was frequently away from Daytona Beach. She never forgot her ability to look ahead, though. "We need vision," she told a group in 1935, "for larger things, for the unfolding and reviewing of worthwhile things."

By the time Nannie Helen Burroughs was born, Lucy Laney had been teaching for ten years and little Mary McLeod was about to enter her first classroom. Nevertheless, Burroughs moved quickly to become their peer, another outstanding educator of the period. She was born in 1883 in Washington, D.C. As an honors high school student, her eye was on a teaching career. However, she was unable to get a job in the Washington public schools. An obstacle like that might have stopped some people, but it only slowed Burroughs slightly.

After a year of office jobs, Burroughs took two important steps. In 1899, at the age of sixteen, she organized a Woman's Industrial Club. The club offered temporary shelter and classes in domestic skills for young black girls, most of whom were Burroughs's age. At that time, hundreds of young women needed jobs to help support their families. Burroughs believed the jobs available to them—mainly as housekeepers and baby-sitters—should still be treated professionally. One year later, she became an administrator and fund-raiser for a coalition of black church groups. For the next nine years, Burroughs's reputation grew as an energetic, bold manager.

Nannie Helen Burroughs

Bethune-Cookman College

In 1909, Burroughs realized her dream. Her school, the National Training Institute for Girls, opened in Washington, D.C., with eight pupils. Twenty years after that first day, Burroughs could point proudly to an eight-acre campus where her students were taking high-school and junior college-level courses and widely varying subjects. Throughout her life, Burroughs continued to reach beyond any limitations placed on her. She encouraged others through speeches, newspaper articles, and her own actions, to work for the future progress of black people.

Lucy C. Laney, Mary McLeod Bethune, and Nannie Helen Burroughs were leading educators of their people. They founded three schools: the Haines Normal and Industrial Institute (now the site of the Lucy C. Laney High School), Bethune-Cookman College, and the National Training School for Girls (now the site of the Nannie Helen Burroughs School). The task of founding a school brought the women several challenges. They were in constant search for funds, for qualified teachers, and for financial and moral support from the outside world. Although their job was difficult, each woman came equipped with strong characteristics such as boldness and unflagging determination.

In addition to their impact on individual students' futures, Laney, Bethune, and Burroughs contributed something else; they shaped great institutions from nothing more than their own dreams. Like most dreamers, these three pioneers looked ahead. Like most outstanding leaders, they created better lives for those around them.

Respond

1. What interested you most in Mary C. Lewis's report? What information did she include that caught your attention?

Discuss

2. Explain in your own words the information that the report presents.
3. List some details that are included to keep readers interested in the report.
4. Which sentences help connect one part of the report to the next?

Thinking As a Writer
Analyzing a Research Report

A research report presents factual information. Its topic and the information within the report are based on current resources. A research report has a **title,** an **introduction,** a **body,** and a **conclusion.**

Writer's Guide

A research report
- presents facts in an organized form.
- has a formal and serious tone.
- is based on source material.
- has a title, an introduction, a body, and a conclusion.

Three Who Looked Ahead

During the late nineteenth century, the idea of educating black people was still so new that schools for them were rare. In many areas there were no public schools at all for blacks to attend. Nevertheless, black Americans viewed education reverently as the tool that would prepare them for better lives. Fortunately, a few pioneers stepped in and founded their own schools for black youth. Among the pioneering educators were three black women: Lucy C. Laney, Mary McLeod Bethune, and Nannie Helen Burroughs.

* * *

By the time Nannie Helen Burroughs was born, Lucy Laney had been teaching for ten years and little Mary McLeod was about to enter her first classroom. Nevertheless, Burroughs moved quickly to become their peer, another outstanding educator of the period. She was born in 1883 in Washington, D.C. As an honors high school student, her eye was on a teaching career.

* * *

In addition to their impact on individual students' futures, Laney, Bethune, and Burroughs contributed something else; they shaped great institutions from nothing more than their own dreams. Like most dreamers, these three pioneers looked ahead. Like most outstanding leaders, they created better lives for those around them.

The **title** sums up the topic of the report in a short, appealing phrase.

The **introduction** states the subject of the report, often using a brief story, a surprising fact, a question, or a quotation to arouse the reader's curiosity. It usually states the main idea of the report and may be one or two paragraphs long.

The **body** includes the writer's research presented in an organized way. It is at least three paragraphs long but may be longer, depending on the topic.

The **conclusion** sums up the paper, often using a final statistic, a quotation, or a question that will make the audience think about what has been presented.

Discuss

1. Look at the title, the introduction, the body, and the conclusion of the report. How is the information in each part different?
2. What does Mary C. Lewis do to capture her readers' interest?
3. If Mary C. Lewis had written only on the education she had as a child, would this have been a good research report? Why or why not?

Try Your Hand

A. Choose an Appropriate Topic Write *yes* for topics that are narrow enough for research reports and *no* for topics that are too broad.

1. The Lost-Wax Method of Bronze Casting
2. The National Costumes of Mexico
3. Why the United States Government Is the Best
4. Fireplace Cooking in Colonial America
5. Indians of North America

B. Analyze Unsuitable Topics Look back at each topic for which you wrote *no*. Explain why it would be unsuitable as a research topic.

C. Add to the Body and the Conclusion Read about zoos in an encyclopedia. Write a sentence about zoos for the body of a report and a sentence for the conclusion.

D. Read a Research Report With a partner, look through magazines for an article that can be classified as a research report. As you skim each article, discuss whether it has or does not have the characteristics of a research report.

Writer's Notebook

Collecting Compound Nouns Did you notice the compound nouns in the report, such as *high school*, *classroom*, and *fund-raiser?* Some compound nouns are spelled as one word, some are spelled as two, and some are joined with hyphens. Read through the report again and record in your *Writer's Notebook* any compound nouns you find. If you are unsure of the spelling of a compound noun, look it up in a dictionary when you revise your writing.

Thinking As a Writer

Connecting Ideas in a Summary

> **Writer's Guide**
>
> To write a research report, good writers
> - always summarize information in their notes.
> - sometimes summarize the main ideas of their report in their conclusion.

To write good research reports, writers summarize information. A **summary** is a brief restatement of the main ideas and important details of a longer work. Usually a summary is about one-third the length of the original material. Read this paragraph, noting the facts you consider important. Then read the summary below it. Finally, study the rules for making a summary.

> The widespread need for useful objects was the principal reason the folk artists and craftsworkers of early America made the things they did. In colonial villages and pioneer settlements, as well as in Indian and Eskimo communities, the home arts, decorative arts, and handicrafts filled an important and logical place in the lives of the people. Folk art was not considered *art* as we know it but was simply an expression of the common people in the form of objects that were intended for their own use and enjoyment.

> Folk art in early America was made for practical rather than artistic reasons. Objects made for personal use were a necessary part of life and were not considered art as we know it.

How to Summarize

1. Read the paragraph, chapter, or article completely.
2. **Paraphrase,** or write your summary in your own words.
3. Identify the main idea and state it in a topic sentence.
4. Add details that support the main idea.

Discuss

Why is it a good idea for summaries to be about one-third the length of the works they summarize?

Try Your Hand

Write Ideas in a Summary Read a newspaper or a magazine article. Summarize the main ideas. Share your summary with a partner.

Developing the Writer's Craft
Capturing the Reader's Interest

Writer's Guide

Good writers
- create a catchy title to capture the reader's interest.
- develop strong beginning and closing sentences.

Clever writers immediately capture the attention of their audience and then hold it throughout their report. Here are five techniques they use.

Anecdote: A short, amusing story.
Interesting statement: A fascinating fact.
General observation: An evaluation of a subject.
Query: A question that invites the reader to read on for the answer.
Quotation: The exact words of a famous person or an expert.

These techniques may be used throughout a research report. Read these sentences from "Three Who Looked Ahead."

1. During the late nineteenth century, the idea of educating black people was still so new that schools for them were rare.
2. Supposedly, when Mary McLeod Bethune was born in 1875, her eyes were wide open, and thus she could see into the future.
3. Like most outstanding leaders, they created better lives for those around them.

The writer carefully used techniques to capture and keep the reader's interest in each part of the report. When you write your research report, try to do the same.

Discuss

1. Look at the sentences from the report, "Three Who Looked Ahead." Which of the five techniques was used in writing each sentence?
2. Look back at the research report on pages 348–353. Find other examples of the five techniques. Was any technique not used? If so, which one?

Try Your Hand

Capture the Reader's Attention Choose a suitable topic for a research report. Write an introduction that you might write for a report of your own on that topic. Remember to write an interesting beginning and to state the subject or main idea of the report.

1 Prewriting
Research Report

Glennette decided to write a research report for her classmates. She used the information in the **Writer's Guide** to help her plan her report. Look at what she did.

Writer's Guide

Prewriting Checklist

- ☑ Brainstorm topics.
- ☑ Limit your topic.
- ☑ Think about your audience and your purpose.
- ☑ Gather information from appropriate sources.
- ☑ Organize the facts.

◆ Brainstorming and Selecting a Topic

First, Glennette thought of possible subjects. Her teacher had asked for a report on an aspect of native heritage. Glennette looked through her history book to get ideas. She thought about her family heritage. Then she jotted down her ideas.

~~Jamaican customs~~
Shakers
~~Southern cooking~~
~~Algonquin Indians~~

Glennette crossed out subjects that would be hard to research. She decided to write about Shakers, because she lived near a Shaker village.

Glennette's next task was to limit her subject. She kept narrowing her topic until she had the right one.

Shakers
Shaker communities
Shaker lifestyle
Shaker products

Glennette chose "Shaker products" for her topic. To help her in her search for information, she phrased the topic as two questions: "What were some Shaker products and designs? Do these products and designs have any influence today?"

Discuss

1. Look at the topics Glennette crossed off her list. Why did she eliminate each one?
2. What problems could arise from choosing too broad a topic?

◆ Gathering Information

After Glennette selected her topic, she gathered information for her research report. To locate information, she first looked in the card catalogue and found several useful books. Next, she checked the *Readers' Guide to Periodical Literature.* For more information on using the card catalogue or the *Readers' Guide,* see the **Writer's Handbook.**

While she was at the library, Glennette checked reference sources. She looked for nonprint media resources too. For more information about using nonprint media, see the **Writer's Handbook.**

Next, Glennette made bibliography cards for all her sources. She knew that it was necessary to credit her sources so that others could find them. She numbered each source for easy reference. Later, Glennette would alphabetize her bibliography cards and use them to make her bibliography.

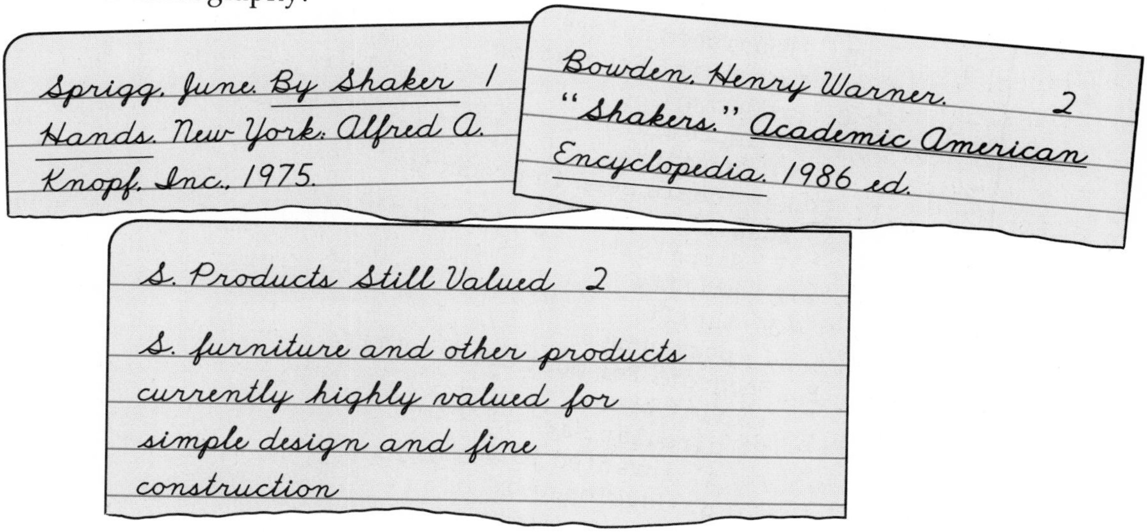
Sprigg, June. By Shaker 1
Hands. New York: Alfred A.
Knopf, Inc., 1975.
Bowden, Henry Warner. 2
"Shakers." Academic American
Encyclopedia. 1986 ed.
S. Products Still Valued 2
S. furniture and other products
currently highly valued for
simple design and fine
construction

Glennette took notes from her sources and recorded them on 3″ × 5″ note cards. For each note card, she put the source number in the upper right-hand corner and a brief heading in the upper left-hand corner. She summarized only one fact from one source on each card.

After her library research, Glennette visited a nearby Shaker village, where she interviewed a resident as part of her research.

Discuss

1. What were some of the sources Glennette used?
2. Where else might Glennette search for information?

◆ Organizing Information

After Glennette had gathered her information, she was ready to use her notes to write an outline. First, she organized her note cards in the order in which she wanted to discuss the facts. Then she wrote her outline, giving it a working title. She wrote a heading for the main idea of each paragraph in her report. She wrote a subheading for each supporting idea that would appear in the detail sentences.

The Shaker Tradition

I. Shakers defined
  A. American society of men and women
  B. Flourished before Industrial Revolution
  C. Products
    1. implements
    2. furniture

II. Shaker ideals seen in products
  A. Ideals
    1. simplicity
    2. utility
    3. thrift
    4. permanence
  B. Products for most areas of life
    1. flat broom
    2. circular saw
      a. invented 1810
      b. developed by Shaker woman

Discuss

In which part of her research report did Glennette plan to explain who Shakers are? Why do you think she placed that information there?

Try Your Hand

Now plan a research report of your own.

A. Brainstorm, Select, and Narrow a Topic Brainstorm a list of possible topics. Think about each topic and your audience.

- Cross out topics for which you cannot get enough information.
- Cross out topics that are inappropriate for a research report.
- Circle the most interesting or stimulating of the remaining topics.
- Form your topic into a question to be answered in your report.

B. Gather Information Locate sources of information by going to the library or another place where you can find material about your topic. Identify each source with a bibliography card and a number. Summarize the important information on note cards. If you are interviewing someone, follow the **Tips on How to Interview.**

C. Organize Your Information Look over your notes.

- Think about your audience. Make sure your notes contain the necessary details that will tell your audience the complete answer to the question you formed when you selected your topic.
- Make an outline for your research report. Show on your outline which facts you will include in the introduction, the body, and the conclusion. Use an appropriate order to arrange your facts.

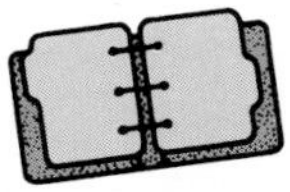

Save your notes and outline in your *Writer's Notebook*. You will use them when you draft your research report.

Listening and Speaking
Tips on How to Interview

You may want to interview local experts as part of your research for your report. Here are the steps you should follow:

1. First, research your topic. This will help you ask better questions.
2. Call or write the expert to arrange a time and place for the interview.
3. Be on time for the interview. Be polite and well-groomed.
4. During the interview, listen carefully to the expert's answers.
5. Take notes carefully. Paraphrase and summarize when possible.
6. Thank the person for the interview.

2 Drafting
Research Report

Glennette followed the checklist in the **Writer's Guide** to draft her research report. Look at what she did.

The Shaker Tradition

The Shakers were a religious society of men and women who lived in nearly twenty locations in the eastern United States. This was before the Industrial Revolution. What they left the world are their designs for implements and furniture. I think Shaker things are neat.

The Shakers were determined to perform each task efficiently. The tasks should be done thriftily too. They therefore contributed inventions or improvements in many areas of everyday life.

Writer's Guide

Drafting Checklist

- ☑ Use your notes for ideas.
- ☑ Draft one paragraph for each Roman numeral in your outline.
- ☑ Write a topic sentence that states the main idea for each paragraph.
- ☑ Write detail sentences for each paragraph according to the subheadings in your outline.

Discuss

Where might Glennette have placed additional details? Why?

Try Your Hand

Now you are ready to write a research report.

A. Review Your Information Think about the information you have gathered and organized. If you need more, recheck your sources.

B. Think About Your TAP Remember that your task is to write a research report. Your purpose is to inform your audience about the topic.

C. Write Your First Draft Use your **Drafting Checklist** to help you write your research report.

When writing the draft, get your ideas onto paper. Do not worry about spelling, punctuation, or grammar. You can correct the draft later.

Task: What?
Audience: Who?
Purpose: Why?

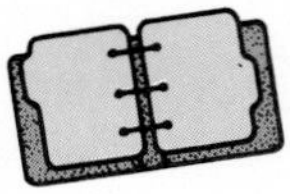

Save your first draft in your *Writer's Notebook*. You will use it when you revise your research report.

3 Responding and Revising
Research Report

Glennette used the checklist in the **Writer's Guide** to revise her research report. Look at what she did.

Checking Information

Glennette realized that she had included a personal comment about the Shakers. She used this mark to cut it.

Checking Organization

Glennette saw that her second paragraph did not flow very well. She used this mark to move the last sentence to the beginning of the paragraph.

Checking Language

Glennette wanted to add variety to her second paragraph. She used this mark to combine two short sentences into a longer sentence. She also decided that her first paragraph was dull. Glennette used this mark ∧ to add an introductory question to the paragraph.

Writer's Guide

Revising Checklist

- Read your report to yourself or to a partner.
- Think about your audience and your purpose. Add or cut information.
- Check to see that your facts are organized correctly.
- Check for monotonous sentences.

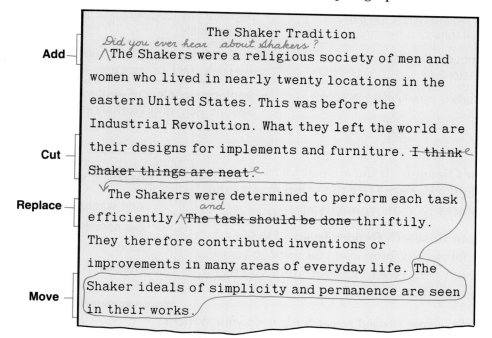

The Shaker Tradition

Add — *Did you ever hear about Shakers?* ∧The Shakers were a religious society of men and women who lived in nearly twenty locations in the eastern United States. This was before the Industrial Revolution. What they left the world are their designs for implements and furniture. Cut — ~~I think Shaker things are neat.~~

Replace — The Shakers were determined to perform each task efficiently ∧*and* ~~. The task should be done~~ thriftily. They therefore contributed inventions or improvements in many areas of everyday life. Move — The Shaker ideals of simplicity and permanence are seen in their works.

Discuss

1. How did Glennette improve the introduction?
2. What other changes might Glennette make? Explain your answer.

Try Your Hand

Now revise your first draft.

A. Read Your First Draft As you read your research report, think about your audience and your purpose. Read your draft silently or to a partner to see whether it is complete and well organized. Ask yourself or your partner the questions in the box.

Responding and Revising Strategies

✔ Respond **Ask yourself or a partner:**	✔ Revise **Try these solutions:**
◆ Have I answered the initial question that I formed when I chose my topic?	◆ Find additional details in your outline and notes and **add** them.
◆ Does my report have an introduction, a body of three or more paragraphs, and a conclusion?	◆ **Add** any sections that are missing or incomplete.
◆ Does my writing reflect the serious and formal tone of a research report?	◆ **Replace** any language that is inappropriate.
◆ Will my introduction catch the reader's interest?	◆ **Add** an interest-catching quotation, anecdote, fact, or question.
◆ Did I include a variety of sentences?	◆ **Replace** monotonous sentences. See the **Revising Workshop** on page 365.

B. Make Your Changes If the answer to any question in the box is *no,* try the solution. Use the **Editor's Marks** to show your changes.

C. Review Your Research Report Again Decide whether there is anything else you want to revise. Keep revising your research report until you feel it is well organized and complete.

EDITOR'S MARKS

- ∧ Add something.
- Cut something.
- Move something.
- Replace something.

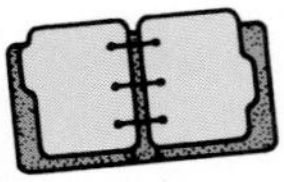

Save your revised research report in your *Writer's Notebook.* You will use it when you proofread your report.

Revising Workshop
Achieving Sentence Variety

Good writers vary their sentences to make them interesting. When they revise, they may change the length, the structure, the word order, or the types of sentences they use. Read the following sentences.

1. "Yankee Doodle" is a national tune. It has a long history. The song has been popular for over two centuries. Its origin remains uncertain. Legends have arisen over the years. One of them credits the British. It singles out one person.
2. "Yankee Doodle" is a national tune with a long history. The song has been popular for over two centuries, but its origin remains uncertain. Legends have arisen over the years. There is one that credits the British. Exactly whom does this legend single out?

In the first example, the writer used a series of short statements in natural word order. In the second, the writer varied the lengths and kinds of sentences. In one place, two short sentences were changed to a longer sentence. To vary the structure, two sentences were combined to form a compound sentence. The word order in one sentence was inverted. Another sentence was changed from a statement to a question. The second set of sentences is more interesting to read than the first.

Practice

Rewrite each group of sentences according to the direction in parentheses ( ).

1. Dr. Richard Shuckburg was British. He was a physician for the army. Supposedly, he composed the words to "Yankee Doodle." This was in the 1750's. (Vary the sentence length.)
2. The legend says the doctor composed the song for a purpose. His intent was to make fun of the untrained Yankee troops. (Change a statement into a question.)
3. Evidence for this theory is scant. (Change the word order.)
4. The British are said to have marched to this tune. This was on their way to Lexington and Concord. (Change one sentence's length.)
5. On their way back, the tables were turned. The victorious Americans sang it loudly as they chased the British. Since then, it has been an American tune. (Change one statement to an exclamation.)

4 Proofreading
Research Report

Writer's Guide

Proofreading Checklist

- Check for errors in capitalization.
- Check for errors in punctuation.
- Check to see that all your paragraphs are indented.
- Check for errors in grammar. Be sure that you have used prepositions correctly.
- Circle any words you think are misspelled. Find out how to spell them correctly.
- ⇨ For proofreading help, use the **Writer's Handbook.**

After revising her research report, Glennette used the **Writer's Guide** and the **Editor's Marks** to proofread it. Look at what she did.

¶They are responsible ~~to~~ for the invention of the flat broom, the pill form of medicine, the circular saw (developed by a shaker woman in 1810), the common clothespin, a revolving oven, a pea sheller, and a tool for paring, coring, and quartering apples, among many other things.

The continued use of many of (there) their inventions and the lasting popularity of Shaker furniture designs ~~is~~ are testimony to both their skillfulness and the ideals behind it⊙ their creations were planned to last, never to become outdated, and to have a look of (simplity) simplicity.

EDITOR'S MARKS

- ≡ Capitalize.
- ⊙ Add a period.
- ∧ Add something.
- ∧ Add a comma.
- ∨∨ Add quotation marks.
- Cut something.
- Replace something.
- Transpose.
- ◯ Spell correctly.
- ¶ Indent paragraph.
- / Make a lowercase letter.

Discuss

1. Look at Glennette's proofread report. What kinds of mistakes did she make?
2. Why did she change the preposition *to* to *for*?

Try Your Hand

Proofread Your Research Report Now use the **Writer's Guide** and the **Editor's Marks** to proofread your research report.

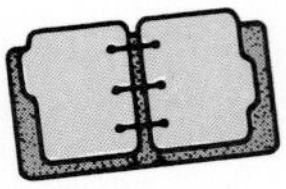

Save your corrected report in your *Writer's Notebook.* You will use it when you publish your research report.

5 Publishing
Research Report

Glennette made a clean copy of her report and checked it to be sure she had not left anything out. Then she and her classmates published their research reports by producing a heritage magazine. You can find Glennette's report on page 60 of the **Writer's Handbook.**

Here's how they published their research reports.

Writer's Guide

Publishing Checklist

- ☑ Make a clean copy of your report.
- ☑ Check to see that nothing is left out.
- ☑ Be sure that there are no mistakes.
- ☑ Share your report in a special way.

1. Working as a group, they decided what size their magazine would be and whether it would be illustrated. Then they designed a cover for their magazine, including a title and an illustration.

2. They planned how each page in the magazine would look. They determined how wide to type every report. Since they intended to include illustrations, they planned where to leave space for them. They retyped their reports to the right width. They added illustrations when their final draft was typed.

3. Glennette and her classmates worked together to organize their reports in the order in which they would appear. They numbered the pages and created a table of contents.

4. They made duplicate copies of each of the finished pages of the magazine. Each student assembled in numerical order his or her own copy of the magazine and then bound it together.

Writing in the Content Areas

Writer's Guide

When you write, remember the stages of the Writing Process.

- Prewriting
- Drafting
- Responding and Revising
- Proofreading
- Publishing

Use what you have learned to write about an aspect of American heritage. You can write a brief report or choose another form of writing. Use one of these ideas or an idea of your own.

Social Studies

The history of the town or city in which you live is an important part of your heritage. Interview historians, political officials, or other citizens who are knowledgeable about your city's or town's past. You might want to find out about the oldest buildings, influential citizens of the past, or other parts of your hometown's history.

Literature

America's literary heritage is one of the richest in the world. American writers and poets have numbered in the thousands. Choose a literary figure of the past, perhaps one who lived in your own state. Find out about his or her background. Tell what the author or poet wrote about.

Fine Arts

Wherever in the world it is played, "Yankee Doodle" has an American sound. Research another American patriotic song. (Other examples are "America the Beautiful" and "The Star-Spangled Banner.") Find out who wrote it and when it became popular. If you like to sing or play an instrument, add music to your presentation.

Physical Education

Whether the game is baseball, football, or another sport, cheering for the home team has long been an American pastime. Choose a sport you like and find out about its history. You might also want to tell about terms from that sport that have become part of the English language, such as *armchair quarterback* and *strike out*.

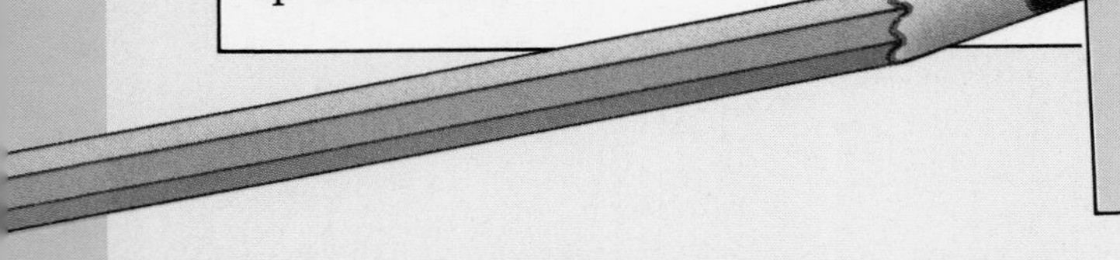

CONNECTING
WRITING ↔ LANGUAGE

Reading a research report may be an interesting learning experience. A research report may tell the reader something he or she did not know before. What do you learn about America's heritage from reading this portion of a research report?

> In the closing years of the nineteenth century in the United States, a major summer event in a small town was the arrival of a traveling chautauqua (shə tȯʹ kwə). The exciting news spread through a small town as the tents of these writers, explorers, politicians, musicians, and storytellers were set up. Interested townsfolk began to gather and to read the signs that announced coming attractions. Singing, storytelling, and dancing seemed to be the favorites of the young people.
>
> Named for a lake in western New York, the chautauqua movement began in 1874.

◆ **Complex Sentences and Verbals in a Research Report** In this excerpt from a much longer report, the variety of sentences keeps the information interesting. The words highlighted in color also make the report interesting. These words are verbals. *Closing, traveling, exciting, interested,* and *coming* are participles, while *Named for a lake in western New York* is a participial phrase. *Singing, storytelling,* and *dancing* are gerunds, and *to gather* and *to read* are infinitives.

◆ **Language Focus: Complex Sentences and Verbals** The following lessons will help you learn more about using complex sentences and verbals in your own writing.

1 Complex Sentences

◆ **FOCUS** A **complex sentence** consists of an independent clause and at least one subordinate clause.

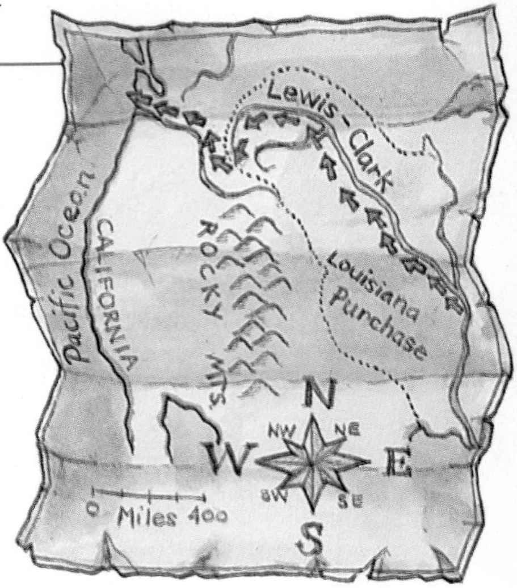

A **clause** is a group of words that contains a subject and a verb. An **independent clause** can stand alone as a simple sentence. When you join two independent clauses, you form a compound sentence.

1. Pioneers had explored west to the Mississippi, but no Americans had mapped the land beyond.

A **subordinate clause** is a clause that cannot stand alone. A subordinate clause appears in color.

2. The land was unexplored by Americans because France owned it.

Subordinate clauses are introduced by such words as *since, because, when, as, if,* and *while,* which are called **subordinating conjunctions.**

A complex sentence contains one independent clause and at least one subordinate clause.

subordinate clause — independent clause

3. When France offered to sell the land, the United States bought it.

Use a comma to set off a subordinate clause at the beginning of or in the middle of a sentence.

4. Since the territory was unknown, President Thomas Jefferson ordered an expedition.

Guided Practice

A. Tell whether each clause is *independent* or *subordinate.*

1. so that they can move fast
2. pioneers canoe down rivers
3. as they blaze new trails
4. explorers suffer hardships
5. because nature worked against them

THINK AND REMEMBER

- Remember that a **complex sentence** has an independent clause and one or more subordinate clauses.
- Use a **subordinating conjunction** to introduce a subordinate clause.

Independent Practice

B. Identifying Kinds of Clauses Write *independent* or *subordinate* to identify each clause.

6. the expedition followed the Missouri River

MODEL independent

7. where they built a fort
8. they hired a fur trader
9. his wife was Sacajawea
10. she was a Shoshone
11. because she could help them
12. when they encountered Shoshone

C. Revising: Combining Sentences Combine each pair of sentences into one complex sentence. Use the subordinating conjunction in parentheses ( ).

13. I see pictures of early immigrants. I think of pioneers. (whenever)

MODEL Whenever I see pictures of early immigrants, I think of pioneers.

14. Pioneers braved the wilderness. They could find farmland. (so that)
15. Settlers found fertile farmland in Oregon. Thousands more headed there. (when)
16. Immigrants also braved the unknown. They came to the United States. (when)
17. Industry boomed here. Thousands of workers were needed. (because)
18. They had escaped poverty and war. They faced hardships here also. (although)

Application — Writing

Journal Captain Meriwether Lewis kept a journal during his trek across the country. Imagine that you are making a journey across the country or across your state today. Write a week of journal entries describing your encounters and the sights. Use at least seven complex sentences in your writing. If you need help writing a journal entry, see page 48 of the **Writer's Handbook.**

2 Adjective Clauses

◆ **FOCUS** An **adjective clause** is a subordinate clause that modifies a noun or a pronoun. It often begins with a relative pronoun.

An adjective clause is a subordinate clause and must appear in a complex sentence with an independent clause. An adjective clause modifies a noun or a pronoun. The words in color are adjective clauses.

1. Each person who enjoys old movies came into the room.
2. Point out those whom you recognize.

An adjective clause is often introduced by a relative pronoun.

Relative Pronouns	Sentence Examples
who, whom, whose (refer to people)	Do you see the man *who* invited you? These are the actors *whom* I described. I met a boy *whose* cousin is an actor.
which (refers to animals or things)	He owns a famous dog, *which* was in a movie.
that (refers to people, animals, or things)	Don't miss the movie *that* won four awards.

Adjective clauses are sometimes introduced by *where* or *when.*

3. This is the location where the movie was filmed.
4. It was filmed on the day when a spectacular rainbow appeared.

An adjective clause is either restrictive or nonrestrictive. A **restrictive clause** identifies the noun or the pronoun it modifies. Do not use commas with a restrictive clause.

5. The film that we saw was *A Night at the Opera.*

A **nonrestrictive clause** gives more information about the noun or pronoun it modifies. It should be set off by commas. If you can leave a clause out of a sentence without losing the basic meaning of the sentence, the clause is nonrestrictive.

6. Groucho Marx , who is my favorite comedian, starred in the movie.

Link to Speaking and Writing

Use *which* in nonrestrictive clauses to refer to animals or things. Use *that* in restrictive clauses to refer to people, animals, or things.

The movie, which was made in 1935, is a classic comedy.
The brothers that made up the comedy team were Groucho, Harpo, Chico, and Zeppo.

Guided Practice

A. Identify the adjective clause in each sentence. Name the relative pronoun that introduces the clause.

1. The films that I like best are old comedies.
2. Have you ever seen *In the Navy*, which stars Bud Abbott and Lou Costello?
3. Bud Abbott, who plays Smokey, keeps outsmarting his friend.
4. Abbott and Costello were two comics whom audiences loved.
5. Comedies that include slapstick humor make me laugh.

B. 6. – 10. Identify whether each clause in **A** is *restrictive* or *nonrestrictive*.

THINK AND REMEMBER

- Remember that an **adjective clause** modifies a noun or a pronoun.
- Remember that the relative pronouns *who, whose, whom, which,* and *that* introduce adjective clauses.
- Remember that an adjective clause can be restrictive or nonrestrictive.

Independent Practice

C. Identifying Adjective Clauses Write the adjective clause, and underline the relative pronoun. Write *restrictive* or *nonrestrictive* to tell what kind of adjective clause it is.

11. Jerry owns posters that advertise old movies.

MODEL that advertise old movies—restrictive

12. His collection, which is huge, has six Marx brothers posters.
13. Look at the one that was used for *Duck Soup*.

14. This is a photograph of Margaret Dumont, who co-starred in the movie.
15. She was the woman who usually was duped by one of the Marx brothers.
16. Do you know of other actresses whose film careers started with the Marx brothers' movies?

D. Using *Which* and *That* Correctly Write each sentence. Choose *which* or *that* to introduce the adjective clause. Add commas where necessary.

17. This show ________ I have seen before has some very tough questions.

MODEL This show, which I have seen before, has some very tough questions.

18. What was the name of the quiz show ________ Groucho Marx hosted?
19. *You Bet Your Life* ________ started on radio later moved to television.
20. Each night the announcer would say the secret word ________ was worth one hundred dollars.
21. The questions ________ stumped many contestants were often quite difficult.
22. I answered a question ________ no one on the show could answer.

E. Writing Sentences Write sentences, using each of the following words to introduce an adjective clause.

23. who

MODEL My sister, who is in the tenth grade, hopes to be a singer.

24. which
25. that
26. whom
27. whose

Application — Writing

Paragraph Write a paragraph telling your classmates about the characters and the story line in a movie. Be sure that you include enough details to help the reader visualize the action. Use at least four adjective clauses in your paragraph.

3 Adverb Clauses

◆ **FOCUS** An **adverb clause** is a subordinate clause that modifies a verb, an adjective, or an adverb. It begins with a subordinating conjunction.

Like an adverb, an adverb clause modifies a verb, an adjective, or an adverb. An adverb clause begins with a subordinating conjunction. The words in color are adverb clauses.

1. Steve laughed when he read the Thurber cartoon . modifies verb
2. James Thurber is funny because his humor is dry . modifies adjective
3. I am reading his stories faster than I should . modifies adverb

Commonly Used Subordinating Conjunctions				
after	as long as	if	though	whenever
although	as soon as	since	unless	where
as	because	so that	until	wherever
as if	before	than	when	while

When you write an adverb clause at the beginning or in the middle of a sentence, use a comma to separate it from the independent clause.

4. When Thurber was in college, he edited a humor magazine.
5. Thurber , although he had poor vision, drew wonderful cartoons.

Guided Practice

A. Identify the adverb clause in each sentence. Name the subordinating conjunction. Then tell what word each adverb clause modifies.

1. When I read "The Secret Life of Walter Mitty," I howled.
2. Although he leads a dull life, Mitty has a wild imagination.
3. He retreats into his fantasy life whenever he can.
4. He daydreams madly until someone interrupts him.

THINK AND REMEMBER

- Remember that an **adverb clause** is a subordinate clause used as an adverb.
- Use commas to set off adverb clauses at the beginning or in the middle of sentences.

Independent Practice

B. Identifying Adverb Clauses Write the adverb clause. Underline the subordinating conjunction.

5. Although it is easy to read, humor is hard to write.

MODEL Although it is easy to read

6. Thurber wrote as if he were speaking.
7. While Thurber wrote about life in America, P. G. Wodehouse wrote humorous tales about English life.
8. His characters are exaggerated so that they become caricatures.
9. Whenever you read about Bertie Wooster, you are also likely to meet the butler Jeeves.

C. Proofreading: Adding Commas Write each sentence, adding commas where necessary.

10. If you ever get a chance you should go to a comedy club.

MODEL If you ever get a chance, you should go to a comedy club.

11. The comedians although they are amateurs are quite funny.
12. Because the clubs are small they are likely to be crowded.
13. If the routines are good you will laugh all night.
14. Comedy though it looks spontaneous must be rehearsed.
15. Comics when they tell a joke should not laugh themselves.
16. While the audience laughs the comic is thinking of the next joke.

D. Revising: Combining Sentences Combine each pair of sentences, using the subordinating conjunction in parentheses.

17. I laughed at the joke. Marlee laughed. (because)

MODEL I laughed at the joke because Marlee laughed.

18. Vince tells a joke. Everyone laughs. (whenever)
19. I usually start to laugh. I hear the punchline. (before)
20. Vince sometimes tells a joke. It happened to him. (as if)
21. We always listen. Vince has more funny stories. (as long as)

Application — Writing

Paragraph of Comparison or Contrast Write a paragraph that compares or contrasts the styles of two comedians. Use at least four adverb clauses in your paragraph. If you need help writing a paragraph of comparison or contrast, see pages 41 and 42 of the **Writer's Handbook.**

4 Noun Clauses

◆ **FOCUS** A **noun clause** is a subordinate clause that is used in the same way as a noun.

A noun clause is another kind of subordinate clause. It is used in the same way as a noun.

Subject **1.** What she made was a doll.

Direct object **2.** I wonder who taught her.

Predicate nominative **3.** The amazing part is that she used a cornhusk.

Object of a preposition **4.** Toys were made from whatever was handy.

These words may introduce a noun clause.

who	whose	whom	which
what	whatever	whichever	whomever
whoever	that	when	where
why	how	whether	if

Some of these words also introduce an adjective clause or an adverb clause. You can recognize a noun clause by its use in the sentence.

5. I know when this toy was made. noun clause—used as direct object

6. This is the toy that was popular. adjective clause—modifies *toy*

7. Adults carved toys when there was time. adverb clause—modifies *carved*

Guided Practice

A. Identify the noun clause in each sentence.

1. I see that you have an old toy.
2. Tell me what it is called.
3. The name is what made me laugh.
4. Whatever you said was funny.
5. I'll repeat it to whomever I see.
6. I know when I should leave.

THINK AND REMEMBER

- Remember that a **noun clause** is a subordinate clause used as a noun.

Independent Practice

B. Identifying Noun Clauses Write the noun clause. Write *subject, direct object, predicate nominative,* or *object of a preposition* to show how the noun clause is used.

7. What makes collectors happy are handmade toys.

MODEL What makes collectors happy—subject

8. I think that mechanical toys are funny.
9. Whoever invented a flipperdinger was clever.
10. He or she understood why it would amuse a child.
11. Look carefully at how this toy was made.
12. What was used was some wire, wood, and string.
13. A pebble was what made the head bob.
14. Worn spots show that a child liked a toy.

C. Distinguishing Between Noun Clauses and Other Clauses Write the subordinate clause in each sentence. Write *noun clause, adverb clause,* or *adjective clause.*

15. Let me explain how you can make furniture with peas.

MODEL how you can make furniture with peas—noun clause

16. Here is some paper that you use for the seat.
17. After you put peas on four toothpick legs, add four toothpick stretchers for the seat.
18. I wonder if raw egg will glue the paper to the stretchers.
19. A paper doll is the only toy that can sit on this stool.
20. Please be careful when you handle it.

D. Writing Sentences Write six sentences that include a noun clause. Begin with each of these words.

21. what

MODEL What you said about the car was the funniest part of the story.

22. whoever
23. why
24. that
25. when
26. which
27. whenever

Application — Speaking, Listening, and Writing

Interview Ask an adult you know to describe a favorite toy or game he or she had as a child. Find out why the person liked it so much. Write a paragraph telling your class what you learned. Use noun clauses in your paragraph.

5 Misplaced Modifiers

◆ **FOCUS** A modifier should be placed as close as possible to the word it modifies.

If a modifier is misplaced, the meaning of the sentence may be lost. The first sentence is unclear. The revised sentence makes more sense.

1. I read about unusual ways to earn a living with great interest.
2. With great interest I read about unusual ways to earn a living.

You should also place adjectives and adverbs close to the words they modify. Notice how the meaning of the sentence changes when you vary the position of the word *just*.

3. I just read that article.
4. I read just that article.

A prepositional phrase should also closely follow the word it modifies.

5. One woman herded sheep from Colorado. modifies sheep
6. One woman from Colorado herded sheep. modifies woman

Place a clause next to the word it modifies.

7. The person is my friend who wrote the article. modifies friend
8. The person who wrote the article is my friend. modifies person

Guided Practice

A. Identify whether the underlined modifier in each sentence is *correct* or *misplaced*.

1. He said in the morning he was going to clean the chimney.
2. It takes about 1½ to 2 hours to clean a chimney.
3. With top hats I read that they wear black suits.
4. More chimney sweeps in our town are needed.
5. Would you climb to the top that is forty feet high of a roof?

B. 6.–10. For each sentence in **A,** put the misplaced modifier in the correct position. Tell which sentences require no change.

THINK AND REMEMBER

- Place a **modifier** as close as possible to the word it modifies.

Independent Practice

C. Identifying Misplaced Modifiers Write *correct* or *misplaced* to describe the underlined modifier in each sentence.

11. A person should join a circus who wants to be a clown.

MODEL misplaced

12. For a year first you will have to attend a challenging and vigorous clown school.
13. Some successful and effective clowns use gestures to communicate only.
14. Clowns may occasionally work in small groups who have separate personalities.
15. With a new painted face, a clown can change personalities.
16. Hilarious clowns frequently entertain children while they're working.

D. Revising: Rewriting Sentences Rewrite each sentence, changing its meaning by moving the word *just* or *only* to a different position.

17. I just stopped by to show you this advertisement.

MODEL I stopped by just to show you this advertisement.

18. I will visit with you for only five minutes.
19. I saw the ad just this morning in the local newspaper.
20. The book in the ad tells just how to set up your own business.
21. The book that may change your financial future costs only $25.
22. Can you lend me $20 just until Monday?
23. I'll only pay you at that time.
24. I just wanted to read about financial planning.
25. I want to share my thoughts only with you.

Application — Writing and Speaking

Oral Report Think of an unusual job that is familiar to you. Write a paragraph describing the job's duties and the qualifications that a person needs for such work. Present your paragraph to your class in an oral report. Use modifiers correctly.

6 Participles and Participial Phrases

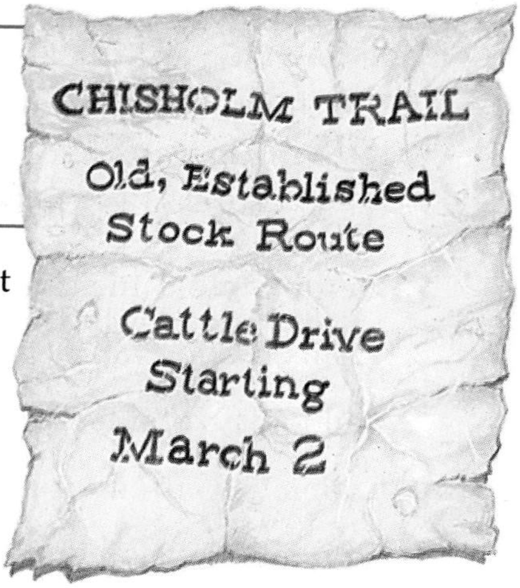

FOCUS

- A **participle** is a verbal used as an adjective.
- A **participial phrase** consists of a participle and its related words.

A **verbal** is a word that is formed from a verb but is used as a noun, an adjective, or an adverb. A participle is one kind of verbal. It functions as an adjective and modifies a noun or a pronoun.

1. A frightened herd might stampede for miles.

A participial phrase is a group of related words that contains a participle and acts as an adjective.

2. The Chisholm Trail, stretching north, started in Mexico.
3. Named for Jesse Chisholm, the trail is famous in folklore.

Use commas to set off participial phrases modifying subjects if the phrase is not necessary to retain the meaning of the sentence.

4. Dodge City, made famous during cattle drives, is historical.

Guided Practice

A. Name the participle or participial phrase in each sentence. Identify the word each participle modifies.

1. Texas longhorn cattle are a vanishing breed.
2. Descended from Spanish herds, they were hardy and tough.
3. Land once roamed by longhorns now supports Herefords.
4. Herefords, known by their white faces, are fine beef cattle.
5. The western grasslands are ideal for these grazing cattle.

THINK AND REMEMBER

- Remember that a **verbal** is formed from a verb but functions as a noun, an adjective, or an adverb.
- Remember that a **participle** is used as an adjective.
- Remember that a **participial phrase** contains a participle and acts as an adjective.

Independent Practice

B. Identifying Participles and Participial Phrases Write each sentence. Underline the participle or participial phrase. Draw an arrow to the word it modifies.

6. Arriving in Kansas, cows were driven into rail yards.

MODEL Arriving in Kansas, cows were driven into rail yards.

7. Herded into cattle cars, they were sent to Chicago.
8. Trains leaving for the stockyards were loaded daily.
9. Railroads crossing Texas ended the cattle drives.
10. Trains, also used for passengers, were cheaper and faster.
11. Two railroads joining the east and west coasts met in 1869.
12. A golden spike driven into the ground marked the junction.

C. Proofreading: Using Commas Write each sentence. Insert commas where necessary.

13. Texas once claimed by Spain became part of Mexico.

MODEL Texas, once claimed by Spain, became part of Mexico.

14. Controlled by Mexico Texans revolted in 1835.
15. Chosen by the Texans Sam Houston became the army commander.
16. His army consisting of 900 soldiers faced 1200 Mexicans.
17. Surprised by the Texans the Mexicans were defeated at San Jacinto.
18. General Santa Anna captured in battle granted independence to Texas.

D. Writing Sentences Write a sentence using each participle or participial phrase.

19. booming

MODEL Booming frontier towns were established in the 1860's.

20. beginning a new life
21. unexplored
22. established by pioneers
23. expanding
24. building
25. creating
26. requiring
27. using new skills
28. unskilled

Application — Writing

Friendly Letter Imagine that you are a cowhand driving a herd north. Write a letter to a friend describing your experiences on the trail. Use at least three participles and two participial phrases in your letter.

7 Gerunds and Gerund Phrases

FOCUS

- A **gerund** is a verbal ending in *ing* that is used as a noun.
- A **gerund phrase** consists of a gerund and its related words.

A gerund uses the present participial form of the verb. A gerund functions as a noun and can be used as a subject, a direct object, a predicate nominative, or the object of a preposition.

Subject **1.** Surviving was difficult during the Depression.

Direct object **2.** The Great Depression halted manufacturing.

Predicate nominative **3.** The most affected industry was banking.

Object of a preposition **4.** Everyone was worried about working.

A gerund phrase is composed of a gerund and any adverbs, adjectives, prepositional phrases, or direct objects that follow it. It also functions as a noun. Like a gerund, it can be used as a subject, a direct object, a predicate nominative, or the object of a preposition.

Subject **5.** Making ends meet was nearly impossible.

Direct object **6.** People tried demanding help from the government.

Predicate nominative **7.** The answer was creating relief programs.

Object of a preposition **8.** Steps can be taken toward preventing another depression.

Guided Practice

A. Name the gerund or the gerund phrase in each sentence. Tell whether each is used as a *subject*, a *direct object*, a *predicate nominative*, or the *object of a preposition.*

1. Saving money will not prevent an economic depression.
2. People should know the dangers of hoarding.
3. Our economy depends on frequent spending.
4. Investing puts dollars into circulation.
5. Another means of circulation is borrowing money.

THINK AND REMEMBER

- Remember that a **gerund** is used as a noun.
- Remember that a **gerund phrase** consists of a gerund and related words.

Independent Practice

B. Identifying Gerunds and Gerund Phrases Write the gerund or the gerund phrase. Write *subject, direct object, predicate nominative,* or *object of a preposition* to tell how it is used in the sentence.

6. Owning stock is one way to learn about business.

MODEL Owning stock—subject

7. Your investment allows sharing in a company's profits and growth.
8. Watching the stock market shows investors which companies are successful.
9. The rising of stock value increases market activity.
10. The business of a stock exchange is buying and selling stocks.
11. Companies may list their stocks for trading.
12. A rapid fluctuation of stock prices often means a lowering of value.

C. Distinguishing Between Gerund Phrases and Participial Phrases Write *gerund phrase* or *participial phrase* to describe each underlined phrase.

13. Talking about money makes some people uneasy.

MODEL gerund phrase

14. Wanting privacy, they never discuss their salaries.
15. Enjoying work was always more important to Grandpa than money.
16. In 1935 the best job he could find was fixing bikes.
17. Having some experience, he was hired immediately.
18. Doing useful work, he was able to make enough money to support his family.

Application — Writing

Personal Narrative Imagine that you are an unemployed worker who has just found a job. Write a personal narrative telling classmates how you found employment. Use at least three gerunds and two gerund phrases in your narrative. If you need help writing a personal narrative, see page 49 of the **Writer's Handbook.**

8 Infinitives and Infinitive Phrases

FOCUS

- An **infinitive** is a verbal consisting of the present-tense form of a verb preceded by *to.*
- An **infinitive phrase** consists of an infinitive and its related words.

An infinitive is another kind of verbal. It can be used as a noun, an adjective, or an adverb.

Using Infinitives in Sentences	
As Nouns	
subject	*To learn* gives me great pleasure.
direct object	Booker T. Washington desired *to learn.*
predicate nominative	One goal of his life was *to learn.*
object of a preposition	He wanted little except *to learn.*
As Adjectives	
modifying a noun	Washington heard of a fine school *to attend.*
modifying a pronoun	His mother wanted him *to attend.*
As Adverbs	
modifying a verb	*To understand,* you must read his story.
modifying an adjective	His ambition is easy *to understand.*
modifying an adverb	You are reading too fast *to understand.*

An infinitive phrase is composed of an infinitive and any direct objects, predicate nominatives or predicate adjectives, adverbs, or prepositional phrases that follow it. It can be used as a noun, an adjective, or an adverb.

1. *To improve Tuskegee Institute* was a huge task.
2. Washington needed money *to build a library.*
3. *To raise funds,* he contacted Andrew Carnegie.

Do not confuse a prepositional phrase with an infinitive. In an infinitive, the word *to* is followed by a verb. In a prepositional phrase, *to* is followed by a noun or pronoun that is the object of the preposition.

4. *Up from Slavery* is an important book to read . **infinitive**
5. It is important to people of all races. **prepositional phrase**

When you use an infinitive with some verbs, such as *help, make, see,* and *dare,* you sometimes drop the word *to.*

6. Washington made his students (to) learn basic skills .

Link to Speaking and Writing
You can combine sentences by forming an infinitive phrase.

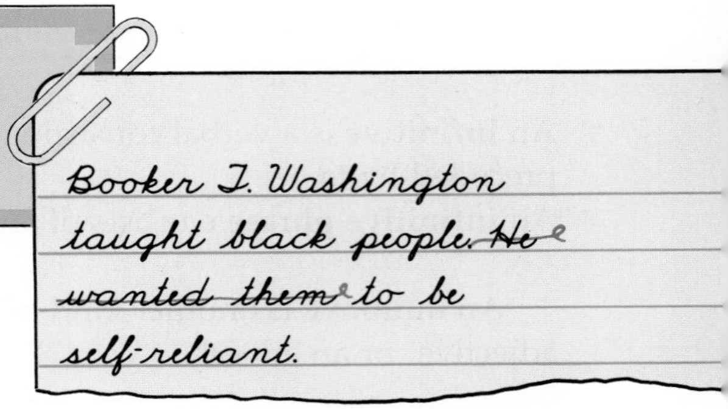
Booker T. Washington
taught black people. He
wanted them to be
self-reliant.

Guided Practice

A. Identify the infinitive or the infinitive phrase in each sentence. Tell whether it is used as a *noun*, an *adjective*, or an *adverb*.

1. Hampton's night school allowed students to work during the day.
2. Washington's friend asked him to go to Tuskegee Institute.
3. The school needed a teacher to take charge.
4. Booker T. Washington was eager to teach at Tuskegee Institute.
5. His purpose was to teach agricultural methods.

B. Tell how to combine each pair of sentences to form a new sentence with an infinitive phrase.

6. New agricultural methods were needed. They could feed the nation.
7. Washington worked hard. He wanted to improve Tuskegee Institute.
8. Many young people attended Tuskegee Institute. They wanted to make better lives for themselves.
9. Washington taught many young people. He taught them to educate themselves.
10. He had many speaking engagements. He delivered addresses throughout the United States.

THINK AND REMEMBER

- Remember that an **infinitive** is the present-tense form of a verb preceded by the word *to*.
- Remember that an **infinitive phrase** consists of an infinitive and the related words that follow it.

Independent Practice

C. Identifying Infinitives and Infinitive Phrases Write the infinitive or the infinitive phrase from each sentence. Then, write *noun, adverb,* or *adjective* to identify its function in the sentence.

11. To improve yourself, you need an education.

MODEL To improve yourself—adverb

12. Some people decide to learn a trade in a technical school.
13. To attend a trade school was my grandfather's ambition.
14. He chose carpentry as the best course to study.
15. He found woodworking easy to learn.
16. His teachers considered him to be quite talented.
17. Grandfather's dream was to build a house for his family.
18. His studies helped to make his dream come true.

D. Revising: Combining Sentences Combine each pair of sentences by using an infinitive phrase.

19. W.E.B. DuBois worked for over 50 years. He fought discrimination.

MODEL W.E.B. DuBois worked for over 50 years to fight discrimination.

20. Black people had been denied their rights. They were entitled to vote and to participate in government.
21. Blacks were not given equal opportunities. They were not allowed to learn skills necessary for better jobs.
22. Many blacks spoke out. They wanted to change the unfair laws.
23. It took many years. The whole country became aware of the problems.
24. DuBois and Washington used vastly different methods. They achieved similar goals.

E. Writing Sentences Write a sentence using each infinitive phrase.

25. to have a united nation

MODEL To have a united nation, we must accept all people as equals.

26. to work toward equality
27. to learn from past mistakes
28. to settle disagreements
29. to write to legislators
30. to improve understanding
31. to defend my beliefs

Application — Writing and Speaking

Personal Philosophy Write a statement that tells other students your feelings about the importance of education. Use at least three infinitive phrases in your writing. Read your statement to a group of classmates.

9 Dangling Participles and Split Infinitives

◆ **FOCUS** Dangling participles and split infinitives should not be used in sentences.

A **dangling participle** is a participial phrase that, because of the structure of the sentence, does not modify any word in the sentence.

1. Hanging in the Statehouse tower, its deep tones echoed across Philadelphia in a celebration of independence. (The tones were not hanging in the bell tower.)

The sentence could be revised in several ways:

2. Hanging in the Statehouse tower, the Liberty Bell sent its deep tones echoing across Philadelphia in a celebration of independence.
3. Across Philadelphia, the deep tones of the Liberty Bell echoed from the Statehouse tower in a celebration of independence.

A **split infinitive** is an infinitive that contains an adverb after the word *to.* To correct it, you can drop the adverb or place it before or after the infinitive phrase.

4. The colonies wanted to proudly proclaim their freedom.
5. The colonies wanted to proclaim their freedom proudly.

Guided Practice

A. Identify the participial phrase or the infinitive phrase in each sentence. Tell whether each is *correct, dangling,* or *split.*

1. Visiting Philadelphia, the tour was complete.
2. We had to quickly return to the bus.
3. Looking at a map, I located the Betsy Ross House.
4. Being a landmark, the first flag was made there.
5. Designed by Betsy Ross, the flag had thirteen stars.

THINK AND REMEMBER

- To correct a dangling participle, place the participial phrase closer to the word it modifies.
- Avoid splitting infinitives with an adverb.

Independent Practice

B. Identifying Split Infinitives and Dangling Participles For each sentence, write the participle or the infinitive. Then write *correct, split infinitive,* or *dangling participle.*

6. Chosen for the Continental Congress, each delegate's trip to Philadelphia was planned.

MODEL Chosen for the Continental Congress—dangling participle

7. The colonies needed to completely unite as a nation.
8. Desirous of avoiding war, a declaration was sent to England.
9. Treating the colonies unfairly, the Congress objected to British policy.
10. Great Britain was unwilling to even consider the American colonies' appeal.
11. After debating for a full year, representatives finally voted for independence.
12. Written by Thomas Jefferson, the Congress approved it.
13. Adopted on July 4, 1776, fifty-six people added their signatures.
14. The Liberty Bell was not to actually ring until July 8.
15. The American people were waiting to eagerly hear the words of the Declaration of Independence read aloud.
16. The American colonies fought to fiercely defend their new freedom.

C. 17.–27. Revising: Correcting Split Infinitives and Dangling Participles Rewrite each sentence in **B,** correcting the split infinitive or the dangling participle. If the sentence is correct, write *no change.*

17. Chosen for the Continental Congress, each delegate's trip to Philadelphia was planned.

MODEL Chosen for the Continental Congress, each delegate planned his trip to Philadelphia.

Application — Writing

Personal Narrative Write a personal narrative of a real or imaginary visit to the Liberty Bell. Describe to others on the tour how you felt as you looked at this symbol of freedom. Use infinitives and participial phrases correctly. If you need help writing a personal narrative, see page 49 of the **Writer's Handbook.**

Building Vocabulary

Context Clues

Finding unfamiliar words in your reading can be frustrating. You cannot fully understand research articles, stories, and other writings unless you know the meanings of most, if not all, of the words. To be a good reader, you need ways of determining the meanings of words you do not know.

Remember that prefixes, roots, and suffixes can give you clues to word meanings. Remember also that you can look up a word in a dictionary. A third way to find clues to word meanings is through context clues in sentences.

Context clues are clues to the meaning of an unfamiliar word. These clues are found in the words and sentences around the unknown word. There are several kinds of context clues: *synonyms, explanations, opposites,* and *further information*. The more skillful you are at finding context clues, the more you will understand what you read.

Type of Clue	Possible Clues or Clue Words	Example Sentences
Synonyms	*or, is*	During the Middle Ages men wore hoods with *liripipes*, or tails.
Explanations	appositives set off by commas	*Wimples*, cloths draped to frame the face, were worn by women.
Opposites (antonyms, contrasts)	*but, however, although, not, instead, despite*	In medieval times there was a *preponderance* of simpler styles, but simple styles were in the *minority* during the Renaissance.
Further information (examples)	*such as, like, for example*	*Tricorns* like the ones worn by Minutemen in paintings of the Revolutionary War were made here.

Reading Practice

Read each sentence. Write the word from the list that matches the underlined word. Then, write *synonym, explanation, opposite,* or *further information* to tell what type of clue was given.

scarves dress hoops glorious severe ever-present

1. The chemise of today developed from several different garments, such as the medieval under-tunic and the loose shirt of the Renaissance.
2. The ubiquitous material today is denim, which can be seen everywhere from classrooms to fields.
3. The large, triangular scarves of today are similar to the fichus worn by women in the early 1700's.
4. Crinolines were worn to expand skirts in many different eras, but such bulky undergarments would be difficult to wear today.
5. In some communities a more ascetic style was adopted; nothing extravagant was allowed.

Writing Practice

For each of the following words, write a sentence using context clues to suggest the word's meaning. You may use the synonym clue provided, or you may create your own clue using explanations, opposites, or examples.

6. panache—swagger
7. cyan—the color blue
8. tractable—willing
9. imperious—dominant
10. plaudit—praise
11. augury—an omen

Project

Choose ten terms from your social studies textbook to use in a crossword puzzle similar to the one shown. Write the number for each word and a sentence with a context clue. Make a copy of your puzzle, but leave out the words. Exchange puzzles.

Example:

DOWN

1. Lincoln and Douglas expressed their views in a series of ________, or arguments.

1 d	e	b	t								
e						2 e					
b						l					
3 a	m	e	n	d	m	e	n	4 t			
t						c		a			
e						t		x			
s						i					
				5 b	l	o	c	k	a	d	e
						n					

Language Enrichment
Complex Sentences and Verbals

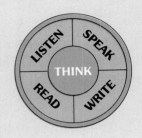

Use what you know about complex sentences and verbals to do these activities.

Choose One from Column A...

Column A
(Subordinate Clauses)
as I was walking home
although the tool seemed useful
since the instructions were lost

Column B
(Independent Clauses)
I had never seen one before.
We went to the library.
I found a strange old tool.

Build complex sentences from subordinate and independent clauses by choosing one from each column. You may put either clause first. Use the sentences you make to begin a paragraph on researching information about the tool.

At the Gerund Factory

Camp Cowabunga needs verbs converted to gerunds for its brochure, which will describe its summer camp activities. Using gerunds, write two additional descriptions for the brochure.

To Make a Wish Come True

What are some things you really want to do in the future? Do you want to travel, to have your own business, to raise a family, or even to go to Mars? Make up your own wish list, using infinitives for the items on the list. Then choose the one thing you want most to do, and write a paragraph explaining how you plan to make this wish come true. Try to use infinitives in your paragraph. Read your paragraph aloud to your class. Ask for ideas about other ways you can make your wish come true.

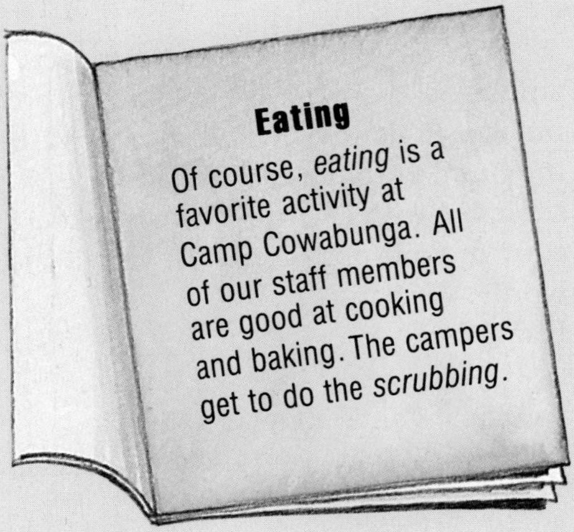
Eating
Of course, eating is a favorite activity at Camp Cowabunga. All of our staff members are good at cooking and baking. The campers get to do the scrubbing.

CONNECTING

LANGUAGE ↔ WRITING

In this unit you learned about complex sentences—sentences that have independent clauses and subordinate clauses. You also learned that some verbs can be transformed into participles, gerunds, and infinitives.

◆ **Using Complex Sentences and Verbals in Your Writing** Knowing how to write complex sentences correctly will make your writing varied and clear. Using verbals can add to the complexity and interest of your writing.

Pay special attention to the complex sentences and the verbals you use as you do these activities.

A Heritage and a Right

You learned on the **Building Vocabulary** pages about using context clues to determine word meaning. You probably also have learned in social studies classes about one of the most important rights of an adult American citizen, the right to vote. Do you think you could explain the voting procedure? Try it by writing a short article for a magazine. Explain what voting in an election is all about. In your paragraph, define these words in context: *candidate, ballot, polling place.*

Dinner at the Home Plate Cafe

The menu at the Home Plate Cafe still features the same past participles with the same nouns. Revise the menu by rearranging the participles and nouns. Then write a one-sentence description for each of your new creations.

8 Unit Checkup

Think Back	Think Ahead
◆ What did you learn about a research report in this unit? What did you do to write one?	◆ How will what you learned about a research report help you record what you learn? ◆ How will knowing how to present factual information help you write a research report?
◆ Look at the writing you did in this unit. How did complex sentences and verbals help you express your ideas?	◆ What is one way you can use complex sentences and verbals to improve your writing?

Research Report *pages 354 – 355*

Read the following titles for research reports. For each title, write a question the report might answer.

1. The Blue and the Gray: The Effects of the Civil War
2. Using Computers for Library Research
3. The Santa Fe Trail: Gateway to the West

Connecting Ideas in a Summary *page 356*

Using the topic sentence, write whether the sentence *would* or *would not* help summarize the information given.

British royalty hold largely ceremonial positions.

4. The Prince of Wales will someday become King of England.
5. Parliament creates and enacts all the laws in England.
6. Royalty often lead extravagant lifestyles.

Capturing the Reader's Interest *page 357*

Read each sentence. Name the technique used to add spice to each.

7. How much do we owe to the Mexican-American culture?
8. The Civil War was the worst period in Texas history.
9. "I only regret that I have but one life to lose for my country."

The Writing Process *pages 358 – 367*

Write the letter for the answer to each question.

10. When gathering information, where would you find titles of books with useful information?
  a. *Readers' Guide* **b.** card catalogue **c.** **Writer's Handbook**

11. What can help you while drafting a research report?
  a. an outline **b.** an interview **c.** *Readers' Guide*

12. What type of sentences should be replaced in a report?
  a. complex **b.** compound-complex **c.** monotonous

Complex Sentences *pages 370 – 371*

Write each sentence. Underline the subordinate clause once, and underline the independent clause twice.

13. When people needed a break, they told tales.

14. Everyone sat around a fireplace as someone told a tale.

15. The tales were legends since they were based on truth.

16. Although some pretended to believe, all knew the tales were fiction.

17. They would hold their laughter until the storyteller had finished.

Adjective Clauses *pages 372 – 374*

Write the adjective clause and underline the relative pronoun. Write *restrictive* or *nonrestrictive* to tell what kind of adjective clause it is.

18. Some people who go to museums refuse to explore because they are unsure what to look for.

19. It is easy to pick out those who have been there before.

20. I remember going to several museums with my uncle, who lives in Galveston, and he knew just what to look for.

21. I know that Galveston, which is one of my favorite cities in Texas, has museums that have historical collections.

22. It is fun to explore with my uncle, who has an interest in history.

Adverb Clauses *pages 375 – 376*

Write the adverb clause. Underline the subordinating conjunction.

23. I often think of my grandmother when I visit the seashore.

24. Although she has never received credit, she has taught me much about respect for sea creatures.

25. Grandmother Chisholm has enjoyed the seashore since she was very young.

26. After writing many poems and stories about the ocean, she decided to illustrate them with paintings.
27. Her genius was not realized until a Palm Beach museum curator put her work on display.
28. Her artistic works are still enjoyed today because they tell tales of our heritage and the sea.

Noun Clauses *pages 377 – 378*

Write the noun clause. Write *subject, direct object, predicate nominative,* or *object of a preposition* to show how the noun clause is used.

29. What has changed in the community is a topic of concern for citizens.
30. I think that less time is being spent on trivial concerns and gossip.
31. Whoever stays in one town for any length of time today wants to know more about its history.
32. Information about their particular place of residence is what people want to know.
33. What some have uncovered about old estates and properties has to be considered interesting.

Misplaced Modifiers *pages 379 – 380*

Write *correct* or *misplaced* to describe the modifier in each sentence.

34. The man wore a costume to the Renaissance Festival with full red sleeves.
35. I thought he looked as though he fit right in by wearing that outfit.
36. He apparently had a job with the festival as a player in skits.
37. People laughed at his skits who came to the show.
38. Standing on the stage, we saw the star and his partners.

Participles and Participial Phrases *pages 381 – 382*

Write each sentence. Underline the participial phrase. Draw an arrow to the word it modifies.

39. Searching family records, people learn something about their heritages.
40. Listed in albums and on marriage and birth certificates, the statistics of a family's marriages and births show the family history.
41. Certificates giving wives' maiden names provide clues to those who seek information about family branches.
42. Also used to verify dates, these marriage certificates are official documents.
43. The certificates giving facts for a family tree must be cared for properly.

Gerunds and Gerund Phrases *pages 383 – 384*

Write the gerund phrase. Write *subject, direct object, predicate nominative,* or *object of a preposition* to tell how it is used in the sentence.

44. Remembering history can instill confidence about the future.
45. People learn about surviving a world war.
46. Keeping the economy strong is very important to citizens.
47. Government officials work on ensuring the peace.
48. Learning history becomes a way to survive disasters.

Infinitives and Infinitive Phrases *pages 385 – 387*

Write the infinitive or the infinitive phrase from each sentence. Then write *noun, adverb,* or *adjective* to identify its function in the sentence.

49. To write your life story is to write an autobiography.
50. The writer sets out to accomplish a variety of goals.
51. Some writers want to defend what they have done.
52. Others just want money to live on.
53. I have found writing a way to order my experiences.

Dangling Participles and Split Infinitives *pages 388 – 389*

For each sentence, write the participle or the infinitive. Then write *correct, split infinitive,* or *dangling participle.*

54. In 1832 there was a need to slowly move toward a free Texas.
55. Feeling the need for self-rule, the struggle seemed certain.
56. They wanted to fully escape any rule but their own.
57. The Anglo-Texans had come to a territory assuming rights.
58. They wanted to enjoy the freedoms that had been won in the East.

Context Clues *pages 390 – 391*

Read each sentence. Write the word from the list that matches the underlined word. Then write *synonym, explanation, opposite,* or *further information* to tell what type of clue was given.

cause spread preventing eager ships

59. The railroad was a <u>catalyst</u>, or stimulus to progress.
60. It <u>disseminated</u> ideas by announcing news throughout the West.
61. Rather than <u>prohibiting</u>, it encouraged the West's growth.
62. Anxious for success, people were <u>keen</u> to ride on the trains to prosperity.

UNIT 9

Creating Drama

◆ COMPOSITION FOCUS: **Play**
◆ LANGUAGE FOCUS: **Mechanics Wrap-up**

The curtain rises and the play begins. How did the leading lady know what her first line was? How did the play come into being in the first place? Play performances begin with a playwright.

Playwrights compose stories to be performed on stage. Sometimes they create a new story for a play, and sometimes they base a play on a previously written story. James Fuller, for example, based his play *The Open Window* on a short story written by H. H. Munro.

Unlike a story, a written play is not a finished product. It is an intermediate step that leads to performance. If a play is to be performed as the playwright intends, it must be carefully written so that the action in the story moves forward and the personalities of the characters are developed. A close reading of *The Open Window* will show how the playwright moves the action forward to its surprising end. In this unit you will learn how to write a play.

Playwright James Fuller created the play *The Open Window* primarily *to entertain* an audience through a stage performance.

Reading with a Writer's Eye
A Play

When a stranger appears at Hampton Heath, a sleepy rural community, it causes quite a stir in the Sappleton household. *The Open Window* tells the story of the stranger's visit and a young girl's effect on the stranger. In this play, based on H. H. Munro's short story, James Fuller leads his audience to a surprising ending. Read the play carefully to see if you can predict what will happen.

The Open Window

A Comedy in One Act
by James Fuller

For One Man, Three Women, and Two Extras

CHARACTERS

Framton Nuttel . . . . a visitor
Mrs. Sappleton . . . . the hostess
Vera . . . . the niece
Maria . . . . the maid
Two Extras

PLACE: The living room of an English country home.
TIME: Recently.

SCENE: *The living room of a country home in England. As the curtain opens, we discover a pleasant English living room. It is furnished rather fully with comfortable old furniture (preferably of some standard period). The walls have prints of hunting scenes or dark oil portraits of ancestors. The room may double as a library, with bookcases along one wall. D R is a sofa with a small table in front of it for serving tea. U C there are French windows, opening on an exterior background that shows several trees in the distance.*

U L is an easy chair, with a table beside it. In the wall D L is a doorway. The whole atmosphere of the room is one of pleasant country charm, perhaps a little heavy and cluttered, and in no sense sophisticated.

AT RISE OF CURTAIN: VERA SAPPLETON, *an attractive, casually dressed young lady of sixteen, is reading a note that has been brought to her on a little silver tray by* MARIA, *the maid, an attractive twenty-year-old, dressed in a maid's costume.*

VERA *(Slowly folding the letter and returning it to its envelope)*: It's a letter of introduction to my aunt from that woman who rented Bellingham Hall the summer before last.

MARIA: My oldest sister, the one that got married, worked for them. Very nice they were, she said.

VERA: What does he look like?

MARIA: I never met him.

VERA: No, no—the young man who brought this letter of introduction.

MARIA: I thought you meant the man my sister worked for, but if it's the person waiting in the hall, he's nice enough. He looks as if he might be an Oxford man except for his tie.

VERA: Well, I'll try and entertain him until my aunt is ready. You better take the letter of introduction to her.

MARIA: Yes, miss.

VERA: But show the young man in first.

MARIA: Yes, miss. *(Goes to door D L.)*

(VERA *straightens her dress slightly and crosses to the chair U L. As soon as she sits in it she looks around to the door—realizes she is poorly placed—gets up and walks a few steps over to the sofa. She seats herself carefully, adjusting her skirts so she presents an attractive appearance. While she is finishing this maneuver the door D L opens and* FRAMTON NUTTEL *walks in. He is followed by* MARIA.)

MARIA *(Announcing the caller)*: Mr. Nuttel. *(Goes out D L closing the door behind her.* FRAMTON NUTTEL *is a well-dressed, attractive young man, perhaps a trifle pale of complexion and nervous of manner.)*

VERA *(Rising and extending her hand, speaking pleasantly)*: How nice to meet you, Mr. Nuttel. I am Vera Sappleton. My aunt will be in presently. In the meantime you must try to put up with me.

FRAMTON *(Crossing, shaking hands with her diffidently)*: It is most kind of you to receive me.

VERA: We're delighted to have you call. We don't get many visitors here in the country.

FRAMTON: My sister recommended Hampton Heath as a wonderful quiet spot. She and her husband had a most enjoyable season here.

VERA: Won't you sit down?

FRAMTON *(Who has been shifting somewhat nervously from one foot to the other)*: Thank you. *(Looks around and decides to settle for the easy chair U L.* VERA *reseats herself on the sofa in the same pose that she had assumed previously.)*

VERA: Everyone will be delighted to meet you. It's lovely here but it does get a bit dull sometimes.

FRAMTON: Dullness! That's just what the doctor ordered.

VERA *(Probing for mutual ground)*: You've been ill?

FRAMTON: Oh, yes, yes. That's why I am here.

VERA *(Moving forward in her seat with interest)*: Was it anything...special?

FRAMTON *(Pompously)*: The pressures of academic life. I was working a little too hard. *(Continues with faint superiority.)* I am afraid it was rather abstruse.

VERA: What effect did it have?

FRAMTON: Well—I became very nervous—easily upset, you know.

VERA: And so your doctor recommended Hampton Heath?

FRAMTON: Not specifically.

VERA: But something like it?

FRAMTON: Yes, exactly. He suggested I find some quiet rural place where nothing ever happens.

VERA *(Firmly)*: I see. So then your sister immediately thought about us?

FRAMTON: Well, not exactly.

VERA: But she did suggest you come down here?

FRAMTON: Certainly. She spoke with much affection of Hampton Heath as a lovely rural part of England, filled with charming people who were interested in hunting and dogs and horses. Things of that sort.

VERA *(Warmly)*: You'll have quiet and a lot of fun, too. There's simply no end of things to do! Really, there are lots of ways of entertaining yourself.

FRAMTON *(Trying to enter into the spirit)*: Entertaining one's self. The very thing my doctor told me. Bracing strolls in the country air. *(Takes several deep breaths, as if in anticipation.)* Early to bed—*(Glumly.)*—early to rise.

VERA *(Dubiously)*: Well—lots of us prefer to hunt instead of just ambling about.

FRAMTON: You hunt?

VERA: A little. I like to ride, but my mare's in foal. I can hardly wait to see what sort of colt she has. I'm hoping for a chestnut, but the Countessa—my mare—is more of a bay herself.

FRAMTON *(Condescendingly)*: It'll be a regular Irish Sweepstake winner, no doubt. *(Ending it.)* Riding isn't for me.

VERA *(Dubiously)*: Well—*(Trying another tack.)* The garden is quite lovely this time of year. Roses do beautifully in this cool weather. As if they were having one last fling before winter. *(Eagerly.)* Would you like to see the garden?

FRAMTON *(Coldly)*: I suppose so. Digging in the ground and all that. *(Sighs.)* Oh, well—my doctor was right. I'll get all sorts of peace and quiet here. *(Not meaning a word of it.)* Of course, I'd love to see your garden—some day. Perhaps—*(Hesitates briefly for an excuse.)*—we had best wait till your aunt…

VERA *(Understanding)*: Of course.

FRAMTON: I suppose there's a village fair that's pretty exciting?

VERA: Now, you're making fun of us.

FRAMTON: I wouldn't think of it.

VERA: There aren't many village fairs anymore.
FRAMTON: I'm just a bit out of my milieu, you know.
VERA *(Brightens)*: The hunt ball comes up next month. We'll see you don't miss that. It is really the most colorful event of the fall.
FRAMTON *(Not wanting to be involved in anything)*: Well, of course, I don't know what my health will be by then. One hopes for the best but...*(His voice trails off.)*
VERA: Certainly.
FRAMTON: With so many friends of my sister to call on, I don't want to get involved with anyone in particular.
VERA *(Realizing he thinks she has been angling for an invitation)*: Oh, I wasn't suggesting...*(Realizing there is no practical way to say it, continues slowly.)*...anything in particular. I'll be there with Henry Hartford. He's got a bay Irish hunter.
FRAMTON *(Trying to be of help)*: Is this your first dance?
VERA *(Stung, but game)*: No, I've been going for years and years. *(Pauses, and then continues in a very bright way.)* It certainly was kind of your sister to give you these letters of introduction. Such an opportunity for us all to meet someone from the outside world.
FRAMTON *(Falling for it)*: She's always thinking of others. She said people hereabouts did so much for her, she really felt quite indebted to them. She gave me several letters and urged me to present them. Really, she's the soul of kindness.
VERA: Then, actually, you know practically nothing about my aunt.
FRAMTON: Aside from her name and address, nothing except that my sister spoke very highly of the whole family.
VERA: Has she been in touch with her recently?
FRAMTON: No, she explained that they had never corresponded. *(*VERA*'s mood alters subtly at this point. She sits back in her chair and speaks more decisively. She's letting him have it now.)*
VERA: It was probably my aunt's fault because of the tragedy.
FRAMTON: A tragedy? I am sorry to hear that.
VERA: Your sister mentioned it to you, of course?
FRAMTON: Never a word!
VERA: Then it would have been since her time.
FRAMTON *(Half rising)*: I am sure she wouldn't have wanted me to intrude on you at a time of difficulty.
VERA *(Motioning him back)*: Oh, no, it happened last year.

FRAMTON *(Delicately alluding to his health)*: I suppose even the quietest of places have their little upsets.
VERA *(Nodding U C toward the open window)*: You may wonder why she keeps the window open on an October afternoon.
FRAMTON: It's quite warm for this time of the year.
VERA: It's Aunt. She insists that it be kept the same way.
FRAMTON: What way?
VERA: The way it was last year. You see, this is the anniversary.
FRAMTON: The anniversary of what?
VERA: The tragedy.
FRAMTON *(Putting a finger in his collar and easing it)*: I am terribly sorry to hear that. Perhaps I had better call some other time.
VERA: Oh, no. Auntie would be very disappointed. Please sit still.
FRAMTON: Whatever you say.
VERA: Perhaps I should prepare you for meeting her.
FRAMTON *(Nervously gulping, and then proceeding)*: Please do.
VERA *(Rising and pointing dramatically U C)*: Out through that window, one year ago to this very day, her husband, her son and their dog went off for a day's shooting. *(Dramatically.)* They never came back. In crossing the moor to their favorite snipe-shooting ground, all three were engulfed in a treacherous piece of bog. It was a dreadful wet summer, you know, and places that were safe in

other years gave way suddenly, without warning. Their bodies were never recovered. That was the dreadful part of it.

FRAMTON: I am terribly sorry to hear this. *(Here* VERA's *voice loses its self-possessed note and becomes falteringly human. She crosses over, standing just behind and downstage of* FRAMTON, *whose attention is now riveted upon the open window. The dramatic quality is gone from her speech and she sounds sympathetic and a little faltering, continuing:)*

VERA: Poor Aunt always thinks they'll come back some day and walk in through that window just as they used to do. That's why it's kept open every evening until it is quite dusk.

FRAMTON: Your poor aunt.

VERA: She often told me how they went out. Ronnie, her husband, was singing "Bertie, Bertie, why do you bound?" to tease her because it got on her nerves.

FRAMTON *(Turning his head to face her)*: A most extraordinary story.

VERA: Of course, we try to humor her.

FRAMTON: Has she been to London to see someone? I mean, they do wonderful things nowadays.

VERA: In every other way she's perfectly all right.

FRAMTON: No nervousness, or anything?

VERA: Not a bit. When she comes in, she'll act perfectly natural. She'll probably even offer you tea.

FRAMTON: Are you sure I should stay?

VERA: Of course. She would be terribly disappointed—besides, it may help to get her mind off things.

FRAMTON: Well, of course, if you think it best.

VERA: I do, unless it makes you nervous.

FRAMTON *(With an effort)*: Oh, no, not at all. Glad to do my bit to help.

VERA: You will have no slightest trouble, but if you watch her you'll notice she keeps looking at the window.

FRAMTON: You don't find it all—a bit unnerving?

VERA: A little. Sometimes on quiet evenings like this, I get a creepy feeling that they all will walk in through that window. *(Steps back from* FRAMTON.*)*

(The door D L opens and MRS. SAPPLETON *enters. She is a woman*

in her thirties, attractively dressed, poised and charming.)

MRS. SAPPLETON: Mr. Nuttel, how nice! *(Shakes hands with him.)* I remember your sister and her husband. I hope Vera has been amusing you. I am Mrs. Sappleton.

FRAMTON *(Rising)*: She's been very interesting.

MRS. SAPPLETON: Maria is bringing tea. I do hope you will join me.

FRAMTON: I will be delighted, Mrs. Sappleton. It is good of you to receive me.

MRS. SAPPLETON: Vera, dear, will you join us?

VERA: Thank you, Auntie, but may I be excused a moment to get my jacket? It's getting quite brisk. *(Goes out D L.)*

MRS. SAPPLETON: I hope you don't mind the open window. My husband and son will be home directly from shooting. They always come in this way. They have been out for snipe in the marshes today so they'll make a fine mess on my poor carpets. So like you men-folk, isn't it.

(They are interrupted by MARIA, *who enters from D L carrying a tea tray with a fairly elaborate tea service. She puts it down in front of* MRS. SAPPLETON, *who proceeds to pour and serve tea.* MARIA *stands in attendance and passes things to* FRAMTON. *During these few minutes we have speeches, as indicated:)*

MRS. SAPPLETON *(to* MARIA): Bring the tray right here, Maria. That's a good girl. It looks simply delicious.

MARIA *(Putting down the tea service)*: Thank you, Ma'am. *(Steps upstage of* MRS. SAPPLETON *and awaits* MRS. SAPPLETON. FRAMTON *sits U L again.)*

MRS. SAPPLETON *(Pouring first the tea and then the hot water)*: Do you like your tea strong?

FRAMTON: Very, please—just a touch of hot water.

MRS. SAPPLETON: Do you use lemon, or cream and sugar?

FRAMTON: Sugar and cream, please.

MRS. SAPPLETON: So much more healthful that way. *(Hands the cup on a plate to* MARIA, *who passes it to* FRAMTON. *He spreads a napkin, which is also offered, on his knee and then takes a biscuit and cream and sugar that are offered by* MARIA.)

FRAMTON: As a matter of fact, I am down here for my health.

MRS. SAPPLETON: This is just the place. We have some of the best hunting in this part of England. Of course, birds have been scarce but the prospects for ducks this winter are excellent. You do hunt?

FRAMTON: No, I am afraid the doctor thinks it would be too exciting.

MRS. SAPPLETON: If your doctor won't let you hunt, perhaps you should find another doctor—unless there's some physical problem.

FRAMTON: Just nerves. After taking a degree at Cambridge, I took the Civil Service exams. But by the time I was through taking exams to prove I would be competent, I was so nervous from lack of sleep, I couldn't take the position they offered.

MRS. SAPPLETON: How sad, to miss out.

FRAMTON: Oh, I still have the job. Civil Service, you know. I'm on an initial leave of absence. It counts against my retirement pay.

MRS. SAPPLETON: I am sure you will find it most calming here. Really, very little of anything happens in these parts. *(Turns and looks out the window, then looks back.)* Tell me, are your dear sister and her charming husband well? We all enjoyed meeting them so much and hoped they would visit again. *(Turns and looks out the window again, and then looks at her wrist watch.* FRAMTON *follows, with exaggerated fascination, her actions, turning his head with hers, and then quickly looking back to her after guiltily realizing there is no point in looking out the window.)*

FRAMTON: They are both quite well, thank you.

MRS. SAPPLETON: Really, the evenings come on so fast this time of year. It is getting quite dark.

FRAMTON: Yes, quite.

MRS. SAPPLETON: You're sure you aren't chilly? The open window doesn't make you nervous?

FRAMTON *(Sitting on edge of his chair and putting a finger in his collar again to loosen it a bit)*: Not at all.

MRS. SAPPLETON: Maria, perhaps you'll partially close the window. Mr. Framton seems a bit chilly.

MARIA *(Moving toward window)*: Certainly, Ma'am.

FRAMTON: I'm perfectly warm. The pleasant atmosphere here, the peace...It's just what the doctor ordered.

(VERA *re-enters from the door D L, wearing a cardigan or jacket of some sort.)*

VERA: I hope I am not too late for tea.

MRS. SAPPLETON: Not at all, dear, it is still quite hot. We have been talking about Mr. Nuttel's health. He is down here for a rest, you know.

VERA: Yes, he told me. (MRS. SAPPLETON *pours a cup of tea for* VERA *and hands it to* MARIA *to pass to* VERA, *along with the biscuits.* VERA *takes it and strolls downstage and around behind the couch, where she sips her tea while standing behind her aunt, a position that also commands a view through the open window. By this time, the lights, which are being dimmed, are quite dim offstage. To her aunt:)* Would you like me to turn on the light, Auntie? It is really quite spooky in here.

MRS. SAPPLETON: By all means, Vera.

VERA: Would you like the window closed? It's quite brisk.

MRS. SAPPLETON: Of course not, Vera. Whatever are you and Maria thinking of?

VERA *(Shrugging her shoulder at* FRAMTON, *who has been following this)*: Of course, Auntie, sorry. *(Suddenly, she points with her left free hand offstage, through the open window, to an area which the audience cannot see.)* Good heavens! Look! *(Sets the cup down, immediately prior to this, on the table behind the couch, with a loud clatter.)*

MRS. SAPPLETON: Maria, step to the window and see.

MARIA: Yes, Ma'am. *(Crosses to window and looks out.)* It's two men and a dog. I can't tell who it is.

VERA: How are they dressed?

MARIA: They're too far away. (FRAMTON *looks nervously back and forth, from* VERA *to* MRS. SAPPLETON *and then to* MARIA.)

VERA: I suppose it's some neighbors.

MRS. SAPPLETON: I doubt that, Vera. After all, it is time your uncle and cousin were coming home.

MARIA: It does look like Mr. Sappleton and young Master Sappleton and the dog, but sure, Ma'am, I can't see—what with the mist and the evening coming on so ghostly.

MRS. SAPPLETON: Bring two more cups. They'll want tea.

FRAMTON: You think—*(Hesitates)*—it might be your husband and son?

MRS. SAPPLETON: Certainly. I've been waiting for them a long time.

FRAMTON: Your niece explained—*(Pauses.)*—all about it. (VERA, *standing behind her aunt, shakes her head to* FRAMTON *and puts her finger to her lips to admonish him not to discuss it. He stares in open-mouthed astonishment at* MRS. SAPPLETON.)

MARIA: I don't think they'll be wanting tea. *(She goes out D L.)*

FRAMTON *(Nervously)*: Whatever did she mean by that?

MRS. SAPPLETON: Usually my husband wants something a little stronger than tea, and my son is interested in food. An afternoon of hunting creates a real appetite.

FRAMTON: I've got to see for myself. *(Steels himself for the ordeal, rising nervously, and crosses to where he can just see out of the window.)* Oh no! They are there.

VERA: Certainly.

MRS. SAPPLETON: Mr. Nuttel, you're pale.

FRAMTON *(Gulping and pulling at his collar again)*: Really, it's nothing, you know. *(Gulps and edges away from the window toward the door D L.)*

VERA: You should remain calm, Mr. Nuttel. Nothing exciting *ever* happens in the country.

FRAMTON *(Pointing dramatically)*: There they are!

(VERA *and* MRS. SAPPLETON *turn, and we see dimly through the dusk two figures, a man and a boy. The boy is leading a springer or cocker spaniel or some other hunting dog on a leash. They are walking toward the house in hunting clothes and carrying shotguns under their arms. They are clothed in pale grays and whites, and have hunting caps pulled down over their faces. The whole effect is indistinct and blurred. One of them is softly singing, "Bertie, Bertie, why do you bound?" to himself. They pause just outside the door.)*

FRAMTON: Oh, no! *(Without turning his back on the window, he edges around his chair toward the door D L, and as soon as he gets near the door, opens it with a rush, and hastily goes out.... We hear his footsteps fading in the distance.)*

(FRAMTON *leaves the door open behind him. The two figures in white Mackintoshes enter through the window U C. They are carrying shotguns, open at the breech and slung casually under their arms;* VERA *goes and turns on the light over the two.)*

MR. SAPPLETON *(The older man)*: Here we are, my dears. I hope we are in time for tea.

FREDDIE *(The younger figure)*: We had a smashing day but really didn't get anything.

MR. SAPPLETON: Who was that who bolted out of the door as we came in?

MRS. SAPPLETON: A most extraordinary man...a Mr. Nuttel. He really didn't talk much of anything—except his health. Then he bolted out of here quite as if he had seen a ghost. Most extraordinary!

VERA: I expect it was the dog. He has a horror of dogs—especially hunting dogs. He was once hunted into a cemetery somewhere on the banks of the Ganges by a pack of Pariah dogs, and had to spend the night in a newly dug grave with the creatures snarling and grinning and foaming just above him. Enough to make anyone lose his nerve. I'll tell you about it. *(The curtain slowly descends as she continues.)* His companion wasn't as lucky. One day when he and a friend were out walking...

CURTAIN

Respond

1. If you were asked to portray one of the characters in the play, which character would you choose? Why?
2. What is Framton's final action in the play? What does Vera do last? Why does the playwright have them act this way?

Discuss

3. What is surprising about the ending of the play? What lines or actions in the play are clues to the surprise?
4. In your own words describe Framton's personality and Vera's personality. How do you think Vera feels about her life in the country? What element in the play leads you to believe this?

Thinking As a Writer

Analyzing a Play

A play is a story that is meant to be performed on stage. The playwright writes the play in a script. A script always has **characters, stage directions,** and **dialogue.**

VERA *(Nodding U C toward the open window):* You may wonder why she keeps the window open on an October afternoon.

FRAMTON: It's quite warm for this time of the year.

VERA: It's Aunt. She insists that it be kept the same way.

FRAMTON: What way?

VERA: The way it was last year. You see, this is the anniversary.

FRAMTON: The anniversary of what?

VERA: The tragedy.

FRAMTON *(Putting a finger in his collar and easing it):* I am terribly sorry to hear that. Perhaps I had better call some other time.

VERA: Oh, no. Auntie would be very disappointed. Please sit still.

FRAMTON: Whatever you say.

VERA: Perhaps I should prepare you for meeting her.

FRAMTON *(Nervously gulping, and then proceeding):* Please do.

VERA *(Rising and pointing dramatically U C):* Out through that window, one year ago to this very day, her husband, her son and their dog went off for a day's shooting. *(Dramatically.)* They never came back. In crossing the moor to their favorite snipe-shooting ground, all three were engulfed in a treacherous piece of bog.

Writer's Guide

A play
- includes characters, stage directions, and dialogue.
- has a plot with an introduction, a complication, and a resolution.

The **characters** are the participants in a play. The characters' names appear in capital letters before every set of lines they speak.

Stage directions indicate how the stage is set up. Stage directions also describe how characters act and feel. Characters' names are printed in capital letters; colons follow characters' names or the stage directions; and abbreviations such as *U C* (upstage center) are used to describe areas of the stage (in this case, the rear and center of the stage).

Dialogue is what the characters say. Also called *lines*, dialogue reveals to the audience the action of a play through what the characters say to each other.

The **plot** is the action in a play. It can be broken down into the **introduction,** the **complication,** and the **resolution.** In a one-act play, the plot is developed in one act. In a play with more than one act, the plot proceeds across the acts. Study this plan for the plot of *The Open Window.*

Introduction

Advised to take a restful stay in the country, Framton Nuttel pays a call on Mrs. Sappleton, his sister's friend. While waiting for her, he is entertained by Mrs. Sappleton's niece, Vera.

The **introduction** reveals the characters and the setting. The introduction may include clues to future action.

Complication

1. Vera learns Framton is suffering from a nervous condition.
2. Framton, a city resident, implies that although he finds it boring, he needs the quiet country.
3. As a mischievous prank, Vera makes up a frightening story of the disappearance of her uncle and her cousin on the moors. She says that her aunt expects them to return through the window that night.
4. Becoming more uneasy after meeting the aunt, Framton begins to believe Vera's story.

The **complication** is the main action of the play. Here, the playwright introduces events that cause dialogue and action to occur. This interaction among characters in the play is part of the play's conflict. The conflict rises to a **climax**, or turning point, in the complication.

Climax

Two figures are seen walking through the fog toward the house. The nervous Framton runs out of the house.

Resolution

Vera's uncle and cousin enter the house. Vera explains Framton's behavior by beginning another strange story.

The **resolution** reveals the solution to the conflict. The resolution may also reveal a character's motives.

Discuss

1. Look at the excerpt of the play in this lesson. What characters appear in this excerpt? What other characters are discussed in the dialogue?
2. Is the section of the play in this lesson taken from the introduction, the complication, or the resolution? Explain your answer.

Try Your Hand

A. Analyze Stage Directions Read the following sections from various parts of a play. For each section, write the stage directions that are given. Then write *moves, speaks,* or *feels* to tell what the character is doing.

1. FIRST TROJAN: Escape through the gates! Troy burns!
   SECOND TROJAN *(Dashing out)*: The Greeks have conquered us. We are only a handful now, but we shall rise to found another great city in this lifetime!
2. SECOND TROJAN *(With hostility)*: I do not trust this Greek or his wooden horse!
   KING PRIAM *(Harshly)*: Hush! Fortune will smile upon us if we are kind to those we have bested. *(Turning to Sinon.)* From today, Troy is your home. Now help us haul the horse into the gates of our city.
3. FIRST TROJAN *(Passes through the gates of the city and voices his relief)*: After ten years of war, at last we have peace here in Troy. The Greeks are gone!

B. Read and Talk About Plays Choose a section from *The Open Window* or from another play. With a partner, identify the characters, stage directions, and dialogue. Decide whether the section you chose is from the introduction, the complication, or the resolution.

Writer's Notebook

Collecting Adverbs Did you notice adverbs such as *nervously*, *dramatically*, and *falteringly* in the stage directions for *The Open Window*? Read the play again and record in your *Writer's Notebook* any directions that have adverbs whose exact meaning you don't know. Look up the words in a dictionary and record their meanings. When you write or speak, try to use adverbs that capture your audience's attention.

Thinking As a Writer
Observing Details

Writer's Guide

To write a play, good writers

- observe the details of how people act in real situations.
- include these details in their stage directions.

In a good play, a writer includes in the stage directions details that make the characters seem real. Read these lines from *The Open Window.*

> FRAMTON *(Who has been shifting somewhat nervously from one foot to the other)*: Thank you. *(Looks around and decides to settle for the easy chair U L.* VERA *reseats herself on the sofa in the same pose that she had assumed previously.)*
> MRS. SAPPLETON: Mr. Nuttel, you're pale.
> FRAMTON *(Gulping and pulling at his collar again)*: Really, it's nothing, you know. *(Gulps and edges away from the window toward the door D L.)*

A writer can make an idea cluster of possible details to include.

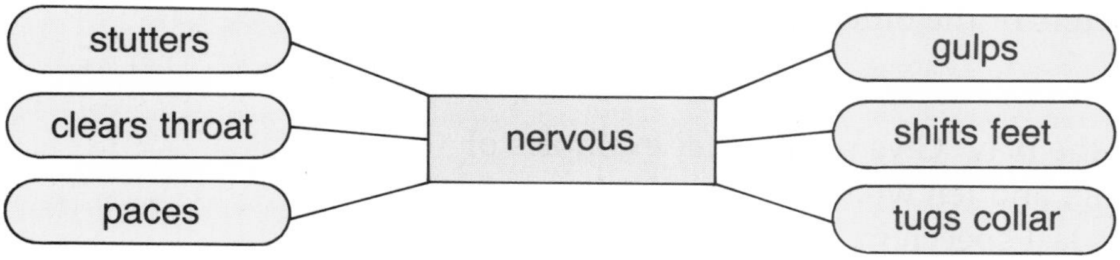

As you write a play, include in your stage directions details that make your characters seem real.

Discuss

Which of the stage directions answers the question *how?* What other questions do the stage directions answer?

Try Your Hand

Observe Details Observe an actor on television portraying a particular emotion. Make an idea cluster of details about how the actor looks, sounds, and moves. Trade idea clusters with a partner. Then discuss with your partner other details that might be added to the cluster.

Developing the Writer's Craft

Storytelling—Foreshadowing

In a good story, poem, or play, writers **foreshadow,** or give clues that allow the audience to predict actions and outcomes.

Read these lines from the play *The Open Window.*

> FRAMTON: You don't find it all—a bit unnerving?
> VERA: A little. Sometimes on quiet evenings like this, <u>I get a creepy feeling that they all will walk in through that window.</u>

Writer's Guide

Good writers

- create clues to foreshadow future actions and outcomes.
- include clues in the dialogue and in the characters' actions.

The underlined words suggest what will happen during the resolution of the play, when Mr. Sappleton and Freddie do come in through the window.

Through foreshadowing, writers build suspense in their plays. Suspense keeps the audience interested because it allows them to anticipate what will happen next.

When you write a play, be sure to include clues that foreshadow actions of characters or the outcome of the plot.

Discuss

1. Look back at the play. Give some other examples of foreshadowing, and tell what they foreshadow.
2. Reread Vera's last speech in the play. What in the play foreshadows this speech?

Try Your Hand

Foreshadow Actions or Outcomes Write a short one-act play about how you and a friend spend the day together. Include clues to indicate the kinds of activities you like to do. Do not write the ending. Trade plays with a partner. Predict how the characters in your partner's play will end their day. Then discuss the clues that foreshadow this outcome.

1 Prewriting
Play

Lorenzo wanted to write a play for his classmates to perform. He used the information in the **Writer's Guide** to help him plan his play. Look at what he did.

Writer's Guide

Prewriting Checklist

- Brainstorm stories.
- Select a story.
- Think about your audience and your purpose.
- Gather events, people, and characters.
- Organize your notes.

Brainstorming and Selecting a Story for a Play

Lorenzo decided to base his play on a folk tale or a legend he had read. First, he brainstormed and listed all the stories or legendary people he thought might make good subjects. Then, he looked at some books for other stories. He added them to the list.

Next, Lorenzo thought about each item on his list. He crossed off some stories. He knew that the right story would have plenty of action. Lorenzo also crossed off stories that were less interesting to him or that he could not find in the library.

Finally, Lorenzo circled the most suitable topic. He decided to write about King Arthur because the legend is full of action and because it interested Lorenzo. A version of it was available in the library for him to look at.

~~''The Lion and the Mouse''~~
~~Fabled Cities from Arabic Mythology~~
John Henry
King Arthur as a boy
~~''The Princess and the Pea''~~

Discuss

1. Look at the stories Lorenzo crossed off his list. Which one probably had too many locations for a play? Why might Lorenzo have crossed off the other topics?
2. What kinds of stories are good to use for a play? What qualities must the story have?

◆ Gathering Information

After Lorenzo selected his story, he gathered information for his play. To begin, he thought about the plot and identified the main **conflict** in it. He knew that every good story has conflict, or struggle between two opposing forces. Sometimes the conflict is a struggle between the main character and an animal or a natural force, such as a wild horse or an earthquake. Another kind of conflict is between two characters or groups that hold opposing views. A story might even place the conflict within the character's own mind. The main conflict in Lorenzo's play is between two characters, Arthur (the protagonist, or main character) and his brother, Sir Kay (the antagonist, or opponent).

Keeping the conflict in mind, Lorenzo then referred to the story to list the events that would show how the conflict arose and how it was resolved. He also listed the places and the characters he would include.

Events
Arthur polishes brother's armor.
Sir Kay fights in tournament.
Breaks sword.
Sends Arthur for new sword.
Places
meadow with green silk tent
armor and rags on ground
town square with sword in anvil
field for tournament
Characters
Arthur
Sir Kay, his brother
Sir Ector, his foster father
Merlin, the magician
a friend

After Lorenzo listed the characters, he made notes.

Protagonist	Arthur—eighteen, blond hair to shoulders, hardworking, loyal, wears page's costume
Antagonist	Kay—brave but dishonest, wears knight's costume
Minor Characters	Ector—In his sixties, stern but fair, wears cloak over knight's costume
	Merlin—long white beard, kind smile, wrinkled old face, wears hooded cloak

Discuss

Look back at Lorenzo's first list of characters. What details did he include about his characters?

◆ Organizing the Information

After Lorenzo had gathered all the information he needed for his play, he was ready to organize his notes. He knew that the plot of his play needed three main sections. He drew a plot diagram.

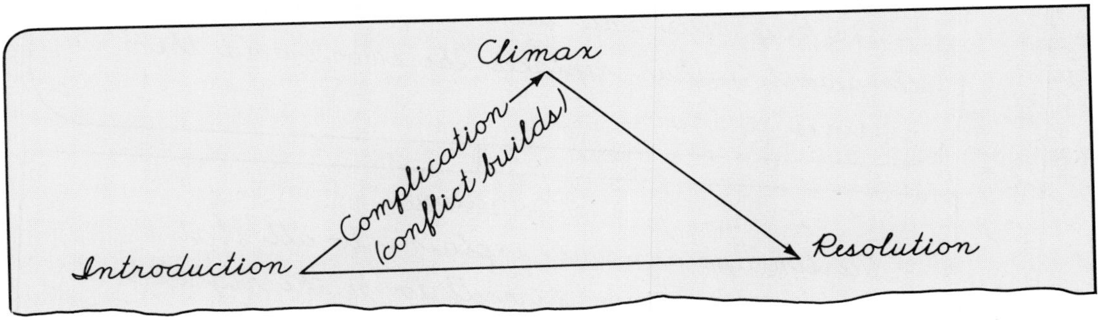

He decided his play needed several **scenes,** or times and places of action, to tell the story. Referring to his notes, he drew sketches of the scenes as a story map. He described what he planned to include in each scene. The story map appears on page 420.

Introduction

Arthur and a friend are polishing armor in a meadow. They are discussing a sword that is stuck in an anvil.

Complication

1. Arthur breaks his brother's (Sir Kay's) sword.
2. Arthur goes to the sword in the anvil and removes it.
3. Arthur gives Sir Kay the sword to replace the one he had broken.
4. Arthur's father enters and sees Sir Kay with the sword. Sir Kay claims he took the sword out of the anvil himself.

Climax

Sir Kay tries and fails to put sword back in the anvil. Arthur replaces the sword and then removes it again.

Resolution

Merlin appears and explains to all that Arthur has proven himself to be the rightful king.

Lorenzo planned one scene for the introduction, in which he would present the main character and set up the situation for the audience. Through dialogue and action he would tell what had happened up to this point. For the complication, Lorenzo planned two scenes to show the conflict between the protagonist and the antagonist. He knew he had to build the conflict to a climax at the end of the complication. In the resolution, Lorenzo planned to resolve and complete the action and to show what finally happened to the characters in the play. Here he planned to make his own ideas clear, since he knew most good plays leave the audience with a message.

Discuss

1. Why did Lorenzo draw the pyramid diagram of the plot? What does it show?
2. Look back at Lorenzo's list of characters, places, and events. How do you think the list helped him when he planned the scenes for each part of his play?
3. In which scene of the play will Sir Kay claim that he pulled the sword from the anvil? Why does his claim appear in this part of the play?
4. Why does the climax occur during the third scene of the play?

Try Your Hand

Now plan a play of your own.

A. Brainstorm and Select a Topic Before planning a plot for a play, brainstorm a list of folk tales or legends you have read. Think about each story and about your audience.

- Cross out stories that are more about thoughts and feelings than about action.
- Cross out stories that do not have interesting or appealing characters.
- If you are going to use a story you have read, cross out those you cannot find at home or in the library.
- Cross out stories that include too many locations or that cover too much time for a play.
- Circle the most suitable story left on your list. This will be the story for your play.

B. Gather Information When you are satisfied with your topic, plan how you can gather information.

- You might want to list the events, the places, and the characters as Lorenzo did.
- If your play is based on a folk tale or a legend, it does not have to include all the events in the story.
- In the list of places, include the props, or the objects the characters will need, for each place.
- For the characters, list the protagonist, the antagonist, and the minor characters who will appear in the play.
- Describe their appearances and their personality traits. Your descriptions will help you write stage directions and dialogue that suit the characters.

C. Organize the Information Review your lists and sketches.

- Make sure you have included ideas that might be useful to you in a play.
- Create a story map showing the introduction, complication, climax, and resolution of your play. You may wish to use a diagram like this one.

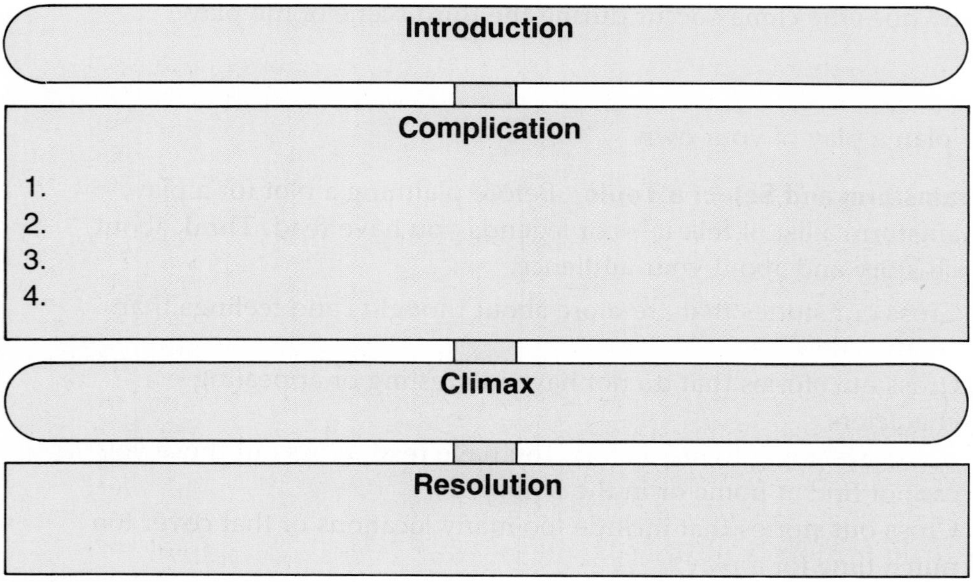

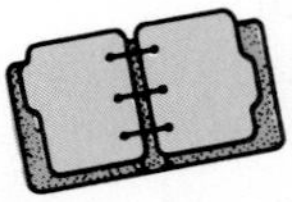

Save your lists and story map in your *Writer's Notebook*. You will use them when you draft your script.

2 Drafting

Play

Lorenzo followed the **Writer's Guide** to draft his play. Look at what he did.

> **Writer's Guide**
>
> **Drafting Checklist**
>
> - ☑ Use your lists and story map for ideas.
> - ☑ First, write the introduction.
> - ☑ Next, write the complication.
> - ☑ Last, write the resolution.

```
SIR ECTOR (Placing a hand on SIR KAY'S shoulder):
  Son, you say you withdrew this sword from the
  anvil. In that case, you are the true king of
  England and should have no trouble placing it
  back in the anvil again.
SIR KAY (Looking guilty and worried): Who could
  possibly put a sword into a block of iron?
SIR ECTOR (Firmly): Whoever drew it out in the
  first place. (KAY responds by taking hold of
  the sword, his face reddening with the effort
  as he tries frantically to thrust it into the
  iron. ARTHUR watches from behind.)
```

Discuss

What action happens? Which words help show the action?

Try Your Hand

Now you are ready to write a play.

A. Review Your Information Think about the information you gathered and organized in the last lesson. Decide whether you need more information. If so, gather it.

B. Think About Your TAP Remember that your task is to write the script for a play. The script is written so that actors will be able to read the play and perform it. Your purpose is to entertain your audience with a live performance.

Task: What?
Audience: Who?
Purpose: Why?

C. Write Your First Draft Refer to your **Drafting Checklist** as you write your play.

When you write your draft, just put all your ideas on paper. Do not worry about spelling, punctuation, or grammar. You can correct the draft later.

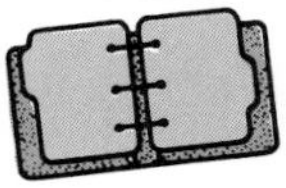

Save your first draft in your *Writer's Notebook.* You will use it when you revise your play.

3 Responding and Revising
Play

Lorenzo used the checklist in the **Writer's Guide** to revise his play. Look at what he did.

◆ Checking Information

Lorenzo added a word to the dialogue to show Arthur's respect for Sir Ector. To make the addition, he used this mark ∧ . Then Lorenzo decided to cut an unnecessary line of dialogue. To show his change, he used this mark ℯ.

◆ Checking Organization

Lorenzo moved a stage direction so that the actor would say the lines correctly. He used this mark ⌒ .

◆ Checking Language

In one of Arthur's speeches, Lorenzo replaced a run-on sentence with two complete sentences. He used this mark ∧‾ to show his change.

Writer's Guide

Revising Checklist

- ☑ Read your play to yourself or to a partner.
- ☑ Think about your audience and your purpose. Add or cut lines.
- ☑ Check to see that your play is organized correctly.
- ☑ Check for sentence fragments and run-on sentences.

Add
Cut
Move
Replace

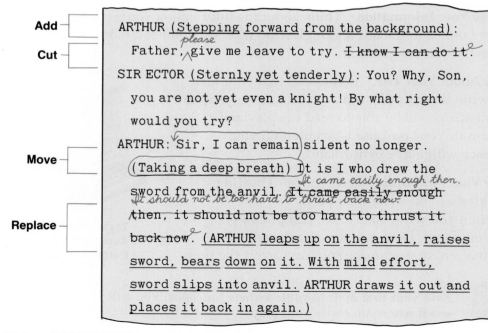

ARTHUR (Stepping forward from the background):
Father, ∧ *please* give me leave to try. ~~I know I can do it.~~
SIR ECTOR (Sternly yet tenderly): You? Why, Son, you are not yet even a knight! By what right would you try?
ARTHUR: ⌒ Sir, I can remain silent no longer. (Taking a deep breath) It is I who drew the sword from the anvil. ~~It came easily enough then, it should not be too hard to thrust it back now.~~ *It came easily enough then. It should not be too hard to thrust back now.* (ARTHUR leaps up on the anvil, raises sword, bears down on it. With mild effort, sword slips into anvil. ARTHUR draws it out and places it back in again.)

Discuss

1. Do you agree with the changes Lorenzo made in Arthur's first speech? Why or why not?
2. Why did Lorenzo make changes in Arthur's second group of lines?
3. Are there other changes he could have made? Explain your answer.

Try Your Hand

Now revise your first draft.

A. Read Your First Draft As you read your play, think about your audience and your purpose. Read your draft silently or act it out with a partner to see if it is complete and well organized. Ask yourself or your partner the questions in the box.

Responding and Revising Strategies

✔ Respond **Ask yourself or a partner:**	✔ Revise **Try these solutions:**
◆ Is there enough action in the play?	◆ **Replace** lines the characters say with actions that they do.
◆ Can my audience predict what will happen in my play?	◆ **Add** clues in the dialogue and stage directions.
◆ Are the characters consistent and believable?	◆ **Replace** actions or dialogue that seem out of place.
◆ Does each part of the play move the action forward to the ending?	◆ **Cut** unnecessary dialogue or scenes.
◆ Have I avoided sentence fragments and run-on sentences in my dialogue?	◆ **Replace** sentence fragments and run-on sentences with complete sentences. See the **Revising Workshop** on page 426.

B. Make Your Changes If the answer to any question in the box is *no,* try the solution. Use the **Editor's Marks** to show your changes.

C. Review Your Play Again Decide if there is anything else you want to revise. Keep revising until your play is well organized and complete.

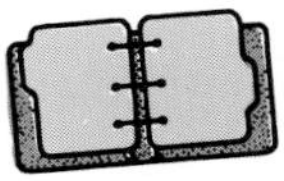

Save your revised script in your *Writer's Notebook.* You will use it when you proofread your play.

EDITOR'S MARKS

∧ Add something.
Cut something.
Move something.
Replace something.

Revising Workshop
Avoiding Sentence Fragments and Run-ons

Good writers express their thoughts in complete sentences. They avoid writing **sentence fragments,** groups of words that do not express a complete thought. Read the following lines from another play about King Arthur.

1. ARTHUR: Now that I am King. My barons beseech me to marry. Give me no rest on the matter.
2. ARTHUR: Now that I am King my barons beseech me to marry. They give me no rest on the matter.

In Arthur's first speech, the writer used two sentence fragments. The writer then corrected the speech. One fragment was joined to the sentence that followed it. A subject was added to the next fragment to make it complete.

Good writers also avoid **run-on sentences,** groups of words that should be written as two or more sentences or as a compound sentence.

3. ARTHUR: I will not marry without your advice, Merlin, help me and I will take heed.
4. ARTHUR: I will not marry without your advice, Merlin. Help me, and I will take heed.

The writer corrected the run-on sentence. The writer divided the thoughts into two sentences. A comma was added to change the second sentence to a compound sentence.

Practice

Rewrite each speech, making complete sentences from each sentence fragment or run-on sentence.

1. MERLIN: A man of your standing. Should not be without a wife. Is there someone whom you love more than any other?
2. ARTHUR: There is a lady. Calls herself Guinevere.
3. MERLIN: I wish I could convince you to look elsewhere it is true that she is fair I warn you that this marriage will be unhappy.
4. ARTHUR: Still, it is my will to marry this fair lady please inform her good father, King Lodegrean, of my intent.

4 Proofreading
Play

After revising the script for his play, Lorenzo used the checklist in the **Writer's Guide** and the **Editor's Marks** to proofread it. Look at some of his changes.

Writer's Guide

Proofreading Checklist

- Check for errors in capitalization.
- Check for proper use of parentheses.
- Check for correct play form.
- Check for errors in your grammar.
- Circle any words you think are misspelled. Find out how to spell them correctly.
- ⇨ For proofreading help, use the **Writer's Handbook.**

SIR ECTOR (Kneeling before Arthur): Oh, now I know who your real father was. Now it is clear why Merlin brought me an Infant to raise secretly as my own.

ARTHUR (Tearfully): Father, your words fill me with fear. Why do you kneel? (The sound of footsteps grows louder.)

MERLIN (Appearing from D L): He kneels because you are the rightful king. Have no fear, Arthur, for you will rule with the advise (advice) of many knights at a great round table, becoming the most glorious king this troubled realm has ever known.

EDITOR'S MARKS

- Capitalize.
- Add a period.
- Add something.
- Add a comma.
- Add quotation marks.
- Cut something.
- Replace something.
- Transpose.
- Spell correctly.
- Indent paragraph.
- Make a lowercase letter.

Discuss

Look at Lorenzo's proofread play. What kinds of mistakes did he make? Why did he add parentheses ( ) before Arthur's speech?

Try Your Hand

Proofread Your Play Now use the **Writer's Guide** and the **Editor's Marks** to proofread your own play.

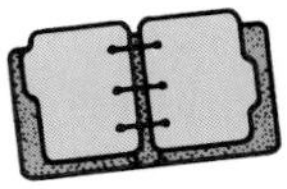

Save your corrected script in your *Writer's Notebook.* You will use it when you publish your play.

5 Publishing
Play

Lorenzo made a clean copy of his script and checked it to be sure he had not left anything out. Then he published his play by having it performed on stage. You can find part of Lorenzo's play on page 51 of the **Writer's Handbook.**

Here's how Lorenzo published his play.

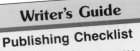

Writer's Guide

Publishing Checklist

- ☑ Make a clean copy of your play.
- ☑ Check to see that nothing has been left out.
- ☑ Be sure that there are no mistakes.
- ☑ Share your play in a special way.

1. First, he duplicated the pages of the play script and stapled them together so that there were enough copies of his script for all the actors.

2. To decide who should appear in the cast, Lorenzo and his classmates held an audition in which actors tried out for the different roles. The director selected the performers.

3. Class members were chosen to create or acquire the scenery, the costumes, and the props.

4. The players rehearsed until they knew their lines comfortably. To learn their lines, they repeated them over and over, both alone and with other actors.

5. Lorenzo and his classmates held a dress rehearsal in which the actors performed in costume.
6. They announced the opening performance by following the **Tips on How to Make Announcements.** Then they performed the play and enjoyed the applause!

Discuss

1. What might happen if the actors did not rehearse the play together?
2. Why is it important to have a dress rehearsal?

Try Your Hand

Publish Your Play Follow the checklist in the **Writer's Guide.** If possible, perform your play, or try one of these ideas for sharing your script.

- Collect into a book plays written by your classmates.
- Submit your play to the school drama club and ask them to offer a critique.

Listening and Speaking

Tips on How to Make Announcements

Giving an Announcement

1. Be sure to announce *what* the event is.
2. Tell *why* the event is being held.
3. State *when* and *where* it will occur.
4. Tell *who* is invited to attend.

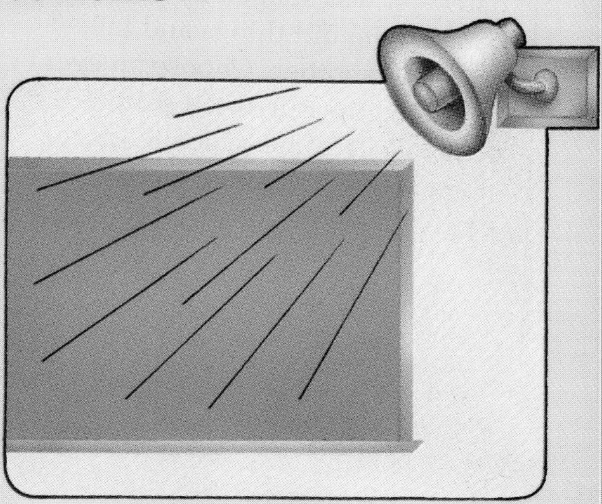

Listening to an Announcement

1. Listen carefully for details.
2. Record when and where the event will be held.

Writing in the Content Areas

Use what you learned to write part of a scene for a play. Let your imagination take center stage as you use one of these ideas or an idea of your own.

Writer's Guide

When you write, remember the stages of the Writing Process.

- Prewriting
- Drafting
- Responding and Revising
- Proofreading
- Publishing

Science

As scientists seek information about new scientific frontiers, their microscopes are trained on incredibly tiny objects. Write some dialogue for actors playing laboratory scientists who are on the verge of a new discovery. You may make their discovery serious, frightening, or funny.

Physical Education

The coach and the players usually have a lot to say to one another during a break in an exciting game. Write some dialogue that might take place at halftime in a sport you enjoy. You could have the characters in your scene discuss what has happened in the game so far and make plans for the rest of the game.

Social Studies

History is more than facts and dates—it was shaped by real people who did things and talked with one another. Choose an event described in your social studies book. Write some dialogue for the characters who helped shape that historical event.

Fine Arts

A Chorus Line, a popular musical play, features dancers telling each other and the audience why they chose their career. Think of something you like to do in the field of fine arts, such as dancing, singing, or painting. Write a scene in which you and your fellow artists tell about your love for that art form.

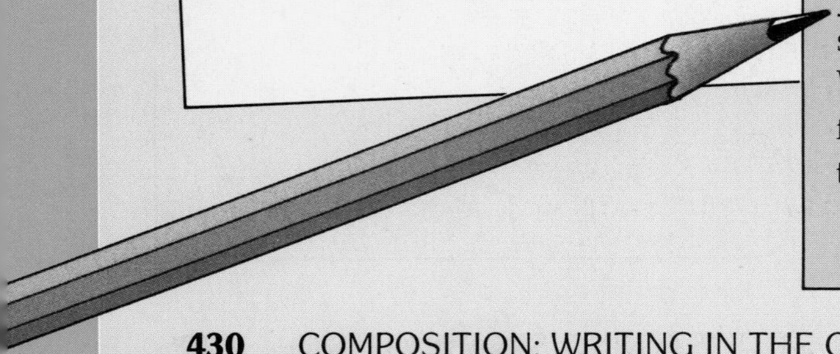

CONNECTING
WRITING ↔ LANGUAGE

Pecos Bill is a legendary hero of tall tales. In the scene below, Pecos Bill claims he will solve a problem. Find out what his solution is.

MAN *(Mopping his head)*: It sure is hot!
WOMAN: And dry! We haven't had a drop of rain in weeks.
FARMER: It is so hot that the corn in my fields is popping right on the cob.
COWHAND: It is so dry that my cows' tongues are hanging down to their knees.
PECOS BILL: It sounds as though we need a little rain.
FARMER: But there isn't a cloud in sight.
WOMAN: There is that little powder-puff cloud way over there, but it's miles away.
PECOS BILL: Well, I'll go get it and coax it over here.
WOMAN: How in the world are you going to do that?
PECOS BILL *(Pulling on the brim of his hat)*: I guess I'll have to go lasso it and drag it back just as I do calves that need branding!

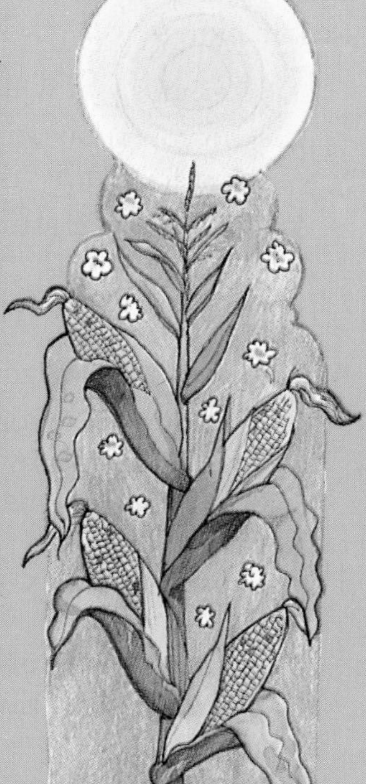

◆ **Mechanics in a Play** Notice that the punctuation and capitalization in the scene help you understand how to read it silently or aloud.

◆ **Language Focus: Mechanics Wrap-up** The following lessons will help you learn more about capitalization and punctuation.

1 Capitalization and End Punctuation in Sentences

◆ **FOCUS** Every sentence begins with a capital letter and ends with a punctuation mark.

Correct capitalization and punctuation help make your writing clearer. Always remember to capitalize the first word of a sentence. End every sentence with a period, a question mark, or an exclamation point.

1. Perhaps you will recognize this poem.
2. Do you know any other poems by Eve Merriam?
3. What a delightful poem that is!

Markings: The Period
by Eve Merriam

Left. Right.
Left. Right.
Absolute black.
Positive white.

Those in the know
march straight in a row
Never a moment's hesitancy.
No raggedy baggy-kneed stragglers like me
who bumble along half-right and
not quite . . .

Guided Practice

A. Tell how to capitalize and punctuate each sentence correctly.

1. what is your favorite poem
2. i like all poems by Robert Frost
3. how many poems did Robert Frost write
4. listen to this one
5. this poem makes you feel warm and peaceful inside
6. frost won the Pulitzer Prize four times
7. can you hear a rhythmic beat when you read this poem
8. poetry with a regular pattern is called bound verse
9. what a wonderful and creative poet Frost was

Eve Merriam

THINK AND REMEMBER
- Capitalize the first word of a sentence.
- End a sentence with a period, a question mark, or an exclamation point.

Independent Practice

B. Proofreading: Using Capital Letters and End Punctuation Write each sentence. Capitalize words where necessary, and insert needed end punctuation.

10. the poems from Old Possum's Book of Practical Cats were made into a play

MODEL The poems from Old Possum's Book of Practical Cats were made into a play.

11. it is a famous Broadway show
12. what wonderful reviews it received
13. we saw that show when it was on tour
14. it is a musical about cats
15. which cat did you like best
16. we both thought that Bustopher Jones was the funniest of the cats
17. we all felt so sorry for Grizabella
18. how surprised T. S. Eliot would be to see his words being presented this way

C. Writing Sentences For each topic listed below, write a declarative sentence, an interrogative sentence, and an exclamatory sentence. Make sure all of your sentences begin with capital letters.

19. dogs

MODEL My favorite dog is the English setter.
Have you seen Buddy, my new dog?
What a smart dog he is!

20. traveling
21. old houses
22. your favorite sport
23. a hobby
24. food
25. rainy days
26. hospitals
27. a special holiday
28. a great vacation
29. finding a treasure
30. the ocean
31. attics

Application — Writing

Friendly Letter Write a letter telling a friend how you feel about a favorite poet or author. You may wish to concentrate on a particular work. Be sure to tell your friend why you find this poet or author so entertaining. Remember to use capital letters and correct end punctuation. If you need help writing a friendly letter, see page 62 of the **Writer's Handbook.**

2 Commas Within Sentences

◆ **FOCUS** A comma is used to separate one part of a sentence from another to make the meaning clear.

Commas indicate pauses in sentences. A comma is used to separate one part of a sentence from another to make the meaning clear.

Use a comma after an introductory word such as *yes, no, why,* or *well.* Also, use a comma after a long prepositional phrase, a series of prepositional phrases, a participial phrase, or an adverb clause at the beginning of a sentence.

1. Yes, I would be glad to attend your graduation.
2. At the beginning of the ceremony, everyone stood.
3. Standing at the podium, Dr. Lucas spoke to the seniors.
4. As their names were called, the students came forward.

Do not use a comma before an adverb clause that comes at the end of a sentence.

5. I felt proud when I watched Ginny's graduation .

When you write three or more words, phrases, or clauses in a series, use a comma after each but the last.

6. Dr. Lucas spoke about dedication, loyalty, and ideals .
7. Awards were given for excellence in math, ability in music, and achievement in science .
8. The students were nervous, the parents were proud, and the young children were impatient .

Remember that appositives are words that rename or explain the meaning of the nouns they follow. Use commas to set off an appositive that is not needed for the sentence to make sense.

9. Mr. Carillo , our principal, presented the diplomas.
10. I sat by Rosita , an exchange student from Mexico .

Use commas to separate a nonrestrictive adjective clause from the rest of a sentence.

11. The ceremony , which lasted two hours, was held outside.

A **noun of direct address** is a person's name or title used in conversation. Use a comma to set it off from the rest of a sentence.

12. Jody, will you take a picture of me with my parents?
13. Look at me , everyone, and smile.

Parenthetical expressions are interrupters such as *in fact, for example, in my opinion,* and *of course.* They are added to a sentence for emphasis or clarity and should be set off by commas.

14. To tell the truth, that speech was rather long.
15. We are getting hungry , by the way .
16. You know , of course, about the graduation brunch.

Use a comma before the conjunction that joins the clauses of a compound sentence.

17. We were early , but most of the seats were already taken.
18. The music began , and the class marched up the aisle.

Guided Practice

A. Tell where commas are needed in these sentences.

1. Holding my yearbook I went looking for my friends.
2. A yearbook is in my opinion good for remembering people.
3. Monica my best friend wrote a long note by her picture.
4. She wrote about our class one of our trips and the fall dance.
5. Wherever I go I will always remember these students.
6. Some will go to the local high school but others will go away to boarding school.
7. Our yearbook has pictures captions poems and anecdotes.
8. Barb Johnson who edited the yearbook wrote this poem.
9. Barb would you sign your name next to your poem?
10. Why I just happen to have a pen with me.

THINK AND REMEMBER

- Use commas after introductory words, phrases, and clauses.
- Use commas between words, phrases, and clauses in a series.
- Use commas to set off appositives, nonrestrictive clauses, nouns of direct address, and parenthetical expressions from the rest of a sentence.
- Use a comma between the two independent clauses of a compound sentence.

Independent Practice

B. Proofreading: Inserting Commas Write the sentences, inserting commas where needed.

11. My brother applied for a scholarship and he is now a finalist.

MODEL My brother applied for a scholarship, and he is now a finalist.

12. He is in my opinion the most qualified candidate.
13. When he applied he was interviewed by the principal.
14. The selection committee a group of high-school teachers will decide.
15. The money will pay his tuition which is quite high.
16. Scholarships will be awarded in math science social sciences and languages.
17. Offered by the hospital one prize goes to a future doctor.
18. In addition the recipient must have hospital volunteer experience.
19. Joanne Farr the winner worked as a volunteer.
20. Joanne has worked hard she has shared her time and she has helped many patients.

C. Revising: Combining Sentences Combine each pair of sentences by forming an appositive, a clause, or a compound sentence. Use commas correctly in your sentences.

21. Lisa is my sister. Lisa just graduated from high school.

MODEL Lisa, my sister, just graduated from high school.
OR
Lisa, who just graduated from high school, is my sister.

22. She is leaving for college. I plan to write to Lisa.
23. Lisa's friends will miss her. Many of her friends are going away to college as well.
24. She will fly home in December. Then we will not see her again until May.
25. I will miss her. I will enjoy having my own room.
26. Her college is Texas Tech. It is located in Lubbock.

Application — Writing and Speaking

Graduation Speech Imagine that you have been asked to speak at a high-school graduation. Write a speech for the graduating class. Give the graduates advice about planning their futures. Use at least one noun of direct address, one interrupter, and one introductory phrase in your address. Deliver your speech to your classmates.

3 Other Punctuation Within Sentences

◆ **FOCUS** Colons, semicolons, dashes, hyphens, and parentheses are used as punctuation within sentences.

There are some rules that will help you to use colons, semicolons, dashes, hyphens, and parentheses correctly in sentences.

Use a colon when you write the time in figures.

9:15 A.M. 2:00 P.M. 6:38 P.M. 11:19 A.M.

Use a colon after phrases beginning with *as follows* or *the following* when they introduce a list. Do not use a colon after a verb or a preposition.

1. We need the following items: pencils, paper, erasers, and chalk.
2. Give the art supplies to Amanda, Rhonda, Bruno, or Chris.
3. The speakers are Ms. Burke, Mr. Fletcher, and Ms. Huntington.

Use a semicolon to join the clauses of a compound sentence when you do not use a conjunction. If you use words such as *therefore, however,* and *furthermore,* place a comma after these words.

4. The meeting is three hours long; we will take a break at 3:00.
5. Our first speaker has not yet arrived; therefore, we will skip to the next part of the program.

Use semicolons to separate items in a series when one or more of the items already include commas.

6. Similar conventions are being held in Dallas, Texas; New York, New York; and Philadelphia, Pennsylvania.

Use a dash to show an abrupt change in thought within a sentence.

7. Mr. Tyson thinks—and I agree with him—that every office should have a computer.

When you break a word at the end of a line, divide it between syllables. Use a hyphen to show the break.

8. New and better equipment has made it necessary to mod-
   ernize dictation machines.

Do not divide a word so that only one letter appears at the beginning or end of a line. Do not divide one-syllable words.

Incorrect: e-jection fo-und **Correct:** ejec-tion found

Use a hyphen when you write out the names of compound numbers and fractions.

thirty-seven   ninety-four   one-fifth   three-fourths

Use parentheses to enclose information not necessary for the meaning of the sentence or information your audience probably knows.

9. Tonight's banquet will be in Ballroom C (next door).

Guided Practice

A. Tell what punctuation is needed in each sentence and where it should be placed.

1. A new convention center we really need one is being built.
2. It will have thirty five large meeting rooms.
3. Each room will have audiovisual equipment a large screen will occupy the front wall.
4. Two thirds of the rooms will have movable walls.
5. The grand opening ceremony is scheduled for 1130 AM on June 15.
6. A committee is planning special fes
   tivities a dedication will be held at noon.
7. They have scheduled the following activities guided tours, a balloon launch, and a party.
8. Anyone who attends all ticketholders may take the guided tour.
9. A light lunch I hope it's good will be served after the tour.
10. After lunch, the convention center will be open to the public until 600 PM or later.

THINK AND REMEMBER

- Use a colon between the hour and the minutes in time designations and after phrases that introduce a list.
- Use semicolons in compound sentences not joined by conjunctions and to separate items in a series that already include commas.
- Use a dash to show a sudden break in thought.
- Use a hyphen in dividing a word at the end of a line and in writing out the names of compound numbers and fractions.
- Use parentheses to set off information not necessary for the meaning of the sentence.

Independent Practice

B. Proofreading: Inserting Punctuation Write each sentence, inserting needed punctuation.

11. Attending a convention can be fun it is also educational.

MODEL Attending a convention can be fun; it is also educational.

12. Knowledgeable speakers present seminars and pro grams about new developments in their fields.
13. You may find ninety five percent of the information useful.
14. Thousands attend conventions they provide an opportunity to meet people who share your interests.
15. From 900 till 500 you can learn how to do your job better.
16. The sightseeing you should try to do some is an added benefit.
17. The following are some fine sites for conventions Augusta, Georgia Austin, Texas Orlando, Florida Portland, Oregon and San Diego, California.

C. Dividing Words Divide each word into syllables, and place hyphens between the syllables. If the word cannot be divided, write it without hyphens. Use a dictionary if you need help.

18. possible

MODEL pos-si-ble

19. criticize	21. strength	23. guarantee	25. advance
20. passport	22. playpen	24. locate	26. stared

D. Using Colons and Hyphens Read each sentence. Write the underlined words as numerals and the numerals as words.

27. At this hotel you cannot check in until eleven o'clock.

MODEL 11:00

28. This hotel has 26 floors.
29. There are 48 rooms on my floor.
30. Let's meet at seven o'clock.
31. Dinner starts at seven-thirty.
32. My meeting starts in 15 minutes.

Application — Writing

Summary of a Meeting Write a summary of a meeting for your classmates who did not attend a computer convention. Include meeting times and the facts you learned. Use colons, semicolons, hyphens, dashes, and parentheses correctly.

4 Numbers in Sentences

◆ **FOCUS** Numbers should be written sometimes as words and sometimes as numerals.

Follow these guidelines for writing numbers and numerals.

Writing Out Numbers
Write out numbers of fewer than three words. The dedication was attended by eighty-one people.
Write out numbers when they begin sentences. Four hundred fifty employees work for this company. *Alternative:* You may rewrite the sentence. This company has 450 employees.

Writing Numbers as Numerals	
Dates	Construction was begun on April 3, 1988.
Times	The dedication ceremony begins at 9:30 A.M.
Addresses	Our old office was at 413 Parkway Drive.
Room Numbers	My office is in Room 346.
Divisions of Reading Materials	Please read Chapter 2, paragraph 6, on page 148.

Remember to use an apostrophe with plurals of numbers.
the late 1900's   two *5*'s in the address

Guided Practice

A. Tell whether each number should be written out or written in numerals.

1. (3) new offices have been built recently in Somerton.
2. The newest is at (712) Market Street.
3. The Bank Tower has (275) offices.
4. Its doors opened for business on November (4, 1989).
5. There are (16) shops on the ground floor.
6. The shops stay open until (9:00) P.M.

THINK AND REMEMBER

- Write out numbers that have fewer than three words or that begin sentences.
- Write numerals in dates, times, addresses, room numbers, and divisions of reading materials.

Independent Practice

B. Proofreading: Replacing Number Words and Numerals in Sentences Rewrite each sentence, changing the numeral to a number word or the number word to a numeral.

7. The middle school has 30 new students.

MODEL The middle school has thirty new students.

8. Most art classes have no more than 25 students.
9. Some students' homes are over 14 miles away.
10. At the end of the day, 13 buses arrive on campus.
11. There are one hundred thirteen rooms in the building.
12. A dance is taking place tonight at eight o'clock.
13. The sponsors graduated in the year nineteen sixty-six.
14. 150 people are expected to attend.
15. That student's picture is on page eighty-two of the literary magazine.
16. Which is the last class to graduate in the nineteen hundreds?

C. Revising: Changing Sentences Rewrite each sentence so that the number does not begin the sentence.

17. 218 people work for this mail-order company.

MODEL This mail-order company employs 218 people.

18. 580 phone calls are received by the switchboard every day.
19. 6,700 catalogues are sent to customers across the country.
20. 950 different items are available for purchase.
21. 425 of them are on sale until the end of summer.
22. 15 days ago I sent an order for pencils.

Application — Writing

Math Problem Imagine that you are the architect who designed a new building. Write a math problem using the number of floors or offices or the dimensions of the building. Use numerals and number words correctly in your problem.

5 Capitalization of Proper Nouns, Proper Adjectives, and *I*

FOCUS

- Proper nouns, proper adjectives, and the pronoun *I* are always capitalized.
- Most abbreviations are capitalized and are followed by a period.

Remember that proper nouns include names of people, groups, geographical areas, and calendar items such as the names of months and holidays. These names always begin with capital letters.

Thomas Jefferson   Richmond   United States Constitution

Capitalize religious terms and names of religions.

Christianity   the Bible   God   Islam

Capitalize and underline the proper nouns that name aircraft, ships, and trains.

Voyager II   the Queen Mary   California Zephyr

Capitalize proper adjectives created from proper nouns.

American   Democratic party   Jeffersonian

Capitalize abbreviations of proper nouns and proper adjectives. Use a period after most abbreviations.

Fifth Ave.   Sept. 23   Gov. Wilson   NATO

Remember that the pronoun *I* is always capitalized.

1. Will I ever see Monticello?   **2.** You run faster than I do.

Guided Practice

A. Identify the word or words that should be capitalized in each sentence.

1. thomas jefferson was a member of the continental congress.
2. In philadelphia he wrote the declaration of independence.
3. This fine patriot became america's third president.
4. He was responsible for the louisiana purchase.
5. He bought from france the area between the mississippi river and the rocky mountains.

THINK AND REMEMBER

- Capitalize proper nouns and proper adjectives.
- Capitalize abbreviations of proper nouns and proper adjectives, and end most abbreviations with a period.
- Capitalize the pronoun *I*.

Independent Practice

B. Proofreading: Capitalizing Proper Nouns Write each sentence. Capitalize words where necessary.

6. Thousands of inventors apply to the u.s. patent office each year.

MODEL Thousands of inventors apply to the U.S. Patent Office each year.

7. Some inventions have changed american lives forever.
8. Imagine life without the inventions of thomas edison.
9. Without the inventions of alexander graham bell, we would have no telephones.
10. Bell was the founder of the bell telephone company.
11. A frenchman, ernest michaux, invented the bicycle.
12. Some inventions, like the bunsen burner, are named for their inventors.
13. Many inventors' names, such as westinghouse, pullman, and diesel, are closely identified with their products.
14. Inventors send patent applications to washington, d.c.
15. The department of commerce controls the patents.

C. Writing Proper Adjectives and Abbreviations Write a proper adjective (adj.) or an abbreviation (abbr.) for each word.

16. Britain (adj.)

MODEL British

17. Corporal (abbr.)
18. President (abbr.)
19. Mexico (adj.)
20. Russia (adj.)
21. Major (abbr.)
22. Greece (adj.)

Application — Writing

Sales Proposal Imagine that you have been hired to sell a machine that copies a letter as it is being written. Write a sales proposal that tells your supervisor details about how, where, and when you plan to sell this machine. Capitalize all proper nouns and proper adjectives in your proposal.

6 Letters and Envelopes

◆ **FOCUS** The parts of a letter and the addresses on an envelope follow rules of capitalization and punctuation.

When you write letters or address envelopes, be sure to use these rules for correct capitalization and punctuation.

Friendly Letter	
Capitalize the street, city, state, and month. Use commas between city and state and the day and year.	993 Briar Lane Akron, Ohio 44311 May 12, 19--
Use a comma after the greeting.	Dear Rick,
Indent each paragraph in the body of the letter.	Thanks for taking me to the museum.
Begin the closing with a capital letter, and end it with a comma.	Your friend,

Business Letter	
Capitalize the names of the company, street, city, state, and month in the return address and inside address. Use commas between the city and state and the day and year.	616 Vine Street Ames, Iowa 50010 May 21, 19-- Hon. John Shea, Mayor City Hall Holmes, Maine 04240
Use a colon after the greeting.	Dear Mayor Shea:
Indent each paragraph in the body of the letter.	I will be visiting Maine in July and
Begin the closing with a capital letter, and end it with a comma.	Sincerely,

Postal Abbreviations

Alabama	AL
Alaska	AK
Arizona	AZ
Arkansas	AR
California	CA
Colorado	CO
Connecticut	CT
Delaware	DE
District of Columbia	DC
Florida	FL
Georgia	GA
Hawaii	HI
Idaho	ID
Illinois	IL
Indiana	IN
Iowa	IA
Kansas	KS
Kentucky	KY
Louisiana	LA
Maine	ME
Maryland	MD
Massachusetts	MA
Michigan	MI
Minnesota	MN
Mississippi	MS
Missouri	MO
Montana	MT
Nebraska	NE
Nevada	NV
New Hampshire	NH
New Jersey	NJ
New Mexico	NM
New York	NY
North Carolina	NC
North Dakota	ND
Ohio	OH
Oklahoma	OK
Oregon	OR
Pennsylvania	PA
Puerto Rico	PR
Rhode Island	RI
South Carolina	SC
South Dakota	SD
Tennessee	TN
Texas	TX
Utah	UT
Vermont	VT
Virginia	VA
Washington	WA
West Virginia	WV
Wisconsin	WI
Wyoming	WY

Envelopes	
Capitalize the names of the company, the street, and the city in the return address and the mailing address. Use commas between the city and the state. Use United States postal abbreviations for state names.	John Myers 20 Russell Lane Salina, KS 67401 Alice Walker-Smith Denver Electric Company 1301 Walton Street Denver, CO 80204

Guided Practice

A. Tell how to capitalize and punctuate each letter part.

1. may 27 1990

2. Ms. Margaret Kelly
Kelly tutoring service
322 sparks street
ames iowa 50010

3. dear Aunt Pat

4. dear Peggy

5. sincerely

6. love

7. dear Ms. Kelly

8. 5801 ellis avenue
chicago illinois 60637

B. Tell how to capitalize, abbreviate, and punctuate these mailing addresses for envelopes.

9. Forbin's recycled books
10. 158 high street
11. jackson mississippi 39205
12. clean cut stylists
13. 42 spruce street
14. smithtown ny 11787
15. home renewal company
16. 129 howell road
17. winter park fl 32789

THINK AND REMEMBER

- Use correct capitalization and punctuation for letter writing.
- Use correct state abbreviations on envelopes.

Independent Practice

C. 18.–24. Capitalizing and Punctuating a Friendly Letter Write the letter with the correct capitalization, punctuation, and indentation.

```
                    1619 rutley circle
                    spring texas 77379
                    june 25 19—
dear Tim
How would you like to visit me here for a week? Mom
said you can come any time in August.
Let me know if you can make it and when you will arrive.
                    your friend
                    Zachary
```

D. 25.–34. Capitalizing and Punctuating a Business Letter Write the letter with the correct capitalization, punctuation, and indentation. Then draw a rectangle and address it as if it were an envelope.

```
                    1416 main street
                    lexington massachusetts 02173
                    september 14 19—
Mr. Richard Cain
the towel hut
875 hamilton drive
pleasant hill california 94523
dear Mr. Cain
I have not yet received the beach towel I ordered
on July 30. Please let me know when it will be sent.
Thank you for your help.
                    yours truly
                    Nancy Martinelli
                    Nancy Martinelli
```

Application—Writing

Business Letter Imagine that you will spend the summer at a basketball camp. Write a letter to your post office informing the postmaster that you will be away and would like to have your mail forwarded. Draw a large rectangle and address it as if it were an envelope.

7 Titles

◆ **FOCUS** The title of a written work or a work of art follows rules for capitalization and punctuation.

When you write titles of written works and works of art, be sure to capitalize and punctuate them correctly. Study the examples in the chart.

Books	The Call of the Wild, Abe Lincoln Grows Up
Magazines	National Geographic
Newspapers	Washington Post, Chicago Tribune
Plays	Sunday Costs Five Pesos, Fiddler on the Roof
Movies	Gone with the Wind
Television series	Sesame Street, Meet the Press
Works of art	American Gothic (painting), The Thinker (sculpture)
Works of music	H.M.S. Pinafore (operetta), "Jingle Bells" (song)
Short stories	"The Most Dangerous Game"
Poems	"My Grandmother Would Rock Quietly and Hum"
Articles	"Texas in Bloom"
Chapters of books	"Getting Started on Your Script"

Capitalize the first, last, and all important words in a title. Do not capitalize unimportant words, such as articles, prepositions, and coordinating conjunctions, unless they are the first or last word in a title.

Guided Practice

A. Identify the words in each title that should be capitalized. Then tell whether the title should be underlined or in quotation marks.

1. the homecoming (play)
2. cry of the crow (book)
3. we are the world (song)
4. albuquerque journal (newspaper)
5. boy's life (magazine)
6. adventures of isabel (poem)

THINK AND REMEMBER

- Capitalize all important words in a title.
- Underline titles of long works, such as books, magazines, newspapers, plays, movies, television series, and works of art and music.
- Place quotation marks around the titles of short works, such as short stories, poems, articles, chapters of books, and songs.

Independent Practice

B. Capitalizing and Punctuating Titles Write each title. Capitalize and punctuate it correctly.

7. an american in paris (movie)

MODEL An American in Paris

8. roll of thunder, hear my cry (book)
9. the cask of amontillado (short story)
10. wall street journal (newspaper)
11. the man from snowy river (movie)
12. two gentlemen of verona (play)
13. the first rose on my rose tree (poem)
14. turkey in the straw (song)
15. the iroquois: keepers of the fire (article)
16. bird in space (sculpture)

C. Proofreading: Writing Titles in Sentences Rewrite each sentence. Capitalize and punctuate titles correctly.

17. I dreamed I wrote a novel called digging to china.

MODEL I dreamed I wrote a novel called Digging to China.

18. A publisher especially liked my first chapter, finding the entrance.
19. Through the earth darkly was an article about my book.
20. The article was carried in the new york times.
21. A studio based its movie subterranean travels on my book.
22. A reporter for famous faces interviewed me for a magazine article.
23. Soon, singing down to china, a play based on my book, was on Broadway.
24. The hit song of the Broadway play was called pack up your gear and smile.
25. When I woke up, I remembered Jules Verne had written my story in journey to the center of the earth.

Application — Writing

Top Ten Write a Top Ten list of your favorite books, stories, movies, and songs. Remember to capitalize important words in each title and to punctuate titles correctly. Compare your list with that of a classmate. Which of your choices are the same?

8 Outlines and Bibliographies

◆ **FOCUS** An outline and a bibliography follow rules for capitalization and punctuation.

To prepare an outline for a research report, follow this format.

```
          Pueblo Pottery
     I. Introduction
    II. Famous Pueblo potters
        A. Nampeyo
        B. Martinez family
           1. Maria Martinez
           2. Popovi Da
           3. Tony Da
   III. Kinds of pottery
        A. Bowls
        B. Pots
        C. Clay figures
           1. Human
           2. Animal
        D. Canteens
    IV. Materials
        A. Clay
        B. Paints
        C. Brushes
     V. Conclusion
```

Rules for Preparing an Outline

1. Give your outline a title.
2. Use Roman numerals for the main topics, capital letters for the subtopics, and Arabic numerals for details.
3. Indent each level of the outline.
4. If you have subtopics under a main topic or details under a subtopic, include at least two. Never have an *A* without a *B* or a *1* without a 2.

A **bibliography** tells the reader where you found information about the topic. Study the sample bibliography entries and the following rules for preparing a bibliography. Notice where commas, colons, and periods are used.

Arnold, David L. "Pueblo Pottery--2000 Years of Artistry." National Geographic, November 1982, pp. 593–605.
Curtis, Natalie. The Indians' Book. New York: Dover Publications, 1968.
"Fossil Recovery." Badlands, Summer 1980, p. 3.
Ortiz, Alfonso. "Pueblo Indians." The World Book Encyclopedia, 1985.

Rules for Preparing a Bibliography

1. Alphabetize the bibliography according to authors' last names. If there are two authors for one work, write the name of the first author (last name first), then the word *and,* and then the next author's first and last names. If no author is given for an article, begin the entry with the title of the article.
2. Underline the titles of books, magazines, newspapers, and encyclopedias. Use quotation marks around the titles of magazine articles and encyclopedia entries.
3. For books, include the place of publication, the name of the publisher, and the latest copyright date on the copyright page.
4. List the date of the issue and the pages you used in a magazine.
5. List the year of publication of an encyclopedia edition.

Guided Practice

A. 1.–3. Identify the parts missing from this outline.

```
______________________
  I. Introduction
 II. Agriculture
     A. Crops
        1. Beans
        2. Corn
        3. Cotton
     ______________________
        1. Irrigation
        2. Tools
III. Arts
     A. Pottery
     B. Jewelry
     C. Basketry
______________________
```

B. Identify what is incorrect or missing in each bibliography entry.

4. Wilbur, C. Keith. The New England Indians. Chester, Conn., 1978.
5. Bean, John Lowell. American Indians. Britannica Macropedia, 1985.
6. National Parkways: A Photographic and Comprehensive Guide to Rocky Mountain and Mesa Verde National Parks. Casper, Wyo.: World-Wide Research and Publishing Co., 1975.
7. Boyer, David S. Warm Springs Indians Carve Out a Future. National Geographic, April, 1979, pp. 494–505.
8. Parsons, Elsie Clews. The Pueblo of Isleta. Albuquerque: University of New Mexico Press.

THINK AND REMEMBER

- Capitalize and punctuate an outline correctly.
- Alphabetize, capitalize, punctuate, and underline correctly in a bibliography.

Independent Practice

C. Proofreading: Correcting an Outline

Rewrite this outline, adding the missing information from the choices on the right.

```
        The Anasazi Culture
     I. Introduction
        A. Development of basketry
        B. Beginning of agriculture
   III. Modified Basketmaker
        period
        A. First examples of pottery
    IV. Developmental Pueblo
        period
MODEL   A. Early
           1. Living in pithouses
           2. Construction of
              ceremonial kivas
           4. Production of cotton
              as a crop
        B. Late
           2. First cooking pots
     V. Great Pueblo period
```

9. A. Early
10. II. Basketmaker period
11. C. Stylized pottery
12. VI. Conclusion
13. 3. Appearance of neck-banded pottery
14. B. Invention of bow and arrow
15. 1. Banding together of "clan kivas"
a. Development of villages
b. Construction of cliff dwellings

D. Proofreading: Correcting a Bibliography Rewrite this bibliography, alphabetizing it and inserting missing punctuation. Make sure each part of the entry is in the correct position.

16. Dutton, Bertha P. "Pueblo Indians." The World Book Encyclopedia, 1965.

MODEL Dutton, Bertha P. "Pueblo Indians." The World Book Encyclopedia, 1965.

17. Kopper, Philip. The Smithsonian Book of North American Indians Before the Coming of the Europeans. 1986. Washington: Smithsonian Books
18. Smith, Gary Utah's Rock Art—Wilderness Louvre. National Geographic January 1980, pp. 96–117
19. LaFarge, Oliver. A Pictorial History of the American Indian. New York: Crown Publishers, 1956.
20. Kingman, Eugene. "Painters of the Plains." American Heritage, pp. 32–42. December 1954.
21. Fleming Paula R. and Luskey, Judith. North American Indians. New York: Harper & Row, 1986.
22. Nichols, Roger I. The American Indian: Past and Present, 3rd ed New York Alfred A. Knopf, Inc., 1985.
23. Spicer, Edward H. A Short History of the Indians of the United States. Melbourne, FL: Krieger Pub. Co., 1983
24. White Jon M Everyday Life of the North American Indians. New York: Hippocrene Books, 1988.

Application — Writing

Outline and Bibliography Make up an outline and a bibliography you might use to write a report about a familiar art, sport, or other topic. Divide your outline into at least five main sections. List at least three references in your bibliography. You may invent the information you need.

9 Direct Quotations and Dialogue

FOCUS

- A direct quotation follows rules of capitalization and punctuation.
- A colon is used after the speaker's name before each speech in a play.

Quotations are used in stories, plays, speeches, or other writing in which what someone said is repeated. A **direct quotation** is the exact words a person said. Enclose these words in quotation marks. Capitalize the first word of a quotation. Separate the quotation from the rest of the sentence with a comma.

1. Nick said, "The movie will start in five minutes."
2. "Here are some good seats," whispered Karen.

If the second part of a divided quotation is a new sentence, begin it with a capital letter. If the second part is a continuation of the same sentence, do not capitalize it. If there are several sentences in the direct quotation, begin each sentence with a capital letter. Place the quotation marks after the last sentence.

3. "Watch this scene carefully," said Paco. "They are fingerspelling."
4. "That is an alphabet," he continued, "for deaf people."
5. "The girl is Helen Keller. She is blind and deaf. Anne Sullivan is her teacher," he explained.

Periods and commas always go inside the quotation marks. Question marks and exclamation points go inside the quotation marks if the quotation is a question or an exclamation. Do not use a comma if you use another end mark.

6. "Who plays Anne Sullivan?" Karen asked.
7. "She's a wonderful actor!" she exclaimed.

Dialogue is a written conversation. Each time the speaker changes, begin a new paragraph. You do not have to write *he said* or *she said* after each quotation.

8. "How much do I owe you for the tickets?" asked Sue.
   Nick shook his head. "It's my treat."
   "That's very generous of you. Let me at least buy the popcorn, then."

Write dialogue for a play by listing each speaker's name before the words he or she speaks. Put a colon after the speaker's name. Show the speaker's movements by including them in parentheses after the speaker's name.

9. SUE: How much do I owe you for the tickets?
   NICK (Shaking his head): It's my treat.
   SUE: That's very generous of you. Let me at least buy the popcorn, then.

An **indirect quotation** tells what someone said but does not use his or her exact words. Do not use quotation marks with indirect quotations.

10. Marta said that she would be five minutes late.
11. I told her we would wait for her.

Guided Practice

A. Tell how each direct quotation should be punctuated.

1. Amy said I enjoy reading the biographies of famous people.
2. I read Helen Keller's biography Paul said She became a lecturer.
3. Someone in the audience once asked Do you close your eyes when you sleep?
4. I never stayed awake to see Helen replied.
5. How Helen's life changed when she learned to write and speak exclaimed Paul

B. 6.–10. Tell how each sentence in **A** can be made into play dialogue and an indirect quotation.

THINK AND REMEMBER

- Enclose a direct quotation in quotation marks.
- Separate the quotation from the rest of the sentence with a comma or other punctuation.
- To write dialogue in a narrative, write each person's exact words within quotation marks, and begin a new paragraph each time the speaker changes.
- To write dialogue for a play, list each speaker's name before his or her words, and put a colon after the speaker's name.

Independent Practice

C. Writing Quotations Write each sentence, adding quotation marks, other punctuation, and capital letters.

11. Dan asked Jean do you know about the college for the deaf

MODEL Dan asked, "Jean, do you know about the college for the deaf?"

12. No she replied where is it what is its name
13. It's called Gallaudet College and it is located in Washington, D.C. he said.
14. Jean said tell me more about the school
15. it was founded in 1864 by Edward Miner Gallaudet, the son of Dr. Thomas Hopkins Gallaudet said Dan Dr. Gallaudet first brought sign language to America
16. Dan continued He founded the Hartford School for the Deaf
17. Jean said I knew about that school in Connecticut
18. that was established in 1817 Dan explained and later other schools for the deaf opened in the United States.

D. 19.–26. Revising: Writing Play Dialogue Rewrite the dialogue in **C** as lines of dialogue from a play.

19. Dan asked, "Jean, do you know about the college for the deaf?"

MODEL DAN: Jean, do you know about the college for the deaf?

E. Revising: Writing Indirect Quotations Rewrite each sentence as an indirect quotation.

27. "Fingerspelling is older than sign language," said Deanna.

MODEL Deanna said that fingerspelling is older than sign language.

28. Ben said, "Sign language is international."
29. "Deanna, with sign language deaf people can communicate across language barriers," he said.
30. Carolyn stated, "I can interpret sign language."
31. Ben asked, "Would you teach me some signs, Carolyn?"
32. "I'll be happy to," replied Carolyn.

Application — Writing and Speaking

Play Dialogue Write dialogue to depict what you remember occurring in a scene from a movie. Write five lines of dialogue for two characters. Use some stage directions to show the actors' movements. Perform your scene with a classmate in front of the class. If you need help writing play dialogue, see page 51 of the **Writer's Handbook.**

Building Vocabulary
How Words Are Formed

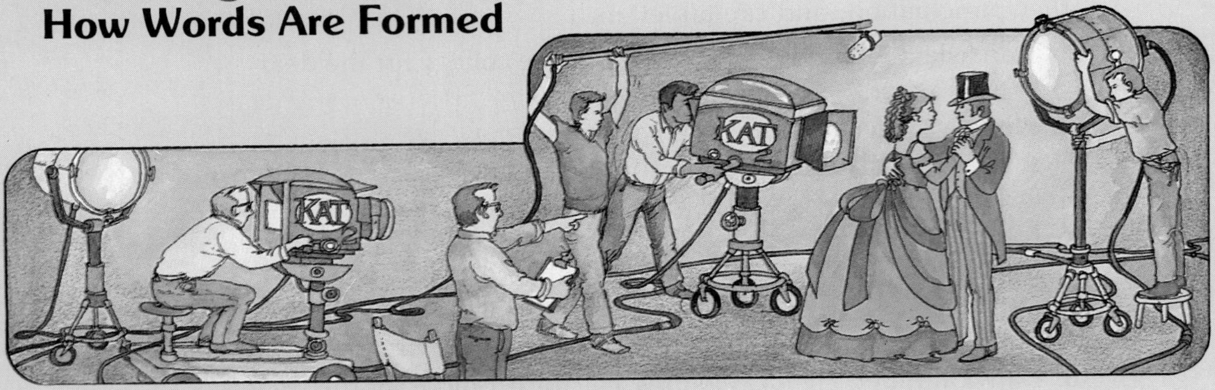

New words are continually coming into the English language. Many are formed from existing words that are shortened in some way.

Clipped words come into use when one or more syllables are dropped from a longer word. Clipped words often start as **slang,** informal shortcuts in conversation that come into and go out of style.

Blended words are formed when two words are combined into one. Blended words are different from compound words in that each of the words loses letters or syllables when combined.

Acronyms are words formed from the first letter or letters of words in compound terms or titles. Some acronyms are written in all uppercase letters, others in all lowercase letters. Often the acronym is known, but the words it represents are not. For example, everyone uses ZIP codes, but did you know that *ZIP* stands for *z*one *i*mprovement *p*lan?

Study this chart for other examples of clipped words, blended words, and acronyms.

	Word	Original Word or Words
Clipped Words	mike prop	microphone property
Blended Words	telecast fortnight	television + broadcast fourteen + night
Acronyms	sonar PBS	*so*und *na*vigation *r*anging *P*ublic *B*roadcasting *S*ystem

Reading Practice

Read the sentences below. Find the shortened word form in each. Write the shortened form and its original word or words. Label the shortened form *clipped word, blended word,* or *acronym.*

1. The new adventure series is sought after by all the networks, including PBS.
2. Negotiations between the producers and the networks have continued for a fortnight.
3. The first episode is slated for telecast in the fall.
4. The set designer is working on some very imaginative props.
5. The plot involves a scuba diver who finds buried treasure.
6. A sunken ship is detected with sonar.
7. The lead part requires an actress with a lot of pep.
8. The crew had trouble getting the underwater mikes to work.

Writing Practice

Rewrite each sentence below, replacing the underlined word or phrase with a shortened form as indicated in parentheses ( ). Use a dictionary if you need help.

9. I watched a fascinating <u>moving picture</u> (clipped word) on television.
10. It was about the history of the space program and the <u>National Aeronautics and Space Administration</u> (acronym).
11. Then, an unusual live <u>television broadcast</u> (blended word) came on.
12. It showed artists using <u>laboratory</u> (clipped word) technology in their art.
13. The two programs were very informative, but there were too many <u>advertisements</u> (clipped word) and station breaks.

Project

With your classmates, write a skit about some friends putting on a telecast from a school television studio. Before you begin writing, brainstorm as many words as possible that are blended words, clipped words, and acronyms. As you write the skit, try to use the shortened word forms in your dialogue. You might create a name and an acronym for the school studio, following the example of television networks.

Language Enrichment
Mechanics Wrap-up

Use what you know about capitalization and punctuation to do these activities.

See Your Name in Lights!

Tonight is opening night for the new play you have written, and the theater worker is ready to climb the ladder to put *your* name in lights. Write directions to tell the worker what letters and punctuation to put on the sign. Then write a short description of your play that will attract theater-goers. Be careful to use correct punctuation and capitalization.

Capital Idea

In a story, a bug uses a typewriter to write its own stories by leaping onto the typewriter keys. It cannot use the shift key to create capital letters, though. Continue the bug's story below. Use words that need capital letters, but write your story in the way the bug would do it. Then use **Editor's Marks** to correct the story.

last monday i saw that there was a full moon. i asked ms. ladybug to go canoeing on the river with me.

O Say, Can You Say?

"Here goes nothing!" said the skydiver.

"Happy landings!" said the instructor.

Would you expect the skydiver to *say* something? Wouldn't she be more likely to *shout*, *stammer*, or *exclaim* her words? How about her instructor?

Here are some words that might take the place of *said* in other situations: *sputtered, whispered, grumbled, drawled.* Add some other synonyms to the list, using your **Writer's Thesaurus.** Then use your list to write some dialogue for the skydiver and the instructor or for two other characters.

You may want to present your dialogue to your class. To do this, read the direct quotations, and have a partner read the words that describe how each quotation is said.

CONNECTING
LANGUAGE ↔ WRITING

In this unit you learned that capitalization and punctuation do more than tell a reader where a sentence begins and ends. Capitalization emphasizes important words in titles. Punctuation, such as commas, colons, dashes, and parentheses, helps readers understand your thoughts.

◆ **Using Capitalization and Punctuation in Your Writing** Knowing how to capitalize and punctuate correctly is important for clear communication. Avoiding errors in mechanics makes your writing easier to read and understand. Pay special attention to capitalization and punctuation as you do these activities.

New Play
"FYI"
Get your tickets now! SRO

New Words

You learned about clipped words, blended words, and acronyms on the **Building Vocabulary** pages. Write a paragraph to tell what might happen on the opening night of a school play. Try to use your own acronyms, blended words, and clipped words as well as established ones. Then trade papers with a classmate, and see if he or she can figure out the meaning of your words.

Invitation

Write a friendly letter to a friend in another city. Invite him or her to attend a performance of your school play. Include the date, time, and address for the play, using the rules for writing numbers and numerals. Then tell about the play and your role.

9 Unit Checkup

Think Back	Think Ahead
◆ What did you learn about a play in this unit? What did you do to write one?	◆ How will what you learned about a play help you follow characters and action? ◆ How will knowing how to observe details help you write a play?
◆ Look at the writing you did in this unit. How did your review of mechanics help you express your ideas?	◆ What is one way you can use mechanics to improve your writing?

Plays *pages 412 – 413*

Read each stage direction. Write *moves, speaks,* or *feels* to tell what is revealed about each character.

1. MAYOR (Raising her fist): Don't let me down! Vote today!
2. WILLIAM (Whispering): If I vote, it won't be for her.
3. ELAINE (Sighing): I don't know. Her promises are vague.

Observing Details *page 415*

Read each stage direction. Write what question is being answered.

4. KING (Saddened, walks slowly with head down): I'll leave.
5. JESTER (Begins a taunting riddle at KING)
6. QUEEN (Moves cautiously from her chair to the corridor)

Storytelling—Foreshadowing *page 416*

Write the following sentences. Insert a clue that would allow the reader to predict an action or outcome.

7. The duke entered. The king ________ inhaled.
8. The duke spoke ________ to the king.
9. The king looked ________ out at his rebellious court.

The Writing Process *pages 417 – 429*

Write the letter for the answer to each question.

10. When drafting your play, what should be written first?
    a. introduction **b.** complication **c.** resolution
11. How can stage directions be revised to make them clearer?
    a. Delete them. **b.** Add dialogue. **c.** Add details.
12. What punctuation mark follows a stage direction?
    a. comma **b.** colon **c.** period

Capitalization and End Punctuation in Sentences *pages 432 – 433*

Write each sentence. Capitalize words where necessary, and insert needed end punctuation.

13. the idea of writing a whole book of poems seems interesting
14. how many poems would that include
15. do you own a book of robert frost's poems
16. "the road not taken" is great
17. robert frost wrote many poems

Commas Within Sentences *pages 434 – 436*

Write the sentences, inserting commas where needed.

18. Writing a book is exciting but it is hard work.
19. Writing in my opinion challenges a person's courage.
20. When an author starts a book he or she must be excited.
21. Then the author needs time energy dedication and ideas.
22. Publishing however requires further work.

Other Punctuation Within Sentences *pages 437 – 439*

Write each sentence, inserting needed punctuation.

23. Writing requires more than a 930 to 530 workday.
24. A writer needs the following tools a dictionary a pen and paper.
25. However writing is ninety nine percent perspiration.
26. Being a writer is important writers are valued.

Numbers in Sentences *pages 440 – 441*

Write each sentence, changing the numeral to a number word or the number word to a numeral.

27. The art class has only 9 students.
28. 15 students were expected to take the drawing class.
29. Perhaps the test every 5th week discouraged students.
30. Nevertheless, the class meets in room fifty-four daily.
31. I need 1 more credit.

Capitalization of Proper Nouns, Proper Adjectives, and *I* *pages 442 – 443*

Write each sentence, capitalizing words where necessary.

32. Writers in america have many possible subjects.
33. Just think of the poems by carl sandburg!
34. He wrote "chicago" about that major city in illinois.
35. robert frost wrote about new england.
36. i enjoy stories by ernest hemingway.

Letters and Envelopes *pages 444 – 446*

37. Write the letter with the correct capitalization, punctuation, and indentation. Then draw a rectangle and address it as if it were an envelope for this letter.

242 princeton road
austin texas 77379
september 16 19--

Ms. Carol Fenwick
1648 bedford avenue
orlando, florida 32887
Dear. Ms. Fenwick
I have received a copy of the script from you, and I will get to work on it right away. Thank you.

yours truly
Jane McCarthy

Titles *pages 447 – 448*

Rewrite each sentence. Capitalize and punctuate titles correctly.

38. I have just finished the draft of my novel learning.
39. The chapter entitled why not me? is too long.
40. I hope the novel is reviewed in the new york times.
41. my agent might schedule me for good morning, america.
42. I might write an article called success.

Outlines and Bibliographies *pages 449 – 452*

Rewrite this outline, adding the missing information from the choices on the right.

Keeping Cockatiels

- I.
  - A. Space
  - B.
- II. Heating and cooling
- III. Feeding
  - A.
  - B. Vegetables
  - C. Fruit requirements
    - 1. Fresh fruits
    - 2.

43. Frozen fruits
44. Perches
45. Seeds
46. Cage requirements

Rewrite this bibliography, alphabetizing it and inserting missing punctuation. Make sure each part of the entry is in the correct position.

47. Duck, Tom Samuel Clemens 1952 Boston: Smith Inc.
48. "Huck Finn." Yale Review pp. 421–431. Lynn, Ken Spring 1968
49. The Adventures of Tom Sawyer. Mark Twain. New York: 1885

Direct Quotations and Dialogue *pages 453 – 455*

Write each sentence, adding quotation marks, other punctuation, and capital letters.

50. The director exclaimed this scene isn't working
51. The lines don't make sense the actor replied.
52. If I could he announced I would ask the playwright myself
53. Isn't Shakespeare dead asked the stage manager.

How Words Are Formed *pages 456 – 457*

Read the sentences below. Find the shortened form in each. Write the shortened form and its original word or words. Label the form *clipped word, blended word,* or *acronym.*

54. Do you watch the soaps on television?
55. I rarely see anyone in an auto on the screen.
56. Even docudramas aren't very realistic.

1-9 Cumulative Review

Simple and Compound Sentences *pages 39 – 41*

Write *simple* or *compound* to identify the type of sentence.

1. Slapstick is a special form of humor.
2. People watch funny movies and television shows, and they often expect to see some form of slapstick.
3. Slapstick is not subtle humor; it is obvious and mostly physical.
4. Falling down and being hit by a cream pie are common occurrences in slapstick.
5. They seem to be getting hurt, but the actors are creating an illusion.
6. Stunt people often take the place of the actors.
7. Slapstick makes people laugh with relief; they themselves are not the victims of the stunts.

Avoiding Sentence Fragments and Run-on Sentences *pages 42 – 43*

Write whether each group of words is a *sentence,* a *sentence fragment,* or a *run-on sentence.*

8. Because the commercials deny us a rational choice.
9. The advertisers create a desire to own something we have to fulfill it.
10. Many officials feel that consumers buy what they do not really need.
11. Money for food and clothing wasted on luxuries.
12. Consumers feel that they must have what is advertised they will be missing out on something.
13. Subliminal advertising that works just below the conscious level.

Kinds of Nouns *pages 74 – 75*

Write the noun or nouns in each sentence. Then write *common* or *proper.*

14. Mr. Diaz and his students seem to have changed this year.
15. The teacher has developed a greater sense of adventure.
16. Students such as Carter and Melanie have taken more responsibility.
17. As a reward, the whole class is going by bus to the Grand Canyon.
18. The Parent-Teacher Association and the Social Studies Department are the sponsors.
19. They appreciate the changes in both the teacher and the students.

Possessive Nouns *pages 84 – 85*

Rewrite each sentence, replacing the underlined phrase with a phrase containing a singular or a plural possessive noun.

20. The changes in a town can be beneficial as well as harmful to the quality of life there.

21. The increase in the population can add to the variety of the people who live together.

22. However, with a greater number of people, the school system of the town could become overcrowded.

23. The elected officials might need to increase the taxes of the citizens.

24. Some of the pleasures of families in the small town may disappear.

Verbs *pages 122–125*

Write the verb or verbs from each sentence. Write whether they are *action*, *linking*, or *helping* verbs.

25. Juan's heroes live in his house.

26. These heroes are not larger than life; they are his mother and his father.

27. They seem like an ordinary mother and father to most people.

28. However, Juan's parents have been working very hard for a long time.

29. They will do whatever is necessary for the happiness of Juan and his brothers and sisters.

30. Juan studies for long hours and works hard so that he can be like his heroes.

Verb Tenses *pages 133–140*

Write the verb or verbs from each sentence below. Next to each verb, write its tense.

31. Antoinette has entered the Tri-County Tennis Tournament again this year.

32. She had made it to the semifinals last year before she lost in straight sets.

33. This year, she practices every day and plays at least three matches per week.

34. I am sure that she will get to the finals and will win the first-place trophy.

35. She has worked too hard for this trophy, and she wants it too badly.

36. Will you be at the tournament when she plays her first match?

Subject – Verb Agreement *pages 141 – 142*

Write the correct form of the verb in parentheses ( ).

37. To be rich and famous is a goal that (drive, drives) some people.
38. Having lots of ambition (is, are) important if riches and fame are what you seek.
39. Getting a great deal of money (require, requires) hard work and good luck.
40. Do not misunderstand me; money can (do, does) some worthwhile things.
41. Money (do, does) help people fulfill dreams such as sending their children to college.
42. Everyone agrees that neither money nor fame (guarantee, guarantees) happiness.

Direct and Indirect Objects *pages 176 – 180*

Write each sentence. Underline each indirect object once and each direct object twice.

43. The Rocky Mountains provide vacationers a perfect place to ski.
44. The altitude and the weather promise families who want to relax ideal conditions.
45. The snow guarantees them ample skiing and a breathtaking view.
46. The majestic mountains show skiers the power and the grandeur of nature.
47. The hotels assure their guests rest, good food, and relaxation.
48. Shouldn't we allow everyone a mountain vacation at least once?

Pronouns and Antecedents *pages 228 – 229*

Write each sentence. Underline the pronoun that agrees with the antecedent in number, person, and gender.

49. People make (his, their) most important decisions in various ways.
50. My college has (his, its) Career Week during the first week of April.
51. I will be glad to introduce you to some of (my, their) former professors.
52. If you are asking me for a suggestion about a college, that is (its, mine).
53. Other recruiters might tell you that the only college for you is (ours, theirs).
54. When you have thought it through, the final decision is (his, yours).

Subject and Object Pronouns *pages 230 – 232*

Write the pronoun or pronouns from each sentence. Next to each pronoun, write *subject* or *object*.

55. Jonathan wanted people to write letters to him over the summer.

56. He made address labels on the printer and passed them out in homeroom.

57. When he offered the labels, many students took them from him eagerly.

58. I wonder how many of them will actually take the time to write.

59. He will definitely be getting a letter from me.

Indefinite Pronouns *pages 237 – 239*

Write the correct form of the verb in parentheses ( ).

60. Many (is, are) interested in success in today's business world.

61. First, one (need, needs) to set a goal.

62. Anyone (is, are) capable of setting a goal.

63. Everyone (is, are) involved in teamwork if the goal is shared by several workers.

64. Each (is, are) responsible for a share of the work.

65. All (achieve, achieves) success by working together toward a common goal.

Adjectives and Adverbs *pages 270 – 282*

Write the adjectives or adverbs from each sentence. Identify each by writing *adjective* or *adverb.*

66. We can stop worrying now because the future of the colony looks bright.

67. We have successfully completed the first phase of our ten-year mission.

68. Our advanced agricultural methods have caught on slowly but surely.

69. We anticipate an ample supply of good foods.

70. This supply will fulfill our needs completely in the approaching years.

71. What we have accomplished here will endure forever.

Comparisons with Adjectives and Adverbs *pages 276–279, 283–285*

Write the adjectives or adverbs from each sentence. Identify each by writing *adjective* or *adverb.* Then write its degree of comparison.

72. The development of leisure time most likely caused a greater increase in readers.

73. People eagerly sought books to fill the many extra hours in the day.

74. The most popular books were novels about exotic heroines and mysterious heroes.

75. People often wanted to escape to more exciting places.

76. They most definitely enjoyed living lives that were wilder and more dangerous than their own.

77. They knew some imaginary worlds better than they knew their own less-interesting world.

Prepositions and Prepositional Phrases *pages 320–322*

Write the prepositional phrase or phrases from each sentence. Underline each preposition and circle its object or objects.

78. Julie and I could spend hours on our surfboards.

79. We always rent a cabin at the beach during our family vacation.

80. For two weeks, we can be seen darting over and around the waves.

81. Mom and Dad sit under an umbrella with their noses buried in long novels.

82. Julie and I are either in the surf or next to each other on a beach towel.

83. Between us, we squeeze every minute of fun from our vacation!

Conjunctions *pages 328–329*

Write the conjunction or conjunctions from each sentence.

84. A long swim in the pool or in the ocean can help stretch out your muscles and improve their tone.

85. Either running or brisk walking will give your heart the workout it needs.

86. Both mental and physical exercises are important to a person's health.

87. Just as you feed your body, so you must feed your mind.

88. You can spend a lot of money, but that will not make you healthier.

89. Neither exercise equipment nor clothing can overcome a lazy attitude about your health.

Clauses *pages 372 – 378*

Write each sentence. Draw one line under each subordinate clause and two lines under each independent clause. Then write *simple, compound,* or *complex* to identify the type of sentence.

90. When you think about it, humor is the major focus in television.

91. Comedy specials and situation comedies have been standards on television for over forty years.

92. Because people watch television to relax, they prefer funny shows.

93. Situation comedies do present problems for the characters, but they are always solved.

94. Although happy endings are nice, they are not enough to make comedies successful.

95. People need to identify with the characters, and they need to laugh.

Participles and Participial Phrases *pages 381 – 382*

Write each sentence. Underline the participle or participial phrase. Draw an arrow to the word or words it modifies.

96. Filled with famous names, American history is the history of American people.

97. The names and faces associated with an event keep history human and memorable.

98. Betsy Ross is America's best-remembered seamstress.

99. Nathan Hale, hanged for spying, is another beloved patriot.

100. Paul Revere, riding into history, warned people of the approach of the British.

Dangling Participles and Split Infinitives *pages 388 – 389*

For each sentence, write the participles or infinitives. Then write *correct, split infinitive,* or *dangling participle.*

101. Do you want to own land and to be a part of your heritage?

102. To quickly buy land would be a mistake.

103. Surrounded by a white picket fence, you could own a house with a down payment and a loan.

104. I could buy a house with borrowed money.

105. Do I want to deeply go in debt?

106. Rising in price though they are, Americans have bought homes.

STUDY SKILLS

Contents

1 Finding Words in a Dictionary

A **dictionary** provides many kinds of information about words. A word listed in the dictionary is called an **entry word.**

To make finding words in a dictionary simple, entry words are listed in **alphabetical order.** A word beginning with the letter *b,* for example, is listed after a word beginning with the letter *a.* Words that begin with the same first letter are alphabetized by their second letters. Words having the same second letter are alphabetized by their third letters, and so on.

A **compound word** is a word made up of two or more smaller words. Compound words are sometimes written as one word, sometimes hyphenated, and sometimes written as two separate words. *Chalkboard* and *black-eyed Susan* are compound words.

To help you locate words easily, the top of each dictionary page displays two guide words. **Guide words** are the first and last entry words found on a page.

Study this model of guide words and entry words.

armadillo 42 arrayal

ar·ma·dil·lo [är′mə·dil′ō] *n., pl.* **ar·ma·dil·los** A small burrowing mammal found from South America north to Texas, having an armorlike shell of jointed plates. Some kinds can roll up, shell and all, into a ball when attacked.

ar·my [är′mē] *n., pl.* **ar·mies** **1** A large group of soldiers, organized, trained, and armed to fight. **2** All the soldiers in the land forces of a country. **3** Any group of people organized to advance a cause. **4** A great number of persons or things: an *army* of insects.

Practice

A. Alphabetize the following groups of entry words.

1. hospital, hose, horseshoe, host

MODEL horseshoe, hose, hospital, host

2. league, leaf, lead, layer

3. push, purple, puddle, purpose

4. flat-footed, flat, flatworm, flesh

5. dessert, desert, destiny, desk

6. blockade, block, blind, blister

7. spin-off, spine, spire, spirit

B. Imagine that the words in each group are located on the same dictionary page. Write the guide words for each page.

8. event, evening, ever, even, eventual, evidence, every

MODEL even, evidence

9. run, rule, ruin, rumba, rug, ruler, ruffle

10. tear, taxicab, teaspoon, tea, taxpayer, teacher, team

11. formula, forbid, four, fork, formal, form, forgive

12. period, perform, perfect, perfume, perch, pep, percent

2 Using a Dictionary for Meanings

One of the most important kinds of information about an entry word in a dictionary is its definition. A **definition** is a word's meaning. Most words have more than one definition. Some words are homographs. **Homographs** are words that are spelled alike but that have different meanings and origins. A *plane* is a flat, even surface. It is also a carpenter's tool. Homographs appear as separate entries in a dictionary. An entry word's definition is sometimes followed by an **example sentence** that illustrates how the word is used.

Dictionaries provide other important information about an entry word. The word's **part of speech,** or function in a sentence (such as noun, verb, or adjective), is shown as an abbreviation. The word's usual spelling and any **alternate spelling** it may have, such as *catalog* and *catalogue,* are listed. Often, an entry's **etymology,** or word history, is explained. Study these entries.

bit¹ [bit] *n.* 1 A metal part of a bridle that fits in a horse's mouth, used to control its movements. 2 A tool for boring or drilling, used with a brace or drill. 3 The cutting part of a tool, as the blade of an ax. 4 That part of a key that enters a lock and moves the bolt.

bit² [bit] 1 *n.* A small quantity; a little: a *bit* of cake. 2 *n.* A short time: Wait a *bit.* 3 *n.* A small part, as in a play or movie. 4 *adj.* Small, unimportant: a *bit* part in a movie. 5 *n.* Twelve and one-half cents, used only in expressions like **two bits,** twenty-five cents. **—a bit** To a certain extent; somewhat: a *bit* tired.

bit³ [bit] The past tense and a past participle of BITE.

bit⁴ [bit] *n.* The smallest unit of information a computer can use for processing; either of the binary digits 0 and 1. ◆ *Bit* comes from *b(inary) (dig)it.*

bite [bīt] *v.* **bit** [bit], **bit·ten** or **bit, bit·ing,** *n.* 1 *v.* To seize, cut, or wound with the teeth: *Bite* the orange; The dog *bites.* 2 *n.* The act of biting. 3 *n.* A wound inflicted by biting. 4 *v.* To sting, or have the effect of stinging: Mustard *bites* the tongue. 5 *n.* A painful sensation; sting: mosquito *bites.* 6 *v.* To take firm hold of; grip: The anchor *bit* the ground. 7 *v.* To take a bait, as fish. 8 *n.* A small bit of food; mouthful. 9 *n.* A light meal; snack. **—bite the hand that feeds one** To mistreat someone who has been kind.

Practice

Use the dictionary entries above to write answers to the following questions.

1. Write the etymology for one of the words listed.

MODEL *Bit comes from binary digit.*

2. Which words are homographs?
3. How many definitions are listed for the word *bite?*
4. Write the example sentence for the word *bit.*
5. What part of speech is listed for the first definition of *bite?*
6. Which word has two past forms?
7. Do any of the entry words listed have an alternate spelling?

3 Using a Dictionary for Pronunciation

You can learn how to pronounce a word by studying its **phonetic respelling** in the dictionary. This spelling with sound symbols can be found directly after each entry word. A **pronunciation key** that explains these sound symbols appears at the beginning of every dictionary. Sometimes an abbreviated key like the one below appears on the dictionary pages.

a	add	**i**	it	**o͝o**	took	**oi**	oil
ā	ace	**ī**	ice	**o͞o**	pool	**ou**	pout
â	care	**o**	odd	**u**	up	**ng**	ring
ä	palm	**ō**	open	**û**	burn	**th**	thin
e	end	**ô**	order	**yo͞o**	fuse	**~~th~~**	this
ē	equal					**zh**	vision

ə = { a in *above* e in *sicken* i in *possible* o in *melon* u in *circus* }

A **syllable** is a word part that has only one vowel sound. When a word has more than one syllable, one syllable is usually spoken with more force than the others. This stressed word part is written with an **accent mark** called a **primary accent (')**. If a word contains more than one stressed syllable, the second strongest syllable is written with a mark called a **secondary accent (′)**.

Practice

A. Use a dictionary to write the phonetic respellings for the following words.

1. block

MODEL blok

2. dentist
3. exercise
4. draw
5. climate
6. telephone
7. radio
8. observe
9. remark
10. easily
11. thunderstorm

B. Divide the following words into syllables, and place primary and secondary accent marks where they belong.

12. reservation

MODEL res′er·va'tion

13. kangaroo
14. conversation
15. lightweight
16. catalogue
17. politician
18. improvise
19. dominate
20. horseshoe
21. absolute
22. disappear
23. terrify

STUDY SKILLS

4 Using a Title Page, a Copyright Page, a Table of Contents, and an Appendix

Knowing a book's parts can help you find information quickly. The **title page** gives the title of the book, the author or the editor, the publisher, and the city of publication. The **copyright page** is often found on the back of the title page. It lists the copyright date, which states when the book was published. The copyright page sometimes lists names of books or people that material or ideas were taken from. This is known as the **acknowledgment section.** The **table of contents** lists chapters or book sections in the order in which they appear in the book and lists their page numbers.

Some books have a section called an appendix. An **appendix** contains materials that illustrate the main text of the book.

title page	copyright page	table of contents
HISTORY OF ASIA by David M. Licht Dixon Media, Inc. New York, NY	Copyright © 1988 Dixon Media, Inc. Acknowledgments Ms. Nancy Diskel Mr. Marc Hallwitz Dixon Media, Inc. Historical Maps of Asia © 1985 All rights reserved. Printed in the U.S.A.	CONTENTS 1. China .... 1 2. Japan .... 55 3. Korea .... 98 4. The U.S.S.R. .... 126 5. Border Lands .... 245 Appendix A .... 325 Appendix B 347

Practice

Use the example pages above to answer the following questions. Then write the name of the page you used to answer each question.

1. Who wrote the book?

MODEL David M. Licht; title page

2. What is the title of the book?
3. On what page does the chapter on Korea begin?
4. How many appendixes does the book have?
5. When was the book published?
6. Who is the book's publisher?
7. What resource did the author use in writing the book?
8. What chapter begins on page 126?
9. Where was the book published?
10. How many pages are devoted to the actual text?
11. How many chapters does the book have?

5 Using Footnotes, a Bibliography, and an Index

A textbook page may sometimes contain footnotes. A **footnote** is a brief note at the bottom of a page that tells more about information stated in the text. Look at these footnotes. Notice the information they contain.

> [1]Sheila Cartwright, *Astronomy Made Easy* (New York: Roebling, 1987), p. 76.
>
> [2] Francis Gregor, "Advances in Modern Telescopes," *Star Flight Magazine,* 20 March 1985, p. 44.

A **bibliography** is an alphabetical listing of books and articles used or recommended by the author. Study these entries.

> Cartwright, Sheila. *Astronomy Made Easy.* New York: Roebling, 1987.
> Gregor Francis. "Advances in Modern Telescopes." *Star Flight Magazine,* 20 March 1985, pp. 42–45.

An **index** is a list of topics in the book. The index lists topics alphabetically and gives their page numbers. Often, when you find a topic in the index, the index will refer you to a related topic. This is known as a **cross-reference.**

Numbers	**topic**
even, 132–133	**subtopic**
ordinal, 130–131	
writing, 44–45	
See also Multi-digit numbers	**cross-reference**

Practice

Use the examples on this page to answer the following questions.

1. Why is an index useful?

MODEL It can help you decide whether a book has the information you need.

2. If you wanted to find the source of a statistic cited in a book, to what would you refer?
3. Name the subtopics in the index on this page.
4. To what topic does the cross-reference refer you?
5. How do the footnotes and the bibliography on this page differ?

6 Using the Dewey Decimal System

The **Dewey Decimal System** is an organizational system commonly used in public and school libraries. In this system, books are arranged according to the ten main subject areas listed below. A book's **call number** tells you where to find the book on the library shelves.

000–099	General works (encyclopedias, atlases, newspapers)
100–199	Philosophy (ideas about the meaning of life, psychology)
200–299	Religion (world religions, mythology)
300–399	Social science (government, law, business, education)
400–499	Language (dictionaries, grammar books)
500–599	Pure science (mathematics, chemistry, plants, animals)
600–699	Applied science (how-to books, radio, engineering)
700–799	Arts and recreation (music, art, sports, hobbies)
800–899	Literature (poems, plays, essays)
900–999	History (travel, geography, biography)

Practice

A. Write the range of Dewey Decimal System numbers in which each of the following books might appear.

1. *A History of England*

MODEL 900–999

2. *The World Book Encyclopedia*
3. *How to Build Your Own Ham Radio*
4. *Berlitz French-English Dictionary*
5. *The Collected Works of William Shakespeare*
6. *An Introduction to Twentieth-Century Music*
7. *Voting Patterns in American Elections*
8. *Myths of the Ancient World*
9. *Mathematics Made Easy*
10. *Philosophies of Native American Peoples*

B. Write the main subject area of the Dewey Decimal System to which the following call numbers belong.

11. 622.75

MODEL Applied science

12. 450.9
13. 987.01
14. 878.64
15. 764.9
16. 20.93
17. 325.45
18. 150.33
19. 289.4
20. 870.9

7 Using the Card Catalogue

The **card catalogue** lists every book in a library. The cards are arranged in alphabetical order. Each drawer is labeled with letters showing the range of book titles listed in that drawer.

There are three types of cards in a card catalogue. The **title card** lists the title of the book first. The **author card** lists the author's last name first. The **subject card** lists the subject of the book first. Each card contains the book's call number. When you know the call number, you can find the book.

author card

329
R **Rosebloom, Eugene Holloway**
A History of Presidential Elections from George Washington to Jimmy Carter / Eugene H. Rosebloom and Alfred E. Eckes, Jr., 4th ed. New York: Macmillan, 1979.

title card

329 **A History of Presidential Elections from**
R **George Washington to Jimmy Carter**
Rosebloom, Eugene Holloway
A history of presidential elections from George Washington to Jimmy Carter / Eugene Holloway Rosebloom and Alfred E. Eckes, Jr. 4th ed. New York, Macmillan, 1979.

subject card

329 **PRESIDENTS, U.S.—Elections**
R
Rosebloom, Eugene Holloway
A History of Presidential Elections from George Washington to Jimmy Carter / Eugene Holloway Rosebloom and Alfred E. Eckes, Jr. 4th ed. New York, Macmillan, 1979.

Practice

A. Use the example cards to answer the following questions.

1. What is the call number of this book?
MODEL 329 R

2. Who wrote the book?
3. When was it published?
4. What company published it?
5. What is the book's title?

B. Write the kind of card you would look for given the information provided in each item.

6. *A Tale of Two Cities*
MODEL title card

7. written by Robert Frost
8. land mammals
9. history of Mexico
10. *The Life of Sir Isaac Newton*

STUDY SKILLS

8 Identifying Kinds of Books

Fiction books, nonfiction books, and reference books are filed separately on library shelves.

Fiction books include novels and short stories and are organized alphabetically by the author's last name.

Nonfiction books contain factual information. These books are arranged by call number under the Dewey Decimal System. Nonfiction represents all the categories in the Dewey Decimal System except literature.

Biographies are nonfiction books that give an account of a person's life. These books are often shelved alphabetically by the last name of their subject.

The **reference section** of a library includes books such as dictionaries, encyclopedias, atlases, and almanacs. These are important research tools that usually cannot be taken from the library. Reference books are arranged by call number.

Practice

A. Write whether the following books would be shelved alphabetically or by call number.

1. a book about the life of George Washington

MODEL alphabetically

2. *Webster's New World Dictionary*
3. a novel by Charles Dickens
4. a historical atlas containing maps of colonial America
5. a book about astronomy
6. *The Wizard of Oz*
7. the life story of William Shakespeare
8. *How to Repair Your Automobile*

B. Write the name of the section of the library in which you would find the following items.

9. *Encyclopaedia Britannica*

MODEL reference section

10. a book on the life of Emily Dickinson
11. a book called *Understanding Biology*
12. a newspaper article about life in New Zealand
13. a map of South America
14. a novel by Gordon Parks
15. the pronunciation of the word *hypotenuse*
16. a book of short stories by Ernest Hemingway
17. *The New York Times*
18. a book about the history of California

9 Using Reference Books

The reference section of the library contains important materials used for research. Atlases, almanacs, encyclopedias, and dictionaries are all located in the reference section.

An **atlas** is a book of maps. A world atlas has maps of every country or region in the world, and a United States atlas has a map of every state. Most atlases include maps and charts that show the size, climate, population, and natural features of the regions. They may also give information on industry, agriculture, and natural resources. Atlas maps usually show country or state capitals as well as other important cities.

An **almanac** gives information on many subjects. This information is often in the form of statistics. For example, an almanac may list the major league records of champion baseball players, the average rainfall of all the countries in the world, the speeds at which different animals can run, or the dates of all the terms of the U.S. Presidents. Almanacs include articles, lists, charts, and tables on such topics as sports, weather, history, politics, and literature.

An **encyclopedia** is a collection of articles on a wide variety of subjects. Encyclopedias often include maps, statistics, and biographies, which may also be found in other reference books.

A **biographical reference** offers brief biographies, or life stories, of many kinds of people. Biographical references are usually organized by category, such as "the most powerful people in the United States today" or "Black Americans in history."

A **dictionary** is a book that gives the meanings and the pronunciations of many words. Some dictionaries tell how to translate words from one language into another. A Latin-English dictionary, for example, will list a word in Latin, tell how to pronounce it, and then tell what the word means in English. Single-language dictionaries may include articles about the history of language, charts of weights and measures, abbreviations, and other useful information.

Practice

Write which type of reference book would include the following information. Give two books if both would have the information.

1. a brief account of the life of George Washington Carver

MODEL biographical reference or encyclopedia

2. a map of Paris
3. the pronunciation of the word *oxymoron*
4. the winner of the 1976 Olympic marathon
5. what life was like in medieval Europe
6. the population and climate of Algeria
7. a listing of last year's hurricanes
8. the origin of the word *king*

10 Using Newspapers

A **newspaper** is an important source of current information. Newspapers contain three kinds of articles.

A **news story** is an account of an important recent event. International, national, and local items of interest are usually reported in this kind of story. The bulk of the story tries to answer the questions *who, what, where, why, when,* and *how* regarding the event being reported.

A **feature story** is a description of a person, a place, or a thing that is of popular interest. A feature story might be about a historical building or the life of an aspiring Olympic athlete.

An **editorial** is an opinion written by a newspaper editor about a topic of current interest or importance. Opposing opinions and letters to the editor are also printed in newspapers.

Most newspapers are divided into sections. Economic information is reported in the business section. Advertisements for jobs and items for sale are listed in the classified ad section. Television and movie listings are printed in the entertainment section. Features on food, health, and fashion can be found in the living section. Editorials and letters to the editor are printed in the editorial section.

Practice

A. Write whether these items would be presented in a news story, a feature story, or an editorial.

1. A hurricane damages a town.

MODEL news story

2. A former mayor celebrates his one-hundredth birthday.
3. Congress has been foolish not to pass more antipollution measures.
4. The President meets with the Prime Minister of Canada.
5. Area artists describe their careers.
6. Michael Jackson's band members give an account of what an international tour is like.

B. Write in which newspaper section each of the following items might be found.

7. an ad for a 1988 car

MODEL classified ad section

8. a stock market report
9. an article about good buys on vegetables
10. an article criticizing a local congressperson

11 Using the *Readers' Guide to Periodical Literature*

Magazines, or **periodicals,** are important sources of information. Publications such as *Time* and *Newsweek* publish articles about news events for a general audience. Other publications, such as *Popular Science, Personal Computing,* and *Architectural Digest,* have more specialized articles for smaller audiences.

The *Readers' Guide to Periodical Literature* is an index to articles published in magazines. This index is updated so that it is easy to locate current articles.

Articles are listed in the *Readers' Guide* alphabetically by subject and author. Each author or subject entry is in bold type. Listed after the main entry and subheadings are the title of the article, the name of the author, and the name of the magazine in which the article appears. Following the magazine's name are its volume number, the pages on which the article appears, and the date of the magazine issue. A key to the abbreviations is listed at the beginning of the *Guide.*

House decoration, French

Allure in the grand manner [J. T. de la Chaume's French-style apartment in Manhattan] J. Kornbluth. il por *House Gard* 159:152-9+ D '87

Fabulous fakery [R. L. Neas uses trompe l'oeil to create French atmosphere in Long Island cottage] E. Greene. il *House Gard* 159:134-43 S '87

A formal balance: cosmopolitan influences in a Toronto setting [home of George and Saundra Mann decorated by Robert Dirstein] D. Lasker. il *Archit Dig* 44:90-5 F '87

Setting the stage: Baroness Philippine de Rothschild in Paris. C. Aillaud. il por *Archit Dig* 44:98-101 Ag '87

House decoration, Georgian

House Democratic Caucus (U.S.)

Bill Gray can't lose in the budget battle. D. Harbrecht. il por *Bus Week* p25-6 S 7 '87

Gray likely appointed to powerful post in Congress. por *Jet* 72:17 Ag 17 '87

House drainage

Downspouts and gutters: how to keep them in good repair. il *Better Homes Gard* 65:114 Ap '87

A drainage problem becomes an asset [manmade creek and drainage swale] il *South Living* 22:96 My 1 '87

Gutters and downspouts. J. Vara. il *Ctry J* 14:19-20 Je '87

How to install vinyl gutters. J. Truini. il *Pop Mech.* 164:131-4 Mr '87

In the gutter. C. Goosen. il *Mother Earth News* 108:118-9 N/D '87

Practice

Use the *Readers' Guide* excerpt to write answers to the questions.

1. Which magazines appear under *House Democratic Caucus?*

MODEL *Business Week* and *Jet*

2. When was the *Business Week* article published?
3. What is the title of the article?
4. On what pages of the magazine does the article appear?
5. Who is the author?
6. How many articles are listed under *French house decoration?*

STUDY SKILLS

STUDY SKILLS

12 Using Audio and Visual Aids

Most modern libraries house more than books and other printed media. Many have filmstrips, slides, films, and videotapes available to patrons. Records and cassette tapes are often available to people who want to listen to musical and theatrical performances as well as book and poetry readings.

Two important reference tools found in many libraries are microfilm and microfiche. Instead of providing old magazines and newspapers that might fall apart if you looked through them, the library photographs the articles and reproduces them in reduced form on microfilm or microfiche. **Microfilm** is plastic film stored on reels. A **microfiche** is a small sheet of plastic film. By using microfilm and microfiche, libraries can easily store vast amounts of information from books and periodicals. Often, recent papers and magazines are photographed just to save space.

Practice

A. Write which audio or visual aid might contain each kind of information. Some items may have more than one answer.

1. a performance of Beethoven's Ninth Symphony

MODEL › record or cassette tape

2. page 23 of *The New York Times* dated May 3, 1957
3. a documentary about the life of Albert Einstein
4. pictures of the Vermont flood of 1927
5. *The Wizard of Oz* starring Judy Garland
6. a performance of Shakespeare's *King Lear*
7. a performance of Romanian folk songs
8. a reading of poems by Robert Frost
9. a radio news broadcast made on December 8, 1941
10. an entire *Newsweek* magazine published four years ago

B. Write one example of what might be on each of these references.

11. filmstrip

MODEL › a documentary about the Great Depression

12. microfilm or microfiche
13. videotape
14. cassette tape
15. film

13 Using the Encyclopedia

An encyclopedia is a good source of general information and an excellent starting point for research. An **encyclopedia** is a set of books containing articles on many subjects.

The books, or **volumes,** of an encyclopedia are arranged alphabetically. A letter or letters on the spine of each volume indicate the starting letters of the subjects in the book.

Subjects, or **entries,** are listed alphabetically within each volume. Articles vary in length, but each presents the most important information that exists on the subject. Each topic in an encyclopedia is called an **entry.** An entry usually includes the name of a topic and an article on that topic. **Guide words** at the top of each page help you find the entries you need. Often, at the end of an encyclopedia article, you will find **cross-references** to articles on related subjects that might also help you in your research.

In every encyclopedia there is an index, which is usually the last volume. The **index** lists the number or letter of the volume and the pages on which information on a subject can be found. Each subject is listed in the index in alphabetical order. The index usually includes **cross-references** to related entries as well.

Practice

Write answers to the following questions.

1. What is an *entry*?

MODEL a topic in an encyclopedia

2. What is a *volume*?
3. What do key words explain?
4. How do you know which entries are listed on a page?
5. Suppose you want information about ship building. You look up *ship* and find the words *See also: boating*. What is the suggestion *See also: boating* called?
6. Name three places where cross-references might be found in an encyclopedia.
7. What is found in the index?
8. Where is the index usually found?
9. In what order are encyclopedia volumes organized?

14 Taking Notes

Note taking is an important study skill. Note taking is especially helpful when you are studying for a test or preparing an oral or written report. As you take notes, you should **paraphrase,** or write the material in your own words.

One good way to organize your notes is to use **note cards.** Start a separate card each time you use a new book or magazine. Write the title, the author, and the page number on the card so that you know the source of each piece of information. Write the topic at the top of each card so that you can easily find the information you want. Study this example note card.

POISONOUS PLANTS AND YOUR HEALTH
Cause headaches, itching, rash if touched
Common examples: poison oak, poison ivy, poison sumac
Wash hands after contact with poisonous plants
Change and wash clothing
Do not burn irritating plants

Accident Prevention by the American Red Cross
pp. 35–44

Practice

Read the following passage about food poisoning. Imagine that it came from the same book shown on the example note card. Take notes that list the most important information from the passage.

To prevent food poisoning, keep a clean kitchen and handle food with clean hands. Keep milk, cream, eggs, fish, chicken, creamy dessert fillings, and all other dairy products and meats in a refrigerator, in a freezer, or on ice.

In some canned foods, a kind of bacterium (germ) can develop that does not need air to grow. If people eat food that has this poison in it, they develop botulism. Botulism is often fatal. One way to prevent botulism is to heat canned foods before eating them. Boiling for 10 minutes or longer will usually prevent botulism poisoning.

15 Writing an Outline

An outline is a great help to students preparing to write research reports. An **outline** organizes main ideas and important details. It helps put facts in logical order.

Tips for Writing an Outline

1. Use Roman numerals for main ideas and capital letters for details.
2. Indent each number or letter and add a period.
3. Capitalize the first letter of each entry.
4. Keep entries short.
5. Never write a *I* without a *II*, an *A* without a *B*, or a *1* without a *2*.

Life in Colonial America

I. Reasons for colonization
   A. Religious freedom
      1. Pilgrims and Separatists—Plymouth, 1620
      2. Puritans—Salem, 1628
   B. Economic freedom
      1. Own their own land
      2. Need game, fish, fertile soil
II. Relationships between people
   A. Indians
      1. Taught settlers skills
         a. Hunting and fishing
         b. Farming
      2. Fought the colonists
   B. Slaves

Practice

Use the outline in writing answers for the questions.

1. What is the first main idea in this outline?

MODEL Reasons for colonization

2. What is the second main idea?
3. Which idea under *Indians* has two details under it?
4. What is the second idea under *Relationships between people?*
5. What would you do about a C entry under *Relationships between people* that reads *Corn*?

STUDY SKILLS

16 Writing a Bibliography

A **bibliography** is an alphabetical listing of sources a writer used in writing a report.

A bibliography is usually organized by type of source. First, list all the books you used. Then, list the magazines, followed by all the newspaper articles. Label each list. Study this bibliography for a report on a symphony orchestra.

BOOKS

Andersen, Denise. *All About the Orchestra.* New York: Charles Press, 1986.

Martin, John. *The Brass Section of an Orchestra.* New York: Drake Publishing Company, 1987.

MAGAZINES

Beck, Francis. "Ludwig von Beethoven." *Music Times.* March 1986, pp. 43–45.

"More Woodwinds, More Percussion." *Music News Magazine.* 7 May 1988, pp. 56–58.

Rodriguez, Ramon. "Modern Classical Music." *Music Appreciation Magazine.* 15 April 1988, p. 10.

NEWSPAPERS

"The Boston Symphony Orchestra Grows Up." *Boston Daily News.* 5 May 1988, sec. B, p. 3, cols. 1 and 2.

Notice that each list in a bibliography is written in alphabetical order. Books are always alphabetized by the last name of the author. Other sources are alphabetized by the last name of the author if there is one listed; otherwise, they are alphabetized by the first letter of the title of the article.

Practice

Use the example bibliography to list the following sources in correct form.

1. *Drought*, a book by Ed James, Paragon Press, 1985, New York.

MODEL James, Ed. *Drought*. New York: Paragon Press, 1985.

2. "Farmers in Crisis" by Jo Taylor, March 1, 1986, *Iola Daily News*, page 2 sec B cols 2 & 3.
3. Lily Anderson's book, *Waiting for the Rain*, Apple Bough Publishers, Minneapolis, 1984.
4. "No Rain Yet," *Weekly World News*, pp. 11–12, July 5, 1986.

STUDY SKILLS

17 Skimming and Scanning

Skimming and scanning are very helpful study techniques. **Skimming** means looking at reading material to note its general subject, its divisions, and its major headings. **Scanning** means looking quickly at a particular passage and searching for specific information. It is useful for finding particular items. Study these tips for skimming and scanning.

Tips for Skimming and Scanning

Skimming

1. Read quickly through a book section, such as a table of contents.
2. Note unit or chapter headings; check definitions in paragraphs.
3. Check subheadings to see if the material might be helpful to you.

Scanning

1. Focus on one or two words that you need.
2. Move your eyes quickly through the material.
3. Check only for those words or words related to them, such as *farming* or *agriculture* for *farm*. Ignore other information.

Practice

A. Read the questions. Find information in the paragraph by skimming. Then write the answers to the questions.

1. What is the main idea of the paragraph?

MODEL Columbus was an important explorer.

2. What conclusion is made?
3. What rules or definitions appear?
4. Name two key words or phrases.

THE EARLY EXPLORERS

Christopher Columbus Christopher Columbus set sail from Spain in 1492. He did not sail to prove that the world was round but simply to find a short sea route to the Indies. The Indies, in Columbus's time, meant China, India, Japan, and the East Indies. Columbus did not, of course, reach the Indies by the western route. However, he *did* discover the New World.

B. Read the questions. Find the information by scanning. Then write the answers.

5. When did Columbus's voyage begin?

MODEL 1492

6. From where did he set sail?
7. Did he discover the New World?

STUDY SKILLS

18 Summarizing

One way to help yourself understand and remember what you read is to write a summary. A **summary** is a condensed version of what you read. It contains main ideas and facts written in your own words (paraphrased). Summaries are usually a quarter of the length of the original material. Read the paragraph and its summary.

> In 1927, Charles Lindbergh made history by completing the first solo flight across the Atlantic Ocean. Lindbergh wanted to win the $25,000 prize offered to the person who made the first nonstop flight from New York to Paris. Lindbergh took off from Roosevelt Field in New York on May 20, 1927. He flew the *Spirit of St. Louis,* the plane named for the city where many people had donated money for his flight. The "Lone Eagle" landed in Paris nearly thirty-four hours later, completing the 3,600-mile trip safely. Tens of thousands of people greeted the pilot in Paris. Lindbergh won the prize of $25,000, earned another $250,000 from *The New York Times* for his story, and was awarded honors and medals from many nations.

> Summary
>
> Charles Lindbergh was the first person to fly solo nonstop across the Atlantic Ocean. In 1927, he flew from New York to Paris in the *Spirit of St. Louis.* The trip lasted nearly thirty-four hours and covered 3,600 miles. Lindbergh won fame and fortune for his brave deed.

Practice

Summarize the following article, using the guidelines for writing summaries.

> The lion and the tiger are the largest members of the cat family. Although the tiger is generally fiercer, the lion is still known as one of the strongest and most feared of wild animals. Lions have powerful bodies. Some lions are more than 9 feet long and weigh about 500 pounds. Lions hunt many kinds of animals, including zebras, giraffes, and wildebeests. Today, lions live wild in Africa and in captivity in zoos all over the world.

19 Writing a Friendly Letter

Friendly letters are written for a variety of reasons. Read this letter from a high-school student named Beth to her Uncle Bill.

812 Aylesworth Court
San Antonio, Texas 78284
February 3, 19-- — **Heading**

Dear Uncle Bill, — **Greeting**

It was good to see you last Christmas. It has been such a long time since I have been able to talk to you and Aunt Elda. Do you remember how we talked about after-school jobs? Well, I wanted to let you know how much I'm enjoying the volunteer job you suggested at St. Luke's Hospital. You said it would show me what being a doctor is like better than any courses I might take in school. Now I think you're right!

I've found out what long hours doctors work. On several occasions I have helped the staff well into the evening when some problems came up. I've also discovered how much training they need. And I've gotten an idea of how satisfying it can be to help people who really need it.

Thanks for giving me such good advice. I'll keep you posted as I get more "on-the-job training"! — **Body**

Love, — **Closing**

Beth — **Signature**

A **friendly letter** is a letter written to a friend or a relative in order to exchange greetings and news. Friendly letters have five parts. The **heading** gives the sender's address and the date on which the letter was written. The **greeting** addresses the person to whom the letter is being sent. The **body** of the letter contains the information that the letter writer wants the receiver to know. The **closing** is the "sign-off," or the writer's way of saying that the letter has come to an end. The **signature,** as a rule, consists only of the writer's first name.

The tone of a friendly letter to a relative or an adult can be formal or informal. The words you choose for your greeting and closing, for example, depend on how close you feel to the person. Generally, the closer you feel, the more informal your words and your expressions become. A more formal letter would not include informal language such as contractions and slang.

There are a variety of different reasons for writing a friendly letter; hence, there are several different considerations to keep in mind, depending upon your audience.

When you have returned from visiting friends or relatives and they have provided you with a place to stay, you should write a letter to your hosts to thank them for their hospitality. This is frequently referred to as a "bread-and-butter" note. It should be written promptly upon your return. The letter does not need to be long, but a simple thank-you and a comment or two on how you enjoyed your stay are in order.

When you receive a gift, a prompt thank-you note should be written and mailed right away. Although this is very much like a "bread-and-butter" note, here you are thanking a person for a tangible object, a gift, rather than hospitality. You should briefly comment upon why you liked that gift. This allows the recipient of your letter to feel that he or she has made a wise gift decision.

Tips for the Friendly Letter Format

1. Write your address and the date in the upper right-hand corner of the page.
2. Write the greeting under it and to the left.
3. Write the body in paragraph form.
4. Write your closing and your signature in line with the heading.
5. Prepare an envelope with your address in the upper left-hand corner and the receiver's address in the lower middle.

Practice

Write a friendly letter to a cousin or to a friend who lives in a distant city and who is about your age. Be informal, but follow correct friendly letter format. Your letter can be written for a real or an imaginary person.

20 Writing a Business Letter

When his rug was not returned on the date promised by the rug cleaners, Thomas Watkins wrote this letter. Notice how it is different in tone from the friendly letter you just read.

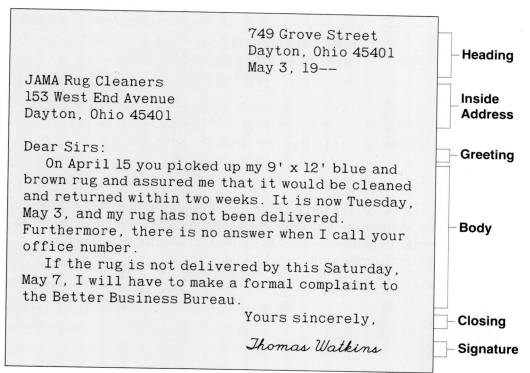

749 Grove Street
Dayton, Ohio 45401
May 3, 19--

JAMA Rug Cleaners
153 West End Avenue
Dayton, Ohio 45401

Dear Sirs:

On April 15 you picked up my 9' x 12' blue and brown rug and assured me that it would be cleaned and returned within two weeks. It is now Tuesday, May 3, and my rug has not been delivered. Furthermore, there is no answer when I call your office number.

If the rug is not delivered by this Saturday, May 7, I will have to make a formal complaint to the Better Business Bureau.

Yours sincerely,

Thomas Watkins

Heading
Inside Address
Greeting
Body
Closing
Signature

Business letters are written to order items, to obtain information, or to issue a complaint. The letter written by Thomas Watkins to JAMA Rug Cleaners is a letter of complaint.

Notice that the writer uses the correct business letter form: *heading, inside address, greeting, body, closing,* and *signature.* The tone of the letter is polite but firm, and his language is businesslike.

Practice

Write the answers to these questions.

1. Why did Thomas Watkins write his letter?
   MODEL The rug company did not return his rug on time.
2. What does he ask the company to do about his problem?
3. Is his request reasonable? Why or why not?
4. Why does he say that he will go to the Better Business Bureau if necessary?
5. Why do you think Mr. Watkins signs his letter with his whole name?

21 Writing Social Notes

When Bob Littlejohn was elected to the honor society at his junior high school, he wanted his relatives and special friends to be present at the ceremony. Here is the invitation he sent out.

```
Mr. Robert Littlejohn
cordially invites you to
his induction into
ARISTA
Saturday, March 3, 19--
at 11 A.M.
Mount Airy Junior High School
Mount Airy, North Carolina
```

Unlike other social notes, the formal invitation has a form that varies little from occasion to occasion. Each line does not have to be centered, as in the above example. Every formal invitation, however, should contain the following information, in the same order as in the example.

1. *who* is issuing the invitation
2. *what* the occasion is
3. *when* the event takes place
4. *where* the event takes place

Practice

Write a formal invitation containing the following information.

- *Who:* Alison Burnham
- *What:* Athletic Awards Dinner honoring her election to the All-County Girls' Basketball Team
- *When:* Wednesday, April 7, 19--, 6:30 P.M.
- *Where:* Mann Junior High School, Brandon, Florida

STUDY SKILLS

22 Writing Book Reports

Study this example book report.

The title of Christopher Lampton's book <u>Astronomy from Copernicus to the Space Telescope</u> is a good description of its topic. The book tells about the lives of some famous astronomers and describes their discoveries.	**Introduction (Author, Title, Main Topic)**
Copernicus was the first to describe the sun as the center of the solar system. Galileo did important work on natural satellites, sunspots, and the laws of motion. Newton's work on the laws of motion and gravity paved the way for Einstein's later theories of the universe. Lesser-known discoveries were made by many others. Yet there are still unanswered questions in astronomy.	**Major Points**
I enjoyed this book. I especially liked the writer's remark that each discovery in this field builds on those that came before it. It must feel good to be a part of such a "team."	**Opinion and Supporting Reasons**

You have probably written book reports on many books of fiction. A report on a nonfiction book is slightly different. It gives the author, the title, and the main topic in the introduction to the report. In the next part of the report, the main points of the book are summarized. At the end, there is an opinion and several supporting reasons.

Practice

A. Write the answers to these questions.

1. Why isn't it necessary to include the main characters and the setting when writing a nonfiction book report?

   MODEL because the emphasis is on the subject of the book, and only incidentally on characters and setting
2. In what ways is a nonfiction book report like a book report on a fictional book?
3. Why does a report on a nonfiction book include a summary of the book's contents?

B. Write a book report on another book of nonfiction, such as a science book (not a textbook) or a book on nature. Follow the format given above.

STUDY SKILLS

23 Studying for Tests

Efficient study habits can be valuable in helping you prepare for tests. If you have studied well, the thought of an upcoming test need not make you nervous. In fact, these few simple rules may help you a great deal.

Tips on Studying for Tests
1. Pay attention to lectures and class discussions.
2. Ask questions when you do not understand something.
3. Organize your schedule so that you have enough time to prepare well for each subject.
4. Work in a quiet place with good lighting and no distractions.
5. Keep any needed books and supplies at hand to avoid unnecessary interruptions, but occasionally take a break to relax and refresh yourself. Studying is hard work!
6. Review all material by going over your study notes.
7. Try to predict what questions will be asked on the test.

One good way to review a subject is to ask yourself questions like the ones you expect on the test. Questions that begin with *who, what, where, when,* and *why* can be helpful. Write each question on a separate sheet of paper. Then make brief notes on each sheet to answer the question. If you know the answers without checking your book, you probably do not have to spend very much time on that part of the material. If you have to look up the answers, take clear, precise notes. Review your notes the next evening. They may be easier to remember than the book itself.

Practice

Rewrite the following study tips to make them more helpful.

1. Always review every word in your book.

MODEL Take study notes from your book and review those.

2. Work while you watch television.
3. Study for an entire evening with no breaks.
4. Before you start studying, remind yourself how hard the test will be.

24 Taking Tests

Having a test-taking strategy can help you do well when you take a test. Here are some general points to follow.

Tips for Taking Tests
1. Carefully read or listen to test directions. **2.** Skim all the test questions and plan your time. Be sure that you have enough time to finish the test and check your answers. Do not spend a lot of time on one item. **3.** Answer easy questions first. Then answer harder ones. In multiple-choice questions, you can do this by first eliminating answers you know are wrong.

Three common kinds of test questions are analogies, multiple-choice, and reading comprehension. An **analogy** is a comparison. In a test an analogy asks you to rely on your knowledge of the relationship between two words to supply a word having the same relationship with a given word.

hot : cold :: summer : ________

This question reads *hot* is to *cold* as *summer* is to ________. The relationship between hot and cold is that they are opposites. For the answer, you must write the word that is the opposite of *summer*. The answer, of course, is *winter*.

A **multiple-choice question** simply supplies you with a statement or a question and a variety of answers from which to choose to complete the statement or answer the question.

A **reading comprehension** question is a question that tests your understanding of a passage. It is important that as you read details, you try to understand the main idea.

Practice

Write the answers to these test questions. Then label each one *analogy*, *multiple choice*, or *reading comprehension*.

1. hand: glove :: head: ________

MODEL hat—analogy

2. When you finish a test, you should a) tell the teacher; b) check your answers; c) study for the next class.
3. arm: elbow :: leg: ________

Skiing has become a popular sport. Millions of tourists visit ski areas for ski vacations. Skiing builds up endurance, tests agility, and challenges the mind. It provides one of the best mind and body workouts.

4. Question: Why has skiing become so popular?

STUDY SKILLS

25 Taking Essay Tests

STUDY SKILLS

On a test you may be asked to answer a question by stating your opinion or by giving reasons or examples to explain a topic. This type of question is known as an **essay question.**

First, read the question and try to determine how to form your response. Look for words in the question telling you what kind of answer is needed. Study these words and expressions.

1. Give an opinion (Tell how you feel about something and give good reasons to support your feeling.)
2. Compare (Show how two things are alike.)
3. Contrast (Show how two things are different.)
4. Explain, Analyze (Give reasons to show why or how something happened; give causes and effects.)
5. Describe (Tell how something looks or how it works.)

Read the way one student answered this essay question: *Compare and contrast the American Revolution with the Civil War.*

> The American Revolution and the Civil War were alike in some ways. Both wars were fought in the land we know as the United States. Officers and troops traveled by horse or on foot. The weapons of war did not change much from one war to the next.
>
> The reasons for the two wars, however, were different. The American Revolution occurred because the colonists had to fight for their independence from Britain's rule and taxation. The Civil War was fought between the states over states' rights.

Practice

A. Write answers to these questions.

1. What key words in the question tell how to answer?

MODEL *Compare and contrast*

2. How did the writer organize ideas?
3. What parts of the question help the student understand the periods of history involved?
4. What is good about the first sentence of each paragraph?
5. Why did the student respond in two paragraphs?

B. Answer this essay question: *Describe farming in America before and after the invention of the reaper in 1831.*

26 Using Graphs and Charts

Graphs and charts are visual aids that can present many facts in a small space. A **graph** displays information in picture form. A **bar graph** is an effective way to display quantities. Study this vertical bar graph showing the yearly earnings of the Drydel Corporation. The **vertical axis**, or vertical line, shows a scale in tens of millions of dollars. The **horizontal axis,** or horizontal line, shows the years that various amounts were earned.

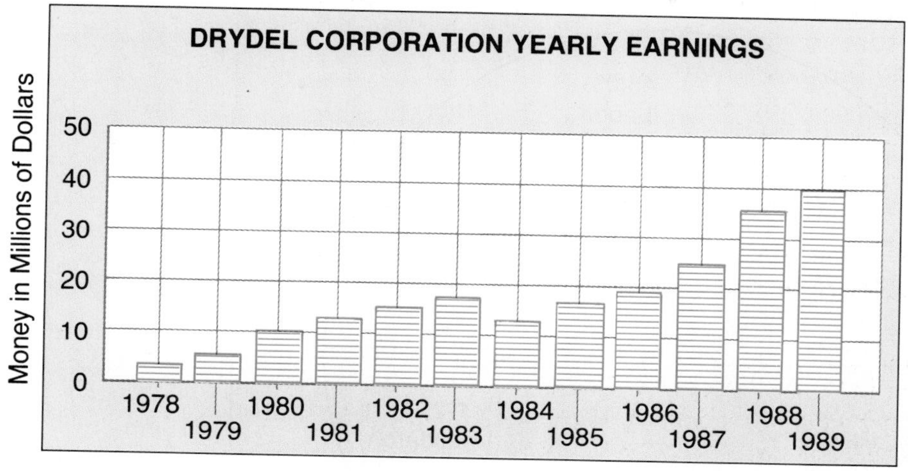

A **line graph** is a convenient way to show changes over a period of time. Study this line graph that shows the same information as the bar graph above. Lines connect points on the scale to show changes in earnings from year to year.

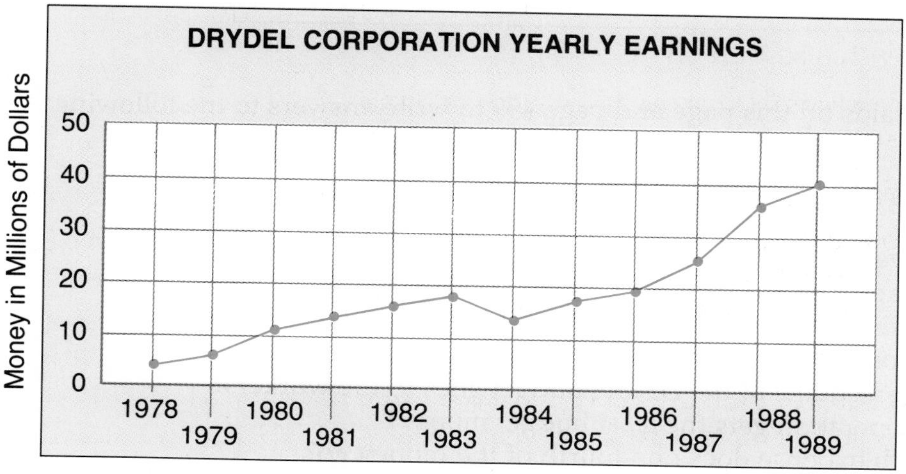

STUDY SKILLS

A **pie chart** is a way of showing how a whole quantity is divided. This pie chart shows what portion of all the available money is spent in each category by the Drydel Corporation. Notice that the parts of the budget are given as percentages.

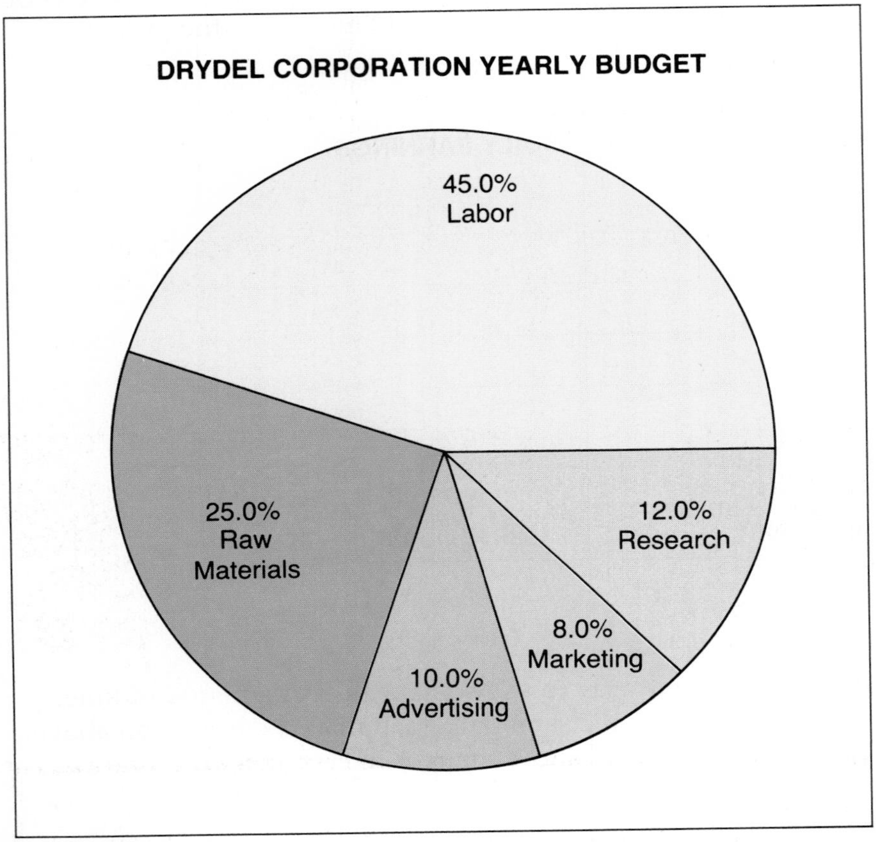

Practice

Use the visual aids on this page and page 499 to write answers to the following questions.

1. What was Drydel's best year for earnings?

MODEL 1989

2. Which year was their worst?
3. What happened to earnings in 1984?
4. Which year showed the greatest increase of earnings from the one before?
5. What percentage of the Drydel budget goes to the workers?
6. Which operation gets the least budget money?
7. To which expense does one-fourth of the money go?

27 Using Tables and Diagrams

Tables and diagrams are two different ways of visually displaying information. A **table** orders information in a set arrangement that usually consists of rows and columns. The table below shows the number of points each player on a high-school basketball team earned during one game.

Ray	Mike	Chuck	José	Chen	Carl	Bill
12	8	2	24	10	8	16

A **diagram** is a sketch, a drawing, or a plan that describes something by outlining its component parts. The diagram below shows the floor plan of a condominium apartment.

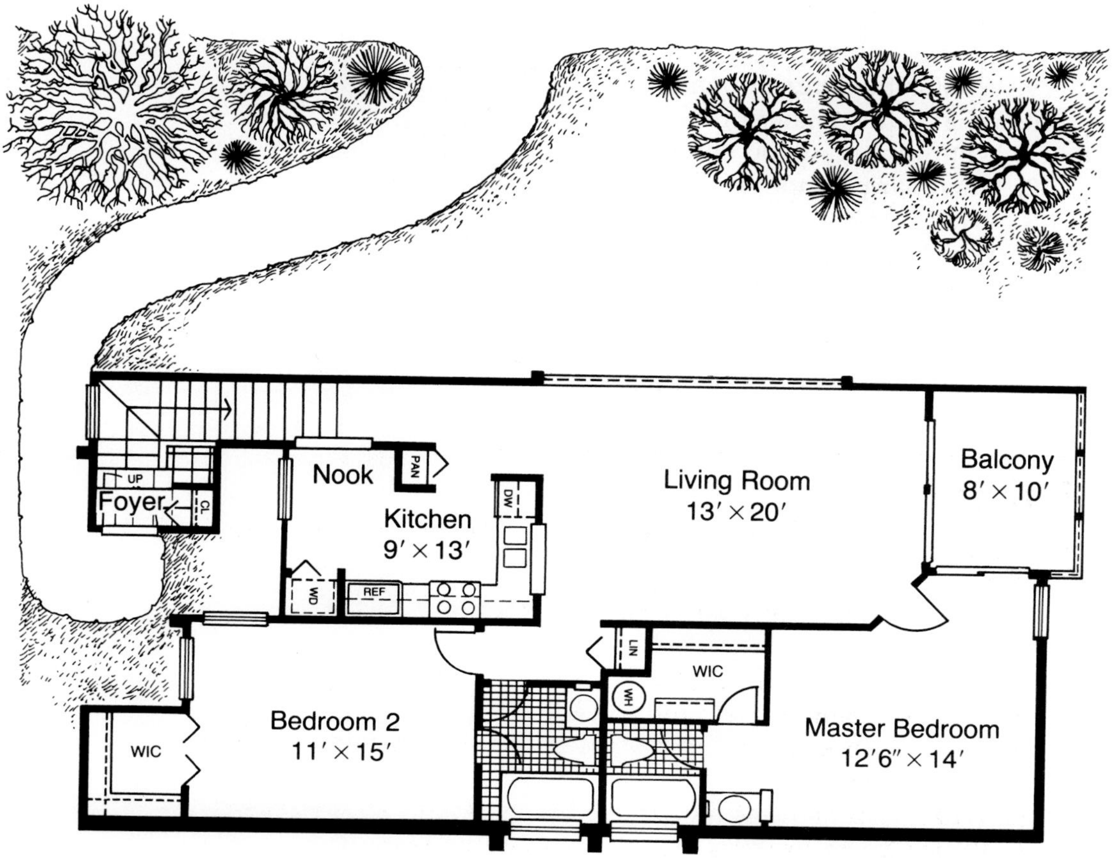

STUDY SKILLS

Practice

A. Use the table to write answers to these questions.

1. Who scored the most points?

MODEL José

2. How many points did Ray score?
3. What two players scored the same number of points? How many points did each score?
4. What was the total number of points that the team scored in the game?
5. Who scored half as many points as José?
6. Who scored the fewest points?
7. Who scored twice as many points as Mike?

B. Use the diagram to write answers to these questions.

8. How many rooms does the condominium apartment have, not including the balcony?

MODEL Four

9. What is the largest room?
10. What is the smallest room?
11. What room can you enter from the kitchen?
12. How many windows does the apartment have?
13. What is the size of the living room?
14. Which room is farthest from the living room?
15. How large is bedroom 2?

28 Using Maps

A **map** is an illustration of a certain geographical area. If you can read a map, you can be in unfamiliar surroundings yet understand where you are and how to get to your destination.

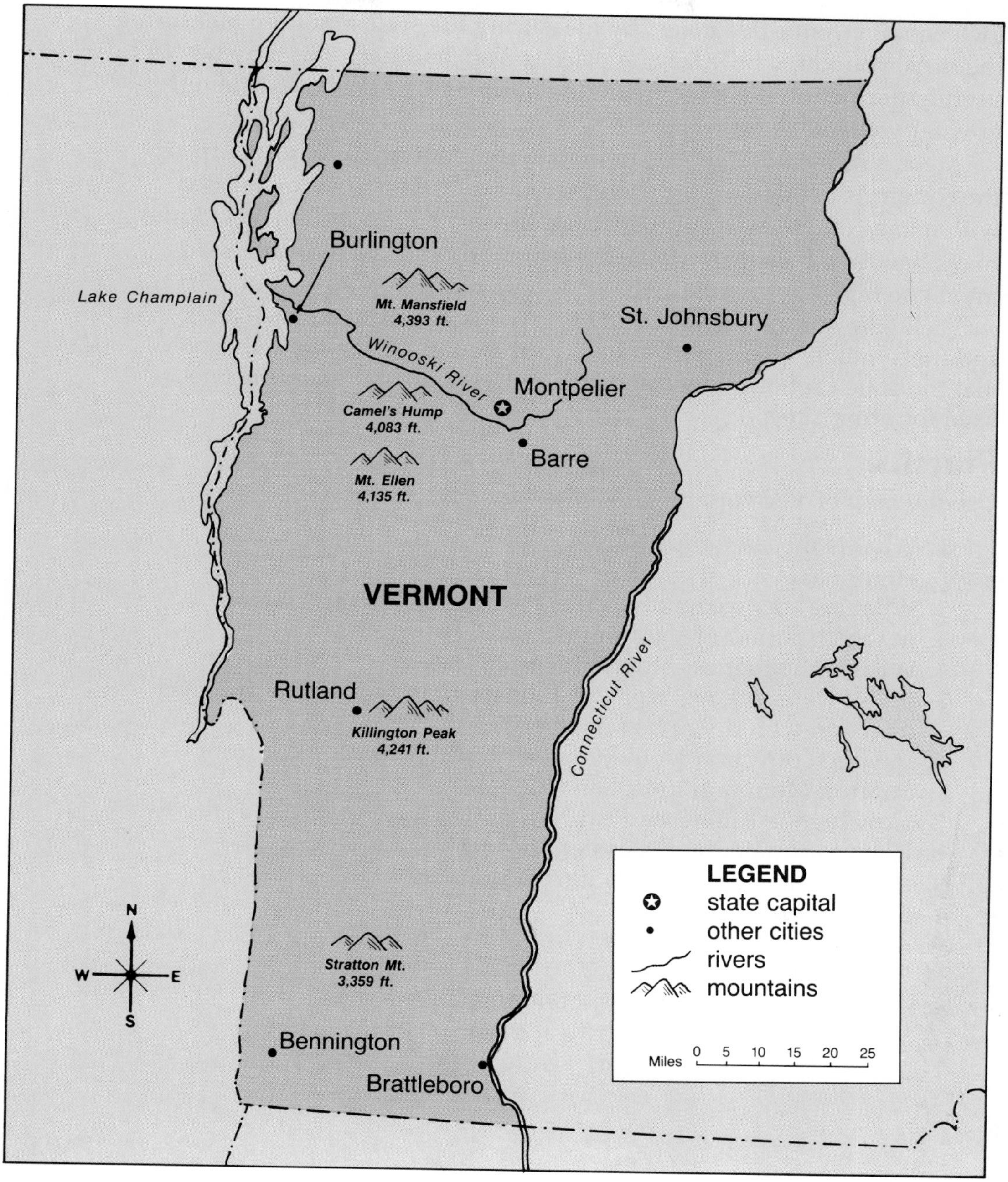

STUDY SKILLS

STUDY SKILLS

Most maps include a *compass rose,* which shows *North, East, South,* and *West.* Some maps also show the in-between points such as *northeast* and *southwest.* On most maps *North* is at the top of the map, but this is not always so. It is necessary to refer to the compass rose to be sure.

Many maps have a distance scale. A *distance scale* shows how to measure distance. The scale on the map on page 503 shows that one inch equals twenty-five miles. By measuring the scale and then measuring the map, you know how far one place is from another. This may be useful information if you are planning a trip and you need to find out how far you will be traveling.

Maps also include *symbols,* or marks, that indicate different parts of the country's or state's geography. On the map thin lines are labeled with names of rivers. You can also see the symbol for mountains. Some maps have symbols for various kinds of roads such as two-lane roads, interstate highways, and toll roads.

Each map should include a legend. The *legend* explains the codes and the symbols the map includes. On this map the legend tells you that the state capital is identified by a different symbol than the one used for other cities.

Practice

Use the map of Vermont to write answers to these questions.

1. What is the state capital?

MODEL Montpelier

2. What are the two southernmost towns shown on the map?
3. In which corner of Vermont is Lake Champlain?
4. What is the highest mountain in the state?
5. If you were to travel from St. Johnsbury to Burlington, in which direction would you be traveling?
6. In which direction would you be traveling if you went from Stratton Mountain to Rutland?
7. How high is Killington Peak?
8. What forms Vermont's eastern border?
9. About how many miles is it from Brattleboro to Bennington?
10. About how many miles is it from St. Johnsbury to Burlington?
11. What is the second-highest mountain in the state?
12. What town is in the southwestern corner of the state?

29 Taking Messages and Using a Telephone Directory

When you take or give a telephone message, it is important that you communicate information accurately and completely. When you take a message, be sure to write down 1) the name of the caller, 2) the time and the date of the call, 3) the reason for the call, 4) the caller's telephone number, and 5) when the caller will be available to receive a return call.

A **telephone directory** is a useful resource for finding telephone numbers. The **white pages** list alphabetically by last name all the residential phone customers. The **yellow pages** list stores and businesses. They are organized alphabetically by type of business. An **index** lists all the headings in the yellow pages. Both white and yellow pages include the phone number and address of each person or business.

Restaurants

B & B FAMILY RESTAURANT
534 River Rd. 555–0098
CHINA JADE
17 First Ave. 555–7692
VILLAGIO ITALIANO
WE DELIVER
Pizza—Calzones—Italian Specialties
34 Baker Rd. 555–7800

Practice

A. Rewrite these telephone messages to make them complete and accurate. You can decide on the details.

1. Jane—A guy called about the bike you have for sale. He wants you to call him back today around 4:00 P.M.

MODEL Jane—Robert Keller called today at 9:00 A.M. about the bike you have for sale. Call him back at 4:00 P.M. to give him the details. His number is 555–5061. Steve

2. Dave—Somebody named Nancy called you at 5:00 P.M. today. Phone number is 555–9879.

B. Use the model directory page to write answers to these questions.

3. If you wanted food to be delivered, which restaurant would you call?

MODEL Villagio Italiano

4. What is the phone number of the restaurant serving Chinese food?

5. Where is the B & B Family Restaurant?

STUDY SKILLS

30 Completing Forms

The ability to fill out forms correctly is a commonly used skill. It is usually a good idea to look over the entire form before you start to fill it out. Some forms ask for your last name first, and others ask for your first name first. Some forms have separate spaces for the different parts of your address. Some forms ask for information above the writing line; some ask for information below the line. If you have looked over a whole form, you will know what to expect and can put the information in the correct place.

APPLICATION FOR TENAKILL SWIM CLUB MEMBERSHIP

Name Brian McDermott Telephone Number 555-0034
Address 45 Hickory Rd. Age 12
Town Warren State Vermont ZIP Code 05674
Do any family members now belong to Tenakill Swim Club? yes
If so, list them: John, Ellen, and Jill McDermott

Practice

Make your own copies of these forms and then complete them. You may invent a name and information if you wish.

JOB APPLICATION FOR BURGERBUN RESTAURANT

Name ______________ Phone Number ______________
Address ______________
City ______________ State ______________ ZIP Code ______________
Date of Birth ______________ Social Security Number ______________
Job you are applying for ______________
List job experience ______________
List high school attended ______________
Did you graduate? ______________ List year of graduation ______________
List reasons why you are qualified for this job ______________
____
Hours available for work ______________

ORDER FORM FOR *SNOW SPORT* MAGAZINE

Name ______________
Address ______________ Apt. ______________
City ______________ State ______________ ZIP Code ______________
Check one _____ one year _____ two years _____ three years
Form of payment: _____ check _____ money order _____ credit card

EXTRA PRACTICE

Contents

1 Four Kinds of Sentences *pages 28 – 29*

A. Identifying Sentences Write *imperative, declarative, exclamatory,* or *interrogative* to identify each kind of sentence.

1. Braille is a code used by blind people.

MODEL declarative

2. Patterns of small, raised dots represent letters.
3. Are there patterns for numbers and punctuation marks?
4. Read the individual patterns by touch.
5. What a wonderful idea this is!
6. How are braille books printed?
7. Metal plates stamp the patterns into paper.
8. Teach me to read braille patterns.

B. Correcting Sentences Write each sentence. Use capital letters, periods, question marks, and exclamation points correctly.

9. do you know sign language

MODEL Do you know sign language?

10. how fast her fingers spell
11. where did you learn sign language
12. sign language is useful to hearing people too
13. does Jackie teach signing to deaf clients
14. look at the chart of the American Manual Alphabet
15. there is a gesture for every letter of the alphabet
16. are there gestures for complete words and phrases

C. Writing Sentences Change each sentence to the type of sentence indicated in parentheses ( ). If necessary, add words.

17. Some computers are voice-activated. (interrogative)

MODEL Are some computers voice-activated?

18. Computers do recognize vocal commands. (interrogative)
19. They translate speech into the alphabet. (exclamatory)
20. Keyboarding is necessary! (interrogative)
21. Is voice processing accurate? (declarative)
22. Such computers do recognize many words. (interrogative)
23. Their capacity expands daily. (exclamatory)
24. Many people will use voice processing. (interrogative)

2 Complete and Simple Subjects *pages 30 – 31*

A. Identifying Subjects Write each sentence. Draw a line after the complete subject.

1. The students are excited about Amy's project.

MODEL The students|are excited about Amy's project.

2. A crew of students is conducting a survey.
3. Specific instructions are available for each student.
4. Carlisle Corners is the chosen interview site.
5. A local news station is tabulating the survey results.
6. The time allotted for interviews is four hours.
7. A goal of ninety interviews is set.

B. Distinguishing Between Simple and Complete Subjects Write the complete subject from each sentence. Underline the simple subject.

8. My sister's club is active in our community.

MODEL My sister's <u>club</u>

9. The group has many members.
10. Funds are being collected for a documentary.
11. A committee of ecologists will review the plans.
12. Many issues are on the agenda for the documentary.
13. A report was compiled by Hale and Barnes Associates.
14. The data reveals high levels of toxic gases.

C. Writing Subjects Write each sentence, adding a complete subject to each word group. Draw a line under each simple subject. If the subject is *you* (understood), write *you*.

15. ________ is sponsoring a debate.

MODEL The <u>Student Council</u> is sponsoring a debate.

16. ________ is the entry fee for the debate.
17. ________ is the location.
18. ________ is the chosen topic.
19. ________ have five minutes for opening statements.
20. ________ applauds for the talented speakers.
21. ________ must speak either for or against an issue.
22. ________ will observe the debate.
23. ________ must decide who wins the debate.

3 Complete and Simple Predicates *pages 32 – 33*

A. Distinguishing Between Complete Subjects and Complete Predicates Write each sentence. Draw a line between the complete subject and the complete predicate.

1. Communication has changed over the centuries.

MODEL Communication|has changed over the centuries.

2. Prehistoric people communicated with gestures.
3. Smoke signals were sent from one village to another.
4. Different languages were developed.
5. Messengers delivered messages verbally.
6. People drew images on cave walls.
7. Alphabets replaced other symbols.
8. Scribes wrote letters, documents, and books.

B. Identifying Simple and Complete Predicates Write the complete predicate in each sentence. Underline the verb.

9. Speaking is one method of communication.

MODEL is one method of communication

10. People use their voices in many different ways.
11. Cheerleaders yell into megaphones.
12. A storyteller changes tone of voice for effect.
13. Auctioneers chant in short, melodic phrases.
14. Professional vocalists sing jingles for commercials.
15. Actors transmit a story to the audience through voice.
16. An audience usually laughs at a comedian.

C. Expanding Predicates Make each word group into a sentence, adding details to each predicate. Underline the complete predicate once, and draw two lines under the verb.

17. Many people communicate

MODEL Many people communicate without speaking.

18. A cyclist gives
19. Police officers direct
20. A ballerina interprets
21. The orchestra conductor waves
22. Crossing guards hold
23. Artists draw
24. Teachers write

EXTRA PRACTICE

UNIT 1

4 Word Order in Sentences *pages 34 – 36*

A. **Identifying Word Order** Write *natural* or *inverted* to describe the word order in each sentence.

1. Do you have a passport?

MODEL inverted

2. Supply proof of citizenship for a passport.
3. Without a passport you cannot enter another country.
4. My family went to the travel agency.
5. Here is my birth certificate.
6. At the top of the passport application are instructions.
7. Under the photograph will appear personal information.
8. In the passport will be a photograph of me.

B. **Identifying Subjects and Verbs** Write each sentence. Underline the simple subject once and the verb twice.

9. Many documents are used for identification.

MODEL Many documents are used for identification.

10. In my wallet are several pieces of identification.
11. On my student passport appears a photograph of me.
12. My signature is written under my photograph.
13. Without this card I cannot enter school.
14. In the side pocket hides my library card.
15. On library books are stamped certain codes.
16. By the library exit is a scanner that reads the codes.

C. **Changing Word Order** Using the word order in parentheses ( ), rewrite each sentence. Underline each simple subject once and each verb twice.

17. To Jeff belongs the deed to this farm. (natural)

MODEL The deed to this farm belongs to Jeff.

18. Have they always lived on the farm? (natural)
19. For his files is needed a copy of the deed. (natural)
20. Another signature is on the mortgage. (inverted)
21. In the office waits a farm manager. (natural)
22. A beneficiary was named in Grandfather's will. (inverted)
23. In my lockbox is a copy of Grandfather's will. (natural)

5 Compound Subjects and Compound Verbs *pages 37 – 38*

A. Identifying Compound Subjects and Verbs Write and label the compound subject or the compound verb from each sentence.

1. Mary and Carla are ham radio operators.

MODEL Mary, Carla—compound subject

2. They organized and operated an amateur radio station.
3. Mary bought a kit and assembled her ham radio.
4. Carla designed and built her ham radio.
5. Citizens of the United States and foreigners talk to them.
6. Sometimes, Carla finds and helps people in trouble.

B. Replacing Compound Subjects and Verbs Replace the underlined compound subjects and verbs with different compound subjects and verbs. Write each new sentence.

7. We rented and played a tape of an old radio program.

MODEL We located and borrowed a tape of an old radio program.

8. A mystery and a comedy were recorded.
9. We chuckled and laughed during the comedy.
10. A clown, a dog, and a magician were the main characters.
11. One character spoiled tricks and mispronounced words.
12. Julie cried and worried during one program.

C. Writing Compound Subjects and Verbs Write each sentence, adding a compound subject or a compound verb to each sentence as indicated in parentheses ( ).

13. ________ and ________ are broadcast on the radio. (subject)

MODEL Music and weather are broadcast on the radio.

14. ________ and ________ play on some radio stations. (subject)
15. I ________ at jokes or ________ along to music. (verb)
16. ________ and ________ usually play soothing music. (subject)
17. Students ________ or ________ portable radios. (verb)
18. I can ________ and ________ radio stations. (verb)
19. ________ and ________ are features of some radios. (subject)
20. ________ and ________ vary from state to state. (subject)

EXTRA PRACTICE

UNIT 1

6 Simple and Compound Sentences *pages 39 – 41*

A. Identifying Simple and Compound Sentences If a sentence is simple, write *simple.* If it is compound, write *compound.*

1. A police officer is directing traffic ahead.

MODEL simple

2. We must take a detour and drive around a minor accident.
3. Warn other drivers; use your flashers.
4. Slow down near busy streets, but don't block the intersection.
5. The flares indicate caution.
6. Watch carefully, and stop for pedestrians.
7. We got a new stop sign; this corner is now safe.
8. I must watch and drive slowly, or I will miss our street.

B. Combining Sentences Combine both simple sentences into a compound sentence.

9. Look at this compass. It indicates directions.

MODEL Look at this compass; it indicates directions.

10. Hold it horizontally in your hand. Look at its face.
11. The *N* represents north. The *S* represents south.
12. The needle is magnetic. It always points north.
13. Turn the compass until the needle points to *N*. You will go in the wrong direction.
14. The sun rises in the east. It sets in the west.
15. This direction is east. That direction is west.
16. Use it if you are lost. Use it to confirm a location.

C. Writing Compound Sentences Think of another simple sentence to add to each sentence. Then write both sentences as a compound sentence.

17. Go to the post office.

MODEL Go to the post office; mail this package.

18. The package is heavy.
19. I can carry it in my backpack.
20. Turn right at the stop sign.
21. I will look for Carnival Avenue.
22. The post office is on the corner.
23. The parking lot is full.
24. Many people are waiting in line.
25. I can return home.

7 Avoiding Sentence Fragments and Run-on Sentences *pages 42 – 43*

A. Identifying Sentence Fragments and Run-on Sentences Write *fragment*, *run-on*, or *sentence* to describe each word group.

1. Read the newspaper, learn what is happening in the world.
MODEL run-on
2. The sensational headline.
3. I read the Style section.
4. The world news in section *A*.
5. The front page is packed.
6. The theater guide.
7. A desk is advertised for sale, I'll look at it.

B. Correcting Sentence Fragments and Run-on Sentences Correct each sentence fragment or run-on sentence.

8. The newspaper article.
MODEL The newspaper article lists community activities.
9. The Asian Club sponsoring a festival.
10. Entertainment will be provided, tickets are available.
11. Folk dancers wearing native costumes.
12. Playing ethnic music and games.
13. Chefs conducting cooking classes.

C. Combining Sentence Fragments and Sentences Combine each set of word groups into one sentence. Write each sentence.

14. I scan newspapers. For items of interest.
MODEL I scan newspapers for items of interest.
15. Stores announce sales. Attract customers with free gifts.
16. Summer clothing appears. In store windows.
17. Exotic vacations are pictured. Now I wish to visit Spain.
18. Camping equipment is displayed. For the adventurer.
19. A beautiful used car. Is advertised for sale.
20. Gardening tips are given. I read them closely.

UNIT 2

1 Kinds of Nouns *pages 74 – 75*

A. Kinds of Nouns Write whether each noun is *common* or *proper* and *abstract* or *concrete*. If the noun is collective, write *C*.

1. computer

MODEL common—concrete

2. The White House
3. mother
4. sadness
5. Niagara Falls
6. honesty
7. audience
8. Nova Scotia
9. country
10. idea
11. Pulitzer Prize
12. grocery store

B. Categorizing Nouns Write the nouns in each sentence. Label each noun *common* or *proper* and *abstract* or *concrete*. If the noun is collective, write *C*.

13. Many decisions and inventions have made life easier.

MODEL decisions—common—abstract; inventions—common—concrete; life—common—abstract

14. John Stevens built the first successful steam engine.
15. The train quickly replaced the Conestoga wagon.
16. People now communicate quickly and efficiently.
17. The sewing machine increased production of textiles.
18. The labor force across America grew.
19. Automobiles replaced teams of horses.
20. Manufacturers in Detroit hired crews of machinists.

C. Writing Nouns Write each sentence, adding a noun to each sentence. Write whether the noun is *common* or *proper* and *abstract* or *concrete*. If the noun is collective, write *collective*.

21. From home you can see the ________.

MODEL From home you can see the Mississippi River. proper—concrete

22. Barges stop in ________ to unload cargo.
23. We watch the ________ of workers on the docks.
24. You can purchase fresh seafood at ________.
25. Mother moved to Louisiana before ________.
26. She remembers when the river was full of ________.
27. She watched ________ of ships sail on the river.
28. Teachers took ________ of children to the river.

UNIT 2

2 Capitalization of Proper Nouns *pages 76 – 77*

A. Identifying Proper Nouns That Are Written Correctly Write *correct* for each proper noun that is written correctly. Write *incorrect* for each proper noun that is not.

1. midwest

MODEL incorrect

2. lisa
3. January
4. french
5. Vietnam War
6. dutch
7. paris
8. first street
9. Monica c. Riley
10. Brooklyn Bridge

B. Capitalizing Proper Nouns Write each sentence correctly.

11. ms. lowery is organizing a field trip to chicago.

MODEL Ms. Lowery is organizing a field trip to Chicago.

12. jefferson high students will land at o'hare airport.
13. They will go to water tower place on north michigan avenue.
14. Is the sears tower next to the chicago river?
15. The sears tower is the tallest building in america.
16. A tour of adler planetarium is scheduled.
17. The museum of science and industry has great exhibits.
18. From the hancock building, lake michigan can be seen.
19. Students will sample food at tung restaurant.

C. Writing Proper Nouns Complete each sentence with the type of proper noun indicated in parentheses ( ). Write each sentence.

20. ________ has changed dramatically. (country)

MODEL America has changed dramatically.

21. Our city of ________ has tripled its population. (city)
22. ________ is a new business in town. (company)
23. ________ has lived in this city for 100 years. (person)
24. Many citizens speak ________ and ________. (languages)
25. The ________ was built this year. (building)
26. A traffic light was installed at ________ and ________. (roads)
27. In ________ we celebrated our town's 150th birthday. (month)
28. The ________ is sponsoring a gala celebration. (government body)

EXTRA PRACTICE

UNIT 2

3 Abbreviations *pages 78 – 79*

A. Identifying Abbreviations Read each pair of abbreviations. Write the abbreviation that is correct.

1. Nov Nov.

MODEL Nov.

2. Ltd Ltd.
3. rpm rpm.
4. Mon Mon.
5. Sgt. Sgt
6. mi mi.
7. Oct Oct.
8. Corp. corp.
9. nasa NASA
10. lb lb.
11. Dr Dr.
12. Inc. inc.
13. Tues Tues.

B. Writing Abbreviations Write each item. Replace each underlined word or group of words with an abbreviation.

14. Charlotte, <u>South Carolina</u>

MODEL Charlotte, SC

15. <u>Central Intelligence Agency</u>
16. 59 <u>North</u> Carver <u>Avenue</u>, Cincinnati, <u>Ohio</u>
17. <u>Bachelor of Science</u>, in physics
18. <u>American Federation of Labor</u> union group
19. Wellington, <u>Incorporated</u>
20. 4 <u>pounds</u> sugar
21. <u>Doctor</u> John <u>Remington</u> Mason
22. <u>Federal Bureau of Investigation</u>

C. Forming Abbreviations Write the abbreviation for each item.

23. Boulevard

MODEL Blvd.

24. Professor
25. February
26. New Jersey
27. East
28. prisoner of war
29. International Business Machines
30. United Nations
31. Esquire
32. Wednesday
33. Rural Delivery
34. Limited
35. Zone Improvement Plan
36. Trans World Airlines
37. unidentified flying object
38. United States Air Force
39. dozen
40. intelligence quotient
41. Circle
42. very important person
43. miles per hour

4 Singular and Plural Nouns *pages 80 – 81*

A. Distinguishing Between Singular and Plural Nouns Write *singular* for each singular noun. Write *plural* for each plural noun.

1. industry

MODEL singular

2. shelves
3. product
4. technologies
5. blintz
6. executives
7. properties
8. employees
9. suffix
10. trios
11. businesses
12. companies
13. galleys
14. address
15. batch
16. policies
17. bureaus
18. engines
19. veto
20. prefixes
21. tariff
22. grouch
23. zeros
24. sheaves
25. man

B. Spelling Plural Nouns Write the plural form of each noun.

26. half

MODEL halves

27. array
28. waitress
29. quartz
30. radio
31. identity
32. key
33. variety
34. bench
35. hero
36. projection
37. mix
38. thief
39. echo
40. knife
41. tomato
42. alley
43. belief
44. duchess
45. prefix
46. rodeo
47. latch
48. ratio
49. loaf
50. potato

C. Using Plural Nouns Write each sentence, changing each underlined noun to its plural form.

51. Rhonda and her friend attended a trial.

MODEL Rhonda and her friends attended a trial.

52. Several attorney arrived with briefcase.
53. Juror were selected after three day of interview.
54. Police chief from two county submitted display.
55. Another display consisted of stereo and knife.
56. All material had been confiscated from three studio.
57. Did the defendant avoid paying tax on all his business?
58. Artist had drawn sketch of the trial.
59. The juror had to distinguish truthful statement from lie.

UNIT 2

5 More Plural Nouns *Pages 82 – 83*

A. Identifying Singular and Plural Nouns Write whether each underlined noun is *singular* or *plural*.

1. Two series of debates will be televised locally.

MODEL plural

2. A special area is reserved for the reporter corps.
3. Economics will be the main topic.
4. All media will have equal representation.
5. My sisters-in-law registered in this district.
6. What are the odds of a tied election?
7. Explain your hypotheses to the campaign manager.
8. Both senators-elect were lieutenants general.
9. Circulate these brochures among passersby.
10. Newsletters were sent to many men and women.

B. Forming Plural Nouns Write the plural forms of these nouns and symbols.

11. father-in-law

MODEL fathers-in-law

12. postmaster general
13. alumnus
14. sergeant major
15. sheep
16. mouse
17. cupful
18. 1750
19. shoe
20. crisis
21. aspirin
22. brother-in-law
23. 5
24. tooth
25. &
26. deer

C. Using Plural Nouns Write each sentence. Use the plural form of each noun in parentheses ( ).

27. The ________ joined a campaign committee. (man)

MODEL The men joined a campaign committee.

28. The parties needed new ________. (headquarters)
29. There were many ________ for the supplies. (bill of sale)
30. Banners would measure 30 ________ by 15 ________. (foot)
31. ________ of nails were used. (handful)
32. Even ________ found things to do. (child)
33. ________ watched the construction. (Passerby)
34. Workers attached tools to their ________. (trousers)
35. ________ and ________ watched curiously. (Goose, deer)

EXTRA PRACTICE

6 Possessive Nouns *pages 84 – 85*

A. Identifying Possessive Nouns For each pair, write the word group that correctly uses a possessive noun.

1. Chris stamp collection
   Chris's stamp collection

MODEL Chris's stamp collection

2. Carlotta's violin
   Carlottas violin
3. antique dolls eyes
   antique dolls' eyes
4. barn's weather vane
   barns weather vane
5. Lee's and Babs's rare coins
   Lees and Babs rare coins
6. books binding
   book's binding
7. Ellis baseball cards
   Ellis's baseball cards
8. Lisas and Kellys game
   Lisa and Kelly's game
9. mirrors' curved glass
   mirrors curved glass
10. neighbors classic car
    neighbor's classic car
11. antique dealer's knowledge
    antique dealers knowledge

B. Forming Possessive Nouns Rewrite each word group, using a possessive noun.

12. cameo belonging to Aunt Amy

MODEL Aunt Amy's cameo

13. stovepipe hat of Abe Lincoln
14. ruby slipper of Dorothy
15. poem of Carl Sandburg
16. script of Robert Redford
17. plane of Wilbur and Orville Wright
18. autograph of Charles Lindbergh
19. gloves of Bette Davis
20. bonnet of Scarlett O'Hara
21. songs of the Andrews Sisters

C. Using Possessive Nouns Write complete sentences correctly using a possessive noun for each word group.

22. treasures of the attic

MODEL We rummaged through the attic's treasures.

23. secrets in the trunk
24. Oriental rug of someone
25. delicate lace of a fan
26. diary of Mother
27. portraits of ancestors
28. medals of Grandfather
29. carved lid of a toy chest
30. porcelain faces of dolls
31. details of a toy train
32. ivory keys of the piano
33. texture of a shawl
34. shrill sound of a whistle

UNIT 2

7 Appositives *pages 86 – 87*

A. Identifying Appositives Write each sentence. Underline the appositive and draw an arrow to the noun it explains.

1. Our guest, Ms. Wade, writes books for children.

MODEL Our guest, Ms. Wade, writes books for children.

2. Mr. McClure, our principal, introduced Ms. Wade.
3. Her characters, lively animals, have crazy adventures.
4. Casey, my friend, shared his book with Ms. Wade.
5. Casey writes great stories, elaborate tales.
6. His illustrator, Kate Edwards, is also a student.

EXTRA PRACTICE

B. Punctuating Appositives Write each sentence, using commas correctly.

7. My favorite painting The Brook is an outdoor scene.

MODEL My favorite painting, The Brook, is an outdoor scene.

8. Its artist John Singer Sargent was an American impressionist.
9. Impressionism a painting style emerged in the 1800's.
10. Artists combined tiny dots splashes of color to create an impression.
11. Light everything seen by the eye was captured on canvas.
12. Mary Cassatt another American artist painted portraits.
13. Claude Monet a French artist was an early impressionist.
14. He often painted flowers water lilies.

C. Writing Appositives Write a sentence using each phrase as an appositive. Underline the noun that is explained.

15. a story about myself

MODEL I am writing an autobiography, a story about myself.

16. a career in art
17. charcoal and paper
18. my sister
19. a masterpiece
20. my impressionistic style
21. my mother
22. the art instructor
23. watercolors
24. beach scenes
25. Denison University

1 Verbs *pages 122 – 123*

A. Distinguishing Between Action and Linking Verbs Write the verb from each sentence. Label each verb *action* or *linking*.

1. Discovery appears ready for orbit.

MODEL appears—linking

2. NASA scheduled the flight for September 29, 1988.
3. Engineers moved Discovery to the launch pad.
4. The crowd grew restless with anticipation.
5. Conditions appeared perfect for the launch.
6. The countdown began with only a minor delay.

B. Using Action and Linking Verbs Write each sentence, adding a verb from the box. Draw an arrow from each linking verb to the word or words it connects to the subject.

7. The astronauts ________ a successful voyage.

MODEL The astronauts completed a successful voyage.

8. A new satellite ________ vital.
9. Discovery ________ the Earth several times.
10. Discovery ________ at Edwards Air Force Base.
11. The landing ________ perfect.
12. The shuttle ________ a legend.
13. Possibilities for the space program ________ endless.

completed
orbited
are
seemed
remains
landed
was

C. Using Action Verbs Write each sentence. Replace each action verb with a more vivid action verb.

14. One day we might send a space station to Mars.

MODEL One day we might ship a space station to Mars.

15. Payload specialists will visit the planet's surface.
16. The astronauts will need special uniforms.
17. The station will circle Mars.
18. The crew will watch the planet's soil.
19. Scientists will see the plant and animal life.
20. Mars has great possibilities for earthlings.

EXTRA PRACTICE

2 Main Verbs and Helping Verbs *pages 124 – 125*

A. **Writing Main and Helping Verbs** Write and label the *main verb* and the *helping verb* in each underlined verb phrase.

1. We were looking for lost treasures.

MODEL were—helping verb; looking—main verb

2. A guide is leading us to the dig site.
3. The sun had crept slowly into the sky.
4. This archaeological expediton can become an adventure.
5. In the dirt we did find something hard.
6. These ancient objects had lost their luster over time.
7. Jackie is pulling artifacts out of the hole!

B. **Identifying Main and Helping Verbs** Write each sentence. Underline the main verb once, and draw two lines under the helping verb.

8. King Ramses II of Egypt did build many monuments.

MODEL King Ramses II of Egypt did build many monuments.

9. During his reign the Luxor Temple was completed.
10. The people did dedicate this temple to Ramses.
11. Six huge statues of the king were carved.
12. The statues would stand at the temple's entrance.
13. Only four of the statues are standing today.
14. Archaeologists have discovered the tomb of Ramses II.

C. **Using Helping Verbs** Write each sentence, adding one or more helping verbs to each.

15. I ________ studied the Seven Wonders of the Ancient World.

MODEL I have studied the Seven Wonders of the Ancient World.

16. The Pyramids ________ become the last of these to stand.
17. The Pyramids ________ located in the desert near Cairo.
18. The Pyramids ________ be renovated.
19. Earthquakes ________ destroyed three of them.
20. The statue of Zeus ________ sit on an elaborate throne.
21. The Lighthouse of Alexandria ________ beckoned ships.
22. Scientists ________ looking for the exact location and ruins of the Hanging Gardens of Babylon.

3 Principal Parts of Regular Verbs *pages 126 – 127*

A. Identifying Principal Parts of Verbs Write each verb or verb phrase. Next to it write whether it is *present, past, present participle,* or *past participle.*

1. worked

MODEL worked—past

2. passed
3. is laughing
4. have planted
5. embrace
6. sleep
7. has lost
8. swim
9. is estimating

B. Writing Principal Parts of Verbs Write the verb or verb phrase in each sentence. Then label the principal part it uses.

10. Farmers have planted crops for years.

MODEL have planted—past participle

11. They are looking for new ways to irrigate the fields.
12. Drought is posing a serious threat.
13. Many fields have dried from drought.
14. Prosperous farmers provide bountiful tables.
15. Insects destroyed many crops last year.
16. Citrus orchards have frozen in Florida.
17. Farmers are replanting acres of orange trees.
18. Citrus canker has also destroyed many trees.

C. Forming Principal Parts of Verbs Replace each verb with the principal part shown in parentheses ( ). Write each sentence.

19. The world's population increase. (present participle)

MODEL The world's population is increasing.

20. Some farmers produce bumper crops. (present participle)
21. Farmers harvest excess grain. (present)
22. Fortunate nations help drought victims. (past)
23. Authorities worry about starvation. (past participle)
24. Organizations ship wheat overseas. (past participle)
25. Grain reach its destination slowly. (present)
26. Nations share technology. (present participle)
27. Agronomists plan irrigation systems. (past participle)
28. Conditions improve in some areas. (present participle)

UNIT 3

4 Principal Parts of Irregular Verbs *pages 128 – 130*

A. Identifying Principal Parts of Irregular Verbs Write the verb or verb phrase from each sentence. Label it with the principal part it expresses.

1. I found a rare stamp!

MODEL found—past

2. Stamp collecting is becoming a popular hobby in the United States.
3. I have sought rare stamps in unusual places.
4. I pay a lot of money for a collectible stamp.
5. I am buying a rare relief-perforated French stamp.
6. Its description and picture came in a stamp catalogue.
7. I had brought my magnifying glass for close inspection.
8. The stamp is costing nine hundred dollars.
9. I lent my commemorative stamps to a friend for analysis.
10. Rare stamps sell at auctions for very high prices.
11. The old imperforate stamps were cut apart with scissors.

B. Forming Principal Parts of Irregular Verbs Write the past, the past participle, and the present participle of each present-tense verb.

12. find

MODEL found, (has) found, (is) finding

13. drink
14. bend
15. fling
16. come
17. shine
18. catch
19. hold
20. cast
21. spring
22. shut
23. hurt
24. leave

C. Replacing Principal Parts of Irregular Verbs Write each sentence, changing the underlined verb to the principal part shown in parentheses ( ).

25. People <u>seek</u> many different treasures. (past)

MODEL People sought many different treasures.

26. I <u>read</u> about Spanish treasures. (past participle)
27. Many ships <u>sink</u> to the bottom of the sea. (past)
28. Explorers <u>seek</u> such bounty for years. (past participle)
29. Many people <u>buy</u> antiques. (present participle)
30. American folk art <u>become</u> popular. (past participle)
31. Antique dolls <u>bring</u> high prices at auctions. (present)

5 More Irregular Verbs *pages 131 – 132*

A. Identifying Principal Parts of Irregular Verbs Write each verb or verb phrase. Label each with its principal part.

1. had gone

MODEL had gone—past participle

2. grow
3. blew
4. wore
5. is lying
6. is rising
7. have ridden
8. had forgotten
9. had chosen
10. have known
11. rode
12. freeze
13. gave

B. Choosing Principal Parts of Irregular Verbs Write the verb or verb phrase in each sentence, and label it with its principal part.

14. Narcissus had chosen no one for a bride.

MODEL had chosen—past participle

15. Never has he known love.
16. The nymph Echo had seen Narcissus.
17. She fell in love with him.
18. Echo had never spoken to Narcissus.
19. The goddess Hera took away Echo's voice.
20. Narcissus has not grown fond of Echo.
21. He broke Echo's heart.
22. Narcissus is going to a pool in the mountains.
23. He saw his own reflection in the water.

C. Forming Principal Parts of Irregular Verbs Write each sentence, using the past participle of the underlined verb or verb phrase. Use *have, has,* or *had* as the helping verb.

24. Who gives a lecture on Roman mythology?

MODEL Who had given a lecture on Roman mythology?

25. The professor speaks on the different mythological gods.
26. He chooses to talk about each god's position in Roman society.
27. Many ancient scholars write about various gods.
28. Most of the ancient statues of the gods break.
29. Statues and temples fall in ruins after Rome was sacked.
30. I am taking a class in Greek mythology.
31. He gets a chart that describes each god in detail.
32. I forget many of the names that were given to them.

6 Verb Tenses *pages 133 – 136*

A. Identifying Tenses Write each verb or verb phrase and the tense it expresses.

1. have invented

MODEL> have invented—present perfect

2. have tossed
3. shouted
4. will have stopped
5. had dressed
6. will provoke
7. computed
8. have pitched
9. had enjoyed
10. will increase
11. arrange

B. Forming Tenses Write each sentence, changing the underlined verb to the tense indicated in parentheses ( ).

12. Jean-Henri Dunant <u>organize</u> the Red Cross. (past)

MODEL> Jean-Henri Dunant organized the Red Cross.

13. In 1862 he <u>ask</u> for volunteers. (past perfect)
14. The volunteers <u>assist</u> victims of war. (future)
15. Sixteen nations <u>answer</u> his plea. (past perfect)
16. They <u>applaud</u> his goal. (present perfect)
17. Representatives <u>travel</u> to Switzerland. (past)
18. They <u>conceive</u> a treaty. (future perfect)
19. They <u>name</u> it the Geneva Convention. (past)
20. Clara Barton <u>support</u> the treaty. (past perfect)
21. Soon the American Red Cross <u>start</u>. (past)

C. Using Verb Tenses Write each sentence, changing the underlined verb to another tense. Use each tense at least once. Identify the new tense.

22. Community service projects <u>attract</u> many students.

MODEL> Community service projects have attracted many students.—present perfect

23. Liz <u>collects</u> clothes for hurricane victims.
24. She always <u>remains</u> calm in a crisis.
25. Organizations <u>turn</u> to the public for assistance.
26. Victims <u>needed</u> the clothing and shelter.
27. Homes and communities <u>suffered</u> greatly.
28. People <u>contribute</u> items willingly.
29. Lance <u>organizes</u> paper drives.
30. He <u>carries</u> the papers to a collection agency.
31. Lance <u>donates</u> the proceeds to his science club.

UNIT 3

7 *Be, Have, Do* pages 137 – 140

A. Identifying Tenses of *Be, Have,* and *Do* Write the verb or verb phrase in each sentence. Underline each helping verb once and each main verb twice. Label the verb or verb phrase with the tense it expresses.

1. What is the legend of King Arthur?

MODEL is—present

2. Arthur had been Merlin's pupil.
3. He was heir to the throne of England.
4. As a youth, Arthur had done unusual deeds.
5. Feats of strength were second nature to him.
6. Arthur had removed Excalibur, a sword, from a stone.
7. He had a plan for a round table.

B. Choosing Forms of *Be, Have,* and *Do* Write the verb or verb phrase in parentheses ( ) that correctly completes each sentence.

8. Knights (were, has been) common during the Middle Ages.

MODEL were

9. Young boys who (has had, had had) training became pages.
10. A page (was, were) sent to another household.
11. There, lessons in courtesy (was, were) taught.
12. In addition, a page (did, do) learn about small weapons.
13. A page (did, do) become a squire.
14. A squire (had, have) duties to perform for a knight.
15. A knight could (have, had) bestowed knighthood on a squire.

C. Using Forms of *Be, Have,* and *Do* Write each sentence, changing the verb to the tense indicated in parentheses ( ).

16. Is Camelot on Broadway again? (future)

MODEL Will Camelot be on Broadway again?

17. We have tickets for Camelot. (past)
18. Tickets are easily obtainable. (past perfect)
19. Camelot was about the legend of King Arthur. (present)
20. The orchestra has a clever conductor. (future)
21. Who has the role of King Arthur? (future perfect)
22. Cole had an old program. (present)
23. Julie Andrews played the role of Guinevere. (past perfect)

EXTRA PRACTICE

UNIT 3

8 Subject-Verb Agreement *pages 141 – 142*

A. Identifying Subjects and Verbs That Agree For each pair, write the sentence in which the subject and the verb agree.

1. In the story, Rikki-Tikki-Tavi is a mongoose.
   His enemies is snakes.

MODEL In the story, Rikki-Tikki-Tavi is a mongoose.

2. The mongoose feeds on snakes.
   The snake fear a mongoose.
3. A mongoose's eyes turn red.
   The red eyes means anger.
4. A mongoose like people.
   They protect people from snakes.
5. Rikki becomes a pet.
   He sleep with the young boy.
6. The snakes prepare an attack.
   Rikki discover the plot.
7. He struggles with one snake.
   The noise wake the people.
8. The man shoots the snake.
   He praise their pet.

B. Choosing Correct Verb Forms Write the verb in parentheses ( ) that agrees with the subject of each sentence.

9. The bear (appear, appears) from nowhere.

MODEL appears

10. The two boys (are, is) not aware of the danger.
11. One boy (leave, leaves) to chop wood.
12. The younger boy (play, plays) in the pond.
13. Suddenly, a bear cub (splash, splashes) into the pond.
14. The boy and the cub (wrestle, wrestles) in the water.

C. Writing Verbs That Agree with Subjects Write a present-tense verb that agrees with the subject.

15. The cat ________ along the deer trail alone.

MODEL walks

16. His two dog companions ________ far ahead of him.
17. A feeling of being followed ________ over the cat.
18. The hairs on his back ________ on end.
19. The cautious steps of a stalking animal ________ distinct.
20. The cat ________ up a slim birch tree for safety.
21. A larger, heavier cat ________ into the lower branches.

EXTRA PRACTICE

9 Tense Changes *pages 143 – 145*

A. Identifying Tense Changes Write *agree* or *do not agree* to describe the tenses of each sentence or pair of sentences.

1. Robert Peary explored. He will find the North Pole.

MODEL do not agree

2. Robert Peary was an American. He was born in Pennsylvania.
3. Peary did explore the country of Greenland and will prove that Greenland was an island.
4. He sailed to the North Pole on his first ship, *Windward,* but does not reach the North Pole.
5. The weather was bitter, and his team returned to America.
6. Peary did try again in 1905 and establishes a record.
7. In 1909 Peary succeeds. He became a national legend.

B. Changing Tenses Make the verbs in each sentence or pair of sentences agree. Write the sentences.

8. Many people came to America and begin new lives.

MODEL Many people came to America and began new lives.

9. America was a new land. The challenges will be tremendous.
10. Immigrants left homelands and achieve religious freedom.
11. The ocean voyages were difficult, and many people die.
12. Pioneers started settlements, and the settlements grow.
13. Early settlements were near the Atlantic coast. The movement west happens later.
14. Pioneers faced the unknown and build a great nation.

C. Using Tenses Write another sentence to follow each sentence, using the appropriate tense and theme.

15. Pioneers and explorers had specific goals.

MODEL Many achieved their quests.

16. Today people have similar quests.
17. Astronomers will locate new solar systems.
18. Space has provided a variety of avenues for exploration.
19. The North Pole still offers many possibilities.
20. Geologists analyze the earth and its materials.
21. Students seek knowledge.
22. Explorers have always charted new lands.

EXTRA PRACTICE

UNIT 4

1 Progressive Forms of Verbs *pages 174 – 175*

A. Identifying Progressive Forms of Verbs Find the progressive form of the verb in each sentence. Write the verb and identify its tense.

1. Dr. Blake has been observing the sky for many years.

MODEL has been observing—present perfect

2. He has been using a powerful telescope.
3. The new computer was processing data.
4. Dr. Blake's article will be appearing in a journal.
5. He is anticipating a major discovery in the solar system.
6. He had been watching a black hole for years.
7. His assistant will have been completing his study of Mars.

B. Writing Progressive Forms of Verbs Write each sentence, using the progressive form of the verb for the tense shown in parentheses ( ).

8. I observed Halley's Comet. (future progressive)

MODEL I will be observing Halley's Comet.

9. People expected disaster from the comet in 1910. (past perfect progressive)
10. Earth passed through the comet's tail. (past progressive)
11. The scientists determine the path of the comet's orbit. (future perfect progressive)
12. The comet travels through the solar system. (present progressive)
13. The comet's light comes from the sun. (present perfect progressive)
14. A hazy cloud surrounds the comet's nucleus. (present progressive)
15. NASA plans further studies of comets. (future progressive)

C. Using Progressive Forms of Verbs Rewrite each sentence, replacing the underlined verb with its progressive form.

16. Astronomers <u>identify</u> many constellations.

MODEL Astronomers are identifying many constellations.

17. The Greeks <u>had named</u> forty-eight constellations.
18. Positions of stars in constellations <u>have changed</u> slightly.
19. Travelers <u>used</u> constellations as direction aids years ago.
20. Now, scientists <u>map</u> constellations to study different stars.
21. A planetarium <u>will show</u> an exhibit on the constellations.
22. We <u>will expect</u> it to open to the general public soon.
23. I <u>enjoy</u> the prospect of watching countless shows.
24. In two weeks I <u>will have studied</u> astronomy for ten years.

2 Direct Objects *pages 176 – 178*

A. Identifying Direct Objects Write the verb and the direct object in each sentence.

1. Volcanoes contain molten lava.

MODEL contain—lava

2. They provide fascinating spectacles.
3. The weight of rock layers suppresses the lava.
4. Fluid lava forms tunnels.
5. Melted rock releases gases.
6. Trapped gas creates tremendous pressure.
7. The gas blasts the magma into fragments.
8. Eruptions produce rivers of fire.
9. Volcanoes shoot hot rock into the air.
10. Volcanoes have destroyed entire towns.

B. Writing Direct Objects Write each sentence, adding the type of direct object shown in parentheses ( ).

11. An avalanche of snow buried ________. (compound)

MODEL An avalanche of snow buried cars, trucks, and other vehicles.

12. The ranger posted ________. (single)
13. Tourists and skiers abandoned the ________. (compound)
14. A mass of wet snow covered our ________. (single)
15. The avalanche barely missed ________. (single)
16. In the evacuation I lost ________. (compound)
17. Many people ignored ________. (single)
18. Rescue teams saved ________. (compound)
19. The townspeople shoveled ________. (single)
20. We planted ________ as natural barriers. (compound)

C. Using Direct Objects in Sentences Write a sentence using each word or word group as a direct object.

21. natural disasters

MODEL Shifting earth causes many natural disasters.

22. earthquake
23. tidal wave
24. endless rain and floods
25. sinkhole
26. sleet and hailstones
27. hurricane or tornado
28. forest fires
29. drought
30. sandstorm
31. rock slide
32. high winds and dark storm clouds

UNIT 4

3 Indirect Objects *pages 179 – 180*

A. Identifying Direct and Indirect Objects Write each sentence. Underline the direct object once and the indirect object twice.

1. The coral reef offers undersea life some shelter.

MODEL› The coral reef offers undersea life some shelter.

2. Warm water furnishes coral a suitable environment.
3. The battering sea brings coral reefs growth.
4. Coral reefs offer various small fish protection.
5. Colorful fish give the reef a beautiful color.
6. Dr. García rented us a touring boat.
7. The guide told our group details about barrier reefs.

B. Placing Indirect Objects Place the indirect object in parentheses ( ) correctly in each sentence. Write each sentence.

8. Laura brings beautiful seashells. (the family)

MODEL› Laura brings the family beautiful seashells.

9. Betty showed her shell collection. (me)
10. I told our beach adventure. (Grandfather)
11. The tide left some sand dollars on the beach. (us)
12. Neil found an oyster shell. (Lilli)
13. The twins showed a small sea horse. (us)
14. We gave some help. (a sea turtle)

C. Writing Indirect Objects Write each sentence, changing the underlined word group to an indirect object.

15. This college offers a course in scuba diving to students.

MODEL› This college offers students a course in scuba diving.

16. Carlos teaches scuba lessons to children and adults.
17. He gives underwater safety tips to his class.
18. Carlos promises underwater adventures to his pupils.
19. Sonja gave her air tanks to André.
20. André loaned his camera to the instructor.
21. Her face mask provides a clear field of vision for Sonja.
22. André gave a slight readjustment to his oxygen tanks.

4 Predicate Nominatives *pages 181 – 182*

A. Identifying Predicate Nominatives Write the predicate nominative and the subject to which it refers in each sentence.

1. Our oceans are natural resources.

MODEL resources—oceans

2. Popular seafoods are crab, lobster, and shrimp.
3. The sea might become a greater food source in the future.
4. Products of the oceans are pearls and sponges.
5. Sponges are water animals that are harvested.
6. Pearls are semiprecious gems that are formed in oysters.
7. The tide is a potential source of power.
8. Salt is one mineral that is found in ocean water.
9. Other minerals are sulfur, calcium, and potassium.
10. Evaporation is the process by which salt is removed.
11. One form of evaporated water is steam.
12. Different forms of water are mist, fog, and spray.

B. Choosing Predicate Nominatives Choose the word or word group in parentheses ( ) that is or contains a predicate nominative. Write each completed sentence.

13. Earth is (an energy resource; changing rapidly).

MODEL Earth is an energy resource.

14. Lightning is (electricity; deadly).
15. Oil is (a mineral resource; pumped by oil rigs).
16. Petroleum is (refined for public use; a source of energy).
17. Plants and trees are (sources of oxygen; producing oxygen).
18. Sources of power are (water and wind; discovered daily).
19. Coal is (energy made from peat; found in America).
20. Precious metals are (platinum, gold, and silver; mined).
21. A form of solar energy is (released by the sun; direct sunlight).
22. Uranium is (a radioactive element; used in nuclear reactors).

C. Writing Predicate Nominatives For each word or word group write a sentence with a predicate nominative.

23. atmosphere

MODEL The atmosphere is a mixture of gases.

24. unusual rocks
25. beautiful islands
26. polar ice cap
27. rainbows
28. thunder
29. canyons and valleys

5 Transitive and Intransitive Verbs *pages 183 – 184*

A. Identifying Transitive and Intransitive Verbs Write whether the verb in each sentence is *transitive* or *intransitive.*

1. Ecology is the relationship among living things in the environment.

MODEL intransitive

2. The environment changes.
3. Many plants provide food.
4. Fruits are eaten.
5. Many animals are consumed.
6. Some species hunt others.
7. Natural imbalances occur.
8. They threaten wildlife.
9. Ecologists monitor specific animal populations.
10. One population is the reindeer.
11. They are isolated naturally.
12. Data are collected.
13. The environment needs plants.
14. Photosynthesis provides oxygen.
15. Plants absorb carbon dioxide.
16. The leaves produce oxygen.
17. Humans breathe the oxygen.
18. They expel carbon dioxide.

B. Changing Intransitive Verbs to Transitive Verbs Write each sentence, adding a direct object that changes the intransitive verb to a transitive verb.

19. Oak trees sprout.

MODEL Oak trees sprout acorns.

20. Acorns develop.
21. A seedling breaks.
22. Rain nourishes.
23. Leaves change.
24. Squirrels hide.
25. Animals seek.
26. Snow freezes.
27. Bees pollinate.
28. Rabbits dig.
29. Owls watch.
30. Beavers build.
31. Raccoons wash.
32. Birds lay.
33. Parents provide.

C. Writing Transitive and Intransitive Verbs Write two sentences for each verb. Use the verb as a transitive verb in one sentence and as an intransitive verb in the other.

34. melt

MODEL The sun melts glaciers.
Glaciers melt.

35. overflow
36. flood
37. erode
38. break
39. increase
40. fill
41. shape
42. carry
43. freeze
44. write
45. collect
46. irrigate
47. navigate
48. contain
49. refresh
50. steer

6 Active and Passive Voice *pages 185 – 186*

A. Identifying Active and Passive Voice Write the verb in each sentence. Then label each verb *active* or *passive*.

1. The Grand Canyon National Park was established in 1919.

MODEL was established—passive

2. The canyon walls are streaked with brilliant colors.
3. The sides of the Grand Canyon reflect the sunsets.
4. The Colorado River flows through the Grand Canyon.
5. The canyon was formed by the flow of the river.
6. The rock formations were also shaped by wind and rain.
7. Many varieties of cactuses grow in the canyon.
8. Beavers, antelope, and snakes are frequently sighted.
9. Elevations range from 1,000 to 9,000 feet above sea level.

B. Changing Passive Voice to Active Voice Revise each sentence, changing the verb from passive voice to active voice.

10. The desert sands were tossed by the wind.

MODEL The wind tossed the desert sands.

11. Only 10 to 20 percent of most deserts is covered by sand.
12. After a rainfall, dried streams are filled with water.
13. Rain is absorbed and stored by roots and leaves of plants.
14. The desert is visited by deer and wolves after rain falls.
15. Salt is carried into desert lake beds by mountain streams.
16. Little vegetation is supported by desert soil.
17. An oasis is nurtured by underground springs.
18. Different land formations can be seen by desert hikers.
19. The largest desert is encountered by travelers in Africa.

C. Using Active or Passive Voice Add a verb to each sentence. Write each sentence, and identify whether the verb is in the *active* or the *passive* voice.

20. Cactuses ________ water in their trunks.

MODEL Cactuses store water in their trunks.—active

21. A tasty fruit ________ by the prickly pear cactus.
22. People ________ the cactus as a source of water.
23. Most cactus plants ________ with sharp spines.
24. Cactuses ________ with their thorns.
25. Cactus plants ________ in dry areas of the world.
26. The saguaro ________ by native Americans for fuel.
27. Cactus roots ________ far out in search of water.

7 Easily Confused Verb Pairs *pages 187 – 189*

EXTRA PRACTICE

A. Identifying Correct Usage of Verbs Write the sentence that is correct in each pair.

1. Tulips bulbs lie dormant in winter.
   We lie tulips bulbs in the ground.

MODEL Tulip bulbs lie dormant in winter.

2. Rivers bring water to this farm.
   Rivers take water to this farm.
3. A harvest moon rose in the sky.
   Smoke raised above the trees.
4. Shoots raised from the seeds.
   We raised different crops.
5. The land lies in the valley.
   The land laid in the valley.
6. Lilacs are set along the hill.
   We sit the lilacs by the hill.
7. Apples lie beneath the tree.
   Lie the apple on the fence.
8. Rain brings our crops relief.
   Rain takes our crops relief.
9. Pumpkins sat among the vines.
   Pumpkins were sat by the road.

B. Choosing the Correct Verb Write the verb in parentheses ( ) that correctly completes each sentence.

10. Spring often (brings, takes) high winds.

MODEL brings

11. The wind often (raises, rises) roofs off buildings.
12. It then (lies, lays) them on the ground.
13. Tornadoes pick up items and (set, sit) them elsewhere.
14. We (set, sit) on our porch and watch the storms.
15. During the storms (leave, let) the pigs go into the barn.
16. The wheelbarrows have (laid, lain) against the fence all month.
17. The wind has (sat, set) the wheelbarrows on the ground.

C. Using Easily Confused Verbs Choose the verb in parentheses ( ) that correctly completes each sentence. Then write the sentence, using the correct form of that verb.

18. New Jersey (lie, lay) between two major river systems.

MODEL New Jersey lies between two major river systems.

19. The Hudson and Delaware rivers (take, bring) fresh water.
20. Cranberries are a crop (raise, rise) in New Jersey.
21. Farmers also (raise, rise) blueberries.
22. People (take, bring) their families to New Jersey's shores.
23. They (sit, set) on the sandy beaches and watch the ocean.
24. Commuters (take, bring) ferry rides to Philadelphia.
25. My family's home (lie, lay) in Trenton, New Jersey.
26. It (sit, set) in a grove of cherry trees.

UNIT 5

1 Personal Pronouns *pages 226 – 227*

A. Identifying Personal Pronouns Write the personal pronoun from each sentence.

1. Danny knows he will graduate from junior high in the spring.

MODEL he

2. I studied many hours for the semester exams.
3. Teachers reviewed the necessary materials with him.
4. They deserve credit for remaining patient.
5. The most difficult test for me was on world history.
6. I was relieved when it was over.
7. Other students thought that they had done well.
8. Test scores were posted, and I read them.

B. Choosing Personal Pronouns Write the pronoun in parentheses ( ) that correctly completes each sentence.

9. (I, Me) will take pictures of the ceremony.

MODEL I

10. Josh will tell (I, you) when the ceremony will begin.
11. Paul waved to (I, me) as the procession started.
12. The crowd anxiously waited for (we, us).
13. The sun came out, and (it, they) made the day brighter.
14. The principal handed diplomas to (we, us).
15. Mother planned a party because (she, it) is so proud.
16. My friends asked me to celebrate with (us, them).

C. Using Personal Pronouns Write each sentence, using a personal pronoun to replace the underlined word or word group.

17. Kara plans to attend Armwood High after Kara graduates.

MODEL Kara plans to attend Armwood High after she graduates.

18. Can you believe Laura will be going to Alaska?
19. The teachers have helped students make important high-school decisions.
20. Mr. Taft thinks Julie and I have chosen courses wisely.
21. Barry and Keith received many notes of congratulation.
22. What Lee and I decide now will have a profound effect on our future.
23. The counselor gave Van the technical school's address.
24. Protect this photograph and put the photograph in a safe place.
25. Have Randi contact Ray and me as soon as she hears from her new counselor.

EXTRA PRACTICE

UNIT 5

2 Pronouns and Antecedents *pages 228 – 229*

A. Identifying Pronoun Antecedents Write each sentence. Draw one line under the pronoun and draw two lines under its antecedent.

1. Corey decided he would study chemistry.

MODEL Corey decided he would study chemistry.

2. Mr. Atha, the guidance counselor, said he approved.
3. Matt and Joe think they will take biology.
4. The laboratory has elaborate equipment in it.
5. Experiments that they do will fascinate Matt and Joe.
6. Corey received a fall schedule and read it immediately.

EXTRA PRACTICE

B. Choosing Pronoun Antecedents From the box, choose a pronoun that makes sense in the sentence. Write the pronoun.

7. The students toured a factory. ________ were amazed.

MODEL The students toured a factory. They were amazed.

8. The factory was modern. ________ had excellent equipment.
9. Holly and I loved the machines. ________ wanted to operate one.
10. Barry examined the product. ________ was very thorough.
11. The workers were knowledgeable. ________ answered many questions.
12. I asked how many people worked there. The answer surprised ________.

they
me
him
I
we
it
us
he
they
she

C. Using Pronouns with Antecedents Write each sentence or pair of sentences, adding a pronoun that renames the antecedent.

13. Victoria, would ________ like to be an engineer?

MODEL Victoria, would you like to be an engineer?

14. The classes are difficult, but ________ are worthwhile.
15. I have studied math, and engineering uses ________.
16. I confuse civil engineering and mechanical engineering. What are the differences between ________?
17. Mrs. Baker is a civil engineer. ________ designs bridges.
18. Mrs. Baker has had many ideas attributed to ________.

3 Subject and Object Pronouns *pages 230 – 232*

A. Distinguishing Between Pronouns Write whether each underlined pronoun is a *subject pronoun* or an *object pronoun.*

1. Teachers sponsor a career camp. They invite the public to attend.

MODEL They—subject pronoun

2. One speaker gave us a seminar on interview strategies.
3. The most inquisitive student at the seminar was I.
4. Counselors gave us clues about future careers.
5. I asked many questions, and they were answered.
6. Ms. Vasquez will help you evaluate a certain company.
7. She can list many companies and careers for you.

B. Choosing Pronouns Write the pronoun in parentheses ( ) that correctly completes each sentence. Then label each pronoun *subject pronoun* or *object pronoun.*

8. Successful graduates talk to students and prepare workshops for (him, them).

MODEL them—object pronoun

9. (I, Me) went to a workshop with a list of questions.
10. My mom is an alumna; (she, her) attended my school.
11. Mom gave (they, us) a speech on publishing.
12. Bradley said (he, him) was happy to meet the graduates.
13. The students wanted (they, them) to answer questions.
14. (They, Them) closed the session on a positive note.

C. Using Pronouns Write each sentence, replacing each underlined word or word group with a pronoun. Then tell whether the pronoun is a *subject pronoun* or an *object pronoun.*

15. Students will confront many challenges.

MODEL They will confront many challenges.—subject pronoun

16. Leaving home gives students new freedom and responsibility.
17. Organization of finances takes time and effort.
18. Ann's counselors recommend college to Ann.
19. Ann will pay the tuition.
20. Several associations interest Margot and me.
21. Gail and I are interested in foreign languages.
22. As a result, travel abroad seems likely for Gail and me.

EXTRA PRACTICE

UNIT 5

4 Possessive Pronouns *pages 233 – 234*

A. Identifying Possessive Pronouns Write the possessive pronoun in each sentence.

1. His goal is to become a pilot.

MODEL His

2. An airplane, with its awesome power, appeals to Daniel.
3. His father has a private pilot's license.
4. Private pilots do not charge their passengers for flights.
5. Our airplane is stored at University Airport.
6. Father often takes Mother and her friends to the city.
7. Daniel receives his flight instruction from Nina Windler.
8. Her students have little trouble obtaining a license.

B. Using Possessive Pronouns Write each sentence, replacing the underlined word or word group with a possessive pronoun.

9. Carmen received answers to Carmen's letters.

MODEL Carmen received answers to her letters.

10. She asked manufacturers about the manufacturers' advertising slogans.
11. Advertising has become Carmen's class project.
12. A man sent brochures from the man's company.
13. The brochures' colors were bright and attractive.
14. Carmen reads Carmen's copy of *Advertising Age*.
15. Don wrote Don's letters to a limousine service.
16. The service places the service's ads in the Yellow Pages.

C. Writing Possessive Pronouns Write each sentence, adding a possessive pronoun.

17. ________ library is an excellent source of information.

MODEL Our library is an excellent source of information.

18. Choose ________ topic before you go to the library.
19. Joe asked the librarian ________ questions.
20. Kaya and Anne found ________ research materials.
21. Kaya compiled ________ list of magazine publishers.
22. Anne found an article on spices and traced ________ author.
23. I quickly found a list of articles about ________ topic.
24. Other students had difficulty finding ________ data.
25. Many people do not have time to do ________ own research.

5 Reflexive, Intensive, and Demonstrative Pronouns *pages 235 – 236*

A. Identifying Reflexive, Intensive, and Demonstrative Pronouns Describe each underlined pronoun as *reflexive, intensive,* or *demonstrative.*

1. John taught himself to refinish wood.

MODEL reflexive

2. You yourself recognize fine craftsmanship.
3. I bought myself a restored wicker rocker.
4. I felt that this was an unusual piece of furniture.
5. Kim herself was the recipient of an antique trunk.
6. That is the piano I have always wanted.
7. Mick himself achieved a miracle when he restored it.

B. Choosing Reflexive, Intensive, and Demonstrative Pronouns Write the pronoun in parentheses ( ) that correctly completes each sentence. Label the pronoun *reflexive, intensive,* or *demonstrative.*

8. (These, This) are outstanding student inventions.

MODEL These—demonstrative

9. Can you believe that (this, those) is my brother's creation?
10. I (myself, ourselves) had no idea he was so talented.
11. He never gives (himself, itself) any credit.
12. I am certain (that, these) inventions are marketable.
13. Didn't you (herself, yourself) create an invention?
14. (These, This) is my own personal creation.

C. Using Reflexive, Intensive, and Demonstrative Pronouns Write each sentence, adding a reflexive, intensive, or demonstrative pronoun. Label the pronoun *reflexive, intensive,* or *demonstrative.*

15. The students ________ rebuilt the car.

MODEL The students themselves rebuilt the car.—intensive

16. Did they teach ________ auto mechanics?
17. This class earned ________ a good reputation.
18. I dropped a wrench and gave ________ a sore toe.
19. We received good advice from my brother ________.
20. ________ is the ratchet set we need for this car.
21. Ms. Brock put ________ through mechanics school.
22. I ________ would like to be an auto mechanic one day.

EXTRA PRACTICE

EXTRA PRACTICE

UNIT 5

6 Indefinite Pronouns *pages 237 – 239*

A. Identifying Indefinite Pronouns Write the indefinite pronoun from each sentence. Label it *singular* or *plural.*

1. Many of Chicago's buildings were destroyed in a fire.

MODEL Many—plural

2. Wood was the material used in most of the buildings.
3. Only a few rain showers fell during the summer.
4. Everyone says the fire started in a barn.
5. The fire burned everything in the downtown area.
6. Many citizens stood in Lake Michigan as the city burned.
7. No one in the fire's path was spared.
8. The rebuilding of Chicago became a challenge for everyone.
9. Chicago boasts that it has architecture for all.
10. Nothing reflects the spirit of America better than Chicago.

B. Choosing Indefinite Pronouns Write each sentence. Choose the indefinite pronoun in parentheses ( ) that makes sense.

11. (Some, Them) use the computer to design houses.

MODEL Some use the computer to design houses.

12. We designed (several, one) houses using the software.
13. The architect showed us (neither, something) new.
14. Tammy carefully drew (most, each) line of her floor plan.
15. (No one, None) of the drawings were on hard disk.
16. I changed (some, such) of my designs several times.
17. Will (most, somebody) help me plot my dimensions?

C. Using Indefinite Pronouns Choose an indefinite pronoun from the box to complete each sentence. Use each pronoun only once.

18. Does ________ want to be an architect?

MODEL Does anyone want to be an architect?

19. Can ________ show me how to design a roof?
20. The museum had ________ models on display.
21. ________ of the teachers discussed foundations.
22. Architecture is one of ________ artistic careers.
23. You had two lessons; do you want ________?
24. I want ________ of my buildings to be skyscrapers.

anyone
several
another
everything
some
all
few
many
somebody
neither
most

7 Interrogative and Relative Pronouns pages 240 – 241

A. Identifying Interrogative and Relative Pronouns Write whether each underlined pronoun is *interrogative* or *relative.*

1. Who won the Newbery Medal for distinguished children's literature this year?

MODEL interrogative

2. To whom was the first Newbery Medal given?
3. Which authors are eligible for the annual award?
4. Is Susan Cooper the one who wrote *The Grey King*?
5. What story tells about a New England girl?
6. *Dicey's Song* is the book that I enjoyed the most.
7. Who won the award for *Sounder* in 1970?

B. Choosing Interrogative and Relative Pronouns Write the pronoun in parentheses ( ) that correctly completes each sentence.

8. An illustrator could win the Caldecott Medal, (which, who) is given yearly.

MODEL which

9. (Whose, Who) illustration is on the medal's face?
10. (What, Who) does the engraving say?
11. To (who, whom) was the award given in 1969?
12. (Who, Whose) won the Caldecott for *Ox-Cart Man*?
13. (Who, Which) author wrote *One Fine Day*?

C. Using Interrogative and Relative Pronouns Write each sentence, using an interrogative or a relative pronoun.

14. To ________ are the Nobel Prizes awarded?

MODEL To whom are the Nobel Prizes awarded?

15. After ________ are the Nobel Prizes named?
16. Alfred Nobel, ________ was a chemist, initiated the prizes.
17. ________ is the reason for Madame Curie's winning in 1911?
18. William Golding, ________ won the Literature Prize in 1983, wrote Lord of the Flies.
19. To ________ was the Medicine Prize given in 1983?
20. ________ won the Nobel Peace Prize in 1983?
21. There are several years in ________ no prize was awarded.

UNIT 6

1 Adjectives *pages 270 – 271*

A. Identifying Adjectives Write the adjective or adjectives in each sentence, including articles. Then write the word that each adjective modifies.

1. Colonial soldiers fought British soldiers in the Revolutionary War.

MODEL Colonial—soldiers; British—soldiers; the—Revolutionary War

2. Unfair taxes and strict laws angered the colonists.
3. Bunker Hill was the first major battle of the war.
4. Energetic colonial leaders soon declared independence.
5. A declaration was written to announce colonial freedom.
6. The Redcoats defeated the Minutemen several times.
7. French troops arrived to help the American cause.
8. In 1783 a peace treaty was signed in Paris, and the colonies rejoiced.

B. Replacing Adjectives Replace each underlined adjective with another adjective. Write the adjective.

9. Brilliant men wrote the Constitution.

MODEL Intelligent

10. The infant country needed a strong government.
11. The states sent insightful delegates to Philadelphia.
12. The delegates were distinguished leaders.
13. They decided to write a better plan of government.
14. The Constitution sets forth fundamental beliefs.
15. It lists the chief aims of the United States government.
16. It divides the mighty government into branches.
17. The Constitution is a wonderful document.

C. Using Adjectives Write a sentence for each noun. Use at least one adjective to describe each noun given. Underline all adjectives in the sentence, including articles.

18. flag

MODEL The American flag has red and white stripes.

19. colors
20. stars
21. symbol
22. country
23. capitals
24. government
25. colonies
26. leaders
27. freedom
28. nations
29. England
30. France

2 Other Parts of Speech as Adjectives *pages 272 – 273*

A. Identifying Parts of Speech The underlined words in these sentences function as adjectives. Write whether each word can also function as a *pronoun*, a *noun*, or a *verb*.

1. This painting shows a wagon train.

MODEL pronoun, noun

2. Many pioneers traveled in covered wagons.
3. It was several years before that trail was established.
4. Those wagon trains carried young and hopeful families.
5. They traveled all day, and at night they slept outside.
6. At sunset the circled wagons protected the families.
7. Another name for the wagons was *prairie schooners*.

B. Choosing Adjectives Write the adjective in parentheses ( ) that correctly completes each sentence.

8. Trains provided quicker transportation to the West (several, neither) years later.

MODEL several

9. The plan was to lay track from (this, these) coast to the other.
10. (Many, One) people worked at laying the railroad track.
11. People and goods needed to travel, and (that, these) trains could carry them.
12. Laying track was grueling work for (most, either) workers.
13. I would rather ride on (any, both) train than fly in a plane.
14. (Such, Some) trees were cut down to be used as railroad ties.

C. Using Pronouns as Adjectives Write a word that functions as an adjective to complete each sentence.

15. ________ people fly from city to city today.

MODEL Most

16. We've flown twice, and ________ trips were great fun.
17. Is it true that ________ airlines just carry cargo?
18. ________ plane is the Concorde?
19. Are there ________ seats left on this flight?
20. After this flight I will plan ________ trip!
21. ________________ day can we take off for Texas?
22. ________ single-engine plane is parked in the hangar.

EXTRA PRACTICE

UNIT 6

3 Predicate Adjectives *pages 274 – 275*

A. Identifying Predicate Adjectives Write each sentence. Underline the predicate adjective or adjectives. Draw an arrow to the word or words modified.

1. The attic was old, dusty, and mysterious.

MODEL The attic was old, dusty, and mysterious.

2. Suzie and I were afraid of the rickety attic stairs.
3. Mother appeared interested in the attic's contents.
4. The treasure hunt soon became worthwhile and exciting.
5. The boxes smelled musty as we opened them.
6. Most of her grandmother's dresses were long and cumbersome.
7. Some photographs were old and yellowed with age.
8. Mom's grandmother seemed proud and graceful in the pictures.
9. She was beautiful in that black evening dress.

B. Choosing Predicate Adjectives Write the predicate adjective in parentheses ( ) that completes each sentence.

10. Nowadays, the idea of pantaloons sounds (funny, bloomers).

MODEL funny

11. In today's age blue jeans are (acceptable, slacks).
12. Elaborate bonnets and veils are not (hats, common).
13. High heels are (impractical, pumps) for long walks.
14. Sweatshirts are (functional and inexpensive, cotton).
15. Good buys are (sales, available) there.
16. My favorite jeans are (old and faded, pants).
17. When shopping, Theresa is (a purchaser, imaginative).

C. Using Predicate Adjectives Replace each predicate adjective with another predicate adjective. Write both adjectives.

18. In the future clothing will be different.

MODEL different—comfortable

19. Shoes of the future may be transparent.
20. Coats could be air-conditioned.
21. Fabrics will feel cushiony and soft.
22. Gloves will be smudge-proof.
23. Suits may be adaptable for any season.

4 Comparisons with Adjectives *pages 276 – 277*

A. Identifying Degrees of Comparison Write *positive, comparative,* or *superlative* to identify the degree of comparison of each adjective.

1. more wrinkled

MODEL comparative

2. warmer
3. more miserable
4. clean
5. most abstract
6. more functional
7. most technical
8. easiest
9. more complex
10. hopeful
11. finest
12. more ridiculous
13. sturdier

B. Choosing Degrees of Comparison Write the form of the adjective in parentheses ( ) that correctly completes each sentence.

14. What are the (more interesting, most interesting) places in town?

MODEL most interesting

15. The museum is (older, oldest) than the train station.
16. However, the station's windows are (more, most) colorful than the museum's.
17. The (finer, finest) stained glass in the world was used.
18. The schoolhouse has an (old, oldest) bell.
19. Of the two bells in town, it rings (louder, loudest).
20. The desk was made of the (harder, hardest) wood available.
21. The park has a (fancier, fanciest) garden than mine.
22. The garden has a (pleasing, more pleasing) design.

C. Using Degrees of Comparison Write each sentence, using the correct degree of comparison for the underlined adjective.

23. We all entered the <u>Creative</u> Student Contest.

MODEL We all entered the Most Creative Student Contest.

24. Of all the students in her class, Mary designed the <u>efficient</u> skyscraper.
25. The outside was <u>simple</u> than the inside.
26. The top floor offered the <u>spectacular</u> view in town.
27. Windows are <u>large</u> on the bottom floor than they are at the top.
28. The roof has <u>beautiful</u> carved beams.
29. Gigi designed an aircraft <u>streamlined</u> than a space shuttle.
30. It would travel the <u>fast</u> of all aircraft.

EXTRA PRACTICE

UNIT 6

5 Irregular Comparisons with Adjectives *pages 278 – 279*

A. Identifying Forms of Comparison For each sentence, write the adjective that shows comparison.

1. Pioneers had the fewest conveniences of all.

MODEL fewest

2. There was little time for recreation.
3. The pioneers could see the farthest hills on clear days.
4. Dust storms had the worst effect of all on the animals.
5. Most time was spent doing chores.
6. Pioneers searched for better ways of life.
7. The pioneers felt good about their achievements.

B. Choosing Degrees of Comparison Write the adjective in parentheses ( ) that correctly completes each sentence.

8. The (better, best) invention is the light bulb.

MODEL best

9. The cotton gin is (best, better) than the hoe.
10. The radio permitted people to hear (many, most) programs.
11. There is (least, little) chance that the radio will be replaced.
12. Which of these two radios is the (less, least) powerful?
13. The computer will evolve (far, further) in future years.
14. (Many, More) inventions are presented at a world's fair.
15. Companies look for the (better, best) products available.

C. Using Degrees of Comparison Write the correct form of each underlined adjective.

16. Cooking food in a microwave oven takes <u>least</u> time.

MODEL little

17. Baking a cake in a convection oven takes <u>much</u> time than baking it in a microwave.
18. Preparing food in a wok takes <u>little</u> time than preparing it in a casserole.
19. Using a Coleman stove when camping requires the <u>little</u> fuss.
20. Jan is the <u>good</u> cook in our group.
21. Ted does a <u>good</u> job in the kitchen than I!
22. I search <u>far</u> than my kitchen for unusual cooking methods.

UNIT 6

6 Adverbs *pages 280 – 282*

A. Identifying Adverbs Write each sentence. Underline each adverb once. If the adverb is an intensifier, underline it twice. Then draw an arrow from each adverb to the word it modifies.

1. Spencer walked very quietly into the crowded room.

MODEL Spencer walked very quietly into the crowded room.

2. Spencer's heart beat furiously as he listened intently.
3. He followed Patrick Henry's speech very carefully.
4. The front door creaked rather noisily.
5. Suddenly, Patrick Henry clamped his wrists together.
6. Then he said, "Give me liberty or give me death!"
7. Spencer glanced curiously at the excited crowd.

EXTRA PRACTICE

B. Completing Sentences with Adverbs Write each sentence, using adverbs that make sense.

8. The doors were locked ________ and the windows were ________ fastened, but Sarah was suspicious.

MODEL The doors were locked tightly and the windows were securely fastened, but Sarah was suspicious.

9. Sarah proceeded ________ through the rooms of the house.
10. ________ she heard footsteps ________.
11. A tree branch tapped ________ against the window.
12. Were the British Redcoats ________ surrounding the house?
13. Sarah saw what looked like a ________ interrupted meal on the table.
14. Someone knocked ________ on the door.
15. Sarah ________ opened it and then stumbled toward the table.
16. Her father and her uncle ________ entered the house.

C. Using Adverbs in Sentences Using each adverb, write a complete sentence. Draw an arrow from each adverb to the word it modifies.

17. strongly

MODEL The cellar smelled strongly of mildew.

18. eagerly
19. inside
20. soon
21. handily
22. always
23. quickly
24. happily
25. out
26. late
27. awkwardly
28. far
29. calmly

UNIT 6

7 Comparisons with Adverbs *pages 283 – 285*

A. **Identifying Degrees of Comparison** Write the adverb in each sentence. Identify its degree of comparison. If the adverb cannot be compared, write *cannot be compared.*

1. Agatha Christie novels sell more steadily than other novels.

MODEL more steadily—comparative

2. Agatha Christie is best known as a writer of mysteries.
3. Hercule Poirot works faster than other fictional detectives.
4. He solves mysteries better than Sherlock Holmes does.
5. The Sherlock Holmes mysteries arrived earliest in bookstores.
6. I immensely enjoyed Christie's novel *Murder on the Orient Express.*
7. Christie's mystery novels also involve Miss Jane Marple.
8. Miss Marple talks more gently to her suspects than Poirot does.
9. Poirot quietly questions suspects.
10. Christie's detectives solve mysteries most often by thinking.

B. **Writing Degrees of Comparison of Adverbs** Write the three degrees of comparison for each adverb. If an adverb cannot be compared, write *cannot be compared.*

11. badly

MODEL badly, worse, worst

12. much	**15.** well	**18.** next	**21.** loudly
13. usually	**16.** fast	**19.** little	**22.** nearby
14. slowly	**17.** always	**20.** away	**23.** far (distance)

C. **Using Degrees of Comparison** Write the correct degree of comparison for each underlined adverb.

24. Sherlock Holmes solved crimes fast than Watson.

MODEL faster

25. The townspeople relied heavily on Holmes than on any other detective.
26. Holmes painstakingly collected every available clue.
27. Professor Moriarty tried hard of all to outwit Holmes.
28. Holmes quickly discovered the first clue in the attic.
29. Watson ran anxiously to Holmes's side than any of the other onlookers.
30. The young child screamed loudly with fear.
31. The strange dog cowered nervously from the crowd than from the child.
32. Dr. Watson ran fast and beat everyone else to the site.

8 Negatives *pages 286 – 287*

A. Identifying Negative Words Write the word or phrase that is negative in each sentence.

1. As a boy, Thor Heyerdahl, the great Norwegian explorer, could not learn to swim.

MODEL not

2. No one in our study group knew that Heyerdahl was born in Larvik, Norway.
3. The *Kon-Tiki* barely made it from Peru to the Tuamotu Islands.
4. Such a trip had never been made before in modern times.
5. The papyrus boat was hardly a sturdy vessel.
6. We may never know if Heyerdahl's theories were correct.

B. Avoiding Double Negatives Write the word or words in parentheses ( ) that correctly complete each sentence.

7. Heyerdahl sailed a raft across the Pacific, though he hadn't (no, any) idea if it could be done.

MODEL any

8. We don't know (nothing, anything) about Heyerdahl's chief motivations.
9. There (wasn't, was) hardly anyone to support his theories.
10. He (couldn't, could) barely inspire a group of seven individuals to accompany him.
11. Nobody knew (anything, nothing) certain about the seaworthiness of a papyrus boat.
12. They (had, hadn't) scarcely enough provisions for survival.

C. Using Negative Words Correctly Rewrite each sentence to include a correctly stated negative idea.

13. Jacques Cousteau never hurts no sea life.

MODEL Jacques Cousteau never hurts any sea life.

14. I don't have scarcely any idea how Cousteau got started.
15. People could not hardly explore underwater before he developed the aqualung.
16. No one has never immortalized sea creatures as Cousteau has done.
17. He hardly had no support in opposing the dumping of radioactive wastes.
18. We cannot never admire another oceanographer more.

UNIT 6

9 Adverb or Adjective? *pages 288 – 289*

A. Distinguishing Between Adjectives and Adverbs Write the underlined words in each sentence. Identify each word as an *adjective* or an *adverb*.

1. Inspector Clouseau is a bumbling detective who does nothing right, but he somehow wins in the end.

MODEL bumbling—adjective; right—adverb; somehow—adverb

2. His clumsy antics slyly hide a determined detective.
3. Desperate fugitives laugh heartily at the assumed good news that Clouseau is on their case.
4. They falsely suppose that Clouseau will undoubtedly ruin his latest assignment.
5. The fugitives are caught by a bewildered inspector who has accidentally stumbled onto their hideout.
6. No mystery fan should casually ignore the outrageous triumphs of Inspector Clouseau.

B. Choosing Adjectives or Adverbs Write the adjective or adverb in parentheses ( ) that correctly completes each sentence.

7. (Clear, Clearly), detectives take daily risks.

MODEL Clearly

8. Readers are (extreme, extremely) fascinated by detective stories.
9. The (intrigue, intriguing) stories are filled with mystery.
10. There are (many, much) writers, but only a few are well known.
11. The detectives are portrayed (most, mostly) as self-employed.
12. The climax (all, always) comes when the criminal is unveiled.
13. The (hero, heroic) detective rarely gets hurt in the story.
14. Later, the criminal (usual, usually) regrets committing the crime.

C. Using Adjectives and Adverbs in Sentences Write each sentence, using at least one adverb and one adjective.

15. "Mystery Mania" is an __________ game when played __________.

MODEL "Mystery Mania" is an interesting game when played correctly.

16. Mary was a __________ competitor who fought __________.
17. Matthew learned __________ because he was __________.
18. The players applauded __________ because they were a __________ group.
19. Boris had a __________ role, which helped him win __________.
20. Competitors move __________ through __________ room.
21. __________ games entertain families who play __________.
22. We won __________ and thanked our __________ rivals.

EXTRA PRACTICE

UNIT 7

1 Prepositions and Prepositional Phrases *pages 320 – 322*

A. Identifying Prepositions and Prepositional Phrases Write the prepositional phrase or phrases in each sentence. Underline the preposition once and its object twice.

1. Mr. Asari wants property on the east side of town.

MODEL on the east side; of town

2. A real estate agent prepared a proposal for him.
3. He will provide affordable housing for city dwellers.
4. This property was not a desirable piece of real estate.
5. After years of neglect, the housing appeared beyond repair.
6. Mr. Asari has restored the buildings with care.
7. Now this area of our city is beneficial for all of us.

B. Combining Sentences with Prepositional Phrases Combine each pair of sentences into a single sentence, using prepositional phrases. Underline the prepositional phrase or phrases.

8. Marcus works at the office. He works on advertising campaigns.

MODEL At the office, Marcus works on advertising campaigns.

9. In the corner stands Marcus's desk. His desk stands under a ton of paperwork.
10. Marcus worked through the night. He worked on a new automobile commercial.
11. Toward morning the commercial took shape. It took the shape of a message about car safety.
12. After writing the script, Marcus slept. He slept late in the morning.
13. In spite of oversleeping, Marcus went to work. He went to work on time.

C. Using Prepositional Phrases Write each sentence, adding prepositional phrases that make sense. Underline each preposition once and its object twice.

14. People who work ________ often commute ________.

MODEL People who work in cities often commute on buses.

15. Some who live ________ must travel ________.
16. If you drive ________, you may find a parking space ________.
17. If you park ________, your car may get towed ________.
18. Pay the fee ________ and move your car ________.
19. I went ________ but stopped ________ for cash.

EXTRA PRACTICE

UNIT 7

2 Prepositional Phrases Used as Adjectives or Adverbs *pages 323 – 325*

A. Identifying Adjective and Adverb Phrases Write whether each underlined prepositional phrase is used as an *adjective* or an *adverb.*

1. Tara has a career in languages at the UN.

MODEL adjective; adverb

2. Since childhood, Tara has been fascinated by communication.
3. She communicates well with people.
4. The study habits of this young woman are disciplined.
5. During morning hours, she practices translation skills.
6. Instead of English novels, Tara reads Spanish and French novels.
7. Like many other translators, Tara is fluent in several dialects.
8. Over the years, Tara has proved efficient as a translator.
9. Her dream of a lifetime is coming true at the UN.

B. Using Adjective and Adverb Phrases Write each sentence, adding prepositional phrases that make sense.

10. ________ many students apply ________.

MODEL At this university, many students apply for admission.

11. The Union Building ________ is a special haven ________.
12. You can work hard ________ and still enjoy activities ________.
13. ________ my high grades, I won a scholarship ________.
14. My acceptance ________ surprised everyone ________.
15. I ran ________ and shared the good news ________.

C. Writing Adjective and Adverb Phrases Write a sentence about each topic given, using the prepositions in parentheses ( ). Draw an arrow from each prepositional phrase to the word or words modified.

16. Arlene's career plans (in, after)

MODEL After college, Arlene will pursue a career in medicine.

17. Dave's study goals (as, with)
18. Sheila's worries (underneath, about)
19. Jane's school life (to, with)
20. the instructor's movements (down, out)
21. the library fire (in spite of, near)

3 Using Prepositions Correctly *pages 326 – 327*

A. Identifying Correct Usage of Prepositions For each pair, write the letter of the sentence that is correct.

1. **a.** Judges went in the gym to choose five cheerleaders.
   b. Judges went into the gym to choose five cheerleaders.

MODEL b.

2. **a.** Jon walked among Mia and Bo.
   b. Jon walked between Mia and Bo.
3. **a.** Mia talked to the judges.
   b. Mia talked at the judges.
4. **a.** Go into the hall for a rest.
   b. Go in the hall for a rest.
5. **a.** Jon jumped to the air.
   b. Jon jumped into the air.
6. **a.** He cheered to the crowd.
   b. He cheered for the crowd.

B. Choosing Prepositions Write the preposition in parentheses ( ) that makes sense in each sentence.

7. Jack chose (between, among) the hockey team and the swim team.

MODEL between

8. He liked the camaraderie (among, between) the hockey players.
9. Jack picked up his uniform (in, into) the coach's office.
10. (Beside, Besides) warming up, the players practiced.
11. They raced from one end of the rink (to, at) the other.
12. After practice, he had them stand (to, at) the goal.

C. Correcting Prepositional Phrases Write each sentence correctly.

13. The photography lab is besides the gym.

MODEL The photography lab is beside the gym.

14. Janet will wait to the photography classroom for us.
15. Kaye went in the camera shop for film.
16. She threaded her film among the two metal guides.
17. Her take-up spool was inserted correctly into the camera.
18. Put the flash prongs for the cameras in the camera cases.

UNIT 7

4 Conjunctions *pages 328 – 329*

A. Identifying Conjunctions Write the conjunction or conjunctions in each sentence.

1. Jan likes sports and competition, but she especially likes to ski.

MODEL and, but

2. Jan lives in Colorado, so she skis a lot in the winter.
3. She enjoys Alpine and freestyle skiing but loves Nordic.
4. Nordic combines cross-country skiing and ski jumping.
5. The term *Nordic* refers to Norway, Sweden, and Denmark.
6. Alpine skiing can be recreational or competitive.
7. Neither Nordic nor Alpine is quite like freestyle skiing.
8. Alpine skiing looks hard, yet it is very easy to learn.

B. Choosing Conjunctions Write the conjunction in parentheses ( ) that makes sense in each sentence.

9. Steve plays golf, (and, but, or) he plays softball.

MODEL and

10. His mother doesn't like softball, (and, but, or) Steve does.
11. Neither Steve (and, but, nor) Brad misses practice.
12. During the game, he (and, but, yet) his team play well.
13. They could win the trophy, (but, or, yet) they could lose it.
14. The umpire was not only accurate (and, but, nor) also fair.
15. Steve accepted the trophy, (but, and, nor) his team cheered.

C. Combining Sentences with Conjunctions Using a conjunction, combine each pair of sentences into one sentence. Write each combined sentence.

16. The violin is a wonderful instrument. It's the one most often played in an orchestra.

MODEL The violin is a wonderful instrument, and it's the one most often played in an orchestra.

17. A violin is made of wood and strings. Many violins are made by hand.
18. The bow is a curved stick. It is strung with horsehair.
19. A bridge stands in the middle of the violin. It raises the strings up.
20. The violin can rest under your chin. It can rest on your arm.
21. The violin is not easy to learn. It takes many years of practice to play well.

UNIT 7

5 Interjections *pages 330 – 331*

A. Identifying Interjections Write each interjection with the correct punctuation. Capitalize the word following the interjection if necessary.

1. Whee this roller coaster is terrific!

MODEL Whee! This

2. Oops my hat flew right off!
3. Whew going so fast scares me.
4. Well don't you think the haunted house was scary?
5. Bravo you are more courageous than I!
6. Ouch I bruised my arm on the twister ride.
7. Gee am I impressed with the band music!
8. Gosh the time went by so fast.

B. Choosing Interjections Write an appropriate interjection from the box for each sentence. Try to use each interjection once.

Oops!
Bravo!
Hurrah!
Whew!
Hey!
Alas!
Hush!
Look!

9. ________ I dropped the baseball!

MODEL Oops!

10. ________ That slide in the mud ripped my jeans.
11. ________ Don't run so slowly when rounding second base.
12. ________ Our last batter struck out!
13. ________ The opposing captain may hear our strategy!
14. ________ Your run saved the game!
15. ________ Our team won the game!
16. ________ That was a close game!

C. Using Interjections Add an appropriate interjection to each sentence. Write each sentence with correct punctuation.

17. We should pack up our picnic gear and go home.

MODEL Well, we should pack up our picnic gear and go home.

18. The sky is black and depressing.
19. We all have sunglasses and there's no sun!
20. Even the ants are disappointed.
21. Do you hear thunder?
22. Don't stand under a tree if there's lightning!
23. The rain started so suddenly!
24. We had hopes of spending a wonderful day here.
25. The sun was beautiful this morning.

EXTRA PRACTICE

UNIT 8

1 Complex Sentences *pages 370 – 371*

A. Distinguishing Between Compound and Complex Sentences Write whether each sentence is *complex* or *compound.*

1. I wanted to become a tour guide when my summer vacation began.

MODEL complex

2. I became interested when I visited Washington Irving's home.
3. I found his stories at the library, and I read them.
4. He wrote many of them while he lived at Sleepy Hollow.
5. Although I was young, my application was accepted.
6. When I stand before a tour group, I feel inspired.
7. Although the tour is short, the tourists enjoy it.
8. I enjoy giving tours, and I might do it again next year.

B. Changing Sentences Change each compound sentence into a complex one. Underline the subordinate clause.

9. Paul juggles well, and he entered a talent show.

MODEL Because Paul juggles well, he entered a talent show.

10. Paul practices with rolled-up socks, but they work well.
11. He juggles often, but he has never juggled on stage.
12. The show was taped Friday, and talent scouts were there.
13. He decided to juggle to music, and he selected a jazz song.
14. He walked onto the stage, and the music started to play.
15. Paul juggled for four minutes, yet he didn't look tired.
16. The audience jumped to their feet, and they applauded.

C. Completing Complex Sentences Add a clause to each word group to make a complex sentence. Write the sentence, and underline the subordinate clause.

17. everyone dressed in a costume

MODEL Everyone dressed in a costume that his or her favorite fictional character might wear.

18. my sister Karen was dressed as Heidi
19. after I saw an old movie
20. we rode the bus in our costumes
21. while the other riders tried not to laugh
22. we arrived an hour late
23. although we were late for the party
24. Karen and I had a great time
25. all Karen could do was talk about the party

2 Adjective Clauses *pages 372 – 374*

A. Identifying Adjective Clauses Write each adjective clause and the word or words it modifies.

1. Ogden Nash, who was a famous humorist, is remembered particularly for his unique poetic style.
   MODEL who was a famous humorist—Ogden Nash
2. Nash was known for using long sentences that included exquisite rhymes.
3. He is a favorite of many who love his amusing verses.
4. His poems, which have lines of unequal length, are satirical.
5. He poked fun at some habits that he considered foolish.
6. Nash, who was born in Rye, New York, died in 1971.

B. Combining Sentences Use a relative pronoun to combine each pair of sentences. Underline the adjective clause.

7. Mark Twain wrote novels. He was a great American humorist.
   MODEL Mark Twain, <u>who was a great American humorist</u>, wrote novels.
8. Samuel Langhorne Clemens used a pen name. Mark Twain was the name he chose.
9. Twain was very successful. He wrote with humor.
10. Twain searched for stories everywhere. He was a world traveler.
11. Twain's writing reflects his complexity. It is often funny yet at the same time serious.
12. Twain kept himself busy. He lectured and traveled frequently.
13. Twain often had a grim outlook. He appreciated comedy.

C. Writing Adjective Clauses Write each sentence, adding an adjective clause. Underline each adjective clause.

14. The students compiled a <u>Limerick Log</u> for publication.
    MODEL The students <u>who won the poetry contest</u> compiled a <u>Limerick Log</u> for publication.
15. A limerick is a type of humorous verse.
16. Limericks cover a wide range of subjects.
17. The <u>Log</u> editors asked us to make contributions.
18. I wrote several limericks.
19. The <u>Log</u> sold out quickly.
20. The popularity of the <u>Log</u> excites us.

EXTRA PRACTICE

UNIT 8

3 Adverb Clauses *pages 375 – 376*

A. Identifying Adverb Clauses Write the word or words that each underlined adverb clause modifies.

1. While we were in Milwaukee, we visited a museum.

MODEL visited

2. We stayed longer than we originally intended.
3. As we wandered in the museum, we noticed sculpture.
4. The sculpture was found where Indians of the Great Lakes once lived.
5. As we learned, little time was spent on creative arts.
6. The exhibit was more interesting than I had expected.
7. I was fascinated when we saw a lacrosse stick.
8. Because we had lingered so long, we exited hurriedly.

B. Combining Sentences Combine each pair of sentences, using a subordinating conjunction. Write each new sentence.

9. The Ohlone Indians formed several villages. Each had its own chief.

MODEL Although the Ohlone Indians formed several villages, each had its own chief.

10. Everyone respected the chief. They owed him loyalty.
11. Traders might visit a village. The chief acted as host.
12. The chief danced. He was dressed elegantly.
13. The chief had to be generous. He could not be wasteful.
14. He kept food and wealth. The villagers criticized him.
15. He gave away too much. Shortages could occur.
16. A new chief was selected. An old chief died.

C. Completing Sentences with Adverb Clauses Add an adverb clause to each sentence. Write each sentence.

17. The Indians camped near a lake.

MODEL The Indians camped near a lake when the sun went down.

18. The children played.
19. All of the adults helped set up the camp.
20. The horses were tied to a long rope.
21. Some women hauled water from the lake.
22. Shelters were quickly erected.
23. The children laughed aloud.

UNIT 8

4 Noun Clauses *pages 377 – 378*

A. Identifying Noun Clauses Write the noun clause in each sentence. Then write how it is used within the sentence.

1. The king knew where the jester was.

MODEL where the jester was—direct object

2. What the jester wore was colorful.
3. Whichever tricks the jester knew were very important.
4. There were never explanations for what the jester said.
5. The problem at court was that the jester was missing.
6. The queen enjoyed how the jester told stories.
7. The joke of the day was how the jester lost his cap.
8. The jester amused whomever he saw.
9. The book does not tell when jesters first appeared.

B. Using Noun Clauses Write a complete sentence for each noun clause. Then write how the noun clause is used.

10. what the knight wore

MODEL What the knight wore was a suit of armor.—subject

11. how a knight climbed on a horse
12. what they used in combat
13. whoever came in contact with it
14. whatever the king wanted
15. who taught the knights
16. what a helmet can do
17. whichever lady asked for his help

C. Completing Sentences with Noun Clauses Write a noun clause to make each sentence complex. Then write how the noun clause is used in each sentence.

18. Castles protected people from ________.

MODEL Castles protected people from whatever enemies invaded the land.—object of a preposition

19. Knights understood ________.
20. ________ was having a strong fortress.
21. The knights defended the castle from ________.
22. ________ warned the people to go to the castle.
23. The peasants repeated the warning to ________.
24. The castle supplies were ________.
25. The enemy knew ________.
26. ________ had to be ready for a long siege.

EXTRA PRACTICE

UNIT 8

5 Misplaced Modifiers *pages 379 – 380*

A. **Identifying Misplaced Modifiers** Write the misplaced modifier in each sentence.

1. The clown was seen by Jamie with blue hair.

MODEL with blue hair

2. Jamie's mother in purple clothes saw an acrobat.
3. The lion approached the trainer with the great mane.
4. The performers from the bleachers looked exotic.
5. I shared popcorn with my grandmother that I bought.
6. The audience in one ring laughed at the clowns.
7. We applauded the clowns from the bleachers.

B. **Correcting Sentences with Misplaced Modifiers** Write each sentence, placing the misplaced modifier where it belongs.

8. The man photographed the elephant with the camera.

MODEL The man with the camera photographed the elephant.

9. His tie can be seen from far away with big blue dots.
10. The actor studied his lines in jeans.
11. The performer was praised by the director who entertained the audience.
12. The director purchased a theater last year in the suburbs.
13. I thought I would be an actor when I was younger.
14. We found a costume backstage with rhinestones.
15. The audience backstage can hear the people.

C. **Writing Sentences Correctly** Write each sentence, adding at least one modifier. Place each modifier where it belongs. Underline each modifier you add.

16. A family watches a comedy.

MODEL A family <u>in the balcony</u> watches a comedy.

17. The youngest son has an orchestra seat.
18. The boy loves comedy.
19. He especially likes slapstick comedy.
20. He laughs when the actors pretend to fall.
21. He listens for every funny line.
22. The boy's mother wonders about him.
23. She sends her daughter to look.
24. The girl returns with her brother.
25. The boy has enjoyed his special seat.

UNIT 8

6 Participles and Participial Phrases *pages 381 – 382*

A. Identifying Participial Phrases Write the participial phrase in each sentence. Then write whether it is a *present participle* or a *past participle.*

1. The Chicano boy walking by is Diego Carlos Valdez.

MODEL walking by—present participle

2. The Olmec Indians living in Mexico from 1200 B.C. to 100 B.C. were a major Mexican civilization.
3. Beginning about A.D. 1200, the Aztec civilization flourished.
4. Arriving in the 1500's, Spaniards settled in America.
5. The Spaniards, introduced to new foods and a new way of life, were indebted to the Indians.
6. Many mission towns established during the 1600's and 1700's became great American cities.

B. Using Participial Phrases Write a sentence for each participial phrase. Underline the word the participial phrase modifies.

7. seeking a better life

MODEL Seeking a better life, Fritz's family came to America from Germany during the 1960's.

8. following the old ways of life
9. shattered during World War II
10. separated by the Berlin Wall
11. living in a single-family house
12. enjoying an excellent standard of living
13. comforted by an old and proud tradition

C. Enriching Sentences with Participial Phrases Add a participial phrase to each sentence. Use commas correctly.

14. Katia's parents visited Russia.

MODEL Longing to research their heritage, Katia's parents visited Russia.

15. Mr. and Mrs. Romanoff began their trip in Moscow.
16. They were impressed by the country's size.
17. It seemed to take forever to reach Leningrad.
18. Mrs. Romanoff's family records were hard to find.
19. Mr. Romanoff finally found some information about several branches of his family.

EXTRA PRACTICE

UNIT 8

7 Gerunds and Gerund Phrases *pages 383 – 384*

A. Identifying Gerunds and Gerund Phrases Write the gerund phrase in each sentence. Underline the gerund.

1. Playing Hawaiian music is Lani's hobby.

MODEL Playing Hawaiian music

2. Hawaiians voted on holding a constitutional convention.
3. Joining the Union became a reality for Hawaii in 1959.
4. Touring the islands is a wonderful experience.
5. Planning ahead assured everyone of a good time.
6. My favorite pastime was snorkeling in the lagoon.
7. Growing orchids is a hobby in Hawaii.
8. I will always remember enjoying these lovely islands.

B. Categorizing Gerund Phrases Write how the underlined gerund or gerund phrase is used in each sentence.

9. Hilda's family keeps its Norwegian heritage alive by speaking Norwegian as well as English.

MODEL object of a preposition

10. Skiing is Norway's national sport.
11. Tourists enjoy seeing the Olympic ski jump in Oslo.
12. Many tourists enjoyed visiting Norway this year.
13. From Oslo they traveled to Bergen by taking the train.
14. Sailing through a fjord called the Sogne Fjord was recommended.
15. The tourists will love remembering their visit.

C. Using Gerund Phrases in Sentences Use each gerund phrase in a sentence. Write how each one is used.

16. cooking Italian food

MODEL Teresa enjoys cooking Italian food for her family.—direct object

17. eating Grandmother's cooking
18. listening to Grandfather's stories
19. learning about their trip to America
20. seeing the Statue of Liberty for the first time
21. settling in Brooklyn
22. raising a family
23. teaching grandchildren the traditional ways

EXTRA PRACTICE

8 Infinitives and Infinitive Phrases pages 385 – 387

A. Identifying Infinitives and Infinitive Phrases Write the infinitive or infinitive phrase in each sentence.

1. Jacy wants to study American Indian culture.

MODEL to study American Indian culture

2. We hope to visit the reservation today.
3. I want to be near the tour guide.
4. Jane was told to address the chief with respect.
5. It is his intention to give our group a lecture.
6. We will be sure to listen attentively.
7. To understand American culture, we must also know American Indian history.
8. I was wrong to assume that tepees were the only type of Indian home.
9. To defend themselves, Indians made their own weapons.
10. The bow and arrow were used to hunt.

B. Using Infinitive Phrases Write an infinitive or an infinitive phrase to complete each sentence. Then write how it is used.

11. Ainaba likes ________ traditional Navajo pottery.

MODEL to make—direct object

12. I plan ________ on a reservation next summer.
13. My desire is ________ everything about the Hopi culture.
14. ________ their naughty children, Indian parents might shame them, not scold them.
15. Our intention is ________ the Sioux way of life.
16. The entire Indian family works ________ the necessities of life.
17. Comanche women learn ________ buffalo hides.
18. ________ their courage, boys undergo an initiation rite.
19. A chief needs ________ confident and in control.
20. ________ weddings was the parents' responsibility.

C. Writing Infinitives in Sentences Use each infinitive in an original sentence. Write how each infinitive is used.

21. to communicate

MODEL Some Indians used smoke signals to communicate.—adverb

22. to visit	26. to grow	30. to call
23. to travel	27. to eat	31. to appreciate
24. to earn	28. to understand	32. to learn
25. to survive	29. to see	33. to know

EXTRA PRACTICE

UNIT 8

9 Dangling Participles and Split Infinitives *pages 388 – 389*

A. Identifying Dangling Participles and Split Infinitives Write *dangling participle* or *split infinitive* to identify what is wrong with each sentence.

1. Driving through the outback, a kangaroo suddenly appeared.

MODEL dangling participle

2. The kangaroo's instinctive reaction was to quickly retreat.
3. Few areas of Australia receive enough rainfall to adequately support a large population.
4. Having a warm, sunny climate, I enjoy the outdoors.
5. Perching in the tree, Grandma discovered a young koala's hiding place.
6. Years ago, Britons settling in Australia had to eventually develop a new vocabulary.
7. The Australian government operates programs to greatly improve the living conditions of the aborigines.
8. Many aborigines want to immediately regain control of their tribal territories.

B. Correcting Dangling Participles and Split Infinitives Write each sentence correctly.

9. In Greece, Damos used to often hike for exercise.

MODEL In Greece, Damos used to hike often for exercise.

10. Greeks prepare to joyfully celebrate holidays.
11. Dancing in the festival, we saw many costumed children.
12. Greeks love to energetically dance to bouzouki music.
13. Sitting in cafes, talk occurs in the evenings.
14. Weaving colorful rugs, the wool created bold patterns.
15. Embroidering linen, Jan admired the skill of the women.

C. Writing Participial Phrases and Infinitive Phrases Correctly Write a sentence for each item. Use each item as noted in parentheses ( ).

16. to visit (direct object)

MODEL Dana wants to visit Japan.

17. to see (subject)
18. hiking (modify the subject)
19. tired (modify the direct object)
20. to view (predicate nominative)
21. to travel (direct object)

1 Capitalization and End Punctuation

pages 432 – 433

A. Identifying Correct Capitalization and Punctuation Write each sentence, using correct capitalization and end punctuation.

1. Here is the poem "The Purple Cow" by Gelett Burgess

MODEL Here is the poem "The Purple Cow" by Gelett Burgess.

2. There is so much to laugh at in so few lines
3. what a wild, strange line this is
4. How many poems did Ogden Nash write
5. this is known as sophisticated light verse.
6. I love his poems about animals

B. Correcting Capitalization and Punctuation Write the letter in front of each sentence part that is incorrect. Then write the sentence part correctly.

7. (a) This poem is "If I Were an (b) Elephant?"

MODEL b—Elephant."

8. (a) Do you like my (b) collection of light verse.
9. (a) My favorite line is (b) the last one
10. (a) you wrote a terrific (b) poem of your own.
11. (a) someday you will see (b) a book of my poetry.
12. (a) I won an award for my poem (b) last semester?

C. Capitalizing and Punctuating Sentences Correctly Write each sentence, using correct capitalization and end punctuation.

13. did you like that Lewis Carroll poem

MODEL Did you like that Lewis Carroll poem?

14. he is known for his stories, too
15. when did Carroll begin his writing career
16. he wrote his first story for a little girl
17. can you understand the joke in that poem
18. why are you laughing so hard

2 Commas Within Sentences *pages 434 – 436*

A. Identifying the Reasons for Using Commas in Sentences For each sentence, write a sentence to explain why commas are used.

1. Yes, Jaclyn's poem won a blue ribbon in the contest.

MODEL › The comma sets off an introductory word.

2. When we filed into the auditorium, Jaclyn crossed her fingers.
3. The poem was imaginative, sensitive, and vivid.
4. No, I have not read the poem yet.
5. Mr. Miller, our English teacher, applauded the loudest.
6. After the awards were announced, I saw tears in Jaclyn's eyes.
7. Jaclyn, did you expect such a crowd today?
8. Her mind, by the way, is full of creative thoughts.

B. Correcting Comma Usage Write each sentence, using commas correctly.

9. The writer Ian, compares lasers, and butterflies.

MODEL › The writer, Ian, compares lasers and butterflies.

10. No I don't think this, is his first poem.
11. It has emotion strength, and vivid, imagery.
12. Did the teacher, Mr. Vic help Ian, develop the poem?
13. Over the weekend Cara, typed her poem.
14. Well you can imagine, how we all felt.
15. I wrote the verses and Jay, drew the illustrations.
16. I, wrote the poem my best one, last summer.

C. Adding Commas to Sentences Add commas to each sentence wherever they are needed.

17. My poem was funny but most of them were dramatic.

MODEL › My poem was funny, but most of them were dramatic.

18. Mr. Collins will you help me with my rhyme scheme?
19. This poem for example is too vague and wordy.
20. Yes I see your point about the opening line.
21. After this semester I will try to go back to writing.
22. Kenny my brother has always supported my efforts.
23. Like a diamond a poem should have clarity.
24. This work has intelligence wit and beauty.
25. My efforts as a matter of fact were very successful.

UNIT 9

3 Other Punctuation Within Sentences *pages 437 – 439*

A. Identifying Correct Punctuation If the punctuation within each sentence is correct, write *correct*. If something is wrong, write the sentence correctly.

1. This book is wonderful I will finish it soon.

MODEL This book is wonderful; I will finish it soon.

2. I went to the library at 530 P.M. yesterday.
3. I was looking for the following kinds of books: adventure, history, and science.
4. We visited New York, New York; Pittsburgh, Pennsylvania; and Chicago, Illinois.
5. There were sixty nine books on a single shelf.
6. We ate the following foods chicken, fruit, and milk.

B. Choosing the Correct Punctuation for Sentences Write the item in parentheses ( ) that is punctuated correctly.

7. We will publish the following poems by (Naomi—) (Naomi:) (Naomi,) "Summer," "Treasure," and "Rain."

MODEL Naomi:

8. Naomi finished reading at (9:15) (91:5) (915) P.M.
9. We checked out the following (books—) (books;) (books:) Hark and Fog.
10. The reading lasted six (hours:) (hours;) (hours) we left exhausted.
11. I don't like poetry (however) (however;) (;however,) I found it interesting.
12. Naomi will visit her relatives in Atlanta, (Georgia:) (Georgia;) (Georgia) Youngstown, Ohio; and Tampa, Florida.

C. Using Punctuation Correctly Within Sentences Write each sentence, using the correct punctuation.

13. Ms. Yarrow says and I agree with her that your poems should be published.

MODEL Ms. Yarrow says—and I agree with her—that your poems should be published.

14. My appointment with the editor was at 915 A.M.
15. She kept me waiting twenty two minutes.
16. I showed her the following poems "Lace," "Phantom," and "Shadows."
17. She liked and it's my favorite too your poem "Lace."
18. The poems weren't even written by me nevertheless I was nervous.

EXTRA PRACTICE

4 Numbers in Sentences *pages 440 – 441*

A. **Identifying Correctly Written Numbers** Write *correct* for each sentence that contains a correctly written number. Write correctly any numbers that are incorrect.

1. The yearbook for 1991 will be available in June.

MODEL correct

2. 41 students paid a deposit on the yearbook.
3. There were 105 pages in the book.
4. Our budget enabled us to include 45 color pages.
5. There are 200 students in the pictures.
6. The editors made one hundred four corrections.
7. The yearbook club meets in Room one hundred sixty-two.
8. The 1989 yearbook was not as nice as this one.

B. **Completing Sentences with Numbers** Write the proper form of each number in parentheses.

9. (50) (Fifty) students contributed to the yearbook.

MODEL Fifty

10. (10) (Ten) teachers assisted the students.
11. I was one of (3) (three) speakers to address the staff.
12. The address was (five seventeen) (517) Bard Road.
13. The office is located in Room (297) (two nine seven).
14. There were (three) (3) 2's in his address.
15. This book was published in the late (1800s) (1800's).
16. The yearbooks were (six) (6) hours overdue.
17. I opened a copy of the yearbook at (nine) (9) o'clock.
18. (Twenty-eight) (28) students unloaded the truck.

C. **Writing Numbers Correctly** Write numbers correctly to complete each sentence.

19. ________ months ago we published a joke book.

MODEL Two

20. The book contained a total of ________ jokes.
21. ________ teachers helped us assemble the material.
22. We had a staff of ________ students.
23. ________ of the pages were illustrated.
24. Our joke book staff met in Room ________.
25. This room held only ________ people.
26. We met at ________ o'clock every Tuesday afternoon.
27. Our chief illustrator lives at ________ Park Place.

5 Capitalization of Proper Nouns, Proper Adjectives, and *I* *pages 442 – 443*

A. Capitalizing Words Correctly Write each sentence. Add capital letters where they are needed.

1. shesota north made a collage called "morning mist."

MODEL Shesota North made a collage called "Morning Mist."

2. The grant art club is the largest art club in the east.
3. On july 10, 1990, we honored the parents' association.
4. david hoffman's collage illustrated purim, a jewish holiday.
5. The local newspaper, the daily sun, sent a reporter.
6. mayor billings invited us to the mayor's mansion.

B. Choosing Correct Capitalization Write the item in parentheses ( ) that is correct.

7. Charles A. Lindbergh flew the (Spirit Of St. Louis, Spirit of St. Louis) to Paris.

MODEL Spirit of St. Louis

8. This American aviator made the first solo nonstop flight across the (Atlantic ocean, Atlantic Ocean).
9. Lindbergh grew up on a farm near (Little falls, minnesota; Little Falls, Minnesota).
10. Lindbergh's father, Charles Augustus Lindbergh, served as a (congressman, Congressman).
11. Lindbergh was trained as an (Army Air Service Reserve pilot, Army Air Service Reserve Pilot).
12. A collection of Lindbergh's writings is called (The Autobiography of values, The Autobiography of Values).

C. Capitalizing Correctly Write each sentence, capitalizing nouns, pronouns, and adjectives correctly.

13. Georgia o'Keeffe painted scenes of the west.

MODEL Georgia O'Keeffe painted scenes of the West.

14. O'Keeffe was an american artist who was born in 1887.
15. This nature artist was born in sun prairie, wisconsin.
16. She studied at the art institute of chicago.
17. O'Keeffe also studied at the art students league.
18. This institution is located in new york city.

UNIT 9

6 Letters and Envelopes *pages 444 – 446*

A. Identifying Correct and Incorrect Mechanics Write whether each item that represents a part of a letter or an envelope address is *correct* or *incorrect*.

1. Southbury Connecticut 06488

MODEL incorrect

2. 62 higging drive
3. January 15, 1990
4. berwyn, pennsylvania 19312
5. 14 bradford circle
6. Very cordially yours,
7. chicago illinois 60606

B. Choosing Correct Mechanics Write the correct form of each pair.

8. Yours Very Truly,
   Yours very truly,

MODEL Yours very truly,

9. *business:*
   Dear Sir or Madam
   Dear Sir or Madam:
10. *return address:*
   Old Bridge New Jersey 08857
   Old Bridge, NJ 08857
11. 62 Wharf Circle
   62, Wharf Circle
12. *friendly:*
   Dear Uncle Joey:
   Dear Uncle Joey,
13. october, 1 1990
   October 1, 1990
14. *mailing address:*
   Cupertino, CA 95014
   Cupertino CA, 95014

C. Using Mechanics Correctly in Letters and on Envelopes Write each of these letter parts or envelope addresses correctly.

15. (inside address) ms dana dombrowski/adventure store/915 jefferson street/ames iowa 50010

MODEL Ms. Dana Dombrowski
Adventure Store
915 Jefferson Street
Ames, Iowa 50010

16. (mailing address) mr arnold baker/super pet shops/ 1316 avenue of the elms/amherst massachusetts 01002
17. (business greeting) dear mr. goldstein
18. (date) may 11 1990
19. (friendly greeting) dear uncle harry
20. (closing) very sincerely yours

EXTRA PRACTICE

7 Titles *pages 447 – 448*

A. Identifying Correct Mechanics in Titles Write *correct* if a title is correctly capitalized and punctuated. If a title is incorrect, write it correctly.

1. Sunday In The Park With George (play)

MODEL Sunday in the Park with George

2. till there was you (song)
3. The apple that astonished Paris (poem)
4. The Rise and Fall of the Third Reich (book)
5. This old House (television series)
6. "Oh, What a Beautiful Morning!" (song)
7. The Spirit of 1776 (play)
8. The journal of Air and Space flight (magazine)

B. Rewriting Incorrect Titles Each title has at least one mistake in it. Write each title correctly.

9. Lad, A Dog (book)

MODEL Lad, a Dog

10. I saw Her Standing there (song)
11. Rosencrantz And Guildenstern are Dead (play)
12. The Chicago sun-times (newspaper)
13. The Wind In The Willows (book)
14. Georgia On my Mind (song)
15. My Candle burns at both Ends (poem)
16. Florence nightingale (play)
17. The Village voice (newspaper)

C. Writing Titles Correctly Write the following titles correctly, using correct capitalization and punctuation.

18. the night the bed fell (short story)

MODEL "The Night the Bed Fell"

19. king of the gypsies (movie)
20. the newark star-ledger (newspaper)
21. sense and sensibility (book)
22. much ado about nothing (play)
23. journal of a tour on the continent (book)
24. ode to a nightingale (poem)
25. You can't take it with you (play)

EXTRA PRACTICE

UNIT 9

8 Outlines and Bibliographies *pages 449 – 452*

A. Identifying Correct and Incorrect Mechanics in Outlines Each outline part is correct except for one error. Write the part the way it should be.

1. Tales of adventure and suspense
   A. American authors

MODEL I. Tales of adventure and suspense
   A. American authors

2. III. American aviation heroes
   1. Charles Lindbergh

3. iv. Stars of the screen
   A. Marilyn Monroe

4. III. Kinds of carpeting
   A. Deep pile
      a. Stain-proof

5. II. Dickens's best-loved novels
   1. Oliver Twist

B. Writing Outlines Write the information given in each item, using correct outline form and mechanics.

6. cartoons/Krazy Kat/Peanuts/daily series

MODEL I. Cartoons
   A. Daily series
      1. "Krazy Kat" 2. "Peanuts"

7. Jeopardy/Television/Wheel of Fortune/Game Shows
8. Modern/Doll Collections/Antique/Collectibles
9. Soap/Uses of oil/Fuel/Mineral oil
10. Television guide/Viewer guides/Movie guide/Sports guide
11. Siamese/Domestic pets/Cats/Abyssinian

C. Correcting Bibliographic Entries Write each bibliographic entry correctly.

12. Richard Peck, Secrets of the Shopping Mall, New York, Delacorte Press: 1979.

MODEL Peck, Richard. Secrets of the Shopping Mall. New York: Delacorte Press, 1979.

13. Robert V. Bruce, September 1988, National Geographic, "Alexander Graham Bell," pp. 358-384.
14. Clem: The Story of a Raven, 1986, Dodd, Mead & Company, New York, Jennifer Owings Dewey.
15. This Delicious Day, Carl Sandburg, "Bubbles," Orchard Books, New York and London, 1987.
16. The World Book Encyclopedia, National Park, 1986 ed.
17. Harper & Row Publishers, New York, 1977, Essays of E. B. White, E. B. White.

9 Direct Quotations and Dialogue *pages 453 – 455*

A. Identifying Direct Quotations If a sentence is written correctly, write *correct*. If a sentence is incorrect, write it correctly.

1. "No! cried Molly." "This painting is perfect!"

MODEL "No!" cried Molly. "This painting is perfect!"

2. "Well, if you say so" Brooke responded reluctantly.
3. Tim asked, "How do we become a part of the picture?"
4. "Touch the wishing well in the center, Molly answered."
5. "It's true! Molly exclaimed. "We've entered the picture."
6. Brooke noted that she wanted to enter the house.
7. Tim replied that he didn't think it was safe.
8. "There are no curtains in the window," Brooke observed.
9. "I'm going in Molly decided, It's probably empty."

B. Correcting Direct Quotations Write each sentence, using quotation marks and punctuation marks correctly.

10. "Look for clues. Molly cried check everything!"

MODEL "Look for clues," Molly cried. "Check everything!"

11. "Exactly who is the painter of this picture" Tim asked.
12. "His name Brooke said hesitantly is Dennis Light."
13. "Do you think that's a clue" Brooke queried.
14. "I think, Tim replied we should check every lamp."
15. Brooke demanded, What are we looking for?
16. "We'll know," Molly said, "When we find it.

C. Using Quotation Marks with Dialogue Write each sentence, adding quotation marks and other necessary punctuation.

17. Molly added, I think it is at the end of the hall.

MODEL Molly added, "I think it is at the end of the hall."

18. It's very dark in here Tim said. Turn on the light.
19. Look Molly exclaimed. It shines in from the outside!
20. She asked, what do all these tiny windows mean?
21. The light is outside of the picture Brooke decided.
22. Hurry! Tim shouted look at these circles.
23. Molly said, We have three clues—gold, tiny, and circles.
24. I know, she announced, they're coins!
25. Look at this unusual coin, Brooke said. It shows the way out of here!

EXTRA PRACTICE

WRITER'S HANDBOOK

Contents

Sentences

- A **sentence** is a group of words that expresses a complete thought. — sentence

  Many people take vacations in the summer.

- There are four kinds of sentences: *declarative, interrogative, imperative,* and *exclamatory.*

- A **declarative sentence** makes a statement and ends with a period. — declarative sentence

  Everyone enjoyed the field trip to the history museum .

  Mr. Gregory accompanied the class .

- An **interrogative sentence** asks a question and ends with a question mark. — interrogative sentence

  Have you heard the good news about Ellen ?

  Did you know that she won the contest ?

- An **imperative sentence** gives a command or makes a request and ends with a period. The subject of an imperative sentence is *you* (understood). *You* refers to the person or persons to whom the command or request is given. *You* is understood, not actually written. — imperative sentence

  (you) Tell me about your trip to England .

  (you) Show us your photographs .

- An **exclamatory sentence** expresses strong feeling and ends with an exclamation point. — exclamatory sentence

  What a wonderful time we had !

  The sights were spectacular !

- A **simple sentence** contains one subject and one predicate. A simple sentence may have a compound subject, a compound verb, or both. — simple sentence

  Lava flowed from the mouth of the volcano.

  Smoke and flames poured into the air.

  The earth rumbled and shook .

compound sentence

- A **compound sentence** contains two or more related simple sentences joined by a comma and a conjunction or by a semicolon.

simple sentence | simple sentence

Brandon looked out the window , but he saw only darkness.

simple sentence | simple sentence

Brandon looked out the window ; he saw only darkness.

complex sentence

- A **complex sentence** consists of an independent clause and at least one subordinate clause.

subordinate clause | independent clause

If you videotape this program tonight, we can watch it tomorrow.

subject

- The **subject** of a sentence names someone or something. The subject of a sentence is the part about which something is being said.

Tourists often come to this resort town.

complete subject

- The **complete subject** is all the words that make up the subject part of the sentence.

A large sign will direct you to the exit.

simple subject

- The **simple subject** is the main, or key, word in the complete subject.

A large sign will direct you to the exit.

compound subject

- A **compound subject** is made up of two or more subjects that have the same verb.

Raymond and his brother wandered through the gift shop.

predicate

- The **predicate** of a sentence tells what the subject is or does.

Belinda was frantic about her lost luggage.

Andrew listened patiently to her story.

complete predicate

- The **complete predicate** contains all the words and phrases in the predicate part of the sentence.

A young deer stood by the maple tree.

- The **simple predicate** is the verb in the complete predicate. It may be one verb or a verb phrase.

  simple predicate

  Your schedule allows one hour for lunch.

  Many of us are becoming hungry now.

- A **compound verb** is two or more verbs that have the same subject.

  compound verb

  Leslie washed and waxed her new car.

- When a sentence has **natural word order,** the subject comes before the verb.

  natural word order

  A smiling waitress stood behind the counter.

- When a sentence has **inverted word order,** the verb comes before the subject.

  inverted word order

  Behind the counter stood a smiling waitress.

- A **complement** is the part of a sentence that completes the thought started by the subject and the verb. A sentence complement may be a direct object, an indirect object, a predicate adjective, or a predicate nominative.

  complement

- A **direct object** is a noun or pronoun that receives the action of the verb. To find the direct object, ask *who* or *what* receives the action.

  direct object

  Krystin tore her new wool sweater. tore what? sweater

  Kwan counted the swimmers and skiers enjoying the lake. counted whom? swimmers, skiers

- An **indirect object** tells to or for whom or to or for what the action of the verb is done. A sentence must have a direct object to have an indirect object. The indirect object is a noun or a pronoun. It is always placed after the verb and before the direct object in a sentence.

  indirect object

  The map showed (V) the hikers (IO) the quickest trail (DO) to the camp.

  A park ranger told (V) them (IO) the best route (DO).

  He gave (V) Bob (IO) and Tim (IO) the directions (DO) to the old cabin.

WRITER'S HANDBOOK • Grammar

predicate nominative

- A **predicate nominative** is a noun or pronoun that follows a linking verb and renames or identifies the subject of the sentence.

  Both of my parents are engineers.

  My first choice for a partner is you.

  The contents of the bag were paintbrushes, rulers, and pencils.

predicate adjective

- A **predicate adjective** is an adjective that follows a linking verb and describes the subject of the sentence.

  The sunset was beautiful.

  Our dog, Sparky, is intelligent and gentle.

Nouns

noun

- A **noun** names a person, a place, a thing, or an idea.

  My brother rushed into the house with a look of surprise.

singular noun

- A **singular noun** names one person, place, thing, or idea.

  Where is your new stereo?

plural noun

- A **plural noun** names more than one person, place, thing, or idea. Add *s* to form the plural of most nouns. For help with the spelling of plural nouns, see the *Spelling* section of this **Writer's Handbook.**

  My parents attend my band concerts.

common noun

- A **common noun** names any person, place, thing, or idea.

  The eagle soared into the sky.

concrete noun

- A **concrete noun** names something that can be seen, smelled, tasted, felt, or heard.

  The right fender was covered with rust.

abstract noun

- An **abstract noun** names an idea, a quality, or a feeling that cannot be experienced with the senses.

  Our primary concern is your safety.

collective noun

- A **collective noun** names a group of things, people, or animals.

  The audience applauded for the winning team.

- A **proper noun** names a particular person, place, thing, or idea. A proper noun is always capitalized. For help with the capitalization of proper nouns, see the *Mechanics* section of the **Writer's Handbook.**

proper noun

Captain T. R. Lee and her family have arrived from Korea.

The Rotary Club will sponsor an auction in August.

James finished his report before Thanksgiving Day.

- A **possessive noun** shows ownership or possession. For more help with forming possessive nouns, see the *Mechanics* section of the **Writer's Handbook.**

possessive noun

- Form the possessive of a singular noun by adding an apostrophe and an *s*.

Kim's guitar is out of tune.

I borrowed Bess's radio to take to the beach.

- Form the possessive of a plural noun that ends in *s* by adding an apostrophe.

The workers' schedules are changed each week.

- Form the possessive of a plural noun that does not end in *s* by adding an apostrophe and an *s*.

The women's clothing department is on the third floor.

- An **appositive** is a noun or pronoun that identifies or renames a noun or pronoun that precedes it.

appositive

My sister, Mary, wears her hair in long braids.

Pronouns

- A **pronoun** takes the place of a noun or nouns. Pronouns can be singular or plural, and they can be masculine, feminine, or neuter. They can be in the nominative or the objective case. The pronouns that are used most frequently are called personal pronouns.

pronoun

Colin said that he has two tickets to the concert.

The Boyds intend to bring two suitcases with them.

antecedent • An **antecedent** is the noun or nouns to which a pronoun refers. A pronoun should agree with its antecedent in number, person, and sometimes gender.

Jack found a surprise when he opened the door.

subject pronoun • A **subject pronoun** is used as a subject of a sentence. Subject pronouns are in the nominative case.

She is the superintendent of this building.

Nominative Case	Singular	Plural
First Person	I	we
Second Person	you	you
Third Person	he, she, it	they

pronoun-verb agreement • A pronoun used as a subject should agree in number with the verb.

She likes to go to the movies on Saturday.

They like to go to the skating rink.

predicate nominative • A pronoun used as a predicate nominative is in the nominative case.

A merry old soul was he .

object pronoun • An **object pronoun** can be used as a direct object, an indirect object, or the object of a preposition. Object pronouns are in the objective case.

Mr. Harmon will drive me to the tennis court. direct object

The announcer told us the reasons for cancelling the game.

indirect object

The firefighters have a tremendous job ahead of them .

object of a preposition

Objective Case	Singular	Plural
First Person	me	us
Second Person	you	you
Third Person	him, her, it	them

- A **relative pronoun** connects a group of words to a noun antecedent or a pronoun antecedent. The words *that, which, who, whom,* and *whose* can be used as relative pronouns.

relative pronoun

Paprika is the spice that you taste in this stew.

- A **possessive pronoun** shows ownership or possession.

possessive pronoun

The weary shoppers carried their bags to the bus stop.

Possessive Pronouns	Singular	Plural
First Person	my, mine	our, ours
Second Person	your, yours	your, yours
Third Person	his, her, hers, its	their, theirs

- A **reflexive pronoun** refers to the subject. The words *myself, yourself, himself, herself, itself, ourselves, yourselves,* and *themselves* can be reflexive pronouns.

reflexive pronoun

Kate allows herself fifteen minutes to walk to school.

- An **intensive pronoun** emphasizes a noun or a pronoun. The words *myself, yourself, himself, herself, itself, ourselves, yourselves,* and *themselves* can be intensive pronouns.

intensive pronoun

My parents built a two-car garage themselves.

- A **demonstrative pronoun** points out a particular person, place, or thing. The words *this, that, these,* and *those* are demonstrative pronouns.

demonstrative pronoun

This is an antique farm tool.

That is not.

These were found in the Midwest.

Those were found on an Indian reservation.

- When *this, that, these,* and *those* are used before nouns, they are adjectives, not pronouns.

I wonder what this tool was used for?

indefinite pronoun

- An **indefinite pronoun** does not refer to a particular person, place, thing, or idea.

Many of these factories have increased production.

Indefinite Pronouns				
Singular			Plural	
all another any anybody anyone anything each either	everybody everyone everything most much neither nobody none	no one nothing one some somebody someone something such	all any both few many	most none several some

- When indefinite pronouns are used before nouns, they are adjectives, not pronouns.

Some jackets will go on sale next week. adjective

Some are available at a discount now. pronoun

- The indefinite pronouns *all, any, most,* and *some* are plural when they refer to things that can be counted. They are singular when they refer to things that cannot be counted.

All of the students have passed. can count students

All of the snow has melted. cannot count snow

interrogative pronoun

- An **interrogative pronoun** is used to ask a question. The words *who, whose, whom, what,* and *which* are interrogative pronouns.

What are the most important natural resources of Yugoslavia?

Who is the leading oil producer?

Which is the most profitable?

Whose is this?

Whom did you choose?

Verbs

- A **verb** expresses action or being. — verb

  Roy drove the tractor toward the hay field.

  The approaching storm clouds were an unwelcome sight.

- An **action verb** expresses physical or mental action. — action verb

  The quarterback hurled the ball down the field.

  He realized his mistake too late.

- A **linking verb** connects the subject of a sentence to a word or words in the predicate. Linking verbs are forms of the verb *be* or verbs that express being, such as *seem, appear, become, look, feel,* and *remain.* — linking verb

  The cost of a new house is very high.

  Construction companies seem busier than ever.

- A **verb phrase** is made up of a main verb and one or more helping verbs. — verb phrase

  We could have been here earlier.

  He is helping me with my homework.

- The **main verb** is the most important verb in a verb phrase. — main verb

  main verb [prefer]

  Nina would prefer the fresh fruit salad.

- A **helping verb** works with the main verb to express action or being. — helping verb

  helping verb [will]

  Mr. Corey will present his report to the group.

  helping verbs [has been]

  The meeting has been postponed.

- A subject and its verb must agree in number. For help with subject-verb agreement, see the *Usage* section of the **Writer's Handbook.** — subject-verb agreement

  A dandelion grows rapidly in warm weather.

  Dandelions grow in lawns all over the neighborhood.

WRITER'S HANDBOOK • Grammar

principal parts of regular verbs

- The **principal parts** of a verb are the *present*, the *present participle*, the *past*, and the *past participle*.

Present	Present Participle	Past	Past Participle
offer purchase reply scan	offering purchasing replying scanning	offered purchased replied scanned	offered purchased replied scanned

tense

- The **tense** of a verb shows time. Verb tenses change to indicate that events happen at different times. The six verb tenses are the *present*, the *past*, the *future*, the *present perfect*, the *past perfect*, and the *future perfect*.

Present: David waits for the bus every morning.

Past: Yesterday he waited for ten minutes.

Future: We will wait a few minutes longer.

Present perfect: Karina has waited with David a few times.

Past perfect: Sue had waited a long time before the bus's arrival.

Future perfect: Soon Gina will have waited longer than anyone else.

progressive verb

- A **progressive verb** expresses action that continues. Each of the present, past, and future tenses has a progressive form. To make the progressive form of a verb, always use the present participle as the main verb with a form of the verb *be* as a helping verb.

Progressive Verb Forms

Present: Luis is saving his money for a skateboard.

Past: Last year he was saving for a catcher's mitt.

Future: With my new job I will be saving ten dollars a week.

Present perfect: Nancy has been saving money by shopping with coupons.

Past perfect: Without the coupons she had been saving very little.

Future perfect: By June, Dan will have been saving his paychecks for six months.

- An **irregular verb** does not have *ed* or *d* added to the present to form the past and the past participle.

irregular verb

- The verbs *be, have,* and *do* are irregular verbs.

Be **Principal parts:** be, was, (have) been, being			
	Present	**Past**	**Future**
I he, she, it we, you, they	am is are	was was were	will (shall) be will be will (shall) be
	Present Perfect	**Past Perfect**	**Future Perfect**
I he, she, it we, you, they	have been has been have been	had been had been had been	will (shall) have been will have been will (shall) have been

Have **Principal parts:** have, had, (have) had, having			
	Present	**Past**	**Future**
I, we, you, they he, she, it	have has	had had	will (shall) have will have
	Present Perfect	**Past Perfect**	**Future Perfect**
I, we, you, they he, she, it	have had has had	had had had had	will (shall) have had will have had

Do **Principal parts:** do, did, (have) done, doing			
	Present	**Past**	**Future**
I, we, you, they he, she, it	do does	did did	will (shall) do will do
	Present Perfect	**Past Perfect**	**Future Perfect**
I, we, you, they he, she, it	have done has done	had done had done	will (shall) have done will have done

contraction • A **contraction** is a shortened way of writing a verb and a pronoun or a verb and the word *not*. Use an apostrophe in place of the letters that are left out when you write a contraction.

he will—he'll	they have—they've	you would—you'd
is not—isn't	were not—weren't	would not—wouldn't
cannot—can't		

transitive verb • A **transitive verb** has a direct object.

Mr. Chin wrapped the parcel in brown paper.

intransitive verb • An **intransitive verb** does not have a direct object.

Suddenly the wrestler grimaced .

active voice • A transitive verb is in the **active voice** when the subject performs the action.

Steam powered the first locomotives.

passive voice • A transitive verb is in the **passive voice** when the subject receives the action.

The first locomotives were powered by steam.

Adjectives

adjective • An **adjective** modifies a noun or a pronoun. An adjective tells *what kind, which one, how much,* or *how many.*

The early inhabitants of America had interesting customs.

proper adjective • A **proper adjective** is created from a proper noun. Proper adjectives are always capitalized.

Camels provide transportation across the African desert.

articles • The words *a, an,* and *the* are special adjectives called **articles.** *A* and *an* are **indefinite articles.** *The* is a **definite article.**

An ambulance needs a siren to warn the other drivers.

demonstrative adjective • A demonstrative adjective points out the noun it modifies. The words *this, that, these,* and *those* are **demonstrative adjectives** when they point out specific persons, places, or things.

This green-headed duck is called a mallard.

I have never seen these ducks before.

WRITER'S HANDBOOK • Grammar

That duck on the other side of the river is a mallard also.

We can watch the ducks from behind those trees.

- A **predicate adjective** is an adjective that follows a linking verb and describes the subject of the sentence.

predicate adjective

The view from the mountaintop was panoramic .

The photograph looks hazy and gray .

- Adjectives can be used to compare nouns. The three degrees of comparison are **positive, comparative,** and **superlative.** Form the comparative and superlative degrees by adding *er* and *est* to one-syllable adjectives and to some two-syllable adjectives. For more help with the spelling of comparative and superlative adjectives, see the *Spelling* section of the **Writer's Handbook.**

adjectives that compare

Positive	Comparative	Superlative
plain fancy	plainer fancier	plainest fanciest

Rick needs sturdy running shoes.

The heel supports make these shoes sturdier than those.

The Supercomets are the sturdiest shoes ever made.

- For some two-syllable adjectives and most three-syllable adjectives, form the comparative degree by using *more* or *less* before the adjective. Form the superlative degree by using *most* or *least*.

more, most, less, least

Positive	Comparative	Superlative
ornate expensive	more ornate less expensive	most ornate least expensive

The early flight will be convenient for you.

Would an afternoon flight be more convenient than a morning one?

This airline offers the most convenient flight schedule of all.

WRITER'S HANDBOOK • Grammar

irregular comparisons • Some adjectives have **irregular forms** of comparison.

Positive	Comparative	Superlative
good, well bad much, many little (small amount)	better worse more less, lesser	best worst most least

Scott has a good knowledge of musical terms.

He is a better piano player than his sister.

His brother Peter is the best musician in the family.

Adverbs

adverb • An **adverb** modifies a verb, an adjective, or another adverb. Adverbs tell *when, where, how, how often,* and *to what extent.*

The sinking sun gradually faded behind the horizon.
modifies verb

Our cabin was barely visible under the huge tree.
modifies adjective

The location of the map is a very closely guarded secret.
modifies adverb

adverbs that compare • Some adverbs have three degrees of comparison: **positive, comparative,** and **superlative.** Form the comparative and superlative degrees by adding *er* and *est* to one-syllable adverbs and to some two-syllable adverbs.

Positive	Comparative	Superlative
loud early	louder earlier	loudest earliest

Lisa knocked hard on the heavy oak door.

When no one answered, she knocked harder than before.

She knocked hardest of all before returning to the car.

- For most adverbs ending in *ly*, form the comparative degree by adding *more* or *less* before the adverb. Form the superlative degree by adding *most* or *least*.

Positive	Comparative	Superlative
seriously	more seriously	most seriously
patiently	less patiently	least patiently
happily	more happily	most happily
nearly	less nearly	least nearly
cautiously	more cautiously	most cautiously
easily	more easily	most easily
confidently	less confidently	least confidently
delicately	more delicately	most delicately

The partners worked diligently on their science project.

Jason studies more diligently than many of his friends.

He reviews his notes most diligently just before the test.

- Some adverbs have **irregular forms** of comparison.

irregular comparisons

Positive	Comparative	Superlative
well	better	best
badly	worse	worst
much	more	most
little	less	least
far	farther	farthest

James swims very well .

Dana swims better than James.

Jaclyn swims best of all.

- Two negative words should not be used together. The most common **negative words** are *no, not, never, hardly, barely, rarely, seldom, nowhere,* and *scarcely*.

double negative

correct: That building will never be occupied again.

incorrect: That building won't never be occupied again.

correct: People hardly notice it as they walk by.

incorrect: People don't hardly notice it as they walk by.

Prepositions

preposition

- A **preposition** relates a noun or a pronoun to another word in a sentence. Some prepositions consist of more than one word.

Some Common Prepositions				
aboard	before	during	next to	till
about	behind	except	of	to
above	below	for	off	toward
according to	beneath	from	on	under
across	beside	in	onto	underneath
after	besides	in back of	out	until
against	between	in front of	out of	unto
along	beyond	in place of	outside	up
among	but	in spite of	over	upon
around	by	instead of	past	with
as	concerning	into	since	within
at	despite	like	through	without
because of	down	near	throughout	

Your supervisor will be checking **with** you.

prepositional phrase

- A **prepositional phrase** is made up of a preposition, the object of the preposition, and all the words in between. The **object of the preposition** is the noun or pronoun at the end of the prepositional phrase.

The last **of the racers** finally came **across the finish line**.

adjective phrase

- A prepositional phrase that modifies a noun or a pronoun is an **adjective phrase.** An adjective phrase tells *what kind, which one, how much,* or *how many.*

The ribbon **on her hat** was yellow. modifies *ribbon*

adverb phrase

- A prepositional phrase that modifies a verb, an adjective, or an adverb is an **adverb phrase.** An adverb phrase tells *when, where, how, how often,* or *to what extent.*

A fierce hurricane swept **through the state**. modifies verb

Simon is true **to his word**. modifies adjective

Lester threw the ball far **to the right**. modifies adverb

Conjunctions

- A **conjunction** connects words or groups of words in a sentence.

conjunction

- The words *and, but, or, so, yet, for,* and *nor* are common conjunctions. These are called **coordinating conjunctions.** They connect words or groups of words that have the same function in sentences.

coordinating conjunctions

The judge and the jury must listen carefully to the evidence.

The lawyer or the judge will speak.

Some jurors are listening, but others are not.

The defense is good, yet few are convinced.

The accused wasn't freed, nor was he sentenced.

- Some conjunctions are made up of pairs of words. These pairs are called **correlative conjunctions.** Correlative conjunctions are used together in the same sentence.

correlative conjunctions

Common Correlative Conjunctions

neither/nor	Neither the swimmers nor the divers scored well at the meet.
either/or	Either they were out of condition, or they had a bad day.
both/and	Both the coaches and the judges agreed on the winners.
whether/or	They must decide whether to compete in the county meet or continue playing intramurals.

Interjections

- An **interjection** expresses feeling or emotion. It has no grammatical relationship to the rest of the sentence. Use an exclamation point after an interjection to show strong emotion. Use a comma to show mild feeling.

interjection

Wow! The Olympic diving competition was wonderful!

Oh, I didn't have a chance to watch it.

Verbals

verbal • A **verbal** is a verb form that functions as a noun, an adjective, or an adverb. Participles, gerunds, and infinitives are the three types of verbals.

participle • A **participle** is a verbal that is used as an adjective. Most participles end in *ed* or *ing.*

The skiers drank cups of steaming cocoa.

Concerned residents should attend the meeting.

gerund • A **gerund** is a verbal that ends in *ing* and is used as a noun.

Swimming strengthens the muscles.

infinitive • An **infinitive** is a verbal consisting of the present-tense form of a verb preceded by *to.* An infinitive can be used as a noun, an adjective, or an adverb.

Her goal is to win. as a noun

Cool nights are the best nights to sleep. as an adjective

We went to the store to shop. as an adverb

Phrases and Clauses

phrase • A **phrase** is a group of words that does not contain a verb or its subject. A phrase is used as a single part of speech.

Wendy swims in the lake.

participial phrase • A **participial phrase** consists of a participle and its related words. A participial phrase is used in the same way as an adjective.

The candidate making the speech favors tax reforms.

gerund phrase • A **gerund phrase** consists of a gerund and its related words. A gerund phrase is used in the same way as a noun.

Ken enjoys conducting scientific experiments.

- An **infinitive phrase** consists of an infinitive and its related words. An infinitive phrase can be used as a noun, an adjective, or an adverb.

infinitive phrase

Henry learned to play the game. as a noun

Football is a game to play outside. as an adjective

They entered the cave to find the treasure. as an adverb

- A **clause** is a group of words containing a verb and its subject.

clause

- An **independent clause** is a group of words that contains a subject and a verb. It can stand alone as a simple sentence.

independent clause

As you type the letter, the words appear on a computer screen.

- A **dependent,** or **subordinate, clause** is a group of words containing a verb and its subject. A subordinate clause cannot stand alone as a sentence and is used with an independent clause to form a complex sentence.

subordinate clause

As you type the letter, the words appear on a computer screen.

- An **adjective clause** is a subordinate clause that modifies a noun or a pronoun. It often begins with a relative pronoun *(who, whom, whose, which, that).*

adjective clause

Clara Barton was a nurse who founded the American Red Cross.

- An **adverb clause** is a subordinate clause that modifies a verb, an adjective, or an adverb. It begins with a subordinating conjunction.

adverb clause

As she combed her hair, she sang cheerful songs.

Common Subordinating Conjunctions		
after although as as if as long as as soon as because	before if since so that than though unless	until when whenever where wherever while

misplaced modifier

- A **misplaced modifier** is a modifier incorrectly placed in a sentence so that the meaning is unclear or distorted. A modifier should be placed as close as possible to the word or words it modifies.

  correct: In the newspaper, she read about the circus that opened.

  incorrect: She read about the circus that opened in the newspaper.

  correct: I watched the polar bear pacing in its cage.

  incorrect: Pacing in its cage, I watched the polar bear.

noun clause

- A **noun clause** is a subordinate clause that is used in the same way as a noun.

  Whoever designed this building included plenty of windows.

Capitalization

- Capitalize the first letter in the first word of a sentence. **sentence**

  The flight from San Francisco will arrive in ten minutes.

- **Proper nouns,** such as titles of people, place names, dates, and holidays, are always capitalized. **proper nouns**

names and titles of people	Mr. Evan Hall; Dr. Julia Martinez; John E. Ridd, Jr.; Captain Kelly; President Jefferson; Aunt Nancy; Ms. Gomez
months, days of the week	August, Monday
events, holidays	World Series, Memorial Day, New Year's Eve
historic events and periods	Civil War, French Revolution, Industrial Revolution, Renaissance, Middle Ages
streets	Park Avenue, Main Street, Route 80
states, provinces, cities, and counties	Kansas, Ontario, Los Angeles, New Orleans, Stark County
countries	Uganda, France
continents	Asia, Europe
heavenly bodies	North Star, Earth, Milky Way, Neptune Exceptions: sun, moon. The word *earth* is capitalized only when it refers to the planet Earth.
geographical terms	New England, Arctic Circle, Pacific Ocean, the West Exceptions: north, east, south, west as compass directions
buildings and bridges	Texas Stadium, Alamo, Wrigley Building, Golden Gate Bridge
monuments	Lincoln Memorial
institutions, clubs, and organizations	Rockefeller Junior High, Dallas Photography Club, Weight Watchers, American Cancer Society

companies	M artinez and A ssociates, F red's F urniture
brand names	C ampbell's soup, P arker pens
government bodies	C ongress, S enate, C abinet, S upreme C ourt
documents	G ettysburg A ddress, B ill of R ights, D eclaration of I ndependence, M agna C harta
school subjects	L anguage A rts III, S ocial S tudies IV
languages	C hinese, E nglish, S wahili, K orean, S panish
races and nationalities	C aucasian, I ndian, S panish, C anadian
religious names and terms	C hristianity, J udaism, I slam, G od, J ehovah, A llah
awards	N obel P rize, C ongressional M edal of H onor

abbreviation • An **abbreviation** is a shortened form of a word. Many abbreviations are capitalized and followed by a period.

titles of people	Mister = M r., Mistress = M rs., Doctor = D r., Junior = J r., Senior = S r., Captain = C apt., Sergeant = S gt., Professor = P rof.
addresses	Street = S t., Road = R d., Boulevard = B lvd., Circle = C ir., Avenue = A ve., Lane = L n., Drive = D r., North = N ., South = S ., Post Office = P . O ., Rural Delivery = R . D .
states	Alaska = AK , Vermont = VT , Alabama = AL
businesses	Company = C o., Corporation = C orp., Incorporated = I nc.
organizations	North Atlantic Treaty Organization = NATO , Parent-Teacher Association = PTA
calendar items	Saturday = S at., Thursday = T hurs., August = A ug., January = J an. (May, June, July are never abbreviated.)
time	midnight to noon = A.M. noon to midnight = P.M.
units of measure	quart = qt., kilogram = kg, pound = lb., mile = mi., feet = ft., kilometer = km, inch = in.

- Proper adjectives are always capitalized. — proper adjectives

  Italian opera Spanish dancing Canadian football

- The pronoun *I* is always capitalized. — *I*

  My sister and I will enter the triathlon.

- Capitalize the first words of the greeting, the closing, and the term used to identify the receiver of the letter. — parts of a letter

  Dear Sirs:

  Yours truly,

- Capitalize the first word, the last word, and all important words in the titles of books, stories, newspapers, movies, and songs. Do not capitalize short or unimportant words such as articles, coordinating conjunctions, or prepositions unless they come at the beginning or end of the title. — titles

  Everyone should read "How to Escape a Fire."

  Pat will never forget reading A Separate Peace.

- Capitalize the first word of a quotation. If the second part of a divided quotation is a new sentence, begin with a capital letter. If the second part is a continuation of the first sentence, do not use a capital letter. — direct quotations

  The teller asked, "What kind of account would you like to open?"

  "A checking account would be best," replied Colleen. "It will be for the money from the paper route."

  "Once you deposit your money," the teller explained, "you can begin writing checks."

- Use a capital letter for the first letter of the first word of headings and subheadings. Write Roman numerals as capital letters. Use capital letters to indicate subtopics in an outline. — outline

  I. Introduction

  II. Sporting dogs

  A. Retrievers

  B. Setters

WRITER'S HANDBOOK Mechanics

bibliography

- In a bibliography capitalize the author's last name and first name, the publishing company's name, the title of the book or magazine, and the place of publication.

  Berger, Gilda. Women, Work, and Wages. New York: Franklin Watts, 1986.

Punctuation

end marks

- End every sentence with a period, a question mark, or an exclamation point.

  Marina spent the day browsing through the mall .

  What is the price of this jacket ?

  What a delicious pie !

period

- Use a period at the end of a declarative or an imperative sentence.

  Jim wants to have a career in politics .

  Vote for a leader with proven ability .

- Use periods after initials that stand for a person's name.

  D. W. Griffith   T. S. Eliot

- Use periods after most abbreviations.

  Prof. Burns

  2:00 P.M., Mon., Oct. 2

  3 ft. 7 in., 1 lb.

- Use a period after each Roman numeral, letter, or number that precedes a topic or a subtopic in an outline.

  Volcanoes

  I. Introduction

  II. Formation

  A. Heat below earth's surface

  1. Geothermal gradient

  2. Melting magma

  B. Pressure

WRITER'S HANDBOOK • Mechanics

- The final period of a direct quotation is written inside the end quotation mark. End each sentence of a direct quotation with the proper end mark.

  The museum guide said, "Feel free to wander around the exhibit. This is a display of modern art . "

- Use commas to separate three or more words in a series. Use a comma after each word except the last.

  comma

  Adam enjoys archery , skiing , hockey , and gymnastics.

- Use a comma before the coordinating conjunction that joins the clauses of a compound sentence.

  I whistled loudly for Rufus , and he came bounding across the yard.

- Use a comma to separate the clauses of a complex sentence if the subordinate clause comes first.

  After we watched the game , we went to a Chinese restaurant.

- Use commas to set off most appositives. Do not use commas to set off appositives that are necessary to identify the nouns they follow.

  Gene Rose , the tennis coach , gave me some good advice.

  Practice your serve , the most important part of the game.

  I have just read the book Misty of Chincoteague .

- Use commas to separate a nonrestrictive clause from the rest of a sentence.

  My brother , who attends Michigan State , is an engineering student.

- Use commas to set off parenthetical expressions, such as *in fact*, *for example*, *in my opinion*, and *of course*.

  Fresh vegetables are , of course , an important part of any diet.

- Use a comma to set off a noun of direct address from the rest of a sentence.

  Beth , please explain the process of photosynthesis.

  Tell us about that plant , Mr. Allen.

  Do you realize , Elda , that the plants need sunlight?

- Use a comma after introductory words, such as *yes, no, why,* and *well*.

No , Mark has not returned from the choral concert.

Yes , he left the hall quite late.

- Use a comma after two prepositional phrases at the beginning of a sentence.

In the alley behind our apartment , Troy learned to ride a bike.

- Use a comma after a participial phrase at the beginning of a sentence.

Glancing at her watch , Mona realized that she was already late.

- Use a comma between the city and the state and between the day and the year.

February 8 , 19––   Steamboat Springs , CO 80477

- Use a comma after the greeting of a friendly letter.

Dear Julio ,

- End the closing of a letter with a comma.

Sincerely yours ,

- Separate a direct quotation from the rest of a sentence with a comma.

Joanna asked , "Do you know how to play this game?"

"Let's read the rules , " Paul suggested.

semicolon

- Use a semicolon to join the parts of a compound sentence when you do not use a conjunction.

The basketball team practiced hard ; they finally won a game.

colon

- Use a colon to set off a list of items when the list is preceded by a noun or a noun phrase to which the list refers.

You may wish to enter the following events : canoeing, tennis, archery, and hockey.

- Use a colon to separate the hour and the minutes in numerals that indicate time.

9 : 30 A.M.   12 : 00 P.M.

- Use a hyphen to divide a word at the end of a line and to write some compound words. **hyphen**

  Each of the forty - seven members of the foresters' associa - tion attended the banquet.

- Use parentheses to enclose explanatory material that is not necessary to the meaning of the sentence. **parentheses**

  First, sauté (quickly fry) the onions in peanut oil.

- Use a dash to show an abrupt change in thought within a sentence. **dash**

  This program — an excellent recycling plan — reduces waste.

- Add an apostrophe and *s* to a singular noun to form the possessive noun. **apostrophe**

  The camel's hump stores its food reserve.

  Charles's dog can perform many tricks.

- Add only an apostrophe to a plural noun ending in *s* to form the possessive noun.

  All the photographers' passes were checked at the entrance.

- Form the possessive of a plural noun that does not end in *s* by adding an apostrophe and *s*.

  Bobbi volunteered to clean all of the mice's cages.

- Use an apostrophe to replace the letters that are omitted when you write a contraction.

  If you'd like to work here, I'll recommend you for the opening we have.

- Place quotation marks around a direct quotation. A period or comma at the end of a quotation is always placed inside the end quotation mark. **quotation marks**

  " There is poison ivy by that tree ," Jeremy warned.

- If the quotation is a question or an exclamation, the question mark or exclamation point goes inside the end quotation mark.

  " How many islands have you visited ?" asked Judy.

  " I left my briefcase in the taxi !" cried Mrs. Yost.

- Use quotation marks to designate titles of short works such as short stories, poems, magazine and newspaper articles, chapters of books, and songs.

  Reading the article " Making Exercise Fun " helped me enjoy my workout.

underline

- In printed works, italics are used to designate the following kinds of titles. However, if you are writing or typing, use underlining.

books	The Red Pony
magazines	Time
newspapers	Miami Herald
movies	Gone with the Wind
plays	Romeo and Juliet
television series	Perfect Strangers
works of art	Mona Lisa
long musical works	Rite of Spring
planes, trains, ships	Queen Elizabeth II

Troublesome Words

- Use *accept* when you mean "to receive."
  Use *except* as a verb that means "to leave out" or as a preposition that means "excluding."

  accept, except

  He has decided to accept the nomination.

  Everyone was pleased except his opponent.

- Use *all ready* when you mean "prepared," "available," or "willing."
  Use *already* when you mean "prior to now," "previously" or "so soon."

  all ready, already

  The actors are all ready to go on stage.

  I have already seen this play.

- Use *complement* when you mean "something that completes."
  Use *compliment* when you mean "to praise or flatter."

  complement, compliment

  A new red tie would complement your outfit.

  I must compliment you on your fine performance.

- Use *formally* when you mean "properly " or "strictly."
  Use *formerly* when you mean "previously."

  formally, formerly

  Nelson dressed formally for the dance.

  Kris was formerly a sports announcer.

- Use *later* when you mean "more delayed" or "beyond the usual time."
  Use *latter* when you mean "the second of the things mentioned."

  later, latter

  Is there a later flight to Tucson?

  I have both records and cassettes, but I prefer the latter .

- *Principal* as an adjective means "main, major, or most important." The noun *principal* means "chief, head, or director."
  Principle means "basic rule, method, or general truth."

  principal, principle

  What were the principal causes of World War II?

  Mrs. Hall is principal of our school.

  Our country was founded on the principle of democracy.

respectfully, respectively

- *Respectfully* means "thoughtfully, politely."
  Respectively means "in the order given."

  Neil addressed the reporters **respectfully**.

  The president and the treasurer are Mark and Lois, **respectively**.

their, there, they're

- *Their* means "belonging to them."
  There means "in that place."
  They're is a contraction meaning "they are."

  The athletes carried **their** equipment to the locker room.

  After reading about Texas, I am eager to go **there**.

  The Driscolls are late because **they're** stuck in traffic.

then, than

- Use *then* as an adverb that tells when.
  Use *than* as a conjunction.

  Back **then**, I was more active **than** I am now.

to, two, too

- Use *to* when you mean "in the direction of."
  Use *two* to indicate the number.
  Use *too* when you mean "also."

  Carla returned the sweater **to** the store.

  Beth and James bought the last **two** umbrellas.

  School was closed today and will be tomorrow **too**.

Easily Confused Verb Pairs

lie, lay

- Use *lie* when you mean "to rest or recline."
  Use *lay* when you mean "to place or put."

  Our dogs **lie** in front of the fireplace on cold nights.

  Would you **lay** the packages on that bench?

sit, set

- Use *sit* when you mean "to take a seat."
  Use *set* when you mean "to place or put."

  Ramón and María usually **sit** in the booth by the window.

  Set the casserole in a convenient place.

bring, take

- Use *bring* when you mean "to carry from there to here."
  Use *take* when you mean "to carry from here to there."

  Did you **bring** your book with you? **Take** your mail out.

- Use *lend* when you mean "to give something that must be given back."
  Use *borrow* when you mean "to take something that must be given back."

  lend, borrow

  They borrow our rake every month.

  We lend it to them because we know they will bring it back.

- Use *rise* when you mean "to get up" or "go up."
  Use *raise* when you mean "to lift" or "to grow."

  rise, raise

  The temperature rises quickly on summer mornings.

  Todd raised his voice in the noisy factory.

- Use *leave* when you mean "to go away from."
  Use *let* when you mean "to allow."

  leave, let

  Mom will leave the meeting at noon.

  Did the coach let you go home early?

Use *learn* when you mean "to gain knowledge."
Use *teach* when you mean "to instruct."

learn, teach

Eventually, he will learn to speak French.

I can only teach him so much in one hour.

Pronouns

- Use *its* when you mean "belonging to."
  Use *it's* when you mean "it is" or "it has."

  its, it's

  Pick up the pitcher by its handle.

  It's wise to check your tires before a long trip.

  It's been a cold winter.

- Use *your* when you mean "belonging to you."
  Use *you're* when you mean "you are."

  your, you're

  Stretch your muscles before you start to run.

  You're eligible to compete in the race.

I, me
- Use *I* as a subject or as a predicate nominative.
Use *me* as a direct object, an indirect object, or the object of a preposition.

My companion and **I** waited for the bus together. **subject**

It was **I** who made the reservations. **predicate nominative**

Last year, he took **me** with him. **direct object**

Dad brought Craig and **me** souvenirs from his trip. **indirect object**

Would you like to go with **me** next year? **object of a preposition**

this, that, these, those
- Use *this, that, these,* and *those* as demonstrative pronouns when they take the place of nouns.

This is an expensive milking machine.

That is an old model.

These are the older cows.

Those are our best cows.

subject pronouns
- Use a subject pronoun as the subject of a sentence or as a predicate nominative. A subject pronoun is in the nominative case.

She won the 100-yard dash. **subject**

It was **she** who broke the state record. **predicate nominative**

object pronouns
- Use an object pronoun as a direct object, an indirect object, or an object of a preposition. An object pronoun is in the objective case.

I helped **him** with his homework. **direct object**

We gave **him** a present. **indirect object**

Billy walks to school with **him**. **object of a preposition**

who, whom, whose
- Use *who* as a subject.
Use *whom* as an object.
Use *whose* as an interrogative pronoun or as a possessive pronoun.

Who is the captain of the team? **subject**

By **whom** was the book written? **object**

Whose is this? **interrogative pronoun**

Whose book is that? **possessive pronoun**

Adjectives

- Use *this, that, these,* and *those* as adjectives when they precede a noun. They point out specific persons, places, or things.

this, that, these, those

This farmer raises cattle.

That farm produces milk and other dairy products.

These cows need to be milked.

Those cows have been milked.

- The adjectives *good, well, bad, ill, much, many,* and *little* (amount) have irregular forms of comparison.

irregular forms of comparison

Positive	Comparative	Superlative
good, well	better	best
bad, ill	worse	worst
much, many	more	most
little	less, lesser	least

Timmy is a good soccer player.

Michael is a better soccer player.

In fact, Michael is the best player on the team.

Adverbs

- Use *really* as an adverb; use *real* as an adjective.

real, really

The last quarter of the football game was really exciting.

Your understanding shows me you are a real friend.

- Use *well* as an adverb; use *good* as an adjective.

well, good

After six years of lessons, Judy plays the piano quite well .

You have given me a good reason to straighten up my room.

- Use *badly* as an adverb; use *bad* as an adjective.

badly, bad

Luckily, Patrick was not badly hurt in the accident.

That little dog has a very bad disposition.

- Use *surely* as an adverb; use *sure* as an adjective.

surely, sure

After weeks of practice, John rode surely and proudly.

Mai is sure she can win the chess tournament.

almost, most

- Use *almost* as an adverb; use *most* as an adverb or as an adjective.

  Pete almost forgot his airline ticket. adverb

  My visit to the beach was most relaxing. adverb

  What do most people think about the upcoming debate? adjective

irregular forms of comparison

- The adverbs *well, badly, much, little,* and *far* have irregular forms of comparison.

Positive	Comparative	Superlative
well	better	best
badly	worse	worst
much	more	most
little	less	least
far	farther	farthest

  Eddie can throw the football far down the field.

  Vince can throw the ball even farther.

  Jack can throw the ball the farthest of all.

Prepositions

at, to

- Use *at* to indicate that someone or something is already in a certain place.
  Use *to* to show movement toward a place.

  Both buses were waiting at the gate.

  Sarah and Bess hurried to the gate.

in, into

- Use *in* when you mean "already inside."
  Use *into* when you mean "moving from the outside to the inside of something."

  The students waited in the classroom.

  The students came into the classroom.

between, among

- Use *between* when you refer to two things.
  Use *among* when you refer to three or more things.

  The chess game between Bob and Ed was a draw.

  The tournament was played among five chess clubs.

- Use *beside* when you mean "at the side of."
  Use *besides* when you mean "in addition to."

beside, besides

The new shopping center is beside the post office.

No one besides my uncle has been there.

Agreement

- A verb must agree with its subject in number. The *number* of a word refers to whether that word is singular or plural. In a sentence, a subject and its verb must both be singular or both be plural.

subject-verb agreement

Edna enjoys hiking in the forest.

They enjoy fishing in the stream.

- Use a plural verb with most compound subjects joined by *and*.

verb agreement with compound subject

The plumber and the electrician are ready to start working.

- Use a singular verb with compound subjects that are normally thought of as a unit.

Spaghetti and meatballs is my favorite meal.

- If a compound subject contains both a singular and a plural subject and uses a conjunction other than *and*, make the verb agree with the subject closer to the verb.

Either my father or my brothers attend my games.

Either my brothers or my father attends my games.

- Collective nouns can be singular or plural. If a collective noun refers to a group as a whole, it is singular. If it refers to individuals in the group, it is plural.

verb agreement with collective noun

The jury are not in agreement.

The jury is in the judge's chambers.

- A noun that states the time of day is singular. A noun that states a block of time can be singular or plural.

verb agreement with time and money nouns

Four o'clock is the best time to play.

Three hours is (are) not enough to get to the game.

- A noun that states a sum of money is singular unless individual units are described.

Five dollars is the admission price.

There are the five dollars I received as tips.

verb agreement with organizations

- The proper name of an organization is singular. If individual members of an organization are referred to, the noun is plural.

The United States Senate is in session this week.

The Boy Scouts of America buy their own uniforms.

titles

- The title of any work, even if plural in form, is singular and takes a singular verb.

One Hundred American Poems is the book required for this class.

irregular noun plurals

- Some nouns that are singular in meaning but written as plurals take plural verbs.

These trousers are my favorite pair.

The scissors are in the top drawer of the desk.

- Some nouns are written as plurals but take singular verbs.

The mumps is a common childhood disease.

Nuclear physics is a controversial branch of science.

subject pronoun and verb

- A verb should agree with the pronoun when the pronoun is the subject of the sentence. The form of a subject pronoun changes, depending on whether it is singular or plural.

He works for the State Department.

They work for the Justice Department.

pronoun and antecedent

- A pronoun should agree with its antecedent in number and gender.

The boys worked together on their science projects. **number**

Albert was pleased with his second-place ribbon. **gender**

Paragraph

- A **paragraph** is a group of sentences that tell about one main idea. A paragraph often begins with a **topic sentence.** The topic sentence expresses the main idea of a paragraph. It tells what all the other sentences in a paragraph are about. The other sentences in a paragraph are called **detail sentences.** Detail sentences add information about the topic. They help the audience understand the main idea.

paragraph

Writer's Guide: Paragraph
1. Write a topic sentence that clearly expresses the main idea of your paragraph. **2.** Indent the first line. **3.** Write detail sentences that support the main idea in your topic sentence.

The solar system is a group of planets that revolve around the sun. It consists of nine planets, four of which are made of solid materials and five of which are made of gases. Nearest to the sun are Mercury and Venus. Then there is Earth, the only planet in the system that has intelligent life. Then there is Mars. Next comes Jupiter, the largest planet in the solar system. Saturn, the giant ringed planet, is followed by Uranus and Neptune. Farthest away from the sun is Pluto, about which little is known. The solar system is only a tiny part of a galaxy, or family of stars, called the Milky Way.

topic sentence

detail sentences

How-to Paragraph

how-to paragraph

- In a **how-to paragraph** a writer gives directions or explains a process.

Writer's Guide: How-to Paragraph
1. Write a topic sentence that identifies the process you are explaining. 2. Write a detail sentence that lists any materials needed to complete the process. 3. Write detail sentences that explain the steps of the process in the order in which they need to be done. 4. Indicate the order of steps with time-order words such as *first, next, then, last,* and *finally*.

topic sentence

time-order words

Treating a snakebite victim requires quick action and immediate medical attention. First, see if you recognize the kind of snake before retreating from its striking range. Next, calm the victim, and splint the bitten body part, remembering to keep the bitten area below the heart. To make the splint, use a stick or other nearby object and a piece of cloth.

Get an experienced person to draw out the poison with a snakebite kit. This is only necessary if the bite is from a rattlesnake and medical care is over an hour away. Then, wash the bite with soap and water, and get the victim to a doctor or a hospital. See that the victim gets an antibiotic.

Paragraph of Comparison

- In a **paragraph of comparison** a writer shows ways in which two subjects are alike. The subjects may be people, places, things, or ideas.

paragraph of comparison

Writer's Guide: Paragraph of Comparison

1. Think of three or more ways your subjects are alike.
2. Write a topic sentence that identifies the two subjects and, if possible, names the qualities you will compare.
3. Write detail sentences that clearly explain the qualities the subjects have in common.
4. Write about the qualities in the same order in which you introduced them in the topic sentence.

The Thames and Hudson tunnels are alike in several significant ways. Just as the first tunnel lies under a river, the Thames, the second one is under a river, the Hudson. In both cases new methods were used to safeguard the builders who bored through the silt and clay. A cast-iron shield protected the Thames workers, while a shaft filled with compressed air was designed to protect the Hudson crew. Yet a dangerous accident occurred in each tunnel, and each accident led to a heroic rescue.

topic sentence

detail sentences explain similarities

Paragraph of Contrast

paragraph of contrast

- In a **paragraph of contrast** a writer explains the key differences between two subjects. The subjects may be people, places, things, or ideas.

Writer's Guide: Paragraph of Contrast

1. Think of three or more ways your subjects are different.
2. Write a topic sentence that identifies the two subjects and, if possible, names the qualities you will contrast.
3. Write detail sentences that clearly explain the differences between your subjects.
4. Write about the differences in the same order in which you introduced them in the topic sentence.

topic sentence

detail sentences showing differences

There are even more differences between the Hudson Tunnel and the Seikan Tunnel, a Japanese passageway opened in 1988. The Hudson Tunnel lies under a river; however, the Seikan crosses the Pacific Ocean from the mainland to Hokkaido. Instead of the Hudson's iron-and-brick lining, cement lines the Seikan Tunnel. Finally, a compressed air shaft that failed the Hudson workers was replaced by a shield in the Seikan project. Its representatives say their losses are considerable, though.

topic sentence

detail sentences showing differences

In other ways the Thames and Hudson tunnels had little in common. The Thames accident ended happily without a single death; however, twenty perished in the Hudson disaster. The Thames workers used picks and shovels, but the Hudson workers used drills and dynamite. After the accident, they, like the Thames workers, had a shield to protect them as they finished the tunnel. Last, there was a sixty-one-year difference between the dates on which the two tunnels opened. The first underwater tunnel ever constructed, the Thames, opened formally in 1843. The ceremonial opening of the Hudson occurred in 1904.

Cause-and-Effect Paragraphs

- In a **cause-and-effect paragraph** a writer focuses on a cause that results in certain effects or on an effect that can be traced back to its causes. This type of paragraph can begin with either the cause or the effect.

cause-and-effect paragraph

Writer's Guide: Cause-and-Effect Paragraph
1. Begin a paragraph that focuses on effect with a *cause*. Write a topic sentence that tells what happened. The detail sentences should all discuss *effects*. **2.** Begin a paragraph that focuses on cause with an *effect*. Write a topic sentence that identifies the effect. The detail sentences should all discuss *causes*. **3.** Write detail sentences in the order in which the effects or the causes happened.

A star called Supernova 1987A exploded in a blast that was visible from Earth on February 25, 1987. Supernova 1987A began as a very large star. Hydrogen in the star changed to helium. Other nuclear reactions occurred and increased until the outside atmosphere fell in on the core and bounced off it. The color of the star changed from blue to red to blue again before it collapsed.

effect

detail sentences discuss causes

The explosion of Supernova 1987A affected the universe in a number of ways. The exploding star sent off a blinding light. It shone as brightly as 100,000 suns. It blew off its outside atmosphere. Particles of the atmosphere formed into a cloudlike mass of dust and gas.

The cloudlike mass grew as the explosion of the star continued. The supernova hurled more debris into space, sent X rays and gamma rays to Earth, and formed into a dense star at the core. In this way the large star left a small remnant of itself at the center.

Persuasive Essay

persuasive essay

- In a **persuasive essay** the writer attempts to convince the audience to share the writer's point of view. Persuasive writing is used in newspaper editorials, speeches, business letters, and essays.

Writer's Guide: Persuasive Essay
1. Include your thesis statement in the introduction. **2.** Develop logical arguments based on reasons. **3.** Have evidence to support conclusions. **4.** Avoid faulty generalizations, bandwagon persuasion, name calling, and other propaganda techniques.

The Advertising Choice: Radio or Magazine?

thesis statement

What is the difference between 28,000 and 10,000? The answer, of course, is a number, the number of people we can reach for the same price through radio or magazine advertising. Research indicates that, for our needs, advertising through a magazine is wiser.

evidence

For our purposes, a major disadvantage of radio advertising is that it does not leave people with an order form they can use.

Also, the expense of reaching a single individual through radio is higher than through magazines. It would cost 2½ cents to reach one listener through a 60-second commercial, according to KISP radio. A commercial is a radio spot. For less than a penny, a ⅓-page magazine ad would reach one reader, says Advertising News.

A magazine advertisement would have an order form and could picture the Lexington Lions T-shirt and logo. In this way we would set up an image of ourselves.

Most important, magazines are a permanent medium. Because they last, the advertisements can be read by people again.

Also our club has the opportunity to attract even more customers by clipping the advertisements and posting them on, for example, supermarket bulletin boards.

In conclusion, magazine advertising is the most effective way of all for our club to spend the money that it has set aside to attract customers.

logical arguments

Description

description

- In a **description** a writer describes a person, a place, a thing, or an event by giving **sensory details**—that is, by using words that appeal to the senses. By using sensory details, the writer allows the audience to see, feel, hear, and sometimes taste and smell what is being described.

Writer's Guide: Description
1. Write a topic sentence that identifies your subject. 2. Write detail sentences that give specific information about your topic. 3. Choose details that contribute to the tone and mood you want to create. 4. Use sensory details to help the audience visualize your subject.

topic sentence

sensory details

The sun began to set across the gulf as I gazed with a smile at the pink sky. Here was exactly where I wanted to be. The smell of the salt spray awakened my senses and left me with a feeling of contentment and peace. I could hear the cry of the seagulls as they flew across the water, occasionally swooping down to catch a splashing fish. The temperature began to drop as the day came to a majestic end. As the fiery orb melted into the salty horizon, I realized how lucky I was and loudly applauded the show.

Dialogue

- In **dialogue** a writer tells the exact words that people say to one another.

dialogue

Writer's Guide: Dialogue

1. Place quotation marks before and after the exact words of a speaker.
2. Use a comma to separate a quotation from the rest of the sentence unless a question mark or an exclamation point is needed.
3. Begin a new paragraph each time the speaker changes.
4. Be sure that the dialogue sounds like real people talking.
5. Use verbs such as *said, called, answered, whispered,* and *shouted* to show how the speaker says the words.

"I'm afraid we are lost at sea, Sir," said Sailor Picardo, discouraged after the long sea voyage.

"Do not despair, Picardo. I do believe it won't be very long before we sight land," replied the captain reassuringly.

Looking out across the endless sea, Picardo muttered, "I wonder if I'll ever find riches and happiness in the new land."

"Picardo, do not let doubt enter your mind," urged the captain. "Once you set foot on the new land, you will know that this long, perilous voyage was well worth taking."

quotation marks

comma

Journal

journal • In a **journal** a writer records a day's significant events and expresses his or her thoughts and feelings about them. Each daily record is called an **entry.** Writers often use journals as idea banks.

Writer's Guide: Journal
1. Begin each entry with the date. **2.** Describe the important events of the day. **3.** Tell *who, what, when, where, why,* and *how* about each event. **4.** Describe your thoughts and feelings about the day's events, or record any special ideas that you might have.

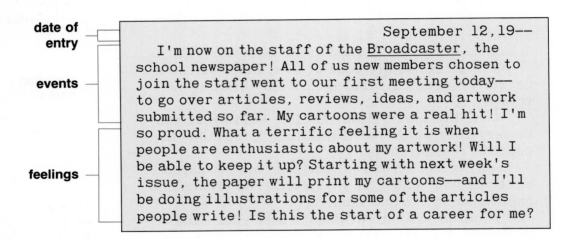

date of entry — September 12, 19—

events — I'm now on the staff of the Broadcaster, the school newspaper! All of us new members chosen to join the staff went to our first meeting today— to go over articles, reviews, ideas, and artwork submitted so far.

feelings — My cartoons were a real hit! I'm so proud. What a terrific feeling it is when people are enthusiastic about my artwork! Will I be able to keep it up? Starting with next week's issue, the paper will print my cartoons—and I'll be doing illustrations for some of the articles people write! Is this the start of a career for me?

Personal Narrative

- A **personal narrative** is a story in which a writer shares a significant experience in his or her life.

personal narrative

Writer's Guide: Personal Narrative
1. Use the first-person point of view in writing a personal narrative.
2. Write the details in sequential order to show the reader what happened.
3. Include details that show how you felt during the event.

I know how much you enjoy baseball, so you should appreciate this story. You know I'm a pinch hitter on the Piermont softball team.

first person point of view

Thursday was the big game against Central Junior High. We were losing 4 to 2 in the 7th inning. Suddenly, Carlota, our star hitter, hurt her ankle stepping in a hole while she ran to catch a fly ball. Then it was our turn at bat, bases were full, and Coach Greenley told me to hit for Carlota. I picked up my favorite bat and stood firmly in place with sweating hands and a racing heart. I waited for the first pitch.

I kept my eye on the ball, but the first pitch was a curve. I swung early and missed badly. I should have been ready for the second pitch, another curve. I prepared for the third pitch.

Now imagine this. It was strike two, my head was pounding, and I felt dazed but determined. I swung my bat to meet the third pitch, a fast ball that sped towards me like lightning. Smack! My hit flew over the first base and into right field. I only reached third, but everyone on base made it home, and the game ended 5 to 4 in our favor.

details written in sequential order

Write and tell me what you are doing on the Fourth of July. I wish we could spend it together. I really miss the fun we used to have here at Piermont.

Short Story

short story

- In a **short story** a writer uses imagination to create a fictional story with a beginning, a middle, and an ending. There are usually one or two main characters, dialogue, and a plot intended to appeal to a particular audience.

Writer's Guide: Short Story

1. With your audience in mind, brainstorm a main idea, characters, a setting, and a plot.
2. Plan the beginning, the middle, and the ending.
3. Use dialogue and concrete, descriptive details to show, rather than just tell, what happens.
4. Title your story.

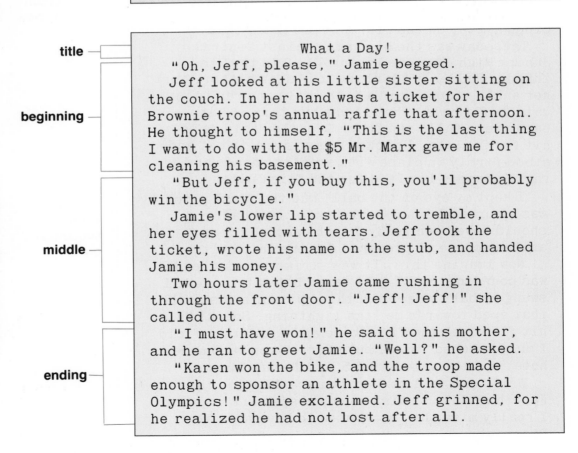

title — What a Day!

beginning —

"Oh, Jeff, please," Jamie begged.

Jeff looked at his little sister sitting on the couch. In her hand was a ticket for her Brownie troop's annual raffle that afternoon. He thought to himself, "This is the last thing I want to do with the $5 Mr. Marx gave me for cleaning his basement."

middle —

"But Jeff, if you buy this, you'll probably win the bicycle."

Jamie's lower lip started to tremble, and her eyes filled with tears. Jeff took the ticket, wrote his name on the stub, and handed Jamie his money.

Two hours later Jamie came rushing in through the front door. "Jeff! Jeff!" she called out.

ending —

"I must have won!" he said to his mother, and he ran to greet Jamie. "Well?" he asked.

"Karen won the bike, and the troop made enough to sponsor an athlete in the Special Olympics!" Jamie exclaimed. Jeff grinned, for he realized he had not lost after all.

Play

- In a **play** a writer tells a story that is intended to be acted out by performers. A play has characters, one or more settings, and a plot. The conversation between characters in a play is called **dialogue.** The writer includes **stage directions,** which tell the actors how to move, act, and speak.

play

Writer's Guide: Play
1. Use dialogue to tell the story. Let the characters' conversations show how the plot develops. When writing a play, do not use quotation marks to show what the characters say. **2.** Write clear stage directions that tell the actors exactly how to move, act, and speak. **3.** Stage directions are written in parentheses and are underlined. **4.** Be sure your play has interesting characters, realistic dialogue, and a well-developed plot. **5.** Give your play a title.

<u>from</u> Arthur's Adventures

SIR ECTOR (<u>Placing a hand on SIR KAY'S shoulder</u>): Son, you say you withdrew this sword from the anvil. In that case, you are the true king of England and should have no trouble placing it back in the anvil again.

SIR KAY (<u>Looking guilty and worried</u>): Who could possibly put a sword into a block of iron?

SIR ECTOR (<u>Firmly</u>): Whoever drew it out in the first place. (<u>KAY responds by taking hold of the sword, his face reddening with the effort as he tries frantically to thrust it into the iron. ARTHUR watches from behind.</u>)

ARTHUR (<u>Stepping forward from the background</u>): Father, please give me leave to try.

stage directions

dialogue

SIR ECTOR (Sternly yet tenderly): You? Why, Son, you are not yet even a knight! By what right would you try?

ARTHUR (Taking a deep breath): Sir, I can remain silent no longer. It is I who drew the sword from the anvil. It came easily enough then. It should not be too hard to thrust back now. (ARTHUR leaps up on the anvil, raises sword, bears down on it. With mild effort, sword slips into anvil. ARTHUR draws it out and places it back in again.)

SIR ECTOR (Kneeling before Arthur): Oh, now I know who your real father was. Now it is clear why Merlin brought me an infant to raise secretly as my own.

ARTHUR (Tearfully): Father, your words fill me with fear. Why do you kneel? (The sound of footsteps grows louder.)

MERLIN (Appearing from D L): He kneels because you are the rightful king. Have no fear, Arthur, for you will rule with the advice of many knights at a great round table, becoming the most glorious king this troubled realm has ever known.

Lyric Poem

lyric poem

- In a **lyric poem** a writer expresses feelings, usually in a songlike manner. Rather than telling stories about people, places, things, or ideas, the writer describes them. A lyric poem usually has a definite rhyme and rhythm. To help the audience see and feel as the writer does, a lyric poem often contains **figures of speech.** Similes and metaphors are figures of speech. In a **simile** a writer makes a comparison between two things, using the word *like* or *as*. In a **metaphor** a writer also makes a comparison but does not use *like* or *as*.

Writer's Guide: Lyric Poem

1. Use strong and colorful words to describe your subject.
2. To help make your feelings clear to the audience, use similes and metaphors.
3. Use rhyme and rhythm to develop feeling in your poem.
4. Give your poem a title.

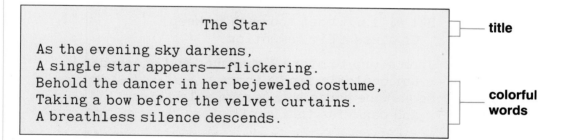

The Star — title

As the evening sky darkens,
A single star appears—flickering.
Behold the dancer in her bejeweled costume,
Taking a bow before the velvet curtains.
A breathless silence descends.

— colorful words

WRITER'S HANDBOOK • Composition

Narrative Poem

narrative poem

- A **narrative poem** tells a story in verse. It may be historical, humorous, or autobiographical.

Writer's Guide: Narrative Poem
1. Use carefully chosen words to create a mood. **2.** Write your stanzas in a sequential order that tells a story. **3.** Give your poem a title.

title

stanzas tell a story sequentially

carefully chosen words create a mood

The Quest
by Kimiko Hanaka

It's very hard to choose a gift
For Dad on Father's Day--
A present that is adequate
For all I want to say,

A present that conveys respect
And filial devotion,
But will not cost too much to keep,
Or cause a big commotion.

From store to store I searched and browsed
But couldn't find a thing.
Bookstore bargains, garage sale tries
And canaries that can't sing.

My dad dislikes my taste in books,
So I save hard-earned cash,
And do not give him my great finds,
Which he'd burn with the trash.

And music's just as bad, as are
Fine prints, and plants, and art.
It's best that I eliminate
Such items from the start.

My dad hates noise; he cringes if
There's buzzing, clacking, squawking.
My dad wears earplugs so he won't
Be bothered by my talking.

WRITER'S HANDBOOK • Composition

So pets are out--from yapping dog
  To soft and woolly monkey.
They take up room, make lots of noise,
  And special feed costs money.

And after-shave is out, and so
  Are razors, brush, and comb.
My father has a beard, you see,
  And no hair on his dome.

I gave my dad a nice new pair
  Of woolly socks with love.
They were his favorite color (black)
  And fitted like a glove.

But Mom has let me know that, since,
  He's used them for a rag.
Next Father's Day, I'll give a card
  Wrapped in a store-bought bag.

And then, just as I left the mall,
  Above the parking lot
I saw a bright hot-air balloon--
  And thought, "Of course! Why not?"

"This is a gift Dad can't return,
  Or burn, or throw away.
A ride in the sky is what I'll buy
  My dad for Father's Day!"

Character Sketch

character sketch

- In a **character sketch** a writer describes a real or an imaginary person. The writer tries to give the audience an accurate account of the person's appearance and personality.

  The writer may state opinions about a particular character or may reveal a character's personality by describing the things he or she does. A writer may also tell about a character by describing the reactions of others around him or her.

Writer's Guide: Character Sketch

1. In the topic sentence, identify the person and try to capture the audience's interest by stating an interesting detail about him or her.
2. In the detail sentences, describe how the person looks and moves.
3. Tell what the person does that makes him or her special. Give clear examples.
4. Describe a situation in which the person showed his or her special qualities.

topic sentence

detail sentences

"Is everyone ready?" asks Dad, his lively eyes expecting a yes. He smiles warmly with a quick flash of his pearl-white teeth. That is Father for you, always on the move, with eyes as quick as a blue jay's and legs that propel him as rapidly as wings. His energy is visible in a tan that never leaves his well-bronzed skin and waves that ripple tirelessly through his brown hair. Always rushing, he dresses somewhat haphazardly. Sometimes the colors don't match, or a shirttail hangs out like an untied bow.

A vigorous handshake is Father's way of greeting the average stranger, whom he is apt to treat like a best friend. In conversation, he clowns a great deal, refusing to take everyday matters too seriously. He speaks hurriedly like someone with a heavy accent who has to catch a plane, and in times of trouble the pace quickens making him less understandable. Sometimes his temper rises and explodes. Then he is a volcano that can't be stopped. Most often, though, he's as calm as water on a windless day.

The energy Father has for others spills over into his own activities, too. His enthusiasm and continual interest in people make him the perfect salesman. I ask myself if he ever feels depressed or dispirited because his energy seems as dependable as the sun. On the tennis court, the man is a tiger, ready to pounce on his prey. Afterward, the person whom he beats gets some friendly advice on how to strengthen his or her game, and then my father suggests a rematch.

special qualities shown

News Story

news story

In a **news story** a writer provides information about a person, a group, an event, an object, or an issue. A news story has three parts: the lead, the body, and the headline. The **lead** is the first paragraph of a news story. It tells *who, what, where, when, why,* and sometimes *how* something happened. The rest of the news story is called the **body.** It gives more details about the lead. The title of a news story is called the **headline.**

Writer's Guide: News Story

1. Write a lead that answers the six news-gathering questions.
2. In the body of the news story, give more details about the lead. Write the most important details first.
3. Write a short, interesting headline. Use a strong verb to attract the attention of the audience.

headline

New Restaurant Offers Student Discount

lead

At the opening ceremonies yesterday for Penny's Pantry, a new luncheonette at 412 Elm Street, Penny Uggins, the owner, announced that she will give Elm Street Middle School students a 10 percent discount on all purchases.

body

Penny's Pantry will be open seven days a week from 7 A.M. until 7 P.M. Specialties of the house include grilled sandwiches, homemade soups, and Penny's homemade bread and muffins.

"I tried the cherry muffins, and they're great!" exclaimed Rick Hartley, an eighth-grade student at Elm Street Middle School.

According to owner Uggins, "If this luncheonette is successful, I am planning to open another Penny's Pantry on the west side of town." Uggins added, "I'm really looking forward to serving students from the middle school."

Book Report

- In a **book report** a writer summarizes the important events in a book. The writer also gives his or her opinion of the book.

book report

Writer's Guide: Book Report
1. In your first sentence, give the title of the book and the name of the author. Remember to underline the title of the book.
2. Write a summary of the important events. Include the main idea, the names of the main characters, and some interesting details. Do not tell the ending.
3. Tell why a person might or might not like the book, or give your opinion of the book. Support your opinion with reasons.

In A Different Season, by David Klass, a strong friendship develops between Jim Roark, star pitcher and captain of his school baseball team, and Jenny Douglas, an outstanding female athlete at the same school. However, when Jenny announces her intention to become the first female player on the varsity baseball team, Jim has difficulty coming to terms with the idea.

Told from Jim's point of view, the novel explores the issues of coed varsity sports, jealousy among friends, and conflicts with a father. In addition, several baseball games are described.

I enjoyed reading A Different Season. The author combines the fast-paced excitement of baseball with the conflicts of real-life relationships. I was left with a lot to think about concerning human interactions.

title
author
summary
opinion

Research Report

research report

- Research reports are written to find out more about a particular subject. To write a **research report,** a writer gathers information from several sources, takes notes from the sources, and organizes the notes into an outline. Then he or she writes the report based on the notes and the outline.

  Research reports are written for the purpose of answering a particular question. The research question should be identified in the beginning of the report. It should be answered by the time the conclusion has been reached.

  It is important that research topics are chosen carefully. Topics must not be too broad nor too limited.

Writer's Guide: Research Report

1. Use your notes and your outline to write your research report.
2. Write an introduction that identifies your topic. Include interesting sentences to capture the attention of the audience.
3. Write one paragraph for each subtopic in your outline.
4. Follow your outline as you write details about your topic.
5. Give your research report a title.

introduction identifies topic

details

The Shaker Tradition

Did you ever hear about Shakers? The Shakers were a religious society of men and women who lived in nearly twenty locations in the eastern United States. This was before the Industrial Revolution. What they left the world are their designs for implements and furniture.

The Shaker ideals of simplicity and permanence are seen in their works. The Shakers were determined to perform each task efficiently and thriftily. They therefore contributed inventions or improvements in many areas of everyday life.

They are responsible for the invention of the flat broom, the pill form of medicine, the circular saw (developed by a Shaker woman in 1810), the common clothespin, a revolving oven, a pea sheller, and a tool for paring, coring, and quartering apples, among many other things.

The continued use of many of their inventions and improvements and the lasting popularity of Shaker furniture designs are testimony to both their skillfulness and the ideals behind it. Their creations were planned to last, never to become outdated, and to have a look of simplicity.

Professor John T. Kirk, a specialist in art history at Boston University and an authority on American furniture, says that Shaker designs have made an important contribution to furniture design in the twentieth century.

Friendly Letter

friendly letter

- In a **friendly letter** a writer sends informal greetings or news to a friend or a relative. A friendly letter has five parts: a heading, a greeting, a body, a closing, and a signature.

Writer's Guide: Friendly Letter

1. Write the heading in the upper right corner.
2. Start the greeting at the left margin.
3. Use paragraph form in the body. Tell personal news, and ask your friend or your relative questions.
4. Think about your reader and your purpose, and choose words accordingly.
5. Write the closing and your signature to line up with your heading. Capitalize only the first word in the closing.

heading

110 East 173rd Street
Chicago, Illinois 60638
October 4, 19--

greeting

Dear Jen,

body

Here's exciting news! Our school has a newspaper, and I'll be drawing cartoons for it each week! In addition to being excited, I'm also a bit nervous about having to think of a different cartoon every week.

Thanks for your letter--your new puppy certainly sounds mischievous. Keep me posted on her antics.

Are you planning to visit your cousins in Chicago during the Thanksgiving holiday? I hope so! We'll make the rounds of the holiday shop windows. Let me know about your plans. Write soon!

closing

Your friend,

signature

Maria

Business Letter

- In a **business letter** a writer usually makes a request or places an order for something. A business letter has six parts: a heading, an inside address, a greeting, a body, a closing, and a signature.

business letter

Writer's Guide: Business Letter
1. Put the heading in the upper right corner. **2.** Write the inside address at the left margin. **3.** Start the greeting at the left margin. If you know your reader's full name, use it. Be sure to precede it with a title (*Mr./Mrs./Ms.*) and follow it with a colon. **4.** Write the body in paragraph form. **5.** Be polite and brief, but be sure to include all the necessary information. **6.** Align the closing with the heading. *Yours truly* and *Sincerely* are appropriate closings. Sign your full name in ink under the closing. Type (or print) your full name under your signature.

403 East 291st Street New York, New York 10052 May 30, 19—	heading
Research and Scientific Services National Park Service Department of the Interior Washington, DC 20240	inside address
Dear Sir or Madam:	greeting
Please send a free copy of "Guide to National Parks of the United States" to the above address. Thank you.	body
Sincerely,	closing
Hannah Hiker	signature
Hannah Hiker	

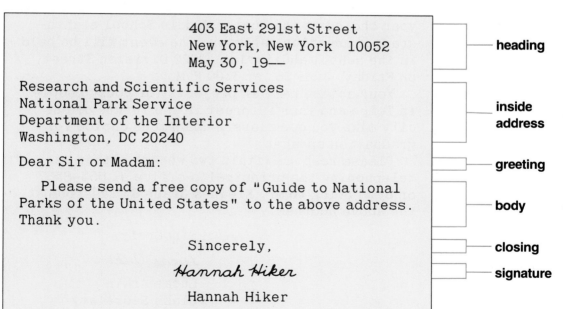

Invitation

invitation

- In an **invitation** a writer invites someone to come to a party or other event or to do something. An invitation has the same five parts as a friendly letter.

Writer's Guide: Invitation
1. Be sure to include a heading, a greeting, the body, a closing, and a signature. **2.** In the body, tell *who* is invited and *what* the invitation is for. **3.** Tell *when* and *where* the activity or the event will take place. Add any other special information your guest must know.

heading

Hunter Middle School
2020 Division Street
Tempe, Arizona 85282
March 15, 19--

greeting

Dear Mrs. Weekly,

body

You are invited to be the speaker on a topic of your choice at the Hunter Middle School eighth-grade graduation ceremony. The event will be held in the school auditorium, 2020 Division Street, on Friday, June 26, at 3:00 P.M.

Your active part in projects for young people in Tempe and your interest in the future of our city make you our class's unanimous choice for graduation speaker.

Please respond within two weeks, either by telephoning the principal's office at 555-8567 or by writing to Mr. Klein's Grade 8 Classroom at the above address.

closing

Sincerely,

signature

Lucas Arkin

Lucas Arkin
Class Secretary

WRITER'S HANDBOOK • Composition

Thank-You Note

- In a **thank-you note** a writer expresses thanks or appreciation for a gift or a special favor. A thank-you note has the same five parts as a friendly letter.

thank-you note

Writer's Guide: Thank-You Note
1. Be sure to include a heading, a greeting, the body, a closing, and a signature. **2.** In the body, tell why you are thanking the person. **3.** If you have been a visitor somewhere, tell why you enjoyed yourself. **4.** If you received a gift, tell how you are using it. **5.** If someone has done a special favor for you, express your appreciation and explain why it was important to you.

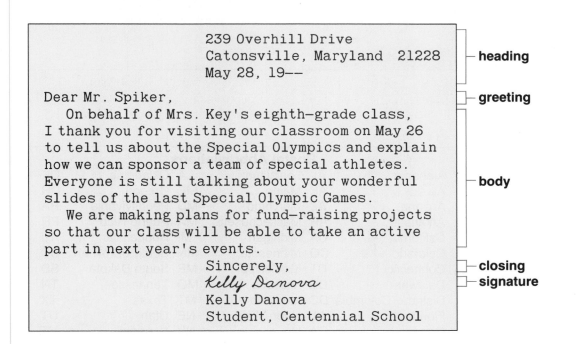

```
                          239 Overhill Drive
                          Catonsville, Maryland  21228      — heading
                          May 28, 19--
Dear Mr. Spiker,                                            — greeting
   On behalf of Mrs. Key's eighth-grade class,
I thank you for visiting our classroom on May 26
to tell us about the Special Olympics and explain
how we can sponsor a team of special athletes.
Everyone is still talking about your wonderful              — body
slides of the last Special Olympic Games.
   We are making plans for fund-raising projects
so that our class will be able to take an active
part in next year's events.
                          Sincerely,                        — closing
                          Kelly Danova                      — signature
                          Kelly Danova
                          Student, Centennial School
```

Envelope

envelope

- An **envelope** is used to send a letter or a note. The **mailing address** is the address of the person who will receive the letter. It is written near the center of the envelope. The **return address** is the address of the person who writes the letter. It is written in the upper left corner. **Postal abbreviations** are used for state names. The **ZIP code** is written after the state abbreviation.

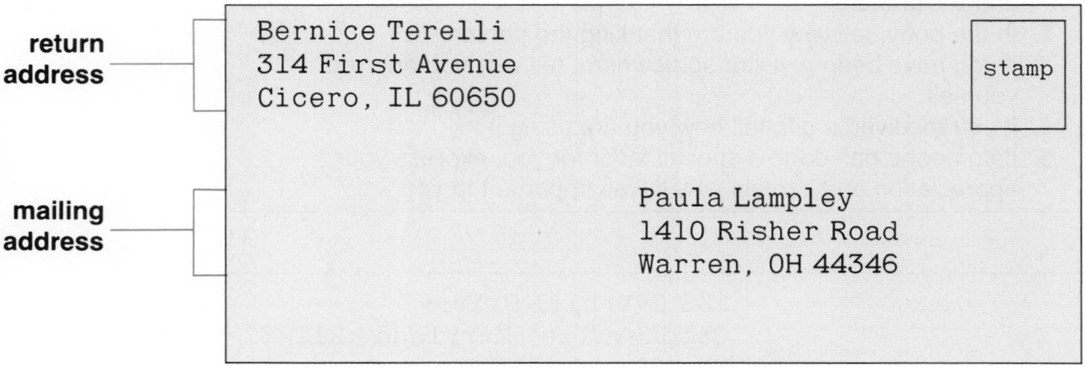

Postal Abbreviations

Alabama	AL	Louisiana	LA	Oklahoma	OK
Alaska	AK	Maine	ME	Oregon	OR
Arizona	AZ	Maryland	MD	Pennsylvania	PA
Arkansas	AR	Massachusetts	MA	Puerto Rico	PR
California	CA	Michigan	MI	Rhode Island	RI
Colorado	CO	Minnesota	MN	South Carolina	SC
Connecticut	CT	Mississippi	MS	South Dakota	SD
Delaware	DE	Missouri	MO	Tennessee	TN
District of Columbia	DC	Montana	MT	Texas	TX
Florida	FL	Nebraska	NE	Utah	UT
Georgia	GA	Nevada	NV	Vermont	VT
Hawaii	HI	New Hampshire	NH	Virginia	VA
Idaho	ID	New Jersey	NJ	Washington	WA
Illinois	IL	New Mexico	NM	West Virginia	WV
Indiana	IN	New York	NY	Wisconsin	WI
Iowa	IA	North Carolina	NC	Wyoming	WY
Kansas	KS	North Dakota	ND		
Kentucky	KY	Ohio	OH		

WRITER'S HANDBOOK • Composition

Vocabulary

- A **base word** is a complete word that cannot be divided into smaller parts and still retain its meaning. Other word parts may be added to base words to form new words.

base word

- A **root** is a word part to which prefixes, suffixes, base words, and other roots are added to form words.

root

Root	Meaning	Example
auto	self	autograph
bio	life	biology
dic, dict	say	dictate
gram, graph, grav	write	engrave
meter	measure	centimeter
micro	small	microfilm
photo	light	photosynthesis
scope, scopy	see	microscope
tele	distant	telescope
therm, thermo	heat	thermometer

- A **prefix** is a word part that is added to the beginning of a word to change its meaning or part of speech.

prefix

Prefix	Meaning	Example
de	down, from	decode
dis	opposite of, not	disagree
ex	out of, former	export
extra	outside of	extraterrestrial
fore	before, in front	foremost
inter	between, among	international
over	too much, above	overfill
post	after	postwar
pre	before	pretest
re	back, again	reconsider

Have you typed the code ?

Mr. Hanks offered to decode the letter.

I'm glad we agreed to see the movie.

Why did she disagree with me?

We visited a national park this summer.

The ranger said many international visitors enjoy the park.

negative prefix

- A **negative prefix** can mean "not," "opposite of," or "wrongly."

Prefix	Meaning	Example
il	not	illegal
im	not	impatient
in	not	inaccurate
ir	not	irregular
mis	wrongly, badly	misinterpret
non	not	nonfiction
un	not, opposite of	uncommon

You have a legal right to erect your sign.

The company was fined for illegal dumping.

Ed is patient with new employees.

He becomes impatient when they are late for work.

Val gave an accurate report of the meeting.

The record of attendance was slightly inaccurate .

suffix

- A **suffix** is a word part that is added to the end of a word. It usually changes the way a word is used in a sentence. Sometimes a suffix changes the meaning of a word. It may also change a word's part of speech.

Adjective Suffix	Meaning	Example
able, ible	able	changeable
al	belonging to, of	national
en	made of, like	golden
ful	full of	gleeful
ish	like, having	selfish
ive	tending to	productive
less	without	timeless
y	showing, having	healthy

The sunny day could change quickly.

The weather is changeable .

The nation heard the program.

An announcer gave the national news.

Hal laughed with glee.

Everyone heard his gleeful shouts.

Noun Suffix	Meaning	Example
ance, ence	act, state of	resistance
er, or	doer	surveyor
ion, tion	state of, action	introduction
ity, ty	quality	rarity
ment	action, result	agreement
ness	state of, quality	eagerness

Mr. Bond will survey our land.

He is a registered surveyor.

These old coins are rare.

Their rarity makes them valuable.

He is eager to make the baseball team.

His eagerness will be rewarded.

Verb Suffix	Meaning	Example
en, n	become, make	thicken
ify, fy	cause, make	mystify
ize	cause to be, make	harmonize

The pudding is thick.

Allow it to thicken some more.

What causes the noises is a mystery.

The sounds mystify everyone.

Listen to the singers' harmony.

They harmonize well.

- **Synonyms** are words that are similar in meaning.

synonyms

Karl was irritated when we arrived ten minutes late.

He was furious to hear we had lost the tickets.

antonyms • **Antonyms** are words that are opposite in meaning.

Howard is generous, but Ron is stingy.

homographs • **Homographs** are words that are spelled alike but have different meanings and sometimes different pronunciations.

The community will present a plaque to the fire company.

Everyone present at the ceremony applauded loudly.

homophones • **Homophones** are words that sound alike but have different meanings and spellings.

My brothers always groan when they are given chores to do.

The rosebush has grown rapidly this summer.

clipped word • A **clipped word** is formed when one or more syllables are dropped from a long word.

The movie star stepped out of a long black limo.
(clipped from the word *limousine*)

blended word • A **blended word** is formed when parts of two words are combined into one.

Amy invited several friends over for brunch.
(*breakfast* combined with *lunch*)

acronym • An **acronym** is a word formed from the first letters of a compound term or title.

She is a technician for NASA.
(National Aeronautics and Space Administration)

initialism • An **initialism** is an acronym in which each of the letters is pronounced.

We adopted a dog from the ASPCA.
(American Society for the Prevention of Cruelty to Animals)

multiple-meaning word • A **multiple-meaning word** has specialized meanings in more than one field or subject.

The two tennis players faced each other across the court.

An attorney will try your case in court.

Lancelot was the strongest knight in King Arthur's court.

Study Steps to Learn a Word

1. **Say** the word. Recall when you have heard the word used. Think about what it means.

2. **Look** at the word. Find any prefixes, suffixes, or other word parts you know. Think about other words that are related in meaning and spelling. Try to picture the word in your mind.

3. **Spell** the word to yourself. Think about the way each sound is spelled. Notice any unusual spelling.

4. **Write** the word while looking at it. Check the way you have formed your letters. If you have not written the word clearly or correctly, write it again.

5. **Check** your learning. Cover the word and write it. If you did not spell the word correctly, practice these steps until the word becomes your own.

Guidelines for Creating a Spelling Word List

You may want to keep your own spelling word list in a notebook. You can organize your spelling word list alphabetically, by subject areas, by parts of speech, or by other categories. Follow these guidelines.

1 Check your writing for words you have misspelled. Circle each misspelled word.

```
a (portible) radio
```

2 Find out how to spell the word correctly.
- Look up the word in a dictionary or a thesaurus.
- Ask a teacher or a classmate.

```
   portable
a (portible) radio
```

3 Write the word in your notebook.
- Spell the word correctly.
- Write a definition, a synonym, or an antonym to help you understand the meaning of the word.
- Use the word in a sentence.

```
portable--easily carried or moved
Kim has a portable typewriter.
```

4 When you write, look at your spelling word list to check your spelling.

```
Sue wants a portable TV.
```

Frequently Misspelled Words

airplane
absolutely
accepted
accidentally
admit
airplane
ankle
announced
apologize
arguing
argument
athlete
attractions
awful
awhile
barely
beginning
business
careful
carrying
castle
ceremony
clothes
commitment
commotion
congratulate
congratulations

cruise
cutest
dangerous
definitely
dessert
diamond
diploma
discipline
discussion
disgusted
double
downstairs
dropped
embarrass
embarrassed
engine
everyday
excellent
exclaimed
frantically
frightened
frustrated
gear
groceries
hobbies
guard

helmet
hopefully
hopped
immediately
incredible
interest
interior
interrupted
jealous
jewelry
license
lifted
losers
model
museum
occurred
opponent
ourselves
paid
picnic
pieces
pilot
preparation
principal
private
probably

receive
received
receiving
relief
restaurant
separated
shiny
skirt
souvenir
spirit
staring
stereo
surprise
teammates
temperatures
tension
themselves
trailer
video
waste
weird
whatever
whenever
whether
whose
wrecked

Vowel Sounds

short vowel sounds

- Each of the short vowel sounds /a/, /e/, /i/, /o/, and /u/ is usually spelled with one letter.

/a/ is spelled **a** as in *gnat*
/e/ is spelled **e** as in *extent*
/i/ is spelled **i** or **y** as in *bliss* or *lymph*
/o/ is spelled **o** as in *prop*
/u/ is spelled **u** or **o** as in *lunge* or *company*
Note: /e/ is sometimes spelled **ea** as in *heavy*

long vowel sounds

- Here are eight ways to spell /ā/.

a as in *gravy*
a-consonant-e as in *crate*
ai as in *explain*
ay as in *stray*
ey as in *whey*
eigh as in *eight*
ei as in *rein*
ea as in *great*

- Here are eight ways to spell /ē/.

e as in *relay*
e-consonant-e as in *impede*
ee as in *fleet*
ea as in *meager*
y as in *hazy*
ey as in *donkey*
ei as in *receive*
ie as in *piece*

- Here are five ways to spell /ī/.

i as in *idol*
igh as in *sigh*
i-consonant-e as in *dice*
y as in *reply*
ie as in *tie*

- Here are seven ways to spell /ō/.

  o as in *oval*
  oa as in *throat*
  o-consonant-e as in *grope*
  ow as in *bestow*
  ou as in *boulder*
  oe as in *doe*
  ough as in *though*

- Here are nine ways to spell /o͞o /.

  oo as in *boot*
  ew as in *chew*
  o as in *do*
  oe as in *shoe*
  u-consonant-e as in *crude*
  ui as in *fruit*
  ou as in *troupe*
  ough as in *through*
  o-consonant-e as in *prove*

Letter Combinations

- Usually when *i* and *e* are combined in a word, they make the sound /ē/, spelled *ie*. *ie, ei*

  belief grieve

  Exceptions: Words with the sound /ē/ after the letter *c* take the spelling *ei*.

  receipt deceive

  Sometimes, the sound /ā/ is spelled *ei*.

  rein skein

- Here are four ways to spell the /ər/ sound at the end of a word. final /ər/

  ar as in *solar*
  er as in *sister*
  or as in *factor*
  ur as in *lemur*

- Here are four ways to spell the /l/ or /əl/ sound at the end of a word. final /l/ or /əl/

  al as in *oral*
  el as in *nickel*
  le as in *handle*
  il as in *civil*

Syllable Divisions

syllable

- A **syllable** is a word or a part of a word. Each syllable in a word has one vowel sound. Knowing how to divide a word into syllables can help you pronounce the word correctly. Correct pronunciation, in turn, can help you spell a word correctly. Some rules for dividing words into syllables are listed below.

- When a word has two consonant sounds between two vowel sounds, divide the word between the two consonants. However, do not divide a consonant digraph.

  tal·cum   sup·per   leath·er

- When a word has two vowel sounds between two consonant sounds, divide the word between the two vowels.

  ru·in   dry·er

- When a two-syllable word has one consonant sound between two vowel sounds and the first vowel sound is long, divide the word before the consonant.

  pi·lot   ba·con

- When a two-syllable word has one consonant sound between two vowel sounds and the first vowel sound is short, divide the word after the consonant.

  prod·uct   civ·il

- When a word ends with a consonant followed by *le*, divide the word before the consonant.

  rus·tle   cra·dle

- When a word has a one-syllable prefix or suffix, divide the prefix or suffix from the base word.

  im·prop·er   dis·qual·i·fy

Verbs

past tense

- Add *ed* to form the past tense of most verbs.

  help—helped   smell—smelled   happen—happened

- To form the past tense of verbs that end in *e*, drop the *e* and add *ed*.

  solve—solved capture—captured trade—traded

- To form the past tense of one-syllable verbs that end with a short vowel sound and a consonant, double the final consonant and add *ed*.

  ship—shipped pat—patted hug—hugged

- To form the past tense of verbs that end in a consonant plus *y*, change the *y* to *i* and add *ed*.

  marry—married hurry—hurried worry—worried

- Add *ing* to form the present participle of most verbs.

  present participle

  match—matching read—reading answer—answering

- To form the present participle of verbs that end in *e*, drop the *e* and add *ing*.

  decide—deciding trade—trading solve—solving

- To form the present participle of one-syllable verbs that end in a short vowel sound and a consonant, double the final consonant before adding *ing*.

  ship—shipping pat—patting beg—begging

Plural Nouns

- Add *s* to form the plural of most nouns.

  plurals

  interview—interviews fortune—fortunes disaster—disasters

- Add *es* to form the plural of nouns ending in *s, z, x, sh,* or *ch*.

  watch—watches boss—bosses radish—radishes

- Add *s* to form the plural of nouns that end in a vowel plus *y*.

  convoy—convoys display—displays

- To form the plural of nouns that end in a consonant plus *y*, change the *y* to *i* and add *es*.

  symphony—symphonies controversy—controversies

- Add *s* if the word is a musical term or ends in a vowel plus *o*.

  soprano—sopranos rodeo—rodeos

- Sometimes, add *es* if the word ends in a consonant plus *o*.

hero—heroes   tornado—tornadoes

- To form the plural of some nouns ending in *f* or *fe*, change the *f* or *fe* to *v* and add *es*.

wharf—wharves   shelf—shelves   wife—wives
life—lives

- Some nouns have irregular plural forms.

man—men   child—children
woman—women   alumnus—alumni
fungus—fungi   alumna—alumnae
tooth—teeth   mouse—mice
ox—oxen   goose—geese

- Some nouns are spelled the same in the singular and the plural forms.

sheep—sheep   deer—deer
trout—trout   moose—moose

Compound Words

compound word

- A **compound word** is two or more words combined to form a new word.

quick + sand = quicksand
thunder + storm = thunderstorm

- A **closed compound** is two words written as one.

countryside   lifeguard   keyboard

- An **open compound** is two words written separately.

home run   space station   fire escape

- A **hyphenated compound** is two or more words joined by hyphens.

hand-me-down   man-of-war   brother-in-law

Contractions

pronoun contraction

- A **pronoun contraction** is a shortened form of a pronoun and a verb. An apostrophe replaces the letters that are omitted.

you + will = you'll   she + is = she's
they + are = they're

- A **verb contraction** is a shortened form of a verb and the word *not*. Write an apostrophe in place of the letter *o* in *not*.

verb contraction

do + not = don't   did + not = didn't
have + not = haven't

Exceptions: will + not = won't
can + not = cannot or can't

Possessive Nouns

- Form the possessive of a singular noun by adding an apostrophe and *s*.

singular possessive noun

author's agent   Louis's book   chimney's foundation

- Form the possessive of a plural noun that ends in *s* by adding an apostrophe.

plural possessive noun

the tourists' schedules   the Martins' station wagon

- Form the possessive of a plural noun that does not end in *s* by adding an apostrophe and *s*.

children's playroom   men's apparel
women's department

Adjectives That Compare

- Add *er* and *est* to one-syllable adjectives and some two-syllable adjectives to form the comparative and superlative degrees.

er, est

clear—clearer—clearest   quiet—quieter—quietest

- In a word with a short vowel sound, double the final consonant before adding *er* or *est*.

hot—hotter—hottest

- In a word that ends in a consonant plus *y*, change the final *y* to *i* before adding *er* or *est*.

filthy—filthier—filthiest

- Drop a final *e* before adding *er* or *est*.

fine—finer—finest

Adverbs That Compare

er, est

- Add *er* and *est* to one-syllable adverbs and some two-syllable adverbs to form the comparative and superlative degrees.

  loud—louder—loudest

- In a word that ends in a consonant plus *y*, change the final *y* to *i* before adding *er* or *est*.

  early—earlier—earliest

- Drop a final *e* before adding *er* or *est*.

  late—later—latest

SENTENCE DIAGRAMMING

sentence diagram

- A **sentence diagram** shows how the parts of a sentence work together. In a sentence diagram, capitalize any words that are capitalized in the sentence, but omit punctuation marks.

simple subject and simple predicate

- The **simple subject** is the main word in the complete subject. The **simple predicate** is the verb in the complete predicate.

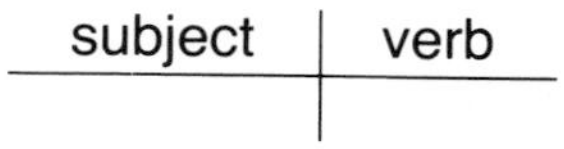

Summer arrived.

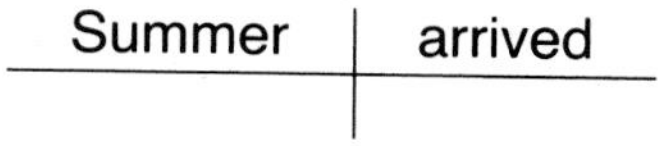

inverted word order

- A sentence has **inverted word order** when the verb comes before the subject. Place the subject before the verb.

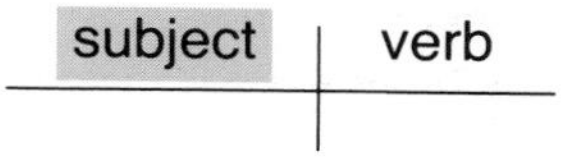

Where is the car ?

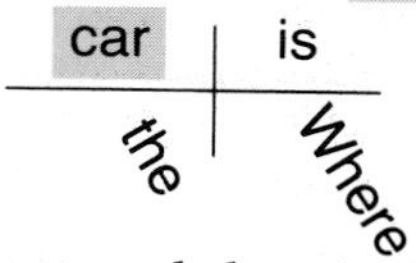

four kinds of sentences

- These diagrams show the simple subject and the simple predicate of each kind of sentence.

Declarative: The team played a good game.

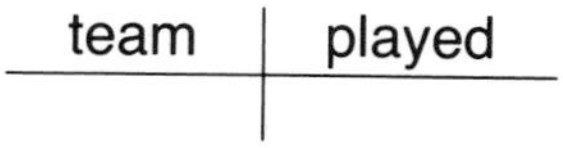

Interrogative: Did the team win the game?

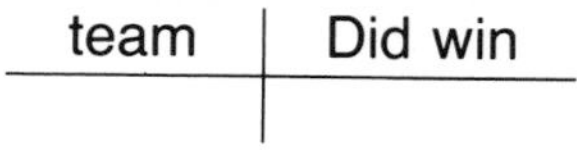

Imperative: Watch the cheerleaders perform.

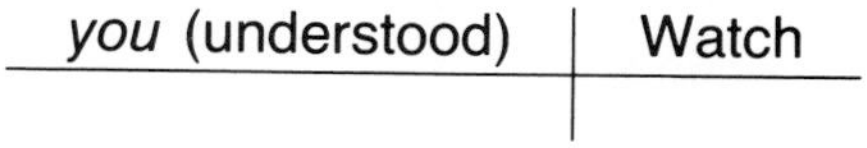

Exclamatory: How loudly everyone cheered!

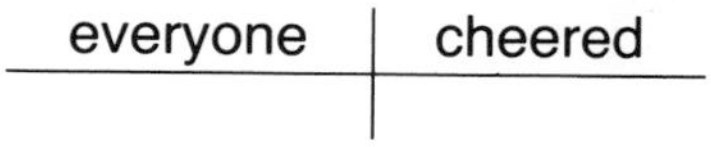

- A **direct object** receives the action of the verb.

The carpenter builds bookcases .

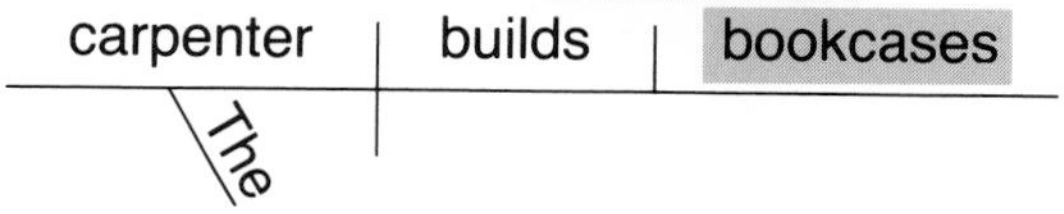

indirect object

- An **indirect object** tells to whom or for whom the action of the verb is done.

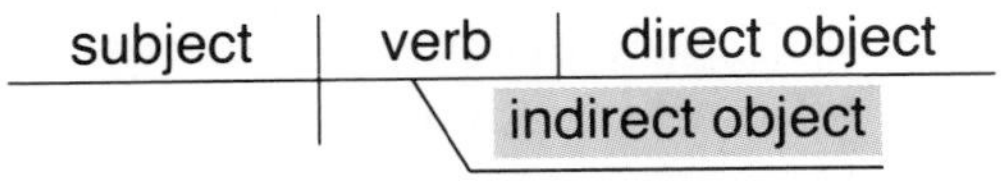

Gary gave me directions.

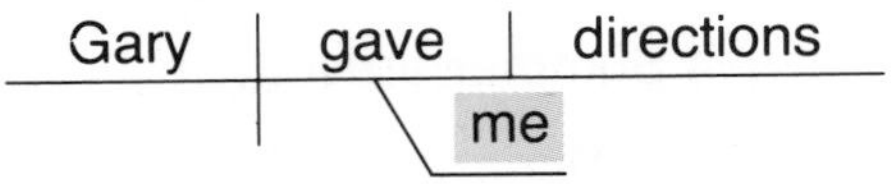

predicate nominative

- A **predicate nominative** is a noun or pronoun that follows a linking verb and renames the subject of the sentence.

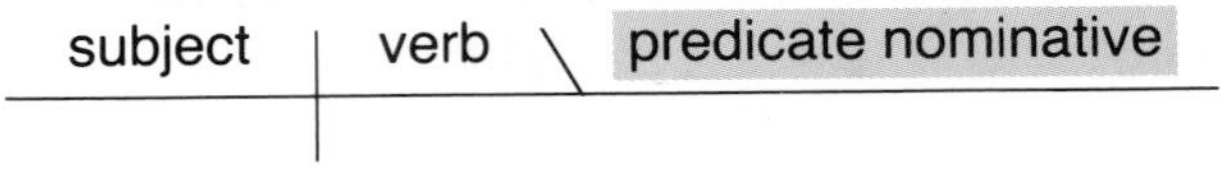

Sally Ride is an astronaut.

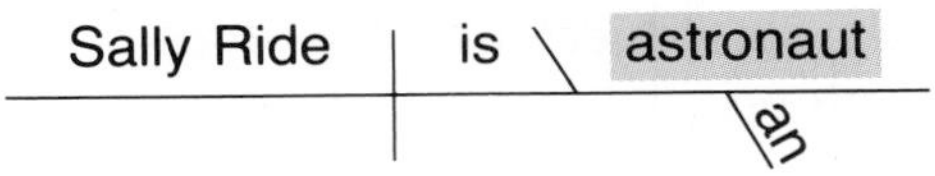

appositive

- An **appositive** is a noun or pronoun, often with modifiers, that identifies or renames the noun or pronoun that precedes it.

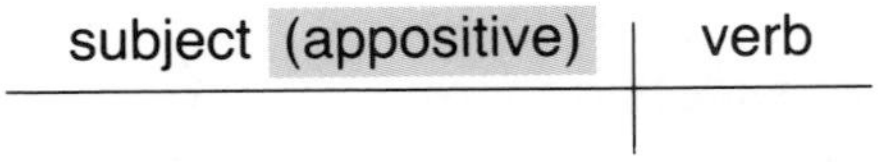

Ellen, my neighbor, won the election.

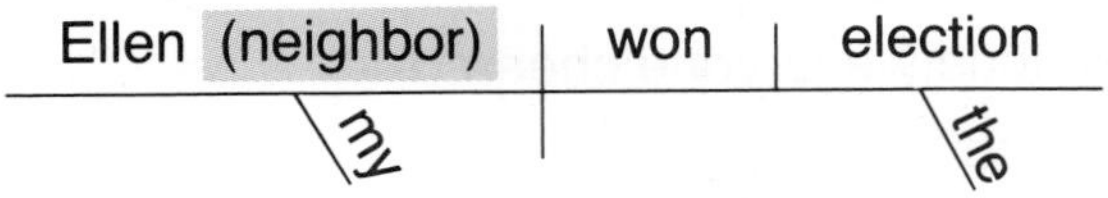

adjective

- An **adjective** modifies a noun or a pronoun.

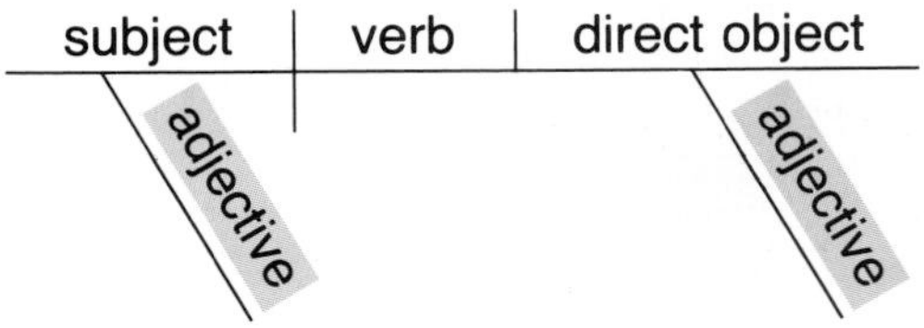

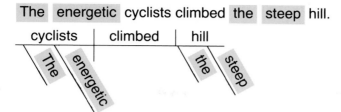

The energetic cyclists climbed the steep hill.

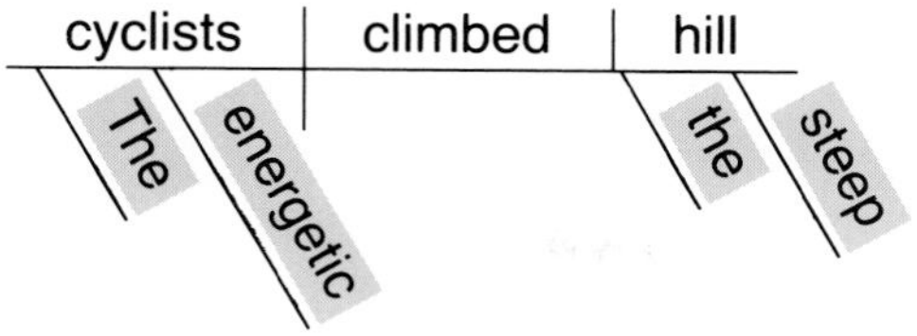

predicate adjective

- A **predicate adjective** follows a linking verb and describes the subject of the sentence.

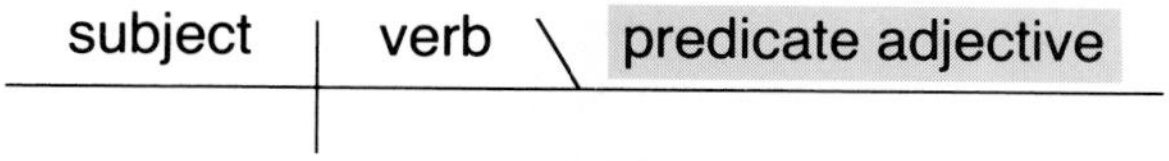

The dessert was delicious.

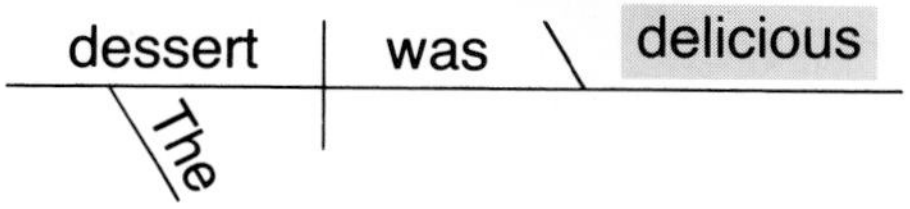

possessives and articles

- **Possessive nouns** and **possessive pronouns** precede nouns to show ownership or possession. The **articles** *a*, *an*, and *the* always signal a noun.

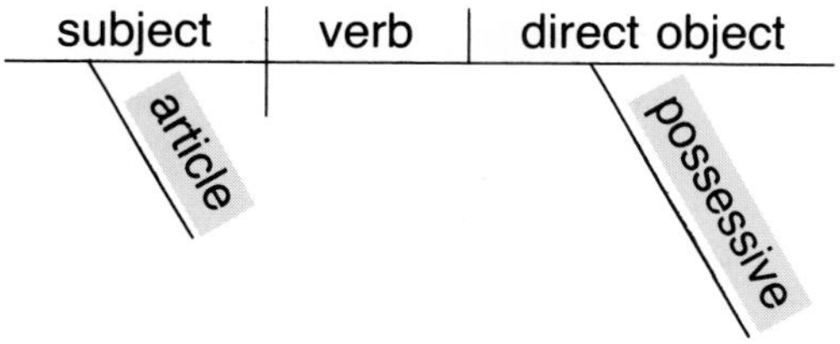

The soldier removed his hat.

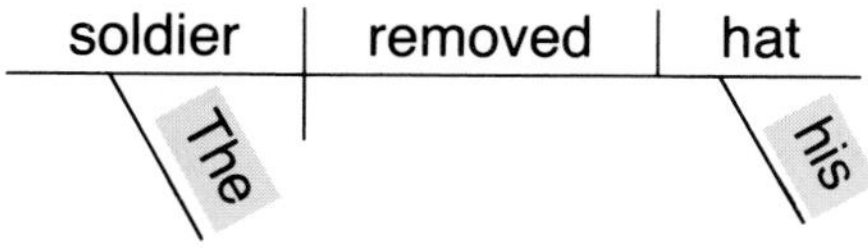

participle

- A **participle** is a verbal used as an adjective.

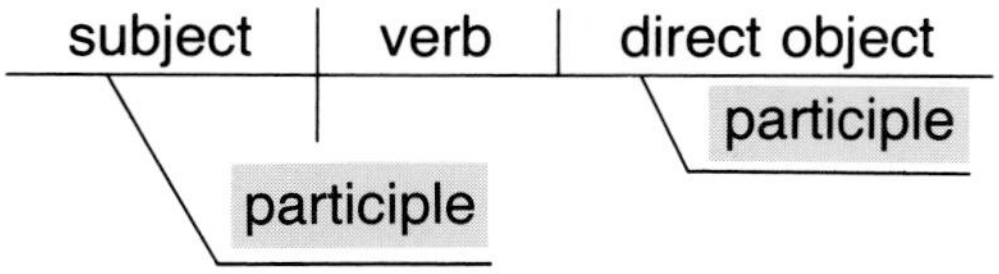

A smiling woman opened the locked door.

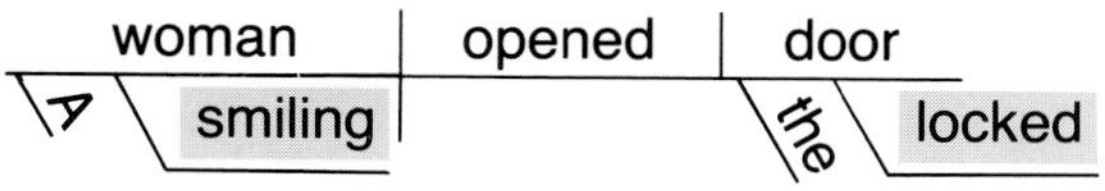

adverb

- An **adverb** modifies a verb, an adjective, or another adverb.

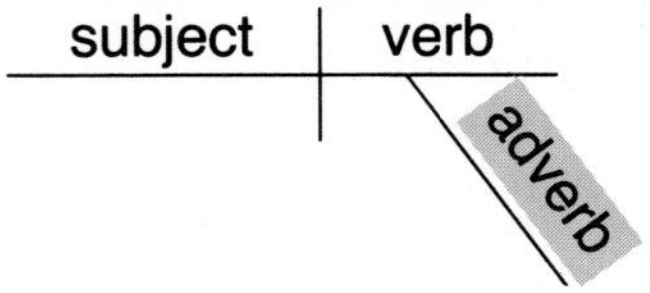

Tien reads the newspaper daily.

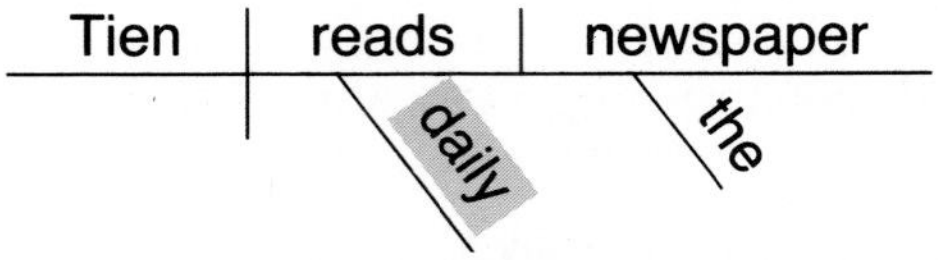

prepositional phrase

- A **prepositional phrase** is made up of a preposition (prep.), the object of the preposition, and all the words in between. The object of the preposition is the noun or pronoun at the end of the prepositional phrase.

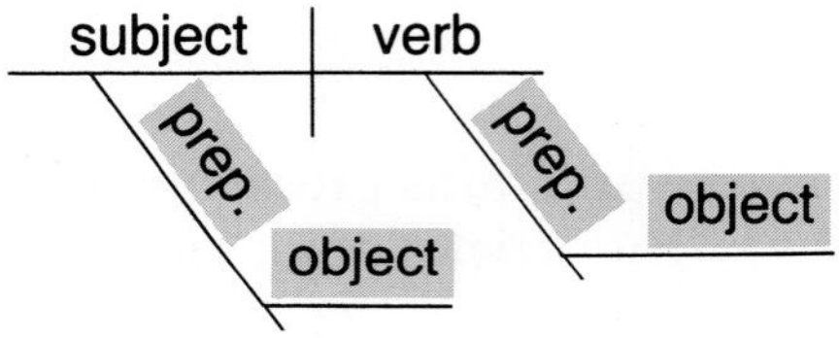

A booklet of instructions came with the chemistry set.

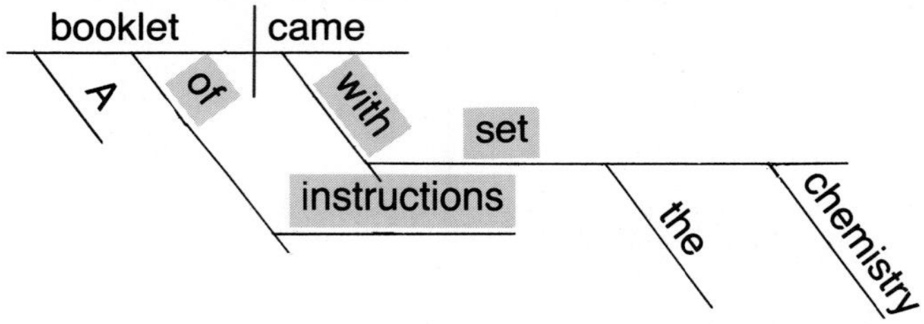

infinitive

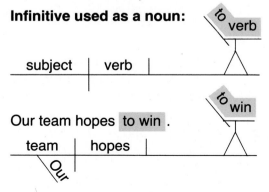

- An **infinitive** is a verbal consisting of the present-tense form of a verb preceded by *to*. An infinitive can be used as a noun, an adverb, or an adjective.

Infinitive used as a noun:

Our team hopes to win.

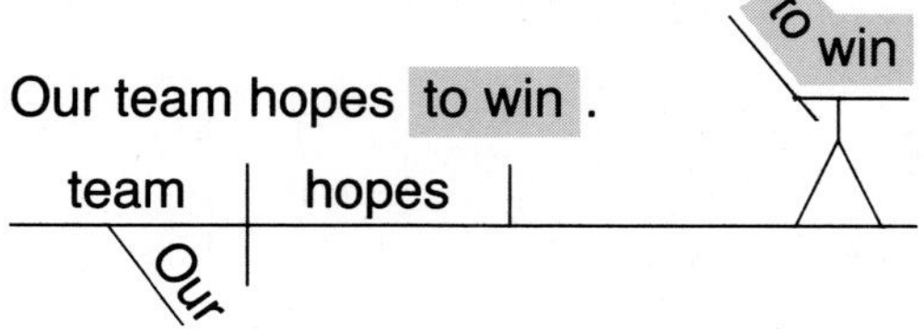

Infinitive used as an adjective:

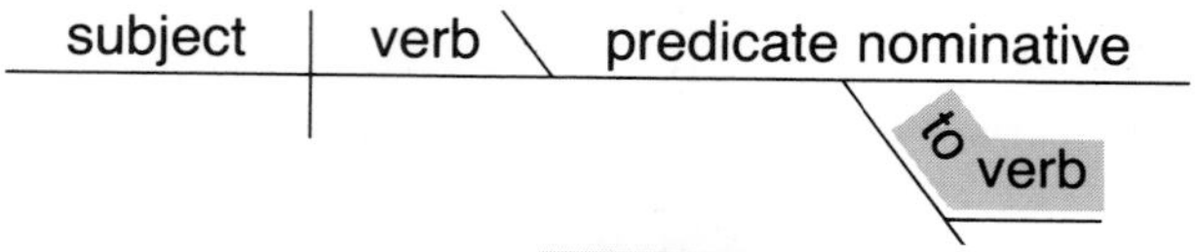

This is the best book to read.

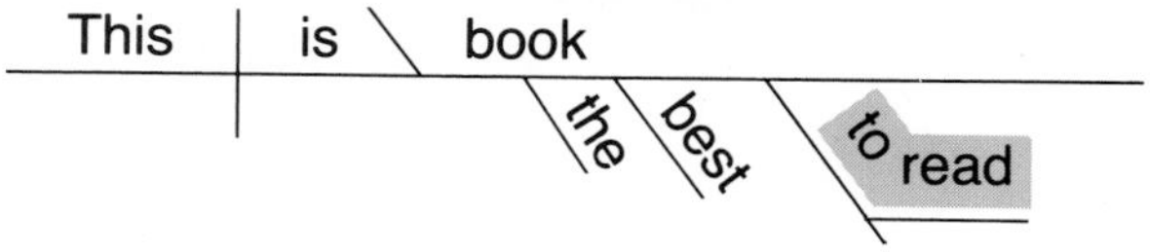

Infinitive used as an adverb:

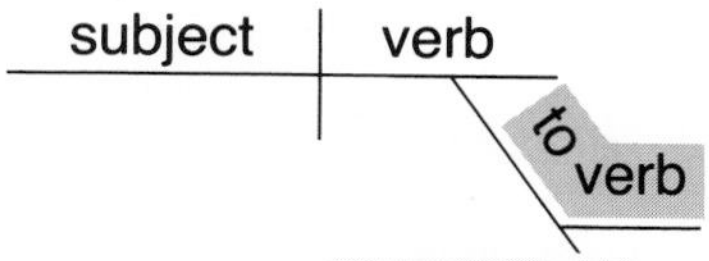

We practice to improve.

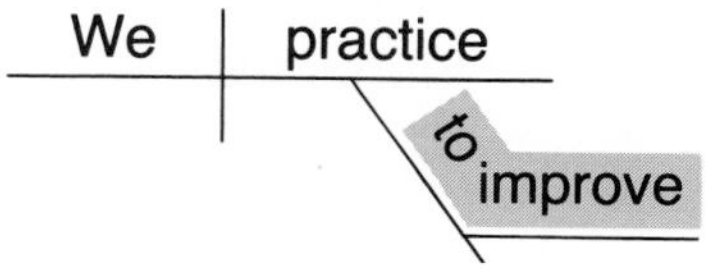

- A **gerund** is a verbal used as a noun.

gerund

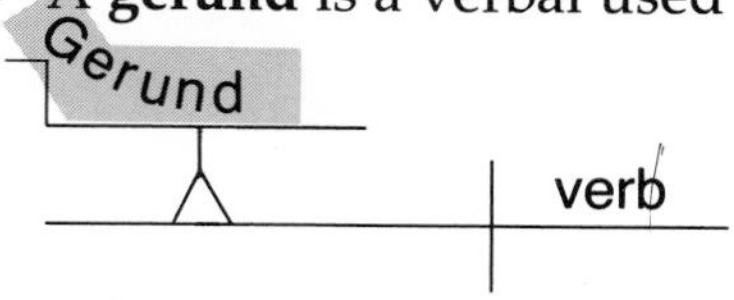

Voting is the obligation of every qualified American.

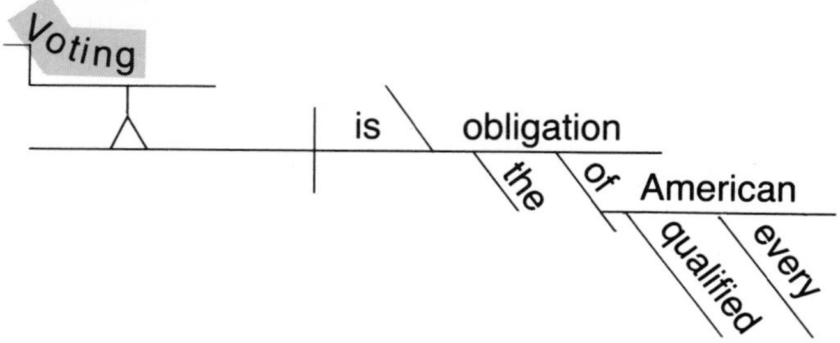

- An **adjective series** consists of three or more adjectives that modify one noun or one pronoun. Notice how a conjunction (conj.) is diagrammed in the following example.

conjunction and an adjective series

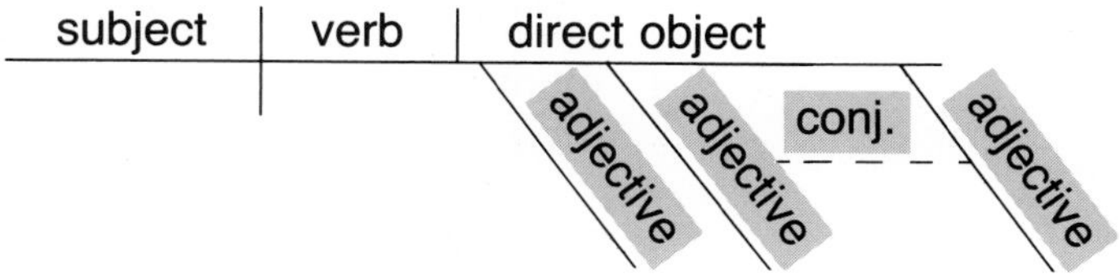

Their restaurant serves delicious, nutritious, and inexpensive food.

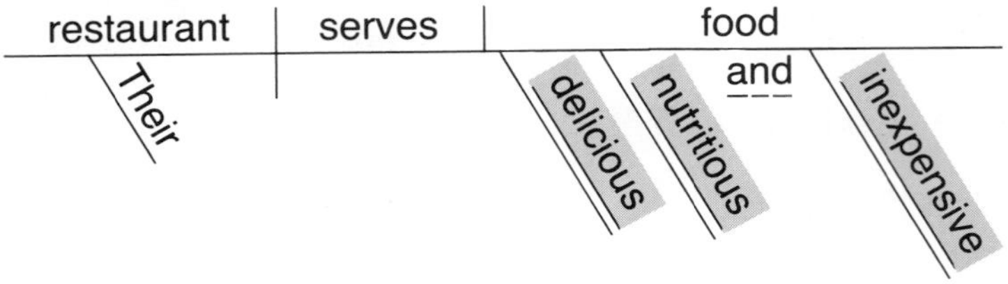

conjunction and a compound subject

- A **compound subject** is two or more subjects that have the same verb. The subjects are joined by a conjunction.

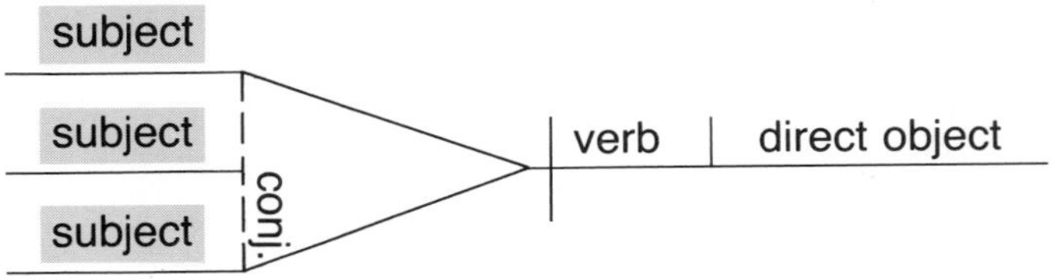

Mr. Tripp, Mrs. Tripp, and her students toured the museum.

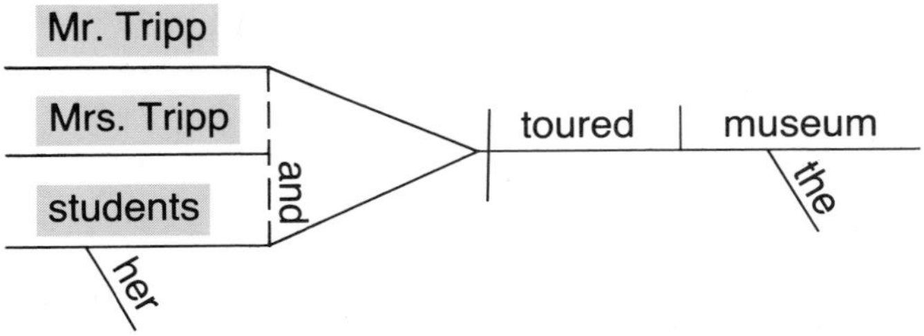

conjunction and a compound verb

- A **compound verb** is two or more verbs that have the same subject. The predicates are joined by a conjunction.

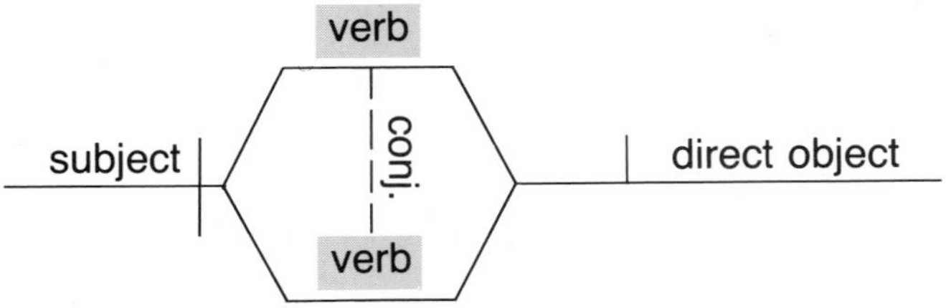

Pat called or visited each member of the committee.

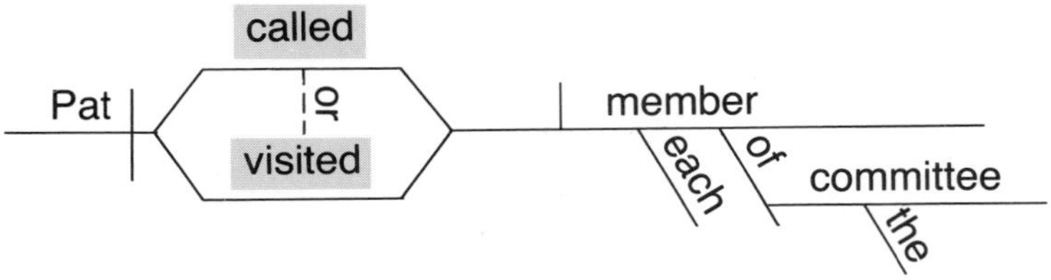

- A **compound sentence** contains two or more related simple sentences joined by a comma and a conjunction or by a semicolon.

conjunction and a compound sentence

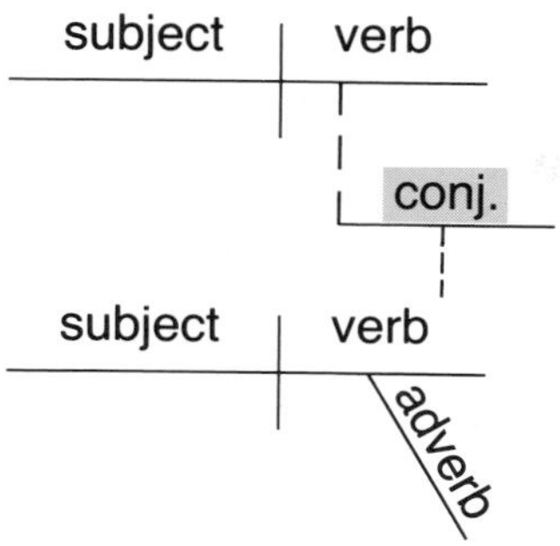

Tomás ordered a new helmet, but it never arrived.

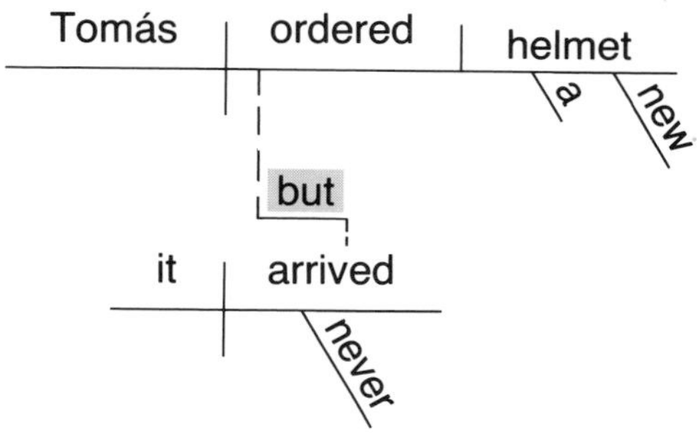

- A **complex sentence** consists of an independent clause and at least one subordinate clause. If the subordinate clause functions as an adjective, diagram the sentence like this.

complex sentence with an adjective clause

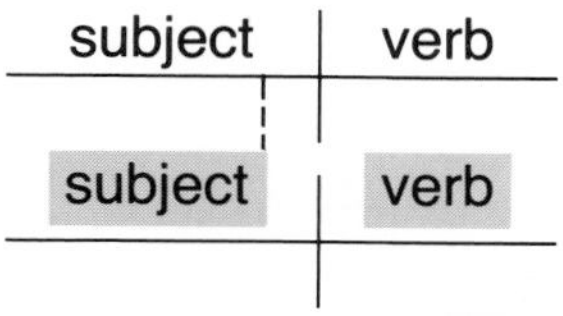

The artist who painted this portrait showed great skill.

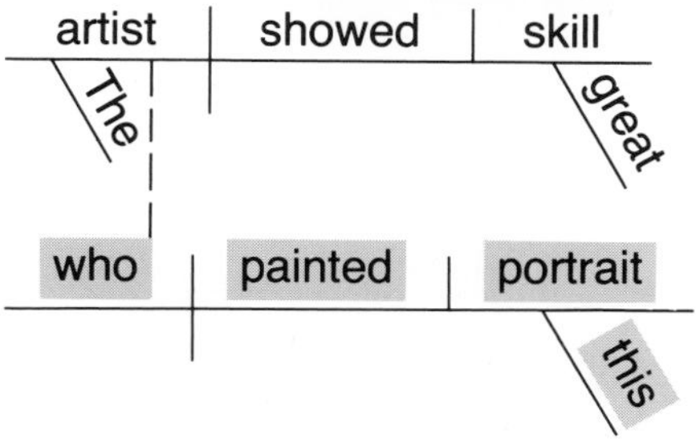

complex sentence with an adverb clause

- If the subordinate clause in a complex sentence functions as an adverb, diagram the sentence like this.

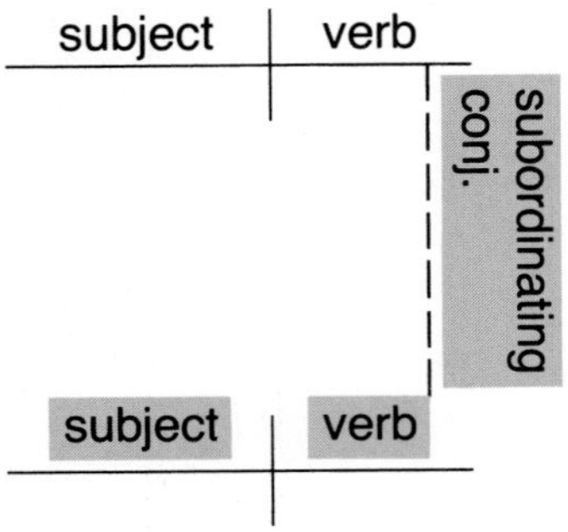

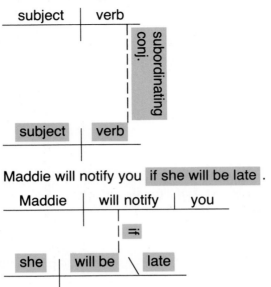

Maddie will notify you if she will be late.

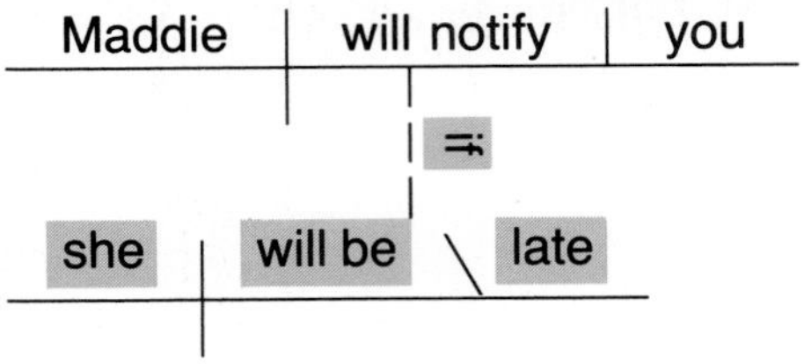

complex sentence with a noun clause

- If the subordinate clause in a complex sentence functions as a noun, diagram the sentence like this.

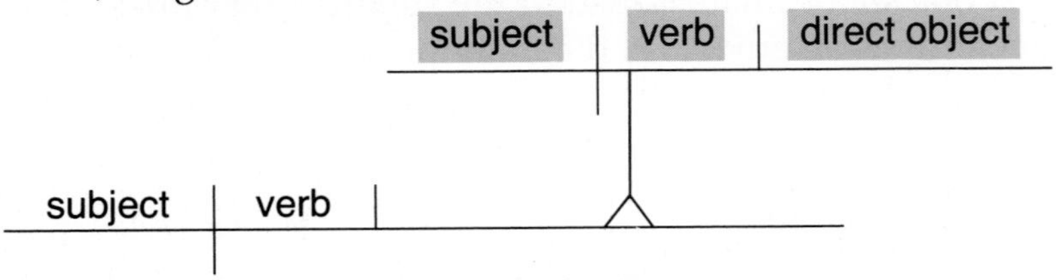

Karim has forgotten where he left his jersey.

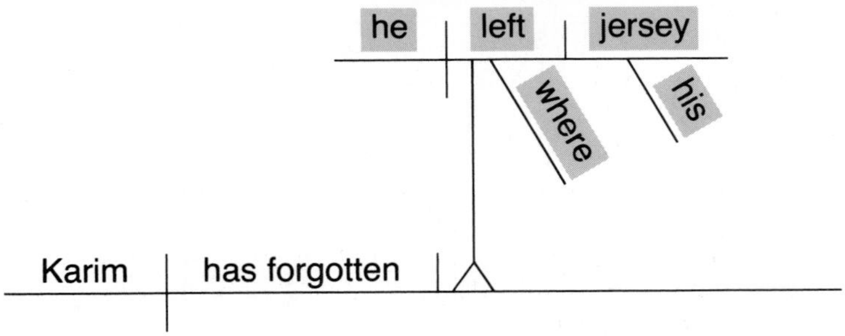

GLOSSARY

Contents

Composition Terms

AUDIENCE *the reader or readers for whom a composition is written* This example from a friendly letter shows that the audience is a friend named Randy.

```
                              19 Orange Street
                              Dallas, Texas 75311
                              December 5, 19--
Dear Randy,
```

CLARITY *the preciseness with which a writer makes the message of a composition understood* Notice the precise words the writer uses in this example.

> The great eagle landed heavily on the nest, grasping in its huge talons the mouse it had caught for its young.

COHERENCE *the orderly arrangement of ideas in a composition* Notice how transitional words make this example smooth and readable. This is one method of achieving coherence.

> First of all, paint the sky a soft blue and add some fluffy white clouds. Next, use warm greens and browns to suggest grass and hills. Then, paint the foreground.

DRAFTING *the writing stage of a composition, which includes the writing of a first draft* This boy is using a prewriting diagram to compose the first draft.

EDITOR'S MARKS *the standard symbols for making changes when revising or proofreading* Use these marks when you revise.

∧ Add something.	Move something.
Cut something.	Replace something.

Use these marks when you proofread.

≡ Capitalize.	Add quotation marks.	Spell correctly.
⊙ Add a period.	Cut something.	Indent paragraph.
∧ Add something.	Replace something.	/ Make a lowercase letter.
Add a comma.	Transpose.	

FINAL DRAFT *the final version of a composition, ready to be published* This example shows one part of a final draft.

```
    At first, the child ran about on the sandy
beach. Then, he found a shell the color of sea
foam. He picked it up and held it to his ear.
```

FIRST DRAFT *the rough version of a composition, in which a writer's ideas are written down* Notice the unfinished quality of the writing in this example.

> The builders of the middel Ages built many cathedruls they are still in use. They workd for hundrds of years on the same biulding.

PREWRITING *the first stage in the writing process, in which the writer thinks of ideas and tries to organize them* This prewriting diagram shows comparison and contrast.

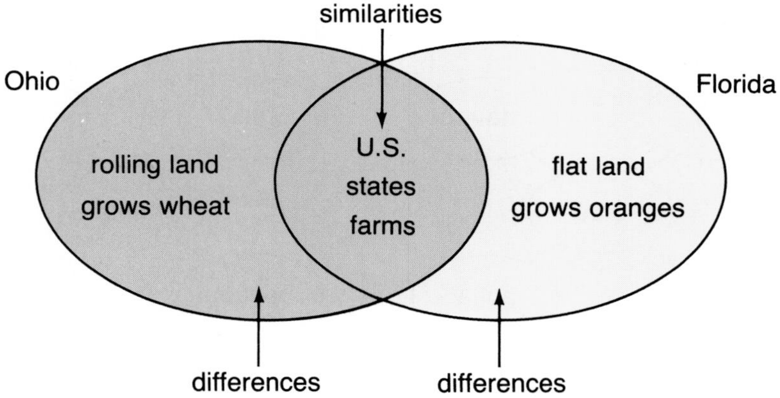

PREWRITING STRATEGIES *the activities or techniques that help a writer gather and organize ideas and information* The following are some examples of prewriting strategies.

- **brainstorming** *an activity that encourages the contribution of ideas from an individual or a group* Here a student records ideas from a brainstorming session.

- **charting** *a visual technique that helps an individual or a group to organize ideas and information* This chart is being written to organize a story.

Chapter 1	Chapter 2	Chapter 3
Bingo is introduced	Bingo runs away	Bingo meets Charlie

- **clustering** *a visual technique to help an individual or a group think of ideas*

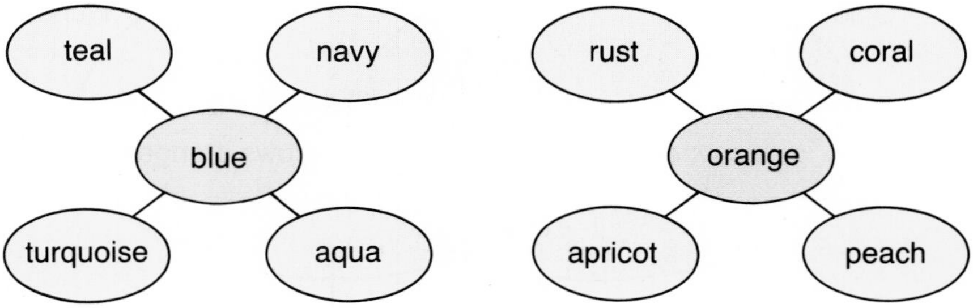

- **diagramming** *a visual technique for putting information in space or time order*

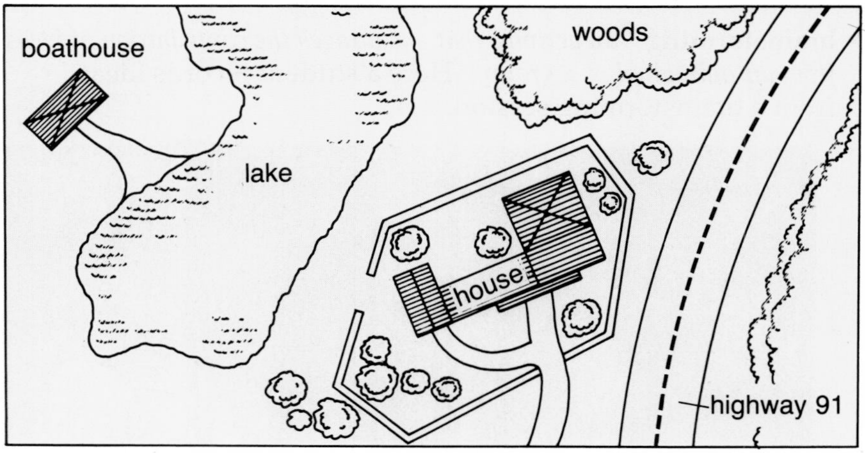

- **using an inverted triangle** *a technique used for narrowing a topic or organizing ideas*

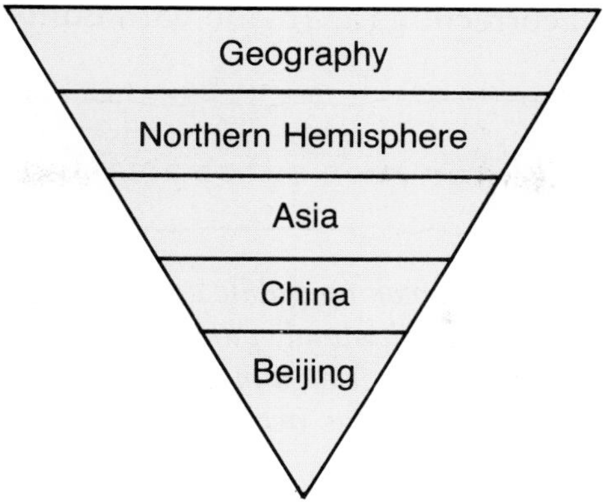

- **list making** *writing, on a chalkboard or on paper, ideas collected in a brainstorming activity*

National Parks		
1. Zion	2. Yellowstone	3. BigBend

- **mapping** *a visual technique for recording or organizing information* This word map shows Carol's relationship to each person or group whose name appears in a square.

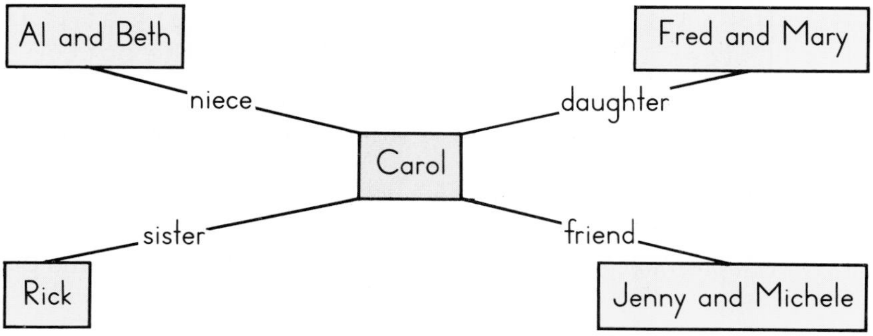

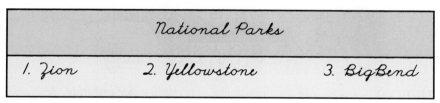

- **slotting** *a brainstorming activity by a group or an individual to find words or word groups to complete a sentence*

Millie ________ the ball into the wall.

slammed pitched

tossed blasted

PROOFREADING *reviewing a composition to correct errors in capitalization, punctuation, usage, grammar, and spelling* In this example, corrections are made with Editor's Marks.

> sight
> did you ever seen sutch a site ?

PUBLISHING *making public a final draft of a composition—for example, by reading it aloud, putting it in a collection of class writing, or displaying it on a bulletin board* These students are putting together a class notebook.

PURPOSE *the reason a composition is written—for example, to inform, to narrate, to describe, or to persuade* The passage in this example was written to inform.

> Take two plastic cups and a string at least six feet long. Punch a small hole in the bottom of each cup.

RESPONDING *a revising activity in which the writer and a partner or the members of a small group ask and answer questions about a composition* Notice the questions this writer asks his partner.

Can you think of any more vivid words? Do I stick to the topic?

RESPONSE GROUP *a group of students who help revise each other's work by asking and answering questions about it* This group is answering a question about coherence.

The part about crickets doesn't fit in here.
The most important detail should come first.

REVISING *the process of editing and proofreading written work to correct errors in organization and language* This girl is reading her composition aloud, a useful revising technique.

OOPS!
I meant to
keep it all in
the past tense!
...when Harriet comes out again...

STYLE *the use of interesting language and varied sentence structure to create a special tone* Notice how changing the words changes the style in these sentences.

A sad-looking girl came into the room.

A disconsolate girl dragged herself into the room.

TASK *the assignment or undertaking of a particular type of composition* Carmen was given the task of writing a how-to paragraph about making a piñata.

You will need a balloon, colored tissue paper, flour, and water. First, mix a cup of flour with two cups of water.

TONE *the language and sentence structure chosen by a writer to express an attitude toward the subject* For example, the tone may be formal, informal, critical, approving, humorous, or solemn. In this passage from a letter to the editor of a newspaper, the writer uses a friendly, approving tone.

Once again, we citizens can congratulate ourselves. The new waterfront plaza is even better than we expected.

UNITY *the orderly arrangement of details in support of the main idea of a composition* A sentence in this passage has been deleted to strengthen its unity.

The dog show will be held next Saturday in Gibson Park. There will be competitions for sporting and working dogs. ~~That park is a popular spot.~~ A prize will be given for the best miniature dog.

GLOSSARY

WRITING PROCESS *the ongoing process of prewriting, drafting, responding and revising, and proofreading a composition until it is ready for publication* A writer can move among these stages until the final draft is completed, as this student is doing.

Now that I've drafted my second paragraph, I need to brainstorm ideas for my conclusion.

Literary Terms

ALLITERATION *the repetition of the same beginning consonant sound in several nearby words* Notice the words that begin with the /s/ sound in these lines of poetry.

Fly away, fly away over
the sea,
Sun-loving swallow, for
summer is done.

ASSONANCE *the repetition of the same vowel sound in several nearby words* In these lines from "The Owl" by William Jay Smith, listen for the repeated long /o/ sound.

The owl that lives in the
old oak tree
Opens his eyes and cannot
see

CHARACTERS *the people (or animals) in a story, a poem, or a play* When authors are concerned mainly with making their characters lifelike, the way the characters feel, act, and change is more important than the plot, or story line. When authors are concerned mainly with the plot, less attention is usually paid to character development. One way in which writers develop their characters is by telling what other characters say or think about them.

Tim usually liked visiting his grandfather, but right now he felt that the old man was ready to spend the rest of his life in a rocking chair.

Another way is by giving a physical description.

Grandpa Shorter ran his fingers through a thinning shock of white hair.

A third way in which characters are developed is by the characters' own speech and actions.

"I ever tell you about the time I caught a trout here that was so long we had to send to Sears and Roebuck for a bigger frying pan?"

CLICHÉ *any expression used so often that it is no longer fresh and interesting* For example, using *"busy as a bee"* in a story has become a cliché.

CONSONANCE *the repetition of similar consonant sounds in several nearby words or at the ends of lines of poetry* The /r/ sound is repeated throughout these lines from the poem "A Modern Dragon" by Rowena Bastin Bennett.

A train is a dragon that
roars through the dark.
He wriggles his tail as he
sends up a spark.

FICTION *a story invented by a writer* Fiction can be broken down into several categories. **Historical fiction** is based on real events, but it involves made-up characters and experiences. **Science fiction** is based on action usually set in the future. It often involves movement in time and space. A **novel** is a book-length story in which the character development and the plot are longer and more complex than those in a short story. **Fantasy** includes stories and novels based on fanciful characters and plots. Fantasy is usually highly imaginative.

FIGURATIVE LANGUAGE *words used in unusual and creative, rather than in literal or usual, ways* The most common forms of figurative language are similes and metaphors. A **simile** uses the word *like* or *as* to compare two very different things. *Dark clouds come rolling in like bowling balls* is an example of a simile. A **metaphor** suggests a comparison by saying that one thing *is* another. In the poem "Spirit of the Grizzly Bear" by Lars Smith and Marc Almond, the first and third lines contain metaphors.

Night its nose,
He follows me.
Stars its eyes,
He follows me.

FORESHADOWING *a technique used by an author to offer hints about future developments in a story* In this passage, foreshadowing is used to create a feeling of suspense.

He wasn't sure he liked the house either. It was painted gray. An owl called and the sound made Eddie feel nervous.

IMAGERY *the use of images, or word pictures, in writing* Authors often use descriptive language to make the reader live the experience. Including sensory details from as many of the five senses as possible makes a word picture more vivid. In "The Main Deep," James Stephens uses sensory details of touch, sight, and hearing.

The long, rolling,
Steady-pouring,
Deep-trenched,
Green billow;

The wide-topped,
Unbroken,
Green-glacid,
Slow-sliding,

Cold-flushing,
On—on—on—
Chill-rushing,
Hush-hushing,

Hush—hushing . . .

NARRATOR *the person who tells a story* All stories have a narrator. It can be either a character in the story or an outsider who tells about events without taking part in them.

NONFICTION *any writing that tells about true events, presents information, or expresses an opinion* Two types of nonfiction are **biography,** the story of a person's life, and **autobiography,** the story of the author's own life. Writing that provides or explains information is called **exposition.** Writing that expresses an opinion is called **editorial.**

ONOMATOPOEIA *the use of words that imitate actual sounds or that suggest by their sounds what the words mean* Notice how Lee Bennett Hopkins, writer of "Valentine Feelings," has used an onomatopoeic word to end each line.

I feel flippy,
I feel fizzy,
I feel whoppy,
I feel whizzy.

PLOT *the action in a story* **Conflict,** the protagonist's struggle against opposing forces, is the most important part of a plot. To hold the reader's attention, a writer plans a sequence of events around a conflict. In the **introduction,** the setting, the characters, and the conflict are presented. The conflict becomes more intense in the **complication,** when the main character tries to resolve his or her conflict. Next, the story moves toward the **climax,** in which the conflict is faced. The ending of the story is the **resolution,** in which the conflict is resolved.

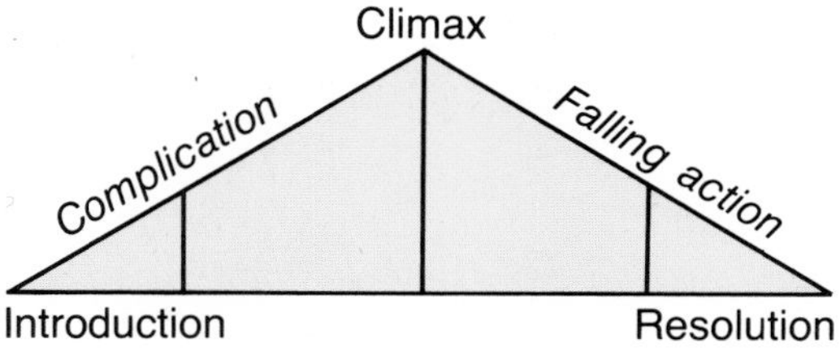

RHYME *the repetition of syllable sounds, especially at the ends of lines of poetry* Notice that in this example the first line rhymes with the second, and the third line rhymes with the fourth.

Half a dozen loaves lie
in the oven of the sky,
round above and flat below.
Who is baking? I don't know.

RHYTHM *a pattern of stressed and unstresssed syllables, especially in poetry* Rhythm in poetry is like the beat in music. In a good poem, the rhythm intensifies what the poet is saying. See how the rhythm in these lines contributes to the image of the dog.

I'm a lean dog, a keen dog,
a wild dog, and lone;
I'm a rough dog, a tough
dog, hunting on my own;

SETTING *where and when a story takes place* A writer can choose any time or place in which to set a story. Sometimes a particular setting is necessary to the plot, as in most science fiction or suspense tales, but when a plot and characters could develop anywhere, the setting is less important.

STANZA *a group of lines in a poem that are read as a unit and are comparable to a paragraph in a work of prose* When a poem has more than one stanza, they are separated by extra space. The stanzas in a poem may all have the same pattern of rhyme and rhythm, or they may be irregular. They may also vary in the number of lines they contain. Notice the differences in these two stanzas from the poem "There Is Danger" by De-Shun Washington.

They sing the harmony of the
forbidden song.
It summons their names
screaming out like lightning
you better be careful because...

They sway back and forth in a winter breeze. A bee follows a bright butterfly.
You better not follow because. . .

SUSPENSE *the feeling of uncertainty about what will happen next* Writers use suspense as a technique to make a story exciting. In this paragraph, the writer has created a feeling of anxiety about what will happen to the character.

As Mimi entered the living room, she suddenly felt cold. Things looked different, somehow, with the curtains drawn. Then she heard a faint rattle upstairs. "Probably just the wind," she thought. Yet she found herself hoping the phone lines would be fixed soon. She did not like being cut off from the outside world.

TONE *the writer's attitude toward the subject as conveyed by language* The tone of a story or a poem may be formal or informal, playful or serious, spooky or matter-of-fact. Notice how the writer has created a tense, worried tone in these lines.

Ellen was exhausted. Rain battered the windshield and lights kept glaring in her eyes. In the driver's seat her mother gripped the wheel and stared at the road.

WRITER'S THESAURUS

Contents

What Is a Thesaurus?

A **thesaurus** lists words and their synonyms. Like a dictionary, a thesaurus lists words in alphabetical order. Each of these words is called an **entry word.** A list of synonyms follows the entry word. Sometimes a thesaurus lists antonyms.

Look at the parts of this thesaurus entry for the word *dark.*

The entry word is in color. It is followed by the part of speech and a definition. An **example sentence** shows how the word can be used.

> **dark** *adj.* Lacking light. During the storm, the sky turned **dark** and cloudy.

Synonyms for the entry word are in italics. Each synonym is followed by a definition and an example sentence.

> *dim* Lacking sufficient light. We could not see well in the *dim* alley.
> *gloomy* Dark and dreary. The daylight made the *gloomy* forest look cheerful.
> *murky* Dark or obscure. The *murky* water was full of mud.
> *shady* Sheltered from the sun. This *shady* spot is cold.

If an **antonym** is given, it is printed in dark letters.

> **ANTONYMS: bright, cheerful, light**

How to Use Your Writer's Thesaurus

Suppose you are writing a scary story for a homework assignment. When you read your first draft, you realize that you have overused the word *dark.* You open your **Writer's Thesaurus** to find some synonyms. Here are the steps you should follow.

1. Look for the word in the Index to the Thesaurus. The Index lists every word in the **Writer's Thesaurus.**

2. Find the word in the Index.

   dark *adj.*

   You know that *dark* is an entry word because it is printed in color.

3. Turn to the page in your **Writer's Thesaurus** on which *dark* is printed in color. Read the entry carefully. Not every synonym will express exactly what you want to say. Choose the synonym that makes the most sense for your story.

Remember: Not every synonym will have the exact meaning you want. Look at the entry for *dark* on page 10. Which synonyms fit your work best?

- Sometimes a word is listed in the Index like this:

  murky dark *adj.*

  This means you will find *murky* listed as a synonym under the entry word *dark.* Since *murky* is not printed in color, it is not an entry word.

- You will also see some lines in the Index that look like this:

  cheerful dark adj.

  This means that *cheerful* is listed as an antonym under the entry word *dark.*

Index to Thesaurus

E

eager *adj.*
easy challenging *adj.*
elements basics *n.*
eliminate *v.*
encumbrance helper *n.*
end finish *v.*
endowed gifted *adj.*
energetic strong *adj.*
enjoy dislike *v.*
enjoy like *v.*
enormous tremendous *adj.*
enter go *v.*
enthusiastic eager *adj.*
eradicate eliminate *v.*
essentials basics *n.*
exhausted strong *adj.*
exhibit show *v.*
exit go *v.*
experience feel *v.*
explorer *n.*
expose hide *v.*
extras basics *n.*
exuberantly *adv.*

F

fall climb *v.*
fast slow *adj.*
feel *v.*
fill pack *v.*
finger feel *v.*
finish *v.*
flow *v.*
forceful strong *adj.*
formidable challenging *adj.*
friendly aloof *adj.*
friendship solitude *n.*
frivolities basics *n.*
frustrating challenging *adj.*

G

gather eliminate *v.*
get give *v.*
giant tremendous *adj.*
gifted *adj.*
give *v.*
give take *v.*
gladly exuberantly *adv.*
glint shine *v.*
glitter shine *v.*
gloomily exuberantly *adv.*
gloomy dark *adj.*
go *v.*
grab take *v.*
guard cherish *v.*
gush flow *v.*

H

halt flow *v.*
hand give *v.*
happily exuberantly *adv.*
hare rabbit *n.*
harmonize argue *v.*
hate dislike *v.*
hate like *v.*
hazardous risky *adj.*
helper *n.*
hide *v.*
hide show *v.*
hindrance helper *n.*
home palace *n.*
hovel palace *n.*
huge tremendous *adj.*
hut palace *n.*

I

ignore look *v.*
imaginative different *adj.*
indifferent eager *adj.*
inept gifted *adj.*
initiate finish *v.*
insignificant tremendous *adj.*
inspect look *v.*
investigator explorer *n.*
isolation solitude *n.*

J

joyfully exuberantly *adv.*
joylessly exuberantly *adv.*

K

keep eliminate *v.*
knapsack pack *n.*

L

lagging slow *adj.*
leave go *v.*
left came *v.*
leisurely slow *adj.*
light dark *adj.*
like *v.*
like dislike *v.*
load pack *v.*
loneliness solitude *n.*
look *v.*
lose take *v.*
love dislike *v.*
love like *v.*
luxuries basics *n.*

M

maneuver move *v.*

mansion palace *n.*
mask hide *v.*
mighty strong *adj.*
minuscule tremendous *adj.*
morning daybreak *n.*
mount climb *v.*
mouthwatering nice *adj.*
move *v.*
murky dark *adj.*

N

nice *adj.*
nightfall daybreak *n.*
nondescript different *adj.*
notice see *v.*

O

obscurity darkness *n.*
odor smell *n.*
open aloof *adj.*
ordinary different *adj.*
original different *adj.*
outbreak storm *n.*
outgoing aloof *adj.*
overlook see *v.*

P

pack *n.*
pack *v.*
palace *n.*
parcel pack *n.*
peace storm *n.*
peculiar different *adj.*
perceive see *v.*
perilous risky *adj.*
pleasing nice *adj.*
plunge climb *v.*
pour flow *v.*
powerful strong *adj.*
preposterous different *adj.*
present give *v.*
prize cherish *v.*
progressed came *v.*
purge eliminate *v.*

Q

quick slow *adj.*

R

rabbit *n.*
radiate shine *v.*
reached came *v.*
receive give *v.*
regard look *v.*
relaxed eager *adj.*
relish like *v.*
remain move *v.*
remove eliminate *v.*
repulsive nice *adj.*
researcher explorer *n.*
reserved aloof *adj.*
restrained aloof *adj.*
retreated came *v.*
reveal hide *v.*
rise climb *v.*
risky *adj.*

S

sadly exuberantly *adv.*
safe risky *adj.*
scatter center *v.*
scent smell *n.*
scout explorer *n.*
scramble climb *v.*
secure confident *adj.*
secure risky *adj.*
see *v.*
separate alone *adj.*
separateness solitude *n.*
shady dark *adj.*
shift move *v.*
shimmer shine *v.*
shine *v.*
short curt *adj.*
show *v.*
show hide *v.*
simple challenging *adj.*
sink climb *v.*
skeptical confident *adj.*
skilled gifted *adj.*
sleep slumber *v.*
slow *adj.*
sluggish slow *adj.*
slumber *v.*
small tremendous *adj.*
smell *n.*
snatch take *v.*
solitary alone *adj.*
solitude *n.*
speedy slow *adj.*
stagnate flow *v.*
stand move *v.*
start finish *v.*
stay move *v.*
stench smell *n.*
stimulating challenging *adj.*
stop flow *v.*
storm *n.*
stream flow *v.*
strew pack *v.*
stroke feel *v.*
strong *adj.*
stuff pack *v.*
subdued aloof *adj.*
sunrise daybreak *n.*
sunset daybreak *n.*
sure confident *adj.*
surge flow *v.*
surrender take *v.*

T

take *v.*

take give *v.*
talented gifted *adj.*
talkative curt *adj.*
tempest storm *n.*
terminate finish *v.*
together alone *adj.*
touch feel *v.*
tranquillity storm *n.*
transfer move *v.*
traveler explorer *n.*
treacherous risky *adj.*
treasure cherish *v.*
tremendous *adj.*

U

unaccompanied alone *adj.*
uncertain confident *adj.*
uninspiring challenging *adj.*
unload pack *v.*
unpack pack *v.*
unpleasant nice *adj.*
unskilled gifted *adj.*

V

value cherish *v.*
various different *adj.*
vast tremendous *adj.*
verbose curt *adj.*
view look *v.*
vigorous strong *adj.*
vivaciously exuberantly *adv.*

W

weak strong *adj.*
went came *v.*
withdraw go *v.*
wordy curt *adj.*
worn-out strong *adj.*

A

alone *adj.* Without other people or things. The horse was **alone** in the empty barn.
separate Apart from others. The twins slept in *separate* rooms.
solitary Without companions. The monk lived a *solitary* life in the mountains.
unaccompanied Without the company of others. None of his friends could go with him, so Sam was *unaccompanied*.

ANTONYMS: accompanied, together

aloof *adj.* Reserved or distant in manner. At first, John kept **aloof** from the other students.
detached Not favoring any side; impartial. A good judge always stays *detached*.
distant Not friendly; reserved. When Pam gets to know us, she will not be so *distant*.
reserved Keeping one's feelings, thoughts, and affairs to oneself. Rose usually remained *reserved* and did not talk about herself.
restrained Held back; repressed. Although Jim spoke calmly, his voice was full of *restrained* emotion.
subdued Not intense. Because she did not feel well, Jaclyn was very *subdued*.

ANTONYMS: friendly, open, outgoing

argue *v.* To give reasons in favor of or against a particular subject. Since Tracy and I have different views on the subject, we often **argue**.
debate To argue for or against something. The two candidates will *debate* on a subject having to do with agriculture.
differ To hold a different opinion. The two girls *differ* on which book they prefer.
disagree To have unlike opinions. Although they are good friends, the two boys sometimes *disagree*.
dispute To challenge in an argument or a debate. Anyone who disagrees with my opinion may *dispute* my findings in next week's debate.

ANTONYMS: agree, concur, harmonize

B

basics *n.* The fundamental parts that make up a particular thing. To achieve success in school, you must master the **basics**.
elements The necessary parts of something. One of the *elements* of a good short story is an interesting plot.
essentials The most important elements. Proper diet and regular exercise are the *essentials* of a healthful daily routine.

ANTONYMS: extras, frivolities, luxuries

C

came *v.* Got near, moved toward. Fran **came** to visit George.
advanced Went forward; approached. The group *advanced* toward the center of town.

approached Came close to. Juan *approached* the sign to see it more closely.
arrived Came to a place. After walking for an hour, Jack *arrived* at the inn.
progressed Went ahead or forward. The hikers *progressed* up the steep hill in single file.
reached Arrived at a place. We *reached* our destination on time.

ANTONYMS: left, retreated, went

center *v.* To focus on something. You must **center** your attention on the lesson.
aim To point in a certain direction. *Aim* the dart directly at the target.
concentrate To direct one's attention completely. Try to *concentrate* on the matter at hand.
direct To aim in a particular direction. We must *direct* the boat toward the shore.

ANTONYMS: disperse, dissipate, scatter

challenging *adj.* Requiring courage or great effort. Mountain climbing can be a very **challenging** sport.
difficult Not easy to deal with or handle. I found the rocky mountain trail *difficult*.
formidable Difficult to accomplish. Learning the long poem by heart was a *formidable* task.
frustrating Tending to produce discouragement. Having our picnic rained out three weekends in a row was *frustrating*.
stimulating Exciting or rousing. The *stimulating* speech filled us with courage.

ANTONYMS: boring, easy, simple, uninspiring

cherish *v.* To regard with great fondness. I will always **cherish** your friendship.
guard To watch over and keep safe. The sentries will *guard* the palace all night long.
prize To recognize the great value of. A collector will always *prize* a rare antique.
treasure To value greatly. We love warm weather and *treasure* every sunny day.
value To regard as having great worth. Many people *value* honesty above all other virtues.

ANTONYMS: belittle, despise, discount

climb *v.* To move upward. To reach the second floor, we must **climb** a flight of stairs.
ascend To rise; to go up. The elevator can *ascend* quickly to the top floor.
mount To step up onto; to ascend. John will *mount* the ladder to reach the top branches of the tree.
rise To go from a lower position to a higher position. The hot-air balloon will *rise* from the ground.
scramble To climb or move quickly. The sudden storm caused the cat to *scramble* up a tree.

ANTONYMS: descend, fall, plunge, sink

confident *adj.* Fully trusting; assured. Having studied the chapter, Helen felt **confident** that she would do well on the test.

assured Certain; sure. José seemed *assured* of his success as an athlete.

certain Having no doubt. The moment Wanda saw the blue jacket, she was *certain* it was the one she wanted.

secure Believing strongly in one's own strength or safety. Although Kim was full of doubt, Pam felt quite *secure*.

sure Free of doubt; certain. Because you are such a fast and strong runner, I am *sure* that you will win the race.

ANTONYMS: doubtful, dubious, skeptical, uncertain

curt *adj.* Abrupt and tersely spoken. Ron spoke in a **curt** manner because he was in a hurry.

abrupt Blunt in manner. Jason is very polite and never *abrupt*.

brief Short in duration. Tanya's *brief* speech lasted barely two minutes.

concise Brief, but full of expression. Please be clear and *concise* when you write your essay.

short Containing few words; brief. The busy politician gave a *short* reply to the question.

ANTONYMS: ceremonious, deliberate, talkative, verbose, wordy

D

dark *adj.* Lacking light. During the storm, the sky turned **dark** and cloudy.

dim Lacking sufficient light. We could not see well in the *dim* alley.

gloomy Dark and dreary. The daylight made the *gloomy* forest look cheerful.

murky Dark or obscure. The *murky* water was full of mud.

shady Sheltered from the sun. This *shady* spot is cold.

ANTONYMS: bright, cheerful, light

darkness *n.* The lack of light. After we pulled the shades down, the room was in **darkness**.

dimness The quality of having insufficient light. In the *dimness* of the cave, Paul could see very little.

obscurity A state of little or no light. The *obscurity* of the darkened room was cool and comforting.

ANTONYMS: brightness, brilliance

daybreak *n.* The first light of morning. We watched the sun rise at **daybreak**.

dawn The time in the morning when daylight appears. The sky remains dark until *dawn*.

morning The period of the day from sunrise until noon. Tim worked all *morning* and took a break at noon.

sunrise The time when the sun appears over the horizon. At *sunrise*, the birds begin to sing.

ANTONYMS: dusk, nightfall, sunset

different *adj.* Unlike another in some way. The twins were as **different** in character as they were similar in looks.
distinctive Having qualities that distinguish or set apart. This city has a *distinctive* skyline.
imaginative Full of originality or creativity. The clever designer arranged the flowers in an *imaginative* way.
original Not produced or copied from another source. We need some *original* ideas for our party.
peculiar Unusual or odd. I have never seen anything quite like that *peculiar* sculpture.
preposterous Going against common sense. He thought his plan was logical, but Marianne found it *preposterous*.
various Of several kinds. The community library contains books on *various* subjects.

ANTONYMS: common, copied, nondescript, ordinary

dislike *v.* To have no fondness for. Although Nancy likes the taste of spicy Mexican food, we **dislike** it.
detest To have a strong aversion to. There are no colors that I *detest*; I like them all.
hate To dislike extremely. I *hate* to be late, so I always wear a watch.

ANTONYMS: enjoy, like, love

E

eager *adj.* Enthusiastic. Vinny was **eager** to see the results of the final exam.
anxious Feeling uneasy. Because Mary was not particularly *anxious* about the test, she remained calm.
enthusiastic Full of passion or interest. Rosa was *enthusiastic* about her exciting new job.
restless Having difficulty controlling one's eagerness. The children were *restless* because they wanted to go swimming.

ANTONYMS: apathetic, indifferent, relaxed

eliminate *v.* To get rid of. If you **eliminate** all the unwanted papers, you will have more room.
eradicate To eliminate completely. Use an eraser to *eradicate* any stray marks on your paper.
purge To remove something unwanted. The admiral intends to *purge* the navy of incompetent sailors.
remove To take off or away. Let's *remove* the old furniture before we paint the room.

ANTONYMS: accumulate, collect, gather, keep

explorer *n.* A person who travels to gather knowledge or to make discoveries. The **explorer** traveled to many distant countries in search of ancient documents.
investigator A person who looks for facts or details. The *investigator* sought information about the abandoned car.

researcher A person who conducts a careful study on a subject. The group hired a *researcher* to study the behavior of whales in the Arctic.

scout Someone who is sent out to gather information. The *scout* returned with important news.

traveler A person who journeys or travels. The *traveler* was glad to rest after her long trip.

exuberantly *adv.* With joy and enthusiasm. The crowd cheered **exuberantly** for the winners.

gladly With a feeling of cheerfulness. Jan accepted the beautiful flowers *gladly*.

happily With joy or contentment. The delighted children danced *happily* in a circle.

joyfully With intense happiness. Ben smiled *joyfully* when he saw the lovely gift.

vivaciously With great vitality. The prancing steed tossed its mane *vivaciously*.

ANTONYMS: dejectedly, gloomily, joylessly, sadly

F

feel *v.* To sense by touching. You can **feel** the texture of the soft fabric.

experience To get a feeling through the senses. We hope to *experience* the welcome coolness of a refreshing breeze.

finger To handle to obtain a physical sensation. When you *finger* this leaf, you can feel the ridges on it.

stroke To rub gently. The pet owner likes to *stroke* the cat's soft fur.

touch To make contact with an object, especially by using one's finger or hands. If your fingers *touch* the sandpaper, you will feel how coarse it is.

finish *v.* To bring to an end; to perform a final step. Jerry will **finish** the project at 10:00.

close To end or conclude. The President will *close* his speech with a famous quotation.

complete To bring to an end. Jill must *complete* her report by next Friday.

end To reach the very last stage. The family will *end* their meal with some fresh fruit.

terminate To end; to expire. The contract will *terminate* on December 31.

ANTONYMS: begin, initiate, start

flow *v.* To come forth steadily and freely. Water will **flow** through an open faucet.

course To flow forcefully. We watched the heavy floodwaters *course* through the streets.

gush To burst out with great force. Everyone hoped that oil would soon *gush* from the well.

pour To transfer in a steady stream. Please *pour* the milk into the bowl.

stream To run freely or abundantly. Clouds of vapor *stream* from the rocket's tail.

surge To flow suddenly or rhythmically with great force. Powerful waves *surge* majestically toward the shore.

ANTONYMS: halt, stagnate, stop

G

gifted *adj.* Full of talent. The **gifted** musician played brilliantly.
endowed Supplied with ability or natural gifts. Don is *endowed* with skillful hands.
skilled Possessing specific abilities. The *skilled* carpenter built a beautiful desk.
talented Having a natural aptitude for a particular activity or craft. We watched the *talented* dancer perform expertly.

ANTONYMS: inept, unskilled

give *v.* To hand over without expecting payment. I will **give** you a bouquet of roses.
bestow To offer as a gift. The company will *bestow* some money on the school.
hand To present something with the hands. The judge will *hand* the trophy to the winner.
present To offer. Pablo can *present* the book to George.

ANTONYMS: get, receive, take

go *v.* To move away from a certain location. I've enjoyed this visit, but I must **go** now.
depart To leave or go away, as on a journey. The train is scheduled to *depart* at 7:30.
exit To leave the premises. Please *exit* through the back door.
leave To go away; to depart. Bill will *leave* for home when the meeting is over.
withdraw To remove oneself from a place. Carla couldn't wait to *withdraw* from the crowded meeting room.

ANTONYMS: arrive, come, enter

H

helper *n.* One who gives aid. The teacher needs a **helper** to assist her with the class.
accomplice A person who assists another, often in a wrongful activity. Jan was Erin's *accomplice* in planning the practical joke.
aide A person who provides assistance. The scientist's *aide* helped with the research.
assistant A person who gives help. The chef worked with an *assistant* who helped prepare the food.
attendant A person employed to serve another. Helen asked the parking-lot *attendant* to retrieve her car.

ANTONYMS: encumbrance, hindrance

hide *v.* To remove from view; to remove oneself from view. Dan's little brother likes to **hide** behind the tree.
conceal To keep from being known or seen. We will *conceal* the document in the secret drawer.

WRITER'S THESAURUS

cover To hide by overlaying something. The painter will *cover* the cracks in the wall with plaster and paint.
mask To disguise so as to prevent discovery. Leo and his classmates felt so happy that they could not *mask* their joy.

ANTONYMS: expose, reveal, show

L

like *v.* To take pleasure in; to find appealing. They **like** taking long walks.
enjoy To derive pleasure from. Barbara and Kim *enjoy* all sports, especially tennis.
love To be extremely fond of. I *love* listening to beautiful music.
relish To appreciate; to find pleasurable. Many great writers and news reporters *relish* a lively conversation.

ANTONYMS: abhor, detest, dislike, hate

look *v.* To direct one's sight toward an object. Let's **look** at the stamp collection.
inspect To examine in detail. Martin will *inspect* the boat for holes.
regard To gaze at attentively. Sally turned to *regard* him coldly.
view To observe closely. The class will *view* the cell with a microscope.

ANTONYMS: disregard, ignore

M

move *v.* To go from one position or place to another. Let's **move** to a quieter spot so that we can talk.
creep To advance very slowly. The hours seemed to *creep* as we waited for the news.
maneuver To move intentionally and skillfully. The captain was able to *maneuver* the boat safely into the harbor.
shift To alter position from one location to another. John tried to *shift* the heavy package from his left shoulder to his right.
transfer To move from one place to another. We need to *transfer* books from the shelf to the attic.

ANTONYMS: remain, stand, stay

N

nice *adj.* Pleasant; likable. It was such a **nice** day that we had a picnic.
agreeable Causing a feeling of happiness or pleasure. I found the tropical island most *agreeable*.
delightful Giving a feeling of great joy. Pam loved her *delightful* garden.
mouthwatering Enticing and highly pleasing to the taste. The dinner guests were eager to eat the *mouthwatering* meal.
pleasing Enjoyable; pleasant to the senses. The living room was decorated in a *pleasing* combination of colors.

ANTONYMS: repulsive, unpleasant

P

pack *n.* A bundle of objects wrapped up for carrying. Jim carried his belongings in a large **pack.**
bundle A variety of things tied or bound up together. Dan arranged the laundry in a *bundle* to make it easier to carry.
knapsack A spacious bag worn on one's back. The camper filled her *knapsack* with supplies for the trip.
parcel A package. Irene received a large *parcel* of gourmet food.

pack *v.* To put items into, often tightly. Jan tends to **pack** suitcases too full.
fill To make something completely full. *Fill* the jug to the brim with fresh milk.
load To place objects into or onto a conveyance. Wendy will *load* the car with our luggage.
stuff To fill by packing tightly. We tried to *stuff* a few more items into the crowded van.

ANTONYMS: strew, unload, unpack

palace *n.* The residence of a monarch or ruler. The king lived in a splendid **palace**.
home A person's dwelling place. We visited the *home* of a famous writer.
mansion A large, stately house. The huge *mansion* contained large, beautiful rooms.

ANTONYMS: hovel, hut

R

rabbit *n.* A small animal with soft fur, long ears, and powerful hind legs. The **rabbit** moved in a series of long jumps.
bunny A pet name for a rabbit, especially a young rabbit. The children discovered one little *bunny* and one adult rabbit.
hare An animal similar to a rabbit, but larger. Unlike the rabbit, the *hare* does not live in a burrow.

risky *adj.* Involving exposure to possible harm. Although John thought the plan was **risky,** Joe believed it was perfectly safe.
dangerous Unsafe. We did not take the steep path because it looked too *dangerous*.
hazardous Involving the possibility of damage or loss. Alex avoided driving in *hazardous* weather.
perilous Full of danger. After the ice melted, the road was no longer *perilous*.
treacherous Involving unforeseen danger. At night, the path through the forest can be *treacherous*.

ANTONYMS: safe, secure

S

see *v.* To perceive by means of the eyes. I would like to **see** the colorful dress you described.
behold To direct one's sight toward. When you *behold* the valley, you will agree that it is beautiful.

notice To take note of. Did she *notice* Jim's new haircut?
perceive To observe or to be aware of through the senses. I can *perceive* two people approaching through the mist.

ANTONYMS: ignore, overlook

shine *v.* To emit light. The light from the lamp will **shine** for hours.
glint To flash with light. We could see the bright sun *glint* off the shiny metal.
glitter To sparkle brightly. A good diamond will *glitter* under any light.
radiate To emit rays of light or energy. The light will *radiate* deep into the darkness.
shimmer To shine unsteadily. The surface of the water seemed to *shimmer* in the sunlight.

ANTONYMS: cloud, darken, dim

show *v.* To indicate or make apparent. The guide will **show** us the interesting sights.
demonstrate To make clear or obvious. The teacher will *demonstrate* the importance of classroom safety.
display To present for viewing. The sales clerks will *display* all the items for sale.
exhibit To put on display. The museum will *exhibit* a rare collection of gems.

ANTONYMS: conceal, cover, hide

slow *adj.* Having a low rate of speed. Carol rode in a **slow** buggy so that she could see all of the scenery.
lagging Moving at a lower speed than desired. The *lagging* hikers arrived at the lodge after their companions.
leisurely Unhurried. Since we were not in a hurry, we rode at a *leisurely* pace.
sluggish Moving less quickly than usual. Although the stream usually flows freely, today it seems *sluggish*.

ANTONYMS: fast, quick, speedy

slumber *v.* To sleep peacefully. Babies **slumber** for short periods of time.
doze To fall asleep briefly. I felt so relaxed that I began to *doze*.
drowse To be partially asleep. Bob's eyes closed as he started to *drowse*.
sleep To rest the mind and body in a state of unconsciousness. Most people need to *sleep* seven or eight hours every night.

ANTONYMS: arouse, awake

smell *n.* A quality perceived by the olfactory sense; odor. Andrea loves the **smell** of popcorn.
aroma An agreeable fragrance. The *aroma* of the fresh roses spread through the room.
odor That which can be perceived by the sense of smell. The cabbage gave off a strong *odor* as it cooked.
scent An odor, usually pleasant. Pat loves the *scent* of this perfume.
stench An intense and unpleasant odor. A skunk protects itself by emitting a powerful *stench*.

solitude *n.* The state of being alone. Ed wanted to spend some time in quiet **solitude**.
isolation The state of being separate from others. Mary never worked in *isolation*; she always had many people around her.
loneliness The feeling of being alone and without friends. There was no risk of *loneliness* in the friendly town.
separateness The quality of acting or being away from others. A strong sense of *separateness* made the islanders yearn for independence.

ANTONYMS: association, companionship, friendship

storm *n.* A forceful outburst. The audience responded to the joke with a **storm** of laughter.
commotion Extreme excitement and confusion. I could not tell what was happening because of the *commotion*.
outbreak A sudden occurrence. Joan witnessed an *outbreak* of activity when she announced the good news.
tempest A violent or sudden disturbance or outburst. The excited fans greeted the celebrity with a *tempest* of wild cheers.

ANTONYMS: peace, tranquillity

strong *adj.* Having great power or force. The **strong** athlete lifted the heavy weight.
energetic Possessing great energy. The *energetic* team played well.
forceful Having much strength and vigor. The *forceful* speaker swayed the audience.
mighty Intensely powerful. The *mighty* elephant carried the burden easily.
powerful Full of strength. A large truck needs a *powerful* engine.
vigorous Displaying much force and energy. The swimmer used *vigorous* strokes to cross the pool.

ANTONYMS: exhausted, weak, worn-out

T

take *v.* To get control or possession of. I will **take** your extra ticket.
capture To obtain by force. I hope they *capture* the wild beast.
grab To seize quickly and forcefully. The children tried to *grab* as many marbles as they could.
snatch To take possession of suddenly and quickly. I tried to *snatch* the ball from my playful dog.

ANTONYMS: give, lose, surrender

tremendous *adj.* Of unusual size or power. The **tremendous** rainstorm caused the streets to flood.
enormous Extraordinarily large. The *enormous* boulder rolled down the mountain.
giant Extremely big or large. The *giant* redwood tree towered above the tourists.
huge Unusually large; immense. The *huge* theater seated more than 20,000 people.
vast Extremely large; expansive. The *vast* desert stretched on for miles.

ANTONYMS: insignificant, minuscule, small

INDEX

INDEX

EP = Extra Practice
G = Glossary
WH = Writer's Handbook
WT = Writer's Thesaurus

A

B

C

D

N

O

P

Q

R

S

T

U

V

W

continued from page IV

Marian Reiner, on behalf of Eve Merriam: "Markings: The Period" from *A Sky Full of Poems* by Eve Merriam. Copyright © 1964, 1970, 1973 by Eve Merriam. All rights reserved.

Richard Rieu, as Executor of the Estate of Dr. E. V. Rieu: From "The Castaways" in *Cuckoo Calling* by E. V. Rieu. Copyright by E. V. Rieu. Published by Methuen & Company, Ltd.

Mary Lee Settle: From p. 70 in *Water World* by Mary Lee Settle. Copyright © 1984 by Mary Lee Settle.

William Jay Smith: From "The Owl" in *LAUGHING TIME: Nonsense Poems* by William Jay Smith. Copyright © 1955, 1957, 1980 by William Jay Smith. Published by Delacorte Press, 1980.

Viking Penguin, a division of Penguin Books USA, Inc.: From "Lone Dog" in *Songs to Save a Soul* by Irene Rutherford McLeod. All rights reserved.

Lloyd Washington, on behalf of De-Shun Washington: From "There is Danger" by De-Shun Washington in *My Skills Are for Survival,* edited by Gail Newman. © 1986 by De-Shun Washington.

The H. W. Wilson Company: Entries "Art, Shaker" through "Art and industry" from *Readers' Guide to Periodical Literature,* February 1987. Entries "House decoration, French" through "House decoration, Georgian" and "House Democratic Caucus (U. S.)" through "House drainage" in *Readers' Guide to Periodical Literature,* 1987. All copyright © 1987 by The H. W. Wilson Company.

Art Acknowledgments

Alex Bloch: 10, 11, 28, 34, 174, 204–205, 307, 401, 405, 411, tap logos (3); Suzanne Clee: 370; Don Dyen: 49, 88, 90, 146, 147, 244, 245, 292; Simon Galkin: 156–157, 286, 290, 349, 390; Anthony Giamas: 70; Richard Loehle: 192, 193, 392; Laurie Marks: 431; Sue Parnell: 245; Dennis Schofield: 148, 280, 334–335, 452–453; Susan Spellman: 450; Gary Undercuffler: 57, 73, 173, 269; Robert Villani: 190, 211, 381; Mel Williges: 252, 301–302; Kit Wray: 102–105.

Cover: Tom Vroman

Production and Layout: Blaise Zito Associates

Photo Acknowledgments

PHOTOGRAPHS: Pages 3, HBJ Photo/Rob Downey; 6(t), HBJ Photo/Rob Downey; (b), HBJ Photo/Rob Downey; 7(t), HBJ Photo/Rob Downey; (b), HBJ Photo/Rob Downey.

UNIT 1: 8, HBJ Photo/Charlie Burton; 16, HBJ Photo/Rob Downey; 25, HBJ Photo/Rob Downey; 28, HBJ Photo/Wiley & Flynn.

UNIT 2: 54, HBJ Photo/Charlie Burton; 62, HBJ Photo/Rob Downey; 70(l), HBJ Photo/Rob Downey; (r), HBJ Photo/Rob Downey; 74, George E. Jones, III/Photo Researchers.

UNIT 3: 100, HBJ Photo/Charlie Burton; 101, The Bettmann Archive; 110, HBJ Photo/Rob Downey; 119(l), HBJ Photo/Rob Downey; (r), HBJ Photo/Rob Downey; 122, AP/Wide World Photos.

UNIT 4: 154, Gregory K. Scott/Photo Researchers; 162, HBJ Photo/Rob Downey; 170, HBJ Photo/Rob Downey; 171, HBJ Photo/Rob Downey.

UNIT 5: 202, HBJ Photo/Rodney Jones; 212, HBJ Photo/Rob Downey; 222(l), HBJ Photo/Rob Downey; (r), HBJ Photo/Rob Downey; 223, HBJ Photo/Rob Downey; 226, Mikki Ansin/Gamma-Liaison.

UNIT 6: 250, HBJ Photo/Charlie Burton; 251, Doug Pizac/AP/Wide World Photos; 258, HBJ Photo/Rob Downey; 267(l), HBJ Photo/Rob Downey; (r), HBJ Photo/Rob Downey; 270, Michael Manheim/The Stock Market.

UNIT 7: 298, HBJ Photo/Rodney Jones; 308, HBJ Photo/Rob Downey; 316(l), HBJ Photo/Rob Downey; (r), HBJ Photo/Rob Downey.

UNIT 8: 346, HBJ Photo/Charlie Burton; 347, Rustam Tahir; 350(l), courtesy of The Atlanta University Center Archives and Special Collections/The Atlanta University Center Woodruff Library; (r), courtesy of Bethune-Cookman College; 352(t), New York Public Library Picture Collection; (b), courtesy of Bethune-Cookman College; 358, HBJ Photo/Rob Downey; 367, HBJ Photo/Rob Downey.

UNIT 9: 398, HBJ Photo/Charlie Burton; 417, HBJ Photo/Rob Downey; 428(tl), HBJ Photo/Rob Downey; (tr), HBJ Photo/Rob Downey; (bl), HBJ Photo/Rob Downey; (br), HBJ Photo/Rob Downey; 429, HBJ Photo/Rob Downey; 432, Bachrach/courtesy of William Morrow & Co., Inc./Publishers.

1
2
3
F 4
G 5
H 6
I 7
J 8